JEWISH COOKERY

LEAH W. LEONARD

JEWISH COOKERY

IN ACCORDANCE WITH
THE JEWISH DIETARY
LAWS

ANDRE DEUTSCH

FIRST PUBLISHED 1951 BY
ANDRE DEUTSCH LIMITED
105 GREAT RUSSELL STREET
LONDON WC1
© LEAH W. LEONARD 1949
SECOND IMPRESSION NOVEMBER 1953
THIRD IMPRESSION JANUARY 1958
REVISED EDITION MARCH 1968
ALL RIGHTS RESERVED
PRINTED IN GREAT BRITAIN
BY EBENEZER BAYLIS & SON LIMITED
THE TRINITY PRESS, WORCESTER AND LONDON

SBN 233 95505 4

To
the loving memory of
MOTHER
who taught me
what I like to call
THE EIGHTH ART

Acknowledgments

My deepest appreciation goes to the hundreds of readers of my weekly columns on Jewish foods for their invaluable suggestions and frequent letters of inquiry about a collection of recipes.

My thanks to relatives and friends for sharing their favourite recipes and testing those submitted by me.

Grateful acknowledgment is hereby given the editors of publications where my food columns and suggestions appear.

For invaluable assistance and encouragement, my thanks and appreciation to the late Rabbi A. E. Halpern of St Louis, Missouri;

The late Dr Joshua Bloch of the Semitics Department, New York Public Library;

Dr Boaz Cohen, formerly of the Jewish Theological Seminary, New York;

Sophie Udin, formerly Librarian of Zionist Archives, New York;

Dr B. A. Botkin, folk-lore authority, for advice and encouragement;

My daughter, Mrs Allen Kanfer, for helping with reading of proofs, and my patient and long-suffering husband, Oscar Leonard.

L.W.L.

Preface

The art of food preparation is limited only by the the cook's ingenuity, educational background and interest in the development of a happy, healthy breed of human beings. Biochemists and nutritionists in this scientific age are pointing the way. But it still remains the duty of one who plans and prepares our daily meals to take an artist's pride in utmost fulfilment. In fact, the art of cooking is the *eighth art*.

There may be a definite relationship between food customs and group continuity which some researcher somewhere will present some day. At any rate, we do know that food customs and food traditions play a significant part in national identity.

The Jewish people, like all other peoples, have food customs traditionally associated with their daily lives, their holidays and festivals, celebrations in the home and out of it. In addition to these, regulations are prescribed in a code of dietary laws, from the slaughter of animals used for food and regulations of other foods, to the kinds of dishes prepared for special holidays and festivals as well as the Sabbath. These food traditions have accumulated through the long, historic experience of the Jewish people. Some food customs and traditions cluster about historic events that have become the basis for annual observance. All of this has contributed to the national continuity of an ancient people.

No one knows the origin of *gefilte fish*. Yet this delicious dish is so definitely a part of Jewish cuisine that it is so designated on menus in all parts of the world.

Chola, the Sabbath loaf, dates back to the *shew bread* (or show bread) of the Temple and the Priestly Blessing.

The annual celebration of *Pesach* (Passover), the flight to freedom from Egyptian bondage, described in the Book of Exodus, has its traditional food customs. A whole section in this book has been devoted to it.

Purim is another festival, a Jewish national holiday, around which has grown a whole set of food traditions. Recipes for foods associated with this festival have been gathered from many countries where Jews have lived and are living today.

With the restoration of the Jewish people to national statehood, other food customs and traditions may develop in the land of Israel. Already there are the beginnings of a distinct cuisine in that land. We have devoted a special section to recipes from Israel.

Some ingenious person may devise a special dish in celebration of the downfall of Hitler and Hitlerism which will become as much a part of Jewish food tradition as *hamantaschen* have become the food tradition associated with *Purim* and the downfall of Haman. Special foods may become associated with the Restoration (after almost two thousand years), and in time develop into an honoured culinary tradition.

While Jewish homes have always been symbols of hospitality, and the Jewish cook famous for skill, it was not until 1826 that a Jewish Cookbook was published in London. It was entitled *The Jewish Manual*, edited 'by a Lady'. In this collection of recipes gathered from many sources there are remarkably few 'traditional' Jewish dishes.

The earliest American Jewish Cookbook was the work of Mrs Esther Levy, published in 1871. It contains very few Passover Recipes, and *not one* for *gefilte fish*!

In *Jewish Cookery* a special effort has been made to present a wide assortment of recipes traditionally associated with the Sabbath, holidays, family celebrations in the home, as well as Jewish national festivals. We have also gathered together favourite recipes and food customs in Jewish homes in almost every country in the world. These recipes, some handed down from countless generations in one country or another, have been tested for accuracy in the light of modern techniques for food preparation plus the most recent kitchen equipment and facilities.

Perhaps *Jewish Cookery* will be a most welcome addition to the kitchen library of the modern homemaker. We hope it will serve as a substantial aid in making the *eighth art* a more significant part of this thing called 'living'.

Leah W. Leonard

Contents

JEWISH COOKERY

Calendar of Jewish Holidays and Food Associations

THE HEBREW CALENDAR

The Jewish year is based on lunar calculations.

The ordinary year consists of 12 months – 355 days.

Some of the months have 29 days and some have 30 days.

Leap Year, an intercalated year called 'eeber yor' in Yiddish, has thirteen months. The thirteenth month is called 'Adar Sheni' in Hebrew, or 'second Adar', and falls between the first Adar and the following month called 'Nissan'.

Because there is this difference of a month instead of one day in leap years of the Hebrew calendar and the calendar used in the Common Era, Jewish holidays do not fall on the same days of the latter calendar every year. The beginning of the Hebrew calendar, marked by the holiday called Rosh Hashana, may come in September or in October.

MONTHS OF THE HEBREW CALENDAR

1	Tishri	7	Nissan
2	Heshvan	8	Iyar
3	Kislev	9	Sivan
4	Tebet	10	Tammuz
5	Sh'vat	11	Ab
6	Adar	12	Elul

JEWISH HOLIDAYS AND FOOD ASSOCIATIONS

Holiday	Hebrew Date	Month C.E.	Traditional Foods
Rosh Hashana (New Year)	Tishri 1, 2	Sept. or Oct.	Honey, Honey Cake, Carrot Tzimmes

Holiday	Hebrew Date	Month C.E.	Traditional Foods
Yom Kippur (Day of Atonement)	Tishri 10	Sept. or Oct.	Total Abstinence from Food (Fast Day)
Succot	Tishri 15–23	October	Kreplach, Holishkes, Strudel
Chanucah	Kislev 25– Tebet 2	December	Grated Potato Latkes, Potato Kugel
Chamiso Oser b'Sh'vat	Sh'vat 15	January	Bokser (St John's Bread) Almonds, Raisins
Purim	Adar 14	March	Hamantashen, Nahit, Apples, Nuts, Raisins
Pesach (Passover)	Nissan 14–22	April	Matzo, Matzo Products, Chremzlach, Wine, Nuts
Lag b'Omer	Iyar 18	May	B'ob (Favah Beans or Broad Beans)
Shavuot	Sivan 6, 7	May	Cheese Blintzes, Kreplach, Dairy Foods

HOLIDAY FOOD CUSTOMS

Culinary customs that have become traditionally associated with Jewish holidays, major and minor, unquestionably originated early in the history of the Jewish people. The origins of some food customs are lost in antiquity. But some customs have been traced to biblical and early post-biblical times.

ROSH HASHANA. On the New Year, it is customary to serve apple slices dipped in a bowl of honey, signifying the heartfelt yearning for a sweet and happy year.

Carrots in some form or other are served to signify the wish for prosperity in the ensuing year. A *carrot tzimmes* is usually served, or a succulent pudding containing carrots, 'sugar and spice and everything nice'.

The Prophet Nehemiah is said to have introduced the Persian custom of eating sweets on this High Holy Day, saying:

'Eat the fat and drink the sweet.'

From the Babylonians, the ancient Hebrews borrowed the

custom of serving a sheep's head for the main course of the meal, signifying a year at the beginning – the head of events to come. Another interpretation of this custom is said to commemorate Abraham's sacrifice of a ram in lieu of his son Isaac.

JEWISH HOLIDAYS

YOM KIPPUR. The High Holy Day of the year is a fast day. The fast is continuous for twenty-four hours, from sundown to sundown. It comes on the tenth day of Tishri.

The beginning of *Yom Kippur*, *Erev Yom Kippur*, is the evening before the Day of Atonement. It is customary to serve no highly spiced or seasoned food before the fast begins. Customary Sabbath or holiday dishes are served following the *Kiddush*, the blessing over wine, at the end of the fast. It is customary to start the meal with *forshpeisse* (appetizers), such as chopped herring, pickled fish or *gefilte fish*. Noodle Soup, poultry, vegetables, salad, fruit compote and *strudel* follow.

SUCCOT. Feast of Booths is celebrated for a whole week beginning the fifteenth day of Tishri. The Booth of Willows, or *Sukkah*, is symbolic of the first stopping place of the Israelites on their flight from Egypt. The inside of the Booth is decorated with festoons of cranberries, grape clusters, red and green apples, ears of corn, pumpkins, squashes and such other harvest fruits and vegetables as are available. It is the ingathering of the harvest.

Meals are eaten in the *Sukkah*. East European Jews include at least one meal of *holishkes* (chopped meat wrapped in cabbage leaves). This dish is called *galuptze* in Russia. In Rumania and other Balkan countries it is called *sarmali in foie de vitza*, grape vine leaves being substituted for cabbage. Dessert is *strudel*.

CHANUCAH. The Feast of Lights is celebrated for eight days beginning the twenty-fifth day of Kislev. This holiday celebrates the heroic battle of the Maccabees in the year 165 B.C.E. (before the common era).

It is primarily a home festival in which the children participate with singing of the traditional *M'Oaz Tzur* (Rock of Ages), and the lighting of candles. One candle is lit the first night, two the second night, etc. The candle that serves to light the others is called the *Shammes*. Grated *potato latkes* (pancakes) are served along with other delicacies on this happy occasion.

CHAMISO OSER B'SH'VAT. Festival of the Trees is a semi-holiday, corresponding to Arbour Day. It is the blossoming time of the trees in Israel. It is celebrated on the fifteenth day of Sh'vat.

Bokser (St John's bread), is the characteristic special food of the holiday. Nuts, dates, figs, raisins, fruits and cakes are customary.

PURIM. The Feast of Esther begins with the reading of the *Megila* (Book of Esther). It comes on the fourteenth day of Adar. It commemorates the downfall of the wicked Haman, trusted councillor of King Ahasuerus (Xerxes) of Persia. Haman's intrigues were disclosed by Mordecai, uncle of Esther, the King's favourite Queen.

This holiday is celebrated with much feasting by adults as well as children. Masquerades, Purim plays, exchange of gifts, special gifts to the poor, are part of the festivities.

The *hamantash*, a three-cornered pastry filled with poppy seed and honey, or prune butter (see p. 369), is the special holiday treat. The three-cornered hat which Haman is supposed to have worn, or, as the name Hamantaschen in German implies, the purse of Haman, is thus commemorated.

In Italy and other Mediterranean countries, Jews have a legend about Haman's ears being shaped like the donkey's – three cornered and slightly elongated. Thus the Haman-cakes are three-cornered and slightly elongated. In Holland and the Low Countries, small cakes in the shape of a man, studded with nuts and raisins like the gingerbread man, symbolize Haman.

In various countries other *Purims* have been celebrated to commemorate some incident of impending disaster to the particular Jewish community at some time in its history. One such Purim is recorded as the *Brandeis Purim* or *Povidl Purim* in 1731 in Bohemia. That may have been the origin of the prune-butter-filled *hamantaschen*. A family named Brandeis was falsely accused of a crime against property, and when proven innocent the whole town made holiday and called it *Brandeis Purim*, which thereafter was celebrated annually.

PURIM FOOD LORE. One of the folk expressions relating to *Purim* customs reflects the significant sociological phenomenon of an extremely small percentage of alcoholism among Jews. On *Purim* it is customary to eat, drink and be merry. Thus the saying: *A gantz yor shikker und Purim nichter!* The literal translation from the Yiddish is: 'All year drunk and sober on Purim!' Thus to chide a Jew for being 'nichter' on Purim and 'shikker' at all other times is the subtlest of pleasantries.

Another folk-saying is the one that taunts the ne'er-do-well with earning lots of money only one day of the year. For on Purim it is customary for plates of Purim pastries, sweets and gifts to be sent by messenger to relatives, friends and neighbours. The recipient of a plate of *Shal Achmonos*, which in Hebrew means a plate of gifts for Purim, tips the messenger who may be a child or an adult. Accumulating lots of money as *Shal Achmonos Traeger* (Purim gift plate bearer) is ironic innuendo.

About good food in general, but Purim delicacies in particular, the folk expression *Tahm Gan Eden*, Hebrew for taste or flavour of Garden of Eden or Paradise, is commonly used.

PESACH OR PASSOVER. The Festival of Freedom from Slavery, or the liberation of the Israelites from Egyptian Bondage, is celebrated for eight days beginning the eve of the fourteenth day of Nissan to sunset of the twenty-second day of Nissan.

This holiday begins with the *Seder* on the evening preceding the first day of the Passover Week. In all countries, except Israel, two *Seders* are observed. The *First Seder* and the *Second Seder* both have the same ritual. The *Seder* is a home festival, and every part of it, from *Haggada* to *Kneidlach*, has been enriched with the traditions that are passed along to the children from generation to generation.

Perhaps a new festival is in the making and the flight or Exodus from excruciating memories in Europe to Israel, Land of Hope, will be recounted to future generations around the family table. Perhaps some special foods will become part of that future festival, too. But for the present, here's what you will need for the traditional *Seder*:

Afikomen. Three *matzos* are placed separately in the folds of a napkin or special *matzo* cover. These represent the Sabbath loaves over which the benediction is pronounced and bear the special significance of symbolizing the 'bread of affliction', or slavery. The child who manages to find the *afikomen*, which has been spirited away and hidden during the service, is awarded a prize.

Roasted lamb bone. A piece of lamb shank or chicken leg bone is browned on the open flame and placed on a plate to symbolize the paschal sacrifice of ancient days when each family brought its special offering.

Roasted hard cooked egg. An egg is roasted in the shell and placed on the plate with the roasted bone. The egg symbolizes Life, the perpetuation of existence.

Bitter herbs. A horse-radish top with some of the green leaves or

2

sprouts, symbolizes the bitterness of Israel's bondage in the Land of Egypt.

Morar. Some grated horse-radish, unflavoured or seasoned, is placed on a small dish. During the service some *morar* is placed between two pieces of *matzo* and passed to each member of the family circle. This is referred to as the 'Hillel Sandwich'.

Charoset. Finely chopped nuts and apple, moistened with wine, represent the morsel of sweetness to lighten the burden of unhappy memory.

Hard cooked egg and salt water. Hard cooked eggs in one dish and salted water in another are passed to everyone at the table during the service.

Greens and salt water. Parsley, watercress, chicory, lettuce or other available greens are the herbs that symbolize Hope and Redemption of Life. There should be salt water in a small bowl for each one at the table and some of the greens placed alongside it.

Wine. This is served in goblets and refilled four times during the service, symbolizing the four-fold promise of Redemption.

Cup of Elijah. A special goblet of wine is placed on the table towards the end of the service. At this time the door is opened and left ajar for the 'coming of Elijah', the coming of a more perfect world of justice and joy for all mankind.

SHAVUOT. Feast of Weeks is celebrated two days in all countries, except Israel, where it is a one-day holiday. Reform Jews celebrate only one day and make this a Confirmation day for boys and girls. It comes on the sixth (and seventh) day of Sivan.

Traditional dishes served on this holiday are *cheese kreplach, cheese blintzes,* and other cheese and dairy dishes.

2 Traditional Ceremonials and Food Customs in the Jewish Home

BEN ZOCHOR. This is a festive occasion for the family and friends of a newborn male child. It is celebrated the Friday evening following the birth of a son. In addition to the traditional wine and cake, *nahit,* boiled and salted, is served, much like salted almonds.

BRIT MILA CELEBRATION. The Rite of Circumcision customarily takes place the eighth day after the birth of a male. *Lekach* and *branfen** (honey cake, whisky or brandy, and wine) is traditional. The menu may be very simple and consist only of chopped herring canapés and tea, or elaborate enough to stretch from soup to nuts.

PIDYAN HABEN. The Redemption of the Firstborn Son is a home ceremonial dating back to the sojourn in Egypt. Observed by many families and made an occasion of rejoicing, it occurs one month after the birth of a firstborn male child. The traditional foods include honey cake and wine or whisky, *nahit,* and holiday dishes ranging from chicken soup to *strudel.*

BARMITZVAH. The attainment of maturity at the age of thirteen for boys is an occasion celebrated in the home after the traditional synagogue or temple service. Sweetmeats of all kinds, honey cake and wine, canapés and *strudel, knishes* and *pirogen* are generally served.

Confirmation for girls as well as boys is customary with Reform Jews. Receptions after the services at temple are held either in the respective homes of confirmants or for the group at temple.

T'NOYIM. This is the writing of a marriage contract on the engagement of a couple. The custom is to serve sweets of all kinds along with the customary cake and wine to parents and relatives of the prospective bride and groom.

---

* *Lekach und branfen* is the customary *kibbet* (Hebrew word for 'treat'). Literally it means honey cake and whisky or brandy. It may include wines, cordials, liqueurs. Also, any kind of cake – small cakes, biscuits or pastries. It has become part of the vernacular in Jewish life to invite friends to a *lekach und branfen* on certain occasions.

CHASSANA. The wedding celebrations have a wide range of food customs depending on the type of wedding. The traditional wine and cake is part of the meal served. Wine is part of the wedding ceremonial.

WEDDING ANNIVERSARIES. Food customs range from simple *lekach und branfen* or wine, to elaborate dinners with a specially prepared and decorated wedding cake.

3 What Every Cook Should Know

One responsible for the selection and preparation of food holds within his or her hand the health of generations to come. On the health of the present generation rests the future of nations. It therefore is essential that such a person know the basic facts of nutrition and the rudimentary values of foods used every day of the week, every week of the month and every month of the year.

Nutritionists have divided foods commonly used into seven basic groups. They serve as a sort of nutritional yardstick that even an amateur at cooking must acquire.

Group 1. Green and yellow vegetables (some raw, some cooked, frozen or canned).

Group 2. Oranges, tomatoes, grapefruit, raw cabbage or salad greens.

Group 3. Potatoes and other vegetables and fruit (raw, dried, cooked, frozen or canned).

Group 4. Milk and milk products (fluid, evaporated, dried milk or cheese).

Group 5. Meat, poultry, fish, eggs, dried beans, peas, nuts or peanut butter.

Group 6. Bread, flour and cereals (natural whole grain, enriched or restored).

Group 7. Butter and fortified margarine (with added vitamin A).

The individual's daily requirements from each of the seven basic food groups are:

Group 1. Two servings daily, one green leafy vegetable and one yellow vegetable.

Group 2. One serving daily of citrus fruit and salad greens.

Group 3. One serving daily of both fruit and vegetables.

Group 4. One quart milk daily for children up to sixteen. One pint milk daily for adults (or cheese equivalent).

Group 5. One serving daily of either one of foods listed.

Group 6. Breads of whole grain are daily essentials.

Group 7. Two or more tablespoonfuls daily.

YOUR BODY NEEDS FOR GOOD HEALTH

Fats. These are found in butter, margarine, cream, cheese, olive oil, vegetable and nut oil, cod liver oil, olives, avocados, egg yolk, poultry, canned fish (in oil), chocolate.

Starches. These are found in flour and grains of all kinds, dried peas, beans, rice, lentils, arrowroot, cornflour, tapioca, potato, sweet potato, Jerusalem artichoke, corn, okra, pumpkin, winter squash.

Sugar. This is found in sugar, honey, molasses, sorghum, maple sugar, maple syrup, corn syrup, jams and jellies, candies, sweet chocolate, beets.

Protein. This is found in milk, cheese, eggs, all grains and nuts, meat, poultry, fish, peas, beans, corn.

Calcium. This is found in milk, cheese, egg yolk, almonds, dried peas, beans, figs, dates, olives, green vegetables (leafy tops included), seafood (salt water fish).

Iron. This is found in fresh meats, liver, egg yolk, almonds, avocado, dates, prunes, raisins, peas, beans, lentils, green vegetables (including leafy tops).

Phosphorus. This is found in cheese, egg yolk, chocolate, peas, beans, meats, poultry, salt water fish, peanuts, walnuts, pecans, whole grain cereals.

Iodine. This is found in salt water fish, cod liver oil, iodized salt.

Copper, Manganese. These are found in oatmeal, whole wheat breads, almonds, dates, pecans, huckleberries, beans, peas, lentils, turnip tops.

PRINCIPAL REASONS FOR THESE ELEMENTS

Calcium. Builds strong teeth, bones, muscles, glands, nerves.

Fats. Cushion nerves and muscles, and provide body heat and energy.

Iodine. Needed for proper functioning of the thyroid gland.

Iron with Copper and Manganese. Makes good blood.

Phosphorus. Needed for bones, glands, muscles, nerves, teeth.

Proteins. Help make flesh and blood.

Starches and Sugars. Needed for body heat and energy.

Water. Regulates body temperature, aids digestion, carries off waste matter.

SUBSTITUTES

Meat Substitutes for a Balanced Diet. Sometimes, for religious reasons, meat may not be used, or is unavailable, or is too high priced to be included in the food budget. Here are some pointers on the subject worth remembering.

1 serving of beef equals:
   $\frac{1}{3}$ of the day's protein
   $\frac{1}{4}$ of the day's iron
   $\frac{1}{10}$ of the day's Riboflavin

Good substitutes for 1 serving of beef:
   2 cups milk and 1 cup whole grain cereal
   2 cups milk and 2 slices whole grain bread
   2 cups milk and 1$\frac{1}{2}$ tablespoons molasses
   1 cup milk and 1 egg
   1 cup milk and $\frac{1}{4}$ pound codfish
   2 cups milk and $\frac{1}{2}$ cup cooked peas or beans
   $\frac{1}{2}$ cup cottage cheese and $\frac{1}{2}$ cup green leafy vegetables
   $\frac{1}{2}$ cup cottage cheese, 2 slices whole grain bread and 6 halves of
      dried apricots
   1 egg, 2 tablespoons nuts and 1 cup whole grain cereal
   1 egg and 1 cup green leafy vegetables

Salt Free foods mean that no salt has been added in preparation. Salt should be eliminated only on medical advice.

Sugar Free prepared foods of any kind from soup to nuts are advised by physicians under certain conditions.

Sugar Substitutes. Be guided by your medical adviser in the use of sugar substitutes.

Fat Free meals mean that no fat of any kind is added in the cooking or baking of foods. Fried foods are generally eliminated completely. Read carefully contents of all prepared, packaged or canned foods.

VITAMINS AND CALORIES

Vitamins. These are chemical elements found in food. They have been isolated and given names. They fall into several basic groups and complexes. The specific vitamins, their uses and the foods in which they are found are listed below.

Calories. These are units of measurement of physical or heat energy derived from foods.

Caloric Requirements per Day. These are as follows:

> 3000 to 3500 for the average man
> 2500 for the average woman
> 3500 for a normally active, growing boy
> 1500 for a child of five

VITAMINS: SOURCES AND USES

Vitamin A. This is essential for good eyesight, teeth, bones, skin.

Sources: Various fish liver oils (the richest sources being halibut liver oil and cod liver oil), green and yellow leafy vegetables. Liver, glandular organs, animal tissues and egg yolks supply small amounts.

Vitamin B Complex. This is essential for good digestion, proper elimination, appetite, growth, energy, nerves, hearing and eyesight.

There are several substances in this group of vitamins, none of which should be used in concentrated form without a competent physician's direction.

Sources: Whole grain cereals, peas, beans, lentils, nuts, fruits, vegetables, lean meat, liver, fish roe, wheat germ, natural or brown rice and yeast.

Vitamin C. This is commonly called *Ascorbic Acid.* It helps the body manufacture that certain substance which holds the cells together. It is essential for building resistance to infection and shock; keeping blood vessels in good condition; preventing bones from becoming porous and fragile; keeping gums and teeth healthy. It is also essential for growth, reproduction and lactation.

Sources: Citrus fruits, tomatoes, potatoes and all fresh vegetables.

Vitamin D. This is referred to as the *Sunshine Vitamin.* The human body cannot get along without it. It affects all glandular functions. It helps the teeth and bones retain and distribute calcium. It helps the skin take oxygen into the body. It prevents rickets in children and bone troubles in adults. It also lengthens the life span.

VITAMINS AND CALORIES IN BASIC FOODS

Key: o indicates a complete lack
1 indicates a fair amount
2 indicates a good amount
3 indicates an excellent amount
4 indicates a super abundance
When referring to vitamin D, 3 indicates an
excellent source when irradiated.

Foods	Vitamin A	Vitamin B	Vitamin C	Vitamin D	Vitamin G	Approximate Calories (Average Serving)
Bread (1 slice)						
Wholemeal	1	2		1	1	100
Rye	1	3			2	100
White		1		1		50
Whole wheat	1	3	0–1	1	2	50
Bread Crumbs						
1 cup, dried	1	1				400
1 cup, soft	1	1				150
Water Biscuits	1	3			2	25
Dairy Products						
Butter, 1 tblsp.	3			1		100
Buttermilk, 1 cup	1	2	1		3	85
Cheese						
Cheddar, 1-inch cube	3				1	110
Cottage, 5 tblsp.	1				1	100
Soft Cream, 2 tblsp.	3				1	100
Double Cream (40% fat), 1 tblsp.	3	2	1		3	60
Single Cream (18½% fat), 1 tblsp.	3	2	1		3	30
Milk						
1 cup whole	3	2	1	1	3	170

VITAMINS AND CALORIES IN BASIC FOODS – *continued*

Foods	Vitamin A	Vitamin B	Vitamin C	Vitamin D	Vitamin G	Approximate Calories (Average Serving)
Dairy Products [Milk] (cont.)						
1 cup skim	2	2	1	1	2	90
¼ cup top	3	3	1	1	3	100
Condensed (sweetened), 1 tblsp.	3	3	1	3	3	65
Evaporated Milk, 1 tblsp.	3	2		3	3	25
Whole Egg	3	2		1	3	70
1 yolk	3	2		1	3	55
1 white					2	15
Fats						
Codliver oil	3			3		
Margarine, 1 tblsp.	1					100
Peanut Butter	1	2			1	
Vegetable Oils, 1 tblsp.	1					100
Vegetable Shortening, 1 tblsp.	1					100
Fish						
Fresh, cooked	1	1		1	1	85–125
Canned						
Salmon, ½ cup	1			1	2	100
Sardines, each	1			1	1	25
Tuna (with oil)	1			1	1	315
Tuna (without oil)				1		135
Fruits						
Apple	1	2	2		2	80
Apricots, dried	2		2		2	75
Apricots, canned, 2 halves	3	3	3			100
Avocado, ¼ medium	2	3	1		2	150
Banana	2	2	2		2	100
Berries, 1 cup	1	1	3			100

VITAMINS AND CALORIES IN BASIC FOODS – *continued*

Foods	Vitamin A	Vitamin B	Vitamin C	Vitamin D	Vitamin G	Approximate Calories (Average Serving)
Fruits (cont.)						
Cantaloupe, ¼ medium	2	2	3		2	25
Cherries, 20 average	2	1	2			100
Cranberries, uncooked, 1 cup	1		2			50
Grapefruit						
Halves	1	2	3		2	100
Juice, 1 cup	1	2	3		2	100
Grape Juice, ⅔ cup		1			0–1	100
Grapes						
Blue, bunch	1	1	1		1	100
Red, 25 – 30	1	1	1		1	100
Lemon, 1 large	1	2	3		2	33
Juice, ¼ cup	1	2	3		2	20
Orange, 1 large, or						
Juice, ¾ cup	1	2	3		2	100
Peach						
Fresh, 1 medium size	2	1–2	2		1–2	50
Canned, 2 halves and syrup	2	1	2		1	200
Pear						
Fresh, 1 medium		2	1		2	50
Canned, 3 halves and syrup		2	1		2	100
Pineapple, canned						
1 slice or ¼ cup crushed	1	2	2		1	100
Juice, ⅔ cup		2	2		1	100
Pineapple, fresh	1	2	2		1	50
Plum, 1 large, ripe	1	1	1			100
Rhubarb, 1 cup diced			1			20
Watermelon, 1 slice	1	1	3		1	100
Grains						
Cornmeal, cooked		1				100
Cornflour, 1 tblsp.		1				35

VITAMINS AND CALORIES IN BASIC FOODS—*continued*

Foods	Vitamin A	Vitamin B	Vitamin C	Vitamin D	Vitamin G	Approximate Calories (Average Serving)
Grains (cont.)						
Farina, cooked		1			2	300
Flour, white, 1 cup		2		1		400
Macaroni, Spaghetti, cooked, plain		2				100
Rice, brown, steamed	1	2			1	100
Rolled Oats, cooked, plain	1	2			1	100
Wheat Cereals						
Puffed	1	2			1	50
Shredded	2	2			2	100
Meats						
Beef	1	2	0–1		2	100
Chicken	1	1			1	100
Lamb	1	1			1	100
Liver, ¼ lb.	3	2	1		3	150
Sweetbreads, 1 pair	1	1				400
Veal	1	1			2	100
Vegetables						
Asparagus, fresh or canned	1		2			20
Beans						
Green	2	2	2		2	25
Dried	1	2			1	345
Lima, dried	1	2			1	275
Beets						
Boiled, plain	1	1	1		1	50
Tops	2	2			3	20
Broccoli	4	2	1		3	50
Brussels Sprouts	1	2	1		2	50
Cabbage						
Raw	2	2	3		2	10

VITAMINS AND CALORIES IN BASIC FOODS – *continued*

Foods	Vitamin A	Vitamin B	Vitamin C	Vitamin D	Vitamin G	Approximate Calories (Average Serving)
Vegetables (cont.)						
Cabbage						
Cooked	1	2	1		2	30
Carrots	3	2	2		2	30–40
Cauliflower	1	2	1		2	20
Celery, green	2	2				25
Chard, cooked	2	1–2				35
Corn, 1 ear	2	2			1	50
Canned	2	2			1	100
Cucumber	0–1	1	2		1	10
Eggplant						
Boiled, plain	1	1	1		2	15
Fried	1	1	1		2	50–60
Salad (oil)	1	1	1		2	75
Kale						
Boiled, plain	3	1	2		3	20
Kohlrabi, creamed		1	1			100
Lettuce, ¼ head						
Plain						12
With Dressing	2	2	2		2	100–150
Onions, cooked	0–1	1	1		1	50–60
Peppers, green, 1	2	2	3			20
Parsnips, plain	0–1	2				50–60
Peas, green, fresh	2	2	3		2	50
Potato, white, 1	1	2	2		1	100
Pumpkin, cooked	2	1	1		1	60–70
Spinach, cooked, plain	3	1	2		2	25
Squash, cooked, plain	2	1			1	30
Sweet potato, cooked, plain	3	2	2		1	200
Tomato	2	2	3		1	25
Turnips	0–1	1	2		1	25
Turnip Tops	3	2	3		2	35

VITAMINS AND CALORIES IN BASIC FOODS – *continued*

Foods	Vitamin A	Vitamin B	Vitamin C	Vitamin D	Vitamin G	Approximate Calories (Average Serving)
Sweets						
Chocolate Cake						200
Chocolate Éclair						250–400
Chocolate Malted Milk, 1 large glass						465
Corn Syrup, 1 tblsp.						75
Cranberry Sauce, ¼ cup						100
Custard, ½ cup						100
Honey, 1 tblsp.						75
Ice Cream, plain						200
Jelly, 1 tblsp.						60
Maple Syrup, 1 tblsp.						65
Molasses, 1 tblsp.						66
Sugar						
Granulated, 1 tblsp.						50
Brown, 1 tblsp.						33

Sources: Sunlight or artificial ultra-violet rays. Food sources are milk, cereals, fresh and canned fish, fish liver oils and concentrates, eggs.

Vitamin E. This is called the *Anti-Sterility* factor. It is the fat-soluble element widespread in foods and necessary for the human body's fertility.

Sources: Whole grain cereals, seeds, vegetable oils, egg yolk, green leafy vegetables, wheat germ and wheat germ oil.

Vitamin K. This is commonly known as the *Surgeon's Friend* because it is the anti-haemorrhage vitamin. It prevents excessive bleeding.

Sources: Tomatoes, cabbage, cauliflower and leafy vegetables like spinach, kale, etc.

Vitamin G (B_2). This is part of the B Complex group. It is also known as *Riboflavin* and is a sort of first aid to longevity. It keeps skin and hair in healthy condition, protects eyesight and promotes growth.

Sources: Milk, egg yolk, liver, some meats, yeast, green and leafy vegetables.

Vitamin B_6. Another in the B Complex group, this is called *Pyridoxine* and is essential in the prevention of pellagra.

Sources: Vegetable fats, cereal grains, peas, beans, lentils, yeast, meat and fish.

In addition to the above-mentioned vitamins, others are being isolated constantly.

CONSERVATION OF VITAMINS

Vitamins A and B can be destroyed by use of baking soda in the preparation of food, but they are not destroyed by boiling.

Vitamin C is lost by boiling or when exposed long to air, except in the case of white potatoes. These retain the maximum when baked in their jackets.

Vitamin G must not be combined with foods containing large amounts of baking soda.

SHOPPING GUIDE

All canned foods as well as quick frozen foods are plainly marked for weight of contents. Be sure to read carefully. In accordance with the *Pure Food and Drugs Act*, all packaged foods (including cereals, processed ready-to-eat breakfast foods, cake, scone, biscuit, popover, muffin mixes, etc.) carry a list of ingredients.

Kosher foods – prepared canned, bottled and packaged – generally bear the stamp of The London Beth Din, or of a recognized Rabbinate. Passover foods are labelled *Kosher for Passover*, or in Hebrew, *Kosher L'Pesach*.

CANS AND CONTENTS

Vegetables, Fruits

No. 1 can	1 lb.	2 cups	3–4 servings
No. 2 can	1¼ lb.	2½ cups	4–5 servings
No. 2½ can	1¾ lb.	3½ cups	4–7 servings

Juices

12½ fluid oz.	1½ cups
1 pt., 2 oz.	2¼ cups
1 pt., 4 oz.	2½ cups
1 pt., 8 oz.	3 cups
1 qt., 14 oz.	5¾ cups

QUANTITIES TO BUY

Vegetable	1 pound	Servings	Cooked	Uncooked
Asparagus	whole	2 or 3	1½ cups	
Beets	minus tops	2 or 3	2 cups, sliced	
Broccoli	untrimmed	3		
Brussels Sprouts	whole	4	3 cups	
Cabbage	trimmed	3 or 4		5 cups, shredded
Carrots	minus tops	3 or 4	3 cups	3½ cups, shredded
Cauliflower	trimmed	3 or 4	2 cups	3 cups, diced
Celery	trimmed	4		3 cups, diced
Cucumbers	whole	5 or 6		2½ cups, sliced
Eggplant		3 or 4	2 cups, diced	
Onions	red, yellow	6 or 7	2½ cups, diced or sliced	
Marrow		3		
Onions (in salads)	green	6		
Parsnips	unpared	3	2½ cups, diced	
Peas, fresh	in pods	2	1 cup, shelled	
Potatoes, white		3	2 cups, diced	
Potatoes, sweet		2 or 3	1½ cups mashed	
Spinach	fresh	3		
Green Beans	3 or 4	3½ cups		
Tomatoes	3			
Turnips		3	2 cups	3 cups, shredded
Zucchini		3 or 4		

Fruit
Apples, Bananas, Oranges, Tangerines – 1 per person.
Grapefruit – ½ per serving.
Pineapple, average size – serves 4.

Meat
Beef	*2 servings*
Chopped	¾ lb.
Roast or stew	1¼ lbs.
Steak	1 lb.

Lamb	
Chops	¾ to 1 lb.
Roast or stew	
Shoulder, unboned	2 to 2½ lbs.
Shoulder, boned	1 lb.
Shoulder steaks	1 to 1¼ lbs.

Veal	
Chops	2 to 4 shoulder chops
Breast, roast or stew	2 to 2½ lbs.
Steak, shoulder	1 lb.
Heart, beef or calf	1 lb.
Liver, beef or calf	¾ lb.
Lung, beef or calf	¾ lb.
Miltz, beef or calf	1 lb.

Poultry
Chicken, spring (broiler)	1½ lbs., dressed
Chicken, spring (frying size)	1½ lbs., dressed
Chicken, roasting	1 to 1½ lbs., dressed
Chicken, stewing	1 lb., dressed
Capons	1 lb., dressed
Goose	1½ lbs., dressed
Turkey	1½ lbs., dressed

Fish
Boned, Fillets	¾ lb.
Dressed, whole	
baking or grilling	1¼ to 1½ lbs.
Dressed, for boiling	1 lb.

3

Fish – continued
  Dressed, for Gefilte Fish $1\frac{1}{4}$ – $1\frac{3}{4}$ lbs.
  Smelts, frying or boiling   1 lb.

Cheese
  Dry or Pressed Cottage Cheese $\frac{3}{4}$ lb.
  Creamed Cottage Cheese $\frac{1}{2}$ lb.
  Cream Cheese for sandwiches $\frac{1}{4}$ lb.
  Cheddar type $\frac{1}{4}$ lb.
  Processed type $\frac{1}{4}$ to $\frac{1}{2}$ lb.

Milk
  Young children require approximately 1 to $1\frac{1}{2}$ pints per day, in
    some form.
  Teenagers $1\frac{1}{2}$ pints or more.
  Adults, approximately 1 pint per day.

Bread
  Depending on age, occupation and appetite, the average
    allowance per day is from 4 to 6 slices of regulation loaf.
  Rolls, muffins, popovers (see p. 136), biscuits – approximately 2
    per person per meal.

DEFINITIONS OF COOKING TERMS

Au Gratin: To bake with a topping of crumbs, butter and cheese.
Bake: To cook food by dry heat, usually in an oven.
Baste: To moisten baked or roasted foods with liquid or fat during
  the process of cooking.
Batter: A pourable mixture of flour and liquid, sometimes thick
  enough to drop from the spoon.
Beating: Mixing or combining with a brisk, even or rotary motion.
Blanching: Submerging or dipping in boiling water and then plung-
  ing into cold water.
Blend: To combine by stirring or mixing to a smooth consistency.
Boiling: Cooking in liquid at boiling temperature (212° F.).
Braising: Browning or searing food in fat before covering to cook
  slowly in its own or added juices or water.
Breading: Rolling in or covering with fine crumbs of crackers or
  bread.

Brewing: Extracting juice and flavour by addition of liquid and gently heating but not boiling.

Broiling: Cooking over or under direct heat. Same as grilling.

Brush: To spread a thin coating of milk, butter, egg or other liquid or semi-liquid over the top.

Chopping: Cutting into very small pieces with a knife or food chopper.

Coating Spoon: A consistency that forms a covering or film over a spoon.

Coddle: To cook slowly in liquid kept just below boiling point.

Combine: To mix or blend ingredients.

Cooking Till Firm: Preparing food by aid of heat until solidified and responsive to pressure of the finger. Or when a knife or toothpick inserted in the centre comes out clean of food particles.

Cooking Till Tender: Preparing food by any cooking method until a fork or toothpick can pierce it with slight pressure.

Creaming: Stirring or mixing to a smooth and creamy softness.

Cubing: Cutting into cubes.

Cutting In: Distributing a creamy mixture through a dry mixture by aid of a cutting motion with a knife, spatula or pastry blender.

Deep Frying: See *Frying.*

Dissolve: To blend together a liquid and solid substance.

Dotting: Scattering small bits over the surface.

Dough: A mixture of ingredients including flour and liquid, blended or kneaded smooth enough to form into desired shapes by rolling or patting.

Drain: To strain off all liquid.

Dredging: Coating with dry substances such as flour or crumbs.

Dressing: Poultry stuffing. Also preparing poultry for oven or pot cooking.

Dusting: Sprinkling lightly over the surface with dry, powdery ingredients such as sugar, spices or flour.

Einbren: German word meaning a thickening made of browned flour and melted shortening blended with liquid.

Evaporate: To heat until concentrated; usually in uncovered pot.

Eviscerate: To remove viscera from poultry, or other animals used for food.

Fleishig: Meat or its derivatives, or combinations containing same.

Flouring: Dusting or rolling in flour.

Folding In: To combine ingredients with a gentle stroke of spoon or fork downward through the mixture, along bottom of container then upwards and over till blended and air incorporated.

Frenching: Breaking up fibres of meat, steaks especially, by cutting, usually in a diagonal or crisscross pattern.

Frying: Cooking food in fat. *Deep frying* means cooking in deep, hot melted shortening till brown on all surfaces.

Garnish: To decorate for colour contrast and attractiveness.

Grating: Reducing to fine particles, usually with a grater.

Greasing: A light coating of shortening.

Grilling: Cooking over or under direct heat. Can be done over charcoal heat, wood or coal embers, gas or electric heat. (Foods to be grilled are placed in a special holder for the purpose.) Can also be done under gas or electric oven. Filled sandwiches are grilled in a Sandwich Toaster.

Grind: To cut into small particles or pulp with the aid of a food chopper.

Infusion: Result of steeping or brewing without boiling.

Julienne: To cut into thin, match-like strips.

Kashrut: Regulations regarding meats, poultry, etc.

Knead: To work into a smooth and elastic mass by pressure of the hand, using the heel of the thumb.

Marinate: To cover and soak in a mixture of oil and vinegar or lemon juice, or other combination as indicated.

Mashing: Reducing to a smooth pulp by beating or pressing.

Masking: Covering with mayonnaise or other dressing.

Melt: To heat until liquid and pourable.

Milchig: Milk derivatives. Foods containing no meat derivative.

Mince: To chop or cut up very fine.

Mixing: Combining ingredients until evenly distributed.

Paste: Combination of liquid and dry ingredients till smooth.

Pan Broil: To cook in an uncovered heated skillet or frying pan without fat, and pour off the fat as fast as it accumulates.

Parboiling: Cooking in boiling liquid until partially soft.

Pare: To remove outer covering with a knife.

Pareve: Neutral – neither meat nor milk nor derivatives thereof.

Peel: To strip off outer covering.

Pesachdig: Prepared for the week of Passover. Approved for Passover use and marked accordingly.

Pinch of: Salt, sugar or spices held between forefinger and thumb.

Planked: Cooked and served on a board made for the purpose.

Poaching: Cooking for a short time in shallow liquid kept at a temperature just below boiling.

Purée: To make a smooth, semi-soft consistency by pressing through a sieve, strainer or fruit press.

Roasting: Cooking without moisture in an uncovered pan in the oven. Or, pot-roasting by first searing then covering and cooking over a slow, steady heat.

Sautéing: Cooking till brown and tender in a small amount of fat in an uncovered pan.

Scalding: Bringing to a temperature just below the boiling point and removing from the heat or flame.

Scoring: Cutting narrow grooves or gashes in the outer surface.

Shredding: Cutting or tearing into thin pieces or strips, with the aid of a knife or a grater.

Simmer: To cook slowly in liquid below boiling point.

Singe: To subject to open flame for brief period.

Skewer: To hold together with thin pieces of wood or metal shaped for the purpose.

Steaming: Cooking in steam generated by boiling water.

Stewing: Cooking in a covered pot, with a small amount of liquid.

Stock: Liquid in which food has been cooked.

Whipping: Whipping with a brisk, rotary motion to incorporate air into a mixture of ingredients. Beating eggs, cream or combinations of both, usually with a fork or rotary beater.

4 *Kosher* Kitchen Questions and Answers (Rules for *Kashrut*)

Question: What is the meaning of *Kosher*?

Answer: The selection and preparation of foods for human consumption in accordance with traditional Jewish ritual (as in the slaughter of animals) and dietary laws.

Question: Who made the rules of *Kashrut*?

Answer: The rules for *Kashrut* came to us through the *Talmud* and the *Shulchan Aruch*.

Question: What animals may be used for food?

Answer: The flesh of quadrupeds that chew the cud and have cloven hoofs such as sheep, goats, deer, cattle.

Question: Can any of these 'permitted' animals become *unkosher*?

Answer: Yes. Animals of any kind, fowl included, not slaughtered in accordance with prescribed regulations would not be *Kosher*, but *treife*. Also, if the flesh of an animal or fowl permitted for consumption has been torn by wild beasts or otherwise mutilated; or if any organs of animals, on post-mortem examination, showed signs of disease or lesions, such would be declared not *Kosher*.

Question: Are all parts of ritually slaughtered animals *Kosher*?

Answer: No. Only the forequarters of permitted quadrupeds are acceptable for *Kosher* use.

Question: Is anyone permitted to slaughter animals for consumption?

Answer: No. An official called a *shochet* who is trained in the laws of *Kashrut* and animal anatomy is authorized.

Question: Is meat from animals or poultry slaughtered by a *shochet* all that is required to make food *Kosher*?

Answer: No. Meat or poultry purchased from a *Kosher* butcher must be *kashered* in the home before preparation for cooking because no blood is permitted in food.

Question: How is meat *kashered*?

Answer: Meat or poultry must be soaked in cold water, in a vessel set aside for that purpose, for a half hour. The meat then is rinsed and sprinkled evenly with coarse salt and placed on a perforated board so tilted as to permit blood to flow off. Salted meat must remain on board for one hour then be washed before cooking.

Question: Are there any exceptions or exemptions to this rule?

Answer: Yes. Meat used for broiling under or over an open fire or flame need not be salted. The broiling process permits free flow of blood from the meat thus prepared. Also, it is not required by laws of *Kashrut* that liver be soaked and salted. But liver must be prepared separately from other meat, only by the process of broiling. After broiling, liver may be used in any manner desired in recipes requiring further cooking.

Question: Does this apply to livers of poultry?

Answer: Yes.

Question: Are any other parts regulated by laws of *Kashrut*?

Answer: Yes. Hearts of animals or poultry must be cut open, veins removed and the blood permitted to flow before soaking and salting.

Question: Can all parts of poultry (such as feet) be used?

Answer: Yes. Poultry that is slaughtered by a *shochet* must be *kashered* by soaking and salting; the neck vein must be removed by cutting lengthwise along the neck between tendons exposing the vein. The claws and skin of feet must be removed.

Question: Are any and all birds regarded as *Kosher*?

Answer: No. Birds of prey and scavengers are forbidden.

Question: Are all kinds of fish and other seafood permitted?

Answer: No. Only fish that have scales and fins.

Question: Do fishes have to be *kashered* in any way?

Answer: No.

Question: Are there any other regulations for the *Kosher* kitchen?

Answer: Yes. Meats must not be cooked with milk or milk derivatives, or otherwise prepared for the table and served together. Utensils, crockery, china, cutlery, pots, pans, containers used for milk and meat dishes must be stored separately, washed separately in separate bowls, dried with separate dish cloths.

Question: Are Jews the only people who have such food laws and regulations?

Answer: No. Until the year 1000 C.E., Christians avoided blood and blood-filled meat.

Moslems do not eat the flesh of swine or carrion.

Buddhists have regulations adopted around the seventh century which forbid the use of all meats.

Vegetarians eat no animal foods.

Question: May fish and meat be eaten together?

Answer: Fish may be eaten with meat if it is not prepared with butter or milk derivatives, but should not be cooked together with meat or eaten from the same dish. Fish is considered *pareve*, neutral, and should be served before the meat course on *pareve* or *milchig* dishes which are kept separate from meat dishes.

Question: May eggs be used in either milk or meat combinations?

Answer: Yes. There is no prohibition against the use of eggs with either meat or milk foods. The only prohibition in connection with eggs is that the yolk of the egg be free of blood.

Note: If there are any further questions on Kashrut, rabbinical authority should be consulted.

5 Sabbath and Holiday Food Traditions and Recipes

Among Jews the world over, the seventh day of the week is the Sabbath, a day of devotions at synagogue and complete freedom from work. Sabbath begins at sundown on Friday and ends when the first star becomes visible Saturday evening.

No preparation of food is done on the Sabbath by observing Jews. Food is prepared on Friday, and such dishes as are to be served hot are kept ready to serve either in a Dutch oven over the pilot light of the gas stove, or over simmer heat turned to its lowest possible point. No lighting of fires of any kind is permitted. The extinguishing of fires or lights is also prohibited.

Recipes for traditional Sabbath dishes follow the food lore connected with these special foods. Also, because food traditions and customs cluster about the Sabbath day, we include those most characteristic.

First and foremost is the good old tradition of inviting an *orach* (Hebrew for guest) to share the Sabbath meals, partake of Sabbath hospitality, now, alas, not practised as often as it might be. 'For you were once strangers in the land of Egypt,' Exodus 22:20, is the biblical injunction which is the basis for this custom.

CHOLA, in twist form or biblical beehive coil, is the Sabbath loaf of white bread. It is customary to place two *cholas* under a special napkin or *chola deckel*, at the head of the table with the decanter of wine and the *Kiddush Cup* over which a blessing is recited. The two loaves are symbolic of the 'two portions of manna' which fell for the Sabbath in place of the single portion for other days of the week. The twist loaves are undoubtedly of comparatively recent origin, most probably with Jews in Germany. In some countries the twist loaf is decorated with a thin braid of the same dough placed lengthwise on top of the loaf. In other countries the decorative part may be short pencil-thin lengths of dough placed ladder-wise and perhaps symbolic of *Jacob's Ladder* which appeared in his dream.

The coiled beehive-shaped Sabbath loaf is reminiscent, in shape at least, of the *shew bread* (or show bread) mentioned in the Bible, which was used for the priestly blessing in the Temple.

Chola is made of white flour, enriched with eggs and a pinch of saffron added to the liquid used in mixing the yeast dough, to lend colour and fragrance. The twist loaves are tapered at each end and glazed with diluted egg yolk, sprinkled with poppy seed. At table a blessing in Hebrew is recited over the *chola* before cutting into the loaf, praising God for bringing forth bread from the earth.

GEFILTE FISH (literally stuffed fish in German) is the first course of the evening meal ushering in the Sabbath. This dish may have originated in Holland, which country welcomed the Jews after their expulsion from Spain in 1492. Or, it may be of Russian or Polish origin, where it was commonly referred to as 'Jewish fish' on hotel and restaurant menu cards. Jews from Rumania and other Balkan countries serve the whole fish with the filleted portion chopped and stuffed back between skin and backbone. In American Jewish families the filleted fish is chopped to a pulp and formed into balls.

Gefilte fish may have originated as an economy dish in any country. However, it is most delectable in any language and remains a traditional Sabbath and holiday dish.

CHOLENT, called *chulent* in some regions and *shalet* in others, is a meal-in-one sort of dish, unquestionably invented by some ingenious homemaker to meet the need for a hot meal on the days when cooking is prohibited. No data on the origin of this Sabbath and holiday dish is available, but it is implied in some writings of ancient times that as far back as the days of the Second Temple, food was kept hot in special vessels. No special name was given to such dishes.

A theory that the word *cholent* may have originated in France from the word *chaud* (meaning hot) is also current. Another theory is that the word may have had its origin in the two German words, *shule ende* (end of synagogue services), and was corrupted in sound to the current term, *cholent*.

Heinrich Heine, in his poem 'Princess Sabbath', refers to this succulent and tasty dish:

> 'Dearest, smoking is forbidden,
>   For today it is the Sabbath.
>
> 'But at noon, as compensation,
>   There shall steam for thee a dish
> That in very truth divine is –
>   Thou shalt eat today of Shalet!'

There are several varieties of *cholent*, depending on regional origin. It may be composed of very inexpensive ingredients, or be expanded to include as lavish items as an opulent budget permits. Whatever the contents of the *cholent pot*, it is the manner of preparation, the slow cooking or baking, that makes it as delectable a meal as the poet Heine described. It is to Jewish cuisine what roast beef and Yorkshire pudding is to English cookery.

KUGEL is another Sabbath and holiday delicacy that has become traditional. It is a pudding that may have got its name from the German *kugel* or ball, because of its shape which is generally round at the bottom. Or, it may have come from the Hebrew word *ke-igul*, meaning 'like a circle', round. Another theory is that *kugel* is traditional Sabbath and holiday food because its shape is like the mound of manna* which fell in time to provide nourishment for the Hebrews in their trek across the desert. Whatever the origin of the name, *kugel* is a pudding enriched with 'sugar and spice and everything nice', including raisins and almonds.†

TZIMMES, of which there are a number of varieties from carrots to prunes, is another Sabbath and holiday meal-in-one. It is particularly associated with *Rosh Hashana*, New Year's Day in the Hebrew calendar, because it is a sweet, succulent combination cooked slowly to a golden richness of colour and taste and symbolizes the wish for a 'sweet and happy New Year'.

Tzimmes, in the vernacular, has come to mean also 'making a fuss over' someone or something, in a purely favourable sense. To *make a tzimmes* over anyone or anything is to specially honour that person, place, thing or occasion.

SABBATH AND HOLIDAY RECIPES

CHOLENT (Basic Recipe)

2 large onions, sliced or diced | 2 tablespoons chicken fat, vegetable shortening or oil | ½ pound dried lima beans, soaked till tender in cold water | 8 to 10 medium potatoes, pared and cut in halves or quarters |

---

* Manna is known currently in countries of the Near East. It falls during June and July from the tamarisk tree and is regarded as a delicacy.

† Raisins and almonds, in Yiddish, *rozhinkes mit mandlen*, has become significant of sweetness and plenty as in the biblical and post-biblical reference to 'the land that floweth with milk and honey'.

CHOLENT (Basic Recipe)—continued

2 pounds beef (brisket, short ribs, chuck or shoulder cut) |
2 tablespoons flour | Salt, pepper, paprika to taste |
Boiling water to cover

Sauté onions in hot fat in the bottom of a heavy pot with a tight-fitting cover. When light brown, add the prepared beans and potatoes and tuck the meat into the centre. Mix flour and seasonings and sprinkle over top. Add boiling water to cover, adjust lid and cook over low heat from 3 to 4 hours. Lift lid to make sure no additional water is needed and then place the pot on an asbestos pad over the simmer flame of a gas stove. The flame should be as low as possible without danger of being extinguished if the cholent is to slow-cook overnight and the following morning, or till noontime. It will be hot enough to serve.

If you have a Dutch oven, the cholent may be placed in this for long, slow cooking over the simmer flame. Cholent should not be stirred with fork or spoon during the whole cooking process. The pot may be given an occasional shake or two before placing into the oven.

If cooking is done on a coal or wood stove where the oven retains heat during the night and following morning hours, the cholent may be placed in the oven after the first 3 or 4 hours of cooking on the back of the stove. If an accommodating baker's brick or tile oven is available, cooking cholent in it when the fires are left to die down during the Sabbath, brings the most desirable results.

Serves 6.

Variation 1: Add ½ cup large barley, rinsed and drained.

Variation 2: Omit potatoes. Increase beans to 1 pound and add 1 cup large barley, making it a Beans and Barley Cholent.

Variation 3: Add a large dumpling to basic recipe or above variations. This is called a *kneidle* and should be added just before placing the cholent on the simmer flame for overnight cooking. The kneidle is placed close to the meat in the centre of pot.

KNEIDLE FOR CHOLENT

1 cup flour | ½ teaspoon baking powder | ⅛ teaspoon salt /
Dash of pepper | ½ cup finely chopped beef suet or uncooked chicken fat/
1 tablespoon minced parsley | 3 tablespoons cold water

Sift together dry ingredients. Cut in suet or mix with a fork. Add parsley and water gradually to make a ball of dough or dumpling.

KASHA CHOLENT (Coarse Milled Buckwheat Groats)

*1½ to 2 pounds brisket of beef | 1 large onion, diced fine |
1 cup kidney beans | 1 cup groats | ½ teaspoon salt |
Dash of pepper | 4 cups boiling water*

Sear the meat in a preheated Dutch oven or heavy pot with tight-fitting cover. Add onion and stir till lightly browned. Add the other ingredients in the order named, cover and cook over moderate heat 1½ hours. Proceed as for Cholent, basic recipe, for serving hot on Sabbath day.
Serves 4 to 6.
Variation: Add 1 cup grated raw carrot and ¼ teaspoon paprika.

TZIMMES. There are several varieties of *tzimmes,* depending on the locale or country and its culinary customs. In Rumania and other Balkan countries it is customary to call a compote of dried fruits, cooked with honey or other sweetening, a *tzimmes,* and to regard a *tzimmes* of lima beans cooked with honey as customary holiday fare. Because *tzimmes* is a composite dish of meat, sweetening and vegetables, we are including recipes in this section, instead of under other categories.

CARROT TZIMMES

*5 large carrots | 5 medium white potatoes | 3 medium sweet potatoes |
2½ to 3 pounds beef brisket | 1 teaspoon salt |
½ cup sugar (more if desired) | Water | 1 small onion (optional) |
2 tablespoons flour browned with
2 tablespoons chicken fat or vegetable shortening*

Scrape and cut carrots into thin rounds or dice. Pare and cut white potatoes into quarters. Pare and cut sweet potatoes into 1-inch thick rounds. Sear the brisket of beef in pot to be used for cooking, turning frequently until evenly browned. Add the vegetables, salt and sugar. Water to cover about 1 inch over all should be added as frequently as required during the cooking process until the meat is tender enough to pierce with a fork. Cook over low heat after bringing to a bubble boil. Cooking time required is from 2½ to 3 hours. Do not stir contents of pot. To prevent possible sticking, shake the pot occasionally.

If an onion is used for additional flavour, it should be left whole, with 1 or 2 cuts at the root end to permit the flow of juice, and removed before it becomes too mushy. Honey may be substituted for sugar.

When the liquid has been reduced by half, turn into a baking pan or casserole. Add an *einbren* or thickening, made by lightly browning flour in hot melted shortening and stirring in some of the liquid from the tzimmes. Shake the casserole to distribute the thickening. Then bake in oven for 30 minutes at 350° F. or gas mark 4, or till brown on top.

Serves 6.

CARROT TZIMMES (Pressure Cooker Method)

Use the above-listed ingredients and directions for preparation. Sear the brisket of beef in the bottom of the pressure cooker, turning frequently until evenly browned. Add the vegetables, salt and sugar, and 1½ cups of cold water. Adjust cover and gauge for 15 pounds pressure. After turning down heat as per instructions for your type of cooker, cook 30 minutes.

Cool under running cold water before removing gauge and lifting cover. Brown flour in hot fat and stir in some of the liquid from the tzimmes to make an *einbren* (see p. 35) or thickening. Return the thickening to the tzimmes and shake the pot to prevent breaking up of vegetable sections and distribute the thickening. Turn into a baking pan and slip under the grill to brown for a few minutes before serving time.

TZIMMES KNEIDLE (Dumpling)

1 *cup flour* | ½ *teaspoon baking powder* |
⅛ *teaspoon salt* | 1 *tablespoon sugar* |
½ *cup chopped beef suet or uncooked chicken fat* |
1 *tablespoon minced parsley (optional)* | 3 *tablespoons cold water*

Sift together dry ingredients. Cut in suet and add water to form a ball of dough. If parsley is used, add before stirring in water. Tuck the dumpling into the centre of tzimmes, close to the meat. If using the *Pressure Cooker Method*, add dumpling to the other ingredients. If cooking is done on top of stove, add dumpling 45 minutes before removing to casserole for baking or browning, and cover the pot during that time to permit dumpling to expand.

Variation 1: Pat dough on a floured board to ½-inch thickness. Cut into squares or rounds. Add as in basic recipe.

Variation 2: For a meatless tzimmes, substitute vegetable shortening, salad oil or butter, and add a dash of nutmeg or cinnamon. Omit parsley.

TZIMMES OF CARROTS (Meatless)

2 pounds carrots, scraped and sliced ¼ inch thick | Cold water to cover |
½ teaspoon salt | ¾ cup honey, syrup or 1 cup sugar |
1 tablespoon lemon juice | 3 tablespoons butter or substitute |
3 tablespoons flour

Cook sliced carrots in water 8 to 10 minutes or till tender enough to pierce with a toothpick. Add salt, honey, lemon juice. Let simmer gently for 20 minutes or until liquid has been reduced to come half way up side of pot. Brown flour in hot melted butter and add, shaking pot to distribute evenly. Cook 5 minutes longer.

Serves 6.

Variation 1: Turn into a shallow casserole and slip under grill to brown lightly before serving.

Variation 2: Tuck a kneidle into carrots just before adding seasonings and sweetening. Cover and let cook as in basic recipe. Brown as in Variation 1.

LIMA BEAN TZIMMES (Balkan Style)

1 pound dried lima beans or baby limas | 2 cups cold water |
1 teaspoon salt | 1 cup honey or syrup | 3 tablespoons butter or substitute

Soak dried beans 3 hours in cold water to cover. Drain and add the other ingredients. Cook in *Pressure Cooker* under 10 pounds pressure for 1 hour. Let cold running water over pot reduce pressure before removing gauge and cover.

Serves 4 to 6.

Variation: Add 2 pounds brisket of beef or sectioned fowl to the above list of ingredients and omit the butter. Braise brisket till lightly browned before adding beans and other ingredients. If poultry is used dredge each piece with flour, then add the ingredients listed. Cook as directed in basic recipe.

TZIMMES OF DRIED FRUITS (Balkan Style)

½ pound each medium prunes, dried apricots, peaches, pears, seeded raisins | 1 cup long grain rice (brown rice may be used) | ½ cup honey | ½ teaspoon salt | ¼ teaspoon cinnamon | 1 quart boiling water

Rinse dried fruits and drain well. Use a colander for best results under running hot water. Combine with rice and add the other ingredients in the order listed. Cook over moderate heat, preferably on an asbestos pad, covered for the first 5 minutes or until it reaches boiling point. Reduce heat to a slow simmer for the next 15 to 20 minutes or until rice is tender and the liquid in the pot almost entirely absorbed. Shake the pot occasionally to prevent sticking, or add a little boiling water if necessary. Serve hot or cold.
Serves 6.

Variation 1: Turn into a casserole, dot with butter and brown lightly under grill just before serving. This dish may be served cold.

Variation 2: Lightly brown 2 tablespoons flour in 2 tablespoons butter and add after turning into casserole. This adds a customary tzimmes thickening and many more calories.

VARIETIES OF PRUNE TZIMMES

PRUNE AND FARFEL TZIMMES

1½ pounds brisket of beef | Cold water to cover | 1 onion | 1 cup farfel (egg barley, packaged) | ½ pound large prunes | 1 teaspoon salt | ½ teaspoon cinnamon | Dash of allspice or nutmeg | Grated rind of 1 lemon | 1 tablespoon lemon juice | ⅓ cup honey or ½ cup sugar

Preheat a heavy pot and braise the brisket on all sides till nicely

Roast Chicken
and
Carrot Tzimmes
(*page 47*)
with Kneidlach
(*page 65*)

browned. No other fat is required. Cut meat into serving portions if desired. Cover meat with cold water, add onion that has been cut into at root to permit flow of juice, cover and bring to a boil. Skim carefully. Cook uncovered for 15 to 20 minutes or till onion is tender. Lift out onion if desired. Add farfel gradually, stirring carefully to prevent lumps. Add more water at this point if necessary so that liquid covers the ingredients.

Reduce heat and simmer 30 minutes with pot lid adjusted. Uncover. Add washed and drained prunes and all the other ingredients in the order listed. Shake pot gently but do not stir contents. Cover and let simmer 1 hour or until the prunes are puffed. Should more liquid be required, use only boiling water added at one side of the pot. Turn into a baking pan or casserole, arranging the meat cuts near the top. The prunes will be well distributed in the process. Bake at 350° F. or gas mark 4 for 15 to 20 minutes or until nicely browned on top.

Serves 4.

PRUNE AND FARFEL TZIMMES
(Pressure Cooker Method)

Braise the meat in the preheated pressure cooker pot, adding finely diced onion. When the meat and onion are lightly browned, add 1½ cups cold water first, then all the listed ingredients. Turn off heat. Shake the pot gently to distribute contents. Adjust cover and gauge to 15 pounds pressure and relight gas burner. Cook 45 minutes after turning down heat as prescribed for pressure cooking. Cool pressure pot under cold running water and remove gauge to permit steam to escape before uncovering. Turn into a casserole and brown lightly under grill just before serving.

PRUNE AND FARFEL TZIMMES (Meatless or Milchig)

*½ pound prunes, washed and rinsed | 1 cup farfel |
3 cups boiling water | 1 teaspoon salt | ½ teaspoon cinnamon |
Grated rind and juice of 1 lemon | ½ cup honey or ¾ cup sugar |
½ cup butter, oil or vegetable shortening*

Soak prunes in cold water to cover for 30 minutes. Turn prunes and liquid into cooking pot for top of stove cooking, or into a casserole

4

for oven baking. Add farfel, then boiling water and the other ingredients as listed. Cook, partly covered, over moderate heat for 30 minutes. Turn into casserole and brown under grill just before serving. Or, bake in covered casserole 45 minutes at 350° F. or gas mark 4. Remove cover and brown under grill. Should added liquid be necessary at any stage of the procedure, add only boiling water and as little as necessary to prevent scorching.

Served 4.

Pressure Cooker Method: Prunes need not be soaked. Reduce water to 1½ cups. Cook 15 minutes under 10 pounds pressure.

PRUNE AND POTATO TZIMMES

2 pounds brisket of beef | 1 onion, diced | 1½ pounds potatoes |
1 pound prunes, rinsed and drained | Cold water to cover |
½ teaspoon salt | ½ teaspoon cinnamon or a dash of nutmeg |
½ cup honey, syrup or brown sugar |
2 tablespoons hot melted shortening (preferably chicken fat) |
2 tablespoons flour

Sear meat and onions together till lightly browned in the pot to be used. If small potatoes are used, pare, rinse and add whole. If large or medium potatoes are to be used, cut into quarters or small pieces. Add potatoes and prunes. Add cold water to cover and cook over moderate heat, uncovered, 45 minutes. Add seasoning and sweetening and continue to cook over low heat, at a mild simmer, with cover adjusted to permit escape of steam. Cook from 45 minutes to 1 hour longer.

This may require the addition of small amounts of boiling water to prevent scorching. Add liquid at side of contents of pot and shake the pot gently to distribute. This must not be a soupy mixture. Just before serving, lightly brown flour in hot melted shortening and add, again shaking pot to distribute evenly. Serve without garnish as a main dish or accompaniment to poultry which has been boiled (lifted from soup), baked or grilled.

Serves 4 to 6.

Pressure Cooker Method: May be used as for Prune and Farfel Tzimmes.

Variation 1: Substitute equal amounts of sweet potatoes and white potatoes to equal 2 pounds. Same procedure as Prune and Potato Tzimmes.

Variation 2: For meatless or milchig tzimmes, follow directions given for Prune and Farfel Tzimmes, omitting meat and substituting butter or vegetable shortening.

PRUNE AND RICE TZIMMES (Without Sweetening)

2 *pounds brisket of beef* | ½ *pound large prunes, rinsed and drained* |
1 *cup rice, converted or brown* | 1 *teaspoon salt* |
¼ *teaspoon cinnamon* | 1 *teaspoon grated rind of lemon* |
2 *tablespoons lemon juice*

Braise the meat in a preheated heavy pot. When nicely browned on all sides, add the ingredients in the order listed and cover with cold water. Cover and cook 30 minutes over moderate heat. Uncover and add boiling water if necessary to prevent sticking, a little at a time, shaking the pot to distribute. Continue cooking over low heat 1 hour or till meat is tender. Turn into a casserole and brown under grill before serving.

Serves 4.

Variation 1: For milchig Prune and Rice Tzimmes (without meat or meat derivatives), omit beef but cook prunes and rice in 1 quart boiling water, adding the other ingredients as soon as it comes to a brisk boil. Turn down heat to simmering point, add ½ cup butter or vegetable shortening, and cook only till rice is tender, approximately 30 minutes.

Variation 2: To make either basic recipe or variation into a sweet tzimmes, add ½ cup honey just before reducing heat.

OTHER SABBATH AND HOLIDAY FAVOURITE DISHES

Recipes for other dishes characteristic of Sabbath and Holiday fare will be found in their respective categories listed in the Index. Some of these are:

Chola	Chopped Liver
Gefilte Fish	Nahit
Pickled Fish	Pitcha (Calf's Foot, Jellied)
Herring, Chopped, Pickled	Strudel and Other Pastries
Shabbos Kugel	

6 Preparations and Recipes for Passover

PASSOVER (PESACH)

Passover or *Pesach*, in modern times, has been referred to as the 'first general strike in recorded history' and the 'first organized flight for freedom from slavery'. During the *Seder* service, contained in the *Haggada*, the story of the 'Exodus' is told and embellished with chants and folk-lore in which all participate, especially the children. The story is essentially a combination of spiritual development, agricultural customs and Jewish history during the time of Pharaoh (the biblical generic title for Egyptian kings of whom there were eleven).

Because Passover is essentially a family celebration in the home, elaborate customs have developed in preparation for the week of festival. The house is cleansed of all *chometz* (leaven) for no leavening agents, except eggs, are used in the preparation of Passover food. Prior to the *First Seder* a 'search for remaining bits of leaven' is customary. This quaint ceremonial consists of gathering up a few crumbs with a brush or goose wing, by candlelight, and casting the crumbs into the fire.

The table is specially prepared for the *Seder* and resplendent with snowy cloth, silverware and candles. At the head of the table, where the person officiating (usually the head of the family) presides, a special plate is placed which holds the *Seder symbols*, explained during the service according to ritual and tradition.

During the service the youngest child of the family participates by asking the 'four questions'. Answers to these, explaining the significance of the *Seder* service and its symbolism, are chanted. Passover is the feast of freedom; and the reading of the *Haggada*, the songs and chants replete with allegory and folk-tale, the questions and answers have all been specially devised to make it a festival for the children. And thus the story of a momentous event in the history of the Jewish people is handed down from generation to generation.

PASSOVER FOODS

During the eight days of Passover meals vary from those of the rest of the year. The same foods are used with these exceptions: all leaven is omitted; dried beans and peas, legumes and grains may not be used; baking powder, baking soda and yeast are not permitted. The customary flour for baking and cooking is replaced by *matzo meal*, potato flour and *matzo meal cake flour* (finely ground *matzo meal*).

All other foods may be used in the same manner as at any other time of the year. Therefore, recipes for meats, poultry, fish, etc., will be found under their proper headings rather than in the *Passover* section. As long as a recipe does not contain any of the prohibited foods, it may be used for Passover. The special *Passover* section does, however, include recipes for mead, beets and black radish preserves, *schmaltz*, beet sour (*beet rossel*) and other foods which are generally prepared in advance of Passover.

In some families it is customary to limit the menus to *fleishig* and *pareve* foods during Passover week in order to eliminate a double set of dishes and kitchen utensils used exclusively for *Pesach*. Various packaged foods, canned goods and sweetmeats, as well as dairy products, are available and labelled *Kosher L'Pesach* (for Passover use). Wines, whisky and soda water for Passover are also marked in the same manner.

Meats, poultry, fish, fresh fruits and vegetables are used extensively for Passover meals. These meals are further enhanced by specially prepared and packaged dried fruits, shredded coconut, almonds and other nuts. Salad oils as well as vegetable shortening are also available for Passover use. Rendered goose fat (*schmaltz*) has been the favourite shortening for centuries. *Schmaltz* of goose fat and chicken fat is usually prepared and stored for Passover use long in advance of the holiday in modern Jewish homes.

The Passover menus are only slightly varied because of the above traditional prohibitions. Specimen menus and substitutes are suggested in the following pages. However, as in all meal planning, individual nutritional needs, tastes, preferences and prejudices must be taken into consideration. With a little ingenuity the cook should have no difficulties in serving well-balanced, nutritious and attractive meals during Passover.

PASSOVER MENUS

Suggested Seder Menus	*Substitutes*

SEDER MENU 1

Gefilte Fish on Lettuce with Beet Coloured Horse-radish	
Chopped-Liver-filled Celery	Chopped Liver
Chicken Soup with Kneidlach mit Neshomes	Chicken Soup with Fluffy Kneidlach
Roast Chicken with Matzo-Prune Dressing, Giblet Gravy	Roast Turkey or Goose with Matzo Farfel Dressing
Asparagus Tips	Carrot Tzimmes
Orange and Grapefruit Salad	Cranberry and Orange Salad
Sponge Cake	Coconut Macaroons
Tea or Black Coffee	

SEDER MENU 2

Gefilte Fish	
Chicken Soup with Egg Noodles	Chicken Soup with Mandlen
Roast Chicken, Matzo-Fruit Dressing, Giblet Gravy	
Red Sea Salad (see p. 92)	Chariot Salad (see p. 92)
Apple Snow	Chremzlach (see p. 73)
Passover Nut Cake	
Tea or Black Coffee	

SEDER MENU 3

Gefilte Fish	
Roast Turkey, Mashed Potato Dressing	Turkey with Sweet Potatoes, Giblet Gravy
Celery, Pickled Beets, Carrot Sticks	Pickled Beets
Tomato and Green Pepper Salad	Waldorf Salad (see p. 333), Ginger Fingers
Prune Whip on Sponge Cake Rounds	
Tea, Black Coffee or Mead	

Suggested Seder Menus	*Substitutes*
SEDER MENU 4	
Gefilte Fish	
Chopped Liver Balls on Lettuce Nests	Chopped Liver in Green Pepper Rings
Chicken Soup, Kneidlach	
Roast Chicken Sections, Gravy	Roast Goose, Matzo Meal Dressing with Prunes
Browned New Potatoes	
Cauliflower, Parsley	Broccoli with Lemon Sauce
Tossed Mixed Green Salad	Cranberry and Orange Salad
Almond Macaroons, Stewed Rhubarb	Sponge Cake
Tea or Black Coffee	Wine, Mead, or Black Coffee
SEDER MENU 5	
Gefilte Fish	
Horse-radish	Hollandaise Sauce or Lemon Wedges
Clear Chicken Soup	
Matzo Meal Kneidlach	Passover Noodles
Grilled, Roasted or Stewed Chicken	
Carrots in Lemon Sauce or Carrot Tzimmes	Asparagus or Cauliflower
Mixed Green Salad	Tomato and Cucumber Salad
Matzo Meal Muffins	Plain or Whole Wheat Matzos
Beet Preserves	Orange Marmalade
Stewed Rhubarb	Compote of Prunes and Apricots
Passover Mandelbrodt	Passover Sponge Cake
Tea or Black Coffee	
BREAKFAST MENU 1	
Orange Juice	Canned Fruit (any kind)
Boiled, Poached or Fried Eggs	Scrambled Eggs
Matzo or Matzo Meal Muffins	Matzo
Butter or Preserves	
Coffee, Tea, or Milk	

Suggested Seder Menus	*Substitutes*
BREAKFAST MENU 2	
Orange or Grapefruit Halves	Stewed Apple Slices
Matzo Brie (fried)	Matzo Meal Pancakes
Coffee, Tea, or Milk	
BREAKFAST MENU 3	
Sliced Bananas with Milk	Strawberries with Milk or Sour Cream
Matzo or Matzo Meal Muffins	
Cottage Cheese	
Coffee, Tea, or Milk	
BREAKFAST MENU 4	
Stewed Prunes or Apricots	Raisins with Matzo Crumbles and Milk
Fried Matzo or Matzo Pancakes	Boiled Eggs
Honey	
Coffee, Tea, or Milk	
LUNCHEON MENU 1	
Fruit Cup	Grapefruit Half
Baked, Grilled or Fried Fish	Cottage Cheese and Fruit Salad
Pickled Beets	
Matzo Meal Muffins	Matzo Meal Pancakes
Coffee, Tea, or Milk	
Macaroons	Sponge Cake
LUNCHEON MENU 2	
Fruit Juice	Spinach Borsht with Sour Cream
Cottage Cheese and Nuts with Sour Cream Dressing	Scalloped Potatoes or Parsley Omelet
Tossed Green Salad	Tomato and Cucumber Salad
Coffee, Tea, or Milk	
Cake	Farfel Balls

Suggested Seder Menus	Substitutes
LUNCHEON MENU 3	
Orange Slices	Fruit Juice (any kind)
Chicken Salad in Lettuce Cups	Flaked Leftover Fish and Celery Salad
Matzo Pancakes	Matzo
Beet Preserves	Sliced Tomatoes
Black Coffee or Tea	Coffee, Tea, or Milk
Coconut Kisses	Nut Biscuits

LUNCHEON MENU 4	
Beet Borsht with Sour Cream	Clear Chicken Soup with Matzo Farfel
Boiled Potato	
Cheese filled Tomato Cups	Chicken Salad, Celery
Matzo Meal Muffins	Matzo
Coffee, Tea, or Milk	Black Coffee or Tea
Sponge Cake	Nut Cake

DINNER MENU 1	
Clear Beef Broth with Matzo Kneidlach	Matzo Farfel (egg coated)
Meat Filled Zucchini, Fresh Tomato Sauce	Boiled Beef with Horse-radish Sauce
Grated Potato Kugelach	Matzo Meal Muffins
Salad of Shredded Cabbage and Carrots on Greens	Raw Cauliflower Salad
Coconut Macaroons	Nut Cake with Stewed Rhubarb
Black Coffee or Tea	

DINNER MENU 2	
Vegetable Soup	Cream of Asparagus Soup
Stuffed Lamb or Veal Breast (Matzo Stuffing)	Cottage Cheese and Sour Cream Matzo Muffins
Harvard Beets (see p. 281)	Tomato and Lettuce Salad or Diced Tomato and Cucumbers
Tossed Green Salad	
Applesauce	Compote of Prunes and Raisins
Black Coffee or Tea	Coffee, Tea, or Milk

Suggested Seder Menus	Substitutes
DINNER MENU 3	
Chicken Soup with Fried Matzo Balls	Spinach Borsht with Sour Cream and Boiled Potato
Browned Chicken with Gravy	Cottage Cheese, Shredded Carrot and Green Pepper Salad (with greens)
Asparagus Tips, Boiled Carrots	
Cabbage and Apple Slaw	
Pinwheel Salad (Orange and Grapefruit)	Matzo Meal Muffins and Marmalade (or butter)
Almond Biscuits	Sponge Cake
Black Coffee or Tea	Coffee, Tea, or Milk
DINNER MENU 4	
Beet Borsht (meat) with Boiled Potato	Cream of Potato Soup
Pot Roast of Beef with Gravy	Grilled Salmon with Lemon Sauce
Grated Potato Pancakes	Broccoli, Asparagus or Beets
Green Salad	Cabbage and Apple Slaw
Apple and Cranberry Compote	Matzo Meal Muffins
Black Coffee or Tea	Stewed Dried Apricots
DINNER MENU 5	
Chicken Soup, Matzo Farfel or Passover Noodles	Meatless Beet Borsht with Diced Cucumber and Parsley
Roast Chicken, Matzo and Prune Dressing	Plaice Fillets (grilled or fried) with Lemon Wedges
Carrot Tzimmes	
Uncooked Cranberry and Orange Salad	Salad
	Matzo Farfel and Prune Pudding with Orange Sauce
Black Coffee or Tea	Coffee, Tea, or Milk

PASSOVER RECIPES

RENDERING CHICKEN OR GOOSE FAT (Schmaltz)

Cut fatty skin and other fat clusters into small pieces. Cover with cold water and cook in a heavy pot or frying pan, uncovered until the water has almost entirely evaporated. Reduce heat and add diced onions, allowing one onion to each cupful of fat. A clove of garlic adds flavour. Also, when rendering a large quantity of fat, the addition of a few slices of raw potato will help clarify the fat. The fat is done when the onion is nicely browned, also the potato, and the cracklings are dry and crisp. Let cool slightly before straining to separate cracklings from clarified schmaltz.

Cracklings are called *greben* or *grebenes* and make excellent additions to mashed potatoes. *Grebenes* also enhance chopped liver dishes. Use some finely chopped cracklings for fillings in Kneidlach mit Neshomes, Mashed Potato Croquettes, and Poultry Stuffings. Cracklings have been called 'Jewish Popcorn'. To store for Passover use, separate from rendered schmaltz and cover with $\frac{1}{4}$-inch layer of melted rendered fat in glass jars, jelly glasses or glazed stoneware. Cover with muslin when cold, then adjust covers. Store in cool place till wanted for use.

PASSOVER BEET PRESERVES

3 pounds beets | 1 pound honey | 1 pound sugar |
2 tablespoons ground ginger | $\frac{1}{2}$ pound blanched, chopped almonds

Cook beets in cold water to cover. When tender, slip skins and cut into thin strips or dice. Bring honey, sugar and ginger to a quick boil in a deep pot and add beets. Turn down heat and cook till the syrup is thick, approximately 30 minutes. Do not stir during cooking but shake the pot gently to prevent scorching or sticking. Stir in chopped or slivered almonds and turn into jelly glasses or a stoneware crock. Store away from light to prevent discoloration.

BLACK RADISH PRESERVES (Russian Style)

3 pounds medium size black radishes | Water | 1 pound honey |
1 pound sugar | 1 cup slivered almonds | 3 tablespoons ground ginger

Scrub radishes, pare and cut into strips like Julienne potatoes. Cover with cold water, bring to a boil and cook 10 minutes. Drain, and cover with fresh cold water, bring to a boil, cook 10 minutes, and drain well. Add honey and sugar while hot and shake the pot to distribute

well. Cook over very low heat the first 10 minutes or till honey and
sugar are dissolved, then turn up the heat slightly and continue
cooking till all the syrup is absorbed and the mass is a heavy preserve
consistency and a rich golden brown. Stir in the slivered almonds
with a fork and add the ginger, a little at a time, while stirring.
Turn into jelly glasses or store in a stoneware crock till wanted.

BEET SOUR (Rossel)

Remove tops and scrub beets thoroughly. Cut in halves or quarters
and place in an earthenware pickling jar that has a cover. Fill the jar
with boiled water, cooled to lukewarm, at least two inches above the
beets. Let stand covered in a warm place from three to four weeks to
form soured beet juice for Passover borsht.

MEATLESS ROSSEL BORSHT

Use 1 cup of beet rossel for each portion to be served. Season with
salt, lemon juice, sugar and onion cut or whole. Boil 10 minutes or
until onion is tender. Strain and serve with beaten egg yolk or sour
cream as a thickening. Garnish with minced parsley, cucumber
diced or chopped, chopped hard cooked egg. Add a medium plain
boiled potato to each serving. Caution: Do not reheat after adding
egg yolk or sour cream.
   Variation 1: Add a dash of ginger for a change.
   Variation 2: Serve ice cold with a hot boiled potato and parsley.

MEAT ROSSEL BORSHT

*1½ pounds brisket of beef | 4 cups cold water | 1 onion | 2 bay leaves |
3 cups beet sour (rossel) | Salt and pepper to taste | Lemon juice (optional) |
Sugar to taste | 6 egg yolks*

Cook the meat, onion, bay leaves, in water at a slow boil until meat
is tender when pierced with a fork. Add the other ingredients, except
egg yolks, and boil 15 minutes longer. Serve hot with 1 beaten egg
yolk per serving (depending on taste), for thickening, and garnish
with parsley, sliced hard cooked egg and plain boiled potato.
   Serves 6.

Variation: The beets from the rossel may be chopped or diced and used with the Soup Meat Recipe, allowing more water and beet sour for the listed ingredients.

ROSSEL BORSHT WITH MEATBALLS

FOR THE SOUP

2 cups diced boiled fresh beets or 3 cups rossel beets |
2 cups boiled water | Lemon juice, salt and sugar to taste

FOR THE MEATBALLS

1½ pounds chopped beef | 1 egg | 1 grated onion |
1 tablespoon water | Salt to taste

Combine the ingredients for soup and boil for 30 minutes. Combine chopped meat with egg, onion, water and salt. Form into balls the size of walnuts and drop into the gently boiling soup. Cook for 1 hour. Serve hot, allowing 2 or 3 meatballs per portion. Garnish with minced parsley or celery leaves.

Serves 6.

Variation: Brown meatballs in a little shortening and add to the soup 5 minutes before serving.

Note

Consult Index for other borsht recipes made of fresh vegetables or fruit.

Borsht for Passover is available in glass jars and is marked accordingly.

CHAROSET (For the Seder Table)

½ cup almonds | ¼ cup walnuts | 1 tablespoon sugar |
1 cup grated apple | ¼ teaspoon cinnamon

Chop all together or run through food chopper. Add enough wine to combine into a paste.

MATZO BRIE OR FRIED MATZO

2 eggs | ½ cup liquid (milk or water) | ¼ teaspoon salt |
Dash of cinnamon | 2 matzos | 3 tablespoons shortening

Beat eggs, add liquid, salt and seasoning, and break the matzo into
this mixture. Stir well and turn into melted fat in a well-heated
frying pan. Cover. Cook over moderate heat about 10 minutes or till
browned on under side. Turn and brown, uncovered, for about 3
minutes. Serve hot, plain or with a sprinkling of sugar and cinnamon, applesauce or honey.
Serves 2.

ZWIEBEL OR ONION MATZO

Rub the cut side of an onion over matzo. Sprinkle with salt and a
little melted chicken or goose fat or butter, and brown in a hot oven
for 3 to 5 minutes. Or slip under grill to brown.

MATZO SCRAMBLES

2 eggs | 2 tablespoons cold water | ¼ teaspoon salt | 2 matzos |
1 onion, finely sliced or diced | 2 tablespoons shortening

Beat eggs till light and creamy. Add water and salt and stir. Break
matzos into small pieces and stir into the mixture. Let stand 15
minutes during which time lightly brown onion in shortening. Add
the mixture and cover. Cook over moderate heat, stirring once or
twice to break the mass into scrambles. Cooking time required varies
with the degree of brownness desired.
Serves from 2 to 3, as an accessory to a meal. Serves 4 to 5 when
used as addition to soup.
Variation 1: Omit browned onion. When scrambles are done,
sprinkle with sugar or sugar-and-cinnamon. Makes a good
breakfast or luncheon dish.
Variation 2: Use milk and fry in butter. Serve with cheese and
sour cream. Season as in basic recipe or as in Variation 1.

MATZO EIRKUCHEN

¼ cup matzo meal | ½ cup water | ½ teaspoon salt |
4 eggs | 2 tablespoons shortening

Pour water on matzo meal and stir in salt. Let stand while beating egg yolks lightly. Combine by stirring. Beat egg whites and fold in. Melt shortening in the frying pan to be used and pour half in the mixture, stirring to combine. Drop mixture from a tablespoon on to frying pan and fry like pancakes. Turn to brown on under side. Serve with preserves or marmalade.

Serves 2 or 3.

GARNISHES FOR SOUP

PASSOVER FARFEL FOR SOUP

1½ cups matzo farfel (package product) | 3 eggs |
½ teaspoon salt

Spread the farfel on a shallow baking dish or sheet and heat in oven till nicely browned, stirring to prevent scorching. Cool. Beat eggs and salt till light. Add farfel. Mix till evenly coated and return to hot oven to dry slightly on same baking pan. The farfel should be separate bits, well coated with egg mixture.

Serves 4.

Variation 1: Add ½ cup lukewarm water to dried farfel before mixing with beaten egg and salt. Form into small balls by dropping from tip of spoon on to slightly greased baking pan and return to heated oven to brown lightly.

Variation 2: Heat a heavy skillet and add 3 tablespoons schmaltz. Turn in either of the above mixtures and stir well over moderate heat till all particles are lightly browned and dry. Add enough hot water or soup stock to permit saturation and let simmer, covered, 5 to 8 minutes. The product, when cool, can be formed into small balls and browned in additional schmaltz before serving in hot clear chicken or meat soup. 3 or 4 farfel balls make an average portion.

MATZO MEAL MANDLEN

2 eggs, separated | Few grains of sugar | 1 tablespoon ground almonds |
1 tablespoon matzo meal | ⅛ teaspoon salt | Shortening for deep frying

Beat egg yolks with sugar and nuts until creamy and add meal
gradually while beating till smooth. Beat egg whites and salt until
stiff enough to hold a peak and fold into the mixture. Drop from the
tip of a teaspoon into deep hot shortening in frying pan and cook
over moderate heat until each of the mandlen is light enough to
float on top, approximately 5 minutes. Skim out with perforated
spoon and drain well on paper towel. May be heated again before
serving in hot soup. Just place the mandlen in a paper bag and heat
in the oven for a few minutes.
Serves 2 or 3.

PASSOVER EGG NOODLES

4 eggs | 4 tablespoons cold water |
1 tablespoon matzo cake flour | Dash of salt

Beat eggs slightly, adding the other ingredients to make a very thin
batter. Beat well until smooth. Pour in a thin stream on a well-
greased frying pan, starting at the centre and tilting the pan to
distribute evenly. Cook over moderate heat until lightly browned
on under side and turn out on a tea towel, bottom side up, to cool
while the second edition is poured and cooked. Roll up each thin
pancake and cut into thin strips or noodles. Drop into boiling hot
soup (clear chicken soup) just before serving.
Serves 6 to 8.

FEATHERLIGHT KNEIDLACH (Basic Recipe)

2 eggs | 4 tablespoons chicken or goose fat | 1 scant cup matzo meal |
¼ to ½ cup water (approximately) | 1 teaspoon salt |
Dash of ginger or cinnamon

Combine eggs, fat and matzo meal and beat well. Add water and
salt, stirring to make a stiff batter. Add seasoning, cover and chill in

Prune and Farfel Tzimmes (*page 48*)
Latkes (*page 299*)

refrigerator for at least two hours. About a half hour before serving, wet hands with cold water to prevent sticking, and form balls of the batter. Drop the dumplings into salted boiling water, cover, and cook 30 minutes. Drain and serve with clear soup or as a substitute for potatoes.

Serves 2 to 4.

Variation: Add marrow, chopped parsley, chopped liver or chopped nuts to batter before chilling.

KNEIDLACH MIT NESHOMES
(Dumplings with Souls – Hebrew)

2 tablespoons matzo meal | 2 tablespoons hot fat |
1 egg yolk | Dash of salt

Dumplings with 'souls' are made by tucking a small ball of this mixture in the centre of each kneidle or dumpling.

Variation: Chopped grebenes or chopped liver or a combination of both make excellent *neshomes.*

KNEIDLACH (Basic Recipe)

2 eggs, separated | ½ cup matzo meal | ½ teaspoon salt

Beat egg whites and yolks separately. Combine, adding salt and matzo meal gradually while stirring till smooth. Refrigerate 30 minutes before forming into small balls with a teaspoon or by rolling in the palms of the hands. Drop one by one into boiling clear soup. Cover and cook at a slow boil for 20 minutes.

Serves 2 to 4.

Variation 1: Add a dash of ginger to the mixture.

Variation 2: Add 2 tablespoons chopped liver just before forming into balls.

Variation 3: Add 2 tablespoons finely chopped parsley.

Variation 4: Add 1 tablespoon uncooked or cooked beef marrow to the mixture, with or without chopped parsley.

Variation 5: 1 tablespoon finely chopped nuts and a dash of cinnamon or ginger lends glamour.

Variation 6: Half of a blanched almond tucked in each ball makes a welcome surprise kneidle.

5

MASHED POTATO KNEIDLACH

*3 eggs | 1 cup mashed potatoes | 1 teaspoon salt | 3 tablespoons fat |
3 tablespoons warm clear soup or water | 1 cup matzo meal*

Beat eggs into hot mashed potatoes and combine with the other
ingredients to make a smooth mixture. If cold mashed potatoes are
used, be sure to mash thoroughly, even diluting with some of the
warm liquid till smooth. Chill for several hours. Form into balls
about a half hour before serving and cook in salted boiling water for
30 minutes. Drain and serve.
Serves 4 to 6.

GRATED POTATO KNEIDLACH

*3 large raw potatoes and 1 cup cooked, mashed potatoes | 2 eggs |
2 tablespoons chicken fat | ½ teaspoon salt | Dash of pepper or cinnamon |
½ cup matzo meal | 1 tablespoon onion juice*

Pare and grate potatoes. Squeeze out as much liquid as possible by
pressing with the hands. Combine with the rest of ingredients, mixing
thoroughly. The mixture should be firm enough to form into balls.
More matzo meal may be added if necessary. Shape into balls the
size of walnuts and drop into rapidly boiling salted water, cooking
for about 1 hour over a moderate heat after the last ball is dropped
in. Drain and serve in clear soup or as dumplings in stew, chicken
fricassée or meat gravy.
Serves 6 to 8.

MARROW KNEIDLACH

*1 tablespoon uncooked marrow from beef bone | Pinch of salt | 1 egg yolk |
1 tablespoon finely chopped parsley | Matzo meal to make a thick batter*

Mash the uncooked beef marrow with a fork. Add salt, egg yolk and
parsley. Stir in just enough matzo meal to make a stiff batter that
will drop from a teaspoon. Or, form the mixture into balls the size
of marbles and drop into boiling soup. Cook over moderate heat
15 minutes.
Yields 4 servings.

MATZO MEAL CHEESE BALLS

½ cup matzo meal | 1 cup cottage cheese or cream cheese |
1 egg, well beaten | ⅛ teaspoon pepper | ½ teaspoon salt

Mix all ingredients thoroughly and roll into small balls. Roll balls
in matzo meal, then deep-fry in vegetable shortening until they are
rich, golden brown. Drain on brown paper, and serve. Matzo meal
cheese balls make an interesting companion to salads and fruit cups,
soups and beverages. As the satisfying main course of a light meal,
serve with sour cream.

Serves 2 to 4.

PASSOVER CHEESE BLINTZES

3 eggs | ¾ cup matzo cake flour | 1½ cups water |
½ teaspoon salt | Butter for frying

CHEESE FILLING

1 pound cottage cheese | 1 egg | ½ teaspoon salt |
½ teaspoon sugar | 1 tablespoon cream

Beat eggs and add flour and water alternately to make a thin batter.
Add salt. Pour about 3 tablespoons of batter on a well-buttered
griddle or frying pan, spreading it as thin as possible. Let fry until
brown and turn out on a tea towel, browned side up.

Mix filling ingredients and spread evenly over the surface, tuck in
ends and roll up. Cut in half. Brown in butter. Sprinkle with sugar
and cinnamon and serve hot.

Makes 6 large (12 cut) blintzes.

Variation 1: Spread a thin layer of preserves over each pancake
and fold over in the same manner. Brown lightly under grill.
Serve with stewed fruit or plain.

Variation 2: Sprinkle with sugar, cinnamon and chopped nuts.
Tuck in sides and roll. Brown. Serve plain or with sugar.

MEAT BLINTZES

Make a batter as for cheese blintzes. Fry in chicken fat until brown and then turn out on a tea towel, browned side up. For the filling use left-over chopped soup meat or boiled chicken, seasoned to taste. To each cupful of filling add 1 beaten egg. Spread filling over surface as for cheese blintzes. Roll and brown in a little chicken fat. Serve with soup or as a main dish. Excellent with stewed tomatoes.

MATZO POLENTA (Milchig)

*3 eggs, separated | ½ cup water | 1 cup matzo meal | 1 teaspoon salt |
Dash of pepper | 1 onion, finely diced | 3 tablespoons butter |
½ pound mushrooms | 3 cups fresh tomatoes, diced, or
2 cups stewed tomatoes | ½ cup cheese*

Beat the egg yolks, add water and half the matzo meal. Fold in the stiffly beaten egg whites, salt, pepper and remaining matzo meal. Fry onion in butter, and lift out as soon as browned. Drop the egg mixture by spoonfuls in the butter and fry till light brown. Arrange in baking dish. Put the onions, washed and cut mushrooms, tomatoes and cheese over the fried batter cakes and bake 45 minutes in a slow oven.
Serves 4 to 6.

SCALLOPED MATZOS (Milchig)

*4 eggs | 6 matzos | 1 pound cottage cheese |
2 tablespoons butter, melted | ½ teaspoon salt |
Optional: 1 tablespoon sugar, ½ teaspoon cinnamon, ¼ cup raisins*

Beat 2 eggs till light and break the matzos into quarters which can be dipped into the eggs. Let stand while you blend the other 2 eggs and seasonings with the cheese. Butter a casserole or pudding dish. Arrange alternate layers of matzos and cheese in the dish. Bake ½ hour at 350° F. or gas mark 4, or till nicely browned. Serve with stewed fruit or plain. An excellent luncheon dish.
Serves 6 to 8.

SPICED MATZOS (Milchig)

3 eggs | 3 matzos, whole or halves | 1 tablespoon melted butter |
3 tablespoons sugar | ¼ teaspoon each cinnamon and nutmeg

Beat eggs well and butter matzos. Mix sugar and spices. Brush
matzos with beaten eggs. Sprinkle liberally with sugar and spice
mixture. Bake 10 minutes till crisp at 350° F. or gas mark 4.
  Serves 4.
  Variation 1: Sprinkle with chopped nuts.
  Variation 2: Sprinkle cheese on top and add more sugar and
    spice.
  Variation 3: Dip each matzo in beaten egg and place in a well-
    buttered baking dish, with the cheese, nuts and seasonings
    between matzos. Pour 1 cup milk over all and bake till milk is
    absorbed and the top lightly brown. Serve like pudding.

BAKED MATZO SANDWICHES (Basic Recipe)

1 matzo | Water | 1 egg | Salt and pepper or cinnamon to taste |
Shortening

SANDWICH FILLING

Boiled chicken or meat (thinly sliced or chopped)

Soak the matzo, broken in half or quarters, 10 minutes in enough
cold water to cover. Press out as much water as possible. Add seasoning to well-beaten egg and pour over matzo pieces. Place in the
bottom of a well-greased baking pan. Cover half the matzo pieces
with thinly sliced or chopped boiled chicken or meat. Place remaining matzo pieces on top, pressing down with bowl of spoon. Dot
with bits of shortening and bake 30 minutes at 350° F. or gas mark 4,
or till nicely browned on top. If quarter sections are arranged
carefully, each matzo makes 2 sandwiches.
  Variation 1: To make a Sweet Sandwich, omit pepper and fill with
    preserves, sliced apples dusted with sugar and cinnamon, or
    chopped raisins and almonds, or soaked and pitted prunes
    finely mashed.
  Variation 2: Cottage cheese, seasoned with sugar, cinnamon, a

dash of salt and mixed with 1 egg yolk to 1 cup cheese, makes a delicious filling.

Variation 3: Use any of the fillings above and make Triple Decker Sandwiches.

Variation 4: Use chopped liver, chopped hard cooked eggs or flaked grilled fish as filling. Arrange in well-greased casserole or baking dish and cover with stewed tomatoes or Creole sauce (see p. 273) (using Passover ingredients) before baking.

Variation 5: Thinly sliced sections of eggplant, seasoned with salt, pepper and paprika makes excellent baked matzo sandwich filling. Bake with or without stewed tomatoes or Creole sauce to cover.

MATZO MEAL MUFFINS (Basic Recipe)

2 eggs | ½ teaspoon salt | 1 cup water | 1½ cups matzo meal | 4 tablespoons chicken or goose fat

Beat eggs. Add salt and water. Stir in matzo meal to make a smooth batter. Heat the fat, grease muffin pans, and stir remaining hot fat into the batter. Fill muffin pans ⅔ full and bake at 350° F. or gas mark 4, 30 minutes or till brown. Serve with clear soup, roast chicken or meat. If any are left over, slice, cover with gravy and heat in oven.

Yields 8 large, or 16 small muffins.

Variation 1: For Sweet Muffins, use butter in place of fat, and milk instead of water. Add sugar and cinnamon, grated rind of lemon. Bake in the same manner.

Variation 2: For a more delicate muffin, omit water and use matzo cake flour. Add ½ cup applesauce, or drained and chopped canned peaches. A dash of nutmeg or cinnamon gives added flavouring. Bake in buttered muffin tins. Serve with sliced canned peaches or with applesauce.

Variation 3: Use 1 cup soaked and pitted prunes, sliced or cut fine.

Variation 4: Finely cut dates, raisins, chopped nuts or a mixture of all three make delicious fruit muffins. Sprinkle with powdered sugar or top with icing.

MATZO MEAL PANCAKES (Crisp and Light)

3 eggs | ½ cup cold water | ¼ teaspoon salt | 1 cup matzo meal |
1 grated onion, medium size | Melted shortening or oil for deep frying

Beat eggs and combine with cold water, salt, ⅔ of the grated onion
and enough matzo meal to make a stiff batter that will drop from the
spoon. Heat shortening in a heavy frying pan and add the remaining
piece of onion for flavour. Drop batter from spoon to form round
cakes and fry till brown before turning over to brown on under side.
Lift out one at a time and drain thoroughly before serving with
applesauce, mixed dried fruits compote, cranberry sauce or just
plain with meat or cheese dishes.
Yields 12 to 14 pancakes.

MATZO MEAL PANCAKES

3 eggs | 1 cup milk or water | 1 cup matzo meal | ½ teaspoon salt |
½ teaspoon sugar / Shortening for deep frying

Beat eggs, add liquid and stir in matzo meal and seasoning to make
a smooth batter thick enough to drop from a large spoon. Drop by
the spoonful into melted shortening deep enough to fry the pancakes.
If fried in deep fat, pancakes will be crisp and absorb less fat. Brown
on both sides, drain well, and serve with applesauce or cheese, or
sprinkle with sugar and cinnamon.
Serves 4.

PANCAKE ROLLS

3 eggs, separated | ½ teaspoon salt | ½ cup matzo cake flour |
1 cup milk or water | ½ teaspoon sugar | Dash of cinnamon or nutmeg |
½ cup jelly or preserves

Beat egg yolks creamy. Add salt and stir in alternately matzo flour
and liquid. Add sugar and cinnamon. Beat to a smooth batter and
fold in stiffly beaten egg whites. The batter should be thin enough

to pour like heavy cream. Pour a thin pancake into a well-greased frying pan or griddle. Fry till nicely browned and turn out on a tea towel, bottom side up. Spread with jelly and roll up. When all pancakes are rolled, sprinkle with sugar and slip under grill to brown before serving.

Yields 6 to 8 rolls.

MATZO PANCAKES

3 matzos | Water | 3 eggs | ½ cup sugar | Dash of salt |
1 teaspoon lemon juice | ½ cup shortening, melted | ½ cup matzo meal

Soak broken matzos in cold water to cover till soft. Drain and squeeze dry. Cream eggs, sugar, salt and lemon juice. Combine and add melted shortening and matzo meal to make a soft batter. Drop from spoon on to hot, greased frying pan or griddle and bake till brown on both sides. Sprinkle with sugar and serve hot. These pancakes are ½ inch thick.

Serves 4 to 6.

Variation 1: Omit sugar and lemon juice. Add an onion, diced and fried light brown, before combining the ingredients. Serve with stewed meat, poultry or fish.

Variation 2: Turn either mixture into well-greased muffin pans. Bake at 350° F. or gas mark 4 till nicely browned.

Yields 8 large or 16 small peaked muffins.

MEAT-FILLED MATZO CAKES

Use recipe for Matzo Pancakes, Variation 1. Add ½ cup matzo meal to the mixture to make it thick enough to mould into ½-inch flat cakes. Tuck 1 tablespoon chopped cooked meat or chicken into centre of each. Flatten into cakes about 1½ inches thick. Fry or bake till browned on both sides. A good way to utilize leftover meat.

BAKED MATZO-VEGETABLE SCALLOP

3 matzos | 1 large onion, sliced | 4 whole tomatoes, medium sized |
½ teaspoon salt | Dash of pepper | 1 teaspoon sugar |
3 tablespoons chicken or goose schmaltz | ½ cup soup or water (if needed)

Grease generously a 9 ×9 ×2-inch baking dish and cover the bottom with thinly sliced onion. Break one matzo into sections and arrange over onions. Cover with slices of tomato, sprinkle with salt, pepper and sugar and top with sections of the second matzo. Cover with the remaining onion slices and top with the third matzo. Cover and bake 30 minutes at 350° F. or gas mark 4. Remove cover and if the top layer of matzo is not softened, add ½ cup soup or water. Continue to bake until lightly browned on top. Serve with meat or fish meal.
Serves 4.
Variations can be made by adding sliced eggplant, green peppers or shredded cabbage between layers of matzos.

CHREMZLACH (Basic Recipe)

*3 tablespoons chicken or goose schmaltz | 6 tablespoons hot water |
1 lemon, juice and grated rind | 4 cups matzo meal (approximate) |
4 eggs, separated | ¼ teaspoon salt |
1½ cups hot melted shortening (approximate) for deep frying*

FILLING

*1½ cups of any fruit preserves (cherry preferred) |
½ cup chopped nuts (almonds preferred) | 2 tablespoons matzo meal*

Combine schmaltz, hot water, lemon juice and grated rind in a large mixing bowl. Stir in matzo meal gradually to make a stiff batter free of lumps. Beat egg yolks with sugar till creamy and stir into batter. Add salt to egg whites and beat stiff. Fold in beaten egg whites as soon as mixture is cold enough to handle. Matzo meal varies in absorptive capacity. Should more moisture be necessary, water or lemon juice (or equal parts of both) may be stirred in a little at a time. The doughy batter should be of a consistency that can be formed into balls after remaining at room temperature 15 to 20 minutes.

Combine the ingredients for the filling – preserves, chopped nuts and matzo meal – and let stand 10 minutes before using. (Honey and slivered almonds may also be used in any desired amounts. Same for sugar and cinnamon.)

Form the batter into balls the size of medium apples and make a depression in the centre of each into which a tablespoonful of filling is tucked and enclosed smoothly. Each chremzle is flattened into a

thick pancake and fried in deep hot melted shortening till lightly
browned on both sides. Lift out and drain on paper towels. When all
of the cakes are fried, arrange on a serving plate and cover with
honey and slivered almonds. Or sprinkle generously with sugar and
cinnamon. Serve hot or cold.

Yields 12 to 14.

MORE CHREMZLE FILLINGS

FILLING NO. 1

1 *cup beet preserves* | ½ *cup chopped walnuts* | 2 *tablespoons matzo meal*

FILLING NO. 2

1 *cup orange marmalade* | ½ *cup ground almonds* | 2 *tablespoons matzo meal*

FILLING NO. 3

1½ *cups grated tart apples (packed firmly)* | ½ *cup finely chopped almonds* |
4 *tablespoons sugar* | ½ *teaspoon cinnamon* | *Dash of nutmeg (optional)* |
3 *tablespoons matzo cake flour*

Combine each of the above filling mixtures in the order listed. Let
stand 15 to 20 minutes before using to permit matzo meal or matzo
cake flour to blend into the preserve, marmalade or fruit and other
ingredients.

CHREMZLACH (Boston Style)

6 *eggs* | 1½ *cups matzo meal* | 6 *tablespoons cold water* |
3 *tablespoons melted shortening (vegetable, oil or schmaltz)* |
½ *teaspoon salt*

FILLING

¾ *cup chopped rossel beets (see p. 60)* | ½ *cup honey* | ¼ *cup chopped nuts* /
¼ *teaspoon ginger* | ⅓ *cup very strong tea*

Beat eggs with rotary beater 3 minutes. Stir in matzo meal and
water alternately and add melted shortening and salt. Chill 2 hours
in refrigerator.

Combine and cook all ingredients for the filling, except the tea, till thick but not scorched. Remove from heat and stir in the tea. When cold use as filling. If same filling is to be used as topping for the chremzlach, reserve ⅓ of the mixture for the topping.

After batter has been chilled in refrigerator for required time, form into 16 flat cakes, 3 inches in diameter. Place 8 cakes on a well-greased baking sheet or in a baking pan and drop a teaspoonful of cold filling in centre of each. Cover with remaining cakes and with the tines of a fork press edges of each filled cake together gently. Bake 20 minutes at 420° F. or gas mark 7, or till nicely browned. Dust with sugar and cinnamon or top each with a gob of the same filling.

Yields 8 filled chremzlach.

PASSOVER DESSERT PUDDINGS

GRATED APPLE PUDDING

6 large apples, pared | 8 eggs, separated | ⅓ cup fine matzo meal | ¼ teaspoon salt | 1 lemon, grated rind and juice | ¼ cup shredded almonds

Grate the apples and add the beaten egg yolks. Stir in matzo meal to which ¼ teaspoon salt has been added. Add grated rind and juice of lemon. Stir well before adding stiffly beaten egg whites. Add nuts. Bake in an ungreased spring form 30 minutes at 350° F. or gas mark 4, or until nicely browned. Serve hot with lemon sauce.

Serves 8 to 10.

Variation: Add 1 cup shredded coconut in place of nuts. Serve with orange sauce.

BANANA PUDDING

2 large tart apples, grated unpared | 2 tablespoons lemon juice | ½ cup sugar | 3 egg yolks | ½ cup matzo meal | ¼ teaspoon cinnamon | ¼ teaspoon nutmeg | 2 large bananas for topping | 3 egg whites | ⅛ teaspoon salt | 2 tablespoons sugar | Dash of grated lemon rind

Combine grated apple and lemon juice. Beat sugar and egg yolks till creamy and add by stirring in quickly, and alternately with matzo meal to which spices have been added. Grease a pudding dish and turn in this mixture. Bake at 325° F. or gas mark 3 approximately 35 minutes, till set. Turn out on serving plate and top with sliced bananas. Beat egg whites with salt and sugar till thick and spread on top just before serving.

May be eaten cold without topping of bananas and beaten egg white meringue. A dusting of sugar and cinnamon may substitute for egg topping.

Serves 6.

CARROT PUDDING

2 cups grated raw carrot (tightly packed) | 2 tablespoons matzo meal |
1 cup sugar | 8 eggs, separated | ½ cup potato flour |
½ cup shredded apple, unpared | ½ cup wine | 1 lemon, grated (rind and juice)

Mix ingredients in the order listed, adding the stiffly beaten egg whites last. Turn into a well-greased pudding dish and bake 45 minutes at 375° F. or gas mark 5. Serve hot or cold.

Serves 6 to 8.

MATZO FARFEL PUDDING (Basic Recipe)

2 cups matzo farfel | Water | 2 eggs | ½ cup sugar |
½ teaspoon salt | 3 tablespoons chicken fat or butter | 2 bananas |
¼ cup chopped walnuts or almonds

Cover farfel with water and drain immediately so that farfel remains moist but not soggy. Add beaten eggs, sugar, salt and fat. Slice one banana and arrange slices in the bottom of a well-greased, heated pudding dish. Add farfel mixture. Top with nuts and other sliced banana. Bake 30 minutes or till brown at 350° F. or gas mark 4. Turn out on serving plate.

Serves 6.

Variation 1: Substitute sliced apples for bananas.

Variation 2: Line the greased pudding dish with sliced pineapple that has been dipped in matzo flour and sugar. Omit the nuts.

Serve with pineapple sauce. This pudding may be turned out
on a heated platter and the sauce poured over it.

Variation 3: Use 1 cup drained canned shredded pineapple instead of other fruit. Sprinkle shredded coconut over the pudding
as soon as turned out on a heated platter. Serve with pineapple
sauce.

Variation 4: Use 2 cups soaked and drained, pitted prunes.
Arrange half the prunes on the bottom of the pudding dish.
Chop the rest and add to pudding batter. Omit the nuts.
Flavour with cinnamon and lemon juice. Serve with wine
sauce, lemon sauce or plain.

MATZO FARFEL PUDDING 2

1 quart boiling water | 3 cups matzo farfel | 2 eggs |
1 lemon, grated rind and juice | ½ cup sugar | 1 tablespoon salt |
3 tablespoons chicken fat or butter

Pour water over farfel and let stand 10 minutes. Drain. Squeeze dry.
Beat eggs. Add lemon juice, sugar, salt and shortening, and fold in
farfel. Turn into a well-greased pudding dish and bake 1 hour at
350° F. or gas mark 4, or till nicely browned. Serve with raisin
sauce or stewed rhubarb.
Serves 6 to 8.

DATE PUDDING

¾ cup sugar | 1 cup matzo meal | 3 eggs, separated and beaten |
½ cup chopped nuts | ¼ pound dates, cut or chopped fine

Mix in the order given, folding egg whites in last. Turn into a well-
greased pudding dish. Set the pudding dish in a pan of hot water and
bake 45 minutes at 350° F. or gas mark 4. Serve with any fruit
sauce.
Serves 8.

VEGETABLE PUDDING

½ *teaspoon salt* | ½ *teaspoon cinnamon* | ¾ *cup sugar* |
½ *cup matzo meal* | ½ *cup seeded raisins, chopped dates or figs* |
1 *large tart apple, cored and finely diced, or grated unpared* |
1 *cup grated raw carrot (tightly packed for measuring)* |
1 *cup grated raw sweet potato* | 1 *cup grated raw white potato*
*(These vegetables may be grated, measured and combined
before preparing the other ingredients)*
1 *lemon, juice and grated rind* |
½ *cup hot melted shortening (chicken fat preferred)*

Begin by combining the dry ingredients. Add raisins and apple,
stirring lightly to coat the fruit. Add the mixed vegetables and lemon
juice, then the grated lemon rind. Heat the shortening in the casserole or baking dish and pour in last, stirring well to combine evenly.
Turn the mixture back into the greased baking dish and bake 50
minutes to 1 hour at 350° F. or gas mark 4, or till firm in the centre
and nicely browned. Serve plain or with a lemon sauce.
 Serves 6 to 8.

CHEESE PUDDING

4 *matzos* | *Lukewarm water* | 1 *pound dry cottage cheese* | 4 *eggs* |
2 *cups milk* | 1 *lemon, grated rind and juice* | ¾ *cup sugar* | 1 *teaspoon salt*

Soak matzos in lukewarm water. Drain and press extra moisture out
carefully so as not to break the matzos. Generously butter square
deep cake pan. Put 1 matzo on bottom of pan, spread with ⅓ of the
cheese, put on another matzo and spread with cheese till 3 matzos
are used. Cover top with fourth matzo. Beat eggs slightly. Add milk,
lemon, sugar and seasoning. Pour over the matzo and cheese. Bake
in oven at 375° F. or gas mark 5 for 1 hour. Can be served hot or
cold.
 Serves 8.

MATZO CHARLOTTE 1

3 *matzos* | *Water* | 1 *teaspoon salt* | 2 *tablespoons chicken fat* |
3 *eggs* | 1 *cup sugar* | 1 *lemon, grated rind and juice*

Soak the matzos in water till soft. Squeeze out excess water. Stir till creamy, adding salt and some of the melted fat (that has been melted in pudding dish to be used). Beat the egg yolks, sugar, lemon rind and juice and add, blending and mixing thoroughly. Fold in the stiffly beaten egg whites. Turn into the greased pudding dish and bake ½ hour at 350° F. or gas mark 4, or till well-browned on top. Serve hot with wine sauce.
Serves 6.

MATZO CHARLOTTE 2

2 matzos | Water | 3 eggs, separated |
¼ pound beef suet or uncooked chicken fat, chopped | ¼ cup sugar |
2 cups sliced apples | ¼ cup chopped almonds |
¼ cup seeded raisins | ¼ teaspoon cinnamon

Soak matzos in cold water to cover till soft. Squeeze out excess water. Stir in beaten egg yolks, sugar, apples, nuts, raisins, cinnamon and chopped suet. Fold in beaten egg whites last and turn into a casserole or well-greased pudding dish. Bake till golden brown on top, about 45 minutes, at 350° F. or gas mark 4. Serve plain or with lemon sauce.
Serves 6.

MATZO KUGEL

3 matzos | Water | 3 eggs, separated | ½ cup sugar | ¼ teaspoon salt |
¼ teaspoon cinnamon | ¼ cup raisins (optional) | 3 tablespoons shortening |
3 tart apples, thinly sliced | Grated rind of 1 lemon or orange |
¼ cup chopped nuts

Soak matzos in cold water to cover. Drain well. Beat egg yolks light, add sugar, salt and cinnamon. Stir in the soaked matzos. Fold in stiffly beaten egg whites and raisins, and turn half the mixture into a heated, well-greased baking dish or casserole. Arrange thinly sliced apples evenly, sprinkle with nuts and grated lemon rind. Cover with the rest of the matzo mixture. Dot with remaining fat, sprinkle with more cinnamon and sugar, and bake at 350° F. or gas mark 4 about 45 minutes or till nicely browned. Serve with applesauce, wine sauce or berries, stewed or fresh.
Serves 6.

Variation 1: Use any dried fruit, chopped or thinly sliced, in place of apples.

Variation 2: Omit the fruit and nuts. Add ½ cup chopped grebenes and browned onion. Serve with poultry or meat.

PASSOVER CAKES

BANANA CAKE

7 eggs, separated | 1 cup sugar | ¼ teaspoon salt | 1 cup mashed ripe bananas | ¾ cup matzo cake flour | ¼ cup potato flour | ½ to 1 cup coarsely chopped nuts (walnuts or mixed nuts)

FROSTING

1 egg white, beaten slightly | ⅞ cup sugar | Pinch of salt | 3 tablespoons cold water

Beat egg yolks with sugar till light and creamy. Combine salt, mashed bananas, cake flour and potato flour. Add to beaten egg yolk mixture. Beat egg whites stiff, adding a pinch of salt for quicker action, and fold into the batter. Fold in chopped nuts lightly and turn the cake mixture into a lightly greased cake pan, spring form or well type. Bake 40 to 45 minutes or till light brown on top, at 325° F. or gas mark 3. Cool on a rack or by placing cake pan so that it rests on 2 separated inverted pans to permit circulation of air under cake pan.

When cold, decorate with an icing that has been made in the following manner: combine icing ingredients, in order listed above, in the top of a double boiler. While the water in the lower pot is boiling, beat the ingredients in the upper pot with a fork or rotary beater for 7 minutes or till it is thick enough to spread.

Makes a medium-size cake.

CHOCOLATE CAKE (Using Cocoa)

7 eggs, separated | 1 cup sugar | ¾ cup matzo cake flour | 3 tablespoons cocoa (for darker cake use 4 tablespoons) | ¼ teaspoon salt | 2 tablespoons cold water | 1 orange, medium size, juice and grated rind | ½ cup chopped nuts

Beat egg yolks with sugar added while beating till creamy. Stir in cake flour, well mixed with cocoa and salt. Combine water, orange juice and grated rind and stir in. Add nuts to the mixture and fold in stiffly beaten egg whites. Turn into an ungreased rectangular cake pan or a round tube cake pan. Bake at 325° F. or gas mark 3 for 45 minutes or till lightly browned on top. Turn off heat and let cake cool in the oven.

Makes a medium size cake.

MYSTERY CAKE

¾ cup matzo cake flour | ¾ cup potato flour | 2 cups sugar | 5 egg yolks |
1 cup orange juice | 2 tablespoons grated orange rind |
1 cup egg whites (7 or 8) | ½ teaspoon salt

Sift together matzo cake flour and potato flour 3 times. Add 1½ cups sugar and sift once more. Use a large size mixing bowl. Make a well in centre of the mounded ingredients and drop in the egg yolks. Add orange juice and grated rind while beating till smooth. Beat egg whites with salt till stiff enough to hold a peak and add remainder of sugar gradually while continuing to beat till smooth. Fold into the batter and turn into an ungreased tube pan.

Bake 1 hour and 20 minutes at 325° F. or gas mark 3. Remove from oven and invert cake in pan over a cake rack. When cold, if cake does not slip out of pan, loosen gently with a knife blade or spatula.

Makes a large size cake.

Variation: Bake in 2-layer cake pans and put together with jam.

NUT CAKE

9 eggs, separated | 1 lemon, grated rind and juice | 9 tablespoons sugar |
1 cup finely ground almonds | 2 tablespoons matzo cake flour

Beat egg yolks till light-coloured and creamy. Fold in grated lemon rind and then lemon juice, a little at a time, till combined. Beat egg whites, adding sugar gradually, till the mixture is stiff. Fold the second mixture into the first with an over and over stroke, adding the finely ground nuts in the final few strokes. Sprinkle the flour over the top and fold in very lightly. Turn the mixture into an ungreased

6

spring form and bake at 325° F. or gas mark 3 for 45 minutes or till lightly browned. This cake must not be disturbed during the baking process if you want it to rise to its maximum height. When done, press lightly with the forefinger in centre to make sure it is not sticky, before removing from the oven.

Makes a large size cake.

SPONGE CAKE (Rectangular Form)

12 eggs, separated | 2 cups sugar |
Grated rind and juice of 1 lemon | ¼ cup cold water |
1 cup each matzo cake flour and potato flour, sifted together

Beat yolks with sugar till thick and creamy. Add liquids and grated lemon rind and stir in sifted dry ingredients. Beat egg whites stiff and fold in lightly. Grease a rectangular baking pan and line with paper. Turn in batter and bake at 325° F. or gas mark 3 for 50 minutes to 1 hour. This cake is done when the edges are crisp and a toothpick inserted in centre comes out dry. Turn out on rack to cool then remove paper.

Makes a large size cake which may be cut into 1½- to 2-inch squares or diamond-shaped pieces.

SPONGE CAKE (With Icing Sugar)

9 eggs, separated | 1½ cups icing sugar | 1 tablespoon lemon juice |
½ cup matzo cake flour | ½ cup potato flour | Pinch of salt

Cream egg yolks with sugar till light and add lemon juice. Sift together matzo cake flour and potato flour at least 4 times and stir into egg yolk mixture very lightly. Beat egg whites, to which the salt has been added, until they hold a peak. Fold into first mixture. Turn into an ungreased cake pan, rectangular or round, and bake at 325° F. or gas mark 3 for 1 hour. Remove from oven and invert to cool, using either a cake rack or resting the inverted pan on 2 separated inverted pans, at least 2 inches above the surface of table.

Makes a large size cake.

Variation: ¾ cup finely ground walnuts may be added to the creamed yolks and sugar before adding the other ingredients. This makes a slightly heavier cake.

POTATO FLOUR SPONGE CAKE (Wheat Allergy Cake)

9 eggs, separated | 1⅔ cups sugar | 1 lemon, grated rind and juice |
1 scant cup potato flour

Beat the egg yolks till light and creamy, adding sugar gradually.
Add grated rind and juice of lemon, beat thoroughly, and stir in
potato flour a little at a time, beating after each addition. Fold in
stiffly beaten egg whites. Turn into a spring form or paper-lined
cake pan and bake at 300° F. or gas mark 1–2 for 45 to 50 minutes.
Makes a large size cake.

ECONOMY ALMOND CAKE

¼ cup potato flour | ½ cup matzo cake flour | 1 cup sugar |
½ teaspoon salt | 1 cup finely chopped almonds | 2 eggs |
Milk to make 1 cup with eggs | 1 tablespoon lemon juice |
2 tablespoons melted butter

Sift together dry ingredients and add almonds. Beat eggs thoroughly
in a cup and add enough milk to fill the cup. Add lemon juice and
melted butter. Combine the two mixtures and bake in a buttered
loaf pan 50 minutes at 350° F. or gas mark 4, or till nicely browned
on top.
Makes a 9-inch loaf.

GINGER FINGERS

2 cups matzo meal | 3 eggs | ¼ cup ground or powdered ginger |
¾ pound sugar | ½ pound honey

Combine matzo meal, beaten eggs and ginger to make a smooth
dough. Let stand at room temperature while bringing to a boil the
honey and sugar. When the sugar and honey combination has boiled
to a reddish colour, add the other mixture, stirring it in with a heavy
spoon. Remove from heat while beating and stir till smooth. This
makes a very thick mixture.

Turn out on a wet board to cool for 15 minutes. Pat flat and cut
into 2- or 2½-inch lengths about ¾ of an inch thick and wide. Or, as

soon as cool enough to handle, cut off parts of the mixture and roll into 1-inch thick sticks and cut to any desired length. Allow to cool thoroughly before serving. These will keep in a well-covered container.

NUT KUCHEN (Light Nut Cake)

6 *eggs, separated* | 6 *tablespoons sugar* | 6 *tablespoons matzo cake flour* | 1 *tablespoon lemon juice* | ½ *cup finely chopped nuts (almonds or walnuts)* | *Pinch of salt*

Cream egg yolks with sugar till light lemon-coloured. Add matzo cake flour gradually by stirring till smooth after each addition. Stir in lemon juice and nuts. Beat egg whites and salt, stiff but not dry, and fold in lightly. Bake in ungreased tube cake pan or a spring form 45 minutes at 300° F. or gas mark 1-2, then increase heat to 325° F. or gas mark 3 for 15 minutes or until set and lightly browned on top. Remove from oven and invert to cool over a cake rack.

Serves 8 to 10.

Variation: Line muffin pans with paper baking cups and fill ⅔ full. Bake 30 to 35 minutes at 300° F. or gas mark 1–2 then increase to 375° F. or gas mark 5 for 5 minutes or till lightly browned on top and firm to the touch. Ice (see Banana Cake recipe) and add chopped or slivered almonds as soon as cold.

SMALL CAKES AND COOKIES

ALMOND MACAROONS

5 *egg whites* | 1 *pound blanched almonds, finely ground* | 4 *tablespoons matzo cake flour* | 1½ *pounds caster sugar (4 cups approximately)* | *Grated rind of 2 lemons*

Beat egg whites stiff. Fold in ingredients in the order listed. Drop mixture from tip of teaspoon on a baking sheet covered with paper, leaving about 1 inch between biscuits. Bake 15 minutes at 300° F. or gas mark 1–2 then increase to 350° F. or gas mark 4 about 15 minutes longer, till nicely browned. Let cool before removing to serving plate.

Yields 36.

PASSOVER PUFFS

½ cup shortening (vegetable, salad oil or butter) | 1 cup water |
1 cup matzo cake flour | 1 cup matzo meal | 2 tablespoons sugar (optional) |
6 eggs, separated | 1 tablespoon lemon juice | 1 teaspoon salt

Bring shortening and water to a boil in a deep saucepan. Remove
from heat and stir in matzo cake flour and matzo meal, with sugar
added if desired. Stir till smooth. Beat egg yolks till creamy and stir
in till blended. Add lemon juice. Beat egg whites, with salt, stiff but
not dry and fold into the mixture, which should be cool. Drop batter
from teaspoon or tablespoon about 2 inches apart on a lightly
greased baking sheet and bake at 350° F. or gas mark 4 for 15
minutes or till lightly browned and puffed. The puffs should double
in diameter, be hollow like cream puffs but not quite as light. Let
cool before filling through a slit in top or side.

Filling may be preserves, stewed dried fruits or whipped cream to
which sugar has been added to suit the taste. Chopped nuts may be
added to any of the mentioned fillings in any quantity suitable to the
occasion.

Yields approximately 24 or 48 small puffs.

PASSOVER INGBERLACH

¾ cup honey | 1 cup sugar | 2 eggs, beaten till creamy | 1 cup matzo meal |
½ cup ground almonds or walnuts | 1 tablespoon ground ginger

Stir honey and sugar together in a deep saucepan and bring to a
quick boil. Cook 10 minutes till it is a deep golden-coloured syrup.
Remove from heat. Combine other ingredients with a fork (making
sure the eggs have been beaten till creamy) and stir into the honey
and sugar syrup.

Place over very low heat and cook approximately 10 minutes,
while stirring mixture to prevent sticking or scorching. The consistency should be thick enough to adhere to sides and bottom of pan
and mixture should be a reddish-gold colour. Turn out on a wet
board and flatten to ½-inch thickness with the bowl of a large spoon
that has been dipped in cold water. Dust with additional sugar and
ground ginger, if desired, and let cool 10 minutes before cutting into
1-inch squares or diamond shapes.

Yields approximately 30.

Variation: Form the egg and matzo meal, nuts and ginger mixture into marbles and drop one at a time into the hot syrup while at almost boiling point. Cook without stirring approximately 10 minutes. Turn out on a platter and let cool enough to touch with the tip of finger. With the tip of a spoon or fork, separate the Ingberlach balls and let dry on a wet board or platter.

MISCELLANEOUS PASSOVER DESSERTS

PASSOVER LEMON PIE

CRUST

1 *cup matzo meal* | ¼ *cup shortening (any suitable kind)* |
Pinch of Salt | *Pinch of cinnamon* | 1 *teaspoon sugar*

FILLING

Juice of 2 lemons | *Grated rind of 1 lemon* | ½ *cup sugar* |
1½ *cups water* | 3 *egg yolks creamed with* ½ *cup sugar* |
3 *tablespoons potato flour moistened with* ½ *cup cold water* |
3 *egg whites, beaten stiff, with a pinch of salt*

Combine the ingredients for the crust in the order given and pat evenly over the bottom of a 9-inch pie pan. Bring the mixture up to the top of the rim as evenly as possible. Bake 10 minutes at 375° F. or gas mark 5, or till lightly browned.

To make the filling for the pie, bring to a boil in the top of a double boiler the first 4 filling ingredients listed. Stir in creamed yolks and sugar as water continues to boil. Then blend in moistened potato flour by stirring till smooth. Let cook 10 minutes or till well blended and creamy. Remove from heat. When the filling is cool, stir in rapidly the stiffly beaten egg whites and turn mixture into the pre-baked pie crust.

Serves 6 to 8.

Variation: Proceed as above, but make a meringue of the beaten egg whites and salt, adding 2 tablespoons of sugar while beating till it holds a peak. Top pie in swirls or peaks and slip under grill to brown lightly before serving.

APPLE SPONGE PUDDING

4 tart apples | 3 tablespoons cold water |
½ cup mixed seeded raisins and slivered almonds | 3 eggs, separated |
1 cup sugar | ½ teaspoon cinnamon | 1 cup matzo cake flour |
¼ teaspoon salt | Grated rind of 1 lemon |
1 tablespoon lemon juice or 2 tablespoons brandy

Pare and core apples. Place in a greased pudding dish or casserole. Cut apples into eighths part way down and spread slightly. Add water and half the amount of raisins and almonds. Cover and cook over asbestos plate at moderate heat 8 to 10 minutes. Uncover and let cool while preparing the batter as follows:

Beat egg yolks, adding sugar gradually. When combined, stir in matzo cake flour to which cinnamon has been added. Beat egg whites and salt, stiff but not dry, and fold in, adding grated lemon rind and juice or brandy, a little at a time during the blending. Turn the batter into pudding dish over the apple sections and top with remainder of raisins and almonds. Bake uncovered 30 minutes at 350° F. or gas mark 4.

Serves 6 to 8.

Variation: Leave pared and cored apples whole and fill with raisins, almonds and grated lemon rind. Proceed as above.

MOCK NOODLE PUDDING

4 matzos | Boiling water | 3 eggs | 4 tablespoons sugar |
5 tablespoons melted butter or other shortening | 4 apples, sliced thin |
1 tablespoon lemon juice | ¼ cup chopped almonds | ½ teaspoon salt

Break matzos into strips 1 inch wide by 3 inches long. Pour boiling water over and drain, using a colander. Let cool.

Beat eggs with 2 tablespoons sugar till light and creamy.

Add butter that has been melted in pudding dish to be used. Add drained soaked matzo strips and stir lightly. Turn half of this into pudding dish. Add apple slices and chopped nuts. Sprinkle with salt and remainder of sugar. Add the other half of matzo mixture and bake 30 minutes at 350° F. or gas mark 4.

Serves 6.

Variation: Substitute well-drained grated pineapple (canned) or thinly sliced fresh pineapple for apples. Sprinkle chopped nuts on top or serve with sauce made by thickening juice from canned pineapple with 1 teaspoon matzo cake flour. Cook sauce till thick over moderate heat, approximately 3 minutes.

BASIC SAUCE

1 cup sugar | 1 cup water | 2 tablespoons lemon juice |
2 eggs, separated | Dash of salt

Combine sugar, water and lemon juice and bring to a boil. Cook 5 minutes over moderate heat. Beat egg yolks in top of double boiler and stir in the hot syrup till smooth. Place over boiling water and cook 15 minutes, stirring occasionally till thick and creamy. Beat egg whites and salt till stiff but not dry. Fold into sauce.
Serves 4.

Variation 1: For *Lemon Sauce,* increase lemon juice to ¼ cup and add 1 teaspoon grated lemon rind. Proceed as in basic recipe.

Variation 2: For *Orange Sauce,* add 4 tablespoons orange juice and 1 teaspoon grated orange rind before folding in beaten egg whites.

Variation 3: For *milchig* puddings or desserts, add 3 tablespoons butter to basic recipe or Variations 1 or 2 while warm. Stir in but do not beat.

PINEAPPLE SAUCE

2 eggs, separated | 1 tablespoon lemon juice |
½ cup pineapple juice (canned) or ¼ cup syrup from canned pineapple |
½ cup sugar | ¼ cup crushed canned pineapple, drained

Beat egg yolks in top of double boiler. Stir in lemon juice, pineapple juice or syrup and sugar. Cook over boiling water 20 minutes, stirring several times till thickened and smooth. Beat egg whites stiff but not dry. Fold in as soon as cold and stir in the crushed pineapple. Serve immediately.
Serves 4.

RAISIN SAUCE

*⅔ cup light or dark raisins (seedless) | 1 cup boiling water |
½ cup honey or ¾ cup sugar | 1 tablespoon lemon juice |
1 tablespoon butter (optional) | 1 tablespoon potato flour |
Dash of salt | 2 tablespoons cold water*

Combine raisins, boiling water, sweetening and lemon juice. Cook
over moderate heat in a covered saucepan 15 to 20 minutes or till
raisins are puffed. Add butter. Combine potato flour and salt and
moisten with cold water, rubbing till smooth. Stir into the raisin
mixture and cook 10 minutes over low heat, stirring constantly till
smooth.
Serves 4.

WINE SAUCE

*½ cup cold water | ½ cup honey | 1 teaspoon potato flour |
2 eggs, separated | 1 cup wine | 1 teaspoon grated lemon or orange rind*

Combine water, honey and potato flour in a saucepan and cook over
low heat, stirring constantly till thickened and smooth. Beat egg
yolks and stir in while hot, beating as soon as well combined and
creamy. Remove from heat. Stir in wine and grated fruit rind. Beat
egg whites and fold in just before serving.
Serves 4 to 6.

MATZO SHALET

*6 matzos | Water | 1 large onion, diced or thinly sliced |
4 tablespoons chicken or goose schmaltz |
2 tablespoons chopped grebenes (optional) | 3 eggs, beaten with
3 tablespoons sugar | 1 teaspoon salt | Dash of pepper or nutmeg (optional)*

Soak matzos in water until soft. Drain off excess liquid. Fry onion
in fat till lightly browned, and if grebenes are to be used, add when
onion is done. Turn this hot mixture into matzos and add the rest
of the ingredients in the order listed. Bake 45 minutes at 375° F. or
gas mark 5, or till nicely browned on top.
Serves 6 to 8.

MATZO FARFEL SHALET

3 cups matzo farfel | Boiling water to cover, approximately 1 quart |
3 eggs, separated | 4 tablespoons sugar | Grated rind and juice of 1 lemon |
4 tablespoons melted fat (butter, chicken or goose schmaltz) |
½ teaspoon salt (optional)

Soak matzo farfel 10 minutes in boiling water and drain off excess
liquid. Beat egg yolks with sugar, add grated lemon rind and juice
and combine with farfel. Melt shortening in pudding dish or
casserole and turn into the mixture as soon as hot. Beat egg whites
with a pinch of salt and fold in lightly. Taste before adding more
salt. Turn into greased pudding dish and bake 1 hour at 325° F.
or gas mark 3. Serve with raisin sauce or lemon sauce.
    Serves 6 to 8.
    Variation: For a Prune Farfel Shalet, add ½ pound soaked and
pitted prunes just before folding in egg whites.

PASSOVER APPLE SNOW DESSERT

1 cup drained applesauce (or sieved steamed apples) |
1 tablespoon lemon juice | 2 egg whites | Pinch of salt |
Honey or sugar to taste | 1 tablespoon slivered or chopped almonds

Combine lemon juice with applesauce and sweeten to taste. Beat
egg whites with salt till stiff but not dry. If sugar is used for sweetening, add gradually while beating egg white, and fold into first
mixture very lightly. Serve in stem glasses and sprinkle almonds on
top.
    Serves 2 or 3.

PASSOVER BAKED APPLES

Unpared tart apples, cored.

FILLING

Equal parts of matzo meal and chopped nuts |
Lemon or orange juice as needed | 1 tablespoon sugar per apple |
1 pitted prune (soaked and drained) per apple, for stuffing in at top

Combine matzo meal and chopped nuts with enough orange juice to hold together (allowing 1 cupful for 8 apples). Press this mixture into the cavity of apple, almost to the top. Add sugar, then pitted soaked prune. Bake 30 minutes in covered casserole at 375° F. or gas mark 5. Uncover and serve hot.

PRUNE JAM KNEIDLACH (Hungarian)

8 medium potatoes | 1 teaspoon salt | 4 eggs |
1 cup matzo meal or ½ cup each matzo cake flour and matzo meal |
¾ cup melted shortening (schmaltz preferred) | 1½ cups prune jam |
½ cup sugar | ¼ teaspoon cinnamon

Pare and dice potatoes. Boil in water to cover, adding salt. When tender enough to mash with a fork, drain and place in a large mixing bowl. Beat eggs slightly and stir in alternately with matzo meal. Combine with the mashed potatoes. Add 2 tablespoons shortening. When cool enough to handle, form into balls the size of an apple. After all balls are formed, bring to boil 2 quarts of water in a large pot. Make a depression in the centre of each ball or dumpling in turn and fill hollow with prune jam, bringing the dough up to cover filling.

Drop dumplings into boiling water one at a time, adjust pot cover partly to permit escape of steam, and keep at a gentle boil for 10 minutes. Dumplings float to the top as soon as done and should be skimmed out with a perforated spoon. Roll dumplings in sugar and cinnamon, baste generously with remaining melted shortening and brown lightly in the oven at 375° F. or gas mark 5 for 10 minutes or under grill. Serve as dessert.

Yields 10 to 15, depending on size.

PASSOVER BAOLAS

6 eggs | ¾ cup matzo meal (approximately) | Pinch of salt |
Hot melted shortening for deep frying | Honey or sugar and water syrup

SUGAR AND WATER SYRUP

1 cup sugar | 1 cup water | ¼ teaspoon cinnamon

Beat eggs with rotary beater till light. Add salt and stir in enough matzo meal to make a batter that will drop from tip of teaspoon. Drop by teaspoonfuls into hot melted shortening and fry till nicely browned. Skim out and drain off excess fat. Use heavy paper towels for the purpose. Serve with honey or sugar syrup. Sugar syrup is made by boiling the above amounts of sugar, water and cinnamon for 5 minutes or till thick.

Serves 4 to 6.

PASSOVER SALADS AND DRESSINGS

Where salad oil for Passover use is not available, use a blend of melted chicken or goose fat, lemon juice, sugar and a dash of salt and pepper.

RED SEA SALAD

2 tablespoons lemon juice | 2 tablespoons honey | 1 egg white | Pinch of salt | 1 large apple, sliced thin | Shredded lettuce or other salad greens | 1 cup diced or thinly sliced cooked beets

Combine lemon juice and honey. Beat slightly salted egg white and blend into honey mixture by stirring well. Arrange thin wedges of apple in pinwheel fashion on a bed of shredded lettuce or other salad greens. Place a mound of beets in centre and spoon lemon, honey and egg mixture over just before serving.

Serves 4.

Variation: Arrange 4 individual salads and garnish with chopped nuts.

CHARIOT SALAD

5 grapefruit segments | 10 thin slices of cooked beets, medium size | Shredded lettuce | Honey | 1 tablespoon chopped nuts

Arrange two slices of beets between grapefruit segments in pinwheel fashion on a bed of shredded lettuce. Drizzle honey lightly over and sprinkle with chopped nuts.

Serves 1.

Variation 1: Substitute thin slices of seedless oranges for either grapefruit or beets.

Variation 2: Make the pinwheels of sliced oranges, unpeeled, and round slices of cooked beets. Use dressing as for Red Sea Salad.

Variation 3: A soaked and drained prune, pitted and filled with chopped nuts, makes a good centre for these individual salads.

PASSOVER FRUIT SALAD DRESSING

2 egg yolks, beaten light and creamy | 1 tablespoon sugar | 2 tablespoons lemon juice | Few grains of salt added to 2 egg whites, beaten stiff | ¼ teaspoon grated lemon rind | 1 to 2 tablespoons orange juice

Combine beaten yolks, sugar and lemon juice and cook over boiling water, stirring till thick. When cool, stir in lightly the stiffly beaten egg whites. Add a little grated lemon rind, and orange juice to thin to desired consistency.

Serves 4 to 6.

MISCELLANEOUS PASSOVER ITEMS

PASSOVER SOUP MANDLEN

3 eggs | ⅔ cup matzo cake flour | ⅛ teaspoon salt | ½ teaspoon potato flour | Hot melted shortening for deep frying

Beat eggs well and add the other ingredients in the order listed to make a batter that will drop from the tip of a teaspoon. Drop from tip of spoon into hot melted shortening and fry till lightly browned. Skim out with perforated spoon and drain on paper towels. To reheat mandlen, place them in a paper bag in the oven at 375° F. or gas mark 5 for 3 to 5 minutes.

Serves 4 to 6.

Variation 1: Increase matzo cake flour to 1 cup and potato flour to 1 tablespoon. The dough should be stiff enough to pat out on a greased platter, ¼ to ½ inch thick. With a thimble cut out rounds. Or cut into ½-inch squares. Fry as in basic recipe.

Variation 2: Add 1 tablespoon ground almonds to Variation 1 and form ½-inch thick rolls. Cut into ½-inch lengths and fry.

HOME-MADE TINY SAUSAGES (for Passover Parties)

1 pound chopped beef (salt added if necessary) | 1 onion, grated |
1 egg | 2 tablespoons cold water | 1 small carrot | Fine matzo meal

Combine chopped meat, grated onion, beaten egg diluted with
water. Grate in the carrot and mix well. Form ½-inch thick sausages
about 2½ inches in length. Roll in matzo meal and fry till browned
on all sides. Drain off excess fat on paper towels.

Yields approximately 24 sausages.

MATZO DRESSING FOR POULTRY (Basic Recipe)

4 matzos broken into small bits | ½ cup cold water |
1 medium onion, diced | 2 tablespoons schmaltz | ½ teaspoon salt |
½ teaspoon sugar | 2 tablespoons chopped grebenes (optional) | 2 eggs |
1 tablespoon minced parsley

Add water to matzo bits and let stand while browning the diced
onion in hot melted schmaltz. Squeeze out excess water from matzo
and add salt, sugar and chopped grebenes. Beat eggs and add,
mixing well before turning into the pan of fried onions. Stir well
over moderate heat till the dressing is free of moisture and light. Let
cool before adding minced parsley.

Variation 1: Add 6 soaked and pitted prunes cut into bits and a
dash of cinnamon.

Variation 2: Add ¼ cup slivered blanched almonds to basic recipe,
or Variation 1.

Variation 3: Add 1 tablespoon grated orange rind and ½ cup diced
dried light prunes, also the kernels from prune pits ground or
finely chopped.

HOME-MADE WINES FOR PASSOVER

RAISIN WINE 1

2 pounds light raisins (specially prepared for Pesach) |
6 quarts cold water (or boiled water, cooled) | 1 pound sugar |
1 lemon, cut rind and juice | 3 sticks cinnamon (approximately 1 ounce)

Chop raisins and add the other ingredients in the order listed, using a large, well-covered crock. Let stand covered at room temperature 1 week. Stir once a day to keep mixture well under the cover. Fermentation will make the liquid rise and bubble over if not given at least 4 inches of space under the cover. Strain at end of week. A muslin cloth placed in a large funnel over another crock makes an excellent strainer. Return to crock. Cover with muslin then adjust cover. Or bottle and store in a cool place away from light at least 2 weeks before using.

Yields approximately 1½ gallons, depending on quality of raisins.

RAISIN WINE 2

2 pounds seeded raisins | 1 pound sugar | 1 lemon, sliced |
6 quarts boiling water

Chop or cut raisins fine. Place in a crock and add the other ingredients. Cover and stir once or twice each day for a week. Strain through muslin, and bottle. Ready for use in 12 to 14 days. Best stored away from light in a fairly cool place.

Yields approximately 1½ gallons.

Variation 1: Combine all ingredients and boil until reduced by one-fourth, approximately. Let cool before straining and bottling.

Variation 2: For a sweeter wine, add 4 quarts cold water to raisins and boil gently until reduced by one-fourth. Add same amount of sugar and substitute 1 ounce cinnamon for the lemon. Proceed as in Variation 1.

CONCORD GRAPE WINE 1

20 pounds stemmed grapes | 10 pounds sugar

Put grapes in an open crock and use two smooth boards with which to squeeze or mash grapes, working the boards like paddles. Cover crock with muslin and let stand at room temperature for 1 week. Stir once or twice during that period. Strain through muslin. *Do not squeeze* mashed grapes. Return wine to the crock and add the sugar, dissolved with some of the grape juice. Cover with muslin and let

stand at room temperature 7 days longer. Fill jars or large bottles
with the wine but do not cover or cork tightly. Store away from light
for 1 month. Taste and add dissolved sugar if desired. The degree
of sweetness depends on the quality of grapes used. Store in a cool
place away from light. If stored in glass containers, a paper bag will
protect the wine. Ready for use after 3 months. Matures and
increases in strength rapidly after that initial period.

Yields approximately 4 to 4½ gallons.

Grape mash may be utilized for a second wine by adding the
following:

1 *gallon cold water | 4 pounds sugar*

Dissolve sugar in water by boiling gently for 10 minutes. Pour over
grape mash as soon as cool and let stand in a crock or open jar one
week. Strain through muslin and bottle. Store as in Concord Grape
Wine 1.

Yields approximately 1 gallon, depending on consistency of mash.

CONCORD GRAPE WINE 2

*20 pounds ripe grapes, stemmed | 6 quarts boiling water |
10 pounds sugar*

Put stemmed grapes in a stoneware crock and pour in boiling water.
When cool enough to handle, squeeze with the hands without
crushing seeds. The grapes need not be mashed to a dry pulp. Cover
with muslin and let stand 3 days. Strain through muslin as in
Concord Grape Wine 1. Squeeze lightly. Add sugar and stir.
Cover and let stand one week. Uncover and skim carefully. Strain,
bottle and cork tightly. Lay bottle on side and store in a cool place
away from light.

Yields approximately 3½ to 4 gallons.

CONCORD GRAPE WINE 3

6 pounds sound but not overripe grapes | 1 gallon cold water

Place stemmed grapes in a cask or large crock and bruise them well with a wooden spoon, stick or hands. Pour water over and let stand 3 days, stirring once or twice a day. Strain through a large jelly bag, if making a quantity, or through a piece of muslin placed inside a funnel over a bowl or crock. Measure strained juice. For each gallon of juice add the following:

3 pounds sugar | ¼ pint good brandy

Dissolve sugar in some of the juice before adding brandy. Pour into cask or return to crock and cover lightly for 3 to 5 days. Do not disturb cask for 6 months. May be stored in bottles tightly corked and sealed if desired. Keep away from light in a cool place.

Yields approximately 2 gallons.

CHERRY WINE

24 pounds small black cherries, or red sour variety |
½ pound sugar to each quart of juice after mashing and straining

Bruise or mash the cherries in an open vessel or crock. Use a wooden spoon. Do not crush pits. Let stand for 24 hours and strain without squeezing. Measure juice and add sugar as directed. Let stand in crock, covered with muslin, another 24 hours and strain. If placed in a cask, adjust the bung loosely and be certain the vent is not too tight. Drain off after 6 months and bottle. Or use as wanted from cask after tightening bung and vent closing.

Yield depends on juiciness of cherries.

CHERRY CORDIAL

12 pounds large sweet cherries | 5 pounds sugar |
1 pint brandy / 1 quart boiled water, chilled

Stem, wash and drain cherries. Place in a crock and add sugar and brandy. Cover with double fold of muslin. Keep at room temperature. Stir each day for 4 to 5 days to dissolve sugar completely. Cover tightly, keep at room temperature 2 weeks and stir in chilled boiled water. Cover and store in a cool place. Can be bottled after

7

6 weeks. The cherries drained from this cordial may be used for preserves. They make a special treat eaten as they are.

Yield depends on juiciness of cherries.

DAMSON PLUM WINE

10 gallons damson plums (approximately 80 pounds) |
10 gallons boiling water | 2½ pounds sugar per gallon of strained juice

Pierce the plums with a knitting needle in one or two places. Put them in a cask and pour in boiling water. Let stand uncorked 48 hours. Draw off juice and measure. Add sugar as directed. When sugar is dissolved, return juice to cask. Cover bung hole with several thicknesses of muslin or cheesecloth. Let stand until all fermentation has stopped. Remove muslin stopper and adjust bung. Standing undisturbed for 3 to 6 months at room temperature before drawing off and bottling is required. Or draw off wine when needed for Passover. The wine is rich in colour and bouquet. And the damson plums, like cherries left from Cherry Cordial, may be utilized for preserves.

Yield depends on juiciness of plums.

Variation: The addition of 1 quart good brandy before adjusting bung in cask gives variation in flavour and is advised by many families who make this wine for Passover use.

PEACH BRANDY

Clingstone peaches | 3 to 4 cups sugar to each quart jar

Use clingstone peaches when ripe but not soft to the pressure of finger-tip. Pack peaches in 2-quart or gallon glass jars with wide openings. Use 3 to 4 cups sugar to each 2-quart jar, or 6 to 8 cups for each gallon jar. Pour sugar into jars and adjust covers loosely. Shake jars once a day for 1 week or till juice begins to form and all sugar is dissolved. The juice should cover fruit by that time. Tighten lids on each jar and store in a cool, darkened place for 3 months. The brandy may be strained and bottled any time after that.

Yield depends on juiciness of fruit.

HOMEMADE MEAD FOR PASSOVER
(Old-Fashioned Recipe)

2 ounces dry hops | 2 gallons strained honey | 8 gallons water |
1½ ounces white ginger (optional) | 2 lemons, sliced very thin

Tie hops in a cheesecloth. Combine water and honey in a large cooking vessel and add ginger, hops and lemon. Bring to a boil, stirring frequently. Reduce heat and let cook gently 30 minutes. Skim as necessary during the cooking process. Let mead cool in the vessel before straining through a double layer of fine cheesecloth into a wooden cask. Do not fill cask more than ⅔ full to permit fermentation without overflow.

Let stand at room temperature uncorked until fermentation stops, approximately 3 weeks. Bottle if desired and store in a cool, dark place until wanted. To produce a dark amber mead add 1 cup of sugar which has been heated over moderate heat till dark brown. This may be added to some of the mead after fermentation stops if 2 varieties of this delicious beverage are desired.

Yields approximately 8 gallons.

For smaller quantity, reduce ingredients accordingly.

7 Food Customs and Recipes in Israel

MODERN CULINARY CUSTOMS IN ISRAEL

Because Jews from many countries have come to live in the Old-New Land of Israel, the food customs vary in accordance with the food customs and preferences in their former environments. For instance, the recent immigrant from the Germanic countries or Western Europe soon enough learns to say *lechem* when she buys or bakes bread. But she does not forget to prepare the various *mehlshpeisse* her family was accustomed to eat 'at home'. Nor has the Jewish home-maker from East European countries like Poland, Russia, Lithuania, etc., discarded *gefilte fish, cholent, tzimmes* or *kishke*.

In the realm of what we like to call 'the eighth art' – cooking – East meets West in Israel. There the Sephardic Jews have a whole set of culinary traditions rooted in biblical times. Lamb roasted in the open on a spit is still the favourite meat. Lentils, the biblical 'mess of pottage' you remember from the story of Jacob and Esau and their father, Isaac, is a part of the average menu. The broad bean or fava, commonly called *ful*, is used sliced through the heavy pod when green and prepared in many delicious ways. When dried, the beans are stored and made into tasty dishes to go with lamb, mutton or poultry. Sometimes *ful* is combined with tomato, pepper, onion and oil into a vegetable meal-in-one.

The Yemenite Jewish woman may live in a primitive dwelling and fetch water from a neighbourhood well, but her kitchen is strictly 'kosher'. Her dinner generally consists of an eggplant dish, green salad, olives and dark bread. Plenty of olive oil and garlic is used in the preparation of her meals which are not examples of elaborate cuisine as a rule.

Soil and water conditions in some parts of Israel produce vege-tables that may have an unfamiliar flavour to newcomers and visitors. The preparation of such produce must be varied to some degree. Instructions on the subject are issued from time to time by the Scientific Department of the Hebrew University and other agencies.

Available grains and fresh vegetables of the region are used in many ways. Rice, for instance, makes the favourite stuffing for breast of lamb. Rice also makes a tempting dish when combined with *bamya*, known to Westerners as okra. A popular name for okra which newcomers from western lands readily adopt is 'lady fingers' – dainty lengths that come to a point like the prevailing fashion in finger-nails. But whether okra is called by the Hebrew name or just plain 'lady finger', it makes a delicious vegetable dish combined with what we would call Spanish sauce – a mixture of onions, garlic, green peppers, tomatoes, diced and stirred in olive oil.

We in the Western World are being educated in the wider use of whole wheat for all purposes, even in the making of pie crusts and cakes. But *borgoul*, crushed whole wheat, is an everyday matter in the land of Israel. Every Sephardic household relies on this staple. It is specially good when combined with lentils, fried onions, a bit of garlic and oil or chicken fat, then served with gravy. *Borgoul* is coarsely milled wheat and resembles buckwheat groats. It is a staple in the Israeli kitchen, high in nutritive value. It can be cooked in salted water much like the rolled oats we know. It is served for breakfast with milk or cream, honey, sugar or raisins, and fruits in season. It is browned in a heavy skillet and then cooked in salted water like buckwheat groats popularly known as Russian *kasha*. It is eaten with vegetable stews, meat dishes and as a substitute for potatoes.

Finer-milled *borgoul* is used in making pancakes, muffins and other baked foods and as a thickening agent in soups, gravies and stews.

The canning industry is constantly expanding in Israel and almost all vegetables and fruits can be had in this convenient form. Jellies and marmalades enhance the cuisine, and are used for puddings and sauces by many housewives.

Honey, date syrup and fruit syrups can also be had in convenient containers and are used extensively in the preparation of cereals as well as in baking.

A neutral vegetable shortening that serves many purposes is called *kokosin*. It is as popular as the vegetable shortenings used in this country. Because it is *pareve* or neutral, it is used with either meat or milk dishes.

Nahit or *nahut* (chick peas) are served much like salted peanuts or almonds. *Nahit* is cooked with honey or other sweetening, sometimes combined with rice, and served on Sabbath and holidays.

Kastanee (chestnuts) is another popular staple cooked with meats or vegetables. It is also used in dessert dishes or roasted, shelled and eaten hot.

Spices and condiments are popular. Among the most popular are: dill (seed as well as leaves), caraway, sesame, cardamon, poppy seed, chervil, marjoram, coriander, paprika, thyme, and curry powder (which is called by the East Indian name of *kurkum*). Mint, called by the Arab name *nana*, is very popular as a garnish for all types of food from stews to beverages. A most familiar sight is the little box or pot of parsley on a window sill or balcony outside the living-room.

Cactus fruit grows along the roadside. Under the prickly skin is a delicious melon-flavoured edible fruit called *sabra*. Yemenite markets sell this fruit 'defuzzed' and ready for eating. It is iced before serving. *Sabra* is the name affectionately applied to native-born Jewish children because they are 'prickly on the outside' – unconquerable but delightful.

Bananas have become so popular, because of their concentrated nutritive value, that 'a banana a day . . .' replaces the popular slogan 'an apple a day keeps the doctor away'.

Citrus fruits such as grapefruit, lemons, oranges are plentiful and popular. These are served in many ways and for all occasions. Citron, used in the Succot ceremonial (the *esrog* and *lulov*), is also popular for preserves and candied fruit.

Dates, figs, nuts (especially almonds) and raisins are traditional *kibbet* served to visitors. Grapes adorn the fruit bowl on every table. Small fruits like berries and cherries of several varieties are found in abundance and are generally popular.

Olives have been an important item in the daily diet since biblical times. Olives may be used as a main dish or garnish. Olive oil is extensively used in cooking, baking and as salad dressing. The olive tree is known to live and bear fruit longer than most fruit-bearing trees and is cared for with special reverence.

Sesame seeds are used in many ways, much like poppy seed. They form decorations for bread, cakes and biscuits as well as filling for *hamantashen* at Purim time. Because these seeds are rich in nutritive values, sesame oil is used for shortening as well as cooking, frying and in salad dressings.

Gelatin, made from a water plant called *kelp*, comes in un-flavoured and fruit flavoured granules ready to use in the making of aspics and fruit desserts. It is *pareve* (neutral) and can therefore be used with either milk or meat preparations.

Preparation of foods may be a bit complicated in certain areas where gas and electric stoves are not available. A popular cook stove called a Primus stove, the contribution of a Swedish inventor, serves many purposes in the kitchen. This little stove is started with alcohol and then burns noisily by virtue of a constant flow of kerosene. It serves for top of stove baking when a 'wonder pot', shaped much like the well type of cake pan used for baking angel food cake, is placed on the 'Primus'.

Pomegranates, a fruit of the oriental countries, extolled in Solomon's *Song of Songs*, and frequently used in the decorative arts to symbolize the lusciousness of fruits of biblical lands, are a favourite item on Israeli tables. They generally form the highlight of a bowl of fruit.

For instance, pomegranate garnish for meat dishes is commonplace with the Sephardic homemaker when she entertains guests. The little globules of garnet-coloured liquid surrounding each seed add a tempting flavour. They are scattered over and around a lamb roast or over chicken. Pomegranate may be added to sliced or diced citrus fruits served in salads or fruit cup.

Pine nuts are fried in oil and used as a garnish like pomegranate seeds. They have a unique flavour.

Fish, Meat and Poultry. Gefilte fish, made of carp which is abundant in Israel, is customary with old inhabitants as well as newcomers. The Sephardic hostess prefers to serve fish fried to a crispy brown and garnished with a mayonnaise over which fried pine nuts are scattered.

Other favourite fish is *buri* and *mussa*, cut into serving portions and fried in olive oil.

Lamb and mutton is preferred meat, used for grilling and roasting over charcoal fires in the open. (See recipes for *kebab* and *shashlik*.) Other meats such as veal and beef are available in large towns and cities.

Poultry is the customary Sabbath and holiday meat.

Breads. Chola is the Sabbath Loaf and is also used for holidays. However, Jews from the Levantine countries in the group commonly referred to as the Near East, bake small flat cakes of dough called *kibbetz*. They have a soft crust and are used to dip into gravies and sauce, or to sop up or spoon up food. Jews from Bulgaria, Rumania and other Balkan countries call these small cakes *peetah* and use them similarly.

POPULAR SOUPS

The most popular soups are made of berries or other native fruits. These are served hot or cold, depending on the occasion, and are thickened with sour cream or beaten egg yolk. Garnishes may be whole berries or slices of the fruit used as the basic ingredients for soup. Berries, cherries, grapes and apricots are used for uncooked soups. Borsht is commonplace and eaten with boiled potato, sour cream or sour milk. (See Index for recipes.)

UNCOOKED FRUIT SOUP (Basic Recipe)

½ *cup berry or other fruit pulp | 1 cup water, skimmed milk or sour milk |*
Sugar or honey to sweeten | Lemon or orange juice to taste (optional) |
1 tablespoon sour cream per serving

Blend together ingredients as listed and thicken by stirring in sour cream.
Serves 1.

COOKED FRUIT SOUP (Basic Recipe)

Stew berries or larger fruit and purée. To each ½ cup pulp add ingredients listed as for Uncooked Fruit Soup and thicken with sour cream, 1 egg yolk per serving or with whole egg slightly beaten and stirred in. Variety can be achieved by thickening with egg yolk and floating beaten egg white on top before serving.
  Variation: Substitute stewed dried fruit or fruits for fresh berries or other fresh fruit.

DRIED APRICOT SOUP

2 cups dried apricots | 3 cups cold water |
3 tablespoons sugar or 1 tablespoon honey | ¼ teaspoon cinnamon |
Dash of nutmeg | 1 teaspoon lemon juice | Pinch of salt |
1 cup light cream and 1½ cups milk, or 1¼ cups evaporated milk
and 1¼ cups water | 3 egg whites or grated lemon rind

Stew apricots in cold water over simmer flame in a covered pot 30

minutes. Put through a sieve or fruit press. Yields approximately
2 cups purée. Add sugar or honey, cinnamon, nutmeg, lemon juice
and salt while hot. Just before serving, hot or cold, stir in cream and
milk or diluted evaporated milk and heat but do not boil. Top with
a little grated lemon rind or float teaspoonfuls of beaten egg white
on top of each serving, using 3 egg whites for the above amount.
Serves 6.

WINE SOUP

1 cup cold water | 2 tablespoons honey | 1 tablespoon lemon or orange juice |
1 tablespoon cornflour | 1 cup table wine (any variety) |
1 beaten egg white | Dash of salt and sugar

Bring to a boil water, honey and fruit juice. Mix cornflour with a
little cold water and stir in. Cook 3 minutes or till clear. Add wine
gradually by stirring into hot liquid just before serving. Float beaten
egg white seasoned with salt and sugar on top in drops or swirls.
Serves 2.
Variation: Serve chilled by refrigerating thickened soup and wine
    separately and combining by quick stirring.

ICED MILK SOUP (Uncooked)

1 cup milk | ½ cup cold water | 1 tablespoon lemon juice | Sugar to taste |
Dash of salt | 1 tablespoon strawberry or other fruit jam or preserves |
Finely slivered or chopped almonds | Mint leaves or pomegranate globules

Combine all ingredients, except nuts, mint or pomegranate. Thicken
with sour cream if desired and garnish with nuts, mint or pomegranate just before serving.
Serves 1 or 2.

BUTTERMILK SOUP (Uncooked)

1 cup buttermilk | 1 tablespoon sugar | Dash of cinnamon |
2 tablespoons dry bread or cracker crumbs |
1 tablespoon light or dark seedless raisins | Grated lemon rind to taste

Combine all ingredients except lemon rind which is floated on top of each serving.

Serves 1.

VEGETABLES

Okra is a popular vegetable in Israel. It grows in abundance and almost every kitchen boasts of strings of okra dried in the sun for out-of-season use. This vegetable is used with rice, chopped meat, tomatoes at any season of the year.

Whether fresh or dried, it is washed and patted dry before removing the stem ends, then cooked in a minimum of water, tomato juice, meat gravy or simply fried in oil till tender. A little salt is all that is required for seasoning. When tomato is added, a little sugar may be required. When combined with cooked rice, cooked meat or meat gravy, no additional flavouring is needed.

Served on a mound of mashed potatoes or boiled rice, it makes a delicious dish.

Squash (marrow) grows in several varieties in Israel and all are very popular. The very small, elongated variety which we are accustomed to call *zucchini* or *courgettes*, is especially plentiful and popular. Here are a few recipes:

MARROW WITH BUTTER SAUCE (Basic Recipe)

*6 to 8 small green marrows | 4 tablespoons cold water or milk |
Salt to taste | 2 tablespoons butter or oil | 2 tablespoons flour |
1 tablespoon lemon juice | Dash of nutmeg (optional)*

Wash and cube the marrows, or cut in quarters lengthwise. Add water and salt. Cook in a tighly covered pot 5 to 8 minutes or till tender. Brown flour in hot melted shortening and stir in the liquid drained from the cooked vegetable till smooth. Cook 3 minutes. Add flavourings and pour over the cooked marrows.

Serves 2 to 4, depending on size of marrows.

MARROW WITH EGGS

1 *onion, diced* | 2 *tablespoons shortening (butter, oil or vegetable)* |
Pinch of salt | 2 *cups diced marrow, cooked* |
4 *tablespoons cold water, approximately* | 4 *to* 6 *eggs, separated* |
$\frac{1}{8}$ *teaspoon salt* | *Minced or sprigs of parsley or dill*

Cook onion in hot melted shortening in a frying pan. When light brown add salt and stir. Turn off heat and skim out fried onion. Cook diced marrow in cold water in a well-covered pot 10 minutes or till tender. Drain off liquid. Add cooked marrow to frying pan and beat eggs separately, adding salt to egg whites while beating stiff but not dry. Combine beaten yolks and egg whites and pour over marrow. Cook over low to moderate heat 3 to 5 minutes or till eggs are set and the top frothy. With a spatula turn up half the omelet over other half and serve with fried onions, parsley or dill. Serve immediately.
Serves 4.

MARROW WITH TOMATO

3 *cups diced marrow* | $\frac{1}{4}$ *teaspoon salt* | 4 *tablespoons cold water* |
1 *cup diced fresh tomato or* $\frac{1}{2}$ *cup stewed* | 1 *teaspoon sugar* |
1 *tablespoon butter* | 1 *tablespoon flour*

Cook in a covered pot marrow, salt, water and tomato 10 minutes. Add sugar. Brown flour in hot melted butter and stir in. Cook 3 minutes longer, uncovered, stirring to prevent sticking.
Serves 4.
Variation: Serve with boiled potatoes, whole or finely diced.

SAUTÉED MARROW

1 *pound marrow (small green variety)* | $\frac{1}{8}$ *teaspoon salt* |
3 *tablespoons fine cracker crumbs or matzo meal* |
3 *tablespoons hot melted shortening* | 3 *tablespoons sugar* |
Pinch of cinnamon

Cut into $\frac{1}{4}$-inch thick rounds (unpared marrow) or lengthwise into

¼-inch thick slices. Sprinkle with salt very lightly and roll each piece in crumbs or matzo meal. Sauté in hot melted shortening on both sides of slices till tender and lightly browned. Sprinkle with sugar and cinnamon as cooked slices are removed from pan to baking dish. Return to hot frying pan and cover till serving time or heat in moderate oven 5 to 10 minutes. This dish is frequently served cold.
Serves 4.

VEGETABLE MEAL-IN-ONE (Sephardic Recipe)

*1 cup diced green beans | 1 cup diced carrots | 1 cup diced eggplant |
1 cup stewed or 1½ cups sliced fresh tomatoes | 1 teaspoon salt |
4 tablespoons butter or other shortening | 4 eggs, well beaten |
2 cups cooked rice, drained, tightly packed*

Wash and drain diced vegetables. Combine and add tomatoes, sprinkle with salt and stir once or twice. Butter baking dish or casserole and turn in vegetable mixture. Melt remaining shortening in a saucepan and drizzle over top of vegetables. Pour beaten eggs over top and bake 25 to 30 minutes at 350° F. or gas mark 4, or till eggs are set. Serve with mounds of cooked rice around or underneath.
Serves 5 or 6.
Variation: Substitute cooked fine noodles or macaroni for rice.

EGGPLANT, of which there are many variations, is included in the menus frequently. Eggplants may form the basis of a meatless meal – a sort of goulash – or they may be served up as a dessert pancake, dusted with sugar.

EGGPLANT PANCAKES

*1 large eggplant | ¼ teaspoon salt | 2 eggs | Icing sugar as required |
Shortening for deep frying (vegetable or salad oil) |
½ cup fine cracker crumbs | Finely ground nuts (optional)*

Pare eggplant and slice into ¼-inch thick rounds. Dust lightly with salt and let stand under a heavy plate while preparing the other ingredients. Beat eggs light, and add a pinch of salt and a few grains of sugar. Heat enough shortening to be $\frac{1}{2}$ inch deep when melted, in a heavy frying pan. Rinse eggplant slices in cold water and pat dry with a towel or paper towels. Dip each slice lightly in cracker crumbs then in beaten eggs, then dip into cracker crumbs on the under side.

Fry until well-browned and crisp at the edges before turning to complete the process. Lift each pancake with a pancake turner and drain free of fat on paper towels. While the second panful is frying, dust each pancake with sugar and roll up. Fasten with a toothpick. Just before serving, dust generously with more sugar. Finely-ground nuts may be added. Or, spread a little preserves of any kind lightly over the tops. If this dessert is served with a milchig meal, heap a tablespoonful of sour cream on each rolled pancake.

These pancakes may be served unrolled with the garnish in the centres, at least two per serving.

Serves 4.

PATLIJAN BOEREG (An Egyptian Eggplant Speciality)

This is a popular dish in Israel, especially with Jews from Near Eastern countries. It is prepared as follows:

> 1 *large eggplant* | *Salt to taste* | $\frac{1}{4}$ *cup flour* | $\frac{3}{4}$ *cup oil* | 3 *eggs* |
> $\frac{1}{2}$ *pound cottage cheese with large curds* | 1 *teaspoon minced parsley* |
> 1 *tablespoon lemon juice*

Cut unpared eggplant into $\frac{1}{4}$-inch thick slices or rounds. Salt lightly and let stand approximately half an hour. Pat each slice dry, dust lightly with flour and fry in hot oil till nicely browned on both sides. Pour off surplus oil, leaving the fried eggplant slices in bottom of frying pan. Remove half the fried eggplant to a plate. Beat 2 eggs, add dry cheese and 1 teaspoon minced parsley and spread over the eggplant slices in the pan. Cover with remaining fried eggplant, and cook over low heat for 3 to 5 minutes. Beat remaining egg till light and frothy. Lift cover and pour beaten egg over top layer of eggplant. Let cook uncovered till set. Garnish with parsley or a sprinkling of lemon juice. Serve hot.

Serves 4.

PATLIJAN ALA NAZ
(Turkish Scalloped Eggplant with Lamb)

This dish is also very popular with Jews from the Near East. It is a meal-in-one type of dish and easily prepared.

10 slices of eggplant, ½ inch thick | Salt to taste |
1 pound chopped lamb, mutton or beef | 1 onion, minced or chopped |
½ cup minced parsley | Pepper or paprika to taste |
½ cup tomato purée | 1 cup water

Salt eggplant and drain or pat dry as soon as softened. Combine chopped meat with onion and parsley and season to taste. Spread on each slice of eggplant and arrange in a well-greased baking dish. Top each piece with tomato purée diluted with water and bake 1 hour at 325° F. or gas mark 3. Slip under grill to brown on top, if desired, a few minutes before serving time. Garnish with parsley or serve on toast, mashed potato or boiled rice.
Serves 5.
Variation: Place 2 meat-topped eggplant slices together and fasten with toothpicks. Arrange in a greased baking dish and cover with diluted tomato purée. Bake till lightly browned on top.

MOUSSAKA (Armenian Eggplant and Meat)

This dish is also popular with Jews from the Near East.

1 pound minced lamb, mutton or beef | Salt and pepper, or paprika to taste |
1 eggplant | ⅔ cup tomato paste | ½ cup dry bread crumbs or
browned borgoul (wheat grains obtainable at Health Food shops)

Season meat to taste and press down into the bottom of a greased casserole or baking dish. Slice unpared eggplant into thin rounds and arrange over meat. Top with tomato paste, cover with bread crumbs or borgoul. Cover tightly and bake 30 minutes at 350° F. or gas mark 4. Remove cover and let brown on top, approximately 10 minutes.
Serves 4.

EGGPLANT WITH EGGS AND ONIONS

1 large eggplant or 6 small ones | 2 onions |
2 tablespoons oil or other shortening | 4 eggs | Salt to taste |
2 tablespoons grated Cheddar cheese | Parsley or dill for garnish (optional)

Pare eggplant and cut into large cubes. Peel and dice onions and fry in oil to a golden brown. Add eggplant. Cover tightly. Let stew over a low flame until the eggplant is tender, about 10 minutes. Remove cover and shake frying pan. Beat eggs, season with salt and pour over eggplant. Cook until the eggs are set. Turn on to a platter and sprinkle with grated cheese. Minced dill or parsley may be used to garnish this very nourishing dish.

Serves 4 to 5.

Variation: Serve with sour cream, omitting eggs. Add more parsley or dill on top.

EGGPLANT IN MARINADE

Small eggplants (4 per serving) | Salt | Vinegar (diluted to taste) |
Sliced onion | Peppercorns | Bay leaf | Whole mixed spices

Cut small eggplants in quarters lengthwise. Do not pare. Cook in salted boiling water 5 to 10 minutes or till tender. Drain well. Dilute vinegar to taste, bring to a boil and add sliced onion, peppercorns, bay leaf and whole mixed spices. Cover eggplant pieces. Store in a covered glass jar or crock for 2 weeks before serving. An excellent condiment for meat, poultry or fish.

EGGPLANT AND RICE SCALLOP

Fried eggplant slices (to make 2 layers) | 1½ cups boiled rice |
1 cup finely cut leftover meat | 1 egg | 1 cup water | Salt to taste

In a casserole or deep baking dish place a layer of fried eggplant slices. Spread boiled rice over evenly, then meat, and top with remaining fried eggplant slices. Beat the egg, add a little water and pour over the top. Add remaining water around the sides. Salt to taste. Bake 30 minutes at 350° F. or gas mark 4. Serve hot.

Serves 4 or 5.

SAVOURY EGGPLANT

2 pounds eggplant | ¼ cup flour | Oil for frying |
2 onions, finely chopped | 1 cup tomato sauce | ¼ cup bread crumbs |
Salt and ginger to taste | 3 tablespoons butter

Slice unpared eggplant. Dip in a little flour and fry in oil till nicely
browned on both sides. Chop or mash the fried eggplant, add onions,
tomato sauce, crumbs, salt and ginger. Arrange in a baking dish, dot
with butter and sprinkle on a few bread crumbs. Bake 30 minutes at
350° F. or gas mark 4, or till browned on top.

Serves 4 or 5.

VEGETABLE STRUDEL (Contributed by Sephardic Jews)

½ cup each finely cut or shredded spinach, cabbage, eggplant, tomato and onions|
Salt and pepper to taste | 4 tablespoons butter or oil |
2 tablespoons flour | 2 tablespoons cold water |
Strudel dough (see Index, homemade stretched Strudel dough) |
Sesame seed

Stew vegetables in a tightly covered pot with only the water which
clings to them. When tender, season to taste with salt and pepper and
1 tablespoon oil. Mix together water and flour till smooth and stir in
lightly, shaking the pot to prevent sticking. Cook over low heat 3 to
4 minutes longer. Let cool before spreading evenly on thin sheets of
strudel pastry dough. Roll up, brush with remaining oil and sprinkle
with sesame seed. Bake at 375° F. or gas mark 5 for 20 minutes or
till nicely browned. Cut the strudel rolls diagonally into 2½- or 3-
inch cuts while warm, before removing from baking pan or baking
sheet. Serve with fish or dairy meals. Or if prepared with oil or
vegetable shortening, serve with meat or poultry.

Serves 4 to 6.

STEAMED LEEK PUDDING

4 large leeks | Boiling water | 1 tablespoon flour |
Salt to taste | 2 tablespoons chicken fat

Dolma (*page 114*)

SUET CRUST

1 *cup flour* | 1 *teaspoon baking powder* | ½ *cup finely chopped suet* |
⅛ *teaspoon salt* | *Water to make stiff dough*

Wash and cut leeks into 1-inch lengths. Scald with boiling water and
drain well. Combine flour, salt and fat. Sprinkle over the leeks.

Make the suet crust by combining ingredients in order listed. Roll
out dough to ½-inch thickness. Place seasoned leeks in the centre of
dough, pinch edges together and tie in a well-greased paper bag or a
muslin cover. Steam 2½ hours.

Serves 4.

FISH AND MEATS

BALUK PLAKKI
(A favourite dish among Jews from Turkey)

3 *pounds cleaned fish (any firm-fleshed fish can be used)* |
½ *cup oil, butter or vegetable shortening* | *Salt to taste* |
2 *large onions* | 4 *large tomatoes (or* 1 *cup strained, canned)* |
1 *cup boiling water* | *Parsley and/or fresh mint* | *Lemon wedges (optional)*

Prepare the fish as for grilling. Rub inside and outside with oil and
salt lightly. Grill under low heat turning when inner side is brown,
then brown outer side. Place the fish in a long baking dish, cover
with sliced onions and tomatoes or the strained canned tomato.
Sprinkle lightly with salt and bake 20 minutes at 400° F. or gas
mark 6. Then add 1 cup boiling water and baste. Bake 5 to 10
minutes longer. Serve either hot or cold, garnished with parsley and/
or fresh mint. Wedges of lemon may be added.

Serves 6.

DA-VO-OD BASHA (Near East Dish)

4 *small eggplants* | ½ *pound chopped lamb or mutton* | *Salt to taste* |
½ *cup tomato purée or* 1 *cup stewed tomatoes* | 2 *tablespoons vinegar* |
2 *tablespoons brown sugar (approximately)*

Cut unpared eggplant lengthwise and scoop out seed sections. Chop
seed sections with the meat and season to taste with salt. Return to

8

eggplant halves, pressing down into the cavities and mounding up slightly. Arrange in a baking pan, add tomato purée and vinegar sweetened to taste. Bake 20 to 30 minutes at 350° F. or gas mark 4, or till the eggplants can be pierced with a fork.

Serves 4.

DOLMA (East Europeans call this dish *Holishkes* or *Praakes*)

Cabbage leaves | Boiling water | 3 large tomatoes |
3 green peppers, cut lengthwise | 1½ pounds chopped meat (lamb preferred) |
Salt to taste | ½ cup borgoul (wheat grains) or brown rice (both
obtainable at Health Food shops)
Lemon juice or vinegar to taste | Brown sugar as required

Cover cabbage leaves with boiling water and let stand till wilted and soft. Cut stem ends from tomatoes and peppers and remove seeds. Add tomato centres to meat, season to taste then add the borgoul or rice. Fill the drained wilted cabbage leaves with the meat mixture and tuck in the ends. Fill tomatoes and peppers. Arrange the cabbage rolls among the stuffed tomato and pepper halves in a casserole or deep baking dish. Add lemon juice, sugar and enough water to prevent sticking to bottom of dish. Cover and cook over low heat 30 to 40 minutes or till gravy has formed. Uncover and cook 10 to 20 minutes longer or till nicely browned on top.

Serves 6.

MEAT-FILLED KIBBAS OR KIBBETS

DOUGH

1 cup fine borgoul (wheat grains) or brown rice | 2 cups boiling water |
¼ teaspoon salt | 1 egg

FILLING

1 pound lamb | 2 tablespoons diced or grated onion | 2 tablespoons oil |
Hot melted shortening for frying (¾ cup approximately)

Stir borgoul into boiling salted water. Cook over moderate heat, stirring till smooth. This mush requires longer cooking than farina.

Stir in beaten egg as soon as mush is cool. Chop meat or put through meat grinder using medium blade. Add onion and stir in hot oil over moderate heat till lightly browned.

When cool enough to handle both mixtures, form 8 thin cakes of the dough, about 3 inches in diameter, and tuck a rounded tablespoon of the meat filling in the centres. Form into elongated rolls pointed at both ends. Fry in hot melted shortening till nicely browned on all sides. Drain well on paper towels. May be reheated in oven or in covered frying pan over low heat on top of stove a few minutes before serving.

Serves 4.

KHIYAR DOLMA
(A favourite among Armenian and Turkish Jews)

10 cucumbers (unpared if small) |
½ cup borgoul (wheat grains) or brown rice | Salt to taste |
1 pound chopped meat | 4 large tomatoes |
Oil or vegetable shortening as needed

Pare and cut cucumbers lengthwise. Scoop out seed section. Steam or boil borgoul or rice in slightly salted water till tender. Season to taste and fill cucumber halves with rice and chopped meat. Arrange in a baking dish, cover with sliced tomatoes, sprinkle with salt and a generous amount of oil or shortening. Bake at 325° F. or gas mark 3 for 40 to 50 minutes or till the cucumbers are tender when pierced with a fork.

Serves 5 (or more if served as a side dish).

SHISH-KEBAB (A special favourite from the Near East)

Lamb or beef (¼ pound per serving) | Onion juice or a grated onion |
Garlic | Wine for flavour | Small tomatoes, mushrooms or cubed eggplant |
¼ cup flour

While lamb is generally used for this dish, beef can be used to advantage and is sometimes preferred by Westerners. Allow ¼ pound per serving and cut meat into small pieces or cubes. Marinate the meat with onion juice or grated onion and a bit of garlic. Sprinkle with wine for special flavour – Sherry is excellent – and let stand two hours or longer in this marinade. When ready to cook, rub individual skewers with a cut clove of garlic and arrange the cubes of meat alternately with small tomatoes or mushrooms, or slightly larger cubes of eggplant. Dust lightly with flour and grill about 10 minutes, turning to brown evenly on all sides. Serve hot.

SHASHLIK (Basic Recipe)

*1½ pounds lamb or mutton, trimmed of fat and rubbed with
1 clove garlic, cut | Halves of egg or plum tomatoes and
sliced small onions | Salt to taste*

Cut into 1½-inch cubes meat that has been trimmed of fat, gristle and bone. Arrange cuts of meat on metal skewers with tomato halves and onion slices between. If long skewers are used, 2 skewers will serve 4. If individual skewers are used, divide meat and vegetables into 4 portions and arrange as for double-portion skewers. Dust lightly with salt and grill over hot charcoal 10 minutes, turning to light brown on all sides, 3 to 5 minutes. The custom is to grill shashlik after dinner guests have arrived.

Serves 4.

Variation 1: Mushrooms may substitute for onion or tomato. Small mushrooms need not have stems removed. Large mushrooms, stems removed, should be peeled, washed and drained well before arranging between meat cubes.

Variation 2: 1½-inch cubes of pared eggplant may be used with mushrooms, with or without tomato halves. Roll eggplant cubes in flour seasoned lightly with salt and pepper before arranging on skewers between meat cubes.

Variation 3: Meat may be pounded to ½-inch thickness before cutting into 1½-inch wide strips. Put point of skewer through one end of strip and twist. Fasten with a toothpick. Grill till lightly browned on all sides then sprinkle lightly with salt and pepper to taste.

NEAR EAST MEAT SAUCE

*1 cup cooked nahit (chick peas) | ½ cup liquid |
1 clove garlic or ⅛ teaspoon garlic salt | 4 tablespoons peanut oil*

Purée nahit, adding liquid in which it has been cooked. Grate or mash garlic and add. Or, use garlic salt. Stir in oil till well combined. Yields 1 pint.
Variation: Add 4 tablespoons peanut butter, combining till smooth.

SARMI (Called *Sarmali* in the Balkan Countries)

This is a favourite dish among Jews from Armenia, Turkey and the Near East. It is made without meat, and is therefore unlike the Sarmali-in-Foie de Vitza that Rumanians prepare. (See Index.)

8 vine leaves the size of a hand | Boiling water |
4 large onions, diced or chopped | Vegetable shortening or oil | 1 cup rice |
⅓ cup cut or chopped seeded raisins | Salt to taste | Parsley

Wash vine leaves and cover with boiling water till the leaves are wilted. Drain well. Fry onions in shortening till light brown and transparent. Add washed rice and raisins and stir well over reduced heat for 2 minutes. Add salt to taste. Let cool before placing a spoonful of the mixture in the centre of each leaf and rolling up, tucking in the ends or forming into a tightly-wrapped ball. Arrange neatly in a heavy skillet, add water to cover and let simmer 30 minutes. Water may be added if necessary to prevent sticking. Slip under grill to brown if desired. Serve with yogurt or sour cream topping, hot or cold, and garnish with parsley.
Serves 4.

FAGGOT SALAD (Probably referring to the Turkish domination of Palestine)

1 cup tiny Brussels sprouts | 1 cup cauliflower florets | Salt |
1 cup cubed cooked liver, beef or chicken | 2 tablespoons shortening |
1 cup sliced mushrooms | 4- to 6-inch lengths of celery stalks |
6 pickled gherkins, cut lengthwise | Lettuce, shredded |
Salad dressing or mayonnaise

Cook the sprouts and cauliflower florets separately in a minimum of salted water until tender. Drain well. Grill liver before cutting into cubes. Sauté the sliced mushrooms. Arrange the celery stalks on shredded lettuce, then the sliced gherkins (or slice lengthwise any pickled cucumbers on hand), and next add the Brussels sprouts and cauliflower. Add the cubed liver and top with mushrooms. Either pass the salad dressing or add it carefully just before serving.

Serves 4.

RED CAPS SALAD (Probably referring to the Spanish Inquisition)

Hard-cooked eggs, 1 per serving | Shredded lettuce |
Small tomatoes (egg or plum), 1 per serving |
Mayonnaise or salad dressing | Fresh mint leaves or parsley

Arrange hard-cooked eggs (one end sliced to permit standing upright) on a bed of lettuce. Top each egg with a scooped out small tomato. With a teaspoon add mayonnaise or salad dressing from the top down, on one side like a tassel. Add fresh mint leaves or parsley for garnish.

Variation: Arrange cooked or canned asparagus spears between the eggs of the Red Caps Salad and decorate with strips of red or green pepper for added colour.

POTATO DOUGH

Potato Dough is used for many attractive dishes. It can be made into balls or croquettes and fried in butter, oil or vegetable shortening. These little balls of dough can also be boiled in salted water and served as a garnish for clear soups or with meat gravy. Potato dough can be cut into strips like broad noodles or thin flat rounds like biscuits, then fried or baked and served as an accompaniment to cottage cheese, with or without fruit sauce or fresh berries.

BASIC RECIPE

1 *egg | 1 cupful cooked mashed potato |*
Enough flour to make a stiff dough

Combine slightly beaten egg with cooled mashed potato. Work in the flour to make a dough stiff enough to roll with a rolling pin on a lightly floured board. Or pinch off a ball of dough and flatten with the hand. Use a small biscuit cutter or a wine glass, and for tiny rounds use a thimble.

Bake, boil or fry as below.

Serves 1.

FRUIT DUMPLINGS WITH POTATO DOUGH (Baked)

Place half an apricot, fresh or canned (well drained), or a dried apricot half, in the centre of a flattened piece of potato dough and bring the edges together, dumpling fashion. Turn upside down, place on a greased baking sheet or in a pan and bake at 350° F. or gas mark 4 till nicely browned. Serve with any fruit sauce or a brown butter and honey combination.

Potato Dough Topping for vegetable or meat pies, or casserole dishes, is very popular and most attractive as well as tasty.

Potato Dough Fingers can be made by forming dough into 1½-inch fingers, frying them till browned, then rolling in finely chopped nuts.

UNCOOKED FRUIT PUDDING MOULD

Fresh or stewed dried fruits | Berries in season | Grated lemon rind | Sugar | Chopped nuts | Rusks or dried bread | Fruit juice

Use either fresh fruits and berries or stewed dried fruits for this pudding. It is best to prepare it on Friday for Saturday serving. Spread a layer of berries or other fruits in season on the bottom of a bowl. Add a sprinkling of grated lemon rind, sugar and chopped nuts. Place rusks or oblong slices of dried bread to cover the fruit. Arrange alternate layers until bowl is filled. Make the top layer of fruit and chopped nuts. Pour in enough fruit juice to come half-way up the side of the bowl. Let stand at least 3 hours before serving. If kept for the Sabbath, be sure to cover and store in a refrigerator.

ERETZ ISRAEL HONEY CAKE

½ cup honey | 1 cup sugar | 1 wineglass raspberry syrup |
1 cup black coffee, warm | 1 cup flour | ½ tablespoon butter |
2 cups finely chopped nuts | ½ cup each finely cut or
chopped candied lemon and orange peel | ½ cup light raisins |
4 teaspoons cinnamon | ½ teaspoon pepper | 2 teaspoons baking soda

Bring honey to boiling point and stir in ingredients in the order given. Turn into a paper-lined cake pan, filling half full, and bake 45 minutes at 350° F. or gas mark 4 until nicely browned. Allow the cake to cool in the pan before turning out. This honey cake should be baked at least 2 weeks before serving. Keep in a cake box or wrapped in a heavy wax paper and covered with a towel.

In Israel this cake is usually baked in a 'wonder pot' over medium heat on top of the stove.

ASHOURAH (A dessert familiar to Near Eastern Jews)

1 cup seeded raisins, chopped fine | 1½ pounds sugar | ¼ cup water |
¼ cup each chopped toasted almonds, walnuts and hazel nuts |
1 pound borgoul (wheat grains) or brown rice (both obtainable
from Health Food shops) | Salt |
1 teaspoon rosewater or almond extract | 1 teaspoon cinnamon or nutmeg

Boil sugar and raisins in ¼ cup water till bubble stage is reached. Remove from heat and add nuts. Cook borgoul in slightly salted cold water to cover and drain when tender. Stir into the raisins and nuts mixture, cool about 5 minutes. Fold in the flavouring. Serve a heaped spoonful of this mixture over more nuts and top with an almond. Add a sprinkling of cinnamon or nutmeg if desired.

Serves 6 to 8.

KATAIYIFF (A sweetmeat classic with Turkish Jews)

1 pound fine noodles | Salt | 4 tablespoons butter or other shortening |
1 cup slivered almonds or hazel nuts | 1 cup honey (approximately)

Cook noodles in slightly salted water till tender and drain thoroughly.

Pack into a shallow oblong pan and when cold and caked, turn out and cut into squares. Arrange on a well-greased baking sheet and cover each slice with nuts. Pour honey over each piece and bake 20 to 30 minutes at 350° F. or gas mark 4. Serve with a sprinkling of nuts on each and drizzle more honey over the nuts. It is a bit sticky, but delicious.

SUM-SUM SQUARES (A Confection)

In Israel at holiday time sum-sum dainties are much in evidence.

*½ cup sugar | ½ cup honey | ¼ cup hot water | Pinch of salt |
1 cup sesame seeds (sum-sum) |
½ cup finely chopped walnuts, hazel nuts or almonds*

Combine sugar, honey and hot water in top of a double boiler. Add a pinch of salt and bring to a boil over moderate heat, stirring to prevent scorching. Let cook till it reaches the soft ball stage – when a drop forms a ball in cold water. Stir in the sesame seeds and chopped nuts and cook over hot water for 3 minutes, stirring constantly. Then return the pot to moderate direct heat, stirring till the colour is a golden brown – approximately 5 minutes. Turn the mixture out on a wet board and pat down to a ½-inch thickness. Dip a knife blade in hot water and cut into 1½-inch squares or diamond shapes. Work fast before the mixture hardens.

8 Breads, Beigels and Rolls

Bread-making in the Home. The baking of bread has become a specialized function, scientifically and professionally performed outside the average home. However, the varieties of bread have multiplied to suit various needs of the modern family. For those whose preferences or requirements demand home-made breads, a number of recipes given here will be acceptable.

Leavening Agents

Yeast is necessary in the making of most breads. It is a microscopic bit of plant life which increases and multiplies when combined with food on which it lives. It is destroyed at 90° F. and ceases to grow in temperatures below 30° F. Yeast increases the vitamin content of food. It can be purchased in convenient granular form in water-resistant packages, stamped with the date beyond which it loses its potency for action as a leavening agent.

Eggs, Salt, Potato Water serve to quicken the action of yeast and are classed as leavening agents.

Baking Powder is used as the leavening agent in quick breads like muffins, popovers and biscuits of various kinds.

Baking Soda is generally used in combination with sour milk, sour cream or buttermilk in the baking of quick breads and coffee cakes.

Unleavened Bread used exclusively by Jews during the week of Passover is called matzo and contains none of the leavening agents used during the rest of the year. Matzo is baked under special supervision and labelled *Strictly Kosher for Passover*. Matzo meal, coarse and finely ground, is made from baked matzos. Matzo farfel is also made from baked matzos. Matzo products are available during the rest of the year but are marked accordingly.

Water and Milk are used as combining elements in the mixing of dough for bread. Water contributes no food value but does produce bread that retains its moisture content and crispy crusts. Milk (used only in some breads) adds food value as well as flavour, helps retain moisture in the loaf, and provides a rich golden brown crust as well as creamy texture.

Other Ingredients in bread-making are used to add flavour, determine texture and stimulate leavening power.

Sugar hastens the activity of yeast and improves the flavour and appearance of bread. Too much sugar retards yeast action.

Salt adds to the flavour of bread but must be used in moderation as too much retards yeast activity.

Shortening improves the keeping qualities of bread and also its texture.

Eggs enrich the loaf's nutritive value, add lightness because of their leavening power, and improve the colour of bread.

Methods of Preparation

Dissolve yeast in lukewarm water to which a teaspoon of sugar should be added to start yeast activity. If dry yeast is used, crumble the yeast into lukewarm water and let stand about 5 minutes to soften. If milk is to be used in the preparation of yeast dough, scald the milk and allow to cool to lukewarm before adding to yeast. Scalding prevents multiplication of bacteria and enzymes which may injure the dough while rising at room temperature. Evaporated milk need not be scalded.

Sift flour and measure the exact amount required in the recipe.

Whole wheat flours are not sifted before measuring, but are stirred lightly to ensure accurate measuring.

To make a Sponge, add sugar to yeast, stir in lukewarm liquid and beat into about half the required amount of sifted flour. Cover and let stand at room temperature until the batter becomes light and bubbly. Add salt, melted shortening, eggs, and flour enough to make dough of the desired stiffness. Knead on a floured board till smooth, folding the dough over and using the heels of the thumbs for pressure. Place the kneaded dough in a bowl 2 or 3 times its size and cover with a folded towel. Let rise till it is double in bulk, and, when pressed with the finger, retains an imprint.

Second Rising of Dough is not essential but improves the texture of bread. When the dough has doubled in bulk, remove to a floured board and knead by pressing down the centre and punching the sides into the depression, working it over several times till smooth and satiny to the touch. Turn the batch of dough smooth side up, cover and let rise the second time.

Shaping of Dough is done on a floured board. Divide the ball of dough according to the type of loaf desired. If a loaf pan is used, grease the bottom and sides of pan and dust lightly with flour. Knead and shape a piece of dough that will half fill a loaf pan. Fold over and over, and punch into oblong shape. Place the creased side of dough down into the pan and brush the top of loaf with melted shortening, oil, water or egg yolk diluted with water, before baking. Cover and let rise in a warm place, not above 70° F. For a *hard crust*, brush with beaten egg white. Start the baking at 400° F. or gas mark 6 and reduce to 375° F. or gas mark 5 after 10 minutes. Baking time should be between 45 minutes and 1 hour, depending on the type of bread and the crust desired.

HOME-MADE CHOLA (for Sabbath and Holidays)

8 cups flour | 1 tablespoon salt | 1 tablespoon sugar |
4 tablespoons vegetable shortening | 2 cups hot potato water |
2 ounces yeast | 3 eggs | Pinch of saffron* added to hot liquid

Sift flour and salt into a large mixing bowl. Mix sugar and shortening with the hot liquid. If potato water is not available, use plain hot water. When cooled to lukewarm, dissolve the yeast in some of the liquid and stir into the flour to make a sponge in the centre of the bowl. Cover and let rise 30 minutes. Add slightly beaten eggs to the sponge and stir in remaining liquid to make a dough. Turn out on a floured board and knead thoroughly until smooth and elastic. The dough should not stick to hand or board. Return to mixing bowl, brush top with shortening or dust with flour, cover, and let rise in a warm place until approximately double in bulk. Knead on floured board for 10 minutes and shape into coils for round loaves. Or, cut in half and divide each into 3 to make braided or twist loaves. Place on greased or floured baking sheet and let rise again till about double in bulk. Brush with egg yolk and water and bake 15 minutes at 400° F. or gas mark 6, reduce heat to 375° F. or gas mark 5 and bake for 45 minutes or till nicely crusted and light brown on bottom.
   Yields 2 loaves.

---

* Saffron is a herb used in baking to lend a yellow colour and fragrance. It is closely associated with the fragrant spices of the 'Psumim' or Spice Box used on Sabbath and holidays. It can be purchased from most grocers.

BASIC RECIPE FOR BREAD (Sponge Method)

1 *ounce yeast* | 1 *teaspoon sugar* | ¼ *cup lukewarm water* | 4 *cups flour* |
2 *teaspoons salt* | 2 *tablespoons shortening* | 2 *tablespoons sugar* |
2 *cups water (or milk and water)* | 2 *eggs (optional) beaten into 'sponge'*

Dissolve yeast and 1 teaspoon sugar in ¼ cup lukewarm water. Add 2 cups flour to make the 'sponge'. Set aside for 10 minutes. Add salt, shortening and sugar to the warm liquid.

Add the rest of the flour alternately with liquid and stir in with eggs, if used, mixing thoroughly to make a soft dough. Turn the dough on to a well-floured board and knead until smooth and elastic. Place the dough in a bowl that has been greased, or invert bowl so it covers the dough. Lift off the bowl. The greased surface of the mound of dough should be sprinkled with a little flour and covered with a cloth. Let stand in a warm place to rise till double its bulk. Punch down the dough or knead lightly and let rise again. Cut the dough in two, knead and shape into 2 loaves. Place loaves in greased and floured bread pans and cover with a cloth. Let rise at room temperature till double in bulk. Bake for 15 minutes at 375° F. or gas mark 5, increase to 400° F. or gas mark 6 and bake for 30 to 45 minutes longer. When done the 2 one-pound loaves should be well crusted on sides and bottom and lightly browned on top.

Yields 2 loaves.

CINNAMON BREAD

When the basic bread dough has risen, divide into 3 parts and roll each into a rectangle. Brush with melted shortening, sprinkle evenly over the surface of each 2 tablespoons brown sugar mixed with ½ teaspoon cinnamon. Roll up like jelly roll and place, seam sides down in a well-greased loaf pan. Let rise till light, brush with melted shortening and bake 15 minutes at 425° F. or gas mark 7, reduce to 375° F. or gas mark 5 and bake for 30 minutes or till nicely browned.

Yields 3.

Variation: Add a generous sprinkling of seedless raisins, chopped nuts, chopped citron over the sugar and cinnamon and roll up.

MILK BREAD (Irma's Never-Fail Method)

2 cups milk (or evaporated milk and water) | 1 ounce yeast |
¼ cup lukewarm water | 1 teaspoon salt | 1 tablespoon sugar |
1 tablespoon butter | 6 cups flour

Put milk in a double boiler and heat till bubbles form around the edge. Put yeast into a cup and cover with tepid water to soften. Place salt, sugar and shortening in mixing bowl.

Add milk and stir with a wooden spoon till shortening is melted. Let cool till tepid and add dissolved yeast.

Stir in 2 cups of flour at a time to make a well-mixed dough. Cover. Let rise in a warm place until double its bulk.

Turn dough on to floured kneading board, adding flour if necessary, and knead by drawing the dough towards you and then pushing away with the heel of the thumb. Turn and fold while kneading until dough becomes smooth and elastic. Divide and form into 2 loaves. Place loaves in well-greased loaf pans and set aside in a warm place to rise till double in bulk. The loaves should be up to the top of the pans when ready for the oven.

Bake for 10 minutes at 400° F. or gas mark 6, reverse position of loaf pans, reduce heat to 375° F. or gas mark 5 and let bake for approximately 40 minutes or till done. Test by tapping moistened finger on bottom of loaf pan. If it pops with a hollow sound, the loaves are done.

Turn out on a cooling rack or raised grill so that air circulates under and around, cover with a tea towel and let cool. This procedure has been followed without failure under various adverse conditions, baked in various types of oven, even in a portable oven on a kerosene stove.

Yields 2 loaves.

POPPY SEED BRAID

1 cup scalded milk | ¼ cup shortening, melted | ¼ cup sugar |
2 teaspoons salt | 1 ounce granular yeast | ¼ cup lukewarm water |
1 egg, beaten | 1 cup poppy seeds | ½ cup chopped cooked prunes |
2 teaspoons grated lemon rind | 4 cups sifted all-purpose flour (approximately) |
Thin icing | Chopped nuts

Combine milk, shortening, sugar and salt. Cool to lukewarm. Dissolve yeast in water 10 minutes. Add to milk mixture. Blend in egg, poppy seeds, prunes and lemon rind. Gradually mix in flour until well blended. Divide dough into five parts. Roll each into 18-inch strips. Place three strips on greased baking sheet and braid. Pinch ends together. Twist the two remaining strips together and place on top of braid. Cover and allow to rise in warm place until double in bulk, about 1 hour. Bake for 45 minutes at 350° F. or gas mark 4. Cool, ice lightly and sprinkle with nuts. Serve thinly sliced. This bread is also good toasted.

Yields 1 large loaf.

SWEDISH LIMPE

½ cup brown sugar | 2 cups water | 1½ teaspoons caraway seeds |
1 teaspoon chopped orange peel | 1 tablespoon shortening |
½ ounce yeast | 3 cups (approximately) wheat flour |
1 teaspoon salt | 2 cups rye flour (approximately)

Boil sugar, water, caraway seeds, orange peel and shortening together for about 3 minutes. Let mixture cool to lukewarm, then add yeast. Stir gradually adding enough white flour to make a soft dough. Let rise in a warm place for 1½ hours. Add salt and enough rye flour to make a stiff dough. Let rise for 2 hours. Knead slightly and shape into a loaf. Put into greased loaf pan and let rise for ½ hour. Bake at 350° F. or gas mark 4 for 1 hour.

Yields 1 loaf.

BEIGEL

(Water Doughnuts)

These doughnuts are as distinctly Jewish as Gefilte Fish.

Beigel-making is a special skill. In East European countries the making of beigel was generally turned over to the skilled fingers of women who formed the circlets of raised dough and passed them on to the master-baker very rapidly. These water doughnuts must be handled with care and processed with precision.

A machine for mixing and forming beigels much like the

machinery for turning out doughnuts has not as yet proved successful. Handmade beigel are still baked and sold by almost all Jewish
bakeries. In the United States it has become a Sunday breakfast or
brunch tradition to serve beigel with cream cheese and lox (smoked
salmon), especially in greater New York.

The following recipe for making beigel on a home-kitchen basis
was extracted from a retired baker, who learned the art in Europe and
practised it in one of our large cities for more than forty years. It has
been kitchen tested and proved successful in spite of the fact that
this baker declared it 'could not possibly be done at home'.

Here is the recipe for beigel. Try it yourself and be convinced.

BEIGEL

*3 cups flour (plus 3 tablespoons for kneading board) | 1½ teaspoons salt |
2 tablespoons sugar | 1 ounce yeast | ⅔ cup lukewarm water |
3 tablespoons salad oil (or shortening) | 1 egg |
4 quarts boiling water to which add 2 tablespoons sugar*

Sift dry ingredients together into a deep mixing bowl. Dissolve yeast
in ⅛ of the lukewarm water. Add oil or melted shortening to remainder of warm water and stir into dissolved yeast. Make a well
in the centre of flour mixture and stir in the liquid, adding slightly
beaten egg when half the liquid has been used. Stir briskly to form
a ball of dough and knead on a lightly floured board 2 minutes.
Return dough to mixing bowl, smooth side up, and punch down
three times. Cover and let rise at room temperature 15 to 20
minutes, or until the dough has come to top of bowl. Knead again
on board till smooth and elastic as for rolls. Divide dough into 12
equal portions. Form into lengths not more than ¾ inch thick,
pinching ends together. Place on a floured baking sheet and slip
under grill 3 minutes. Drop each beigel into rapidly boiling water
in a deep pot and cook over moderate heat 15 to 20 minutes. Skim
out and place on a baking sheet. Bake at 375° F. or gas mark 5 for
10 minutes, then increase heat to 400° F. or gas mark 6 for 5 to 6
minutes or till beigels are browned and crust golden brown and crisp,
approximately 15 minutes.

Yields 12.

Variations are made by sprinkling beigels with poppy seed or
coarse salt before baking.

Shish-Kebab (*page 115*)

ZEMMEL (Crisp Rolls)

Use basic recipe for bread. When ready to shape the dough, cut into pieces the size of an apple. Knead each piece and shape into flat cakes 1 inch thick and about 3 inches in diameter. Place on a greased and floured baking sheet 2 inches apart. Press a crease in the centres with back of a knife. Let rise in a warm place. Before baking, brush with egg yolk and water, sprinkle with poppy seeds or sesame seeds. Bake for 20 minutes at 400° F. or gas mark 6, or until crisp and nicely browned.

Yields approximately 18.

Variation: Form into tiny braids like miniature Chola. Cut dough into pieces the size of walnuts. Form 3-inch rolls, stretch slightly while braiding 3 together. Pinch together at ends. Let rise on the baking sheet. Brush tops with milk, add poppy seeds, or brush with diluted egg yolk.

ONION ZEMMEL

Use basic recipe for bread. Pinch off pieces the size of medium apples. Flatten into 3- or 4-inch cakes $\frac{1}{2}$ inch thick. Brush with water or egg yolk diluted with water. Sprinkle with coarse salt and add 1 teaspoon finely diced onion to top of each cake. Let rise at room temperature till double in bulk. Press down centres with the fingertips. Bake on ungreased baking sheet for 15 to 25 minutes at 350° F. or gas mark 4, or till onions are lightly browned and the under crust of rolls firm and light brown.

Yields approximately 18.

REFRIGERATOR ROLLS (Basic Recipe)

1 *ounce yeast* | 1$\frac{1}{2}$ *cups lukewarm water or scalded milk* | 2 *eggs* |
$\frac{1}{3}$ *cup sugar* | 2 *teaspoons salt* | $\frac{1}{2}$ *cup melted shortening* |
1 *cup water from boiled potatoes* | 1 *teaspoon vanilla* |
6$\frac{1}{2}$ *cups sifted flour* (*approximately*)

Dissolve yeast in lukewarm water or milk. Beat eggs, add sugar and salt. Combine shortening with potato water and vanilla. Make a well in centre of sifted flour in a large mixing bowl and stir in dissolved

9

yeast, adding egg mixture mixed with potato water and flavouring. This forms a loose dough. Sift a little flour over top and cover with aluminium foil or doubled tea towel. Chill in refrigerator overnight.

When ready to bake, shape dough into a round ball on a floured kneading board. Knead 1 to 2 minutes. Form into 36 rolls and arrange on a greased baking pan or on a baking sheet. Let rise at room temperature until double in bulk. Brush tops of rolls with melted shortening, evaporated milk or water. Bake at 400° F. or gas mark 6 for 15 to 20 minutes or till lightly browned.

Yields 36 rolls.

TEA PUFFS (Beaten Batter)

½ ounce yeast | 2 tablespoons lukewarm water | ½ cup milk |
2 tablespoons sugar | ½ teaspoon salt | ¼ cup shortening |
1½ cups flour / 1 egg / ¼ teaspoon vanilla extract

TOPPING

½ cup sliced almonds | ¼ cup sugar | ½ teaspoon cinnamon

Soften yeast in lukewarm water. Scald milk. Add sugar, salt and shortening. Cool to lukewarm. Add ½ cup flour. Beat well. Add softened yeast, egg and vanilla extract. Beat well. Add remaining flour to make a thick batter. Beat thoroughly till smooth. Cover and let rise until double in bulk, about 1 hour. When light, stir down. Drop by spoonfuls into small greased tart tins. Combine ingredients for topping. Sprinkle over muffins. Let rise till doubled in bulk, about 45 minutes. Bake for 25 minutes at 375° F. or gas mark 5.

Yields about 16 puffs.

ORANGE ROLLS

1 ounce yeast | ¼ cup lukewarm water | 2 eggs, beaten | ⅓ cup sugar |
1 teaspoon salt | ⅓ cup shortening | 3 cups sifted enriched flour |
1 egg | 2 tablespoons sugar

Soften yeast in lukewarm water. To eggs add sugar, salt, and shortening and mix well. Add 2 cups flour. Mix well. Add softened yeast. Beat well. Add more flour, enough to make a soft dough. Turn out on lightly floured board and knead until smooth. Place in greased bowl. Cover and let rise in warm place until doubled (about $1\frac{1}{2}$ hours). When light, punch down. Form dough into small balls about the size of walnuts. Place on baking sheet and flatten balls slightly. Place ball of orange topping on each roll. Brush with egg yolk. Sprinkle with sugar. Let rise until doubled, about 45 minutes. Bake for 15 minutes at 350° F. or gas mark 4.

Yields 2 dozen.

ORANGE TOPPING

$\frac{1}{2}$ *cup sifted flour* | $\frac{1}{4}$ *cup sugar* | 1 *teaspoon grated orange rind* |
1 *tablespoon orange juice* | $\frac{1}{4}$ *cup shortening* | 1 *egg yolk*

Mix together ingredients in order given. Form into small balls and flatten. Press 1 ball into top of each roll.

QUICK BREADS

SCONES (Basic Recipe)

2 *cups flour* | 3 *teaspoons baking powder* | 3 *tablespoons shortening* |
1 *teaspoon salt* | $\frac{3}{4}$ *cup water or milk (iced)*

Sift together dry ingredients, cut in shortening with knives or finger-tips till crumbs the size of peas are formed. Combine with liquid a little at a time to make a stiff dough, handling as little as possible. Pat or roll to $\frac{1}{2}$-inch thickness. Cut into 12 rounds with biscuit cutter or into squares or diamond shapes. Brush with milk, water or melted shortening. Bake for 10 to 15 minutes at 400° F. or gas mark 6 till lightly browned. Serve hot.

Yields 12.

Variations:

Orange Scones are made by adding 1 tablespoon sugar, juice and grated rind of orange to liquid. Increase the flour to $2\frac{1}{2}$ cups. Cut into larger rounds, brush with melted shortening and fold over, pocketbook fashion. Brush tops with orange juice.

Cinnamon Scone Ring is made by adding $\frac{1}{2}$ teaspoon cinnamon and 4 tablespoons sugar to a double recipe. Cut scones. Brush with shortening. Arrange scones three deep in a ring pan. Sprinkle sugar and cinnamon between layers. Bake at 350° F. or gas mark 4 for 15 minutes, then turn up heat to 375° F. or gas mark 5 for 10 minutes or till nicely browned.

Cheese Scones, plain or in fold-over style, are made by sprinkling generously with grated Cheddar cheese after brushing with melted shortening.

BUTTERMILK SCONES

*2 cups sifted flour | ½ teaspoon baking powder | 1 teaspoon salt |
¼ cup shortening (chilled) | 1 cup buttermilk | ½ teaspoon baking soda*

Sift together flour, baking powder and salt. Cut in shortening. Combine buttermilk and baking soda and work into flour mixture. Pat or roll out to ½-inch thickness, cut with a biscuit cutter and bake 15 minutes at 425° F. or gas mark 7.
Yields 12.

SOUR CREAM SCONES

*2 cups flour | ½ teaspoon salt | ¼ cup shortening |
1 cup sour cream | ½ teaspoon baking soda*

Sift flour and salt and cut in shortening. Add baking soda to sour cream and combine with first mixture to make a soft scone dough. Turn on to well-floured board and pat or roll out to ½-inch thickness. Cut with a biscuit cutter and bake for 15 minutes at 425° F. or gas mark 7, or till nicely browned.
Yields 12.
Variation: Drop from a tablespoon on a floured baking sheet. Bake till nicely browned.

CRESCENTS

*2¼ cups flour | 3 teaspoons baking powder | 1 teaspoon salt |
4 tablespoons shortening | 2 eggs | 2 tablespoons sugar |
⅔ cup milk or water | 2 tablespoons caraway seeds,
1 tablespoon celery seeds or 1 teaspoon poppy seed*

Sift together dry ingredients except sugar, cut in shortening. Beat eggs with sugar, add milk or other liquid. Stir into flour mixture to make a scone dough. Divide into 3 parts. Pat or roll lightly into 3 half-inch-thick rounds. Cut into 6 wedges, pie fashion. Roll up starting with wide outer edge and shape into crescents. Brush tops with liquid, sprinkle with seeds and bake for 15 minutes at 425° F. or gas mark 7, or till nicely browned on top.
Yields 18 crescents.

POT-O'-GOLD SCONES

2 cups sifted wheat flour | 3 teaspoons baking powder | 1 teaspoon salt |
4 tablespoons shortening | ½ cup grated raw yams |
¾ cup milk or orange juice

Sift together flour, baking powder and salt into a mixing bowl. Blend in shortening with a pastry blender or use two knives to cut until the mixture forms small peas. Stir in grated yams alternately with about half the amount of liquid, adding more liquid as necessary. The dough should be stiff enough to handle easily on a lightly floured board. Pat or knead gently for half a minute then roll out lightly to ½-inch thickness. Cut into small squares with a knife and bake on a well-greased baking sheet at 450° F. or gas mark 8 for 10 to 12 minutes. Serve hot with orange marmalade at tea time or with any meat or poultry meal.
Yields approximately 18.

CHEESE TWISTS

2 cups sifted flour | 1½ teaspoons salt | ¾ cup shortening | 2 eggs |
3 tablespoons milk | 1 cup grated Cheddar cheese (or Swiss cheese) |
1 tablespoon caraway seed

Sift together flour and salt and cut in shortening. Add 1 egg and 1 egg white, beat until smooth, then stir in milk. Chill until firm, approximately 1 hour. Roll dough on a lightly floured board to ½-inch thickness and cut into ½-inch-wide strips, using a fluted cutter or a pastry wheel. A sharp knife will do if these are not among your kitchen equipment. Cut the strips into 5-inch lengths and twist two together as lightly as you can. Place on a well-greased baking sheet and brush with slightly beaten egg yolk. Sprinkle generously with grated cheese and top with caraway seed. Bake 15 minutes at 425° F. or gas mark 7.

Yields 36 twists.

MUFFINS

MUFFINS (Basic Recipe)

2 cups sifted flour | 1 teaspoon salt | 1 tablespoon sugar |
4 teaspoons baking powder | 1 egg | 1 cup milk or water |
4 tablespoons melted shortening

Beat egg, a few strokes with a fork, add milk or water, stir into the sifted dry ingredients and beat lightly till smooth. Do not beat too much. Fold in melted shortening. Fill well-greased individual tart tins half full and bake for 20 minutes at 400° F. or gas mark 6, or till lightly browned.

Yields 16 muffins, average size, or 24 small muffins.

Variations:

Blueberry Muffins. Add 1 scant cup of blueberries, washed, drained and rolled in flour. Add sugar if berries are not very sweet.

Caraway Muffins. Use wheat flour, add 2 tablespoons caraway seeds. Sprinkle seeds on top of each muffin.

Cheese Muffins. Add 4 tablespoons grated Cheddar cheese and a dash of paprika. Top with a little grated cheese.

Date Muffins. Add ½ cup finely-cut unsweetened dates, double the amount of sugar and flavour with vanilla.

Holiday Muffins. Add ½ cup mixed dried fruits, finely cut or chopped and rolled in a little flour before folding into the mixture. Increase sugar to 3 tablespoons.

Raisin-Bran Muffins. Use 1¾ cups wheat flour and ½ cup bran. Roll raisins in flour before adding.

Rice Muffins. Use 1½ cups flour, proceed as usual and add 1 cup cooked rice and ¼ cup seedless raisins.

Soybean Muffins. Use ¾ cup soybean flour and 1¼ cups wheat flour.

CORNMEAL MUFFINS (Basic Recipe)

*1 cup cornmeal | 1 cup flour | ½ teaspoon salt |
4 tablespoons baking powder | 2 tablespoons sugar | 1 egg |
1 cup milk or water | 3 tablespoons shortening, melted*

Sift together dry ingredients. Beat egg, add liquid and melted shortening. Combine only till flour is moistened. Fill greased individual tart tins ⅔ full and bake for 20 to 25 minutes at 400° F. or gas mark 6.
Yields 12.

BRAN MUFFINS (Basic Recipe)

*2 cups bran | ½ cup wheat flour | 1 teaspoon baking soda |
1½ cups sour milk (or buttermilk) | 1 egg | 3 tablespoons molasses |
½ teaspoon salt | 2 tablespoons shortening, melted*

Combine bran and flour in a mixing bowl. Dissolve baking soda in sour milk and stir into lightly beaten egg. Add molasses, salt and shortening. Beat only till smooth. Fill well-greased individual tart tins half full. Bake at 375° F. or gas mark 5 for 20 to 25 minutes or till nicely browned on top.
Yields 16 medium muffins.
Variation: Add ½ cup chopped seedless raisins or pitted dates rolled in a little flour just before turning into tins.

RYE FLOUR MUFFINS

*1½ cups rye flour | 1 teaspoon baking soda | ½ teaspoon salt | 1 egg |
½ cup dark molasses | ¼ cup melted shortening |
¼ cup chopped seedless raisins*

Sift together dry ingredients. Beat egg and combine with molasses and melted shortening. Combine mixtures, adding chopped raisins during the process. Turn into well-greased tart tins, filling ⅔ full and bake for 25 minutes at 375° F. or gas mark 5, or till nicely browned.
Yields 9 medium muffins.

POPOVERS

*1 cup sifted flour / ¼ teaspoon salt / 2 eggs / 1 cup milk /
1 tablespoon melted shortening*

Sift together dry ingredients. Beat eggs, add milk and melted
shortening. Combine the two mixtures and beat with a rotary
beater till smooth. Fill greased tart tins half full. Bake at 400° F. or
gas mark 6 for 20 minutes. Reduce temperature to 350° F. or gas
mark 4 for the next 15 minutes.
Yields 8.

BANANA NUT BREAD

*½ cup butter / 1 cup sugar / 2 eggs / 1 cup mashed bananas /
1 teaspoon lemon juice / 2¾ cups sifted flour / 3 teaspoons baking powder /
½ teaspoon salt / 2 cups crushed toasted Brazil nuts*

Cream the butter and sugar till light and fluffy. Add the well-beaten
eggs, crushed bananas and lemon juice. Sift together flour, baking
powder and salt. Combine dry ingredients with the other mixture
and blend thoroughly. Fold in the crushed (or rolled) Brazil nuts.
Line greased loaf pan with waxed paper. Fill ⅔ full. Bake at 375° F.
or gas mark 5 for 1¼ hours.
Yields 1 large loaf or 2 small loaves.

9 Breakfast Begins the Day

FRUITS AND FRUIT JUICES FOR BREAKFAST

Citrus Fruit Juices. Orange, grapefruit, tomato juice, or a combination of any two of these, adds that precious and indispensable vitamin C to your daily diet. In addition, canned or fresh citrus fruit juices make a good 'refresher course' with which to start any meal!

Grapefruit Halves. Whole grapefruits cut through the centre between stem and blossom end, straight or star pointed (if you have the time), with seeds removed and the segments separated and loosened from the outer skin by aid of a curved blade knife, make good starters for any meal, especially breakfast. Drizzle a little honey or syrup over the top, or add a sprinkling of sugar a few minutes before serving.

For luncheon or dinner, add a canned cherry or a maraschino (red or green) to the cored centre for special eye-appeal. Or, slip under the grill for 2 minutes.

Large Orange Halves. These should be served in the same way as grapefruit halves.

Small Oranges. The seedless varieties, especially, should be served whole, with the outer skin cut down in sections from stem to blossom end and the skin points turned in at the top. Specially pleasing to eye as well as palate.

COOKED CEREALS FOR BREAKFAST

Cereals in packages are of two kinds – *quick cooking* and *standard*. Be sure to read labels for cooking time on each type. There is a difference in cooking directions as well as preparation time. *Follow directions on package.* Add raisins or other dried fruit in cooking. Serve with milk, cream or fruit juices.

Ready-to-Eat Cereals. These require no preparation but are enhanced by the addition of fresh, canned or quick frozen berries or other fruit and milk or cream. Dried fruits of any kind may be added.

Sweetenings for Cereals. Try honey, molasses, syrup, light brown sugar or maple sugar, or use the sweetened canned-fruit syrups for novelty.

Cooked Cereals are more essential in a cold weather diet.

Ready-to-Eat Cereals make a better choice for warm or hot weather.

Whole Grain, Coarse Milled Cereals include kasha or groats, oatmeal, or whole wheat.

Finely Milled Cereals include cornmeal, cream of wheat, farina, quick cooking oatmeal.

BREAKFAST BREADS

Toast. This is by far the most popular. It may be made on a table electric toaster, a top-of-the-gas-stove toaster, or under the grill of a gas stove, especially when quantities of toast are required at the same time. It can be toasted on both sides or on one side then buttered, turned and browned.

*Rolls.** Plain hard or soft crusted, fresh baked at home or reheated when bought from the bakery, may be served plain or cut and toasted then spread with butter or jelly, jam or preserves. Or, served with honey or any of the syrups available.

*Muffins.** Whether these are bought at the store or fresh baked at home, they make special holiday breakfasts most festive.

*Scones.** When baked in time for breakfast, these are still popular in many families and can be made in very little time if breakfasts are planned ahead.

TABLE-MADE BREADS

In this electric age, griddle cakes and waffles are generally prepared in the kitchen and cooked at table on electric plate or waffle iron. Here are some basic recipes that will serve for either breakfast or luncheon, or even for an afternoon or pre-bedtime snack. Also, already prepared 'mixes' are available at all groceries. Read the labels on packages to make sure contents meet your needs.

* See Index.

GRIDDLE CAKES (Basic Recipe)

2 eggs | 2 cups milk | 2 cups wheat flour | 3 teaspoons baking powder |
¾ teaspoon salt | 3 tablespoons sugar |
4 tablespoons butter or vegetable shortening | ½ teaspoon vanilla

Beat eggs with rotary beater till fluffy and stir in milk. Sift together dry ingredients twice and add half the melted shortening to the mixture with a fork. Stir in small amounts of the liquid to make a stiff batter before adding the rest of the liquid and flavouring. Beat with a fork to remove any possible lumps. Heat the electric griddle or sandwich toaster and grease well before pouring on the batter in as many rounds as space permits (or make the cakes on top of the hot plate or in a pan). Let cook till brown on under side before turning with spatula or pancake turner to brown on other side. Serve hot with butter, honey, corn or maple syrup, or marmalade, jelly or jam. Serves 6.

Variation 1: For thin cakes reduce dry ingredients by a quarter or thin batter by adding ¼ cup additional liquid.

Variation 2: Use 1 cup sour cream and 1 cup milk for a richer griddle cake and flavour with 1 tablespoon orange juice, and some grated orange rind.

Variation 3: For special holiday occasions, add ½ cup finely chopped nuts to the batter and serve with preserves or cranberry sauce.

WHOLE WHEAT GRIDDLE CAKES

2 eggs | 2 cups buttermilk | 1 teaspoon salt | 2 tablespoons shortening |
3 cups whole wheat flour | 1 teaspoon soda | 3 teaspoons baking powder

Beat eggs well, and to them add buttermilk, salt, shortening and flour. Mix well, beating for lightness. Just before baking, add soda and baking powder and beat until batter is foamy and light. Have griddle hot and well-greased.
Serves 6.

FRENCH PANCAKES

3 eggs, separated | ¼ cup flour | ¼ teaspoon of salt |
1 cup milk | 2 tablespoons melted butter

Beat yolks slightly and stir in flour, salt and milk to make a smooth
batter. Add stiffly beaten egg whites by folding in lightly. Add hot
melted butter and bake like any poured batter on hot, well-buttered
griddle or in frying pan. Brown on both sides and spread with
currant jelly. Roll up like jelly rolls, dust with sugar and serve hot.
Serves 2 to 3.

WAFFLES (Basic Recipe)

2 eggs, separated | 1¼ cups milk | 1½ cups wheat flour |
2 teaspoons baking powder | ¼ teaspoon salt |
2 tablespoons melted butter or vegetable shortening | ¼ teaspoon vanilla

Beat egg yolks till creamy and stir in the sifted dry ingredients
alternately with the liquid, using a fork or rotary beater till the batter
is smooth and thick. Beat egg whites stiff and fold in, then fold in the
melted shortening and flavouring.

Grease the waffle-maker lightly and pour batter on. The waffle is
done when the steam ceases to come from the sides. Waffles should
be crisp and evenly browned. Serve hot with butter, honey, maple
syrup or any other syrup.

Serves 6, making 6 seven-inch waffles.

Variation 1: Use half sour cream and half milk, stirring ½ teaspoon baking soda in the sour cream and 1 teaspoon baking
powder in the dry ingredients. Serve with sour cream and
cottage cheese, with or without honey or preserves.

Variation 2: For Cheese Waffles, add ½ cup grated Cheddar
cheese and a dash of paprika to the basic recipe.

Variation 3: To make Orange Waffles, add 1 cup orange juice
and ¼ cup evaporated milk to the batter in place of milk. A
tablespoon grated orange rind and 1 tablespoon honey should
be folded in last. Serve with orange marmalade.

TOAST FOR BREAKFAST OR LUNCHEON

BROWNED BUTTERED TOAST

Toast one side of bread. Spread the untoasted side with butter and slip under grill to brown.

Variations can be made by spreading browned buttered toast with honey, jam or jelly, grated cheese, or sugar mixed with cinnamon or nutmeg.

If toast is made with an electric toaster, toast both sides and butter while hot. Spread with topping quickly and keep hot till served by placing on top of toaster.

CINNAMON TOAST 1

Toast one side of bread. Spread untoasted side generously with butter, sprinkle with sugar mixed with cinnamon. Slip under grill to brown lightly.

CINNAMON TOAST 2

Spread thin slices of bread with butter. Sprinkle other slices generously with sugar and cinnamon. Put together one sugared slice with one buttered slice, press together lightly, and brown lightly under grill on both sides. Cut diagonally or into finger sections. Good for afternoon tea parties.

MILK TOAST

Toast ¾-inch slices of bread, spread lightly with butter and place in a bowl. Pour in hot milk to cover. Season with salt or sugar. Or, to tempt a flagging appetite of child or invalid, add a drop or two of vanilla in addition to sugar or honey. A dash of grated orange rind sometimes helps.

FRENCH TOAST

2 eggs | 1 tablespoon sugar | Dash of salt | ¼ teaspoon cinnamon | ⅔ cup milk | 6 slices stale white bread

Beat eggs lightly, add salt, sugar and cinnamon, and stir in milk.
Dip the slices of bread in this mixture and fry on a well-buttered
griddle or in frying pan till nicely browned on both sides. Serve hot
sprinkled with sugar and cinnamon, or spread with currant jam,
plum butter (see p. 522) or berry preserves.

   Variation: Cut rounds with biscuit cutter before dipping and
   frying.

ORANGE TOAST

Omit milk from French Toast recipe. Substitute $\frac{1}{2}$ cup orange juice,
a $\frac{1}{4}$ teaspoon grated orange rind. Dip and fry. Spread with orange
marmalade.

TOMATO TOAST

Substitute $\frac{1}{2}$ cup condensed canned tomato soup for other liquid,
season with salt and paprika. Fry. Serve hot with cheese sauce or
sprinkle generously with grated cheese.

MELBA TOAST

Slice white, rye or other bread very thin. Cut into $1\frac{1}{2}$-inch by 1-inch
pieces and dry on a baking sheet in a hot oven until evenly browned
but not burnt. Or remove crust from bread sliced $\frac{1}{4}$ inch thick and
cut diagonally or into fingers and dry out in a hot oven.

FRITTERS

Method of Frying. Be sure to use enough melted shortening to amply
cover fritters. Fritters should be fried at 365° F. and turned as soon
as brown on the under side.

   A frying basket in a deep skillet or frying pan is most satisfactory.
Drain fritters on paper towels and sprinkle with icing sugar while
warm.

FRITTER BATTER (Basic Recipe)

1¼ cups flour | ¼ teaspoon salt | 2 tablespoons sugar |
1 teaspoon baking powder | 2 eggs | 3 tablespoons liquid (water,
milk or fruit juice) | ¼ teaspoon nutmeg or cinnamon |
Shortening (corn, soybean or vegetable oil) for frying

Sift together all dry ingredients. Add beaten eggs blended with
liquid to make a batter.

Serves 4.

Variation 1: For a thicker batter, additional flour should be used.
Thick batters are necessary for juicy fruits like oranges, pineapple (canned) or berries, to be dipped.

Variation 2: Use grated rind of lemon or orange instead of nutmeg
or cinnamon for flavouring.

APPLE FRITTERS

2 eggs, separated | ½ cup water | 1 cup flour |
1 tablespoon melted butter or oil | 1 tablespoon lemon juice or wine |
¼ teaspoon salt | 4 large apples (pared, cored and sliced) |
Flour | ¼ cup lemon juice | ½ cup sugar

Beat the egg yolks till light yellow. Add water and stir in flour.
Combine the lemon juice and melted butter or oil and blend into
batter mixture. Beat egg whites stiff, add salt, and fold into the
batter.

Dip each apple slice in flour, then dip into the batter. Lift out
with a fork and fry in deep fat until a delicate brown on both sides.
Drain on paper and serve with lemon juice and sugar dusted on top.

Yields 20 fritters.

BANANA FRITTERS

Peel and cut bananas lengthwise then in halves. Dip in thin batter
and fry till brown. Or use batter of a stiffer consistency by adding
3 tablespoons flour to basic recipe and fry in deep fat. Serve with
lemon juice and powdered sugar, or lemon sauce.

Vegetable Fritters (see Index).

10 The Egg and You

Eggs hold a most important position in the realm of essential foods. They serve in many ways – through breakfast, luncheon, dinner or as special colour or flavour factor. In baking they are leavening agents. They decorate salads, giving colour contrasts and added nutritional value.

You don't have to learn to boil water, but you do have to know how to cook eggs. Here are some know-hows to remember:

Low Temperature prevents toughened egg whites, keeps yolks from turning green around their rims when hard-cooked, and makes any style egg a delight to your digestive equipment.

Use Salted Water when cooking eggs to forestall leakage in case of a crack in the shell. Salt is not absorbed no matter how long eggs are immersed.

TIME TABLE FOR EGGS

Soft boiled	212° F.	2 min.
Medium	212° F.	3 min.
Coddled	180° F.	5–8 min.
Hard cooked	212° F.	10–20 min.

Eggs for Garnishing salads or to be served sliced or devilled, should be placed in cold water to which salt has been added, then cooked at very low temperature for 20 to 30 minutes, turning them carefully with a spoon once or twice during the process. This will prevent 'lopsided' yolks. Hard-cooked eggs should be chilled immediately, in the shell. Then let plenty of cold water run over them. You'll find their shells will come off without difficulty. Incidentally, quick cooling after gentle cooking will keep the yolks clear to their white frames.

TIPS ON EGGS

Tests for freshness of eggs can be made in your kitchen this way:

Assorted Breads: Chola and Beigel
(*pages 124-128*)

Place the egg in cold water three times its depth. If it remains at the bottom it is fresh. If it lifts at the large end, it is not. The staler the egg the higher it will rise. Fresh eggs are heavy because they fill the shell. Stale eggs shrink from their shell. The staler the eggs are, the more they rattle when shaken.

Don't wash off the natural 'bloom' from fresh eggs before storing them in your refrigerator. Stale eggs wear a tell-tale shiny look – beware!

Break eggs into the same bowl with caution. One bad egg may prove the undoing of all the rest. Break *each* one into a saucer first.

To separate yolks from whites easily and without danger of getting a bit of yolk into the whites, use one of those handy gadgets called an egg separator. Just in case you haven't one, when some of the yolk slips into the whites, use the half shell of an egg to remove the offending bit of yolk. Otherwise the whites will not beat up stiff.

When adding beaten eggs to a hot mixture, be sure to stir the liquid into the beaten egg slowly and use a clockwise stroke, with fork or spoon close to the bottom.

If you must keep egg yolks for use the following day, be sure to cover them with about $\frac{1}{8}$ inch cold water. It will prevent a hardened film. Or cook them hard in salted water and use for salad garnish.

Egg whites that must be kept over will not evaporate if stored in a tightly covered dish in the refrigerator.

Egg whites beat faster at room temperature, with a pinch of salt or a small amount of cream of tartar added. Use rotary beater.

Don't try to remove egg stains from dishes with hot water. It only hardens the egg particles. Soak dish in cold water for a few minutes then wash in the usual way.

Eggs as main dishes rate high with the Jewish cook. There's one special reason if the household maintains a strictly kosher kitchen. That reason is, egg dishes can be prepared *milchig, fleishig*, or *pareve*.

Egg dishes fit into luncheon menus. They are adaptable for menus that range from utter simplicity to the most elaborate and artistic creations. Here are some suggestions that leave room for application of your own culinary artistry.

Luncheon egg dishes that must be served as soon as prepared include the omelet, many variations of which you will find on the following pages. Cook-and-serve egg dishes should not be started before the table is set. In fact, it is best to prepare them after preliminaries around the table, and then work fast. But one can have all the ingredients ready in the kitchen. Eggs whip better

10

when cold and in chilled bowls. Use a rotary beater or an electric mixer. Failing these, use a fork.

Egg dishes that can be prepared in advance are best when serving a number of persons.

Remember that winter egg dishes should always be served piping hot while the summer egg dishes should be just the opposite.

EGG DISHES

EGGS IN RICE NESTS

*1 diced onion or 1 tablespoon onion juice | 3 tablespoons butter or
vegetable shortening | 1½ cups brown or long grain rice |
3 cups cold water | 1 teaspoon salt | 6 hard-cooked eggs |
1 green pepper, strips | Parsley for garnish | ¼ cup mayonnaise*

If you use a *pressure cooker*, brown the diced onion in butter first and then add rice, water and salt. If you do not use a pressure cooker, then cook the rice in salted water in the top of a double boiler for 30 minutes till tender. Drain, add browned onion or onion juice, and pack into 6 greased teacups for individual servings. Unmould and serve cold with quartered egg in each nest of rice. Garnish with pepper strips, parsley, and top with mayonnaise.

Serves 6.

Variation: For a large nest pack cooked rice and onion in buttered ring mould. Unmould on lettuce and fill with diced eggs. Garnish.

CREAMED EGGS

*4 hard-cooked eggs | 1 cup thin white sauce (see Index) |
1 tablespoon minced parsley | Salt, pepper, paprika |
Buttered toast points, 4 slices*

Remove shells from hard-cooked eggs. Slice and add to white sauce with seasonings to taste. Heat 3 to 5 minutes. Serve on toast. Garnish with parsley.

Serves 4.

Variation 1: Sprinkle liberally with grated hard cheese.

Variation 2: Garnish with strips of pimento and stuffed olives.

Variation 3: Add 2 tablespoons minced green pepper to hot white sauce, cook one minute before adding eggs. Garnish with un-cooked green pepper ring.

Variations can be made by combining creamed eggs with asparagus tips, cooked green peas, flaked or diced leftover fried or baked fish. Serve on buttered toast, toasted muffin halves or on beds of hot mashed potato.

POACHED EGGS

Heat salted water to boiling point in a shallow pan. Break egg in a saucer and slip into the water very gently to avoid breaking. When all the eggs are in the water, remove pan from fire, cover and let stand until set. Be sure the water covers the eggs. Remove with a skimmer to toast or bread.

RUMANIAN FRIED EGGS

Preheat fat in frying pan and slip the egg from saucer into which it has been broken. Cook slowly to prevent toughening of edges. Baste with fat in the pan if yolk does not cook as rapidly as desired. *Do not baste* for Sunny-Side-Up Eggs.

SCRAMBLED EGGS

Preheat frying pan, add butter or other shortening, then beaten whole or separated eggs, salt added. With a fork, scramble the eggs as soon as they begin to set or cook through. Cook slowly to preserve softness and fluffiness.

BAKED EGGS

Use individual baking dishes or ramekins. Melt a scant teaspoon of butter in each, break 1 or 2 eggs into each dish, sprinkle with salt and top with a bit of butter. Bake at 275° F. or gas mark ¾ until set but not hard. Serve in same dishes.

SHIRRED EGGS

Use ramekins. Grease each dish, add a layer of buttered crumbs and break one or two eggs over the crumbs. Season with salt and pepper, cover with buttered crumbs and bake at 275° F. or gas mark ¾ until browned on top.

CROWN ON TOAST

Moisten the edges of toast, allowing one slice to each egg. Spread with butter. Separate the eggs and poach the yolks in salted water till firm. Place 1 egg yolk on a piece of toast, make a crown around it with stiffly beaten egg white seasoned with salt and pepper. Slip under grill to brown and set the whites, or bake in oven at 350° F. or gas mark 4 till nicely browned on top. Serve hot.

PAN-AMERICAN EGGS

Grease ramekins and place 1 or 2 tablespoons of thick tomato sauce in bottom of each. Slip 1 or 2 poached eggs into each ramekin, cover with grated sharp cheese, sprinkle with crumbs and slip under grill to brown lightly. Serve hot.

EGGS NEAPOLITAN

2 tablespoons butter | 1 cup fine crumbs (bread or cracker) |
6 tablespoons mushroom sauce | 6 eggs | Salt to taste | Pepper to taste

Butter the inside of individual ramekins and sprinkle with crumbs. Add a teaspoonful of sauce then break into each 1 egg and sprinkle with salt and pepper. Cover with crumbs and set the ramekins in a shallow pan of hot water. Bake at 350° F. or gas mark 4 until the yolk of egg is set, approximately 10 minutes.
Serves 6.

DEVILLED EGGS

Cut hard-cooked eggs into halves lengthwise. Remove yolks and mash. Season with salt, pepper, a little dry mustard and a few drops of lemon juice. Or mix with salad dressing. Form into small balls and fill the cavities. Press 2 halves together.

EGGS À LA BENEDICT

4 eggs, poached | 4 slices sausage | ⅛ teaspoon salt |
4 slices toast or halves of toasted biscuits | 1 cup Hollandaise sauce

Fry lightly each slice of sausage and place on top of toast. Slip a poached egg on top of sausage. Place each on individual serving plate, cover with hot Hollandaise sauce and garnish with minced parsley or a dash of paprika.
Serves 4.

EGGS GOLDENROD

3 hard-cooked eggs | 1 cup thin white sauce | Salt, pepper and paprika |
Toast, 3 slices | Parsley

Cut the whites from yolks. Chop whites fine and add white sauce. Season to taste. Press the yolks through a tea strainer. Lay hot buttered toast on a platter and pour the heated wine sauce mixture over. Scatter the sieved egg yolk over top and garnish with parsley.
Serves 3.

EGGS ROMANOFF

Cut a slice from the large end of each hard-cooked egg (use 2 per serving). Remove the yolks and mash with a fork. Add 1 teaspoon caviar and dash of onion juice. Refill the eggs with this mixture. Serve each egg cut side down on a slice of tomato placed on a bed of shredded lettuce. Serve with Russian dressing (see Index) and garnish with anchovies, more caviar or slices of cucumber marinated in lemon juice or vinegar and oil.

OMELETS

PLAIN OMELET

4 eggs, separated | 4 tablespoons hot water or milk |
Butter or margarine | Salt and pepper, ¼ teaspoon

Beat yolks till thick and creamy, add water. Season. Beat egg whites
stiff and fold in. Melt butter in frying pan, butter the sides, turn in
the egg mixture and cook over low heat to achieve a fluffy omelet.
If an omelet pan is used, grease the inside of pan top and bottom. An
omelet should be light, springy to the touch and not stick to the pan
when done.

Do not overcook or the omelet will shrink and be tough.

Loosen the edges with a knife if necessary, or use a spatula in
turning out on a heated platter. Serve as soon as cooked.

Serves 2 to 3.

Variations can be made by adding any of the following to omelet
mixture before cooking:

    1 tablespoon minced parsley
    2 tablespoons finely chopped green onions
    2 tablespoons finely chopped young dandelion greens
    2 tablespoons chopped green pepper
    2 tablespoons minced olives
    ½ cup leftover fish, flaked and seasoned.

Other Variations can be made by turning the egg mixture over
browned sliced onions, boiled and sliced potatoes, sautéed cubes
of sausage, diced cooked meat or chicken, diced grilled beef
liver or minced chicken livers.

FRUIT OMELETS

These are made by adding preserves or well-drained canned fruit
or berries. Sprinkle top with icing sugar before serving.

PERFECT FLUFFY OMELET

4 eggs, separated | ¼ cup milk | ½ teaspoon salt |
⅜ teaspoon pepper | 1 tablespoon butter

Beat whites until stiff enough to hold shape but not dry. Overbeating causes the omelet to fall during cooking. Beat yolks thick and lemon-coloured, stir in milk, salt and pepper. Add this yolk mixture slowly to the whites, combining the two with a spoon, using a folding motion. Don't be too vigorous. Heat a heavy frying pan, drop in the butter, allow to melt, but not brown, as the flavour of the browned butter will detract from the taste of the egg. Tip pan gently from side to side until it is well-greased and the fat bubbling.

Pour in the egg mixture, cover now with a second frying pan, which permits the omelet to rise above the edge of the first. Cook over low heat for 5 minutes or until omelet puffs up. Slowly, gently, lift the edge to see if the bottom has turned to light amber and is evenly coloured. Transfer omelet to a moderate oven (300° to 350° F. or gas mark 2 to 4) and cook uncovered for 10 minutes or until the top is done. The total cooking time will vary according to the thickness of the omelet.

Hold skillet in left hand, with the right make a cut, perpendicular to skillet handle, across omelet and half through its thickness. With the spatula loosen half of omelet, and slide the folded omelet to a hot platter.

Serves 2.

PUFFY OMELET FOR TWO

2 eggs, separated | ½ teaspoon salt | Dash of pepper |
2 tablespoons milk | 1½ teaspoons butter

Beat egg yolks until thick and lemon-coloured. Stir in salt, pepper and milk. Beat egg whites until peaks form. Gently fold in yolk mixture with a rubber scraper or spatula. Melt butter in hot 7-inch omelet pan. Pour in egg mixture all at once. Cook over low heat, without stirring, 3 to 5 minutes, or until browned on bottom.

Then place pan in moderate oven (350° F. or gas mark 4) 5 to 10 minutes, or until top springs back when pressed with finger. Make a crease down the centre of omelet at right angles to the omelet pan handle. Fold carefully on crease towards side of pan opposite the handle. Grasp the handle with the left hand; tilt the pan up and over the serving dish until the omelet gently tips over on to plate.

Serves 1 large or 2 average portions.

CURRIED EGGS

6 *eggs, hard-cooked | 2 tablespoons butter | ¼ cup flour | ½ teaspoon salt |*
⅛ teaspoon pepper | ¼ teaspoon curry powder | 2 cups milk

Remove shells and cut eggs lengthwise in halves or quarters. Melt butter in saucepan, blend in flour, salt, pepper and curry powder, but do not brown. Remove from heat and stir in milk gradually till smooth. Return to heat, stirring till creamy smooth. Arrange the cut eggs on toast, toasted muffins or biscuits, or on a bed of mashed potatoes. Pour the white sauce over all just before serving. Garnish with parsley or minced green pepper.
Serves 4.

EGGS IN TOMATO CUPS (Individual Serving)

Cut stem ends from tomatoes and scoop out pulp. Drop a whole raw egg into each tomato, season with salt and pepper, top with buttered crumbs and sprinkle with grated cheese. Bake at 350° F. or gas mark 4, 20 minutes or till egg is set. Serve with buttered toast points, beds of hot mashed potatoes or boiled rice.

EGG ROLLS

PFANNKUCHEN (German Egg Rolls)

These have a definite German origin but have been adopted widely for their versatility. The most popular variation among Jewish cooks is what is perhaps better known as *blintzes* when cheese filled (commonly attributed to Russian or Polish origin called *blinchiki* or *blini*). Here is the basic recipe and a number of variations.

BASIC RECIPE

4 *eggs, separated | Dash of salt | 2 tablespoons flour |*
4 *tablespoons milk or water | 1 tablespoon butter | Icing sugar*

Beat egg yolks with salt till well blended and creamy. Stir in flour and liquid. Add stiffly beaten egg whites. Pour batter on well-buttered heavy skillet, starting at centre and tipping pan to distribute over whole bottom of pan. Do not pour on too much at a time. Cook over moderate heat till nicely browned on under side and the edges begin to curl up. Turn out browned side up on a hot plate or folded kitchen towel. Cut into 4 or 6 wedges, dust with icing sugar and roll up each from outer edges. When all rolls are made, return to brown lightly on buttered pan. Dust with more icing sugar and serve hot.

Serves 3.

Variation: Use a small frying pan for individual pfannkuchen.

EGG ROLLS INTERNATIONAL

1 cup flour / ¼ teaspoon salt / 3 eggs / ⅔ cup milk or water /
1 tablespoon melted shortening

Sift together flour and salt. Beat eggs till light. Stir or beat in dry ingredients alternately with liquid till a smooth batter is formed. Melt shortening on frying pan and add to batter. Pour batter in a thin stream on to greased pan, tipping to distribute over entire surface evenly as possible. Cook over moderate heat till lightly browned on under side. Turn bottom side up on a kitchen towel. Spread with filling, roll up like jelly roll, tucking in both ends. When all rolls are made, brown under grill or in well-greased frying pan. Cut rolls in half to facilitate handling. Serve hot.

Yields 6 rolls or 12 halves.

EGG ROLL FILLINGS

Chinese Style (known to Chinese as *Chu Pa Pa*). Spread with fried onion, green pepper, bean sprouts or other greens like celery, parsley and celeriac in any desired combination. Fold over filling and tuck in both ends. Cover with hot melted shortening and bake till brown and crisp.

Mexican Style. Spread with finely chopped leftover meat seasoned with onion juice or browned onion and mixed with an egg yolk. Meat filling should be at least a half inch thick. Tuck in sides and

fold over or roll. Brown lightly and serve hot. These are called
cariocas.

Norwegian Style. Spread with strawberry preserves or jam and
sprinkle with finely chopped nuts. Brown the rolls and dust with
sugar. Serve as a dessert.

11 Dairy Dishes and Meatless Meals

In the strictest sense of the term, dairy dishes should mean only foods made of milk and milk products. But we find that it has become a very elastic term and covers many types of meals. These may range from strictly vegetarian menus to meatless meals.

To those who, out of principle, abstain from the eating of flesh foods of any kind, the suggestions in this section on dairy dishes will be of help in planning meals. Other suggestions may be found in the sections on vegetables and pulses, and other parts of this book.

To all who prefer meals that exclude meats and poultry but include fish, this section will also be of great help in extending menus. Consult the Index for fish recipes.

Those who must at some time or other eliminate meats and fish of all kinds for health reasons will find dairy dishes a first aid in solving their diet problems.

SUGGESTIONS FOR MEATLESS MEALS

MENU 1

Tomato Juice, Crackers
Potato Latkes (p. 299) with Cream Cheese and Sour Cream or
    Cottage Cheese and Applesauce
Mixed Green Salad, Dressing
Compote of Dried Fruits, Biscuits
Coffee, Tea or Milk

MENU 2

Orange or Pineapple Juice
Cheese Blintzes (p. 161) with Sour Cream
Tomato and Cucumber Salad, Dressing
Canned or Fresh Sliced Peaches
Coffee, Tea or Milk

MENU 3
Cream of Tomato Soup, Croutons
Meatless Prune and Potato Tzimmes (p. 50)
Raw Carrots and Grapefruit Salad, Dressing
Canned or Quick Frozen Berries, Dry Skim Milk Topping
Coffee, Tea with Lemon or Orange Slices

MENU 4
Lentil Soup, Crackers, Croutons or Matzo Wafers
Chopped Herring (p. 218), Hard-Cooked Egg Garnish
Lettuce and Tomato Salad, Dressing
Gingerbread, Whipped Cream Topping
Coffee, Tea, Milk or Buttermilk

MENU 5
Meatless Cabbage Soup with Boiled Potato
Pirogen with Tomato Sauce
Waldorf Salad (p. 333), Sweetened Salad Dressing
Coffee or Tea

MENU 6
Cream of Mushroom Soup, Crackers or Matzo Wafers
Kasha-Varnitchkes (p. 311), Parsley Garnish
Shredded Raw Carrot, Celery and Green Pepper Salad, Dressing
Canned, Quick Frozen or Stewed Dried Pears
Cake or Biscuits
Coffee, Tea or Milk

MENU 7
Chilled Beet Borsht (p. 183) with Sour Cream Thickening
Scalloped Potatoes
Baked Acorn Squash with Green Peas Filling
Pinwheel Salad, Dressing
Sponge Cake
Coffee, Tea or Milk

MENU 8
Chilled or Hot Schav (p. 184) with Sour Cream Thickening
Noodle-Cheese Ring (p. 165), with Raisin Sauce
Sweet-Sour Green Beans
Sliced Tomato and Chicory or Romaine Lettuce Salad, Dressing
Apple Strudel (p. 409)
Coffee, Tea or Milk

MENU 9
Cherry Borsht with Egg Drops
Beans and Barley Kasha (p. 312)
Eggplant Salad in Lettuce Cups with Maslinas or Canned Black
Olives
Applesauce Cake
Coffee or Tea

MENU 10
Blueberry Soup with Sour Cream Topping, Crackers
Cheese Filled Potato Knishes (p. 296), Creole Sauce
French Fried Carrots and Parsnips
Diced Orange and Avocado Salad, Shredded Lettuce, Dressing
Mandelbrodt (p. 347)
Coffee, Tea or Milk

MENU 11
Chopped Green Bean 'Liver' on Crackers or Rye Bread Triangles
Baked Macaroni and Cheese
Gelatin Beet Ring on Shredded Greens, Mayonnaise or Salad
  Dressing
Compote of Dried Mixed Fruits, Biscuits
Coffee, Tea or Milk

MENU 12
Cream of Celery Soup with Caraway-Cheese Wafers
Baked Rice Filled Green Peppers, with Tomato Sauce
Raw Carrot Curls, Maslinas or Stuffed Olives
Apple Pie
Coffee or Tea with Lemon or Orange Slices

MENU 13
Barley and Mushroom Soup, Crackers or Matzo Wafers
Eggs in Mashed Potato Nests, Baked
Creamed Peas
Shredded Cabbage and Carrot Salad, Dressing
Prune and Apricot Pie
Coffee, Tea or Milk

MENU 14

Pineapple Juice
Mamaliga (p. 313) with Dry Cottage Cheese and Sour Cream
Diced Cucumber and Tomato Salad, French Dressing
Cheese Beigelach
Coffee, Tea or Milk

MILK FACTS

Pasteurized Milk has been heated to destroy all harmful germs without affecting the flavour. This is the most usual grade supplied.

Homogenized Milk has been heat-treated and processed so as to break up the fat into such tiny particles that they do not rise to the top to form a cream-line. It has a richer, creamier taste and is good for milk puddings.

Sterilized Milk is homogenized milk which has been bottled and heat-treated at a higher temperature to ensure that it will keep (while still sealed) for at least seven days.

T.T. Milk comes from cows of any breed which have passed the tuberculin test. It is of superior hygienic quality but has no specially high butterfat content.

Channel Islands T.T. comes from cows of the Channel Islands breeds (Jerseys and Guernseys) which have passed the tuberculin test. It is of superior hygienic quality and must have a butterfat content of at least 4%.

South Devon T.T. is similar to Channel Islands T.T. milk but comes from cows of the South Devon breed.

Channel Islands and *South Devon* are similar to their T.T. counterparts but do not necessarily come from cows which have passed the tuberculin test. Their hygienic quality is superior and butterfat content is at least 4%.

Farm-bottled Milk is milk from the above grades which has been bottled at the place of production.

Buttermilk is the by-product from the churning of sour cream into butter. It is usually pasteurized and has a similar 'solids not fat' content to that of whole milk. Its fat content, however, is between 0.1 and 1.5%.

Skim Milk is milk from which the cream has been removed – thus reducing its butterfat content to somewhere in the region of 0.1%.

Evaporated Milk is milk from which approximately half the water has been removed by heat. After evaporation it is homogenized, canned and sterilized.

Condensed Milk is also heat-treated to remove much of the water but sugar is added so that the finished product contains about 42% sugar. This acts as a preservative and it is not necessary to apply heat-treatment after canning.

Dried Milk has been so treated that practically all the moisture (about 95–98%) has been removed and the milk becomes a powder. It may be made from whole or skimmed milk. It will keep for a much longer time but, once it has been opened, care should be taken to see that the lid is always replaced. After reconstitution, evaporated, condensed and dried milks require the same care as fresh milk.

Yoghurt, though described in some dictionaries as 'a thick fermented liquor made by the Turks from milk', is what is known as cultured milk. Often prescribed for special diets, it is healthy for everyone. It is slightly tart in flavour and makes an excellent dessert either flavoured or with fruit.

Kosher or Kedassiah Milk is specially prepared in accordance with Jewish orthodox requirements.

Sour Cream can be made quickly by adding 1 tablespoon of white vinegar or lemon juice to each cup of cream. Undiluted evaporated milk makes good sour cream. Jews have long known its versatile uses. Russian and Polish Jews serve sour cream with fresh vegetables, herring, as a thickening and garnish for meatless soups and as a topping for salads and desserts.

Here are a few suggestions for the use of sour cream:

Serve with cottage cheese on lettuce, with or without chives or green onions.

Mix with diced cucumbers and tomatoes, serve on lettuce.

Combine diced or sliced radishes, green onions and boiled potatoes, and top with sour cream.

Pickled herring is delicious with sour cream.

Pancakes of any kind, especially grated raw potato pancakes, are served with sour cream.

Cheese blintzes or kreplach, browned in butter, are served with a generous topping of sour cream.

Fresh fruits and berries may be served with sour cream in place of sweet cream for breakfasts or desserts.

Fruit salads are delicious with sour cream topping.

COTTAGE CHEESE RECIPES

Cottage Cheese applies to at least three kinds of cheese commonly used by the Jewish people. These are not processed cheeses like the Cheddar type of cheese which is also used in many of the recipes in this collection. Cottage cheese is usually served with sour cream as a main dish for luncheon or supper. It is usually made of skimmed milk, with cream added after separation of curds from whey.

Farmer Cheese is cottage cheese squeezed dry and pressed into form in a muslin cloth or bag.

Pot Cheese is similar to cottage cheese, but curds are larger.

PRESSED COTTAGE CHEESE (Polish Style)

1 *quart cottage cheese | 2 tablespoons caraway seeds |*
Salt to taste | Dash of white pepper

Combine all ingredients, turn into a muslin bag and twist the bag to form a heart shape. Tie. Hang point down, in open air if possible, for about a week or ten days. Unmould and serve with sour cream, mixed, diced green vegetables or both.

WHIPPED COTTAGE CHEESE

1 *pint cottage cheese | ½ cup cream or top milk | Salt to taste*

Beat cheese with fork or rotary beater, adding cream slowly while beating until mixture is light and smooth. Serve on shredded lettuce, diced mixed green vegetables, potato pancakes, waffles, or whole rye or pumpernickel bread.

Variation: Serve on canned pineapple, peaches or pears and garnish with chopped nuts. A bed of shredded lettuce enhances this delicious summer salad.

COTTAGE CHEESE IN GREEN PEPPERS

Cut nicely-shaped green peppers lengthwise through the centre. Do not remove stem, but do remove seeds and fibres. Fill pepper halves

Cheese Blintzes (*page 161*)

with cottage cheese seasoned with salt, pepper, minced parsley or chives and as much sour cream or beaten egg white as needed to make a fluffy mixture. Allow ½ cup cheese for two pepper halves of medium size. Sprinkle with chopped nuts or decorate with mint leaves or parsley.

Variation 1: Use long green sweet peppers, cut away stem ends. Remove seeds and fill with the cheese combination. Serve one stuffed pepper on each salad plate, with sandwiches, radish roses, tomato wedges.

Variation 2: Fill pepper halves or whole peppers with seasoned cottage cheese and top with sour cream.

Variation 3: Fill whole peppers with cottage cheese. Chill and slice into 1-inch thick rounds. Serve on lettuce and top with an olive or radish rose, minced parsley, fresh dill or fresh mint.

COTTAGE CHEESE–FILLED TOMATO

Slice off stem ends of tomatoes, remove pulp and fill with seasoned cottage cheese. Top with sour cream and minced parsley and serve on a bed of lettuce, green pepper rings, other greens.

COTTAGE CHEESE AND NUT BALLS

Season cheese with salt, sugar, a dash of cinnamon. Form into balls and roll in finely chopped nuts. A tiny mint leaf on each ball adds a party touch. Or top with maraschino cherry, red or green.

CHEESE BLINTZES

2 eggs | ½ cup sifted flour | ¾ cup water (or milk and water) | 1 tablespoon melted butter | Pinch of salt

Make a thin batter of beaten eggs, flour added alternately with the liquid while beating with a fork, then working in the melted butter and salt until smooth. Heat a heavy frying pan and butter well before pouring in a thin stream of batter, starting at centre and tilting pan to spread the mixture evenly across the bottom. Reduce the heat as soon as you begin pouring on the batter to achieve a

11

well-baked pancake layer for the first blintze. As soon as the under-side is lightly browned, turn out on a double layer of kitchen towel, browned side up. Start the second blintze layer, buttering the pan before pouring batter. While the second (and successive) blintzes are baking on the frying pan spread the browned side just turned out with the following mixture:

FILLING FOR CHEESE BLINTZES

1 *pound cottage cheese (or cream cheese)* | 1 *egg yolk* | 2 *tablespoons sugar* | *Dash of salt* | *Dash of cinnamon (or few drops of vanilla)*

Mix with a fork to a spreadable consistency. Spread evenly and roll up each blintze, tucking in at the ends. Cut in two, and when all are filled and rolled up, and cut, fry them in butter until nicely browned on both sides. Serve with sour cream, stewed berries, cherries, rhubarb, or compote of prunes and dried apricots.

Yields 12 blintzes if a 10-inch frying pan is used. Serves 4 (three per serving).

CHEESE KNISHES

1 *package granulated yeast* | 1¼ *cups warm water* | 2 *tablespoons sugar* | 1 *teaspoon salt* | 2 *eggs* | 4 *tablespoons melted shortening (butter preferred)* | 3½ *cups flour*

Let yeast granules stand in warm water a few minutes before adding the other ingredients in the order listed, stirring until thick enough to form a ball of dough. Add additional flour if necessary. Let rise in bowl covered with a kitchen towel. At room temperature this dough should rise to double its bulk in about 3 hours. Punch down and knead on a floured board until smooth and elastic. Pinch off a ball of dough the size of an apple and roll to ½-inch thickness. Fill with the mixture given below and pinch together to form a crescent. If you have a fluted cutter, use it to scallop the edges. Place each knish on a well-buttered baking pan or baking sheet and let rise at room temperature. Brush the tops with diluted egg yolk and water, evaporated milk or melted butter. Bake in a preheated oven at 350° F. or gas mark 4 until nicely browned. Serve with fruit salad, fish dishes of any kind, or as an accompaniment to coffee, tea or cocoa.

SWEET FILLING FOR KNISHES

*1½ pounds dry cottage cheese | 2 eggs | ½ teaspoon salt | ¼ cup sugar |
¼ cup dry bread crumbs (or crushed cereal) | Grated rind of 1 lemon |
1 tablespoon lemon or orange juice*

Mix in the order listed.

UNSWEETENED CHEESE FILLING

*1½ pounds dry cottage cheese | 2 eggs | ½ teaspoon salt |
1 large onion, diced | 4 tablespoons melted shortening (oil or butter) |
¼ cup crushed dry cereal or crumbs*

Fry onion in hot melted shortening until light brown. Combine all
the ingredients as soon as onion is cool.
Yields 12 to 14.

CHEESE KREPLACH

DOUGH

*Pinch of salt | Flour enough to make a stiff dough as for noodles (see
Index, Noodle Dough) | 1 egg | 1 tablespoon cold water*

Make a well in the centre of sifted flour and salt and add egg and
water. With a fork stir together to make the noodle dough. Roll out
to ⅛-inch thickness, cut into 2½-inch squares and fill each with the
following cheese mixture, pinch two points together to form puffed
triangle.

CHEESE FILLING FOR KREPLACH

*1 pound dry cottage cheese | 2 egg yolks or 1 whole egg and
2 tablespoons sour cream | ¼ teaspoon salt |
Sugar and cinnamon to taste (if served with sour cream) |
Or dash of white pepper (if served with hot milk)*

Drop prepared kreplach into rapidly boiling water, one at a time.
Cook, covered for 10 minutes. Uncover and reduce heat for 5
minutes. Drain. Drizzle with additional butter and brown under
grill. Serve with cream cheese and sour cream.
Serves 4 to 6.

CHEESE DUMPLING (Viennese)

4 eggs | 3 tablespoons butter or fortified margarine | 1 cup cottage cheese |
¾ cup flour | ¼ cup bread crumbs, fine, dry | 2 teaspoons salt |
¼ teaspoon pepper

Separate eggs. Cream butter or margarine, add egg yolks one at a time, beating well after each addition. Press cottage cheese through sieve. Add to egg mixture with flour, bread crumbs, salt and pepper; mix well. Beat egg whites until stiff and fold into cottage cheese mixture. Drop by spoonfuls into several inches of boiling salted water (2 teaspoons salt to 1 quart water), cover and cook 10 minutes. Do not remove cover while cooking. Drain well and serve at once.
Yields 10 to 12 dumplings.

COTTAGE CHEESE SOUFFLÉ

½ cup butter | ½ cup sugar | 4 eggs, separated |
½ pound cottage cheese, sieved | ⅓ cup seedless raisins |
1 teaspoon lemon juice | 1 cup sour cream

Cream butter, add sugar and egg yolks. Stir in sieved cottage cheese, raisins, lemon juice and sour cream. Fold in beaten egg whites and turn into a buttered casserole set in hot water. Bake uncovered 1 hour at 350° F. or gas mark 4 and serve immediately.
Serves 6.

NOODLE CHEESE (Casserole)

1 tablespoon butter, creamed | ½ cup sugar | 1 teaspoon salt |
¾ cup cottage cheese | ¼ cup sour cream | ¼ cup raisins, chopped, if desired |
Grated rind of ½ lemon | Juice of ½ lemon |
One 8-ounce package of wide noodles, cooked and drained | 4 eggs, separated

Mix the butter, sugar and salt together. Add the cottage cheese, sour cream, raisins, lemon rind and juice. Add noodles. Beat egg yolks until thick and lemon-coloured. Fold into cheese mixture. Fold in

stiffly beaten egg whites. Turn into oiled casserole, set in pan of hot water, bake in moderate oven (350° F. or gas mark 4) 1 hour or until set.
Serves 8.

CHEESE AND NOODLE RING (Shavuot Dish)

3 cups boiled noodles | Salted water |
1½ cups cottage cheese or half this amount and ½ cup cream cheese |
2 eggs | ½ teaspoon salt | Dash of pepper |
3 tablespoons dry cracker crumbs | 3 tablespoons butter

Boil broad noodles in salted water 7 to 10 minutes. Drain and rinse with hot water. To 3 cups boiled noodles add 1½ cups cottage cheese or ½ cup each cottage cheese and cream cheese. Add salt, pepper and eggs. Turn into a well-buttered ring mould, sprinkle with cracker crumbs and bake at 375° F. or gas mark 5 for 30 minutes or till lightly browned on top.
Serves 4.
Variation: Turn into a buttered heavy frying pan and cook over moderate heat 5 minutes, stirring lightly to prevent sticking. Brown more cracker crumbs in hot melted butter and sprinkle on top.

HOME-MADE CHEESE

KOCH KAESE (German Boiled Cheese)

1 quart cottage cheese | 1 teaspoon caraway seed | 1 teaspoon salt |
1 tablespoon butter | 1½ cups water | 2 egg yolks

Press cheese through a coarse strainer. Mix with salt and caraway seeds. Place in an earthenware dish, cover well and set in a warm place. Stir the cheese thoroughly evey day for one week, or until it is ripe and clear. Use a wooden spoon or fork for stirring. Heat water with butter and stir in cheese. Boil slowly for 20 minutes, stirring constantly. Remove from stove and beat in egg yolks until the mixture becomes smooth and glossy. Pour into cups or bowls that have been rinsed with cold water and set away in a cool place. Serve cold. To keep this cheese for a length of time, cover it with a cloth saturated with beer and wrung out. Makes an appetizing spread for ryebread sandwiches.

RUSSIAN CHEESE (Called *Pashka*)

2 pounds cottage cheese | ½ cup sour cream | ½ pound butter |
1 cup sugar or less | 1 egg | ½ cup chopped almonds, if desired |
½ cup chopped fruit or raisins, if desired

Force cottage cheese through strainer. Mix with butter and sour cream. Add sugar, egg, almonds and chopped fruit and beat until smooth. Place napkin in wooden mould, pour in mixture, fold napkin over top and put under press for 24 hours. If you have no wooden mould, mixture can be tied in napkin and hung over the sink for 24 hours. Unmould.
Serves 6.

HOME-MADE COTTAGE CHEESE

Heat sour milk over low heat until the whey rises to the top. Pour off whey and put the curd into a bag to drip slowly. *Do not squeeze.* It may take 6 hours or overnight to drain the liquid from the curds.
Turn the cheese into a bowl, season with salt to taste and form into balls. Keep covered with a cloth. This is the foundation cottage cheese.
1 quart sour milk yields 1 cup cottage cheese.

OTHER CHEESE DISHES

CHEESE-RICE CASSEROLE

1 cup rice | 2 quarts boiling water | 1½ teaspoons salt |
1 tablespoon butter | 1¼ cups grated Cheddar cheese |
2 eggs, beaten slightly | 1 cup milk

Drop the rice in the boiling salted water and cook till tender, from 20 to 25 minutes. Drain well. Arrange in buttered casserole in alternate layers with the grated cheese. Combine the eggs and milk and pour over the rice mixture. Set the dish in a pan of hot water and bake for 30 minutes at 350° F. or gas mark 4. It is done when a knife inserted in the centre comes out clean.

Serves 6 to 8.

CHEESE SOUP (A Quickie)

2 tablespoons butter | 3 tablespoons flour | 1 quart milk, scalded |
¼ teaspoon salt | ¼ teaspoon celery salt | 2 egg yolks, beaten slightly |
¼ cup grated Cheddar cheese

Melt the butter and blend in the flour but do not brown; add the scalded milk gradually, stirring until smooth. Cook 5 minutes and add seasonings. Add a small amount to the egg yolks, being careful to blend well, then stir into soup. Cook 1 minute longer, add the cheese and serve.

Serves 6.

ENGLISH CHEESE MONKEY

1 tablespoon butter | 1 cup grated cheese | 1 cup milk |
1 cup bread crumbs | 1 egg | ½ teaspoon salt |
Dash of cayenne pepper or paprika

Melt butter and cheese in a double boiler. Add crumbs and milk. Stir in beaten egg and seasonings. Cook 5 minutes. Serve on toast.

Serves 4.

CHEESE CASSEROLE

6 slices stale bread | 1 tablespoon butter or margarine |
½ pound sliced Cheddar cheese | 2 eggs | 1 cup milk |
½ teaspoon salt | Pinch of pepper

Arrange 2 pieces of bread in bottom of a buttered casserole. Add sliced cheese to cover and repeat the layers, ending with bread.

Beat eggs, add milk and seasoning. Pour into casserole and dot with butter. Bake 15 to 20 minutes at 350° F. or gas mark 4.

Serves 5 or 6.

Variation: Utilize stale rolls, biscuits or muffins. Grated cheese may be used in place of sliced.

CHEESE TRIANGLES

4 sandwiches of whole wheat bread | Butter | Sliced Cheddar cheese (4 slices) |
3 tablespoons melted shortening | 1 can tomato soup |
Minced parsley or green pepper | 1 cup cottage cheese

Butter enough bread for 4 sandwiches, putting a slice of Cheddar cheese in each sandwich. Cut cheese sandwiches into 4 triangles each and brown on both sides in hot melted shortening. Remove triangles to a heated platter.

Heat the tomato soup in the frying pan and pour over browned sandwiches. Add minced parsley and balls of cottage cheese. Serve hot.

Serves 4.

CHEESE PEGS

2 cups mashed potatoes | 2 tablespoons butter |
1 cup grated nippy cheese (Cheddar) | 1 egg | 1 cup cracker crumbs |
Dash of nutmeg | Salt and pepper to taste | Oil or vegetable shortening

Combine the hot mashed potatoes, butter, cheese, beaten egg. Add ¼ cup of cracker crumbs and season to taste. Toss on to a bread board sprinkled with the remaining crumbs and roll into cylinders 1 inch thick. Cut into 2½-inch lengths. Fry in deep fat till brown. Drain well. Serve with vegetable platter or with the salad.

Serves 4 to 6.

HOT CHEESE STICKS

½ cup butter | 1½ cups sifted flour | 1 teaspoon salt |
1 egg yolk, slightly beaten | 2 tablespoons sour cream |
¼ cup grated Cheddar cheese

Cut the butter into the flour until it is like coarse sand. Add salt. Mix the egg yolk with the sour cream and add a little at a time to the flour mixture to make a stiff dough. Blend in the grated cheese. Roll out on a well-floured board to $\frac{1}{8}$-inch thickness and cut in narrow strips. Prick the cut pieces with a fork and place them on a baking sheet. If desired, cut into fancy shapes or twist the strips. A quarter of an hour before serving, put them into a moderate oven (350° F. or gas mark 4) and bake 10 minutes or until lightly browned.

Yields 3 to 4 dozen sticks.

CHEESE-NUT LOAF

1 tablespoon butter | 2 tablespoons minced onion | Salt and pepper to taste |
1 cup grated cheese | 1 cup chopped English walnuts |
1 cup dry bread crumbs | 1 tablespoon lemon juice | $\frac{1}{2}$ cup milk or water

Sauté onion in butter till light brown. Combine all ingredients, stirring in liquid last, add browned onions and turn into a buttered baking dish. Brown top under grill or in oven and serve hot.

Serves 4.

CHEESE-RICE LOAF

2 eggs | 1 cup cooked rice | 1 cup grated cheese or cottage cheese |
Salt and pepper to taste | 1 tablespoon butter | 1 tablespoon minced onion |
2 tablespoons cracker crumbs | Tomato sauce

Beat eggs, add cheese and rice and blend well. Add seasonings and onion browned in butter. Turn into a greased loaf pan and bake at 350° F. or gas mark 4 about 45 minutes. Top with buttered crumbs, return to brown lightly under grill and serve with tomato sauce.

Serves 4.

GRILLED CHEESE TOAST DE LUXE

2 eggs | $\frac{1}{2}$ cup syrup from any canned fruit | Dash of cinnamon |
1 tablespoon butter | 8 slices bread | 4 thin slices Cheddar cheese

Beat eggs slightly and stir in fruit juice and cinnamon. Butter bread

on one side and let slices absorb the egg and fruit mixture. Put two slices together with cheese between and place in electric sandwich toaster till browned. If electric sandwich toaster is not available, fry these sandwiches in hot melted butter till browned on both sides.
	Serves 4.

CHEESE FONDUE

*8 slices bread | 3 eggs | ½ pound Cheddar cheese | 2 cups milk |
1 teaspoon salt | ½ teaspoon paprika | ¼ cup butter or margarine, melted |
1 teaspoon Worcestershire sauce or ½ teaspoon dry mustard, if desired*

Place bread in a shallow baking dish. Pour melted butter over it and arrange cheese, cut in thin slices, on top. Beat the eggs, add the remaining ingredients and pour over all. Let stand in refrigerator at least several hours. Bake at 350° F. or gas mark 4 about 30 minutes, till it puffs and browns.
	Serves 6.

CASHKAVAL A'CAPAK (Rumanian Cheese Dish)

Cashkaval cheese is similar to Cheddar. Cut cheese ½ inch thick in oblongs or squares. Dip in slightly beaten egg then in cracker or fine bread crumbs and fry till brown on one side before turning to brown the other side.
	Allow 2 squares 2½ × 2½ inches per serving.

PARMESAN CHEESE PUDDING

*6 eggs, separated | ¼ cup flour | 1 cup milk | ¼ teaspoon salt |
Dash of pepper | ¼ cup grated Parmesan cheese*

Beat egg yolks and stir in flour; add milk, salt and pepper. Cook in double boiler until thickened, stirring constantly. Add cheese and stir until cheese is melted. Fold in stiffly beaten egg whites. Turn into greased mould. Cover tightly and steam for ¾ hour. Serve with melted butter, additional grated Parmesan cheese, sautéed mushrooms, or Creole sauce.
	Serves 6.

CHEESE PUFFS WITH SPANISH SAUCE

*4 egg whites | 1 pound Cheddar cheese, shredded | Salt and pepper | 1 egg |
1 tablespoon water | Fine dry bread crumbs | Shortening for deep frying |
Toast rounds*

Beat egg whites until stiff. Carefully fold in shredded cheese and
season. Form into croquettes and chill in the refrigerator 30 minutes.
Beat the whole egg and add water. Roll the croquettes in fine
crumbs, dip in the beaten egg and roll in crumbs again. Fry in deep
fat heated to 375° F. or gas mark 5. Drain and serve on buttered
toast rounds topped with hot Spanish sauce.
 Yields 10 puffs.

SPANISH SAUCE

*½ green pepper, shredded | 1 small onion, chopped | 2 tablespoons butter |
2 cups canned tomatoes | ½ cup button mushrooms | Salt and pepper*

Cook green pepper and onion in butter 5 minutes. Add tomatoes and
simmer until sauce is thickened. Add mushrooms and seasonings.
Cook 5 minutes longer.
 Yields 2½ cups sauce.

CHEESE AND VEGETABLE RING

*2 tablespoons butter or vegetable shortening | 2 cups fine noodles, cooked |
1 cup grated Cheddar cheese | 2 cups each cooked green beans, peas,
carrots (canned may be used) | ½ cup chopped spinach or other greens |
½ cup dry skim milk or 2 cups milk | 2 cups water (if using dry skim milk) |
2 tablespoons flour | ½ teaspoon salt | Dash of white pepper (optional) |
3 eggs, well beaten | Minced parsley for garnish*

Use a 9-inch ring mould (or a casserole dish). Grease the inside and
bottom well and cover with half the cooked noodles. Sprinkle half
the amount of grated cheese evenly, add half the amount of mixed
vegetables then repeat, reserving some of the grated cheese to
sprinkle over the top. Combine milk, flour and seasonings in a
saucepan.
 Cook over low heat till sauce begins to thicken. Stir in the well-
beaten eggs till smooth and pour into the ring mould slowly, turning

so that the sauce is absorbed evenly by the layers of noodles and vegetables. Bake 30 minutes at 350° F. or gas mark 4, or till lightly browned on top. Turn off oven heat. After 5 minutes remove from oven and turn out on serving plate. Fill centre with cooked diced carrots, peas or both and garnish with minced parsley. If a casserole is used surround with mounds of alternating carrots and peas.

Serves 5 or 6.

GRATED CHEESE SOUFFLÉ

*2 tablespoons butter | 3 tablespoons flour | ¾ cup milk |
Dash of cayenne (or paprika) | 3 eggs, separated | ½ teaspoon salt |
1 cup grated cheese | ½ teaspoon cream of tartar*

Melt butter in saucepan and rub in flour until smooth. Add the milk and seasonings slowly, stirring constantly until thickened. Beat egg yolks and combine with ¼ of the hot sauce. Add to the remaining sauce. Add grated cheese, stirring until it melts. Beat egg whites and cream of tartar until it holds a peak. Fold egg whites into cheese mixture carefully. Pour into a buttered baking dish or a casserole. Place in a pan of hot water and bake 15 minutes at 325° F. or gas mark 3, then raise temperature to 375° F. or gas mark 5 for 20 minutes. Serve at once.

Serves 4.

FRUITED CHEESE RING

*1 package lemon gelatin | 1 tall can crushed pineapple and juice |
1 pound cream cheese | 1 green pepper, minced |
1 cup almonds, blanched and chopped | 1 cup mayonnaise |
1 cup whipped cream | Lettuce*

Dissolve gelatin in heated juice drained from crushed pineapple. Blend with the other ingredients, folding in the whipped cream.

Fill a ring mould rinsed in cold water and place in refrigerator at least 3 hours or overnight.

Unmould on a round serving plate. Garnish with lettuce. Cut like cake when serving.

Serves 10 to 12.

LUNCHEON LOAF

1 *loaf white bread, unsliced* | 1 *can tuna fish* | 1 *carrot, grated* |
1 *green pepper, chopped fine* | *Lemon juice, salad dressing or mayonnaise* |
1 *package cream cheese (8 ounces)* | 3 *tablespoons sour cream* |
2½ *cups tomato juice* | 2 *packages lemon gelatin* |
3 *hard-cooked eggs* | *Salad greens* | *Black olives*

Cut away the crust from bread on all four sides, then slice lengthwise into three parts. Flake tuna fish and combine with grated carrot, green pepper and enough lemon juice, salad dressing or mayonnaise to form a spreadable consistency. Spread evenly over one long slice of bread. Spread the cream cheese which has been combined with 1 tablespoon of sour cream and some of the carrot and green pepper over the second slice of bread. Place on top of the covered slice and top with the third slice. Heat 1 cup of tomato juice and dissolve the lemon-flavoured gelatin in it. Add the rest of the tomato juice and stir well. Rinse a loaf pan in cold water, turn in some of the tomato juice mixture – about 1 inch deep – and let stand or chill until firm.

Place the filled loaf of bread in the pan and press down slightly to contact the jellied mixture in bottom. With a rotary beater whip the balance of jellied tomato juice, adding the remainder of sour cream while beating. Arrange the filled loaf in pan so there is a little space on all sides and turn in the beaten mixture. When firm unmould on serving platter and garnish with sliced hard-cooked eggs over top and sides. Watercress, shredded lettuce or chicory, makes a nice contrast around this luncheon loaf. A few black olives give an excellent accent. To slice, use a cake knife and cut into six or eight pieces about 1 inch thick.

Serves 6 to 8.

MISCELLANEOUS MEATLESS DISHES

DAMPF NUDELEN (German Dumplings—sometimes called *Pompushki* in Russian)

1 *ounce yeast* | 1 *cup lukewarm milk* | 1 *teaspoon sugar* |
3 *cups flour (approximately)* | 1 *teaspoon salt* | 1 *egg* |
¾ *cup additional milk* | 4 *tablespoons melted butter*

Dissolve yeast in cup lukewarm milk. Add sugar. Sift together flour and salt into a bowl and stir in yeast and milk mixture lightly. Add

whole egg and continue stirring, adding additional milk gradually
to form a soft dough. Dust with flour and cover with a tea cloth. Let
rise at room temperature 30 to 45 minutes. Melt butter in a shallow
casserole, 2 to 2½ inches deep. Turn out dough on a lightly floured
kneading board and pat into 1-inch thickness. With a small biscuit
cutter make rounds and dip each into the melted shortening as you
place it in the bottom of casserole. Pile these up and brush top layer
of rounds with melted butter. Add milk enough to come half-way
up the side of casserole. Bake at 375° F. or gas mark 5 for 25 to 35
minutes or till top layer is lightly browned and the milk absorbed.
Serve with lemon sauce.

Serves 6.

Variation: Melt shortening on a shallow baking pan and dip each
    round into it, placing it butter side up at least 1 inch from the
    next. Bake at 375° to 400° F. or gas mark 5 to 6 till lightly
    browned top and bottom. Serve like scones. These should
    double in height during baking process.

VEGETABLE FRITTERS WITH SOUR CREAM

*2 eggs | ½ teaspoon salt | 4 tablespoons flour |
2 cups of any mixed cooked vegetable (except beets) |
1 tablespoon lemon juice | 1 teaspoon grated onion or onion juice |
4 tablespoons shortening | 1 cup sour cream*

Be sure the vegetables are well drained and cut as fine as possible –
not mashed. Beat eggs, add salt and stir in flour to make a thick
batter. Add vegetables, lemon juice and onion juice and blend
smooth. Drop from the spoon into hot melted shortening and fry till
browned on both sides. Remove to a casserole, cover with sour cream
and bake 10 minutes at 350° F. or gas mark 4. Serve hot.

Serves 4.

RICE AND NUT CROQUETTES

*3 tablespoons butter or margarine | 4 tablespoons flour | ½ teaspoon salt |
Dash cayenne | 1 cup milk | 2 teaspoons grated onion |
½ teaspoon dry mustard | 2 cups boiled rice |
1 cup chopped pecans or other nuts | Fine dry bread crumbs |
1 egg | 1 tablespoon water*

Melt fat, blend in flour, salt and cayenne. Add milk. Cook, stirring constantly, over a low flame till mixture is very thick. Add onion and mustard. Cool. Add rice and nuts. Add additional salt to taste. Chill.

Shape into 10 or 12 balls and roll in crumbs. Blend egg with 1 tablespoon water. Coat croquettes well with egg and dip again into crumbs. Fry in deep hot fat (380° F. – a cube of bread turns light brown in 40 seconds) till brown. Drain on unglazed paper. Serve with tomato sauce.

Serves 5 to 6.

NOODLES AND ALMONDS

An 8-ounce package noodles (about 4 cups cooked) | 1½ quarts water |
1 tablespoon salt | 1 cup chopped salted almonds |
4 tablespoons butter, melted | 1 tablespoon celery seed |
2 teaspoons poppy seed | 2 teaspoons grated orange rind |
2 teaspoons grated lemon rind

Cook noodles covered in boiling salted water until tender. Drain and rinse under hot water. Heat almonds in butter but do not brown. Combine remaining ingredients with almonds and add to noodles. Salt to taste.

Serves approximately 6 to 8.

NOODLES AND APPLES

3 cups cooked noodles (6 ounces uncooked) | 3 tablespoons butter |
3 tablespoons grated Swiss cheese | 3 cups sliced tart apples |
8 cooked prunes, pitted and cut in quarters | ½ teaspoon salt |
¼ teaspoon cloves | 3 tablespoons brown sugar

Combine all ingredients and pour into well-oiled 2-quart casserole. Cover and bake in a moderate oven (350° F. or gas mark 4) 30 minutes. Remove cover and bake 15 minutes longer, or till lightly browned.

Serves 6 to 8.

POPPY SEED NOODLES (Dutch Style)

*1 package (8 ounces) broad noodles, cooked and drained |
3 tablespoons poppy seeds | ½ cup slivered blanched almonds, toasted |
1 tablespoon butter | 1 teaspoon lemon juice |
1 cup sour cream, if desired | Salt, dash of cayenne pepper |
1 teaspoon minced parsley or watercress, if desired*

Keep cooked noodles warm while preparing sauce. Toss poppy seeds and slivered almonds in butter or dripping. Then add lemon juice. Pour over hot noodles. Add remaining ingredients. Toss together lightly. Serve piping hot.
Serves 6.

CREOLE STYLE NOODLES

*4 cups cooked broad noodles | 1 onion, chopped | 2 tablespoons butter |
1 green pepper, chopped | 6 tomatoes | 1 cup green beans, cooked |
4 okra pods | 1 teaspoon salt*

Parboil the noodles. Cook onion in butter. Add peeled and quartered tomatoes, chopped pepper, beans and prepared okra. Prepare the okra by washing, removing both ends, cutting into ¼-inch pieces and blenching. Simmer sauce 20 minutes, add noodles and cook till tender, replacing water if necessary.
Serves 6 to 8.

NOODLE RING

*2 eggs, beaten | ½ cup undiluted evaporated milk |
1 tablespoon Worcestershire sauce | ¼ cup ketchup |
¼ cup grated Swiss cheese | ¼ cup chopped red pepper (optional) |
¼ cup chopped green pepper (optional) | ½ teaspoon salt |
Pepper to taste | 2 cups cooked noodles (4 ounces uncooked)*

Combine all ingredients and blend well. Pour into oiled 8-inch ring mould. Place in a pan of hot water. Cover and bake in moderate oven (350° F. or gas mark 4) 30 minutes or until inserted silver knife comes out clean. Turn out on to platter and serve with creamed fish or freshly cooked vegetables heaped in the centre.
Serves approximately 4 to 6.

Beet Borsht (*page 183*)

MACARONI (Basic Recipe)

6 ounces macaroni | 2 quarts boiling water | 1 teaspoon salt |
½ pound grated hard cheese | ¼ cup buttered crumbs

Drop broken macaroni into rapidly boiling salted water. Cover and
cook 10 to 15 minutes or till tender. Drain in colander and pour
boiling water through to rinse. Add grated cheese and top with
buttered crumbs.
Serves 4 to 6.
Variation: After rinsing with hot water and draining, add grated
cheese and 1 cup milk. Turn into well-buttered baking pan or
casserole and top with buttered crumbs. Bake 15 minutes at
350° F. or gas mark 4 uncovered or till lightly browned on top.

MACARONI CASSEROLE

½ pound macaroni | 1 quart boiling water | 1 teaspoon salt | 4 eggs |
½ cup each minced green pepper, celery, and onion |
2 tablespoons grated Cheddar cheese | 1 can cream of mushroom soup or
1 cup sliced fresh mushrooms | 1 cup milk

Cook macaroni in salted water 8 to 10 minutes. Drain. Boil eggs for
10 minutes, remove shells and slice. Add the other ingredients.
Arrange egg slices on top and sprinkle with grated cheese. Add the
liquid. Bake in an open casserole 30 minutes till the liquid has been
reduced by half and then slip under the grill to brown slightly before
serving.
Serves 4.

MACARONI WITH MUSHROOMS

½ pound macaroni | 1 quart boiling water | Salt | 1 onion, sliced |
2 tablespoons butter or oil | ½ pound fresh mushrooms or 1 can mushrooms |
Salt and pepper to taste | 1 tablespoon dry crumbs | 1 cup milk

Boil macaroni in salted water till tender. Drain. Brown onion in
shortening, add mushrooms and sauté. Combine with macaroni.
Add seasoning to taste. Turn into buttered casserole, top with dry
12

crumbs and add milk. Bake 30 minutes at 350° F. or gas mark 4, or
till browned on top.

Serves 4 to 5.

Variation: Substitute boiled or roasted chestnuts for mushrooms.

MACARONI WITH CHEESE AND OLIVE SAUCE

½ pound macaroni | 1 quart boiling water | 1 tablespoon salt

SAUCE

*4 tablespoons butter | 3 tablespoons flour | 2½ cups milk |
1 teaspoon salt | 2 cups grated Cheddar cheese | ⅛ teaspoon pepper |
½ to 1 cup sliced, stuffed green olives*

Cook macaroni in rapidly boiling salted water 15 to 20 minutes, or
till tender. Drain and run hot water through macaroni.

Make the sauce, as follows: Melt butter, add flour and blend until
smooth. Add milk and cook in top of double boiler until sauce
thickens, stirring constantly. Grate cheese, keeping a little out to
garnish top if desired. Add cheese and seasonings to sauce and stir
until cheese is melted. Add stuffed green olive slices. Arrange
macaroni on serving plate and pour sauce over it. Garnish top with
grated cheese.

Serves 6.

SPAGHETTI (Basic Recipe)

*6 ounces spaghetti (gluten, when preferred) | 1 teaspoon salt |
1 quart boiling water*

Drop spaghetti into rapidly boiling salted water and cook 8 to 10
minutes or till tender. Drain. Serve with melted butter or grated
cheese.

Serves 3 to 4.

Variation 1: Serve with hot tomato sauce, grated cheese.

Variation 2: Serve with tomato and chopped meat sauce (see
Index).

Variation 3: Add chopped meat balls and cover with tomato sauce. Bake 20 minutes.

Variation 4: Add sliced frankfurters and tomato sauce, and bake 15 minutes in a covered casserole.

BROAD NOODLES WITH CHEESE

Use same amounts of ingredients as for Marcaroni and same procedure.

Variations can be made by serving boiled noodles with cottage cheese and buttered crumbs; grated cheese and cooked mushrooms.

WELSH RAREBIT (Basic Recipe)

½ cup milk | 2 eggs | 1 teaspoon dry mustard | Dash of cayenne | 2 cups diced Cheddar cheese | 1½ tablespoons butter | ¼ teaspoon salt

Scald milk in top of double boiler. Beat eggs and add seasonings. Stir into hot milk till it begins to thicken. Add cheese and butter, stirring till smooth. Cook 1 minute and serve on toast.

Serves 4.

Variation 1: Add 1 teaspoon Worcestershire sauce.

Variation 2: Blend in ½ cup beer or ginger ale just before serving.

WELSH RAREBIT 2

1 pound grated sharp cheese | 1 tablespoon butter | 1 teaspoon dry mustard | 1 teaspoon cornflour | ¾ cup milk | 1 egg | 1 tablespoon Worcestershire sauce

Melt cheese and butter in double boiler. Moisten cornflour and mustard with a little milk and rub smooth. Blend in. Combine slightly beaten egg with the rest of milk. Stir into melted cheese, add Worcestershire sauce and cook over hot water till thickened. Serve on toast.

Serves 4.

EGGPLANT STEAK WITH ONIONS

1 eggplant | 1 teaspoon salt | 2 eggs, beaten | 1 cup bread crumbs |
4 tablespoons oil or shortening | 2 tablespoons grated cheese |
1 tablespoon minced parsley | 1 large onion

Slice the eggplant in rounds $\frac{1}{2}$ inch thick. Do not peel. Salt the slices
lightly and allow to stand for 30 minutes. Drain or wipe each slice
dry. Dip in beaten egg then in crumbs and fry till brown on both
sides. Serve with grated cheese and minced parsley. Cut the onion
into rounds and fry till light brown. Serve with the eggplant steaks.
Serves 4 or 5 (depending on size of eggplant).

GARNISHES FOR SOUPS

Kinds of Soups	*Garnishes**
Chicken Clear Beef Broth	Einlauf (Egg Fluff) Farfel (Egg Barley) Kreplach (Meat-Filled Dump- lings) Kasha (Buckwheat Groats) Lokshen (Noodles) Mandlen (Soup Nuts) Rice
Borsht (Sweet and Sour Soups)	Boiled Potato Sliced or Diced Hard-Cooked Eggs Sour Cream or Egg Yolk
Creamed Soups (Vegetable)	Croutons Grated Cheese Salted Crackers
Fruit Soups (Cooked and Un- cooked, Served Hot or Chilled)	Einlauf (for hot soups) Fresh Mint or Self Fruit or Berries Uncooked
Purées (Legumes or Vegetables)	Crackers Croutons Minced Parsley or Dill
Vegetable (with or without Meat)	Crackers or Croutons

CHICKEN SOUP (Basic Recipe)

In the Jewish home chicken soup is associated with Sabbaths and holidays. Specially rich clear chicken soup is commonly called *Gilderne.*

Fowl that has had the fatty portions removed is best for soup.

* Minced parsley or fresh dill are always acceptable garnishes.

Sections of chicken should include the gizzard, heart, neck and feet. A 4½- to 5-pound fowl will make 8 to 10 servings of soup. After preparing chicken parts for cooking, add the following:

> 1 *large onion* | 1 *large carrot diced, sliced or strips* |
> 2 *stalks celery including leaves* | 1 *bay leaf* | 6 *peppercorns (optional)* |
> *Boiled water (1 quart per pound of chicken)*

Cook slowly after bringing to a quick boil. Skim carefully. Add vegetables after 30 minutes of simmering. Cooking time depends on tenderness of fowl.

Pressure Cooker Method: Cook all ingredients listed 25 to 30 minutes under 15 pounds pressure or as directed in the booklet accompanying your particular type of pressure cooker.

Strain soup while hot just before serving.

BEEF SOUP (Basic Recipe for Clear Soup)

> 2 *pounds lean beef* | 1 *marrow bone* | 4 *quarts cold water* | 1 *large onion* |
> 1 *carrot* | 2 *stalks celery and leaves* | 1 *bay leaf* |
> *Peppercorns (optional)* | *Salt to taste*

Bring water with meat and marrow bone to a quick boil and skim carefully before adding vegetables and seasonings. Simmer gently 2 to 2½ hours or until meat is very tender. If marrow bone has plenty of marrow, mix cooked marrow with salt and a little paprika and spread on toasted squares of bread or crackers as a special accompaniment. Serve soup hot after straining. Beef stock or clear soup may be used as a basis for borsht, meat and vegetable soups, purées, gravies, etc.

Store left-over clear soups in covered glass jars in the refrigerator. Remove chilled fat from top of soups for use with vegetables, etc.

LAMB BROTH (Basic Recipe)

With 2½ pounds shoulder of lamb use same vegetables in same quantity as Beef Soup recipe. Cook until lamb is tender enough to fall away from bones. Cut meat into tiny bits and serve with strained soup.

Use of Left-over Soup Meat. Meat may be cut from bones and chopped for use in making Kreplach, Piroshki, Pirogen, and other meat-filled garnishes (see Index).

BEET BORSHT

4 medium size beets and tops | 1 onion, peeled | 4 cups boiling water |
1 tablespoon salt | ½ cup mild vinegar or ¼ cup lemon juice (or
¼ teaspoon citric acid crystals) | 3 tablespoons brown sugar (or to taste)

Cut tops from beets 2 inches from the roots. Scrub beets thoroughly, cover with cold water and boil 15 minutes or until tender enough to pierce with a toothpick. While beets are boiling, wash leaves and chop fine in a wooden bowl. The stems may be used, too. Strain the liquid from beets into a bowl or soup pot. Slip skins from beets and grate them, using a fine grater. Grate onion into grated beets. Add this to the strained beet juice, boiled water and chopped beet tops. Add salt and bring to a quick boil. Reduce heat and cook 5 minutes. Add vinegar sweetened to taste with brown sugar. Or sour salt cystals dissolved in ½ cup beet soup and sweetened to taste with brown sugar. Cool and chill in closed jars. Add a boiled potato, 3 tablespoons diced cucumber and 1 heaped tablespoon sour cream to each plateful just before serving. If you have fresh dill, use it for garnish.

Serves 6 to 8.

Variation 1: Add 1 hard-cooked egg, diced or sliced, to each serving in addition to, or in place of, the other garnish.

Variation 2: For a fleishig (meat) borsht, use diced or grated cooked beets with 1½ to 2 pounds brisket of beef. Cook 1½ hours or until meat is tender. Add the same ingredients including tops and seasoning 15 minutes before serving. Thicken hot borsht by stirring in 1 egg yolk per serving. Add boiled potato. Or substitute garnish of sliced hard-cooked eggs.

Variation 3: Cook 1 cupful diced rhubarb with borsht and omit vinegar or lemon juice.

Variation 4: For a delicious summer-time cooler, serve strained meatless beet borsht (with or without rhubarb), in tall glasses topped with fresh mint after thickening with a little sour cream.

Variation 5: A borsht cocktail that is delicious on a hot summer day is made by adding soda water or lemon soda to strained chilled borsht.

CRANBERRY AND CABBAGE BORSHT

*1 cup picked-over cranberries | 1 cup cold water |
2 cups shredded white cabbage | 3 cups water |
3 tablespoons lemon juice or vinegar | 4 tablespoons brown sugar |
2 tablespoons white sugar | 1 teaspoon salt*

Cook cranberries in 1 cup water, covered, 3 to 5 minutes or till they pop. Remove from heat and put through strainer or fruit press. Add the other ingredients in the order listed and cook 8 to 10 minutes over moderate heat. Serve hot or cold with a thickening of egg yolk or sour cream, allowing quantities as for other borsht.
Serves 4.

Variation: Brown 1 onion, finely diced or sliced, in 2 tablespoons butter or other shortening. Stir shredded cabbage in frying pan 3 to 5 minutes. Combine with all the ingredients as listed in basic recipe. Serve hot with a boiled potato per serving added.

SCHAV BORSHT (Sorrel or Sour Grass)

*1 pound schav (sorrel grass) | 1 quart cold water | 1 onion |
1 teaspoon salt | ½ cup vinegar or ¼ teaspoon citric acid crystals |
½ cup brown sugar*

Wash leaves in several waters. One good method is to pick over leaves and place them in a colander. Dip up and down into a filled pot of cold water larger than the colander. Drain well. Cut fine or chop leaves coarsely. Add the other ingredients listed and cook 10 minutes over moderate heat. Taste and add vinegar and sugar to suit the taste. Lemon juice may be substituted if vinegar and citric acid is omitted, and added a few minutes before removing from heat.

Chill Schav Borsht in refrigerator. Serve cold with a hot boiled potato per serving, or sliced hard-cooked eggs.

Thicken with sour cream or beaten egg yolks, just before serving.
Serves 4 or 5.

SPINACH BORSHT

Quantities of cleaned spinach and other ingredients same as for

Schav Borsht. Cook, chill and serve with same garnish and thickenings.

SPINACH AND RHUBARB BORSHT

Prepare same as above. To each pound of spinach add 1 cup finely diced tender rhubarb, omitting sour flavouring.

KRUPNIK

¾ cup pearl barley | 6 cups water or vegetable juice |
1 onion or 2 leeks, cut fine | 1 carrot, grated | 1 small turnip, grated, or
½ cup mushrooms (dried or diced fresh) | 1 stalk celery, diced fine |
4 tablespoons butter | Salt and pepper |
Sour cream as desired for thickening and topping

Cook barley over moderate heat in half of the vegetable juice or stock. When tender add the other ingredients and remaining liquid. Season to taste with salt and pepper and cook 15 to 20 minutes or until vegetables are tender. When ready to serve thicken with sour cream and top with a little of same. A bit of minced parsley adds a festive look.
Serves 6.

RUMANIAN BEAN SOUP WITH TAYGLACH
(Egg Drops)

SOUP

1 quart cold water | 1½ cups dry lima beans | 1 teaspoon salt | 1 onion |
2 tablespoons chicken fat, oil, vegetable shortening or butter

TAYGLACH

1 egg | 2 tablespoons flour | A pinch of salt

Soak beans in cold water to cover, overnight preferably, but at least 3 hours. Drain. Add fresh cold water and salt. Cook over moderate heat in a covered pot 45 minutes or till beans are tender. Drain, reserving liquid. Reduce beans to pulp, through strainer or food press.

Add the bean pulp to liquid. There should be about 1 quart of thickened soup. Thin with boiled water if you wish, and add diced brown onion. Bring to a boil and drop from the tip of a spoon the tayglach or egg drops made by combining to a paste the beaten egg, flour and salt, one at a time while the soup is at moderate boiling point or bubbling slightly. After the last egg drop is put in, turn down heat and let cook 5 to 7 minutes.

Serves 4.

VEGETABLE MEDLEY

1 *cup diced potato | 1 cup finely cut green beans | 4 okra pods, sliced thin |*
1 *cup skinned and cut tomato | 4 cups cold water | 1 teaspoon salt |*
1 *onion, diced fine | Parsley | 2 tablespoons butter or other shortening*

Combine all vegetables except onion and parsley. Add water and salt and cook, covered, 10 minutes. Brown diced onion in hot melted butter and add just before serving. Serve with crackers or croutons.

Serves 4.

CABBAGE SOUP

2 *pounds cabbage | 1 large onion | Salt to taste |*
2 *or 3 pounds brisket of beef | 2 quarts boiling water | 1 carrot |*
½ *cup vinegar or lemon juice (citric acid crystals may be used) |*
4 *tablespoons brown sugar*

THICKENING

1 *tablespoon browned flour | 1 tablespoon shortening | ½ cup soup*

Shred or chop the cabbage and onion. Salt lightly and let stand about 45 minutes or until it 'sweats'. Squeeze out the moisture. Sear the meat in the pot in which soup is to be cooked. When brown on all sides, add the cabbage and continue to sear meat and vegetables. When light brown, stir in the boiling water, add grated or diced carrot and the seasonings. Cook over a low heat about 1½ hours or until meat is tender. Make a thickening of 1 tablespoon browned flour and 1 tablespoon shortening, adding ½ cup soup and stirring till smooth. Add this einbren 15 minutes before serving time. Serves 6.

Variations: Add 1 cup stewed tomato, or ½ cup tomato paste, or ½ cup seeded raisins, or 1 tart apple diced or grated.

LENTIL SOUP (Basic Recipe)

1½ to 2 pounds soup meat | 2 quarts cold water | 1½ cups lentils |
1 carrot, diced | 1 medium size potato | 1 onion | 2 stalks celery, diced |
Salt to taste | Parsley

Bring meat and water to a quick boil and skim carefully. Add the other ingredients and cook over reduced heat 1½ hours or till meat is tender. Serve hot with minced parsley for garnish.

Serves 6 to 8.

Variation 1: Lentil and Barley Soup is made by adding ½ cup small, medium or pearl barley to the above.

Variation 2: Add ½ cup canned tomato purée or 1½ cups canned or fresh tomato pulp 15 to 20 minutes before serving time.

Variation 3: Meatless Lentil Soup is delicious and nourishing. Cook with or without tomato, with or without barley or farfel, but use the other ingredients as in basic recipe. Observe one variation, however – brown the diced onion in butter or other shortening and add just before serving. Meatless Lentil Soup requires cooking only till lentils are tender, approximately 45 minutes. Serve hot or cold.

POTTAGE OF LENTILS

Christian missionaries in the Near East wrote that this is said to be the very dish for which Esau sold his birthright. Jews and Arabs alike prepare this dish today.

½ cup shortening | 6 onions | 1 pound finely cut or chopped lamb or veal |
2 carrots | 1 parsnip | 2 stalks celery | 1 green pepper |
2 cups tomatoes | 1 cup of cold water | 1 pound lentils |
Salt to taste | Dash of pepper (optional)

Melt shortening and add onions, diced or sliced fine. Sauté the onions till light brown before adding meat. Simmer 10 minutes while preparing the vegetables. Dice carrots, parsnips, celery and green pepper, add tomatoes and about 1 cup of cold water. Add meat mixture and lentils and simmer at least 1½ hours or until lentils are tender. Add salt and pepper to taste. Shake the pot occasionally to prevent sticking.

Serves 4 to 6.

MOTHER WOLFF SOUP

2 pounds lean beef | ½ pound marrow bones | 4 quarts cold water |
1 large onion | 1 cup each diced potatoes, diced carrot, celery, yellow or
white squash, green beans, peas (fresh or dried), parsnips and
1 cup canned tomato sauce | ½ cupful dried lima beans |
¼ cup each rice, barley, yellow split peas | Salt and pepper to taste |
½ cup uncooked fine noodles | ½ cup minced parsley or dill

Boil meat and bones in water, skim carefully, then add all ingredients except noodles. Cover and simmer 2 hours. Season with salt and pepper to taste, add noodles and boil 10 minutes longer. Serve hot, garnished with parsley or fresh dill. This is a very hearty soup, full of **vitamins** and minerals. May be stored in a covered dish in the refrigerator for several days. If too thick, add boiling water and reheat.

Serves 8 to 10.

PURÉES

These are thickened soups generally made of legumes, cooked till tender in water with or without the addition of vegetables. Purées may be milchig or fleishig, depending on the addition of milk or cream and butter for the former, and meat or bones, or schmaltz, in the preparation of the latter.

LEGUME PURÉE (Basic Recipe)

1 cup dried beans (any variety), or lentils, or split or whole green or
yellow peas | 1 onion | 6 cups water | 1 tablespoon salt | 1 or 2 bay leaves

Dry legumes should be soaked in cold water to cover at least 2 hours.
Drain. Add onion, water, salt and bay leaves. Cook in a covered pot
1½ hours over moderate heat. Or in a pressure cooker from 20 to 30
minutes in 2 to 3 cups of cold water under 15 pounds pressure.
Consult time table used for your particular pressure cooker.

Cooked legumes are pressed through a coarse sieve or strainer,
forcing the purée through by addition of some of the liquid from
pot during the process to eliminate skins (in the case of beans and
peas).

Purées may be enriched by the addition of milk, cream or butter.
Allowing 1 teaspoon per serving for milchig purée is a good basis.
Chicken or goose schmaltz may substitute for butter or cream when
no addition of milk is made, or when legumes are cooked with meat
or bones, for fleishig purées.

Serves 6.

ONION PURÉE

3 large onions | 2 cups water | 3 tablespoons butter | 3 tablespoons flour |
2 cups milk | Salt and white pepper to taste

Peel onions and cook in cold water till tender. Press through a sieve.
Make a white sauce by blending the flour in hot melted butter and
stirring in the milk till smooth. Combine, season with salt and pepper
and beat with a rotary beater 2 minutes in soup pot. Serve hot with
crackers, buttered toast or pretzels.

Serves 4.

POTATO PURÉE

3 medium potatoes, pared | 1 onion | 1 small carrot |
1 small green pepper (optional) | 2 cups cold water | 1 cup milk |
Salt and pepper to taste | 2 tablespoons butter |
Minced parsley or celery tops

Dice vegetables. Cook in water 20 minutes. Press through a sieve,
add milk and seasoning to taste. Heat and add butter. Garnish with
minced parsley or celery tops and serve with toast or croutons.

Serves 4.

TOMATO AND BARLEY PURÉE

½ cup fine barley | 2 cups canned or stewed tomatoes | 1 onion |
4 cups water | ½ teaspoon salt | 2 tablespoons butter or chicken fat |
2 tablespoons flour

Rinse barley in cold water, add all ingredients except fat and flour. Cook over moderate heat 45 minutes or till barley is tender. Put through a sieve. If thickening is desired, blend the hot fat with 2 tablespoons flour and stir in some of the soup. Cook for 3 minutes and add to soup. Serve hot.

Serves 4 to 6.

CORN CHOWDER

2 cups diced raw potatoes | 1½ cups water |
1 cup canned corn (cream style) or 1½ cups fresh corn cut from cob |
1½ cups milk | Salt and pepper to taste | 2 tablespoons butter |
1 onion | Minced parsley

Boil potatoes in water till tender. Mash in water. Add corn, milk, salt and pepper. Cook 5 minutes if fresh corn is used, or 3 minutes if canned corn. Dice onion and cook in butter till light brown. Combine, add minced parsley and serve hot.

Serves 4.

FISH CHOWDER

1½ cups diced raw potatoes | 1½ cups water | 1½ cups milk |
2 cups flaked left-over fish (boiled, grilled or baked) | Salt and pepper to taste |
2 tablespoons butter | 1 tablespoon flour | Minced parsley

Boil potatoes in water till tender. Add milk, fish and season to taste. Blend flour in hot melted butter and thin into a smooth paste with 3 tablespoons of liquid from pot. Cook 5 minutes longer and serve. Garnish with minced parsley.

Serves 6.

Variation: Canned salmon or tuna fish may be substituted.

CREAM SOUP (Basic Recipe)

2 tablespoons flour | 2 tablespoons butter | 1½ cups milk or milk-and-water |
Pinch of salt | 1 cup cooked diced or mashed vegetable

Blend melted butter and flour in a saucepan over a moderate heat,
rubbing with bowl of spoon till smooth but not brown. Stir in milk
slowly and cook 1 minute. Add salt and 1 cup of cooked, diced or
mashed vegetable. Bring to a slow boil. Stir while cooking to prevent
a skin formation on top.
Serves 2.

Variations:
Asparagus – cut tender stalks and tips ¼ inch thick.
Broccoli – cut or chop fine, using some leaf sections.
Celery – cut fine, including ¼ part leaves.
Corn – cut from cob or use creamed style canned.
Mushroom – cut tender parts of stems with tops very fine.
Mushroom and Potato – add equal amount of potato, diced fine.
Potato – dice, cover with water or milk-and-water.
Spinach – chop carefully washed leaves and stems.
Tomato – peel fresh whole tomatoes or use canned variety.

Flavouring Cream Soups:
1 tablespoon minced onion browned in 1 tablespoon butter.
Grated Cheddar cheese sprinkled on top just before serving.
1 teaspoon lemon juice plus 1 tablespoon brown sugar for Tomato
Soup (optional).
A dash of white pepper.

Garnishes for Cream Soups:
Tiny croutons browned in butter, dry croutons, crackers.
Minced parsley.
A dash of paprika sprinkled on each serving.
Chopped hard-cooked egg yolk.

Fruit Soups are especially delicious for perking up appetites on warm
days. But any time of the year you'll find them a welcome starter for
any meal. (See Israeli section for additional recipes.) Use fresh
berries, cherries or other fruit in season. Canned, quick frozen or
dried mixed fruits or berries can be used any time of the year.

CHERRY SOUP WITH EGG DROPS

SOUP

1 *quart stemmed and pitted cherries (canned or fresh)* |
1 *tablespoon lemon juice* | 2 *tablespoons sugar (more with sour cherries)* |
1 *quart cold water* | *Pinch of salt*

EGG DROPS (MINUTE DUMPLINGS)

1 *egg* | ¼ *cup cold water* | 3 *tablespoons flour* | *Pinch of salt* |
Pinch of nutmeg

If soup is to be served hot, then prepare the egg drops first. Beat egg well. Stir in water then add flour, salt and flavouring and beat vigorously with a fork or spoon till smooth. Bring the combined soup ingredients to a boil and drop the egg mixture from the tip of a teaspoon into the rapidly boiling soup. Cook for 5 minutes and the dumplings will rise to the top when done.

If soup is to be served iced, do not cook it with the egg drops. After bringing soup to a boil and cooking for 5 minutes, let it cool. Then chill it in the refrigerator in a glass jar for at least 2 hours before serving. Just before serving, cook the egg drops in slightly salted water, using the same procedure as above. Drain them well before adding to the soup. A spoonful of sour cream may be added to each serving, stirred in or floated on top.

Serves 6 to 8.

GARNISHES FOR SOUP

Noodles. The art of making noodles at home has become almost obsolete in a day when factory-made varieties are available in convenient packages. There may be some home-makers who want to add this achievement to their culinary skill.

There are varieties of noodle dishes, from main dishes to desserts. Noodle dough is also used for the making of Kreplach, a traditional dish in Jewish cuisine. Below is a recipe for making noodle dough in the home kitchen. Measurements of the two ingredients used are approximate. Flour absorption varies. And eggs are of various sizes. Rolling dough evenly requires skill and experience.

However, with a little patience and practise, this art can be mastered.

Chicken Soup
(*page 181*)
with Kneidlach
(*page 65*)
Chicken
Casserole
(*page 261*)

HOME-MADE NOODLE DOUGH (Basic Recipe)

2 cups sifted flour (approximately) | 2 eggs | 2 or 3 teaspoons cold water

Sift flour into mixing bowl or on kneading board. Make a well in the centre. Add eggs and combine with a fork adding spoonfuls of water as necessary to form a ball of dough that is compact but not hard. Knead dough until as smooth and elastic as possible. Roll out on a lightly floured board. Use the rolling pin from the outer edges towards the centre, turning the board as necessary in order to achieve easier rolling. When dough is rolled *evenly thin* through the whole round, let stand 10 to 20 minutes in order to dry so that it will not stick together when rolled up. Roll up lightly. Use a sharp knife to cut fine. Shake to loosen and spread noodles on lightly floured cloth. Let dry at room temperature. Store in jars when dried. *Do not try* to make noodle dough in damp weather, especially if you are a novice at it.

Uses for Home-made Noodle Dough:
   It may be cut fine and used with clear chicken or meat soup.
   The dough may be cut into broad noodles and used with cheese or other combinations and for *kugel*.
   When cut into 1-inch squares and pinched together like bowknots, the noodles are called *shpaetzlen* (see recipe below for complete instructions). These are used for soups and goulashes.
   Noodle dough can also be used for making kreplach filled with cheese or chopped and seasoned cooked meat, liver, or chicken. (See Index for kreplach recipes.) Rolled out dough must not be dried out before cutting into 2½- to 3-inch squares for filling.
   Recipes using home-made noodle dough are given below.

SHPAETZLEN are like the scalloped, bow-knot, dried noodles that can be bought in packages. They can be made at home, minus the scalloped edges, by cutting the noodle dough as soon as it is rolled out. Cut into 1-inch squares and pinch together with thumb and forefinger. Let dry about a half hour before dropping one by one into rapidly boiling salted water. Cook over moderate heat about 10 minutes after the last one has been dropped in. Skim out with a perforated spoon or drain thoroughly in a colander.

FAVOURITE SHPAETZLEN

3 tablespoons butter | ½ cup dry bread crumbs (matzo meal or cracker crumbs) |
4 cups cooked shpaetzlen

Melt butter in a heavy frying pan and stir in crumbs till nicely
browned. Turn in the cooked shpaetzlen and stir lightly for 1
minute. Serve hot.

> *Variation 1:* Turn into a shallow casserole or baking dish and slip
> under grill to brown on top. Or cover with grated Cheddar.

> *Variation 2:* Fry 2 diced onions in 3 tablespoons fat till light
> brown. Add ½ cup vinegar and ½ cup water or soup stock, 3
> tablespoons brown sugar and cook 1 minute before pouring
> over the shpaetzlen. Brown on top under grill, top with
> minced parsley and serve as a vegetable substitute with meat or
> poultry.

NOODLE SQUARES

Noodle dough may be cut into ¼-inch squares, dried out and stored.
Cook in rapidly boiling salted water 8 to 10 minutes. Drain well.
Add 1 beaten egg to each cup of cooked noodle squares, ½ cup
chopped greben and onions, and ½ cup dry crumbs. Bake in a thin
layer in a well-greased shallow pan 10 minutes at 400° F. or gas
mark 6, or till brown on top. Serve as a substitute for potatoes with
roast meats or poultry.

KASHA-VARNITCHKES

Cut noodle dough into ½- or ¾-inch squares. Cook till tender in
rapidly boiling salted water. Drain thoroughly and combine with
prepared buckwheat groats (*Kasha* – see Index for method of
preparation). Add butter or schmaltz. Bake 10 minutes at 400° F.
or gas mark 6, or till browned lightly.

HOME-MADE FARFEL

Farfel, or egg barley, comes in convenient packages like commercial noodles of all varieties. But just in case you care to make your own at home, just add ½ cup sifted flour to basic noodle dough to make ball of dough hard enough to grate or chop fine. Let stand for half an hour before grating or chopping the dough in a wooden bowl as fine as necessary. Chop in a wooden bowl with a single- or four-blade chopping knife. Dry out the farfel on a board or shallow platter, stirring occasionally to facilitate thorough drying by exposure to air. May be stored in a glass container.

BITE-SIZE KREPLACH (for Purim)

Use the basic noodle dough. Roll out thin. Do not dry. Cut into 1½-inch squares. Place ½ teaspoon meat filling in centre of squares and pinch together securely into triangular puffs. Pinch together 2 points. Drop into boiling salted water. Cook 10 to 15 minutes. When done kreplach rise to the top. Skim out. Serve with clear soup or meat gravy.
Yields 24 to 36.

CHICKEN FILLING

1½ *cups finely cut left-over chicken* | 1 *egg* | 1 *tablespoon minced parsley* | 1 *teaspoon onion juice*

Blend together in the order given.

CHICKEN LIVER AND EGG FILLING

Chop together grilled chicken livers and as many hard-cooked eggs as desired to make a smooth mixture. Season with minced parsley, poultry seasoning, salt and pepper.
Variation: Greben and grilled liver, chopped fine and seasoned to taste.

CHEESE FILLING (FOR SHAVUOT KREPLACH)

1 *cup dry cottage cheese* | 1 *egg* | ¼ *teaspoon salt* | *Dash of pepper* | 2 *tablespoons fine crumbs*

Blend together with a fork.

LIVER DUMPLINGS

*1 egg | ½ cup dry bread crumbs | ½ cup hot mashed potatoes |
1 tablespoon minced parsley | ½ cup chopped liver (chicken,
goose, beef or calf's liver) | Salt and pepper to taste*

Blend together in the order given. Form into balls the size of
walnuts and drop into rapidly boiling salted water. Cook 7 minutes.
Skim out or drain and serve with clear soup. Or, drop directly into
boiling clear soup.

Serves 4.

MARROW DUMPLINGS

Substitute cooked or uncooked beef marrow for chopped liver and
follow procedure for Liver Dumplings.

SOUP NUTS (Mandlen)

3 eggs | 2 tablespoons salad oil | 1 teaspoon salt | 2 cups sifted flour

Beat eggs slightly, add oil and salt while beating. Stir into sifted
flour gradually to make a dough stiff enough to handle. Form into
pencil thin rolls on a floured board or between the palms of both
hands. Flatten slightly and cut into ¼- or ½-inch pieces. Bake on a
baking sheet or in a shallow baking pan at 375° F. or gas mark 5
for 10 minutes until nicely browned. Shake the pan or stir occasionally to brown evenly on all sides. When cold and dry these
mandlen may be stored for several days and heated before serving in
clear soup or with meat gravy.

Serves 6 to 8.

Variation: Drop the mandlen into hot melted shortening and cook
like doughnuts until nicely browned and crisp. Skim out with a
perforated spoon as soon as brown. It is best to drop in only as
many as will not crowd the pan and skim out as fast as browned.
Drain on paper towels. Reheat by enclosing in a paper bag
twisting top to close and placing in a preheated, 350° F. or gas
mark 4, oven for 5 minutes.

GRATED POTATO DUMPLINGS (Halkes)

*1½ cups well-drained grated raw potato | ½ cup flour (approximately) |
1 egg | ¼ teaspoon salt | Dash of grated onion or onion salt |
2 tablespoons dry crumbs*

Combine in the order given to make a batter thick enough to form
into balls the size of a hazelnut or walnut. Drop into rapidly boiling
soup 20 to 25 minutes before serving time. The dumplings will rise
to the top when done. Turn heat down to a simmer. Or, drop
dumplings in rapidly boiling salted water and cook till done. Drain
or lifted out with a perforated spoon and serve separately with soup
or meat gravy.
Serves 4 to 6.

BAVARIAN KARTOFFEL KLEISS
(Mashed Potato Dumplings)

*4 boiled potatoes, mashed | 2 eggs, slightly beaten |
2 slices toast, crushed | Salt and pepper to taste | 1 tea poon cornflour |
1 teaspoon minced parsley | Dash of nutmeg or cinnamon (optional)*

Combine ingredients in the order listed and form into balls the size
of hazelnuts or walnuts. Drop into rapidly boiling salted water one
at a time. Lift out as soon as they rise to the top, using perforated
spoon. Add chicken fat or other shortening and brown lightly in a
frying pan. Serve with soup or meat gravy.
Serves 6.

PIROSHKI

Use well-kneaded yeast dough or any of the pie crust doughs. Roll
or pat dough ½-inch thick. Cut into 3-inch rounds, brush with
melted shortening and place a spoonful of chopped cooked meat,
liver, lung, chicken or kasha in the centre and pinch edges together
securely. Shape into half moons and scallop the edges with a fluted
cutter if you desire. Let rise 1 to 1½ hours on a well-greased baking
sheet if yeast dough is used. Brush with melted shortening or diluted
egg yolk with equal amount of water before baking at 375° F. or gas
mark 5 for 20 to 30 minutes or until nicely browned. Serve with
clear soups or with the meat course. These baked dumplings may

be made in any desired size. For afternoon teas or receptions small ones are recommended if they are to be served with cocktails.

PIROGEN

These are made just like Piroshki but much larger. Yeast dough (see *Bread* section) should be used. The 5- or 6-inch rounds of rolled or flattened dough may be 1 or 1½ inches thick before filling with well-seasoned meat mixtures. Fold over. Pinch edges of dough together securely in a fluted design. Brush with melted shortening or diluted egg yolk after pirogen have risen at room temperature to about double in bulk. Bake at 350° F. or gas mark 4 for 30 to 35 minutes or till nicely browned. Serve hot. These are specially good with stews and roasts.

VARENIKES (Russian, Polish and Ukrainian)

Roll basic noodle dough to ⅛-inch thickness and cut into 4-inch rounds. Fill centres and pinch edges together securely. If you have a fluted cutter use it to make a scalloped edge. Drop these filled dumplings into rapidly boiling slightly salted water and turn down heat to a moderate boil. These dumplings rise to the top when done and should be skimmed out with a perforated spoon and placed in a buttered baking dish. Drizzle melted butter or vegetable shortening over them and bake 15 minutes at 350° F. or gas mark 4 till lightly browned. Serve with sour cream, or stewed fruit.

FILLINGS FOR VARENIKES

Berry or Cherry. Stew pitted cherries or hulled berries with enough sugar or honey to sweeten to taste. Thicken with cornflour or cracker crumbs and let cool before filling.

Cheese. To each cup of dry cottage cheese or farmer cheese add ½ cup mashed potatoes, 1 fried diced onion, salt and pepper to taste. Combine well, cool before using as filling.

Kasha or Chopped Meat. Add to the cooked kasha (see Index) or chopped meat, a browned diced onion and seasoning to taste. Add 1 egg yolk for each cupful of filling. Cool before using as filling.

13 Fresh Fish and Good Herring

METHODS OF PREPARING FISH. The most popular ways of serving fish from fresh caught to quick frozen are: baking, boiling, grilling, frying and pickling.

Fresh fish is generally dressed when purchased, that is, scales, fins and viscera removed. If fish is to be dressed at home, it should be placed on a cleaning board and a sharp-pointed knife applied under the scales, working towards the head. The scales, fins and tail are removed next. If head is to be used, remove eyes and gills before severing from body of fish. Remove entrails by slitting fish about a half inch into the underbody. If roe or milt is to be used, separate from the rest. Salt lightly the roe, milt and the whole fish or cut sections, and prepared head.

Filleted Fish. To fillet fish there are 3 steps that must be followed – clean, skin, and bone the fish.

To skin fish (after cleaning) insert the point of a sharp knife close to the backbone at the tail end, but do not detach skin from the backbone. Cut the skin from the flesh, working towards the head and keeping the knife blade close under the skin. Turn fish and remove skin from other side in the same manner.

To bone the fish (after it has been cleaned and skinned) cut the flesh from the bone structure, using the point of a knife to remove the flesh that adheres between the bones.

Filleted fish may be used whole or cut into small pieces. Whole fish is best for boiling, stuffing and baking.

Gefilte Fish. It is best to cut through whole fish to make sections conveniently large enough for filling, as directed in the recipe. Fillet each cut of fish separately.

Grilled Fish. The skin should be left on and the fish trimmed of fins, tail and head, and split lengthwise through under side. Grill whole fish with the cut side towards heat.

Quick Frozen Fish. Like all quick frozen foods, directions for treating contents are printed on carton or wrapping of fish. These directions must be followed precisely as given and fish prepared for cooking after complying with defrosting instructions.

Canned Fish. These varieties are the most popular among Jews: salmon, tuna, pickled herring (in sour cream or wine sauce), kippered herring and sardines. Canned fish of any kind is ready to serve but can be used in various recipes that require flaking, as in salad, or combining with other ingredients for grilling, baking or frying.

Smoked Fish. There are a number of varieties of Smoked Fish from Carp to Salmon and White Fish. These are favourite delicatessen specialties.

Salted and Dried Herrings. Herrings that are choice have thick, meaty bodies. The favourite varieties are Bismarck and Milch herring. Salt herring should be soaked in cold water to cover, several hours or overnight, then rinsed and cleaned of scales and entrails as well as head. The milt or roe of salt herring is used in many ways along with the sectioned herring for dressing with oil, lemon juice (or vinegar), sour cream, etc. Several favourite recipes for herring dishes are given.

Left-over Fish. Many uses can be found for this from salads to croquettes. But when using left-over fish of any kind for main dishes, it is a good point to remember that much of the original nutritive value has been lost. Therefore, to restore the possible loss of nutritive elements, combine the left-over fish with milk and/or eggs, whole wheat crumbs or wheat germ.

ABOUT GEFILTE FISH

Gefilte Fish may have originated in Germany or Holland some time after the expulsion of Jews from Spain in 1492. Or, it may have been invented in Russia or Poland. Or, perhaps, it was only the culinary ingenuity of a housefrau-on-a-budget in need of a food stretcher. One thing *is* certain, Gefilte Fish is Jewish.

Gefilte Fish in German means 'filled fish' or stuffed fish. However, it is usually associated with Jews from Eastern Europe. Jews from almost every country know its tempting fragrance and flavoursome taste.

The techniques for preparing Gefilte Fish have changed since the invention of the food chopper. In the old days Granny used a wooden bowl and chopping knife to reduce the filleted fish to a smooth pulp. Today the electric mincer makes short shrift of what was a customary Friday morning kitchen ceremonial.

Gefilte Fish is served chilled, with beet-juice flavoured and coloured ground horse-radish. Carrot slices cooked with the fish are usually used for garnish. It is the first course of Sabbath eve meals and occupies first place on holiday menus as well.

GEFILTE FISH (Basic Recipe)

3 *pounds fish (any firm-fleshed fish, preferably yellow pike, carp, bream, roach, or any combination of these) | Salt (as required) | 2 large onions, 1 diced | 2 eggs | Pepper to taste (optional) | 1 large carrot, sliced | 2 stalks celery, diced | 2 slices white bread, soaked and squeezed | Parsley | Cold water to cover*

Skin and bone the fish (see Filleted Fish), leaving skin attached to bones of each part or cut. After the whole fish has been dressed and sectioned, salt evenly skin-bone cuts to be stuffed. Let stand in a covered glass bowl in the refrigerator while chopping the filleted parts or flesh. Grate in one onion, add eggs, salt and pepper to taste, and soaked bread if desired as a 'stretcher'. If no bread is used, add 2 tablespoons cold water and combine thoroughly. Wet the hands and return pulp to bones, covering with the attached skin. Place the head bones and diced vegetables in the bottom of a deep pot. Place filled fish sections neatly on top, add cold water to cover. Cover pot. Bring to a quick boil, remove cover and turn down heat, keeping the fish at a slow boil 1½ to 2 hours. The liquid should be reduced by half. When cool, remove to a platter carefully, to retain shape of each section. Strain the liquid over the fish or into a separate bowl. Chill thoroughly before serving, using the carrot for garnish. The jellied sauce may be cut and served separately or as an additional garnish.

Serves 4 to 6.

Variation 1: Grate a raw carrot into chopped filleted fish after grating in an onion. Add the ingredients as listed. After forming and arranging balls or filled sections in cooking pot, add 1 carrot thinly sliced.

Variation 2: Place bones, head and skin removed in the process of filleting fish on the bottom of pot. Arrange several stalks of celery across and arrange fish balls on top to make removal easier when cooked. The bones and skin add flavour to the fish sauce. Discard bones after removing fish and straining sauce.

Variation 3: Form 3-inch patties of pulp, dip in fine crumbs and fry. Or bake 12 to 15 minutes at 375° F. or gas mark 5.

Variation 4: Remove all bones from skin cuts and fill with chopped fish pulp as in basic recipe.

GEFILTE FISH (Pressure Cooker Method)

Whether formed into balls or stuffed into sections of fish between bones and skin, Gefilte Fish can be cooked successfully in a pressure cooker in 10 minutes at 10 pounds pressure. Arrange bones and vegetables in bottom of pressure pan and cover with the perforated disc or trivet which fits snugly inside the vessel. Arrange fish balls or portions on the trivet and add 1 cup of cold water or just enough to come up to layer of fish balls. Close pot and adjust pressure gauge to 10 pounds. Cook over moderate heat until the gauge 'jiggles'. Turn down heat as directed for your type of pressure cooker and cook 10 minutes. Reduce pressure by letting cold water run over covered pot before removing gauge and cover. Remove fish and cool before refrigerating.

GEFILTE FISH (Rumanian Style, Using Oval Fish Pot)

Do not section the fish. Leave head attached. After cleaning, remove the flesh from the skin and bones (see Filleted Fish). Prepare and chop filleted fish as in basic recipe. Restore pulp between bones and skin. Lay whole filled fish on fish cooker tray or trivet over prepared vegetables. Cover with cold water and cook slowly over low heat. An elongated roasting pan, with a perforated trivet can be used. Follow procedure as in basic recipe.

BAKED STUFFED FISH (*Not to be confused with Gefilte Fish*)

½ cup chopped onion / 1 cup finely diced celery / ½ cup butter /
6 cups soft bread crumbs / 1 teaspoon salt (and pepper if desired) /
2 eggs / 3 pounds trout (or any other firm-fleshed fish) / 1 tablespoon flour /
Parsley, lemon wedges, melted butter for garnish

Stir the onion and celery in hot melted butter for 5 to 7 minutes over moderate heat. Add bread crumbs and seasoning and stir well till light brown. Remove from heat. When cool add well-beaten eggs. Have the fish thoroughly cleaned, with scales, entrails, gills and eyes removed. Wipe inside of fish with a towel. Fill the opening with above stuffing and place fish in a well-buttered baking dish. Dust with flour. Add a few dots of butter or drizzle melted butter over the top. Bake at 375° F. or gas mark 5 for 40 to 45 minutes.

Serve hot with melted butter, lemon wedges and parsley. Or eat it cold, with horse-radish.

Serves 6 or 7.

BAKED FISH FILLETS IN MILK

1 pound fish fillets (any kind) | 2 tablespoons flour | ½ teaspoon salt |
Dash of pepper | ¾ cup evaporated milk and
¾ cup water (or 1½ cups whole milk) | Butter or vegetable shortening

Wash and dry fillets. Arrange in a well-greased baking dish and dust with flour, salt and pepper. Cover with combined milk and water. Bake 25 minutes at 375° F. or gas mark 5, or till fish is tender. Garnish with parsley or watercress.

Serves 4.

BAKED WHITE FISH WITH TOMATO SAUCE

4 pounds whitefish | Salt | 2 tablespoons flour | 1 onion | 1 green pepper |
1 clove garlic | 4 tablespoons butter or oil | 1 large can tomatoes |
1 tablespoon lemon juice | 1 teaspoon brown sugar |
Salt and pepper to taste | Minced parsley

Remove scales and head from fish. Split in half and salt inside and outside. After 20 minutes, wash and dry fish portions and dust with flour.

Mince onion, garlic and green pepper and sauté in hot shortening in the baking dish to be used. Place fish on top and cover with tomatoes. Add sugar dissolved in lemon juice and bake 20 to 30 minutes at 375° F. or gas mark 5. Serve from the baking dish. Sprinkle with salt and pepper and garnish with parsley.

Serves 6 to 8.

BOILED FISH WITH EGG SAUCE

*2½ to 3 pounds fish (plaice, halibut, pike, pickerel, salmon or
any other firm-fleshed fish) | 1 carrot | 1 parsnip | 2 stalks celery |
1 large onion | Water | 3 bay leaves | 6 peppercorns |
2 tablespoons lemon juice | 2 teaspoons salt | Dash of white pepper | 3 eggs*

Clean fish. Split head. Remove gills and eyes. Cut body of fish into
5 or 6 serving portions. Wash under cold running water and drain
thoroughly. Place the split head of fish in the bottom of a deep pot.
Scrape carrot and parsnip and cut into thin slices. Dice celery. Peel
and slice onion. Add the vegetables to the fish head, spreading
evenly around and over it. Place the cut portions of fish cut-side up
over vegetables. Add cold water to come half-way up portions of
fish, and then add bay leaves, peppercorns, lemon juice, salt and
pepper. Heat slowly over moderate heat till the liquid begins to
bubble. Reduce heat to simmer and cook the fish 15 to 20 minutes.
The fish must not cook to the point where the flesh separates from
the bone. Remove from heat. Lift fish carefully to a platter. Strain
the fish liquid into another pot or saucepan and bring to a boil.
Beat eggs with rotary beater and stir in the boiling hot fish sauce,
stirring rapidly while pouring until the sauce is thickened. Pour
over fish or serve separately. Garnish with lemon slices or wedges,
and parsley.

Serves 5 to 6.

Variation: Add 1 tablespoon prepared mustard to the egg sauce.
Cook 1 minute.

FRIED FISH FILLETS

*2 pounds fillets | 2 eggs | ½ cup matzo crumbs |
Salt as required | Shortening for frying*

Cut fillets of any desired fish into serving portions. Beat eggs
thoroughly in a shallow bowl. Dip fish sections in matzo crumbs
then in beaten egg. Return to crumbs to coat on one side as each
piece is placed in hot melted shortening. Fry over moderate heat till
brown on under side. Turn to brown other side, using a spatula or
small pancake turner. Lift fish from fat as soon as browned and drain
on paper towels. Sprinkle with salt.

Serves 4 to 6.
Variation: Cook 1 sliced or halved onion in the fat before frying
fish. Adds flavour.

DEEP FRIED FISH

Allow ⅓ or ½ pound of prepared fish per serving. Heat shortening
in a deep frying pan while preparing serving portions of fish as for
Fried Fillets. Fry fish in hot melted shortening that comes to top of
fish, or use a frying basket in deeper fat. Fried fish should be lifted
from fat as soon as well browned and placed on paper towels to drain
off excess fat. Sprinkle with salt and pepper before serving with
lemon wedges and other garnish.

GEVETCH DE PESHTE
(Rumanian Fish and Vegetable Dish)

4 to 5 pounds cleaned pike or trout (or any firm-fleshed fish) |
3 tablespoons oil or vegetable shortening | 4 tablespoons flour or fine crumbs |
1 cup each diced green beans, cabbage, carrots, celery, eggplant |
1 cup fresh limas, fresh peas, diced green pepper |
4 medium potatoes, 1-inch slices | 4 medium tomatoes, skins removed,
sliced or diced | 4 small white turnips, finely diced or sliced small |
3 onions or 4 green onions, diced | 1 cup water |
Salt and pepper as required (approximately 1 tablespoon combined)

Rub fish inside and outside with oil or shortening. Dust with flour or
crumbs. Mix prepared vegetables and arrange in bottom of an oval
baking pan large enough and deep enough to hold all the ingredients
listed. Place the fish on the bed of vegetables, filling fish with some.
Scatter diced onions over top and add water. Bake 45 to 50 minutes
at 350° F. or gas mark 4, or till potatoes and limas are tender. The
sauce should be even with the fish but not over it. Add salt and
pepper to taste in a cupful of sauce and return seasoned sauce to
top of fish. The fish should be lightly browned on top and all the
vegetables tender. Lift fish out carefully to a large serving platter
and surround with vegetables. Or, serve vegetables and gravy
separately.
Serves 8 to 12.

Variation 1: Omit tomatoes. Add 1½ cups tomato sauce 15 minutes before turning off heat.

Variation 2: Fish may be cut into serving portions for more convenient handling when serving. Follow directions for vegetables and baking. Turn fish portions before adding tomato sauce.

HALIBUT RING

2 pounds halibut | Cold water to cover | ½ cup diced celery |
2 small carrots, diced | 1 tablespoon grated onion |
1 tablespoon lemon juice or vinegar | 1 teaspoon salt |
¼ teaspoon pepper (optional) | 2 eggs, separated | 1 cup whipped cream |
Parsley | Green pepper strips and carrot strips (as many as desired)

Simmer fish in water 3 minutes. Add prepared vegetables and seasonings. Cover and cook 10 to 15 minutes or until fish is firm but tender when tested with a fork. Let cool. Lift out fish and remove skin and bones. Purée vegetables after straining through a colander. Beat eggs separately and combine, folding in whipped cream. Arrange pepper and carrot strips in any desired formation in a well-buttered ring mould and turn in the beaten egg and cream mixture carefully and evenly. Arrange fish in this and add purée, distributing as evenly as possible without disturbing decorative vegetable strips at bottom of mould. Set in a pan of boiling water and bake 30 to 35 minutes at 375° F. or gas mark 5, or till set. Lift from hot water container and invert serving plate over ring mould. Turn quickly to unmould. Garnish with parsley and more green pepper and carrot strips. Add lemon wedges if desired. May be served cold.
Serves 6 to 8.

HALIBUT IN SOUR CREAM

1 pound halibut fillets | 1 egg | 4 tablespoons matzo meal |
1 onion, sliced thin | ¼ cup melted shortening |
Salt and white pepper to taste | 1 cup sour cream

Cut fish into 4 serving portions. Beat egg slightly and dip each piece of fish into matzo crumbs then in beaten egg. Let stand while cooking onion slices till light brown in melted shortening. Remove onion to baking dish. Fry prepared fish in shortening till light brown and turn to brown other side. Dust with salt and pepper and arrange fried fish on onions in baking dish or casserole. Cover with sour cream and bake 10 minutes at 350° F. or gas mark 4. Serve hot. Serves 4.

ICRE DE CARP (Rumanian Fresh Caviar)

1 carp roe, average size | 1 tablespoon salt | ¼ cup lemon juice |
¼ cup salad oil | Black olives for garnish |
Sliced black radish (optional) | Minced onion (optional)

Salt fresh carp roe and let stand overnight in a covered glass dish in the refrigerator. Rinse with plenty of cold water to remove excess salt. Remove membrane if possible. Beat with a rotary beater in a deep bowl. Remaining membrane will adhere to the beater and can be removed. Add lemon juice and oil alternately while beating until a thick creamy consistency, like mayonnaise. Chill and serve with any or all of the garnishes listed. Excellent for canapés.

PICKLED FRIED FISH

Fry any firm-fleshed fish till nicely browned. Drain on paper towels. When cool, arrange in a crock or deep glass dish. Cover with the following:

MARINADE

1 cup white or cider vinegar | 2 tablespoons brown sugar |
¼ cup cold water | 2 bay leaves | 2 cloves garlic |
½ teaspoon sage or mixed herbs | 1 lemon, sliced thin

Boil all except lemon 3 minutes. Pour over fish. Add lemon. When cold, cover tightly and store in the refrigerator. Ready for use after 48 hours. Will keep several weeks. Marinade sufficient for 3 pounds fish.

PICKEREL OR SALMON MARINADE

Boil 2 pounds fresh fish steaks in salted water to cover 15 to 20 minutes. Add the following:

MARINADE

2 cups equal parts vinegar, white wine and fish liquid |
Add 1 teaspoon mixed whole spice containing mace,
ginger root, whole peppers, coriander

Boil 3 minutes, strain and pour over cooled cooked salmon or
pickerel. Serve cold.
Serves 4 to 6.

BAKED SALMON STEAKS

2 pounds salmon, fresh or quick frozen (cut ¾ to 1 inch thick) |
2 tablespoons melted butter or oil | 2 onions, sliced (optional) |
1 cup milk | ½ teaspoon salt | ¾ cup fine cracker or dry bread crumbs |
Dash of white pepper (optional) | Lemon wedges for garnish

Melt the shortening in shallow glass baking pan in oven while
preparing the fish steaks. If onions are to be used, arrange the slices
in bottom of pan. Dip the steaks in milk (or water) to which salt has
been added, then roll in crumbs to which pepper has been added.
Place the salmon steaks on top of sliced onions and bake, uncovered,
15 to 20 minutes at 475° F. or gas mark 9, turning up the heat for
2 minutes just before serving. The fish should be golden brown on
top and easily pierced with a fork. Transfer to a heated serving
platter or serve in the baking dish, garnished with lemon.
Serves 4 to 6.

GRILLED FISH (Halves or Fillets)

When using halves of any fish like bass, trout, porgy, etc., save the
heads for chowder or as the French say, *bouillabaisse.*
   Be sure to have all scales and fins removed before dipping in cold
salted water each half of the fish to be grilled. Wipe dry with a towel
or absorbent paper. Heat the grill compartment to 350° F. or gas
mark 4 for 10 minutes (about the time it takes to prepare fish for
grilling). Dust fish halves with flour and place on preheated grilling
pan about 2 inches below source of heat. Dot with butter or vegetable shortening, or drizzle with oil and grill from 8 to 10 minutes,

Chopped
Herring
(*page 218*)
Chopped
Calf's Liver
(*page 219*)

depending on thickness of fish. Basting with melted shortening once or twice during the process adds flavour and nourishment.

Serve on a preheated platter with a garnish of lemon wedges or slices, parsley or watercress.

FISH ROLL-UPS

1 onion, diced or thinly sliced | 2 tablespoons oil or vegetable shortening |
1 cup dry bread crumbs | 1 egg | Paprika | ¼ cup milk |
½ pound fillets of plaice (use 1 thin fillet about 8 inches long per serving) |
Flour

Fry onion in shortening until light brown and add dry crumbs. Stir constantly for 1 minute. Beat egg lightly and add the crumb and onion mixture as soon as cool. Season with salt and paprika. Stir in milk and let stand 5 minutes. Spread the mixture over the fish fillets and roll up. Fasten with toothpicks. Dust with flour and sprinkle lightly with paprika. Arrange on greased baking dish and cover with wax paper. Chill in refrigerator until ready to bake 15 to 20 minutes at 375° F. or gas mark 5, or till lightly browned.

Serves 4 to 6.

BAVARIAN SCHARFE FISH

4½ to 5 pounds fish (any firm-fleshed fish is good but lake trout is best) |
Salt | 4 onions | 3 carrots, sliced |
1 cup each cut green beans, cauliflower, celery | 3 egg yolks |
3 tablespoons butter | Salt and pepper to taste | Parsley

Clean fish (see *Methods of Preparing Fish*) of scales, remove head and fins and viscera. Cut into 2½-inch portions. Clean the head thoroughly, remove gills, eyes, etc. Salt all lightly, cover and keep in refrigerator while preparing vegetables. Cut carrots lengthwise, and dice other vegetables. Wash the fish head and cook with vegetables in enough water to yield 2½ cups liquid when done. Let boil about 20 minutes. Wash the cut portions of fish and place carefully with the vegetables to avoid crowding. Boil ½ hour. Remove fish carefully to a platter. Continue cooking the vegetables in the liquid until the liquid is reduced to approximately 2 cupfuls. Strain liquid into top

14

of double boiler and fold in beaten egg yolks. Add butter and let thicken over hot water, stirring to prevent curdling. Do not boil. Season to taste with salt and pepper and pour over the cooked fish. Decorate with cooked carrot and parsley sprigs. Serve cold.

Serves 8 to 10.

SOUTHERN FISH DISH

2 pounds of any firm-fleshed fish (sea bass, grey mullet, etc.) | Salt to taste |
Matzo meal or cornmeal | 1 medium eggplant, sliced | 2 eggs |
3 tablespoons butter or other shortening | 1 sliced onion

After cleaning and preparing fish, dust it lightly with salt and matzo meal or cornmeal. Pare and slice the eggplant into ½-inch thick rounds and parboil in a minimum of water for 8 minutes, using a covered pot. Drain well and dip each slice first in the meal then in the beaten eggs, salted to taste, and arrange slices in a well-greased baking pan. Cover with thinly-sliced onion and place the fish dipped in remaining beaten egg on boiled eggplant. Dot with shortening and bake 45 minutes at 350° F. or gas mark 4, or till nicely browned on top.

Serves 4.

FINNAN HADDIE SCALLOP

1 onion | 3 tablespoons butter or salad oil |
3 medium size potatoes, pared and sliced thin |
1 pound finnan haddie (smoked haddock) |
Milk (approximately 1 cup) | 2 tablespoons minced parsley

Slice or dice onion and spread over bottom of a glass casserole. Add 2 tablespoons shortening and about ⅓ of the sliced potatoes. Cut portions of finnan haddie should be placed over the layer of potato slices and topped with a second layer of potatoes. If you have any of the fish left, cut it into thin strips and place in a sunburst design, topping with remainder of potato slices.

Add milk slowly from the side of casserole to half-way up. Cover with crumbs and dot with shortening or drizzle with remaining oil. Cover and bake at 375° F. or gas mark 5 for 45 to 50 minutes or till potatoes are tender. Remove cover and brown under grill. Sprinkle with minced parsley and serve hot.

Serves 4.

PLANKED SHAD (OR HERRING)

Butter the plank (which may be any clean board) and heat it in the oven about 5 minutes. Grill the split shad, skin side down on the warm, buttered board. It should be nicely browned in 20 minutes. Add dots of butter, sprinkle with minced parsley and serve with mashed potato mounds right on the plank. Pass wedges of lemon.

SHAD ROE

Dip roe in seasoned flour or bread crumbs and fry in hot melted shortening.

PICKLED SMELTS

4 dozen small smelts | 2 cups shortening | 1½ cups vinegar | 1 onion | 1 stalk celery | Bay leaves, cloves, peppercorns | 1 tablespoon chopped carrot

After frying smelts in oil or other shortening, place them in a deep casserole. Simmer the other ingredients together 15 to 20 minutes. While warm, pour over the fried smelts. Let stand overnight before serving. Serve cold with hot boiled potatoes.

Serves 4 to 6.

SWEET-SOUR SMELTS

24 medium size smelts (2½ pounds) | Water to cover | 1 onion, sliced | 1 carrot, sliced | 1 stalk celery and leaves | Salt and pepper to taste | ½ cup vinegar | ½ cup brown sugar | 4 gingersnaps | ¼ cup light raisins

Boil smelts 5 minutes in enough water to cover. Add vegetables, salt and pepper to taste. Cook for 10 minutes. Remove fish carefully to a platter. Strain fish liquid and add vinegar and brown sugar, crushed gingersnaps and raisins. Bring to a boil and add the fish. Cook 5

minutes before removing from heat. There should be enough liquid
to cover the fish. Let cool before removing from the pot. Chill.
Serves 4 to 6.

FISH SOLIANKA (Russian Style)

*1½ pounds fish (pike, pickerel, trout or other firm-fleshed variety) |
½ pound fresh or frozen salmon steak | 4 cups cold water | 1 bay leaf |
1 teaspoon salt | 2 medium onions | 4 medium dill pickles |
6 tablespoons tomato paste | 6 each green olives and black olives |
3 tablespoons butter (optional) | Lemon wedges | Parsley sprigs*

Cook fish in water 20 minutes over moderate heat, adding bay leaf
and salt after it begins to boil. Remove salmon first and flake or cut
into small pieces in a separate bowl. Strain off sauce and remove
remaining fish to a platter. Flake fish and return sauce and fish to
pot, adding salmon strips or flakes after boiling begins. Chop together onions and dill pickles and combine with tomato paste. Let
stand while cutting up green and black olives, discarding pits. Add
these mixtures to the fish and enough hot water to cover. Cook over
moderate heat 10 minutes. Garnish with lemon and parsley, and
more of either or both kinds of whole olives.
Serves 6.

SWEET-SOUR FISH

*4½ to 5 pounds trout or pickerel | Salt | 2 cups vinegar | ½ cup water |
½ cup brown sugar | 3 tablespoons butter |
¼ teaspoon each cinnamon and cloves | 4 onions | 6 lemons, sliced |
1 cup seedless raisins | ¼ cup blanched and sliced almonds |
3 egg yolks | Salt as required*

Clean fish and remove the head. Cut into 2½-inch cuts and salt
lightly. Cover and let stand in the refrigerator for 2 hours. Boil together water, vinegar, sugar, raisins, almonds, butter and seasonings
until raisins are puffed. Arrange sliced onions in the bottom of the
cooking pot. Wash and clean the head, removing gills and eyes.
Place over onions. Rinse fish and arrange neatly around the head.
Cover with cold water. Add half the sliced lemons and boil 15

minutes, then add other ingredients. Cook over moderate heat 45 minutes. When cool, lift the pieces of fish out and arrange on a platter deep enough to hold at least 1-inch depth of liquid. Cook contents of pot 10 minutes.

Strain the gravy. Stir into beaten eggs. With a fork remove some of the raisins and almonds and use as a garnish with remainder of sliced lemon. Chill.

Serves 8 to 10.

BAKED FISH RING

1½ pounds cooked, flaked and boned fish (any variety) |
2 cups cooked, drained rice | ⅔ cup mayonnaise |
1 tablespoon finely chopped onion | 1½ teaspoons Worcestershire sauce |
¼ teaspoon salt | ¼ cup dry bread crumbs | Dash of pepper |
Lettuce, green pepper rings, parsley, lemon slices for garnish

Combine flaked fish, 1 cup of rice, mayonnaise and seasonings with a few whisks of a fork. Line a well-greased ring mould (or any other shape of mould or baking pan) with the remaining rice. Turn in the fish mixture and cover with seasoned crumbs. Bake at 400° F. or gas mark 6 for 20 minutes. Unmould on a large platter, garnish and serve hot.

Serves 6.

TUNA FISH RING

2 cups flaked canned tuna fish | 1 cup grated raw carrot |
½ cup finely cut celery | 2 tablespoons minced parsley |
1 cup soft bread crumbs | 2 eggs | 1 tablespoon lemon juice |
¼ teaspoon salt | Dash of white pepper | 1 cup milk |
3 tablespoons melted butter | 1 cup crushed breakfast cereal (cornflakes)

Flake tuna and combine with all ingredients listed except butter and cereal. Mix thoroughly. Melt butter in ring mould over low heat and add crushed cereal flakes evenly over bottom of mould. Turn in the fish mixture carefully. Set ring mould on a baking pan to facilitate removing from oven after baking 40 minutes at 350° F. or gas mark 4. To unmould, place a serving plate or platter over mould as soon as removed from oven. Invert quickly and the fish ring will come out evenly. Fill centre with creamed carrots and peas or other cooked vegetables and serve hot, with or without cream sauce.

If necessary to keep ring mould warm for more than 15 minutes, place an ovenproof plate over the baked ring and unmould. Slip the Tuna Fish Ring from hot plate to serving plate or platter just before filling centre as directed and serve with vegetables or cream sauce around ring.

Serves 8 to 10.

Variation: Fill centre of ring with French fried potatoes and garnish with parsley sprigs around the ring.

FISH TETRAZINI EN CASSEROLE

2 pounds halibut | Salt | Butter | 1 large onion | 1 large green pepper |
1½ pounds mushrooms, slices | 1 can tomato soup |
2 cups cream sauce (see Index) | Sugar, salt and pepper |
2 cups cooked spaghetti | Grated cheese or minced parsley

Cook the fish in a little salted water about 15 minutes till tender. Cool and remove skin and bones. Melt butter and sauté minced or sliced onion, green pepper and mushrooms till light brown. Combine all ingredients, season to taste and turn into a buttered casserole. Bake uncovered, 30 minutes at 350° F. or gas mark 4. Sprinkle top with either grated cheese or minced parsley and serve hot.

Serves 8.

BAKED LAKE TROUT

Clean and prepare fish. (See *Methods of Preparing Fish*.) Remove fat along the backbone. Salt lightly and let stand about ½ hour. Wash with cold running water and drain. Lay the whole fish in a buttered baking pan and dust with flour or fine matzo crumbs and a dash of pepper. Dot with butter or vegetable shortening. Cover with slices of onion. Bake at 375° F. or gas mark 5 for 45 minutes or till nicely browned. Garnish with parsley and lemon wedges.

Allow 3 pounds for 6 servings.

BAKED FISH CAKES (Basic Recipe)

*1 cup flaked or chopped fish (fresh, quick frozen or canned) |
1 cup dry bread crumbs | 2 cups milk | 4 tablespoons butter |
⅛ teaspoon salt and pepper, mixed | 4 eggs |
2 tablespoons melted butter for greasing pans*

Flake or chop the fish very fine. Combine bread crumbs, milk, 4
tablespoons butter and salt and pepper. Cook in top of double boiler
10 minutes. Stir in fish. Beat eggs till light and stir into the hot
mixture. Remove from heat. Grease 8 individual baking dishes with
hot melted butter, and turn in the fish and crumb mixture. Bake 30
minutes at 350° F. or gas mark 4, or till firm and lightly browned on
top. Unmould. Serve with Creole sauce, horse-radish, lemon sauce,
mushroom sauce, Cream of Mushroom Soup, heated, or tomato
sauce.
Serves 4.
Variation 1: Drop the fish and crumbs mixture on a well-greased
baking dish, 2 inches apart each way. Bake as in basic recipe.
Variation 2: Substitute 1½ cups left-over baked, grilled or cooked
fish, boned and chopped, for the amount in basic recipe. Bake
as above.
Variation 3: Fry fish and crumbs mixture like pancakes, using ⅓
cup of oil or melted vegetable shortening in a heavy frying pan.
Turn the cakes as soon as brown on under side and brown on
other side. Drain on paper towels. Serve with sour cream.

UKKHA (Russian Puréed Fish)

*4 pounds fresh water fish, filleted | 2 quarts cold water | 1 large onion, diced |
2 stalks celery, leaves, cut fine | 1 parsnip, diced | 1 small carrot, diced |
2 bay leaves | Salt to taste | 2 tablespoons lemon juice*

Divide the fish in half. Cover one half the amount of fish with cold
water and add prepared vegetables and bay leaves. Cook 5 minutes
and taste before adding salt as desired. Reduce heat and let simmer
till the fish begins to fall apart, approximately 15 minutes. Force
through a coarse strainer and bring the purée to a quick boil. Add

remaining fish cut into serving portions if desired. Cook 15 minutes and remove from heat. Add lemon juice and serve hot.

Serves 8 to 10.

HERRING DISHES

Herrings also called *milch herring* are desirable for all purposes, including pickling. These are large, have white flesh and make the best Herring Salad (chopped herring).

Herrings should be soaked in cold water to cover, from 6 to 12 hours. Glass containers are best for this purpose because they do not retain herring odour after cleansing.

Wash soaked herring thoroughly under cold running water to remove scales. Remove entrails and rinse inside. Do not discard roe or milt. They may be used in various ways. Milt is mashed with a fork for preparing Pickled Herring sauce or marinade. Roe is combined with chopped hard-cooked eggs for canapés.

To remove skin from herring easily, use the point of a paring knife, starting at the tail end and loosening skin so that it can be pulled off towards the head.

Skinned herring is used for several dishes in the following recipes. For pickling whole or sectioned, it is only necessary that the herring be washed of scales, eviscerated and trimmed of fins.

BAKED HERRING IN VINEGAR

1 cleaned and prepared herring | 1 onion, sliced thin |
6 peppercorns and a few mustard seeds | 1 bay leaf | ¾ cup vinegar |
4 tablespoons water | 4 tablespoons brown sugar | Flour for dusting over top

Place herring in a glass baking dish. Add onion slices around whole or sectioned herring. Combine peppercorns, bay leaf, vinegar, water and sugar in a cup. Stir till sugar is dissolved and pour over herring. Dust with flour very lightly. Bake 20 minutes at 375° F. or gas mark 5, or till onion is tender and tinged a light pink.

Serves 2.

MARINIERTE HERRING (Pickled Herring)

*3 medium or 2 large cleaned and prepared herrings (skin not removed) |
1 large onion, sliced thin | 1 cup vinegar | ¼ cup water |
1 tablespoon brown sugar | 3 bay leaves |
1 teaspoon mixed whole spice (optional) | 12 peppercorns |
6 thin slices of lemon, seeds removed | Milt, mashed |
2 tablespoons sour cream (optional)*

Place whole herrings or sections into a quart jar. Add onion. Bring
to a quick boil vinegar, water, sugar and cool till lukewarm. Add
liquid to jar with bay leaves, spices, lemon slices. Combine mashed
milt with sour cream and stir in lightly, or shake jar to distribute.
Cover and let stand 24 hours before serving.

Yield depends on size of sections.

RUSSIAN HERRING BALLS (*Kotleti Sledziowe*)

*5 herrings, filleted | 1 onion, finely diced | 3 tablespoons butter or oil |
3 small hard-crusted rolls, grated (1 cup, approximately) | 2 eggs |
½ cup matzo crumbs | Dash of pepper (optional) |
Melted shortening for frying*

Chop herring fillets. Brown onion in hot butter and stir in grated
rolls (or equivalent in dry bread crumbs). Beat eggs and blend in as
soon as onion and crumbs are cool. Add to chopped herring. If more
moisture is required, a few drops of lemon juice or cold water may
be added. The mixture should be thick enough to mould into balls
the size of walnuts. Roll each ball in matzo crumbs, seasoned with
pepper if desired, and fry in hot melted shortening till browned on
all sides.

Serves 6 to 8.

HERRING AND POTATO SALAD

*1½ cups finely cut herring fillets | 3 cups diced boiled potatoes |
1 teaspoon chopped or grated onion | 1 cup finely cut celery, including leaves |
½ cup sour cream | 2 tablespoons lemon juice |
1 tablespoon minced parsley | Dash of paprika*

Combine by mixing with two forks. Serve on lettuce.
Serves 4.

HERRING SALAD (*Gehackte Herring*)

1 *large prepared herring, filleted* | 2 *hard-cooked eggs* | 1 *tart apple, pared* |
1 *small onion (optional)* | 2 *tablespoons lemon juice or*
3 *tablespoons vinegar* | 2 *tablespoons salad oil* |
2 *tablespoons sugar (or to taste)* | 3 *tablespoons dry bread or cracker crumbs* |
Dash of pepper (optional)

Chop herring fillets and eggs to a smooth pulp. Grate in apple and
onion. Add lemon juice or vinegar and oil. Taste and add sugar.
Stir in dry crumbs and add pepper. Cover and refrigerate ½ hour.
   Serves 2 to 4 as an appetizer, or 6 to 8 spread on crackers or thinly
sliced toasted cuts of bread for canapés.

HERRINGS IN WINE SAUCE

Do not remove skin from prepared herring. Remove fins and tail.
Cut into 1-inch sections, discarding head. Make a marinade of equal
parts vinegar, brown sugar and wine. Add well-mashed milt and a
bay leaf for each herring. Place herring sections in a glass jar and
cover with the marinade. Let stand 2 to 3 hours before serving. A
toothpick in each section facilitates handling, and can be inserted
just before serving.

LIVER RECIPES

CHOPPED CALF'S OR BEEF LIVER (Basic Recipe)

Slice liver 1 inch thick and grill 5 to 10 minutes or till light brown on both sides. Remove veins and skin. Put through food chopper using fine cutting blade. Or chop to a smooth paste in a wooden bowl.

For each pound of liver fry $\frac{1}{4}$ cup finely diced onion in $\frac{1}{4}$ cup hot melted schmaltz or other shortening till nicely browned and add to liver paste with salt and pepper to taste. Use a fork for mixing till smooth. The fat as well as fried onion is added.

Variation 1: To each pound of liver add 2 hard-cooked eggs before chopping.

Variation 2: To basic recipe add $\frac{1}{2}$ cup peanut butter and blend well.

CHOPPED CHICKEN OR GOOSE LIVERS

Follow same procedure as for Calf's or Beef Liver in basic recipe and variations.

MOULDED CHOPPED LIVER

Press chopped liver in a well-greased round or ring mould. Chill at least 2 hours. To unmould, dip bottom of mould in hot water for 1 to 2 minutes. Invert on serving plate. After inverting on plate and unmoulding, it may be served with a garnish of shredded lettuce, parsley, watercress. Shredded greens may be piled loosely into the centre and thin strips of green pepper used to garnish the ring. Radish roses make a nice garnish, as do green stuffed or whole olives, black olives in brine, and/or tiny pickled gherkins.

LIVER OMELET

Add ¼ cup Chopped Liver, basic recipe or Variations 1 and 2, to each 3- or 4-egg omelet just before turning cooked omelet.
Serves 2.

SAUTÉED LIVER (Basic Recipe)

Cut grilled liver slices into cubes. Salt lightly and sprinkle with flour or fine matzo crumbs. Sauté in hot melted shortening 3 to 5 minutes, allowing 4 tablespoons shortening to each pound of diced liver, and cook over moderate heat approximately 5 minutes or till lightly browned. Allow ½ pound liver per serving.
   Variation: Add 1 cup sliced fresh or canned mushrooms after sautéing cubed liver. Cook 5 to 6 minutes, stirring lightly with fork or spoon.

GOOSE LIVER WITH APPLES AND ONIONS

2 large goose livers | 2 large tart apples | 2 large onions |
4 tablespoons goose schmaltz | ½ cup Madeira wine or sherry |
Salt and pepper to taste

Grill livers, 10 to 15 minutes or till lightly browned and firm. Core and slice apples, unpared. Slice onions. Sauté onions in hot melted fat till light yellow, add apple slices and fry on both sides in the same pan. Cut livers and add. Add wine, cover pan and keep over moderate heat 5 minutes. Serve immediately.
Serves 4 to 6.

CHOPPED GOOSE LIVER AND GREBEN

1 pound goose liver | 1 cup greben | Salt and pepper to taste

Put liver and greben through a food chopper. Add seasoning. Combine and serve with hard-cooked egg wedges and parsley garnish. Use as a *forshpeisse*, or for canapé spread.

OTHER ORGAN MEATS

GRILLED SWEETBREADS

Prepare sweetbreads for cooking like any other meat. Cover with cold water to which 1 tablespoon vinegar has been added. Cook over moderate heat 20 minutes and drain. Remove membrane as soon as cool enough to handle. Slice ½ inch thick. Place slices in a shallow glass baking pan, dot with shortening, dust lightly with salt, pepper and paprika and slip under grill for 10 minutes or till lightly browned. Serve hot or keep hot in heated oven till serving time.

Two pairs of sweetbreads of beef will serve 4.

FRIED SWEETBREADS

Cook prepared sweetbreads as for grilling. Remove membrane and slice. Dip both sides in slightly salted flour, bread crumbs or matzo meal. Fry in hot melted chicken or goose schmaltz till nicely browned on both sides. Garnish with minced parsley or fresh dill.

Two pairs of sweetbreads will serve 4.

STEWED SWEETBREADS WITH MUSHROOMS

2 pairs beef sweetbreads, parboiled as for grilling |
2 tablespoons hot melted shortening | 2 tablespoons flour or
fine dry bread crumbs | 1 cup sliced fresh mushrooms or
1 small can button mushrooms | 1 tablespoon onion juice |
Dash of soy sauce or Worcestershire | Salt and pepper to taste |
2 hard-cooked eggs, sliced or diced | 2 tablespoons minced parsley

Trim parboiled sweetbreads of membrane. Dice and sauté in hot melted shortening 10 minutes over moderate heat. Dust with flour or crumbs, add mushrooms, onion juice, soy sauce and cover. Simmer 20 minutes over moderate heat. Taste and add salt and pepper if desired. Serve with sliced or diced hard-cooked eggs and parsley garnish.

Serves 4.

FRIED CALF'S BRAINS

1 set calf's brains | Cold water to cover | 1 clove garlic |
4 tablespoons shortening | ¼ cup matzo crumbs | Salt and pepper

Scald brains. Drain. Remove membrane. Add cold water to cover
and a cut clove of garlic. Cook over moderate heat 20 minutes.
Drain. When cool enough to handle, slice into ½-inch thick pieces.
Heat frying pan over a moderate heat, add shortening. Dip each
slice of brains in cracker crumbs and fry till nicely browned on both
sides. Dust with salt and pepper. Serve hot.
Serves 2.

BRAINS WITH SCRAMBLED EGGS

1 set calf's brains | Boiling water to cover | ¼ cup flour or fine crumbs |
4 tablespoons hot melted shortening | 3 eggs | Pinch of salt |
2 tablespoons minced parsley | 3 slices of toast

Scald brains and drain. Remove ·membrane and cut into ½-inch
thick cubes. Roll in flour or crumbs and fry till nicely browned. Beat
eggs slightly and add salt. Turn over fried brains, reduce heat, cover
and let cook 20 minutes. Uncover, stir with a fork to break up into
small pieces. Cover toast with the brains and scrambled eggs and
top with minced parsley.
Serves 3.

BRAIN FRITTERS

1 set calf's brains | Cold water to cover | 2 tablespoons vinegar |
½ teaspoon salt | 2 eggs | ¼ cup flour | 3 tablespoons cold water |
Pinch of salt and pepper | Hot melted shortening for frying

Cook brains in water with vinegar and salt 25 to 30 minutes over
moderate heat. Drain. Remove membrane. Slice ¼ inch thick. Beat
eggs, stir in flour and cold water to make a thick batter. Add salt and
pepper and beat 2 to 3 strokes. Dip sliced brains in batter and fry in
hot melted shortening till nicely browned on both sides.
Serves 2 to 3.

BRAINS WITH EGG SAUCE

1 *set beef or calf's brains* | *Boiling water to cover* |
1 *onion, diced or sliced thin* | 1 *green pepper, diced* |
1 *tomato, skinned and diced* | 1 *cup hot water* | $\frac{1}{4}$ *teaspoon salt and pepper* |
Dash of ginger | 2 *eggs* | 2 *tablespoons lemon juice* |
1 *tablespoon cornflour* | 1 *tablespoon cold water*

Cover brains with boiling water and cover for 5 minutes. Drain.
Remove membrane. Place brains, uncut, in a saucepan and add
vegetables, hot water, salt, pepper and ginger. Cover and cook over
moderate heat 30 to 35 minutes. Lift out brains and put the sauce
through a coarse strainer. There should be about 1 cup of sauce.
Return sauce to saucepan and stir in well-beaten eggs and lemon
juice. Blend cornflour with cold water and add. Cook over low heat,
stirring till smooth. Add the brains and cover. Simmer 10 minutes.
Serves 4.

SWEET-SOUR BRAINS

1 *set calf's brains* | *Boiling water to cover* | 1 *onion, sliced* | 2 *bay leaves* |
2 *or* 3 *cloves* | $\frac{1}{4}$ *teaspoon mixed whole spice* | $\frac{1}{4}$ *cup seedless raisins* |
$\frac{1}{4}$ *cup vinegar* | 3 *tablespoons brown sugar* | *Sliced lemon for garnish*

Place brains in boiling water for 5 minutes in a covered saucepan.
Drain. Remove membrane. Leave whole or cut into cubes. Add cold
water to barely cover. Add onion, bay leaves, cloves and spice, cook
over moderate heat 30 minutes. Remove brains and strain sauce.
Add raisins, vinegar and brown sugar to strained sauce and replace
brains. Cook 10 minutes over moderate heat. Garnish with lemon
slices. Same procedure for Beef Brains.
Serves 2 or 3.

BEEF HEART CHOW

1 *pound of beef heart* | 2 *tablespoons flour* |
3 *tablespoons hot melted shortening* | 1 *onion, finely diced* |
$\frac{1}{2}$ *cup diced green pepper* | $\frac{3}{4}$ *cup brown or long grain rice* |
1 *cup canned tomato sauce with* 1 *cup water or* 1$\frac{1}{2}$ *cups stewed tomatoes* !
1 *teaspoon salt* | $\frac{1}{8}$ *teaspoon garlic salt* | *Dash of paprika*

Cut heart free of fat and membrane. Remove veins. Cut into 1-inch cubes and dredge with flour. Sauté in hot melted shortening 5 to 10 minutes or till lightly browned. Remove from frying pan. Sauté onion and green pepper in remaining fat for 2 to 3 minutes. Return sautéed heart and add the rest of listed ingredients. Cover and simmer 35 minutes, adding hot water to prevent sticking if necessary. Do not stir ingredients. Shaking the pan once or twice will be sufficient. The rice should be tender and the combination not too dry. Before serving, slip under grill for 3 to 5 minutes to brown on top.
Serves 4.

SWEET-SOUR HEART

2 veal or 1 beef heart, cut into cubes | 4 tablespoons hot melted shortening |
1½ cups stewed fresh or canned tomatoes | ½ cup vinegar |
4 tablespoons water | 4 tablespoons brown sugar | 2 tablespoons flour |
2 tablespoons hot melted shortening | 1 teaspoon salt |
Dash of paprika (optional)

Sauté heart in hot melted shortening 5 to 10 minutes over moderate heat. Add tomato, vinegar, water and sugar. Cover and simmer 35 to 40 minutes or till beef heart is tender enough to pierce with a fork. Brown flour in hot melted shortening in a separate saucepan and stir in some of the gravy from heart combination till smooth. Cook 5 minutes. Combine and taste. Add salt and paprika. Cook 5 minutes longer before serving.
Serves 6.

LUNG

BEEF LUNG is added to soup meat or soup bones in the making of soup. When tender, it may be used in several ways. It may be put through the food chopper with beef heart or cooked meat of any kind and form the basis for filling of Pirogen or Piroshki (see Index). Or it may be used with other meat in a stew.

Gefilte Fish (*page 201*)

LUNGEN STEW (Basic Recipe)

1 beef lung, cut into small pieces | 1 pound lean beef |
3 tablespoons chicken schmaltz or other shortening | 1 clove garlic, minced |
3 medium onions, diced | 1½ cups stewed or canned tomatoes |
1 tablespoon brown sugar | Salt and pepper to taste |
½ cup soup stock or hot water if necessary

Cut away veins from lung and slice or dice. Dice beef, not too fine. Sauté lung and beef in hot melted shortening 3 to 5 minutes. Add garlic and onions and cook over moderate heat 8 to 10 minutes, stirring till onion begins to turn yellow. Add tomatoes, brown sugar, salt and pepper to taste. Cover and cook 45 minutes over moderate heat or till beef is tender. Stir once or twice during the cooking process and add soup stock or hot water if necessary. Thicken if desired with an einbren (see Index) or serve as it is.

Serves 3 to 4.

Variation 1: Add ½ cup diced celery and 1 cup shredded carrot when adding tomatoes and seasoning. Cover and cook as in basic recipe.

Variation 2: Add 1 pound potatoes cut into 1-inch cubes to basic recipe and/or Variation 1. Follow same procedure. To thicken the stew, mash some of the potato in the gravy before serving. Garnish with parsley.

SWEET-SOUR LUNG AND HEART

1 pound calf's or beef heart | 1 cooked lung (from soup) |
3 tablespoons finely diced onion | 3 tablespoons hot melted shortening |
2 tablespoons flour | ¼ teaspoon paprika | 1 cup tomato purée |
¼ cup vinegar or lemon juice | 2 tablespoons molasses |
Salt and pepper to taste | 1 cup soup stock | Minced parsley for garnish

Trim calf's or beef heart of fat and veins. Cut into 1½- or 2-inch cubes. Cut cooked lung into pieces of similar size. Brown onions in hot melted shortening and sprinkle with flour and paprika. Add diced heart and lung, tomato purée, vinegar and molasses. Cover and cook over moderate heat 30 minutes. Taste and add salt, pepper and soup stock. Simmer 30 minutes. Garnish with parsley.

Serves 4 to 6.

STUFFED MILTZ

1 *beef miltz, cut for stuffing* | 1 *clove garlic, minced* |
4 *medium onions, sliced* | ½ *teaspoon salt* | 2 *tablespoons shortening*

FILLING

1½ *cups dry crumbs* | 1 *egg* | 1 *onion, diced* | 2 *tablespoons, shortening* |
¼ *teaspoon poultry seasoning* | *Dash of nutmeg or ginger*

Ask the butcher to make the incision in the side of a beef miltz as
large as you desire. Prepare miltz for cooking like any other meat.
Trim away particles of fat or loose skin. Combine minced garlic,
sliced onions, salt and shortening in the bottom of roasting pan.
Combine ingredients listed for filling in a bowl and stuff into
incision of miltz. Sew together the long opening or fasten with
polished toothpicks or metal skewers. Place filled miltz on the bed
of garlic and onions in pan. Prick it in several places with the tines
of a fork to prevent curling up at the edges or bursting open. Roast
at 350° F. or gas mark 4 for 45 to 50 minutes, or till the top is
brown and firm.
Serves 4.

STUFFED KISHKE
(Beef Casings—also called Stuffed Derma)

Beef casings purchased from the butcher shop are only partially
cleaned. Casings have to be washed in cold water and scraped free of
fat. It is best to have casings cut to 12-inch lengths for easier facility
in handling for cleaning and stuffing. For final rinsing, use lukewarm
water, turning casings inside out. Sew together one end of each
length and fill with the following mixture:

STUFFING FOR EACH 12-INCH LENGTH OF CASING

1 *cup flour* | ½ *cup chopped beef suet (fat from casings may be used)* |
1 *small onion, grated* | ⅛ *teaspoon salt* | *Dash of pepper* |
2 *tablespoons fine bread or cracker crumbs*

Combine ingredients in the order listed. Stir well in a shallow bowl.
Place the sewed up end of casing in the centre of flour mixture and

begin stuffing by turning in the end with the mixture as you proceed to fill the entire length of casing. The casing should not be stuffed too full as the filling expands and the casing shrinks during cooking process. Tie or sew up and rinse free of flour mixture that has adhered to outer surface. Plunge into boiling water for 1 minute. This helps shrink casing. It is ready to be tucked into the midst of a Tzimmes (see Index) or placed with meat of any kind to be roasted or stewed.

Stuffed Kishke may be roasted with chicken, duck, goose or turkey. Or, it may be roasted independently on a bed of sliced onions to which schmaltz and grebenes have been added. Roast 1½ to 2 hours at 350° F. or gas mark 4, or till nicely browned.

Stuffed Kishke is sometimes added to Cholent (see Index).

15 Beef, Lamb and Veal

TIME-TABLE FOR ROASTING BEEF, LAMB AND VEAL

Meat	Weight	Oven Temperature		Minutes Per Pound
Beef Roast, Rib or Boned, Rolled	3–5 lbs.	325° F. or gas mark 3	Rare Medium Well done	25 min. 25–30 min. 30–35 min.
Chuck or Shoulder	3–5 lbs.	325° F. or gas mark 3	Medium Well done	25–30 min. 30–35 min.
Lamb Shoulder, Stuffed Breast or	Average weight	325° F. or gas mark 3		30–35 min.
Rib Crown	Average weight	325° F. or gas mark 3		30–45 min.
Veal Shoulder or Breast Stuffed with Dressing	Average weight	325° F. or gas mark 3		25–30 min.

Use a Meat Thermometer for best results.
Rare – 140° F.   Medium – 160° F.   Well done – 170° F.

TIME-TABLE FOR PRESSURE COOKING OF MEAT

(Consult instructions accompanying your pressure cooker)

Left-over Meat. When using left-over meats of any kind for main dishes, it is a good point to remember that much of the original nutritive value has been lost from the original product. To restore that possible loss of nutritive elements, combine the left-over meat with eggs, whole wheat bread crumbs or wheat germ.

BEEF

Steaks. Because Jewish dietary laws prohibit the use of hind quarters of animals, steaks are limited to cuts from the chuck, flank, rib and shoulder. These cuts are the less tender parts and must be given special consideration.

GRILLED STEAK

Grilled meats do not require *kashering* (soaking and salting – see Chapter 4). The best grilled steaks are made over charcoal grills and have a special place in Jewish cuisine.

Preparation of Steak for Grilling. Pound the surface of steak with a wooden cleaver or the bottom of a heavy bottle. Rub a cut clove of garlic over the steak if desired. For grilling over open heat (charcoal grill) dust top of steak lightly with flour. For grilling under gas or electric heat, dust the under side of steak. Have charcoal glowing red and place steak in a wire grill with long handles. Grill until the juices begin to rise to top of meat. Turn to brown on under side. Season with salt, pepper and paprika. For grilling under gas or electric heat, be sure to keep the meat 4 inches from source of heat. Proceed as for charcoal grilling, turning to brown under side when the upper surface is browned. Add seasoning before serving.

FRIED STEAK

Use a heavy frying pan over moderate heat. Preheat pan, add shortening and fry steak to desired stage before turning to brown the other side. Add thinly sliced onions, minced garlic, sliced mushrooms (fresh or canned). Cover and cook 3 to 5 minutes or till onions are tender. Serve on a heated plate.

Variation: Fry sliced onions till transparent then add steak cut into serving portions. Add mushrooms and cook till tender.

PAN-GRILLED CHUCK OR FLANK STEAK

Have steak cut 1 inch thick, allowing $\frac{1}{3}$ pound per serving. Preheat a heavy frying pan and sear the meat on both sides, turning quickly to prevent escape of juices. Dust with flour, salt, pepper and paprika. Cover and cook over reduced heat 25 to 30 minutes. This is very much like a stewed steak but should be served with fried onions, green pepper and/or sautéed fresh or canned mushrooms, separately prepared.

STEWED STEAK (Chuck, Flank or Rib)

1½ *to 2 pounds steak | Flour for dredging | 3 tablespoons shortening |*
1 large onion, sliced or diced | 1 carrot, shredded or thinly sliced |
1 cup diced celery | 1 green pepper, thin strips (optional) |
1 cup canned or stewed tomatoes | 1 tablespoon vinegar or lemon juice |
1 tablespoon brown sugar | ½ cup hot water | Salt and pepper

Cut steak into serving portions and dredge with flour. Melt shortening in a heavy frying pan. Add steak and fry 3 to 5 minutes on each side. Add vegetables, vinegar, sugar and water to cover the meat. Cover and cook over moderate heat 15 to 20 minutes. Reduce heat and simmer 10 to 15 minutes uncovered. Test with a fork for tenderness. The steak should be turned and cooked for 5 to 10 minutes longer if not tender enough at this point. Add salt and pepper to taste before serving.
Serves 4 to 6.

ROULLADEN (Rolled Shoulder Steak)

Cut beef shoulder ½ inch thick, making slices as large as desired. Pound each cut of steak with a cleaver or heavy bottle, or french (see p. 36) on one side only, using a sharp knife for cutting across the grain in one direction then in the opposite direction. One rolled steak per serving is customary.
Prepare a stuffing of the following:

STUFFING FOR ROULLADEN

2 cups dry bread crumbs | 1 egg, slightly beaten |
2 tablespoons hot melted shortening | 1 teaspoon onion juice (or minced onion) |
¼ teaspoon salt | Dash of poultry seasoning | Dash of paprika |
2 tablespoons water to moisten if necessary

Stir egg into crumbs and add the other ingredients in the order listed. The stuffing should be soft enough to spread, and sufficient for 6 medium pieces of steak. Spread a layer of stuffing on a piece of meat, roll up and tie securely, then proceed to do the same with the rest of the steaks. Brown each roll in hot melted shortening in a heavy frying pan. Add 1 cup boiling water or soup stock and simmer 1 hour on top of stove or bake at 325° F. or gas mark 3 for the same length of time.

SAUERBRATEN

1 cup cider vinegar | ½ cup cold water | 6 bay leaves |
1 teaspoon peppercorns | 1 tablespoon mustard seed | ⅓ cup brown sugar |
4½ to 5 pounds brisket, first cut | 2 cloves garlic, minced |
2 large onions, sliced fine | ½ cup seeded raisins | 8 to 10 gingersnaps |
1 cup concentrated tomato sauce (canned)

Make a marinade of vinegar, water, bay leaves, peppercorns, mustard seed and brown sugar. Place meat in this and keep well covered in the refrigerator overnight. Lift meat from marinade and sear quickly in a preheated heavy pot. Add garlic, onions, raisins and gingersnaps. Cover and cook over moderate heat 30 minutes. Reduce heat and simmer 2½ to 3 hours. Add tomato sauce and ½ cup of the marinade. Cook 10 minutes.
    Serves 8.

SWEET-SOUR BRISKET AND SAUERKRAUT
(Irma's Recipe)

3 pounds brisket of beef or shoulder cut | 3 pounds sauerkraut |
1 onion, diced | 1 cup cider vinegar | ½ cup brown sugar |
1 teaspoon caraway seed | Parsley for garnish

Sear meat in a heavy pot or Dutch oven. Cover with sauerkraut, add all ingredients except parsley. The vinegar should come half-way up the cut of meat. Cover. Preheat oven to 375° F. or gas mark 5. Reduce heat to 325° F. or gas mark 3 and bake 45 minutes before basting. Continue oven heat at 325° F. allowing a total cooking time of 1½ hours. There should be enough gravy in the pot, but hot water may be added if desired, and thickening of browned flour stirred with some of the water before adding. Cook on top of stove

10 minutes if thickening is added. Slice meat, arrange on a heated serving platter and mound up the sauerkraut around it. Garnish with parsley. Serve with baked potatoes.

Serves 6.

SWEET-SOUR BEEF AND CABBAGE

2½ to 3 pounds brisket of beef or short ribs |
2 pounds cabbage, shredded or chopped | 1 teaspoon salt |
1 onion, diced fine | ¾ cup vinegar | ½ cup brown sugar |
½ cup seeded raisins | 2 tablespoons matzo crumbs or flour |
2 tablespoons shortening

Sear meat in pot in which it is to be cooked, over moderate heat. Sprinkle cabbage with salt. Let stand while preparing onion. Squeeze out liquid from cabbage, add onion and stir into the pot, moving seared meat to one side. When cabbage and onion are lightly browned, add the remaining ingredients except crumbs or flour and shortening. Cover pot and cook over reduced heat 1 hour. Lift cover and turn meat. If additional liquid is needed, add ¼ cup of boiling water at a time. The cabbage should be light brown and the meat beginning to be tender when pierced with a fork. Reduce heat and simmer 45 minutes longer. Thicken with crumbs or browned flour and shortening 10 minutes before serving time.

Serves 5 to 6.

BOILED BEEF

3 pounds lean beef, middle chuck cut or short ribs crosscut | 1 carrot, diced |
2 stalks celery, diced | 1 large onion, peeled | 1 parsnip, diced |
1 small white turnip, diced | 3 bay leaves | 6 peppercorns |
1 tablespoon salt | ¼ teaspoon paprika | 2½ quarts boiling hot water |
1 cup skinned fresh or canned tomato | ¼ cup minced parsley

Braise the meat in the pot in which it is to be cooked until it is lightly browned on all sides. Add the vegetables and cook for 5 minutes, stirring once or twice. Add remaining ingredients and cook over moderate heat, uncovered, for 1½ to 2 hours or till meat is very tender. Remove meat and cut into serving portions. Serve hot with horse-radish, mayonnaise or tomato sauce. Strain the liquid and use for soup stock or serve with vegetables as a soup foundation.

Serves 5 to 6.

BEEF STEW (Basic Recipe)

3 pounds beef cut from shoulder or chuck |
3 tablespoons schmaltz or vegetable shortening | 3 onions, diced |
2 carrots, thinly sliced | 1 parsnip, diced | 1 cup green onions, cut fine |
1 cup green beans, cut fine | 1 cup fresh or stewed tomatoes |
1 teaspoon salt | Dash of paprika

Brown meat whole in hot melted shortening, or cut into large cubes and sear quickly till browned. Add vegetables, salt and paprika. Cover and cook over moderate heat 45 minutes. Uncover and turn or stir meat and vegetables. Simmer 45 minutes or till tender.

Serves 6.

Variation 1: Add diced potatoes after 45 minutes, allowing ½ pound per serving, or less. Simmer as in basic recipe.

Variation 2: Omit green beans and add 1 cup soaked and drained dry lima beans, or 1 cup soaked navy beans.

Variation 3: Add 1 cup diced sweet potato and 2 cups diced celery root to basic recipe. Same procedure as in basic recipe.

SHORT RIBS OF BEEF STEW (Basic Recipe)

3 pounds short ribs, bones cracked | 3 tablespoons flour |
3 tablespoons melted shortening | 1 onion, diced | 1 carrot, diced |
1 cup diced celery | Salt and pepper to taste | 1 cup canned tomato sauce

Ribs may be cut apart before dredging in flour. Brown quickly in hot shortening and add onion. Stir 2 minutes over moderate heat. Add carrot and celery, taste and add salt and pepper if desired. Cover and cook 30 minutes over moderate heat. Uncover and add tomato sauce diluted with water if desired. Cover and simmer 1 hour.

Serves 4.

GOULASH (Basic Recipe)

4 pounds lean beef | 4 tablespoons flour |
4 tablespoons hot melted shortening | Water to cover |
1 cup canned tomato sauce | 2 tablespoons onion juice |
1 clove garlic, minced | 6 peppercorns | 2 bay leaves

Cut meat into 1½-inch cubes. Dredge in flour and brown on all sides in hot shortening. Add water to cover. Simmer 1 hour. Add tomato sauce, onion juice, minced garlic and spices. Add salt to taste, if required. Continue cooking over moderate heat 30 to 40 minutes. Serve with mashed potatoes, steamed rice or baked sweet potatoes.
Serves 6.

Variation 1: Brown onion, sliced or diced, and add meat dredged in flour. Omit water. Substitute 1½ cups tomato juice for tomato sauce and add a dash of red pepper. Omit bay leaves, peppercorns and garlic. Add 1 pound diced potatoes and ½ teaspoon salt. Simmer without stirring contents of pot 1½ hours.

Variation 2: Omit bay leaves and peppercorns from basic recipe. Add ½ teaspoon paprika. Add 2 cups cooked elbow macaroni 10 minutes before serving time.

BEEF ROAST (Non-Fatty)

4½ to 5 pounds shoulder cut or middle chuck | 2 cloves garlic |
3 tablespoons flour | ¼ teaspoon salt | Dash of pepper | Paprika |
3 tablespoons hot melted shortening | 3 onions, sliced |
2 carrots, cut lengthwise

Rub the meat with cut cloves of garlic and dredge with flour. Sprinkle with salt, pepper and paprika. Place in roasting pan in which shortening has been melted. Arrange onions and carrots around or under meat. Place in a preheated oven and roast at 325° F. or gas mark 3, allowing 25 to 35 minutes per pound (see *Time Table for Roasting*). Do not turn roast with a fork. Piercing the seared outer coat releases juices that should remain inside. Do not baste. Thicken gravy after roast is done and lifted from the pan.
Serves 8.

ROAST OF BRISKET, RIB (Not Rolled)

4 onions, sliced or diced | 2 carrots, sliced | 1 parsnip, cut into strips |
1 cup diced celery | 10 peppercorns | 3 bay leaves | 3 tablespoons flour |
½ teaspoon salt | Dash of pepper | 6 pounds brisket or ribs of beef

Place the vegetables in bottom of roasting pan. Add peppercorns and
bay leaves. Combine flour, salt and pepper. Pat into the cut side of
roast and sprinkle rest on top. Place meat on the bed of vegetables·
Preheat oven to 375° F. or gas mark 5 and reduce heat 10 minutes
after placing roast in oven. Roasting time will depend on whether
the meat is desired rare, medium or well done (see *Time Table for
Roasting*). Baste once or twice. Turn 30 minutes before end of
roasting time.
Serves 8 to 10.

POT ROAST WITH CIDER

2 cups cider | 2 tablespoons molasses | 2 large onions, sliced thin |
1 clove garlic, minced | 2 bay leaves | ⅛ teaspoon each ginger and allspice |
4 to 4½ pounds chuck or brisket (first cut) | 3 tablespoons shortening |
3 tablespoons flour | ½ teaspoon salt | Dash of pepper (optional)

Make a marinade of cider, molasses, onions, garlic, bay leaves and
spice. Place the meat in this, cover and let stand in the refrigerator
overnight. Turn and keep in marinade until ready for roasting in a
heavy pot or pressure cooker. Melt shortening in pot. Lift meat from
marinade and dust with flour, salt and pepper. Sear meat in hot
melted shortening, turning once or twice to brown all parts. Add
the marinade and cook over moderate heat 2 hours. Reduce heat and
simmer 30 minutes.
Serves 8 or 9.
Pressure Cooker Method: Follow same procedure but cut down the
marinade by half after lifting meat from it. Add half to meat in
cooker after searing. Adjust cover and gauge and cook under 10
pounds pressure 45 to 50 minutes. Add remainder of marinade 10
minutes before serving and cook over moderate heat on top of
stove, uncovered. Thicken gravy with an einbren made of 2 tablespoons flour browned in 2 tablespoons hot shortening and stir in
½ cup of gravy from pot. Cook 5 minutes and add to pot, stirring in

after removing meat to platter. Serve with Potato Latkes (see Index) or mashed potatoes.

OLD-FASHIONED POT ROAST (Gedaempfte Fleisch)

4 pounds beef shoulder, top cut brisket or middle chuck cut |
3 onions, diced or sliced |2 cloves garlic, minced | 1 carrot, shredded |
1 stalk celery, diced | 1 green pepper, diced | 3 tablespoons chicken schmaltz |
2 teaspoons salt | ½ teaspoon paprika | 4 bay leaves | 10 peppercorns |
1 tiny red pepper (optional) | 1½ cups soup stock or tomato juice |
2 tablespoons brown sugar

Heat a heavy pot and braise the meat till evenly browned on all sides. Add remaining ingredients in the order listed, cover and simmer 1½ to 2 hours. Or, follow same procedure for *Pressure Cooker Method*, reducing liquid to half the amount. Consult chart for time. Slice when tender and serve with gravy from pot.
Serves 6 to 8.

CHOPPED MEAT COMBINATIONS

Chopped meat with an addition of rice as an 'extender' is used extensively by the Jewish home-maker, especially if her background is European. In addition to hamburgers, called *kotletti* in some countries, chopped mixtures are used for stuffing vegetables. These meat-stuffed vegetables may be boiled or baked, usually with a sweet-sour sauce, the basis of which is tomato.

HOLISHKES (Meat-filled cabbage leaves, also called *Praakes* and *Galuptzi*, depending on locale)

1 pound chopped beef | ¼ cup uncooked rice | 1 egg | 1 onion, grated |
1 carrot, grated | ¼ teaspoon salt | 10 or 12 cabbage leaves |
¼ cup lemon juice, vinegar or ⅛ teaspoon citric acid crystals |
½ cup brown sugar | 1 cup tomato sauce, canned | Water to cover

Combine chopped meat, rice and egg. Grate in onion and carrot. Add salt. Blanch cabbage leaves by covering them with boiling water for 2 to 3 minutes. Drain cabbage leaves. Place a ball of the meat mixture in the centre of each cabbage leaf and roll up, tucking in the ends securely. Place close together in a heavy frying pan, add the other ingredients and enough water to cover. Cover tightly and cook over moderate heat 30 minutes. Reduce heat and simmer 20 minutes. Bake in the oven 20 minutes at 350° F. or gas mark 4 to brown on top, turning once to brown under sides. Hot water may be added in small quantities if necessary during the baking period.

Serves 4 to 5.

SARMA

This is the name for Holishkes in the Near Eastern countries. Usually ½ cup raisins are added to the sweet-sour tomato sauce. Procedure is the same as for stuffed cabbage leaves.

SARMALI IN FOIE DE VITZA

This dish is popular in Rumania and other Balkan countries. It is also a favourite with the Greeks. It is made of a chopped meat mixture wrapped in fresh or salted vine leaves.

Salting of Vine Leaves. When the leaves are tender on the grape-vine, they are picked and packed in a glazed crock. Each overlapping layer of leaves is generously sprinkled with salt, and salt forms the top layer. No water is added. The salt forms moisture and the leaves turn colour but do not dry out. They may be kept for months.

Cooking of Sarmali in Foie de Vitza. Use 1 large vine leaf or 2 small ones for each meat ball. Fresh or salted vine leaves are blanched with boiling water, drained and filled with the same meat mixture as for Holishkes. The wrapped balls of meat mixture are placed close together in a large frying pan and water to barely cover is added. Cook on top of stove, covered, 30 minutes over moderate heat. Uncover, add the same sauce ingredients as used for Stuffed Peppers. Add raisins as in that recipe. Cover with several vine leaves and bake 30 minutes at 350° F. or gas mark 4. Remove covering of vine leaves and brown on top or under grill 2 to 3 minutes.

1 pound of chopped beef mixture will serve 4 to 5.

STUFFED PEPPERS (Basic Recipe)
[Called *Ardei Implut* in Rumania and other Balkan countries]

*Six 5-inch sweet green peppers | Boiling water for blanching |
1 pound chopped beef | ¼ cup uncooked rice or ½ cup cooked rice or
bread crumbs | 1 onion, grated | 1 carrot, grated | ½ teaspoon salt |
Dash of pepper | 2 eggs | Water to cover*

SAUCE

*1 cup tomato purée | ½ cup water | 3 tablespoons vinegar, or lemon juice |
3 tablespoons brown sugar | ⅛ teaspoon paprika | ½ cup raisins (optional)*

Cut away stem end of peppers. Remove seeds. Blanch and invert to drain while preparing the meat mixture for filling. Combine all ingredients except water. Mix thoroughly. Stuff peppers compactly and even with the top. Stand upright in a casserole and cover with water. Bake 45 minutes at 350° F. or gas mark 4. Remove cover and increase heat to 400° F. or gas mark 6 for 15 minutes.

Cook sauce on top of stove, stirring continuously till thick, approximately 10 minutes over moderate heat. Add to the peppers in casserole, turn off heat. The heat of the oven is sufficient to lightly brown tops of pepper stuffing and cook sauce with liquid in casserole.
Serves 6.

BAKED MEAT LOAF

*1½ pounds chopped beef | ½ cup soft bread crumbs or boiled rice |
1 large onion, grated | 1 large carrot, grated | 1 clove of garlic, grated |
2 eggs | ¼ cup water or soup stock |
3 tablespoons hot melted shortening | Paprika*

Combine all ingredients except shortening and paprika. Form into a loaf. Melt shortening in loaf pan and place meat loaf in, pressing into shape of pan. Dust with paprika. Bake in a preheated oven at 375° F. or gas mark 5 for 45 minutes or till evenly browned on top. Serve with Creole sauce or tomato sauce.
Serves 4 to 6.

GRILLED HAMBURGERS (Basic Recipe)

1½ pounds flank steak, minced fine | 1 grated onion | 1 grated carrot |
1 teaspoon salt and/or ¼ teaspoon garlic salt | 2 eggs |
3 tablespoons flour | ⅛ teaspoon paprika

Combine chopped meat, grated vegetables, seasoning and eggs.
Form into ½-inch-thick patties. Dip in flour mixed with paprika and
place on a wire grill over glowing charcoal fire. Grill until brown
and turn to brown other sides. A handy long-handle wire grill is
available at any hardware or housewares store. This type of grill can
be held by the handle while turning the hamburgers or, grease the
grill of gas stove and grill hamburgers under moderate flame 3 to 4
inches from heat, turning as soon as browned on top to brown under
sides.

An electric table grill may be found convenient. Follow same
procedure as for charcoal or cooker grilling.

Serves 6.

Variation 1: Form chopped meat combination into 1½-inch-thick
rolls. Cut roll into 4-inch lengths. Roll each in seasoned flour.
Grill till evenly browned.

Variation 2: Add 1 minced clove of garlic and ½ tablespoon mixed
herbs (or poultry seasoning) to basic mixture. Add a dash of
cayenne if desired. Form into 1-inch-thick rolls, 3 to 4 inches in
length. Taper rolls at both ends. Roll in seasoned flour and grill
over charcoal fire. These are called *carnatzei* in Rumanian.
When made into smaller rolls they are called by the diminutive,
carnatzlach.

GLAMOUR PATTIES

Use same ingredients as for basic recipe for Meat Loaf or Hamburger.

Form into ½-inch-thick patties and dust with seasoned flour. Cut
3-inch tomatoes in half through the centre, crosswise. Place a pattie
on the cut side of a tomato. Place topped tomato halves in a baking
pan. Add ½ to ¾ cup soup stock or water. Bake 30 minutes at 375° F.
or gas mark 5, or till browned on top and the tomato is tender but
still holding its shape.

Serve in mashed potato nests, 2 per serving.

STEWED MEAT BALLS

2 pounds chopped beef | 1 cup dry bread crumbs | 2 eggs |
1 onion, grated | 1 small carrot, grated | ½ teaspoon salt |
Dash of pepper | Shortening for frying |
1 cup tomato sauce, fresh or canned | 1 cup sliced mushrooms

Combine chopped meat, crumbs and eggs. Add grated onion and
carrot, salt and pepper. Mix thoroughly. Form into balls 1½ inches
in diameter. Fry in hot melted shortening till nicely browned.
Add tomato sauce and mushrooms. Cover and simmer 5 to 10
minutes.
Serves 4 to 5.

SWEET-SOUR MEAT BALLS (Basic Recipe)

1 pound chopped beef | ¼ cup brown or long grain rice | 1 onion, grated |
1 clove garlic, grated or ¼ teaspoon garlic salt | ½ teaspoon salt |
2 eggs | 1 tablespoon minced parsley |
4 tablespoons schmaltz or vegetable shortening

SAUCE

1 cup tomato soup (concentrated, canned) | ¼ cup cider vinegar |
3 tablespoons brown sugar | 1 cup finely cut celery |
1 green pepper, chopped

Combine all ingredients except shortening. Form into balls the size
of walnuts and sauté in hot melted shortening till browned on all
sides. Add ingredients for sauce in the order listed. Cover and
simmer 20 minutes over moderate heat. Uncover and cook 5 to 10
minutes longer. Serve with cooked spaghetti or wide noodles.
Serves 4 to 5.
Variation: Cook ½ pound elbow macaroni or shells in salted water
10 to 15 minutes or till tender. Drain and rinse with hot water.
Divide in half, placing 1 portion in bottom of a greased casserole, adding browned meat balls. Top with remainder, add
sauce ingredients and bake 20 minutes at 375° F. or gas mark
5, or till browned on top.

PICKLING MEATS IN THE HOME

To pickle meats means to place them in a solution for a length of time, during which time the meat is 'cured' or preserved for later use. The meats that are especially used for pickling are *brisket of beef* from outer or first cut to the more fatty and bony sections. These are called *corned beef* and require cooking before serving. The corned beef sold in delicatessen and other food shops is the cooked and/or smoked product after it has been processed in a pickling solution.

For pickling *beef tongue*, the same procedure is followed as for corned beef. The meat selected for pickling is made Kosher first (see *Kosher Kitchen Questions and Answers*). The following pickling solution is prepared and added to the meat which remains submerged in it for a period of 10 days to 2 weeks. It is then ready for cooking in accordance with the recipe directions. Pickled meat requires longer cooking than fresh meat.

PICKLING SOLUTION FOR HOME-MADE CORNED BEEF

4 quarts cold water | 1½ pounds coarse salt |
½ ounce saltpetre (purchased at chemists) | 1 tablespoon brown sugar |
1 tablespoon mixed whole spice | 12 bay leaves

Combine ingredients and boil 5 minutes. This amount is sufficient to cover 5 pounds of meat or tongue. Place the meat to be pickled in a stoneware crock fitted with a tight cover. Add 4 or 5 cloves of garlic and pour in the pickling solution as soon as cold. Weight the meat with a heavy plate or flat rock. A board that fits inside the crock may be weighted with a rock to keep meat well under the solution. Cover with a double layer of muslin tied securely around crock. Store the covered crock in a cool place 10 days to 2 weeks. The crock cover may be adjusted, providing it is propped up so that air circulates between it and the muslin cover.

BOILED CORNED BEEF (Home-made Variety)

5 pounds corned beef | 1 large onion | ½ cup cider vinegar |
6 bay leaves | 1 large clove garlic |
1 tablespoon whole mixed spice (optional) | Cold water to cover

16

Soak corned beef in cold water 1 hour. Drain well. Place corned beef in a deep pot, add the other ingredients listed and cover with cold water. Bring to a quick boil, skim, and cook over reduced heat allowing 30 to 40 minutes per pound. Test with a fork for tenderness before removing from heat. Let the meat remain in the liquid 20 minutes before draining sauce. Slice and serve hot. If the meat is to be served cold, add about 1 cup of the strained sauce and store in a well-covered glass container in the refrigerator.

Serves 10 to 15.

Pressure Cooker Method: Cook in pressure cooker after soaking. Allow 15 minutes per pound at 15 pounds pressure, and add only 1 cup cold water.

CORNED BEEF AND CABBAGE

*2 pounds cabbage | 2 pounds boiled corned beef | 1 onion, diced |
1 clove garlic, minced | 2 cups cold water*

Removed wilted outer leaves from cabbage. Cut into quarters or eighths and remove core. Place half the cabbage in the bottom of a deep pot, add onion and garlic with the corned beef. Cover with remaining cabbage and add 2 cups cold water. Cover and simmer 30 minutes or till top layer of cabbage is tender. Serve hot with boiled or baked potatoes.

Serves 4.

Variation: Add 1 teaspoon caraway seeds and 2 tablespoons dry bread crumbs. Thicken the sauce with an einbren made with 2 tablespoons flour browned in 2 tablespoons hot melted shortening.

CORNED BEEF CASSEROLE

*3 tablespoons shortening | 3 tablespoons flour | 1 onion, minced or diced |
1 green pepper, diced | 1 clove garlic, diced fine |
1 pound potatoes, pared and thinly sliced |
2 cups cooked diced or chopped corned beef | 2 eggs |
3 tablespoons minced parsley*

Melt shortening in bottom of casserole or other baking dish. Stir in flour till lightly browned. Add onion, green pepper and garlic and sauté 5 minutes, stirring constantly, till the onion is yellow. Arrange a layer of potato slices and add the corned beef. Top with remaining potato slices. Beat eggs well and add. Cover and bake 25 to 30 minutes at 350° F. or gas mark 4. Remove cover and slip under grill for 3 minutes to brown on top. Garnish with minced parsley.

Serves 4.

CORNED BEEF HASH

2 cups cooked corned beef, diced or chopped |
4 medium boiled potatoes, diced fine | ½ cup cold water |
3 tablespoons dry bread crumbs | 3 tablespoons shortening

Combine corned beef and potatoes. Add water and turn into a shallow baking pan. Sprinkle bread crumbs on top and dot with shortening. Bake 25 to 30 minutes at 350° F. or gas mark 4, or till nicely browned on top. Serve hot.

Serves 4.

CORNED BEEF AND VEGETABLES

2 pounds corned beef | Cold water to cover | 1 onion, diced or sliced |
4 medium size beets, pared and diced |
4 medium size carrots, scraped and sliced or diced |
1 pound cabbage, shredded or cut into sections |
4 medium size potatoes, pared and quartered | 2 tablespoons shortening |
2 tablespoons flour

Cover corned beef with cold water. Cook in a deep pot over moderate heat 1 hour. Add vegetables, cover and cook 35 to 45 minutes. Test meat for tenderness, and if necessary, continue cooking 10 to 15 minutes longer till meat is tender. Melt shortening in a saucepan and brown the flour, stirring constantly. Stir in 1 cup of the sauce from pot and cook 5 minutes. Add to the cooked corned beef and vegetables and shake the pot gently to distribute evenly. Cook 5 minutes. Serve hot.

Serves 4 to 6.

PICKLED TONGUE

This may be cooked in the same manner as Boiled Corned Beef (see Index).

After the tongue is cool, remove the skin. Slice and serve.

FRESH BEEF TONGUE

*A 4- to 4½-pound fresh beef tongue | Cold water to cover |
1 clove garlic, minced | 1 onion, sliced | 2 bay leaves |
10 peppercorns | 1 scant teaspoon salt*

VEGETABLES TO BE ADDED

*½ cup diced carrots | ½ cup diced celery | 3 onions, sliced |
4 cups strained liquid*

Combine all ingredients and bring to a brisk boil. Reduce heat and simmer 1½ hours. Remove tongue from liquid, remove skin and trim away parts from base. Strain the liquid and reserve. Place the vegetables in a roasting pan. Top with trimmed tongue and add strained liquid. Cover and bake approximately 2 hours at 300° F. or gas mark 1–2, or till tender.

Serves 8.

BEEF TONGUE ORIENTALE

*A 4- to 4½-pound fresh beef tongue | Cold water to cover |
1 large onion, diced | 2 cloves garlic, minced | 2 bay leaves |
2 tablespoons vinegar or lemon juice | 2 tablespoons sugar |
2 tablespoons honey or corn syrup | 1 cup seedless raisins |
¼ teaspoon ginger or 6 gingersnaps*

THICKENING FOR SAUCE

2 tablespoons cornflour | 2 tablespoons cold water

Cook tongue in water to cover over moderate heat for 30 minutes. Add onion, garlic and bay leaves. Cover and continue cooking 30 to 45 minutes. Test with a fork. If tender, lift out tongue to a plate.

Strain liquid. Remove skin from tongue and trim away excess fatty part at base of tongue. Return skinned tongue to liquid. Add vinegar, sugar, honey, raisins and ginger. Cover and simmer 45 minutes. Test again for tenderness. If not soft enough to pierce easily at centre of top, cook 15 to 20 minutes longer. The sauce may be thickened with 2 tablespoons cornflour mixed with cold water and added to the gravy after lifting out tongue. Cook gravy 5 to 10 minutes, stirring once or twice.

Serves 8.

SWEET-SOUR TONGUE

A 4- to 4½-pound fresh beef tongue | Cold water to cover | 1 clove garlic |
1 tablespoon whole mixed spice, tied in a bag | 1 cup cider vinegar |
¾ cup brown sugar | ½ cup seedless raisins |
6 gingersnaps or ¼ teaspoon ground ginger

Boil tongue in cold water 10 minutes. Skim. Add garlic and whole spice. Simmer 2 hours. Remove tongue from liquid. Remove skin and trim away fatty parts at base. Strain liquid. Return tongue to strained liquid, add remaining ingredients and simmer 20 to 30 minutes.

Serves 8 to 10.

CALF'S TONGUE

Prepare like recipes for beef tongue, reducing cooking time to 1 hour approximately. Bake 30 minutes at 325° F. or gas mark 3.

PITCHA (Calf's Feet Jelly—also called *Sulze*)

2 calf's feet, cleaned and sawed to fit pot | Cold water to cover |
1 onion | 1 clove garlic | 3 bay leaves | 1 teaspoon peppercorns (optional) |
Salt to taste | 2 tablespoons lemon juice or ½ cup vinegar |
3 hard-cooked eggs, sliced | Sliced lemon for garnish or parsley

Cook feet in water 10 minutes. Skim and add onion, garlic, bay leaves, peppercorns. Cook over reduced heat for 1 hour. Skim again.

Simmer for 3 hours or till bones stand away from gristle and meat.
Strain. Cut usable meat and gristle into fine cubes. Add to strained
liquid. Taste and add salt if necessary. Add vinegar. Cook 5
minutes after bringing to a quick boil. Turn into an oblong glass dish
about 2 inches in depth. Let cool until partly jellied. Place some egg
slices on the top and stand remaining egg slices upright inside the
dish along the sides. Chill in refrigerator. When completely jellied
and firm to the touch, unmould on serving plate. Cut into squares if
desired. Garnish with parsley and/or lemon. Chicory, shredded
lettuce or watercress makes a nice base on which to serve this dish
as an appetizer.

Serves 4 to 6.

Variation 1 : Add 1 wine glass of sherry before turning into dish or
other mould. Do not stir the wine in while hot.

Variation 2 : Add 2 egg whites, stiffly beaten with a pinch of salt,
after straining the liquid into a bowl. Put aside gristle and meat
particles for later addition. Cook over moderate heat combined
liquid and beaten egg whites for 20 minutes or till clear. This
makes a clear jelly. When cool, add sherry without stirring.
Place the gristle and meat bits in the bottom of mould or dish
and add the clear jelly. Chill. Use sliced hard-cooked eggs for
garnish.

LAMB

BREAST OF LAMB (Rice-Stuffed)

1 *breast of lamb, with pocket for stuffing* | 1 *clove garlic* |
¾ *cup brown or converted rice, parboiled* 15 *minutes in salted water* |
1 *teaspoon salt* | ¼ *cup chopped peanuts, pecans or any mixed nuts combination* |
2 *tablespoons minced parsley* | 4 *tablespoons flour or fine crumbs* |
4 *tablespoons olive or other oil* | 2 *cups boiling water or soup stock*

Rub the cut clove of garlic into inside and outside of meat. Trim
off bits of fat from meat and chop or cut fine. Combine with rice
that has been drained, salt, chopped nuts and parsley. Fill pocket
in breast of lamb and fasten opening with polished toothpicks or
metal skewers. Pat bottom and top with flour or crumbs. Heat oil
in roasting pan and place filled breast in centre, spooning some of
the oil over top. Add 2 cups boiling water or soup stock. Roast at

325° F. or gas mark 3, allowing 30 to 35 minutes per pound of meat. Baste occasionally with the gravy in pan.

Serves 4 to 6.

Variation: Omit chopped nuts. Add 1 pound chopped beef, prepared as for Hamburger or Meat Loaf, to ingredients listed. Stuff cavity with the mixture. Proceed as in basic recipe.

Serves 6 to 7.

CROWN ROAST OF LAMB (Basic Recipe)

Have the butcher tie together a side of lamb ribs from shoulder joint down. Then cut 2 inches down between ribs and into other portion. The weight is usually about 5 pounds. Prepare meat and rub well with a cut clove of garlic. Dust with flour inside the well and fill with your favourite poultry dressing or chopped beef that has been prepared as for Stewed Meat Balls (see Index). Roast in a preheated oven at 325° F. or gas mark 3, allowing 35 to 45 minutes per pound including meat filling. Serve with mint sauce (see Sauces) spooned over each serving. Or serve with Creole sauce.

Serves 8 to 10.

LAMB SHOULDER ROAST (Basic Recipe)

4 to 4½ pounds shoulder of lamb | 1 clove garlic |
3 onions, sliced thin | 3 tablespoons flour | Dash of pepper |
½ teaspoon salt | ⅛ teaspoon paprika

Rub meat well with cut clove of garlic. Arrange onion slices in bottom of roasting pan and place the meat over. Combine flour, pepper, salt and paprika and dust top of roast generously. Roast 2 hours at 325° F. or gas mark 3, or till nicely browned on top.

Serves 6.

Variation 1: Add 12 or more small potatoes, boiled in their jackets till tender then peeled and rolled in seasoned flour mixture, 20 to 25 minutes before roast is done. Potatoes should be turned once during that period.

Variation 2: Roast lamb shoulder on a bed of the following mixed vegetables:

2 carrots, quartered lengthwise | 2 parsnips, quartered lengthwise |
1 cup diced green pepper | 1 cup diced white turnips (tender greens included) |
3 medium fresh tomatoes, sliced or diced (optional)

Add to sliced onions in the order listed. Sprinkle lightly with salt, pepper and paprika. Proceed as in basic recipe or Variation 1.

LAMB STEW (Basic Recipe)

3 pounds breast or shoulder of lamb, cut up |
3 tablespoons hot melted shortening (schmaltz preferred) |
2 large onions, diced | 1 large carrot, diced or sliced |
1 large parsnip, diced or sliced | 2 medium white turnips, pared and diced |
1 cup finely cut green beans | 1 pound potatoes, pared and cubed |
1 cup finely cut celery and leaves | 2 tablespoons minced parsley |
¼ teaspoon powdered garlic | 1 teaspoon salt | ¼ teaspoon paprika

Braise the meat in hot melted shortening in the pot in which it is to be stewed. Add diced onion and as soon as light brown, add the remaining ingredients in the order listed. Cover pot and cook over low heat, allowing 25 minutes per pound. Shake the pot once or twice during the stewing time to prevent sticking. Water that adhered to vegetables provides sufficient moisture to form a rich gravy.

Serves 4 to 5.

Pressure Cooker Method: Braise meat in hot melted shortening in pressure pot. Place pot in cold water to cool rapidly. Add vegetables and seasoning, and ½ cup cold water or soup stock. Adjust cover and gauge and cook under 10 pounds pressure for 30 minutes after reducing heat. Tomato sauce may be added after reducing pressure as directed for your type of cooker. Reheat 3 to 5 minutes uncovered.

FRIGARUI (Rumanian equivalent of Turkish *Shish Kebab*)

Cut 1-inch-thick lamb, veal or beef steak into 1½- or 2-inch squares. Dredge with flour that has been seasoned with garlic salt, onion salt and paprika in amounts to suit the taste. Fasten each square of meat on a metal skewer, allowing ¼ inch space between, 5 or 6 per skewer. Grill over charcoal fire or under gas or electric heat, turning to brown evenly on all sides.

BREADED LAMB CHOPS

Pat shoulder or rib chops dry with towel. Dust with fine matzo crumbs. Dip in well-beaten egg, then in crumbs. Heat shortening in frying pan and fry prepared chops till brown before turning. Fry over moderate heat. Drain off excess fat by placing chops on paper towels as soon as removed from frying pan. Allow 2 chops per serving, or 1 shoulder chop ¾ inch thick. 2 eggs for 4 to 6 chops is generally sufficient.

LAMB SHOULDER CHOPS (Basic Recipe)

4 chops, ¾ inch thick | 4 tablespoons hot melted shortening |
2 large onions, thinly sliced | Salt and pepper to taste

Dry each chop before frying in hot melted shortening till browned on both sides. Lift fried chops to platter covered with paper towel. Fry onions in same frying pan till light brown. Return chops to pan on top of onions. Cover and turn off heat. Serve chops topped with onions and dusted with salt and pepper.

Serves 4.

Variation: Make a dressing of the following:

2 cups dry bread crumbs | ½ cup cold water | 1 egg |
1 tablespoon minced parsley | ⅛ teaspoon garlic salt | Dash of paprika

Combine well. After frying shoulder chops, spread with dressing and top with fried onion. Place in a greased baking pan and bake 15 minutes at 350° F. or gas mark 4.

PAN GRILLED LAMB CHOPS

Use either rib or shoulder chops. Preheat a heavy frying pan and brown chops on one side before turning to brown the other. Dust with salt or garlic salt and serve, allowing 2 rib chops or 1 shoulder chop, ¾ inch thick, per serving.

CHARCOAL GRILLED LAMB CHOPS

Dust chops lightly with seasoned flour if desired. Arrange chops on a greased wire grill with a long handle. Grill over charcoal fire, turning as soon as lightly browned to brown on other side. Or, grill under gas or electric heat till nicely browned. Turn and brown other side of chops.

GRILLED LAMB PATTIES

1 pound lean lamb, chopped | 1 tablespoon grated onion |
1 clove garlic, minced fine | 1 egg | 1 tablespoon fine matzo crumbs

Combine chopped lamb, onion, garlic and egg. Form into 4 patties, 1 inch thick. Dip in crumbs on one side only. Arrange on a greased wire grill with long handle and grill over charcoal fire till lightly browned on the crumbed side before turning to brown the other side.
Serves 2.

SMOTHERED LAMB CHOPS AND ONIONS

4 rib chops or 2 shoulder chops (1 inch thick) | 4 onions, sliced |
3 tablespoons hot melted shortening | Salt and pepper | ⅛ teaspoon paprika

Place the chops between sliced onions while heating shortening in a heavy frying pan. Place sliced onions in centre of pan and sauté 2 or 3 minutes. Move lightly browned onion to one side of pan and fry each chop first on one side then on the other. Cover the fried chops with onions, dust with salt, pepper and paprika. Reduce heat and simmer 15 minutes with or without a cover on pan.
Serves 2.

VEAL

Breast of veal for roasting or stewing is prepared very much like the same cuts of lamb (see *Time Table for Roasting Beef, Lamb or Veal*). Veal chops and steaks require somewhat different treatment. Longer and slower cooking is required.

VEAL SHOULDER ROASTS

See recipe for Lamb Shoulder Roast.

ROAST BREAST OF VEAL WITH GRATED POTATO STUFFING

Have the butcher cut a deep pocket in the breast of veal.

FILLING

6 *medium potatoes | 1 onion | 2 eggs | ½ cup flour | 1 teaspoon salt | Dash of white pepper | Minced parsley | ½ cup hot melted shortening | Clove of garlic | Flour*

Grate pared potatoes into a deep bowl Squeeze out excess water. Grate onion into bowl. Add eggs, flour, salt, pepper and parsley. Stir till well combined. Heat shortening in roasting pan and pour into the potato mixture, stirring rapidly till combined. Let the mixture stand for a few minutes before filling pocket in veal breast. Fasten with polished toothpicks or metal skewers. Rub the meat with a cut clove of garlic, dredge with flour and place in greased roasting pan. Consult *Time Table* for oven temperature and roasting time.

VEAL STEW

See basic recipe for Lamb Stew. Simmer after adding vegetables, allowing 30 minutes per pound. Also see *Pressure Cooker Method* for same recipe.
   Variation: Add 1 cup thinly sliced fresh mushrooms 20 minutes before serving time, simmer in uncovered pressure pan, stirring once or twice.

VEAL BIRDS

2 veal chops | Garlic | Matzo crumbs | Shortening

Have butcher cut 2 chops together and slice between bones to permit spreading open to resemble a pair of wings. Allow 1 pair of wings

(Veal Bird) per serving. Rub meat with a cut of garlic, dust with fine crumbs on both sides and brown in hot melted shortening, turning to brown under side. When all the Veal Birds have been browned place them in a baking pan and top each wing with a ball of the following:

DRESSING

1½ *cups dry bread crumbs* | 1 *tablespoon onion juice* | 1 *egg* |
1 *tablespoon minced parsley or* 1 *teaspoon poultry seasoning* |
⅛ *teaspoon salt* | *Dash of pepper or paprika*

Combine by mixing in a bowl. Form into 8 balls. Bake Veal Birds 1 hour at 325° F. or gas mark 3. Increase heat to 350° F. or gas mark 4 for 20 to 30 minutes or till browned on top. Serve with tomato sauce.

Serves 4.

BONED VEAL SHOULDER POT ROAST (Basic Recipe)

4½- *to* 5-*pound boned shoulder*
3 *tablespoons hot melted shortening, chicken schmaltz preferably* |
1 *cup diced onions* | 1 *large carrot, diced* | 1 *cup diced celery* |
2 *bay leaves* | 10 *peppercorns* | 1 *clove garlic, diced fine* |
1 *teaspoon salt* | ¼ *teaspoon paprika*

Sear meat in hot melted fat in roasting pot or Dutch oven. Lift out meat and add the other ingredients. Stir 1 or 2 minutes over moderate heat or till onions begin to soften. If possible, place a perforated rack over the vegetables and place the pot roast on it. Add enough water to come ½ inch over vegetables, approximately 1 cup. Cover and cook over moderate heat 2½ hours. Reduce heat and simmer 20 minutes uncovered. Thicken gravy with an einbren made of 2 tablespoons flour browned in 2 tablespoons melted shortening and ½ cup of gravy from pot stirred in till smooth. Cook 5 minutes. Lift out meat and rack, combine thickening with gravy and vegetables in the pot. Put gravy with vegetables through a coarse strainer for smooth gravy. Or serve unstrained over sliced pot roast.

Serves 6 to 7.

Variation: Substitute 1 cup cider for water. Do not use perforated rack in pot. Turn pot roast once or twice during the first hour of cooking. Slice meat when done and return to pot for 10 minutes before serving.

VEAL ROULLADEN

Pound well eight ½-inch thick cuts of shoulder steak with a cleaver or heavy bottle. Follow directions as in basic recipe for Beef Roulladen. Spread dressing in a thin layer, roll up and tie. Allow 1½ hours for top of stove simmering or oven baking at 325° F. or gas mark 3.
Serves 8.

VEAL SHORTCAKE

2½ pounds diced veal | 2 tablespoons hot melted shortening |
1 onion diced fine | 1 bay leaf | 6 peppercorns | 2 cups boiling water |
Salt, pepper, paprika to taste | 2 tablespoons dry crumbs |
1 recipe scone dough (see p. 131) | Mushroom or tomato sauce

Sauté meat in hot melted shortening. Add onion and stir frequently while cooking over moderate heat for 10 to 15 minutes. When onion turns yellow or light brown, add bay leaf, peppercorns and water. Stir and taste. Add salt, pepper and paprika to suit the taste. Simmer 1½ hours or till meat is tender. Thicken gravy with 2 tablespoons dry crumbs or flour and water paste, stirring 3 to 5 minutes till smooth. Pat out scone dough on a lightly floured board. Divide in 2 and roll out 1 piece to fit into bottom of an 8 × 8 × 4-inch baking pan. Remove bay leaf and peppercorns. Spread meat on dough. Roll out second square of dough and place on top. Bake in a preheated oven at 425° F. or gas mark 7 for 30 minutes or till top crust is lightly browned. Serve with mushroom or tomato sauce added to gravy left in pot.
Serves 4 to 6.

VEAL STEAKS (Bombay Style)

4 veal shoulder steaks ½ inch thick (approximately 8 ounces each) |
1 clove garlic | 4 tablespoons flour | ⅛ teaspoon salt and pepper |
4 tablespoons hot melted shortening | 1 large onion, sliced or diced

Rub meat with cut clove of garlic. Dredge with flour seasoned with salt and pepper. Reserve 1 tablespoon melted shortening. Brown steaks on both sides in 3 tablespoons hot melted shortening in a heavy frying pan. Remove steaks from pan. Wipe pan with a paper towel and add reserved tablespoon of fat. Sauté onions till light yellow, return browned steaks to pan and add:

SAUCE

1 *small can tomatoes (including juice)* | *4 tablespoons canned tomato paste* |
½ *teaspoon salt* | 1 *teaspoon brown sugar* | 1 *teaspoon curry powder* |
½ *teaspoon thyme or poultry seasoning* | 1 *teaspoon soy sauce* |
4 medium size canned pimentos, diced or cut in strips

Cover and simmer 45 minutes or till steaks are tender. Arrange steaks on a heated platter and pour gravy over. Garnish with parsley.
Serves 4.

WIENER SCHNITZEL (Basic Recipe)

6 *veal shoulder steaks*, ½ *inch thick* | ½ *cup flour or dry crumbs* |
2 *eggs* | 4 *tablespoons hot melted shortening* |
Salt, pepper and paprika | *Minced parsley*

Pound steaks, dip in flour or crumbs and pat with the fingers till smoothly coated on both sides of meat. Beat eggs in a bowl. Heat a frying pan and shortening, dip prepared steaks in beaten egg. Fry till brown on one side. Turn and reduce heat while frying steaks on under side. Cover pan and cook over very low heat 30 to 40 minutes. The steam that gathers under the cover will be sufficient to keep steaks from becoming dry. Dust with salt, pepper and paprika and garnish with minced parsley.
Serves 6.
Variation: Add a 6-ounce glass of currant jelly, 2 tablespoons lemon juice and 6 slices of lemon. Cover steaks and proceed as in basic recipe.

16 Poultry

Preparation of Poultry. In this modern age it is limited to *kashering* in the home kitchen of the average Jewish family. The poultry dealer generally presents to his customer cleaned, drawn and even sectioned birds on order. There are, however, a few details for the cook to carry out. (See *Kosher Kitchen Questions and Answers.*)

A berry huller is a handy gadget for removing pin feathers. The gas burner is convenient for singeing almost invisible hairs. The eviscerated poultry is easily made ready for the pot, grill or oven in accordance with the recipe.

If it is necessary to store *kashered* poultry in the refrigerator, it is advisable to wipe it with a towel before placing it in the coolest part, or wrapping it in aluminium foil if stored in the freezing compartment.

If the chicken is to be used for soup, excess fat from the inside and outside should be removed and rendered. Schmaltz and greben or grebenes (cracklings), are utilized in a number of the recipes given in this and other sections of this book.

Rendering Chicken or Goose Fat. To make schmaltz, cut the fat clusters and fatty skin portions into 1-inch cubes or strips. Cover with cold water and cook in a covered pan or pot for 20 to 25 minutes. Uncover and continue cooking over reduced heat until the water has evaporated and only the melted or cooked fat and cracklings remain. Cracklings, greben, begin to turn light brown at this point and diced onion should be added for flavour. Allow 1 cupful of onion for each pound of unrendered fat. The addition of a clove or two of garlic is also recommended by some cooks. The fat is ready for straining when the onion turns a light brown and cracklings curl up and become crisp and brown. Strain when boiling has stopped. Cracklings and onion may be utilized in many ways. Rendered schmaltz as well as greben can be stored for months in glass containers or glazed covered crocks, in the refrigerator or other cool place. Goose schmaltz for Passover use is generally prepared months in advance.

The skin of the neck can be cut and used for stuffing. (See Gefilte Helzel.) The giblets may be used for enriching soup or dressing for roasted poultry. The liver, carefully separated from the gall sack, can be used for chopped liver. Eggs found inside the bird, without shell, should not be used with milk or milk derivatives, but dropped into soup or boiling salted water to cook. Eggs with shell may be used without restriction.

Spring Chicken. This is best for frying. It is also the only kind used for grilling, either in the cooker or table grill, or over a charcoal grill.

FRIED CHICKEN

Cutting into small sections or disjointing is the best procedure. For frying large quantities, a frying pan with wire basket such as is used for French Fried Potatoes, is recommended. For frying 1 or 2 spring chickens, a heavy aluminium frying pan serves very well. Sections of chicken to be fried should be wiped dry and rolled in fine crumbs or flour. Have the frying pan hot and the fat melted before frying chicken. A small clove of garlic and/or a few slices of onion in the hot fat adds flavour and can be lifted out and discarded. Turn each piece of fried chicken to brown on all sides. Lift out as soon as fried and drain off excess fat on paper towels.

KENTUCKY FRIED CHICKEN (Basic Recipe)

A 1½-pound spring chicken, sectioned | 1½ cups flour |
1½ teaspoons baking powder | ½ teaspoon salt | Dash of pepper |
1 egg | ½ cup water | Fat for deep frying | 1 small onion, sliced

Dust each section of the cut-up chicken with flour using about 2 tablespoons. Sift together flour, baking powder, salt and pepper. Beat egg and stir in water. Stir the egg and water into the flour mixture to make a smooth batter. Melt shortening in a deep frying pan and add onion slices. When the onion is light brown, lift out and begin to dip each piece of chicken in batter, transferring to the hot fat to fry at 380° F. or gas mark 5 till nicely browned. If possible, use a frying basket. After all the pieces of chicken have been fried, place in a covered casserole and bake 20 to 30 minutes at 350° F. or gas mark 4. Uncover for 10 minutes before serving.

Serves 3.

Variation 1: Chicken from which soup was prepared may be

used. After cutting chicken into sections, let cool before proceeding as for spring chicken in basic recipe.

Variation 2: After chicken has been fried, pour off remaining fat. Sauté canned pineapple slices till lightly browned on both sides. Arrange around the fried chicken.

STIR-FRIED CHICKEN WITH RICE

2 tablespoons schmaltz or vegetable shortening | 2 onions, diced |
1 green pepper, cut fine | 3 cups steamed rice |
2 cups diced or finely cut cooked chicken breast | 2 tablespoons soy sauce |
Dash of ginger (optional)

Brown onions in hot melted shortening. Add ingredients listed and stir lightly while cooking over moderate heat 25 to 30 minutes.
Serves 4.

GRILLED CHICKEN

Cut in halves or quarters. Prepare as for frying by dusting or rolling in fine crumbs or flour to insure a crisp outer crust. Chicken sections may be rubbed lightly with a cut clove of garlic or dusted with powdered garlic if desired. Grilling time for a split spring chicken should be about 45 minutes. The grill rack should be 4 to 5 inches from electric element or gas flame. It is best to turn portions once or twice during the process.

Pan Grilling or Pan Frying. This is recommended only for very tender chickens, weight not to exceed 2 pounds. For heavier birds, grilled or pan fried, it is safer to cover and keep at 350° F. or gas mark 4 in the oven or on top of stove over moderate heat for 15 to 20 minutes before serving. Grilled and fried chicken can be served hot or cold.

TIPS ON ROASTING CHICKENS, DUCKS, GEESE, TURKEYS

Prepare poultry for roasting whole. Wipe inside with a towel before rubbing with garlic and filling with desired stuffing. Dressing should be sufficient to make the bird look plump and the opening fastened

17

with metal skewers or sewed together. Sew together skin at the neck or pull skin over breast and fasten with skewers.

Dust the stuffed bird with seasoned flour or fine crumbs and pat gently before placing breast down in a metal roasting rack fitted into roasting pan. The rack helps circulation of heat around every part of the bird during the roasting process and assures an even brown coat.

Geese and ducks are rubbed with garlic on the outer parts as well as inside.

If an uncovered roasting pan is used, with or without rack or trivet, no need for turning of bird will be required. Basting will not be necessary if oven temperature is maintained as indicated in the chart. No addition of water will be needed for basting.

If the skin of bird is very fat, prick with a fork in several places.

ROASTING CHART FOR POULTRY

CHICKEN AND DUCKS

Weight (Dressed, Drawn)	Oven Temperature	Approximate Time Per Pound
3 –4 lbs.	325° F. or gas mark 3	45–50 min.
4½–5 lbs.	325° F. or gas mark 3	45 min.
5 –6 lbs.	325° F. or gas mark 3	40 min.

GEESE

| 8–10 lbs. | 325° F. or gas mark 3 | 35 min. |
| 11 lbs. and over | 325° F. or gas mark 3 | 30 min. |

TURKEYS

| 10–15 lbs. | 300° F. or gas mark 1–2 | 20–25 min. |
| Over 18 lbs. | 300° F. or gas mark 1–2 | 15–18 min. |

STUFFING, TRUSSING AND ROASTING

Sew up at neck before stuffing or fasten skin over breast with small metal skewers or polished toothpicks. Fill the cavity lightly with desired dressing and sew up or fasten as at the neck. Bend wings under securely, tie legs together with string, and bring string around tail before tying close to body. Dusting the outer surface of stuffed bird just before placing it in the roasting pan helps to form a crisp, evenly browned roast. A V-shaped wire rack that fits into a roasting pan is recommended for roasting poultry breast-side down, ensuring juicier breast meat.

BRAISED CHICKEN (Basic Recipe)

A 5½- to 6-pound fowl, dressed | 1 clove garlic |
1 large onion, diced or sliced | 1 cup finely cut celery |
1 cup diced or sliced carrot | Flour for dredging |
Salt, pepper, paprika | 1 cup hot water

Section or disjoint dressed chicken. Rub each piece with garlic. Heat pot and braise a piece or two at a time until lightly browned on the surface. Remove braised chicken to a plate. Add onion, celery and carrot to pot. Return chicken after dredging with seasoned flour. Add hot water, cover and cook 10 minutes at moderate heat. Reduce heat and simmer 1½ hours approximately, or till the dark meat is tender and begins to leave the bone. Turn into a covered baking dish or casserole and add ½ cup hot water if necessary. Chicken must not be dry. Bake 30 minutes at 350° F. or gas mark 4.

Serves 6 to 8.

BRAISED CHICKEN (Pressure Cooker Method)

Follow same procedure for braising as in basic recipe, using the pressure pan over moderate heat. Return braised chicken pieces to pan without dredging with flour, but salt and pepper each piece lightly before adding to the vegetables in the pan. Add ½ cup cold water. Cover and adjust gauge to 15 pounds pressure and turn down heat when gauge begins to jiggle, as directed in instructions for your cooker. Cook 45 minutes approximately. Reduce pressure quickly under running cold water. Thicken gravy with flour and water paste if desired and cook 5 to 8 minutes on top of stove over moderate heat.

Note: If pressure cooker is used for preparation of the various chicken dishes, consult booklet for your particular type of cooker for procedure and cooking time.

CHICKEN PILAF

1 *cup rice, brown or white* | 2 *cups chicken stock or cold water* |
½ *teaspoon salt if water is used* | 1 *medium size onion, chopped or diced* |
2 *tablespoons schmaltz or vegetable shortening* |
2 *cups diced cooked chicken, white meat* | *Diced cooked gizzard* |
1 *cup tomato juice or thin sauce* | 4 *tablespoons hot melted schmaltz*

Rinse rice and drain. Cook in chicken stock or water in double boiler
until the liquid has been absorbed. The rice should be tender when
pressed between finger and thumb. Sauté onion in schmaltz and add
diced chicken and sliced gizzard as soon as light brown. Stir lightly
1 minute over moderate heat. Add cooked rice and tomato juice.
Turn into a well-greased pudding dish, topping with remaining hot
melted shortening. Bake 20 to 30 minutes at 350° F. or gas mark 4,
or till lightly browned on top.
Serves 4.

CHICKEN STUFFED APPLES

6 *large apples for baking* | 2 *cups crushed dry cereal* |
1 *cup finely diced cooked chicken (breast preferably)* |
3 *English walnuts, cut fine or chopped* | 1 *tablespoon sugar* | *Dash of salt* |
3 *tablespoons chicken schmaltz* | 1 *cup cold water* |
1 *tablespoon lemon or pineapple juice*

Wash apples and slice off stem ends. Remove cores with a coring
knife and scoop out as much of the apple as you can with a teaspoon.
Put cores and apple centres into a saucepan and add ¼ cup water.
Cover and stew till soft enough to put through a coarse strainer.
Reserve this pulp to add later. Combine crushed cereal with diced
chicken, nuts, sugar and salt, reserving 3 teaspoons of cereal for
topping. Fill cavities in apples with this mixture and place in a
shallow baking dish. Add apple pulp, schmaltz, remaining water and
fruit juice to pan. Bake 30 to 45 minutes at 350° F. or gas mark 4,
or till apples are tender. Baste once or twice with the sauce in the
pan. Top with cereal after removing from oven.
Serves 6.

CHICKEN CASSEROLE

A 5- to 5½-pound chicken, sectioned | 2 onions, diced |
1 green pepper, finely cut | 3 tablespoons schmaltz or vegetable shortening |
4 medium potatoes, sliced thin | 2 tablespoons flour | 1 teaspoon salt |
1 cup chicken soup or boiling water

Place chicken in casserole. Brown diced onion and green pepper in hot melted schmaltz and add. Cover with sliced potatoes, tucking around chicken. Sprinkle with flour and salt. Add liquid, cover and bake 1½ hours at 375° F. or gas mark 5. Uncover and leave in oven for 5 minutes before serving. Garnish with raw carrot curls, parsley and green pepper strips.

Serves 6 to 8.

Variation 1: Boiled chicken from which soup was prepared can be used in place of young poultry. Bake 45 minutes at 350° F. or gas mark 4.

Variation 2: Substitute 3 cups boiled rice for potatoes. Omit flour. Add 1 cup finely diced carrots and 1 cup fresh or quick frozen peas. Same procedure as in either basic recipe for uncooked chicken, or above variation for cooked chicken.

CREAMED CHICKEN ON TOAST

3 cups diced cooked chicken | 1 teaspoon onion juice or grated onion |
Dash of celery salt | Dash of powdered garlic | 1 tablespoon soy sauce |
3 tablespoons chicken schmaltz | 3 tablespoons flour | 1 cup chicken soup

Combine diced chicken with onion juice, celery salt, garlic powder and soy sauce. Heat schmaltz in a small frying pan and stir in flour till lightly browned. Add chicken soup, stirring till thick while cooking 3 to 5 minutes over moderate heat. Add chicken combination and cover for 5 minutes or till warm enough to serve. Do not stir. Serve on toast points.

Serves 3 or 4.

CHICKEN WITH DUMPLINGS (Pressure Cooker Method)

A 4½- to 5-pound chicken | 1 onion, diced | 1½ cups cold water |
1 cup shredded carrot | ½ cup finely diced celery | ½ teaspoon salt |
Dash of paprika (optional)

DUMPLINGS

*1½ cups sifted flour | 2 teaspoons baking soda | ½ teaspoon salt |
3 tablespoons shortening | Dash of nutmeg | 4 tablespoons water*

Section chicken or cut into serving portions. Heat a heavy frying pan and sear chicken pieces on all sides. No other fat is required. Add diced onion and stir till onion is light yellow, stirring with chicken while pan is over moderate heat. Or, sear chicken and onion in pressure cooker pan. Add the other ingredients listed and cook under 10 pounds pressure 40 minutes. Reduce pressure quickly under running cold water. Add dumplings and adjust cover and gauge. Return to moderate heat for 5 minutes.
Serves 6.

Dumplings

Combine dry ingredients listed and cut in shortening. Add water and mix with a fork to form a light dough that will drop from a spoon. Drop from a tablespoon into pot on top of chicken and proceed as directed for cooking.

CHICKEN WITH DUMPLINGS (Top-of-Stove Method)

For top-of-stove cooking, follow directions as in previous recipe except that a heavy deep pot is used. Increase water to 3 cups and cook over moderate heat, tightly covered, 1½ hours or till chicken is tender. Add dumplings. Cover and simmer 15 minutes.

CHICKEN FRICASSÉE

*A 4½- to 5-pound chicken | 4 tablespoons flour | 1 teaspoon salt (optional) |
4 tablespoons chicken schmaltz | 1 quart water (hot if fowl is used) |
1 onion | 1 carrot, diced | 1 small turnip, diced*

Section chicken. Dredge with flour and brown lightly in hot melted schmaltz. Add water gradually. Add vegetables, cover and simmer 1½ to 2 hours or till tender. Lift out chicken. Put gravy and vegetables through a strainer. Mashing vegetables thickens gravy. Or, make an einbren (see Index) for thickening and add to strained gravy, cooking 5 minutes or till thick. Use strained vegetables for garnish. Combine gravy with chicken and simmer 10 minutes.

Serves 5 or 6.

Variation 1 : Add 3 beaten egg yolks to strained gravy and cook 3 to 5 minutes over moderate heat, stirring till smooth.

Variation 2 : Substitute 1 cup canned or stewed tomatoes for an equal amount of water in cooking chicken. Add 1 cup diced celery and ½ cup diced green pepper, with the other vegetables. Mash vegetables through strainer and omit other thickening.

CHICKEN AND NOODLES

A 5½- to 6-pound fowl, cooked | 4 tablespoons schmaltz or vegetable shortening |
1 large onion, diced | 4 cups cooked broad noodles |
½ teaspoon paprika | 2 tablespoons minced parsley

Remove fat and skin from cooked chicken that has been used for making soup. Melt schmaltz and brown onion in it. Add cooked noodles that have been drained and rinsed with hot water, stirring with the onions 2 to 3 minutes. Combine chicken and noodles and sprinkle with paprika. Turn into a baking dish or casserole. Cover and bake 30 minutes at 375° F. or gas mark 5. Uncover and let brown in top of oven for 10 minutes or under grill for 2 minutes. Garnish with parsley.

Serves 8.

CHICKEN PAPRIKA WITH RICE

1 large onion, diced | 4 tablespoons schmaltz |
A 4½- to 5-pound chicken, sectioned | 2 tablespoons flour |
¼ teaspoon salt | Boiling water | 1 cup uncooked rice | 1 teaspoon salt |
Dash of garlic salt | ½ teaspoon paprika

Sauté onion in hot melted shortening till light brown. Dredge sections of chicken in flour seasoned with ¼ teaspoon salt. Brown each piece in pan in which onion has been cooked, pushing onion to one side. Add boiling water to cover, adding a little at a time. Add rinsed rice and seasoning, cover tightly and simmer 1½ hours. Turn into a casserole or baking pan and bake 30 minutes at 325° F. or gas

mark 3. It should have absorbed all the gravy and be lightly browned on top. The rice should be puffed and brown.
Serves 6.

CHICKEN CACCIATORE

2 frying chickens (2 pounds each) | ⅓ cup olive or salad oil |
2 onions, finely diced | 1 large green pepper, chopped |
1 large clove garlic, minced | 3 medium size fresh tomatoes, skinned and diced |
1½ cups canned tomato soup | 3 tablespoons white wine or cider |
1 teaspoon salt | Dash of white pepper | ⅛ teaspoon paprika

Cut chickens into serving portions. Pat each piece dry with a paper towel. Heat oil and brown chicken on both sides. Add onions, pepper and garlic and stir till nicely browned. Add tomatoes, tomato soup, wine and seasonings. Simmer ½ hour or till chicken is tender. Serve with the sauce poured over chicken.
Serves 6.

STEWED CHICKEN (Basic Recipe)

A 5½- to 6-pound fowl | 4 tablespoons flour | ½ teaspoon salt |
Dash of pepper | 4 tablespoons diced onion | 4 tablespoons schmaltz |
1 large carrot, diced | 1 parsnip, diced | 1 green pepper, minced |
2 cups soup or boiling water

Section the fowl or cut into serving portions. Dredge each piece with flour seasoned with salt and pepper. Lightly brown onion in hot melted schmaltz in pot in which chicken is to be stewed. Add chicken, vegetables and soup or water. Cover and simmer 2 to 3 hours or till tender.
Serves 8.

Pressure Cooker Method: Follow same procedure but reduce liquid by half. Cook 45 minutes at 15 pounds pressure.

Variation 1: Add 1 cup dried limas that have been soaked 2 hours in cold water to cover, and cook as in basic recipe.

Variation 2: Omit carrot, parsnip and green pepper. Add lima beans as in Variation 1 and ½ cup brown sugar or ¼ cup honey. Same procedure.

CHICKEN POT PIE (Basic Recipe)

2 tablespoons schmaltz in casserole, heated | A 4-pound chicken, cooked |
1 cup diced carrot | ½ cup diced celery | 1 finely sliced onion |
1 diced green pepper | 1 diced parsnip (optional) |
½ cup fresh or canned mushrooms (optional) | ¼ teaspoon salt |
2 tablespoons fine matzo crumbs | 1 pie pastry (see Index for recipe) |

Use soup chicken, including giblets, or other cooked chicken. Cut into sections or remove from bones in large pieces. Add vegetables and chicken to greased casserole. Dust with salt and cracker crumbs. Cover with rolled out pie pastry and press down around edges firmly. With the tines of a fork prick pastry at top and mark the edges. Bake in a preheated oven 45 minutes at 325° F. or gas mark 3, or till crust is nicely browned.
Serves 4.

TCHULAMA (Rumanian or Turkish equivalent of Chicken à la King)

1 cooked chicken (from soup) | 1 onion, thinly sliced | 1 green pepper, diced |
1½ cups sliced fresh mushrooms | 3 tablespoons chicken schmaltz |
3 tablespoons flour | Dash of salt and pepper | 1 cup chicken soup | Parsley

Section cooked chicken in serving portions. Combine onion, green pepper and mushrooms and sauté in hot melted schmaltz. Sprinkle with flour, stir till vegetables are coated and begin to become tender. Add salt and pepper and stir in chicken soup. Cook 5 minutes. Add chicken, cover and cook 10 minutes over moderate heat. Serve on toast, with mashed potatoes or steamed rice. Garnish with parsley and cooked carrot lifted from soup, or add a dash of paprika in place of carrot.
Serves 5 to 6.

OTHER POULTRY

ROASTED FRUIT-STUFFED DUCKLING

A 4- to 4½-pound duckling, drawn and dressed | 2 cloves garlic |
2 cups grated tart apple | 12 to 18 large pitted prunes |
4 tablespoons dry bread crumbs | 1 egg | 2 tablespoons brown sugar |
Dash of salt, after tasting dressing

After preparing duckling for roasting (see *Preparation of Poultry*), rub inside and outer skin with cut garlic. Combine dressing by mixing ingredients in the order listed, adding salt if desired after tasting. Fill cavity and sew together or close with metal skewers or toothpicks. Dust lightly with flour seasoned with paprika if desired. Roast in preheated oven, allowing 40 minutes per pound of duck. If the neck has been stuffed (see Stuffed Helzel), it should be roasted along with the duck. Place the duck breast-side up on a wire rack or trivet inside roasting pan. If the duckling is fat and melted fat collects in bottom of pan, spoon out once or twice during roasting process. A duckling need not be basted or turned if roasted on a rack. An even brown surface is most desirable and can be achieved by keeping the oven temperature at 325° F. or gas mark 3 until taken from the oven.

Serves 5.

CASSEROLE OF DUCK AND ORANGE

A 4- to 4½-pound duckling | 2 tablespoons flour |
3 large seedless oranges, sliced | 1 cup orange juice |
2 tablespoons lemon juice

Cut duck into serving portions or section at joints and cut breast and back. Dust each piece with flour and arrange in a casserole. Tuck orange slices between parts and over top. Add orange juice, and lemon juice sprinkled over top. Roast at 325° F. or gas mark 3, allowing 40 minutes per pound.

Serves 4 to 5.

DUCKLING WITH A BLUSH

A 4½- to 5½-pound duckling, prepared and disjointed | 2 cloves garlic |
3 tablespoons flour | ⅛ teaspoon each celery salt, onion salt, paprika |
3 tablespoons chicken schmaltz or other shortening |
2 cups stewed fresh cranberries or 1 tall can whole cranberry sauce

Rub each piece of duck with garlic. Combine flour and seasoning. Roll each piece of duck with flour mixture till well coated. Melt fat in bottom of casserole and add duck pieces. Top with cranberry sauce, cover and bake 45 to 50 minutes per pound at 325° F. or gas mark 3.

Serves 5 to 6.

MOCK DUCK

Most families want more dressing out of the roasted chicken, duck, goose, or even turkey. Prepare a double recipe of dressing the next time you roast poultry of any kind and follow these directions:

Cut the skin carefully across breastbone and back. Cut under each wing through the joint next to the body, and pull wings and skin loose from body and over neck bone. Be careful not to break the skin at any point. Sew up the neck end and fill with dressing. Sew up the large opening and pat with both hands to distribute the dressing inside the Mock Duck. Roast with skinned poultry.

> *Variation 1:* To make this the main dish, surround with meat balls prepared as for Hamburgers. Bake 45 minutes at 325° F. or gas mark 3 in a covered pan, uncover and continue roasting 45 minutes or till nicely browned.
>
> *Variation 2:* Arrange Mock Duck and meat balls on a bed of thinly sliced onions. Bake as in Variation 1. Add sliced or diced, carrots, parsnips, potatoes. Cover and proceed with baking 20 minutes. Uncover and bake till brown.

ROAST GOOSE-IN-A-BLANKET

To roast a goose after skinning it and removing inside soft fat, it is necessary to give it a protective covering during the baking process, in order to prevent dryness of the breast meat.

After preparing the goose by removing all feathers, singeing it, soaking and salting in accordance with Laws of Kashrut (see *Kosher Kitchen Questions and Answers*), cut off the heavy layers of skin and fat and cut fat into small pieces. Reserve neck skin for stuffing, separately.

Rub the inside cavity of goose as well as the outside with plenty of garlic. Stuff with dressing and place the trussed goose in roasting pan. Make a 'blanket' as follows, of thinly rolled biscuit dough:

Biscuit Dough

*2½ cups sifted flour, sifted again with 1 teaspoon salt and
1 teaspoon baking powder | 3 tablespoons rendered goose schmaltz |
¼ cup ice water (approximately)*

Sift together dry ingredients and cut in schmaltz. Add ice water to make a dough stiff enough to pat or roll out to ½-inch thickness or thinner if desired. Cover the goose breast, tucking around and under the body. With the tines of a fork prick the 'blanket' in any design.

It is ready for the oven and should be baked or roasted in an open pan at 325° F. or gas mark 3, allowing 30 minutes to the pound, if 11 pounds or over (see *Roasting Chart for Poultry* for goose under 10 pounds). Brush with fat that collects in the pan several times during the baking period. (Excess fat in the pan cannot be used for Passover schmaltz.)

STEWED GOOSE (After Skinning)

Cut goose wings and legs from body. Cut up breast and back into serving portions. Rub each part with garlic and dredge with flour. Proceed as for Stewed Chicken, basic recipe or variations (see Index), allowing 30 minutes per pound for top of stove cooking.

If using *Pressure Cooker Method*, consult book of instructions for your type of cooker for time and pressure per pound.

Sauce

*Gravy (from stewed goose) | 1 tablespoon wine for each cup gravy |
1 tablespoon cider vinegar for each cup gravy | 2 tablespoons flour |
2 tablespoons hot melted goose fat | Brown sugar to taste |
Dash of cinnamon or nutmeg*

For a piquant sauce, strain the vegetables from the gravy. Add wine and cider vinegar to gravy in the required proportions. Make an einbren by stirring the flour into the hot melted shortening. Stir in gravy while cooking till thick. Add sugar and cinnamon or nutmeg. Serve hot in a gravy boat or add to goose meat and cook 2 to 3 minutes before serving.

POULTRY DRESSINGS

BREAD CRUMB DRESSING (Basic Recipe)

1 *large onion, diced* | 4 *tablespoons chicken schmaltz* |
3 *stalks celery, diced fine* | ½ *large green pepper, diced fine* |
½ *cup shredded carrot* | ½ *cup thinly sliced fresh or canned mushrooms* |
3 *cups grated stale chola or other bread* | 2 *eggs* |
½ *teaspoon powdered garlic* | 1 *teaspoon salt* |
Dash of ginger, paprika and white pepper

Sauté onion in hot melted schmaltz for 2 minutes before adding celery, green pepper and carrot. Stir while cooking over moderate heat 5 minutes. Add bread crumbs and mushrooms and stir for 1 minute over increased heat. Beat eggs in a bowl. Add the cooked mixture in frying pan and stir well. Add seasoning as soon as cool. If the mixture is too dry, ½ cup of hot water or chicken soup may be added, stirring well.

Yields an amount sufficient for stuffing a 5½- to 6-pound fowl. For stuffing turkey or large goose, double amounts of all ingredients.

Variation 1: Add ½ cup finely cut dry prunes to basic dressing.

Variation 2: Add ½ cup thinly sliced or diced apple and a dash of cinnamon or nutmeg, 1 tablespoon lemon juice, 2 tablespoons sugar.

Variation 3: Add ½ cup diced roasted chestnuts to basic dressing and/or variations.

WHOLE WHEAT CRUMBS DRESSING (Basic Recipe)

3½ *to* 4 *cups dry crumbs of whole wheat bread* | 1 *large onion, finely diced* |
4 *tablespoons chicken schmaltz, melted* | ½ *cup finely diced celery* |
½ *cup sliced fresh mushrooms* | 1 *teaspoon salt* |
½ *teaspoon powdered garlic (optional)* | ⅛ *teaspoon paprika* | 2 *eggs*

Dry crumbs should be kept in the heated oven with door open while preparing the other ingredients. Sauté onion in hot fat till nicely browned. Add celery and mushrooms and stir 1 to 2 minutes over moderate heat. Put dry bread crumbs into a bowl, add sautéed vegetables and fat. Stir in seasonings. Add eggs and mix well. Yields an amount sufficient for stuffing a 5- to 6-pound chicken. Double recipe for stuffing a large goose or turkey.

CHESTNUT DRESSING FOR POULTRY

6 to 8 slices of stale bread | 1 large onion, diced |
3 tablespoons schmaltz or vegetable shortening |
1 cup sliced roasted chestnuts or ½ pound boiled chestnuts | 2 eggs |
Salt to taste | 1 tablespoon sugar | ¼ cup dry bread crumbs |
¼ cup chicken soup

Soak bread in cold water to cover. Squeeze dry. Brown diced onion in hot melted shortening and add soaked bread. Stir with onions over moderate heat 5 to 10 minutes. Add sliced chestnuts or put boiled chestnuts through a coarse sieve and stir in. Add slightly beaten eggs, salt to taste, sugar and dry crumbs. Moisten with soup stock. When cool, stuff into cavity of chicken or duck.

Yields an amount sufficient for a 5½- to 6-pound chicken.

If any dressing remains after stuffing a duck, make balls of dressing and add to roasting pan after pouring off fat. Continue to roast until browned.

Double the listed ingredients for 18-pound turkey.

Increase by one half the listed ingredients for goose.

FRIED CROUTON DRESSING WITH GIBLETS

8 slices of stale bread (white or wholewheat) |
4 tablespoons hot melted shortening | 1 large onion, diced or sliced fine |
Giblets chopped or thinly sliced (cooked gizzard, heart, grilled liver) |
1 teaspoon poultry seasoning | 1 cup soup stock

Cut sliced bread into cubes and sauté in hot melted shortening till lightly browned. Lift out to a bowl, using a perforated spoon. Add onion to remaining fat in pan and stir till lightly browned. Add chopped giblets and stir 3 minutes over moderate heat. Combine all ingredients by tossing lightly in pan or bowl. Sprinkle with poultry seasoning and moisten with soup stock.

Yields an amount sufficient for a 6-pound chicken or duck.

NOODLE DRESSING

2½ cups boiled broad noodles | 2 eggs | ¼ cup dry bread or matzo crumbs |
1 onion, diced | 2 tablespoons hot melted chicken schmaltz |
Salt and pepper to taste | 2 tablespoons minced parsley

Combine cooked noodles, eggs and crumbs. Brown diced onion in fat and add. Season with salt and pepper. Add parsley.
Yields amount sufficient for a 5½- to 6-pound chicken or duck.

POTATO DRESSING (For 16-Pound Turkey)

7 cups cooked mashed sweet potato | 1 cup dry bread crumbs | 2 eggs |
1 tablespoon grated rind of lemon or orange | ¼ cup juice of either fruit |
1 teaspoon poultry seasoning (optional) |

Combine in the order listed as soon as mashed potato is cool.
Variation 1: Add 1 cup thinly sliced prunes.
Variation 2: Add 2 grated tart apples to basic dressing. Omit poultry seasoning and add ¼ cup sugar and 1 teaspoon cinnamon.
Variation 3: Combine 2 cups mashed white potatoes with 5 cups mashed sweet potatoes and beat well till smooth. Combine with fruit as in Variation 2.

RAISIN AND RICE DRESSING (For Goose or Turkey)

3 cups parboiled long grain rice | 2 cups dry bread crumbs | 3 eggs |
1 cup diced onions | ½ cup chicken or goose schmaltz |
½ cup seedless raisins, plumped | 2 tablespoons flour |
1 teaspoon salt | 2 tablespoons sugar

Drain parboiled rice. Combine with crumbs and eggs. Cook onions in hot melted fat till light brown. Plump raisins by placing them in a soup strainer over boiling water for 10 minutes. Roll raisins in flour. Combine all, taste and add salt and sugar.

Gefilte Helzel (Stuffed Neck). Chicken, duck, goose or turkey neck skins may be stuffed and either roasted with the bird or prepared separately. A stuffed chicken neck may be cooked with Tzimmes, baked with Kasha, Nahit, etc. (see Index).

GEFILTE HELZEL (Basic Recipe)

1 *cup flour | ⅛ teaspoon salt | ¼ cup chopped uncooked chicken fat or melted shortening | 2 tablespoons grated onion | Dash of nutmeg (optional)*

Combine all ingredients listed. Sew up the small end of chicken neck and fill ¾ full. Sew up other end. Wash with cold water then pour boiling water over. This will bring a smoothness to skin. Cook with other food or place in roasting pan with the bird. Remove thread at both ends before slicing for serving.

For stuffing the necks of geese or turkey, double or triple the amount of ingredients according to size of neck skin.

OTHER HELZEL STUFFINGS

Bread Crumb : Substitute dry crumbs for flour. Add salt. Brown diced onion in hot melted shortening. Combine and stir the crumbs till saturated with fat. Add ⅛ teaspoon mixed herbs (poultry seasoning).

Chestnut and Crumb : Add 3 roasted chestnuts, finely cut or mashed, to basic recipe or Bread Crumb Stuffing. Substitute a dash of cinnamon for nutmeg or poultry seasoning.

Almond and Greben : To either basic or Bread Crumb recipe add 1 tablespoon slivered almonds and 1 tablespoon finely chopped greben.

Turkish Stuffing for Turkey Neck : To basic recipe (in required quantity) add ¼ cup chopped almonds or walnuts. Add hardcooked eggs end to end after filling the neck an inch, pushing the dressing in around each egg. Fill the last inch of neck with dressing and sew up. Slice diagonally when serving. A cut of egg will be in the centre of each slice.

17 Sauces for Meats, Poultry, Fish and Vegetables

Note: Replace butter with schmaltz or a pareve shortening in any sauce to be used with meat.

BARBECUE SAUCE

½ cup vegetable shortening | 2 tablespoons finely chopped onion |
1 medium green pepper, chopped | 2 tablespoons Worcestershire sauce |
2 tablespoons chili sauce | ½ cup hot water | ½ teaspoon salt |
¼ cup vinegar or lemon juice | 1 tablespoon brown sugar |
1 tablespoon cornflour and 2 tablespoons cold water | Dash of cayenne

Melt shortening in frying pan and sauté onion and pepper 2 minutes or till tender. Add the other ingredients except cornflour and cayenne. Cook over moderate heat 3 to 5 minutes, stirring once or twice. Dissolve cornflour with cold water, add cayenne and stir into hot sauce. Cook 5 minutes or till clear gravy results.

Yields approximately 1½ cups.

CREOLE SAUCE

2 medium onions, sliced or diced | 2 medium green peppers, diced fine |
2 tablespoons shortening | 2 tablespoons flour |
½ cup thinly sliced fresh mushrooms | 2 large tomatoes, skinned or ½ cup purée |
¼ teaspoon salt | Dash of pepper |
1 teaspoon prepared mustard or horse-radish

Brown onions and peppers in hot melted shortening. Stir in flour. Add remaining ingredients except mustard. Cook over moderate heat 5 minutes and add 1 cup hot water and mustard. Stir 1 minute and remove from heat.

Yields 2 to 2½ cups.

MINT SAUCE

½ cup chopped fresh mint leaves | ½ cup cider vinegar, heated | 2 tablespoons brown sugar

Combine and cover. Keep in a warm place to steep 20 to 30 minutes before serving. Vinegar may be diluted with hot water to make a weaker infusion.

Yields approximately ¾ cup.

Variation: Mint Sauce may be thickened by mixing 1 teaspoon cornflour with 1 tablespoon cold water and adding to hot vinegar. Cook 3 to 5 minutes before combining with mint and sugar. Serve hot.

PAN GRAVY (Basic Recipe)

4 tablespoons schmaltz or vegetable shortening | 4 tablespoons flour | 2 cups beef or chicken soup | ¼ teaspoon salt | ⅛ teaspoon paprika

Melt shortening in a frying pan. Stir in flour till deep brown. Stir in soup gradually till thickened. Cook 5 minutes over moderate heat. Add salt and paprika.

Yields 2 cups.

Variation 1: Add chopped chicken giblets that have been cooked in chicken soup.

Variation 2: Add ¼ cup finely chopped greben to basic recipe.

Variation 3: Add 1 tablespoon grated onion or onion juice. Cook 1 minute longer with basic recipe or variations.

MUSHROOM SAUCE

Add 1 cup thinly sliced fresh mushrooms to Pan Gravy or variations. Cook 5 to 10 minutes. If using canned mushrooms, cook 3 minutes. Yields 2½ cups.

TOMATO SAUCE

2½ cups stewed or canned tomato | 1 cup finely diced celery |
2 tablespoons grated onion | ½ teaspoon salt |
2 tablespoons hot melted shortening | 2 tablespoons flour |
1 tablespoon lemon juice | 1 tablespoon brown sugar |
½ teaspoon soy or Worcestershire sauce

Cook the first 4 ingredients over moderate heat till celery is tender, stirring occasionally. Put through a sieve. Brown flour in hot melted shortening and stir in tomato mixture, lemon juice, sugar and soy sauce. Stir till smooth over moderate heat approximately 10 minutes or till smooth.
Yields 2 cups.

EMERGENCY TOMATO SAUCE

1 can tomato soup | ¼ cup hot water |
1 tablespoon soy or Worcestershire sauce | 1 tablespoon lemon juice or vinegar |
1 tablespoon brown sugar | Dash of salt and pepper

Combine and bring to a boil, stirring till sugar is dissolved.
Yields 1½ cups.

EGG SAUCE

½ cup melted butter | 1 tablespoon lemon juice | 1 egg yolk |
Salt and pepper to taste | 1 tablespoon minced parsley

Melt butter in saucepan, stir in lemon juice and egg yolk. Add seasoning and parsley or chopped green onions for garnish. Add to 1 cup medium White Sauce. Stir.
Variation: Add 2 finely chopped hard-cooked eggs and omit egg yolk.

LEMON-BUTTER SAUCE

3 tablespoons butter, melted | 3 tablespoons lemon juice |
½ teaspoon grated lemon rind | 1 tablespoon brown sugar |
Dash of salt and pepper | 1 tablespoon minced parsley

Combine by stirring well in a saucepan after butter has melted. Serve with fish or vegetables.

HOLLANDAISE SAUCE

2 egg yolks | ½ cup butter or margarine | 1 tablespoon lemon juice | ¼ teaspoon salt | Dash of cayenne | ½ cup boiling water

Add egg yolks one at a time to melted butter in top of double boiler over hot water, blending each thoroughly. Add lemon juice. Cook over hot water till thick stirring constantly till smooth. Just before serving add seasoning and boiling water gradually, stirring and beating constantly to keep consistency smooth.

Yields ¾ cup.

Variation 1: Stir in gradually 1 tablespoon sherry just before serving.

Variation 2: Blend in a little anchovy paste for fish salad.

Note: Should Hollandaise Sauce separate, beat in more lemon juice and 1 or 2 tablespoons boiling water drop by drop, stirring till smooth.

MOCK HOLLANDAISE SAUCE

2 egg yolks | 2 tablespoons butter | 1 teaspoon cornflour | ½ cup lemon juice | ¼ teaspoon salt | ¼ teaspoon paprika or dash of cayenne

Beat egg yolks light. Blend butter and cornflour with lemon juice, salt, paprika and combine. Cook over boiling water, till thick and smooth, stirring constantly.

Yields 1 to 1¼ cups.

ONION SAUCE

4 large boiled onions | 2 tablespoons minced parsley | Salt and pepper to taste | 1 cup thin white sauce

Mash cooked onions through a strainer. Add other ingredients as listed. Serve with fish or vegetables.

Yields 2 cups.
Variation: Substitute finely cut chives or green onion tops for parsley.

WHITE SAUCE (Basic Recipe—Milchig)

2 tablespoons butter | 1 tablespoon flour | 1 cup milk |
¼ teaspoon salt | Dash of white pepper

Melt butter in saucepan over low heat. Blend in flour but do not brown. Add milk gradually, stirring till smooth. Cook 3 minutes. This makes a sauce thin enough to pour over or cook with vegetables.
Yields 1 cup.
Variations:
Medium White Sauce can be made by doubling the amount of flour and using part cream, or ¾ cup evaporated milk and ¼ cup water. Use for creamed vegetables, fish and scalloped dishes.
Thick White Sauce can be made by blending 4 tablespoons butter with 4 tablespoons flour. Add 1 cup milk or ¾ cup evaporated milk.
Cheese Sauce can be made by adding ¼ to 1 cup grated cheese to either Medium or Thick White Sauce. Season with celery salt or onion salt and use with vegetables, fish and egg dishes.
Curry Sauce can be made by adding 1 teaspoon curry powder to Medium White Sauce. ⅛ teaspoon garlic salt or powdered garlic and/or ½ teaspoon minced onion may be added.
Caper Sauce can be made by adding 1 tablespoon capers to basic recipe or variations.
Brown Sauce can be made by melting butter until brown, blend in flour. Stir till as brown as desired. Do not scorch. Proceed as in basic recipe. For meat meals, substitute vegetable shortening, chicken fat or oil for butter, and thin out with soup stock or gravy.
Lemon Sauce can be made by adding 1 teaspoon lemon juice to basic recipe for White Sauce.

18 Vegetables

Because vegetables, whether fresh, quick frozen or canned, constitute a group of edibles essential to our daily diet for good health, we serve them in addition to meats, poultry, fish, eggs and dairy products. They contain valuable mineral salts and vitamins. These elements must not be destroyed in preparation.

Pressure-cooked vegetables retain vitamins. Long cooking is wrong cooking for all except starchy vegetables. Use as many un-cooked vegetables as possible. Here is a list of those which can be eaten raw in salads or as garnish:

Cabbage	Cucumber	Parsley
Carrots	Dandelion Greens	Radishes
Cauliflower	Dill	(all varieties)
Celery (stalks and leaves)	Endive	Scallions
Celery Cabbage	Fennel or Finocchi (bulb & tender tops)	Spinach
(Chinese Cabbage)	Lettuce (all varieties)	Tomatoes
Celeriac (Celery Root)	Mint Leaves	Turnips
Chicory (Curly Endive)	Onions (green, yellow or Spanish)	Watercress
Chives		

Leftover Vegetables. In order to make up for the nutritive value that has been lost, left-over cooked vegetables may be combined with milk, cheese, eggs, butter or vegetable shortening in the form of sauces.

Appeal to both taste and eye as well as additional variations may be achieved by the use of sauces. See Chapter 17 for the sauces, both milchig and fleishig, which may be added to the vegetables.

ARTICHOKES

Soak artichokes, stems up, in salted cold water at least 10 minutes. Drain and plunge into boiling salted water to cover. Cook covered 30 to 45 minutes, depending on size. They are done when a tooth-pick will easily pierce the stem end. Drain and serve hot with melted butter, mayonnaise or Hollandaise sauce, or serve plain.

Allow one medium artichoke per serving, or cut large one into halves through stem. The leaves are dipped into the sauce and only the tender inside layer of pulp is eaten. The fuzzy part near the stem is called the 'choke' and is discarded.

JERUSALEM ARTICHOKES

These vegetables are very unlike the other artichokes. They are edible roots that look like small clusters of new potatoes. Italians call it *girasole*, but it must have been some early American Puritan colonist who named it Jerusalem Artichoke. If you have to combat a starch allergy or plan a diabetic diet, this starch-free vegetable will be of great help.

Wash, scrape and boil, in very little salted water, till tender. Drain. Add butter or grated cheese. Or cream with a white sauce made of butter, flour and milk or vegetable liquid (see Sauces).

ASPARAGUS (Basic Recipe)

Cut away hard, fibrous part of stalks. Tie together and place in a tall covered pot, or use top of double boiler. Add about $\frac{1}{2}$ cup of boiling water and $\frac{1}{2}$ teaspoon salt. Cover and cook over moderate heat 8 to 10 minutes. Allow 3 to 5 tips per serving, depending on size.

Variation 1: Serve with hot melted butter poured over tips.

Variation 2: Cover with Hollandaise sauce or cream sauce.

Variation 3: Serve plain with meat or poultry. Or add chicken fat or meat gravy to thickened vegetable liquid.

CREAMED ASPARAGUS ON TOAST

Steam tips of asparagus as in basic recipe. Make a cream sauce, using the vegetable liquid and milk, add grated cheese and asparagus tips just before serving on toast points. Dust with paprika or minced parsley.

Variation: Place 3 or 4 steamed asparagus tips on toast and cover with sliced hard-cooked eggs. Top with cream sauce and a dash of paprika.

STEAMED GREEN BEANS

1 *pound beans* | ½ *cup water* | ¼ *teaspoon salt* | 2 *tablespoons butter*

Wash. Cut beans slantwise or lengthwise. Cook in pressure cooker, or cook in top of double boiler without additional water until steamed through and tender. Or cook in a well-covered saucepan with a little water 5 to 8 minutes. Season with salt and butter before serving.

Serves 6.

Variation 1: Add Creole sauce after beans are tender. Simmer 3 minutes and serve hot.

Variation 2: Add thick white sauce and top with grated cheese and a dash of paprika.

Variation 3: Add canned tomato sauce or stewed tomatoes, season with lemon juice and brown sugar, simmer 5 minutes and serve hot or cold.

Variation 4: Combine with steamed brown rice, season with butter and grated Cheddar cheese.

Variation 5: Add browned sliced onions and green peppers.

SPICED GREEN BEANS

1 *pound green beans* | 2 *tablespoons vinegar or lemon juice* |
Brown sugar to taste | 1 *clove garlic* | 1 *bay leaf* | *Dash of allspice*

Cut beans diagonally or lengthwise. Cook in very little water 5 minutes, in a covered saucepan. Add the other ingredients, cook 3 minutes longer. Remove garlic and bay leaf. Serve hot or cold. Excellent with cold meats or fish.

Serves 6 to 8.

BEETS (Basic Recipe)

Scrub beets well after removing tops 2 inches from root. Cook beets of uniform size in cold water to cover, adding ½ teaspoon salt to 1 quart of water. The smaller the beets the less time it takes for boiling till tender enough to pierce with a toothpick. Drain and use beet liquid for borsht. Slip skins from beets, cut away stems and slice or dice. Add butter and serve hot.

Variation 1: Add 1 tablespoon prepared horse-radish. Omit butter.

Variation 2: Add 1 tablespoon lemon juice or vinegar for each cup sliced beets, 1 tablespoon sugar and 1 tablespoon flour or corn-flour. Cook 3 to 5 minutes without stirring but shaking the saucepan to prevent scorching. Add butter or other shortening and serve hot. Known as Harvard beets in America.

CREAMED MASHED BEETS

3 cups cooked, mashed beets | 1 tablespoon lemon juice | ½ teaspoon salt | ½ cup heavy cream or sour cream | ½ cup crumbs | 1 tablespoon butter

Cooked or canned beets, drained, put through the sieve may be used. Add lemon juice and salt, fold in sour cream or stiffly beaten heavy cream. Top with crumbs and dot with butter. Slip under grill to brown lightly and serve hot.

Serves 4.

GINGER BEETS

1 tablespoon flour | 1 tablespoon shortening | ½ cup beet liquid |
2 cups cooked beets, cut in strips | 1 tablespoon lemon juice or vinegar |
2 tablespoons brown sugar | ¼ teaspoon salt | 1 teaspoon ground ginger |
¼ teaspoon dry mustard (optional)

Blend flour and shortening and brown lightly. Add beet liquid and stir till smooth. Add the other ingredients. Cook 3 to 5 minutes. Fine with lamb, veal or fish meals.

Serves 5 or 6.

BEET TOPS (Important part nutritionally!)

Wash leaves and stems thoroughly in cold water. Drain. Cut into inch pieces. Cook without additional water in a well-covered pot 5 minutes. Add ⅛ teaspoon salt to each cupful, 1 tablespoon butter, oil or schmaltz, 2 tablespoons dry bread or matzo crumbs. Toss lightly. Serve hot.

Variation: Add 1 tablespoon brown sugar and 2 tablespoons mild vinegar to above. Cook 2 minutes over moderate heat. Garnish with diced hard-cooked egg.

BROCCOLI (Basic Recipe)

2 pounds broccoli | 1 teaspoon salt | 1 small onion

Remove fibrous section of stems. Wash and drain well. Cover with cold water and let stand 10 minutes before cooking. Pour off half the water, add salt and onion, boil 20 minutes in a well-covered pot. Drain when ready to serve.
Serves 6.
Variation 1: Add Hollandaise sauce and a dash of paprika.
Variation 2: Serve with cheese sauce and garnish with parsley.

BROCCOLI FLORETS

*1 onion | 1 clove garlic | 2 tablespoons oil or vegetable shortening |
3 pounds broccoli | 1 teaspoon salt | 2 tablespoons lemon juice |
1 cup water*

Use tender parts of stems with the flower or head. Cut stems into ¼-inch rounds, and separate the heads into florets. Brown diced onion and garlic in shortening. Remove the garlic. Add broccoli, salt and lemon juice and water. Cover and simmer 15 to 20 minutes. Garnish with boiled or roasted chestnuts.
Serves 6 to 8.

BOILED NEW CABBAGE

Remove wilted outer leaves, cut into quarters or eighths through the core. Soak 5 minutes in cold water to which salt has been added so that any insects may be drawn out. Drain. Add 1 cup cold water to 2 pounds of cabbage, and 1 teaspoon salt. Cover and cook 5 minutes, or till tender. Cabbage that is not overcooked is most digestible. Add melted butter or margarine just before serving, and serve hot.

CREAMED NEW CABBAGE (Milchig)

Pour hot white sauce (see Sauces) over drained cooked cabbage, add a dash of grated cheese and a sprinkling of paprika.

HEALTH CABBAGE

Grate or shred cabbage, allowing 1 cupful per serving. Melt 1 tablespoon butter in a heavy frying pan for each cupful of cabbage. Add grated cabbage, season with salt and grated onion to taste. Stir 5 minutes till steamed through. Serve at once. This loses flavour if cooked too long or allowed to stand overlong before serving.

CABBAGE IN SOUR CREAM

1 *medium head cabbage (3 to 3½ pounds)* | ½ *cup cold water* |
2 *cups sour cream* | 2 *tablespoons butter* | ½ *cup flour* |
½ *cup mild vinegar* | ½ *cup sugar* | *Salt to taste*

Shred cabbage and add water. Cook in frying pan for 5 minutes. Drain off excess liquid. Add sour cream and butter. Blend flour, vinegar and sugar and stir in. Cook 3 minutes longer. Add salt.
Serves 6.

GLAZED CARROTS

6 *medium carrots* | ½ *cup brown sugar* | 3 *tablespoons butter*

Scrape carrots. Cut into thin rounds or quarter lengthwise. Parboil in enough salted water to prevent sticking. Drain. Reserve liquid. Add butter, sugar and bake 25 to 30 minutes at 350° F. or gas mark 4, basting with the liquid till glazed.
Serves 4.

CARROT AND TURNIP

6 *young carrots (approximately 1 pound), diced* | 6 *young white turnips, diced* |
Water | ½ *teaspoon salt* | ¼ *teaspoon sugar* | 2 *tablespoons butter or other fat* |
Dash of paprika | *Greens (tender tops of carrots and turnips) cut fine*

Wash carrots and turnips after removing tops. Do not scrape or pare them. Dice, then cover with cold water, add salt and sugar and cook in a covered pot 6 to 8 minutes or till tender. The liquid should be reduced by half. Turn into a large bowl and mash with a fork. Add the melted shortening and serve hot, heaped up in a vegetable dish or in individual portions, garnished with greens and a sprinkling of paprika. Or form into balls and garnish.

Serves 4 to 6.

CARROT AND TURNIP WHIP

1 *cup cooked, mashed carrot* | 1 *cup cooked, mashed turnip* |
⅛ *teaspoon salt* | ½ *teaspoon sugar* | ½ *cup heavy cream*

Combine vegetables while hot, add salt and sugar and beat with a rotary or electric beater 2 to 3 minutes or till fluffy. Fold in stiffly beaten cream and serve at once. Fine with baked fish.

Serves 3 to 4.

CAULIFLOWER WITH BROWN RICE

1 *cup brown rice* | 1 *quart water* | 1 *teaspoon salt* |
2 *tablespoons butter or vegetable shortening* | 1 *head cauliflower (trimmed)* |
1 *tablespoon lemon juice* | 2 *tablespoons bread crumbs* |
1 *tablespoon minced parsley*

Boil rice in salted water, in double boiler 30 minutes till tender. Drain well, return to upper part of boiler and let steam till dry. Add 1 tablespoon butter. Cook whole cauliflower in very little water in a tightly covered pot. Lemon juice and salt should be added after boiling starts. Boil 5 minutes, or till tender. Drain. Place the whole head of cauliflower on serving platter, dot with remaining butter. Surround with rice and top with crumbs. Sprinkle with minced parsley.

Serves 4 to 6.

CREAMED CELERY

2 cups diced celery | ¼ cup water | Salt and white pepper to taste |
1 tablespoon flour | 2 tablespoons butter |
½ cup milk or ¼ cup evaporated milk

Remove strings from celery stalks before cutting. Wash and drain.
Add water, salt and pepper to taste. Cook 3 minutes in a covered
saucepan. Blend flour in hot melted butter. Add milk slowly, stirring
till smooth. Add celery and cook 3 minutes. Serve hot. Garnish with
sliced hard-cooked eggs or parsley or both.
Serves 2.

CREAMED CELERIAC (Celery Root)

Pare celeriac and dice or cut into strips or thin slices. Cover with
cold water, add a little lemon juice and let stand 10 minutes before
cooking 8 to 10 minutes. Drain. Add cream sauce (see Index), sour
cream or meat gravy. Season with salt and pepper, add minced
parsley and serve hot. One medium sized celery root will yield 1 cup,
diced or sliced, and serve 2. Garnish with sliced hard-cooked eggs or
grated cheese.

CORN-ON-THE-COB

Tender corn should spurt milk when kernels are pressed. Remove
husks and corn silk. Cover with boiling water, adding ¼ teaspoon salt
and ⅛ teaspoon sugar to each cupful. Cover and cook 15 minutes.
Serve with butter. Allow 1 or 2 ears per serving.

CORN O'BRIEN

2 cups corn, cooked | 1 onion | 1 large green pepper | 2 tablespoons butter |
1 tablespoon flour | ½ cup milk | ¼ teaspoon salt | Dash of white pepper

Cut corn from cob or use canned whole kernels. Dice onion and
green pepper. Sauté in butter till lightly browned. Blend in flour,
stirring lightly 1 to 2 minutes, add milk slowly to blend smooth. Add

cooked corn and season to taste. Cook 3 minutes. If uncooked corn kernels are used, sauté with browned onion and pepper before adding milk in which flour has been blended smooth. Cook over low heat 5 to 10 minutes till corn is tender.
Serves 4.
Variation: To serve with meat, omit butter and milk. Use vegetable shortening or chicken fat and add soup stock or water.

CORN FRITTERS

2 cups cooked corn kernels | 2 eggs | ½ teaspoon salt | ½ cup flour | ½ cup milk or water | Shortening for frying

Beat eggs, add salt, flour and liquid to make a smooth batter. Add corn kernels and drop by the spoonful in deep hot melted shortening. Fry till nicely browned on both sides. Drain well.
Serves 4.

SUCCOTASH (Basic Recipe)
[A Southern Favourite]

1 cup cooked fresh corn, cut from cob | 1 cup cooked fresh lima beans | 2 tablespoons butter | ½ teaspoon salt | Minced parsley

Combine corn and beans and cook 3 minutes with the other ingredients.
Serves 4.
Variation 1: Add ½ cup stewed tomatoes, and ½ teaspoon brown sugar.
Variation 2: Substitute cooked green beans for limas, cutting them into ½-inch lengths or smaller.
Variation 3: Use same proportions of canned corn kernels and baby limas, well drained.

BAKED EGGPLANT

Cut eggplant in half, lengthwise. Scoop out centre, leaving a ½-inch wall. Fill with seasoned chopped meat, fresh or cooked, as for

Hamburgers. Bake 30 to 40 minutes at 350° F. or gas mark 4, or till tender. Serve with tomato sauce or stewed tomatoes. One medium eggplant and 1½ cups meat will serve 4.

Variation 1 : Make a stuffing of breadcrumbs, egg and cheese, seasoned with salt, pepper and melted butter. Fill eggplant shells and bake 20 to 30 minutes, or until tender.

Variation 2 : Combine 1 cup cooked rice with leftover flaked or diced meat, chicken or fish, seasoned with onion juice, minced parsley, poultry seasoning, salt and pepper. Stuff eggplant shells and bake till tender.

EGGPLANT CAVIAR

Here's a favourite among most Europeans, especially the French and Italians. You'll agree it's worth the time and effort. Just be sure the eggplant you select for the purpose is ripe, deep purple, light in weight and without brown spots.

Wrap the eggplant in heavy wax paper and brush the exterior with salad oil. Bake at 350° F. or gas mark 4 about 25 to 30 minutes, or till soft to the pressure of fingers or fork. Unwrap, remove the skin and chop fine in a wooden bowl. Add grated onion, garlic and two or three skinned tomatoes while chopping to a fine pulp. Work in some salad or olive oil and season to taste with salt and pepper. Chill thoroughly and spread on rounds of hot toasted biscuits, crackers or pumpernickel cut thin.

EGGPLANT SALAD (Russian Style)

Remove stem and peel. Slice, cut into cubes. Cook over moderate heat in very little water 5 minutes or till transparent. Drain, chop and add sliced or diced hard-cooked eggs, lemon juice or vinegar, salt and pepper to taste. Add minced or sliced onion, sliced black radish, black olives or minced parsley as garnish.

EGGPLANT SALAD (Roumanian *Patlajele Vinete*)

Select a 1- to 2-pound eggplant. It should be ripe and unblemished or the salad will be dry, dark and lumpy. Grill eggplant over or under flame till tender. Plunge grilled eggplant into cold water till cool enough to handle. Remove peel and stem. Chop in a wooden chopping bowl till smooth. Add oil, chopped onion, chopped green pepper, fresh or grilled (seeds and stem removed). Or serve with black olives and/or sliced black radishes.

Serves 4 to 6.

EGGPLANT AU GRATIN

Peel and dice a ripe eggplant. Cook covered in very little water till tender. Drain. Fill a well-buttered casserole with alternate layers of dry bread or matzo crumbs, grated Cheddar, cooked eggplant, the top layer being bread crumbs. Dot with plenty of butter, add liquid in which eggplant was cooked, or milk half-way up casserole. Bake 30 minutes at 350° F. or gas mark 4, or till nicely browned on top.

EGGPLANT FRITTERS

A 1½- to 2-pound eggplant | 1 teaspoon salt | 2 eggs | 6 tablespoons flour | 4 tablespoons water | Melted shortening for deep frying

Slice unpared eggplant into ¼-inch rounds. Sprinkle lightly with salt, place a heavy plate over and weight down if necessary. Let stand 30 to 45 minutes. Drain well and dip in batter made of beaten eggs, salt, flour and water. Fry in deep hot melted shortening till light brown. Turn to brown on both sides. Drain well.

Serves 6.

KALE

These greens are at their best after frost. Wash and drain well any amount required. Cut or chop. Cook with very little water in a covered saucepan. Season with salt, pepper and plenty of fat. Serve with meat or fish, like spinach.

1 pound serves 4.

KALE WITH MEAT (Bohemian Style)

2 pounds brisket of beef | 2 pounds kale | ½ cup dry rice |
2 medium potatoes, diced | 2 onions, chopped or sliced | 1 teaspoon salt

Cut meat into serving portions. Wash, drain and chop kale. Combine, add washed and drained rice, potatoes, onions and salt. Cook in covered pot over moderate heat 1½ hours. Do not add water unless necessary to prevent scorching. The water which clings to greens is usually sufficient. Do not stir during cooking, but shake the pot occasionally to prevent sticking. When the meat is tender and the rice soft, this nourishing dish is ready to serve.
Serves 6.

KALE WITH RICE

2 cups chopped kale | 1 cup cooked rice | 1 grated onion |
½ teaspoon salt | 3 tablespoons butter or chicken fat

Combine all ingredients, turn into buttered baking dish and bake 30 minutes at 375° F. or gas mark 5, or till nicely browned on top.

SCALLOPED KALE

1½ pounds kale | 1 onion, diced | 2 tablespoons butter |
½ cup grated cheese | ½ cup dry crumbs | 1½ teaspoons salt |
1 cup thin white sauce (see Sauces) | 2 hard-cooked eggs

Cut away fibrous stems and wilted tops from kale. Wash well. Drain. Chop or cut fine. Cook in a tightly covered pot over moderate heat 8 to 10 minutes. Sauté onion in butter till light brown. Combine cooked kale with onion and turn into a casserole or baking dish. Top with grated cheese mixed with crumbs. Bake 15 minutes at 375° F. or gas mark 5. Pour on white sauce and garnish with sliced cooked eggs.
Serves 4.

GRILLED MUSHROOMS (Basic Recipe)

Select large mushrooms, allowing 2 or 3 per serving. Wash, remove stems and drain. Combine 1 cup dry bread or matzo crumbs with

19

2 tablespoons melted butter and 1 tablespoon grated cheese. Season
with onion salt or salt and pepper. Stir in egg. Place a ball of this
mixture in each mushroom cup. Grill 3 to 5 minutes or till lightly
browned. Drizzle melted butter over each before serving.

> *Variation 1:* Slice large or medium mushrooms and sauté in hot
> butter, chicken fat or oil. Season with minced parsley, a dash of
> salt and pepper or paprika.
>
> *Variation 2:* Sauté and serve with sour cream. Garnish with
> minced parsley or fresh dill.

CREAMED MUSHROOMS

Cut woody parts from button or small mushrooms. Wash and drain
well. Cook 3 minutes, without water if tightly covered. Add a dash of
salt, pepper, paprika and combine with thick cream sauce (see
Creamed Onions) just before serving. Serve on toast points or
rounds and garnish with minced parsley and/or sliced hard-cooked
egg.

> *Variation:* Dice hard-cooked eggs, add sliced mushrooms and cook
> 3 minutes in a thin cream sauce. Serve on toast, on nests of
> mashed potato or in patty shells. Top with grated cheese and
> brown lightly under grill.

MUSHROOMS À LA RUSSE

4 cups sliced fresh mushrooms | 1 heaped tablespoon flour |
¼ teaspoon salt | 1 cup sour cream | 1 teaspoon onion juice or
2 tablespoons chopped chives or green onion tips | Generous dash of paprika

Do not peel fresh mushrooms but cut away the woody, fibrous stem
section. Slice from the top down as thin as desired. Wash in slightly
salted water and drain well. Enough water will cling to the slices to
form sufficient steam. Place in saucepan or heated frying pan and
cook over low heat 3 to 5 minutes. Rub the flour and salt with a little
sour cream until smooth then stir into the remaining sour cream.
Add to steamed mushrooms, stirring lightly to combine, then add
the onion juice or chives. Cook 1 minute longer and serve hot on
toast or Holland rusks. Garnish with a dash of paprika or a few bits
of parsley.

Serves 4.

OKRA AND RICE

2 cups cut okra | ½ cup dry rice | 1 cup cold water | ½ teaspoon salt |
2 tablespoons butter or oil | 1 cup tomato sauce (see Sauces)

Use only tender okra pods. Remove stem ends and tips. Cut into
½-inch slices. Add washed and drained rice, water and salt. Cook in
double boiler 30 to 45 minutes. Turn okra and rice into a greased
baking dish and add tomato sauce. Bake 10 minutes at 375° F. or
gas mark 5.
Serves 4.

STEWED OKRA AND TOMATOES

1 pound okra | 1 cup tomatoes, stewed | 2 tablespoons butter, oil or chicken fat |
1 tablespoon lemon juice | 1 tablespoon brown sugar |
½ teaspoon salt | Boiling water

Remove stems and tips from pods. Wash and drain. Slice pods if
large. Add boiling water to barely cover and cook 15 minutes.
Add the other ingredients and cook 5 minutes longer.
Serves 4.

BAKED ONIONS

Use large yellow onions, 1 per serving. Peel under water and cut in
half, crosswise. Cut away stem. Arrange onion halves around meat
roast, dust with fine matzo crumbs or flour. Bake 45 minutes to 1
hour before serving time. Baste with some of the meat gravy just
before serving.

PAN-FRIED ONIONS

Peel and slice large yellow onions. Dust lightly with flour and fry
in shortening till light brown. Serve with grilled liver or grilled steak.
Makes a good garnish for mashed potatoes.
Variation 1: Combine equal amounts of onion slices with green
pepper rings. Fry till tender and lightly browned.

Variation 2: Fry sliced onions and apple rings together, adding a little salt and a sprinkling of brown sugar just before serving.

CREAMED ONIONS

8 medium size white or yellow onions | Cold water to cover |
¼ teaspoon salt | 3 tablespoons butter | 3 tablespoons flour |
1½ cups milk | 4 tablespoons grated cheese, sharp or mild Cheddar type |
Dash of paprika (optional)

Peel onions and cut away root and stem ends. Cover with cold water, add salt and bring to a quick boil. Reduce heat and cook, uncovered, 20 to 25 minutes or until the onions are tender enough to pierce with a toothpick. Drain. Make a cream sauce by melting butter in a saucepan and rubbing in the flour till smooth. Stir in milk and cook over moderate heat 5 to 8 minutes, stirring constantly till thick. Add grated cheese and stir till smooth. Remove from heat. Add the cooked onions. Heat before serving. Add a dash of paprika for colour if desired.

Serves 4.

Variation: White pickling onions 1 inch in diameter may be used, allowing 4 to 6 per serving. Proceed as in basic recipe.

PARSNIPS

This root vegetable is very flavourful when young and tender. It should be scraped like carrots, cut lengthwise into quarters, and soaked in salted cold water 5 minutes before cooking. Allow 2 slender parsnips per serving, if fairly large. Cook parsnips 10 minutes in just enough water to prevent sticking. Add melted butter or schmaltz.

CREAMED PARSNIPS

Cook parsnip strips in salted water 10 minutes or till tender enough to pierce with a fork. Cover with cream sauce (see Creamed Onions). Prepare 10 minutes before serving time.

SAUTÉED PARSNIPS

Parboil parsnips 5 minutes in slightly salted water. Drain well. Roll in flour or fine crumbs and fry in butter or oil till nicely browned on all sides.

FRENCH FRIED PARSNIPS

Cut parsnips in strips or ¼-inch-thick rounds. Soak in salted water. Drain and dust lightly with flour or fine crumbs seasoned with salt and pepper. Fry like French Fried Potatoes.

MINTED GREEN PEAS

2 cups shelled fresh peas or 1 tall can | ¼ teaspoon salt | Few grains of sugar |
⅓ cup cold water | 2 tablespoons chopped fresh mint leaves |
1 tablespoon butter

If canned peas are used, heat with liquid from can. If quick frozen peas are used, follow directions on the package. For fresh peas, add cold water, salt and sugar and cook in tightly covered saucepan 5 to 7 minutes over moderate heat. Or 2 minutes in pressure cooker. Just before serving add butter and chopped mint, shake the pan to distribute evenly.

Remember when shopping that it takes about 3 pounds unshelled peas to serve 4.

POTATOES

Scrub potatoes and boil with jackets on, in enough water to prevent burning or sticking. Use a covered pot or saucepan and do not cook over a high flame. Boiling time depends on the size of potatoes. Add salt after boiling begins, ⅓ teaspoon to 1 pint water. Drain when tender.

1 pound serves 4.

Variation 1: Add butter, salad oil, chicken fat or other shortening to peeled boiled potatoes and garnish with minced parsley or fresh dill.

Variation 2: Serve with thin or thick cream sauce (see Index) to
which grated cheese or minced parsley is added.

Variation 3: Roll peeled, boiled potatoes in flour seasoned with
salt and white pepper. Brown in butter or other shortening.

Variation 4: Add enough meat gravy to cover boiled potatoes and
heat before serving.

Variation 5: Serve cooked whole small potatoes or diced large
ones, hot or cold with sour cream and/or creamed cottage
cheese. Garnish with minced celery, chives, finely cut green
onion or green pepper.

Variation 6: Fry thinly sliced cooked potatoes in hot melted
shortening till lightly browned on both sides. Add 1 beaten
egg for each cupful potatoes. Cover and cook over low heat
3 minutes. Turn out on heated platter underside up.
1 cupful per serving.

MASHED POTATOES

Wash and peel, allowing one large potato per serving. Quarter or
slice. Cover with cold water. Add 1 teaspoon salt per pound. Cook
15 to 20 minutes over moderate heat. Drain and reserve liquid.
Mash and beat with a fork or rotary beater till light and fluffy.
The potato liquid may be added while beating. For each pound add
1 tablespoon buttermilk, sour cream, sour milk or schmaltz.

MASHED POTATO NESTS

To 2 cups cold mashed potatoes add 1 egg, and ½ cup flour. Form
into balls 3 inches in diameter and place them 2 inches apart on a
well-greased baking pan. Make a depression in the centre of each
and fill with 1 tablespoon or more of chopped and seasoned leftover
diced chicken, meat, or creamed mushrooms. Bake 10 to 15 minutes
at 375° F. or gas mark 5, or till lightly browned.
Serves 2.

BAKED POTATOES

Scrub large baking potatoes and wipe dry. Rub a little butter or
oil into the skins. Bake at 350° F. or gas mark 4 for 1 hour or until

soft enough to pierce with a toothpick. Slash lengthwise and across. Insert 1 teaspoon butter or schmaltz and a few grains salt.

Variation 1: Cut baked potatoes lengthwise. Scoop out. Mash thoroughly and season with butter or chicken fat, salt and pepper. Return to the half shells. Brush with melted butter, milk, or chicken fat. Brown lightly under grill.

Variation 2: Top filled half shells with grated cheese. Return to hot oven for 3 to 5 minutes before serving.

Note: Wrap baked potatoes in aluminium foil to keep hot if serving time is delayed.

FRENCH FRIED POTATOES

Allow 1 large potato for each serving. Wash and pare potatoes. Slice or cut lengthwise into 2½- by ¾-inch pieces. Dry between towels and fry in deep hot shortening until a rich golden brown, using a frying basket. Drain well and sprinkle with salt.

POTATO CHIPS

Slice potatoes very thin. Pat dry and fry as for French Fried Potatoes until crisp and golden brown. Drain well and sprinkle with salt while hot. Leftover Potato Chips can be restored to crispy goodness by heating in a shallow pan in a moderate oven.

JULIENNE POTATOES

Cut potatoes into shoestring or match-like strips and fry like French Fried Potatoes. These take less time to cook than potato chips. Do not let them become too dry.

POTATO GOLD

4 medium potatoes, sliced | 4 medium carrots, diced | 1 medium onion, diced |
2 tablespoons butter or vegetable shortening |
2 tablespoons milk (or soup stock) | Salt and pepper to taste

Cook potatoes and carrots together in about 2 inches of water in a tightly covered saucepan. When tender, press through a colander or coarse sieve. Brown onion in shortening and combine, adding milk or soup stock and seasoning. Remove from heat. Mix or beat well. Mound up the Potato Gold and garnish with a sprig of parsley.
Serves 6.

POTATOES AU GRATIN

2 tablespoons butter | 4½ cups diced cooked potatoes |
4 tablespoons grated cheese | ½ cup dry crumbs | 1 egg |
¼ teaspoon paprika | Salt and pepper to taste

Melt shortening in a shallow baking dish. Toss cheese, crumbs, egg and seasonings with potatoes. Bake 10 to 20 minutes at 400° F. or gas mark 6.
Serves 4.

POTATO KNISHES (Basic Recipe)

1 cup mashed potato | 1 egg | Flour to make a stiff dough | Salt to taste |
1 tablespoon schmaltz, butter or vegetable shortening

Combine ingredients thoroughly. Form into 2 mounds. Brush with diluted egg yolk or evaporated milk and bake 20 minutes at 350° F. or gas mark 4, or till nicely browned.

Variation 1: Same proportions for larger quantities. Make a depression in centre and fill with 1 tablespoon chopped greben, and/or left-over meat or chicken, chopped liver and hard-cooked eggs. Or, cottage cheese seasoned to taste with salt and white pepper and combined with 1 egg per cupful. Bake.

Variation 2: Add chopped nuts, raisins and sugar, a dash of cinnamon or nutmeg, or grated lemon rind to cottage cheese to which egg has been added and combine well. Brush top of filled knish with melted butter, sprinkle with sugar and cinnamon or chopped nuts and bake.

POTATO PATTIES

Add 1 teaspoon caraway seeds (*kimmel*) to each cup of Potato Knishes dough and form 2-inch flat cakes. Brush with milk, melted shortening or diluted egg yolk. Sprinkle with caraway seed and bake 10 minutes at 375° F. or gas mark 5, or till browned. Serve like biscuits or muffins.

POTATO-CHEESE PUFFS

1½ *cups mashed potatoes (hot or cold)* | 3 *tablespoons hot milk* | ½ *cup grated cheese (or dry cottage cheese)* | 2 *eggs, separated* | 1 *teaspoon salt* | ¼ *teaspoon paprika* | 1 *tablespoon finely chopped green pepper (or parsley)* | 1 *small grated onion (or* 1 *tablespoon juice)* | 2 *tablespoons melted butter*

Beat mashed potatoes with milk. Add egg yolks to cheese and beat till fluffy. Combine other ingredients. Fold in stiffly beaten egg whites and melted butter. Drop in small mounds on a well-greased baking sheet and bake 20 minutes at 350° F. or gas mark 4, or till nicely browned. Excellent with a fish or vegetable dinner.
Serves 6.

SCALLOPED POTATOES

1 *large onion, thinly sliced or diced* |
3 *tablespoons melted shortening (butter, preferably)* |
5 *pounds potatoes, pared and thinly sliced* | 1 *pound Cheddar cheese* |
½ *teaspoon salt and* ⅛ *teaspoon white pepper* | *Milk as required*

Use a large casserole of earthenware or glass ovenware with a tight cover. Melt the shortening in the baking dish, scatter onion bits over the bottom then arrange alternate layers of sliced potato and sliced cheese dusted with salt and pepper combination. The casserole may be filled to the top and pressed down before adding enough milk to come ¾ of the way up the side. Arrange strips of cheese in a sunburst over the top and bake, covered, 45 minutes at 375° F. or gas mark 5. Uncover and bake 15 minutes longer or till nicely browned on top.

When reheating, cover the dish till hot then remove cover 5 minutes before serving.

Serves 8 to 10.

BAKED SWEET POTATOES (Yellow or Red)

Select well-rounded sweet potatoes, allowing 1 per serving. Wash thoroughly and dry. Bake at 375° F. or gas mark 5 till tender enough to pierce with a toothpick. With the point of a paring knife slit each potato lengthwise then across. Press the pulp till it shows between the cuts. Insert $\frac{1}{4}$ teaspoon of butter or other shortening. Slip under the grill to brown.

SWEET POTATO AND APPLE CASSEROLE

Arrange alternate layers of parboiled and sliced sweet potatoes and $\frac{1}{4}$-inch slices of cored tart apples in a well-greased casserole. Pour in maple or corn syrup diluted with hot water to come half-way up the side of casserole. Top with a layer of crumbs or cornflakes. Dot with butter or other fat and bake 40 minutes at 350° F. or gas mark 4, or till nicely browned.

SWEET POTATOES WITH CHESTNUTS

2 pounds sweet potatoes, pared | 1 pound chestnuts | $\frac{1}{2}$ cup brown sugar | $\frac{1}{4}$ cup water | $\frac{1}{2}$ cup bread crumbs | 2 tablespoons butter or substitute

Slice sweet potatoes in 1-inch-thick rounds. Boil 5 minutes in enough water to cover, adding $\frac{1}{4}$ teaspoon salt and covering the pot while boiling. Remove the shells from chestnuts and parboil at least 10 minutes. Drain and remove brown skins. Drain water from sweet potatoes, saving $\frac{1}{4}$ cup to mix with brown sugar and shortening. Arrange layers of sweet potato rounds and chestnuts in a baking dish or casserole, add the sugar mixture, top with crumbs and bake 30 to 40 minutes at 350° F. or gas mark 4 till brown.

Serves 6.

Yam is the name for the Southern sweet potato which is less dry and much sweeter than the lighter coloured ones. Both varieties can be used in these recipes.

BAKED YAMS ON THE HALF-SHELL

6 yams | ⅓ cup seedless raisins | 1½ teaspoons salt |
1½ tablespoons sugar | 2 tablespoons butter or margarine

Bake yams in jackets 50 minutes at 375° F. or gas mark 5. When done, cut lengthwise and scoop out pulp. Be careful not to break the skins. Mash pulp, add raisins, salt, sugar, butter. Mix well and pile lightly back into potato shells. Brown. Serve hot.
Serves 6.

LATKES (Grated Potato Pancakes)

6 medium size potatoes | 1 onion | 2 eggs | ½ cup flour |
1 teaspoon salt | Vegetable shortening or oil for deep frying

Pare and grate potatoes into a mixing bowl. Squeeze out liquid. Peel and grate onion into potatoes. Add eggs, flour and salt and stir to make a smooth batter that will drop heavily from the spoon. Heap the shortening in a heavy frying pan using enough to cover the pancakes amply. Drop the batter from a spoon into the hot shortening, making pancakes 3 inches in diameter. Fry over moderate heat until brown on the underside, turn to brown. Lift out and drain off excess fat on paper towel. Pancakes fried in deep fat should be puffed and crisp. Serves 4 to 6.

Variation 1: Use same mixture in greased shallow baking pan (8 × 12-inch baking pan), bake 45 minutes at 350° F. or gas mark 4, or until nicely browned. Cut into squares and serve hot.

Variation 2: Add ½ cup well chopped greben to grated potato batter. Substitute fine matzo meal for flour and fry as in basic recipe.

Variation 3: Turn either basic recipe or Variation 2 into well-greased small baking tin and bake 45 minutes at 350° F. or gas mark 4.

YAM PUFFS

*4 medium sized cooked yams | 1 egg, well beaten | ½ teaspoon salt |
Dash of pepper | Dry bread crumbs*

Peel the potatoes and put through a sieve or mash. Combine
ingredients. Cool the mixture. Drop by teaspoonfuls into bread
crumbs. Toss with a fork until completely covered. Then drop into
deep hot fat. Fry until browned.

GREEN PEPPERS AU GRATIN

*4 cups green or red sweet peppers | 1½ cups thin white sauce (see Sauces) |
½ cup shredded cheese | 2 tablespoons fine dry bread crumbs |
1 tablespoon melted butter*

Core and cut peppers in strips before measuring. Cook in boiling
salted water about 10 minutes or until tender. Drain. Add hot white
sauce and cheese. Add salt and pepper if needed. Pour into 1½ quart
casserole and top with crumbs mixed with butter. Bake 20 minutes
at 350° F. or gas mark 4.
Serves 4.

GREEN PEPPER SAUTÉ

*6 large green or red sweet peppers | ¼ cup vegetable shortening |
Salt and pepper*

Core and cut peppers in eighths. Cover with boiling water and cook
3 minutes. Drain and sauté in hot melted shortening until lightly
browned.
Serves 4 to 6.

BAKED PUMPKIN

Select medium sized pumpkin. Cut into 2-inch wedges, melon
fashion. Remove seeds and stringy part. Sprinkle each piece with a
little brown sugar, add a dash of nutmeg. Bake 45 minutes at 350° F.
or gas mark 4. Bake the seeds, too. Just sprinkle a little salt on them
and bake till nicely browned. The Balkan peoples eat baked
pumpkin seeds much like roasted chestnuts.

MASHED PUMPKIN

Pare and cube pumpkin. Boil in salted water to cover till tender.
Mash and season to taste with salt, nutmeg and butter.

Variation: Place mashed and seasoned pumpkin in a shallow
baking dish and brown under grill before serving. Or, dot with
butter and bake in the oven till lightly browned on top.

SALSIFY

Wash and scrape 1 bunch of salsify. Cut into ½-inch slices and drop
into cold water. Add juice of half a lemon to prevent discoloration.
When ready to cook, drain and cover with boiling water. Add salt to
taste and cook 10 minutes or till soft. Serve in a rich cream sauce
(see Sauces) to which minced parsley has been added and sprinkle
a dash of paprika on top. For individual servings, place 3 tablespoons
on a slice of buttered toast.

CREAMED SPINACH

1 pound spinach, cleaned and chopped fine | ½ cup heavy cream, whipped |
⅛ teaspoon salt

Cook chopped spinach 2 minutes in a tightly covered pot, without
water except what clings to leaves. Cool. Fold into whipped cream
lightly, adding salt. Garnish with sliced hard-cooked eggs.

Serves 3 to 4.

BAKED SPINACH AND WHITE SAUCE

4 tablespoons flour | 4 tablespoons butter | 1½ cups milk |
¼ cup light cream | 3 eggs | 3 cups chopped raw spinach |
Salt and pepper to taste

Make a white sauce of flour, melted butter, milk and cream. Beat
eggs lightly and stir into sauce. Add spinach and seasoning. Turn
into a buttered mould. Set mould in a pan of hot water and bake

45 minutes to 1 hour at 375° F. or gas mark 5. Unmould and serve
hot.
Serves 3 to 4.

SWEET-SOUR SPINACH

1 pound spinach | 1 large onion | 2 tablespoons shortening |
2 tablespoons flour | ½ cup cider vinegar | 2 tablespoons brown sugar |
1 teaspoon salt | 1 cup drained canned tomatoes

Wash and drain spinach. Shred or chop leaves and stems. Brown
diced onion in shortening. Stir in flour and blend till light brown.
Add vinegar in which sugar has been dissolved. Add salt. Stir till
smooth. Add tomatoes and chopped spinach and cook 3 minutes.
Serves 4.

SPINACH RING 1 (With Cream)

2 eggs | 1 tablespoon cornflour | 1 tablespoon brown sugar |
Salt and pepper to taste | 1 cup whipped cream |
3 cups finely chopped spinach | 1 tablespoon butter

Beat eggs light. Combine with sugar and cornflour. Fold into cream
and add seasoning. Stir in spinach. Pour in buttered ring mould.
Set ring in a pan of hot water and bake at 375° F. or gas mark 5,
40 minutes or until set. Unmould just before serving.
Serves 6.

SPINACH RING 2

4 eggs, separated | 1 cup crushed cornflakes | 3 cups chopped spinach |
Salt and pepper to taste | 2 tablespoons shortening

Beat egg yolks light and fold in half the cornflakes. Add well drained,
chopped spinach, add seasoning and fold in stiffly beaten egg whites.
Turn into greased ring mould that has been lined with remaining
cornflakes. Set ring mould in a pan of hot water and bake 30 to 45
minutes at 350° F. or gas mark 4. Unmould and serve with a garnish
of sliced hard-cooked eggs.
Serves 6.

BRUSSELS SPROUTS

1 pound sprouts | ½ teaspoon salt | Water to cover |
2 tablespoons butter or oil

Pick off wilted outer leaves and soak sprouts in cold water 10 to 15 minutes before cooking. Drain well. Cover with cold water, add salt, bring to a boil and cook 10 minutes or until sprouts can be pierced with a toothpick. Add shortening and serve.

Serves 2 to 3.

Variation 1: Drain and serve with white sauce (see Sauces).

Variation 2: Combine with ½ cup boiled chestnuts, adding butter to taste before serving.

Variation 3: Serve Brussels sprouts with well-seasoned tomato sauce (see Sauces).

Variation 4: Cover Brussels sprouts with meat gravy and cook 2 minutes before serving.

BAKED MARROW

Cut the tops off small marrows, allowing 1 per serving, or use the larger variety and serve filling only. Scoop out centres, leaving ½-inch-thick shells. The seeds of young marrows are very tender and need not be discarded. Cook the scooped-out portions in a little salted water, in a tightly covered pot, till soft. Mash thoroughly and combine with ½ the quantity bread crumbs. Add 1 egg, per cupful, 1 tablespoon grated cheese, minced parsley and a dash of cayenne. If additional liquid is necessary, add cream or evaporated milk. Fill the cavities of marrows, adjust the tops and bake 30 to 40 minutes at 350° F. or gas mark 4. Remove the 'lids' and slip under grill to brown lightly. Serve with 'lids' on to retain the heat.

BOILED MARROW

Select very young and tender marrow. Do not peel but cut into cubes or ½-inch wedges. Salt lightly and let stand 10 minutes. Rinse and drain. Add boiling water to cover and cook, covered, 5 minutes over moderate heat. Add butter, cream or evaporated milk, and salt to taste. Cook 5 minutes.

1 pound serves 2 or 3.

SWISS CHARD

Wash carefully in several waters to remove dust, dirt, insects. Or cut into 2-inch lengths, using stems and leaves, and soak 10 minutes in cold water to which a little salt has been added. Drain well. Cook 5 minutes in very little water, adding lemon juice and salt to taste. Cook like spinach, and serve it in the same way. Allow 1 pound for 2 to 3 servings.

TOMATOES, STUFFED AND BAKED

6 tomatoes | 1 cup chopped meat (leftover or fresh) |
½ cup boiled rice or bread crumbs | Salt and pepper to taste |
¼ teaspoon poultry seasoning | 1 tablespoon onion juice | 1 tablespoon fat

Slice off stem ends of tomatoes, scoop out centres and invert tomatoes to drain. Make a stuffing of meat, rice and seasonings and add the scooped-out part of tomatoes if desired. Press enough into each tomato to fill, make small balls to place on top of each, dot with a little fat and bake 30 minutes at 375° F. or gas mark 5, or till tender and the tops browned. Serve from the baking dish.
Serves 6.
Variation: Use any other stuffing such as rice and cheese; bread crumbs, eggs and cheese; canned salmon and rice or bread crumbs; cooked soybeans and cheese.

TOMATOES, STUFFED AND GRILLED

4 tomatoes | 1 cup flaked salmon, sardines, tuna | ¼ cup bread crumbs |
1 tablespoon butter or oil | 1 tablespoon minced parsley |
1 tablespoon lemon juice

Remove stem ends and cut tomatoes in half lengthwise. Scoop out pulp carefully without breaking walls. Combine flaked fish with buttered crumbs and parsley, season with lemon juice and fill the tomato halves. Grill 5 minutes and serve hot.
Serves 4.

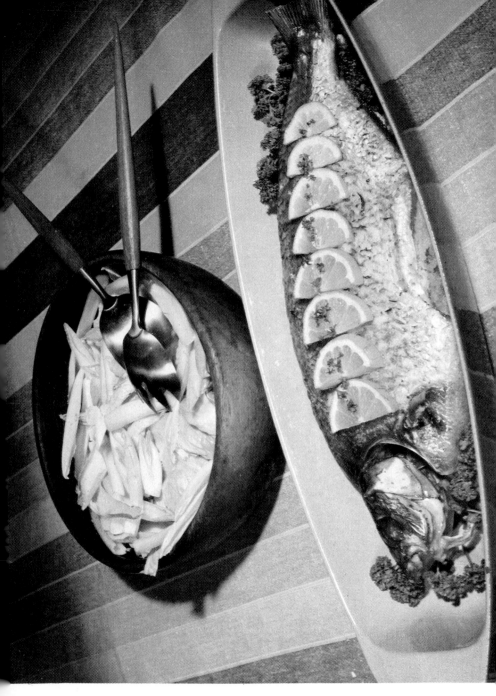

Baked
Stuffed Fish
(*page 202*)

TOMATO FRITTERS

4 slightly under-ripe tomatoes | 1 egg | ¼ cup water or milk |
¾ cup flour | ¼ teaspoon salt | Melted shortening

Cut tomatoes into thick slices and dust with flour. Make a batter of
beaten egg, salt, flour and liquid. Dip tomatoes in batter and fry in
deep hot melted shortening till nicely browned on both sides.
Serves 4.

GRILLED TOMATOES

Cut large firm tomatoes in halves crosswise. Dust with salt and
matzo crumbs. Add a dot or two of butter and grill 3 to 5 minutes
under grill to melt butter and brown crumbs. Allow 1 tomato for
two servings.

Variation: Mix equal portions of dry bread crumbs and grated
cheese. Season with salt and pepper. Cover tomato halves
generously and grill 5 to 10 minutes under a very moderate
flame. For meat meals, omit cheese. Add vegetable shortening
to bread crumbs instead of butter.

TURNIPS

Select young, small size white turnips. Pare and slice or dice. Cook
5 minutes in a minimum of salted hot water or till tender. Drain and
mash with butter or other shortening. Serve hot.
Allow ½ pound per serving.

CREAMED TURNIPS

2 cups boiled diced turnip | 1 cup cream sauce (see Creamed Onions) |
1 tablespoon minced parsley | Dash of white pepper

Combine and cook 3 to 5 minutes.
Serves 4.

20

TURNIP GREENS

Wash and cut tender turnip greens. Cook in very little water for
5 minutes. Season with salt and butter to taste. They're full of
mineral substance – calcium, phosphorus, iron and copper – all
essential body requirements. Add to cooked turnips or ½ cup portions
per serving.

VEGETARIAN CHOPPED LIVER

> 1½ *cups finely chopped or ground cooked green beans (packed tight)* |
> 1 *hard-cooked egg* | 1 *chopped onion* | 2 *tablespoons butter or oil* |
> *Salt and pepper to taste*

Mash hard-cooked egg with the beans. Lightly brown chopped
onion in hot melted shortening and add seasoning to suit the taste
with salt and pepper. This should be a compact mass and look just
like chopped beef or calf's liver. Tastes as good, too!

Use for filling celery, on crackers for canapés, or form into tiny
balls (like marbles) and serve as a salad on shredded chicory or
mixed greens. Garnish with black or pitted green olives. Or dot with
a bit of mayonnaise and sprinkle with paprika.

VEGETABLE LOAF

> 2 *tablespoons melted shortening* | 1 *cup diced or chopped onion* |
> 1 *cup minced celery* | 1 *cup grated raw carrots* |
> 1 *cup finely ground English walnuts (or mixed nuts)* |
> 1 *cup dry whole wheat or rye bread crumbs* |
> 1 *teaspoon each salt and poultry seasoning* | 2 *eggs* |
> 1 *cup evaporated milk or cream* | 1½ *cups tomato or mushroom sauce*

Cook onions in hot melted shortening till light brown and add
vegetables, nuts, crumbs and seasonings. Sauté. Beat eggs and stir
in cream. Combine both mixtures and turn into a well-greased loaf
pan or shape into balls or patties for individual portions. Bake at
350° F. or gas mark 4, 40 to 45 minutes or till nicely browned. Turn
out loaf and serve with tomato sauce or fresh mushroom sauce. Or,
use a can of cream of mushroom soup, heated just before serving.

Garnish with sliced hard-cooked eggs or cooked green peas around the loaf.

Serves 4 to 6.

ZUCCHINI (Basic Recipe)

1 pound zucchini | ½ teaspoon salt | 1 tablespoon butter

This small green marrow is exceptionally good when young and tender. Do not pare. Remove stem end and blossom point. Cut into ¼-inch slices and cook 5 minutes in very little water in a covered saucepan. Season with salt and butter while hot.

STUFFED ZUCCHINI

Select the larger variety. Wash and cut into 2½-inch sections. Scoop out centres. Dust with salt while preparing the filling. May be stuffed with chopped and seasoned left-over meat, chopped beef prepared as for Hamburgers, or any dressing as for poultry (see Index). Rinse the scooped out zucchini and pat dry before filling. Fill. Bake in a shallow baking pan 45 minutes at 350° F. or gas mark 4, or till browned on top. Serve with tomato sauce, stewed tomatoes or meat gravy.

19 Pulses and Grains

Pulses, especially dried beans, peas, lentils and soybeans, are included in this section. They may be served as a meat substitute or with other foods. Steaming in a pressure cooker, or soaking in cold water before cooking to restore the moisture, is the usual method used.

Canned Pulses are already cooked and require heating only.

Quick Frozen Pulses are generally the fresh varieties and require cooking unless marked otherwise.

Grains, such as barley, kasha, and all varieties of rice, may be served as separate dishes or cooked with other foods.

BAKED BEANS (Basic Recipe)

2 cups haricot beans | ½ teaspoon salt | 1 onion |
4 tablespoons shortening | ¼ tablespoon molasses | ½ cup tomato sauce

Beans should be soaked in cold water for several hours or overnight. Drain, cover with fresh cold water, add salt and onion and cook over moderate heat until the skins of beans fill out and beans begin to soften enough to crush between thumb and forefinger. Add molasses and tomato sauce. Turn into a casserole, cover and bake 1 to 1½ hours at 325° F. or gas mark 3. Uncover and bake 10 to 25 minutes longer till reddish brown on top.

Serves 4 to 6.

Variation 1: Use tenderized haricot beans (marked on package). These do not require soaking. Cook as above.

Variation 2: Add 1½ to 2 pounds brisket of beef to the ingredients listed. Omit shortening. Cook over low heat 1½ hours, then add molasses and tomato sauce just before turning into casserole, leaving the fat part of meat exposed. Bake 1 to 1½ hours at 300° F. or gas mark 2.

Variation 3: Black-eyed round beans or red kidney beans may be substituted.

FRESH LIMA BEANS

2 cups fresh limas | Water to cover | 1 teaspoon salt |
2 tablespoons butter or other fat

Cook limas in salted water over moderate heat 45 minutes or till
tender. Add butter just before serving.
Serves 4 to 5.

DRIED LIMA BEANS (Basic Recipe)

1½ cups dried lima beans | Water to cover |
1¼ teaspoon salt | 1 onion

Soak dried beans overnight. Drain and cover with cold water. Boil
slowly 2 to 2½ hours in a covered pot, adding onion and salt after 1
hour of cooking. Remove onion, drain, and serve with gravy or
butter.
Serves 4 to 5.

HONEYED LIMA BEANS

1½ cups lima beans (dried) | Water to cover |
½ cup honey or molasses | 1 teaspoon salt

Proceed as for Dried Lima Beans, basic recipe. After 1 hour of slow
cooking, add sweetening. Uncover and continue cooking 45 minutes
or until tender and golden brown.
Serves 4.

LIMA BEANS IN TOMATO SAUCE

Proceed as for Dried Lima Beans, adding ½ cup tomato sauce or 1
cup stewed fresh tomatoes, onion and 1 tablespoon brown sugar
after the first hour of cooking. Canned limas may be used in the
same quantities as given in these recipes. Follow same procedure and
reduce cooking time to 20 minutes.

Soybeans. There are many varieties of edible soybeans, an Oriental staple which has become a favourite in the Western world. These beans rank high in protein and low in carbohydrates, but contain elements similar to fats. They are an invaluable item in a diabetic diet. Any variety from the tiny green, round soybean to the large haricot bean kinds may be used in the following recipes:

BOILED SOYBEANS (Basic Recipe)

½ cup soybeans per serving | ⅛ teaspoon salt |
Cold water to cover | Onion (optional)

Cook till tender and serve whole, with or without liquid, with butter or grated cheese added while hot.

> *Variation 1:* Mash or put through sieve and add butter or other shortening.
> *Variation 2:* Drain cooked soybeans and add ¼ cup tomato sauce, Creole sauce, fried onion rings. Slip under grill to brown lightly.

SOYBEAN LOAF

2 cups cooked, mashed soybeans combined with liquid | 1 cup fine crumbs |
1 egg | ½ cup evaporated milk or cream | 1 onion, diced and fried |
Minced parsley | Salt and white pepper to taste

Combine. Turn into greased loaf pan and bake at 350° F. or gas mark 4 till nicely browned.

> Serves 4 or 5.

Kasha is the generic term for food cooked to a mushy consistency. 'To make a kasha of something' is derived from a Yiddish phrase used to denote mixing up things or matters – making a mess of something. Kasha, in kitchen parlance, generally refers to cooked buckwheat groats. Kasha made of groats is used in various ways from soup garnish to filling for specially prepared soup or stew accessories. Kasha may be the filling for Kreplach, Knishes, Pirogen and Piroshki, or may be combined with noodle squares or bowknots and the dish called Kasha-Varnitchkes. It serves as a substitute for potatoes. There also are dishes called kasha that are not made of groats. Such dishes generally are a combination of beans and barley or lentils and barley. But the name has been applied to mashed potatoes also. This section, however, will present kasha of buckwheat first in the series of recipes for kasha.

Fine milled groats are used like farina or other cereal for breakfast. Cook in salted water as directed on the package and serve with sweetening and milk or cream.

KASHA (Basic Recipe)

1½ cups coarse buckwheat groats | 2 egg yolks | 3 to 4 cups boiling water | 1 teaspoon salt | 1 onion, diced | 4 tablespoons shortening

Heat a heavy frying pan over moderate flame and add groats. Stir to prevent too rapid browning or scorching. Stir in beaten egg yolks and continue stirring till groats are egg coated and dry. Add water gradually, stirring steadily. Add salt. Cover and reduce heat for 10 to 15 minutes or till the grains are tender. If necessary to prevent sticking, more boiling water may be added, a little at a time. The groats should have doubled in bulk before adding browned diced onion and fat in which it has been prepared while the groats were being cooked.

Turn cooked kasha into a shallow baking dish and bake 10 minutes at 350° F. or gas mark 4, or till nicely browned.

Yields 3 cups.

Variation: Spread groats in a thin layer on bottom of a shallow baking pan. Brown in the oven at 350° F. or gas mark 4 approximately 10 minutes, stirring once or twice. Beat eggs in a bowl and stir in browned groats. Return to hot oven to dry, leaving oven door open, and stirring 2 or 3 times to prevent scorching. Cook in boiling salted water as directed in basic recipe and combine when tender with browned onion, chopped greben and same amount of fat.

KASHA-VARNITCHKES

1 cup coarse buckwheat groats | 2 egg yolks | 4 cups boiling water | 1 teaspoon salt | 4 tablespoons chicken fat or butter | 1 cup cooked noodle squares or bow-knots

Brown the groats in a heated heavy skillet or frying pan, stirring constantly to prevent burning. Stir in the egg yolks till grains are coated. Add the hot water slowly, stirring constantly. Add salt. Cook till tender over moderate heat. Add shortening and cooked noodle squares. Turn into a casserole and brown under grill till nicely and evenly browned. Serve with meat gravy or plain.

Serves 3 or 4.

BEANS AND BARLEY KASHA

1 *cup haricot beans | Water to cover | ½ cup large barley | ½ teaspoon salt |*
1 *large onion, diced | 2 tablespoons chicken fat or butter*

Soak beans in cold water overnight or at least 4 hours. Drain and cook till almost tender before adding washed and drained barley. Cook slowly in enough water to prevent sticking. Avoid stirring. Add salt when beans and barley are tender. Brown onion in fat and add when the water has been absorbed and the beans tender but not mashed. Turn into a casserole and bake 20 minutes at 350° F. or gas mark 4, or until nicely browned on top.

Serves 3 or 4.

LENTILS AND BARLEY KASHA

1 *cup lentils | ¼ cup large barley | Water | ½ teaspoon salt |*
1 *onion | 2 tablespoons butter*

Cook lentils and barley in cold water to cover 45 minutes or until tender. Add salt and enough boiling water if necessary to prevent sticking. Brown sliced or diced onion in butter and add, stirring in lightly.

Serves 3 or 4.

Variation 1: Substitute chicken fat for butter.

Variation 2: Add 1 cup fresh or stewed tomatoes, 1 tablespoon brown sugar and a minced clove of garlic. Simmer without stirring 15 to 20 minutes or until all liquid is absorbed.

Farfel can be bought in neat little packages these days. But just in case you adhere to the old-fashioned method, make farfel by mixing an egg with a tablespoonful of cold water and stirring in sifted flour till you have a ball of dough, stiff and hard enough to grate or chop into tiny bits.

LENTILS AND FARFEL

1 cup lentils | ½ cup farfel | ⅛ teaspoon salt | 3 cups boiling water | 1 onion, diced | 3 tablespoons chicken fat or butter | Greben or grated Cheddar

Brown the diced onion in hot melted shortening while the other ingredients are cooking till tender over moderate heat. Turn into a casserole, add a generous sprinkling of greben or cheese – then bake covered 20 minutes at 350° F. or gas mark 4. Uncover and brown slightly under grill. Makes an excellent meat substitute.
Serves 4.

SWEET-SOUR LENTILS

1½ cups lentils | 1 quart cold water (¾ cup if using pressure cooker) | 2 tablespoons butter or vegetable shortening | 2 tablespoons flour | ¼ teaspoon salt | Juice of 1 lemon (a bit of grated rind) | 2 tablespoons sugar

Cook lentils in cold water 45 minutes to 1 hour or till tender. Drain, reserving liquid. (Cooks in 10 minutes in pressure cooker.) Heat shortening in saucepan and add flour, stirring till deep brown. Add some of the liquid strained from cooked lentils, stirring smooth. Add salt, sugar and lemon juice and rind. Cook 1 minute before adding to lentils. Turn into a casserole and bake 15 minutes at 350° F. or gas mark 4, or till the liquid has been absorbed. Garnish with minced parsley or sprinkle with paprika and serve hot.
Serves 4.

MAMALIGA (Roumanian Style)

2 cups coarsely milled yellow cornmeal or farina | 4 cups water | ½ teaspoon salt | 2 tablespoons butter

Moisten the cornmeal with 1 cup of cold water, stirring well to

prevent lumps. Bring 3 cups of water to the boiling point in top of a double boiler. Add salt and stir moistened cornmeal into water gradually while cooking over moderate heat. Continue to stir vigorously for 10 minutes. Add butter. Place over boiling water, cover and let cook over moderate heat 20 minutes. Turn out on a heated platter. Make a well in the centre and add ⅓ to ½ pound *Brunza Alba*, Roumanian cheese, mashed with a fork and additional butter if desired. Cottage cheese may be substituted for the Roumanian cheese, and additional salt and pepper added.
Serves 4.
   Variation: For serving with pot roast and gravy, substitute schmaltz for butter in basic recipe. Omit cheese and additional butter.

Nahit or Chick Peas. This is called by various names, depending on the country of origin. Spanish *garbanzos*, Italian *cecci*, and *nahit* or *nahut* are one and the same. Boiled and salted nahit is served on holidays and Sabbaths, like salted nuts.

NAHIT (Basic Recipe)

Soak dry chick peas in cold water to cover 10 to 12 hours. Drain, rinse in cold water. Add fresh water to come 2 inches over top. Cook in a covered pot 30 to 45 minutes, add salt to taste and continue cooking uncovered till tender. Drain, dust lightly with salt and serve hot or cold.
   Pressure Cooker Method: Soak peas 2 hours. Drain and rinse as in basic recipe. Add cold water to cover and 1 teaspoon salt for each 1½ cups of peas. Cook under 15 pounds pressure, 15 minutes.

NAHIT WITH RICE (Roumanian Style)

1 *cup cooked nahit* | ¼ *cup rice* | 3 *cups water* | 1 *teaspoon salt* |
½ *cup honey* | ¼ *cup brown sugar*

Combine and cook over moderate heat 20 to 30 minutes or until rice is tender. Turn into a casserole. Bake at 400° F. or gas mark 6 for 15 minutes or till nicely browned on top.
   Variation: Cook chick peas with 2 pounds brisket of beef and an onion 1½ hours or till meat is tender. Remove onion, add an

einbren (see Index) and brown in the oven, with or without adding honey and sugar.

Rice. There are several varieties on the market. The directions on package include proportions of liquid and grains, in accordance with the variety. A general and basic rule is to use 2 cups water to 1 cup rice.

Brown rice is the unpolished variety that is advocated by nutritionists. *Converted*, long grain, rice retains most of the original vitamin content. *Polished rice* is the least desirable variety. *Wild rice* is an American grain in the luxury class.

BOILED RICE (Pressure Cooker Method)

1½ cups rice, rinsed | 1¼ cups boiling water | 1 teaspoon salt |
1 teaspoon lemon juice or vinegar

Cook at 5 pounds pressure 15 minutes and reduce heat quickly under running cold water or by setting cooker in deep cold water.
Serves 4 or 5.

BOILED RICE (Double Boiler Method)

1½ cups rice | 1¼ cups boiling water | 1 teaspoon salt |
1 teaspoon lemon juice or vinegar

Cook in covered double boiler 45 minutes or till liquid has been absorbed.

SPANISH RICE

1½ cups rice | 1 onion, diced | 3 tablespoons shortening |
1 cup finely cut green pepper | ½ cup finely cut celery |
½ cup tomato sauce or 1 cup canned or fresh tomato

Boil rice as directed above. Fry or sauté onion in shortening, stirring several times till light brown. Add other ingredients. Add to cooked rice with tomato sauce, canned or fresh tomato. Cook over low heat 5 minutes.
Serves 4 or 5.

CURRY OF RICE

Add ½ to 1 tablespoon curry powder and ½ cup hot soup stock to cooked or Spanish Rice and cook 3 minutes longer.

PEAS AND RICE CASSEROLE

1 cup rice (brown or converted) | 3 tablespoons butter or substitute |
2 cups peas, fresh, frozen or drained canned | ½ teaspoon salt |
1 tablespoon sugar | 3 cups boiling water

After washing rice under running water and draining it thoroughly, add to the melted shortening in a heated, heavy frying pan. Stir constantly until lightly browned. Add peas, salt and sugar and stir in gradually the boling water. Cook only 5 minutes uncovered, then turn into a casserole. Cover and bake at 350° F. or gas mark 4 for 45 minutes. Uncover, and if rice is tender, place a few strips of Cheddar cheese on top. Bake until cheese is melted. Or, slip under the grill long enough to melt the cheese and brown lightly on top.
Serves 4 to 6.

VIENNESE RISI BISI

1 cup rice | 2 teaspoons salt | Few drops of lemon juice |
1 cup canned or fresh peas | 6 cups boiling water |
3 tablespoons oil, butter or schmaltz | 1 onion, diced fine |
Minced parsley

Cook rice in salted water (adding lemon juice for whiteness) over moderate heat 30 minutes or until tender. Drain rice and add peas. If fresh peas are used, return rice and peas to pot and cover well, allowing the steam to tenderize peas. Top of a double boiler is fine for the purpose. If a *pressure cooker* has been used for boiling rice, add fresh peas when pressure has been reduced, cover again and adjust gauge. Keep pot over very low heat for 3 minutes.
Brown diced onion in shortening and stir into the rice and peas, using 2 forks.
Serves 5 or 6.

20 Salads for Health

Salads may be any combination of uncooked or cooked vegetables, marinated with dressing and served with or after the fish, poultry or meat course. Or, as in European countries, piquant salads may be served before a meal to stimulate the appetite.

Salads may also serve as the main course for luncheon, in which case more proteins and carbohydrates should be included. Also, a richer dressing may be used.

Salads for desserts should be made of fruits – fresh, canned or frozen – and combined with a sweetened, mild salad dressing.

Thanks to rapid transportation, fresh salad greens, fruits and vegetables are available throughout the year. Seasonal variations in diet have also been eliminated by our canneries and frozen food techniques. Salads made of fruits, greens or vegetables grown hundreds of miles away can be served every day of the year.

Dressings for various types of salads are available in glass jars and bottles. For the sake of variety, we offer some recipes which can be made in the home kitchen.

The following recipes for salads fall into three categories: luncheon salads, dessert salads, and 'year round' or all-purpose salads.

For *uncooked vegetables* that can be used for salads see Chapter 18, Vegetables.

Salad Greens are: Celery (stalks and leaves), chicory or green endive, dandelion greens, dill, endive (French stalks), fennel (bulbs and tops), lettuce, all varieties, watercress. Tender beet tops, carrot greens, turnip greens, horse-radish greens and mint leaves add variety as well as mineral content.

Salad Hints
All vegetables and greens to be used for salads should be chilled and crisp.

A sharp scissors helps quick cutting.

Use a sharp-pointed knife for paring and slicing vegetables.

Score the sides of carrots and cucumbers. The sawtooth edge of a potato peeler will serve better than a fork for scoring.

Remove skins from tomatoes by placing them in a colander and pouring boiling water over them. Be sure to chill them thoroughly after peeling.

Carrots, cabbage and turnips can be shredded coarse or fine on a grater.

HOME-MADE SALAD DRESSINGS

BASIC MARINADE

½ cup salad oil (corn, peanut or soybean) | ¼ cup olive oil (optional) | ½ cup lemon juice or wine vinegar | 3 tablespoons brown sugar | Dash of salt and pepper | ¼ teaspoon paprika | Clove of garlic (cut and left in Marinade)

Combine all ingredients in a tightly covered bottle or jar and shake well. Beat when prepared in advance and chilled. Yields approximately 1½ cups. Store in refrigerator.

Variation: For *Fish or Meat Salads,* add horse-radish, a dash of curry, and/or minced parsley and green pepper.

For *Vegetable or Egg Salads,* add onion juice or grated onion, minced parsley, chopped pickle relish, chopped stuffed olives.

For *Fruit Salads,* add well-mashed cream cheese mixed with sour cream, light cream, evaporated milk and/or pineapple juice to taste. Add icing sugar as desired and a few drops of almond extract.

For *Greens Salads,* add grated Parmesan or Roquefort cheese.

A POPULAR RUSSIAN DRESSING

Add to Basic Salad Marinade chopped cucumbers, mixed pickles, olives, chili sauce and a dash of cayenne or Worcestershire sauce.

BOILED SALAD DRESSING

3 egg yolks | 1 tablespoon flour | 1 teaspoon dry mustard | ¼ teaspoon salt | ¼ teaspoon paprika | 1 tablespoon sugar | ¼ cup vinegar or lemon juice | ¾ cup cold water | 2 tablespoons butter or oil

Beat egg yolks slightly. Stir in the mixed dry ingredients. Blend water and vinegar and add a little at a time, stirring to blend smoothly. Cook over hot water until thickened and stir in butter or oil after removing from heat. Chill before using.

Yields 1½ cups.

Variation 1: Thin with sour cream, whipped cream or evaporated milk before using.

Variation 2: Thin with cider, pineapple juice or onion juice.

EGGLESS SALAD DRESSING

2 tablespoons butter | 2 teaspoons sugar | ⅛ teaspoon salt and pepper |
1 teaspoon prepared mustard | ½ cup cream or milk |
½ cup vinegar | 1 tablespoon cornflour

Combine butter, sugar, salt and pepper, mustard, cream or milk, and vinegar. Add flour mixed to a paste with a little cold water. Cook over low heat until thickened.

Yields 1½ cups.

EGGLESS MAYONNAISE

½ teaspoon each salt, dry mustard, paprika | 1 tablespoon sugar |
Dash of pepper | ½ cup evaporated milk |
3 tablespoons vinegar or lemon juice | 1½ cups salad oil

Mix dry ingredients and stir in the milk. Add vinegar and oil alternately while beating till smooth and creamy. May be thinned out with more evaporated milk and lemon juice as needed. Store in covered glass jar in refrigerator.

Yields 1 pint.

FRUIT SALAD DRESSING (Without Oil)

3 tablespoons mild vinegar, orange or pineapple juice |
3 ounces cream cheese | 1 egg, separated | 3 tablespoons honey

Combine cheese and liquid till smooth and creamy. Beat egg yolk well and add honey while beating till well blended. Combine the two mixtures and fold in stiffly beaten egg white.

Variation: Omit vinegar. Blend cheese with ¼ cup canned fruit syrup, preferably pineapple, and 1 tablespoon lemon juice. Beat with rotary beater, adding egg yolk while beating till thick. Fold in stiffly beaten egg white.

COOKED FRUIT SALAD DRESSING

¼ cup sugar | 1 tablespoon cornflour | ⅛ teaspoon salt |
1 cup pineapple juice | 2 tablespoons lemon juice |
4 tablespoons orange juice | 2 eggs | 1 cup heavy cream, whipped

Combine dry ingredients. Add fruit juices. Cook in top of double boiler over boiling water, stirring till smooth. Remove from heat. Beat eggs well and stir in. Return to cook 5 to 10 minutes, stirring constantly. Remove from heat. When cold, stir in beaten cream till smooth. Store in a covered container till chilled. Serve as a topping for fruit salads, frozen cheese salads or gingerbread.

Yields approximately 2½ cups.

SOUR CREAM SALAD DRESSING

2 teaspoons sugar | ½ teaspoon salt | ½ teaspoon dry mustard |
3 tablespoons lemon juice | ⅛ teaspoon paprika | 1 cup heavy sour cream

Combine ingredients in the order listed, stirring till smooth. Cover and store in refrigerator to use on frozen cream cheese salads. Can be used with fresh or canned fruit salads, vegetable salads, fish salads. Will keep for a week or two in a covered container in refrigerator.

Yields 1¼ cups.

Hints for Gelatin Base Salads
Kosher Gelatins are available in most food markets and in some department stores. They come in various fruit flavours as well as unflavoured and can be used for vegetable, fruit or other aspics and salads. Kosher gelatin is made of a vegetable called kelp and can be used with meats, fish, cheese and fruit combinations.

Directions are generally supplied with the packaged gelatin, but in adding any liquid or semi-liquid (mashed fruits or whipped cream

Avocado
Crescent Salad
(page 322)
Beet Salad
(page 323)
Cheese and
Carrot Salad
(page 324)
Carrot and
Green Pepper
Salad
(page 325)

and cheese), the total quantity must be taken into consideration. It is therefore best to follow the recipes for gelatin salads as given in this collection. Too much liquid may prevent proper congealing.

It is wise to remember that *fresh pineapple* is the only fruit which *cannot* be combined successfully with gelatin.

Other points to remember in making gelatin salads or desserts are as follows:

Rinse the mould in *cold water* before turning in gelatin base mixtures.

Unmould by dipping the bottom of pan or ring mould in *hot water* and lifting it out before the congealed mixture liquefies. Place the serving plate or platter on top of mould and invert quickly. The salad will drop evenly on to the plate. If it does not, place a towel wrung out in *hot water* over the mould and let stand about 1 or 2 minutes.

SALAD RECIPES

APPLE AND CHEESE SALAD RING

PART 1

1 *tablespoon plain gelatin* | ¼ *cup cold water* | 1½ *cups hot water* |
¼ *cup lemon juice* | 4 *tablespoons sugar* | 8 *slices apple*

PART 2

1 *tablespoon plain gelatin* | ¼ *cup cold water* | 2 *cups cottage cheese* |
⅛ *teaspoon paprika* | ¾ *teaspoon salt* | ½ *cup light cream* |
3 *apples, sliced* | 2 *oranges, sectioned* | 1 *grapefruit, sectioned* | *Lettuce*

Part 1. Soften gelatin in cold water and dissolve in 1½ cups hot water. Add lemon juice and sugar. Cool. Arrange apple slices in bottom of ring mould, rinsed in cold water. Pour gelatin mixture over apples and place in refrigerator. While setting, make the rest of the salad.

Part 2. Soften gelatin in cold water in a small saucepan. Combine cheese, paprika, salt and cream. Set saucepan containing gelatin over hot water until dissolved. Add to cheese mixture. Pour this into mould and chill until firm. When firm, unmould on lettuce and fill centre with rest of fruit. Serve with dressing.

Serves 6 to 8.

21

AVOCADO CRESCENT SALAD

*2 avocados | 1 tablespoon lemon juice | Dash of salt |
2 bananas, peeled, sliced | 1 cup diced apple |
1 cup cubed orange, seeded or seedless | French dressing |
1 head shredded lettuce*

Cut avocados into 6 rounds before removing skins. A slight twist
with a knife edge will loosen the seed and separate the rounds.
Remove skins. Cut small openings in the solid ends. Cut the rounds
across to make crescents. Sprinkle with lemon juice and a little salt.
Sprinkle lemon juice on apples and bananas. Marinate in French
dressing. Arrange shredded lettuce on a large serving plate. Mound
the apple and banana mixture in centre. Arrange orange and
avocado crescents around.
Serves 6.

AVOCADO SALAD ON THE HALF-SHELL

Cut avocado lengthwise. Remove pit, and with a fork mash the fruit
in the half shells, adding a little lemon juice and a pinch of salt, or
top with any dressing.
1 filled half-shell per serving.

AVOCADO SALAD

*1 package orange or lemon gelatin | 1½ cups water | 1 avocado, mashed |
3 ounces cream cheese | ½ cup mayonnaise | ½ green pepper |
¼ cup celery heart | Pinch of salt | Few drops onion juice*

Dissolve gelatin in 1 cup hot water, then add ½ cup cold water.
Combine avocado with cheese and mayonnaise. Dice pepper and
celery. Add seasonings and combine with gelatin. Turn in to 9-inch-
square pan. Cut into 1-inch cubes when firm. Serve on a nest of
shredded lettuce.
Serves 6.

AVOCADO AND GRAPEFRUIT SALAD

1 teaspoon lemon juice | 1 avocado | 1 large grapefruit |
2 tablespoons mayonnaise | 1 tablespoon finely chopped green pepper

Cut avocado in half lengthwise and remove pit. Slip the point of a knife between the outer shell and meat without removing from the shell. Cut into narrow strips. Remove skin from grapefruit and membrane from individual segments. Arrange 3 segments of grapefruit on a bed of shredded lettuce on individual salad plates. Place strips of avocado between grapefruit in wheel fashion. Place a spoonful of mayonnaise in centre and top with chopped green pepper.
Serves 4.

JULIENNE BEET SALAD

1 can Julienne beets | 1 lemon, grated rind and juice |
1 tablespoon brown sugar | 1 tablespoon peanut oil | Salt and pepper

Drain liquid from beets. Make a dressing of lemon juice, grated rind, sugar and oil. Add salt and pepper. Marinate beets 10 minutes in this before serving on lettuce.
Serves 4.

BEET SALAD

2 cups diced cooked beets | 4 tablespoons prepared horse-radish |
2 tablespoons salad oil | Salt and pepper to taste

Combine horse-radish, oil and seasoning. Add to beets. Serve on lettuce.
Serves 4.

MOULDED BEET SALAD

2 cups beet juice | 2 packages lemon gelatin | 1½ cups water |
1 cup shredded or grated cooked beets | ½ pound cream cheese |
1 cup whipping cream or evaporated milk (chilled)

Heat beet juice. Dissolve gelatin in boiling water and add beet juice and grated beets. Whip chilled evaporated milk with a rotary beater. Add cheese and beat a few minutes together. Combine. Chill in cup moulds. When set, unmould on lettuce or other salad greens.

Serves 6 to 8.

BEET BORSHT SALAD (Basic Recipe)

2 cups Beet Borsht (shredded beets included) | 1 package lemon gelatin | Pinch of ginger | 3 tablespoons mayonnaise or sour cream | Shredded lettuce or endive | 3 hard-cooked eggs

Heat 1 cup of Beet Borsht liquor and stir in gelatin till dissolved. Add the rest of the borsht as soon as it begins to thicken. Add ginger. Fill 6 moulds rinsed in cold water and chill till firm. Unmould on shredded greens mixed with mayonnaise or sour cream. Top each salad with slices of hard-cooked eggs.

Serves 6.

Variation 1: Use canned diced beets put through a coarse strainer. Omit ginger. Add ⅛ teaspoon salt. Same procedure. Same proportions. Same servings.

Variation 2: Use wedges of hard-cooked eggs for garnish and arrange around beet gelatin mould. Top with sour cream. Serve in lettuce cups or on endive leaves.

CHEESE AND CARROT SALAD

¾ pound cottage cheese | ½ pint sour cream | ¼ teaspoon salt | 8 walnuts, halves or chopped | 3 medium carrots, shredded | Lettuce

Mix cheese with 2 tablespoons sour cream and salt to taste. Form into 4 balls and roll in chopped nuts or press halves into cheese balls. Place the shredded raw carrot on a nest of lettuce and arrange the cheese balls in centre. Serve with sour cream heaped on top of each cheese ball.

Serves 4.

CARROT AND CABBAGE SLAW

1 *large carrot | 1 pound cabbage | ¼ teaspoon salt |*
2 *tablespoons lemon juice or vinegar | 4 tablespoons evaporated milk or cream*

Shred carrot and cabbage into a large bowl. Add salt, lemon juice or vinegar and evaporated milk or light cream. Stir lightly with 2 forks and serve.

Serves 4.

Variation: To serve with meat or poultry meals, substitute 2 tablespoons oil for milk.

CARROT AND GREEN PEPPER SALAD

1 *cup shredded raw carrots | ¼ cup mayonnaise or salad dressing |*
1 *medium size green pepper, diced or chopped | 3 walnuts coarsely chopped |*
Salad greens (lettuce, chicory, endive, parsley)

Combine shredded carrots with dressing, chopped nuts and green pepper. Serve on mixed greens on individual salad plates. Top with dressing.

Serves 4.

COLE SLAW AND CARROT SALAD
(This is a tempting accompaniment for fish)

2 *cups finely shredded cabbage | 1 large carrot, scraped and shredded |*
1 *small green pepper, diced or chopped | ¼ teaspoon salt |*
½ *cup salad dressing*

Combine. Serve on endive.

Serves 4 to 6.

CRANBERRY AND CABBAGE SLAW

3 *cups shredded cabbage, crisped | 1 tablespoon minced onion |*
1 *cup cranberry-orange relish | 1 teaspoon salt | 2 tablespoons vinegar*

Mix ingredients together lightly with a fork. Chill for 1 hour. Serve as a salad.

Serves 4.

RED CABBAGE AND PINEAPPLE SALAD

1 small head red cabbage | 1 tablespoon lemon juice | ¼ teaspoon salt |
8 slices canned pineapple | 2 tablespoons chopped nuts |
½ cup sour cream | Lettuce or salad greens

Shred cabbage, add lemon juice and salt and let stand about ½ hour before serving. Place a generous spoonful of cabbage on top of each slice of drained pineapple. Top with sour cream mixed with pineapple syrup. Garnish with salad greens and chopped nuts.

Serves 8.

CAULIFLOWER SALAD

Cut raw cauliflower into tiny flowerets, add mayonnaise or other dressing and seasoning to taste. Serve on lettuce.

Variation 1: Combine cauliflower with shredded carrot, minced green pepper and parsley. Add mayonnaise and seasonings.

Variation 2: Combine leftover cooked cauliflower with peanuts. Add French dressing.

Variation 3: Combine cooked cauliflower with cooked peas or green beans. Add Russian dressing.

CELERY ROOT SALAD

Select firm celery roots. Scrub clean and pare. Cut into strips or dice. Add mayonnaise or French dressing. Serve on lettuce and garnish with parsley.

Variation 1: Add sour cream to salad dressing.

Variation 2: Add shredded blanched almonds or pecans for added calories.

Variation 3: Boil celery root first. Dice or cut fine and add mayonnaise.

CHANUCA SALAD

Use canned asparagus tips for candles. Arrange flat on a flattened lettuce leaf or finely shredded lettuce. Make tips of carrot to represent flame, garnish with watercress, olives, radishes and parsley. Serve with French dressing.

Serve individual salads or arrange on a long platter.

CHANUCA CANDLE SALAD

2 bananas | 4 slices canned pineapple | 4 orange gumdrops |
4 strips green pepper | Lettuce | Mayonnaise

Cut bananas in half and remove tips. Stand upright in pineapple centres. Top with gumdrop to represent flame. Pour a little mayonnaise from tip of each candle to represent melted wax. Arrange strip of pepper for handle, making a loop fastened into pineapple at base of candle.

Serves 4.

Variation: Cut red apples in 2 without paring and remove cores. Set a half banana into centre to represent candle, top with gumdrop and pour mayonnaise down side of candle.

CUCUMBER IN LIME GELATIN

1 package lime gelatin | 1 cup boiling water | 1 large cucumber |
1 cup grated raw carrot | 1 cup finely chopped cabbage |
1 cup chopped apple | ¼ cup chopped nuts or peanuts |
½ cup canned shredded pineapple | Salt to taste | Shredded salad greens

Dissolve gelatin in boiling water. Grate unpared cucumber, combine with carrot, cabbage, apple, nuts, drained pineapple and salt to taste. Combine with gelatin. Turn into a ring mould rinsed in cold water. Chill till firm. Unmould and serve on shredded salad greens marinated with dressing. This salad may be turned into individual moulds.

Serves 8.

CUCUMBER AND FRESH PINEAPPLE SALAD

Diced cucumber and fresh pineapple bits mixed with mayonnaise makes a delicious salad.

CUCUMBER AND PINEAPPLE ASPIC SALAD

1 *package lemon flavoured gelatin* | 1 *cup boiling water* |
1 *cup grated cucumber* | ½ *cup crushed canned pineapple* |
¼ *cup chopped nuts* | ¼ *cup each mayonnaise and evaporated milk or cream* |
1 *green pepper minced fine* | *Shredded lettuce*

Dissolve gelatin in water. Cool. Combine ingredients and chill in a ring mould till firm. Unmould on shredded lettuce.
Serves 8.

CUCUMBER BOATS

Cut unpared cucumbers lengthwise. Scoop out centres to form boats. Fill with a mixture of cream or cottage cheese seasoned with mayonnaise, salt, paprika and minced parsley. Decorate with paper sails held with coloured toothpicks. Serve 1 boat on each salad plate. Use finely shredded lettuce or white cabbage around the boat to simulate water.

DESSERT SALADS

BIRD'S NEST SALAD

½ *pound cream cheese* | *Salt to taste* | ¼ *cup chopped nuts* |
2 *tablespoons mayonnaise* | *Minced parsley* | *Shredded lettuce or chicory*

Combine cheese, salt, nuts, mayonnaise and parsley. Form into balls the size of walnuts. Arrange in nests of lettuce or chicory.
Serves 4.

BLACK MAJESTY SALAD

*24 large prunes | 1 cup cream or cottage cheese | ½ cup chopped nuts |
Mayonnaise (½ cup approximately) | 8 slices canned pineapple |
1 small head lettuce*

Soak prunes. When soft, remove pits and drain well. Combine
cheese, nuts and 1 tablespoon each mayonnaise and pineapple
syrup. Stuff centres of each prune with cheese mixture. Arrange 3
prunes on each slice of pineapple. Chill at least a half hour before
serving. Arrange on shredded lettuce on serving plate or as individual
salads.
Serves 8.

CHERRY AND GRAPE SALAD

*Pitted canned or ripe cherries (large size can) | Small seedless grapes |
Cream cheese | Lettuce or chicory | Pecans or English walnuts, chopped |
French dressing*

Insert a small grape in place of cherry pits; make a nest of cream
cheese in the centre of salad greens and place cherries in it. Sprinkle
with nuts. Serve with French dressing.
Allow 6 cherries and 1 ounce cheese per serving.

CHEESE-FILLED FRUIT SALAD

*1 cup cream or cottage cheese | ¼ cup chopped pecans |
Candied cherries or preserved ginger | 2 tablespoons mayonnaise |
Dash of salt | Sugar to taste | ¼ teaspoon vanilla |
1 tablespoon fruit syrup (canned) | 8 canned peach or pear halves (drained) |
Salad greens | ½ green pepper (8 strips)*

Combine cheese, nuts, candied cherries (finely cut or chopped),
mayonnaise. Add vanilla, salt and sugar to taste. Add about 1 tablespoon fruit syrup. Arrange drained fruit halves on shredded lettuce
on a serving plate or individual salad plates. Press balls of cheese
mixture into fruit centres. Arrange strips of green pepper for stems.
Serves 8.

CRANBERRY DELIGHT

1 package lemon gelatin | 1 cup boiling water | ¼ cup pineapple juice |
1 cup canned crushed pineapple | 1 cup dry cottage cheese |
½ cup chopped nuts | ¼ cup mayonnaise | 1 tall can cranberry sauce |
Shredded lettuce

Dissolve gelatin in boiling water and add pineapple juice. When cool
and beginning to thicken, add pineapple, cheese, nuts, and mayonnaise. Chill thoroughly. Cut cranberry sauce into 8 slices. Arrange
a ring of shredded lettuce on each salad plate. Fill centre with gelatin
mixture topped with a cranberry round.
Serves 8.

PINEAPPLE-CHEESE RING (With Whipped Cream)

1 package lemon or lime gelatin | ½ cup boiling water |
1 cup pineapple juice | 1 cup cream or evaporated milk |
½ pound cream cheese | ½ cup chopped almonds |
½ cup minced green pepper | ½ cup mayonnaise | Dash of salt |
1 cup canned crushed pineapple, drained | Green pepper slices |
Mint leaves, watercress, shredded lettuce

Dissolve gelatin in boiling water and add the pineapple juice. Cool
while preparing the rest of the ingredients. Chill and whip cream
(or evaporated milk) and combine with well-mashed cheese. Add
all the other ingredients except green pepper slices and greens and
stir in cold gelatin mixture. Turn into a rinsed ring mould and chill
in the refrigerator till set about 2 hours. When ready to serve, dip
bottom of ring in hot water and invert on serving plate. Garnish with
green pepper slices or strips and greens. In centre of ring place a tall
stemmed compote dish of salad dressing. Cut the ring and serve like
cake, spooning some of the dressing over each serving.
Serves 8.

DRESSING 1

Combine 1 cup sour cream with 2 tablespoons lemon juice or
pineapple juice and sweeten to taste with icing sugar.

DRESSING 2

Beat 3 ounces cream cheese with ½ cup pineapple juice till smooth, using rotary beater. Add 1 tablespoon lemon or orange juice and enough honey to taste. Add finely chopped almonds or pecans if desired.

GRAPEFRUIT SURPRISE

1 cup finely diced apple | ¼ cup chopped nuts |
¼ cup chopped or cut seeded raisins, dates or figs |
1 tablespoon mayonnaise | Bed of lettuce | 6 segments grapefruit

Combine apple, nuts, raisins and mayonnaise. Form into a ball by pressing into a cup rinsed in hot water. Turn out on lettuce. Arrange grapefruit segments by pressing into the mound lengthwise to hold in place. Garnish with chopped nuts or top with cut raisin or date.
Serves 2.

MIDWINTER SALAD SUGGESTIONS

TANGERINE SALAD

With a sharp-pointed scissors cut through the skins of tangerines to make the petals. Six petals, cut almost to the bottom and turned in about an inch from the pointed tops is about right. With the fingers, spread the tangerine segments slightly apart and place a small ball of cream cheese rolled in minced parsley in the centre. Place each tangerine on a bed of shredded lettuce or in a lettuce cup and serve with a sweetened salad dressing. A few biscuits or cheese spread on toasted crackers make a delicious accompaniment to this dessert salad. Add some canned pineapple juice or orange juice, freshly squeezed, to mayonnaise dressing. A few drops of rum or sherry may be added.

Use 1 tangerine per serving plus a tablespoon of your favourite cheese.

SUNBURST SALAD

Arrange grapefruit and large orange segments (from which seeds and membrane or fibre has been removed) in alternating rows on a bed of shredded lettuce or chicory. Combine mayonnaise or commercial salad dressing with sour cream or evaporated milk. Add chopped nuts and grated orange rind to suit the taste and serve separately or spoon over the salad just before serving. Garnish the large salad plate with maraschino cherries, red or green, or use canned Royal Anne cherries.

Allow 1 large grapefruit and 1 large orange for 2 servings.

SHREDS AND PATCHES SALAD

1 cup each shredded cabbage, raw carrots, cauliflower bits |
½ cup each chopped green peppers, canned crushed pineapple |
¼ teaspoon salt |
1 tablespoon French dressing mixed with 2 tablespoons pineapple juice

Combine, toss and serve on lettuce leaves in a large salad bowl. Parsley and carrot wheels for garnish.

Serves 4 to 6.

RAW SPINACH SALAD

¼ cup peanut butter | 3 tablespoons orange or pineapple juice |
2 cups washed, drained and chopped spinach (tightly packed) |
3 hard-cooked eggs, sliced or cut in wedges | ⅛ teaspoon salt |
Lettuce or chicory leaves | Radish roses or black olives for garnish (optional)

Mix to a smooth paste peanut butter and fruit juice and combine with chopped spinach. Season to taste with salt. Arrange in lettuce cups or on chicory leaves and garnish with hard-cooked egg and radish roses or olives.

Serves 6.

SPLIT RAIL SALAD

1 medium size yellow turnip | Shredded lettuce | 4 slices of canned pineapple |
½ cup each pineapple syrup and orange juice | 1 tablespoon rum or sherry

Pare the turnip and cut into strips $\frac{1}{4}$ inch thick (as for Julienne potatoes). Arrange these 'split rails' horizontally, then in the opposite formation in 3 layers of 4 or 5 strips, on a bed of shredded lettuce. (It is best to make individual salads.) Cut pineapple slices in halves or quarters and insert between 'rails' or at side of plate.

Make a dressing by combining fruit juice, fruit syrup and rum and drizzle it over each salad just before serving. Or serve separately to be added at table.

Serves 4 to 6.

SPRING SALAD

3 tender endive leaves | 3 small green onions | 3 wedges of tomato | 1 green pepper ring | 1 tablespoon salad dressing

Arrange endive leaves on one side of salad plate. Place the green onions (tips removed) on opposite side of the plate. Arrange the tomato wedges between and place the green pepper ring where the onion greens and endive meet. The salad dressing gob in the centre of the pepper ring completes the picture. Add a dash of paprika if you like.

Serves 1.

WALDORF SALAD

2 apples | 1 tablespoon lemon juice | $\frac{1}{2}$ cup raisins | $\frac{1}{2}$ cup chopped nuts | 1 cup diced celery | $\frac{1}{2}$ cup mayonnaise | 1 tablespoon sugar | Lettuce

Dice apples and add lemon juice. Combine with raisins, nuts, celery and dressing to which sugar has been added. Serve in lettuce cups.

Serves 4.

LUNCHEON SALADS

FARMERS' CHOP SUEY

1 cucumber | 2 tomatoes | 1 green pepper | 4 stalks celery and leaves | 2 spring onions | Sprig of parsley | 2 cups shredded lettuce | Sour cream

Score unpared cucumber and slice very thin. Dice tomatoes. Cut pepper, celery and onions fine. Add parsley and shredded lettuce. Combine all in a salad bowl, add a dash of salt and pepper. Serve with plenty of sour cream.

Serves 4.

Variation: Add diced boiled potatoes.

SALMON SALAD

1 *large can red salmon | 1 tablespoon prepared mustard | ¼ cup salad oil |*
¼ cup lemon juice | 2 hard-cooked eggs, mashed | 1 tablespoon onion juice |
Salad greens | 1 cup diced celery | Celery cabbage |
3 tomatoes or 1 cucumber | 1 green pepper | Parsley

Drain liquid from salmon reserving liquid. Remove skin and bones and flake the fish. Rub mustard, oil and lemon juice to a smooth paste. Add mashed eggs, onion juice, and a little of the fish liquor. Combine with salmon and arrange on a bed of salad greens. Garnish with diced celery, ½-inch slices of celery cabbage, topped with slices of cucumber or tomatoes and pepper. Use plenty of parsley to garnish.

Serves 6.

Variation: Substitute 1 cup flaked canned tuna fish for salmon.

COUNTRY CLUB SALAD

1 *oval can kippered herring (in tomato sauce) | ¼ cup lemon juice |*
1 *tablespoon brown sugar | 3 hard-cooked eggs, chopped | Parsley |*
2 cups shredded carrot | 1 cup diced celery | 1 head lettuce |
1 *can peas, drained | 1 green pepper | 2 medium cucumbers, sliced*

Remove bones from herring. Flake fish. Add lemon juice, sugar and eggs to the tomato sauce. Add minced parsley, shredded carrot and celery. Arrange on bed of lettuce placing peas in centre of mound. Garnish with cucumber slices and pepper strips.

Serves 8.

MACARONI OR SPAGHETTI SALAD

Combine cooked macaroni or spaghetti with any salad dressing. It will require 1 pound of dry macaroni or spaghetti and 1 cup dressing to serve 10 to 12.

Variation: Press into a buttered ring mould. Chill. Unmould on a bed of lettuce and garnish with strips of canned pimento.

MEAT LUNCHEON SALAD

1 *cup diced cooked chicken* | 1 *cup diced cooked lamb* |
1 *cup diced cooked veal* | 1 *cup diced celery* | 3 *hard-cooked eggs, diced* |
1 *cup mayonnaise* | *Salt, pepper and celery salt* | 8 *beets* |
2 *green peppers (8 rings)* | *Olives, radishes, small pickles* |
Lettuce, endive, chicory

Combine the meats, celery and chopped eggs with mayonnaise and season to taste. Arrange on a large serving plate and garnish with beet and pepper rings, radish roses, pickles, olives, parsley sprigs. Arrange lettuce and other greens around and under the edges of the salad mound. Chill before serving. To make beet and radish roses, make cuts into but not through tops to simulate petals.

Serves 8.

POTATO SALAD

10 *medium potatoes* | 1 *cup diced celery* | ½ *cup minced onion (optional)* |
½ *cup minced parsley* | 3 *hard-cooked eggs* |
2 *tablespoons prepared mustard* | 1 *cup salad dressing*
Salad greens or lettuce |

Boil potatoes in jackets in salted water till tender. Drain. Peel as soon as cool. Dice or slice, add celery, onion and parsley and season to taste. Chop or dice eggs, add mustard and dressing. Combine and chill before serving in a bowl lined with greens. Garnish with parsley, sliced hard-cooked eggs and radishes.

Serves 8 to 10.

Variation 1: For additional protein and calories, serve with cubes of Cheddar cheese.

Variation 2: For a fish meal, add bits of canned herring fillets in wine sauce, or add anchovy paste to dressing.

Variation 3: For a meat meal, add diced sausage, smoked tongue or bits of corned beef mixed with dressing before combining. Or, garnish with rolls of thinly sliced sausage fastened with coloured toothpicks. Black or green olives, radish roses and raw carrot curls make attractive garnishes.

STUFFED TOMATOES (Basic Recipe)

Cut off the stem ends of as many tomatoes as required. One to a serving is customary. Cut down but not through, making 6 or 8 sections, held together at the blossom end. Place a large spoonful of filling on top and press down gently. Top with mayonnaise or thick salad dressing. Or use a topping of sour cream with a garnish of parsley or a dash of paprika for colour. Add a few slices of pimento-stuffed green olives if you like.

STUFFINGS

Chicken salad.
Tuna fish or canned salmon salad.
Cottage cheese mixed with chopped nuts and raisins.
Creamed cottage cheese mixed with diced celery, green pepper, sweet red pepper and enough dressing to combine.
Chopped hard-cooked eggs combined with diced Marinierte Herring and dressing.
Flaked leftover baked, grilled or fried fish mixed with diced cucumber and dressing.
Eggplant salad Roumanian style, topped with parsley. Add an olive.
Flaked cooked chicken, diced celery and peppers combined with dressing.
Chopped liver, chicken or beef, to which has been added chopped greben. Top with a sprig of parsley.

TOMATO AND CHEESE ASPIC

1½ packages unflavoured gelatin | 1 cup boiling water |
1 tablespoon lemon juice | ¾ pound cream cheese | Dash of salt |
2 tablespoons chopped green pepper or parsley | 1 can tomato soup

Combine gelatin, boiling water and lemon juice and chill while preparing other ingredients. Combine cheese, salt, chopped greens and add to tomato soup. Add gelatin mixture and turn into 6 rinsed individual moulds or a loaf pan. Chill until solid and unmould on lettuce topped with salad dressing or mayonnaise.
Serves 6.

RAW TURNIP SALAD

2 cups shredded raw turnips, white or yellow | ½ cup shredded raw carrot | ½ cup celery, diced | ½ cup French dressing | Salt to taste

Combine and serve on lettuce leaves as soon as prepared.
Serves 6.

21 'Let Them Eat Cake'— Many Kinds

General Rules for Cake Making

Follow directions carefully.

Measure ingredients accurately.

Combine as directed in the recipe.

Oven temperature for baking is important. If oven is not equipped with temperature control, an inexpensive oven thermometer will be very helpful.

Types of Cakes

Angel cakes are made without shortening, egg whites only.

Butter cakes are cakes made with butter or vegetable shortening.

Sponge cakes are also made without shortening but include whole eggs, beaten separately.

Types of Cake Batters

Pour batter is made with 1 cup liquid to 1 cup flour.

Drop batter is made with 1 cup liquid to 2 cups flour.

Soft dough is made with 1 cup liquid to 3 cups flour.

Stiff dough is made with 1 cup liquid to 4 or more cups flour.

Coffee Cakes and Kuchens are generally made of yeast dough.

Tips on Baking of Cakes

All-Purpose Flour should be sifted before measuring, then sifted as directed in recipe.

Shortening should be measured in a cup indicating amount of contents in quarters. If the measuring cup is $\frac{1}{2}$ filled with water, adding butter to bring contents up to the cup line indicates $\frac{1}{2}$ cup of butter.

Creaming of shortening and sugar is important if a fine-textured cake is desired. An electric mixer is best for this purpose. Next best mixing technique is using a wooden spoon in a deep bowl.

Combining separately beaten egg yolks with the creamed mixture is best achieved with the use of a fork (in the absence of an electric mixer).

Flavouring is added by folding in after all ingredients are mixed.

Adding Beaten Egg Whites must be done carefully, with a fold-over motion, in order to avoid destroying the air pockets and thereby taking a chance on a heavy cake.

Leavening

Single-action baking powder (tartrate and calcium-phosphate).

Double-action baking powder (so indicated on container).

Tartrate, composed of cream of tartar in addition to other ingredients.

Baking soda, used in combination with sour cream, sour milk, or buttermilk. It is not a balanced leavening agent in itself. Follow recipe directions.

SUGAR SUBSTITUTES IN BAKING

(With honey, honey and sugar and molasses, use $\frac{1}{4}$ less of liquid called for in recipe. With corn syrup, sugar and corn syrup, use $\frac{1}{3}$ less of liquid called for in recipe.)

$\frac{3}{4}$ cup honey	takes the place of 1 cup sugar
$\frac{1}{2}$ cup sugar plus $\frac{1}{2}$ cup honey	1 cup sugar
$\frac{3}{4}$ cup molasses plus 1 teaspoon baking soda	1 cup sugar
1 cup corn syrup (in cakes, biscuits, muffins)	1 cup sugar
$\frac{3}{4}$ cup sugar plus $\frac{1}{4}$ cup corn syrup (in sweet cakes and candies)	1 cup sugar
$1\frac{1}{3}$ cups maple sugar	1 cup sugar

Size of Cakes: In the following recipes, unless otherwise noted, ingredients are specified for a 9-inch diameter cake pan or an 8 × 12-inch oblong or rectangular pan.

CAKE RECIPES

BASIC CAKE RECIPE

1 cup sugar | $\frac{3}{4}$ cup shortening | 2 eggs, separated | 2 cups sifted flour |
2 teaspoons baking powder | 1 cup milk (or other liquid) |
1 teaspoon flavouring | Pinch of salt

Cream sugar and shortening. Add egg yolks and continue creaming until sugar particles are thoroughly dissolved. Sift dry ingredients together two or three times. Combine creamed mixture with dry ingredients and liquid, adding a little of each alternately while mixing with a rotary motion. Fold in stiffly beaten egg whites. Fill well-greased cake pan ½ to ⅔ full. Bake for 20 to 30 minutes at 350° F. or gas mark 4. Cool on a wire cake rack.

Variations:

Chocolate Spice Cake. Can be made by adding 1 teaspoon each cinnamon and allspice and 2 tablespoons cocoa to dry ingredients before sifting. Bake in a loaf pan and top, when cold, with chocolate icing (see Index). For a 2-layer cake, put layers together with chocolate or white icing. Or fill with white icing and decorate with chocolate icing.

Raisin Cake. Add ½ cup seeded raisins dusted with a little flour. Bake in a loaf pan. Dust with icing sugar when cold.

Filled Cake. Bake in 2 round layers. Cut the centre from one layer, leaving a rim about 2 inches wide. Put the cake rim on top of the other, spreading a little jam or icing to hold together. Fill with fresh berries and top with whipped cream.

Apricot Cut-Out Cake. Apricot or prune whip (see Index) makes a delicious filling.

Lemon-Custard Cake. With a biscuit cutter or thin glass, cut 6 circles out of top layer. Put together and fill with thick lemon custard (see Index). Allow time for custard to cool before serving.

Petit Tea Cakes. Bake in a large shallow pan. Let cool in the pan and cut into small squares, oblongs, crescents, diamonds, etc. Cover with several different icings and decorate with chopped nuts, cinnamon candies, candied fruit peel, sliced gum drops, almond halves or chopped nuts.

Frostettes. Bake in greased individual baking tins and ice as desired.

Marble Cake. Divide batter in two. Add 1 ounce melted chocolate to one portion. With a spoon make swirls of the dark batter in the light batter in pan.

Black and White Cake. Bake in a tube or spring-form cake pan. When cold, ice half of cake with white and the other half with chocolate icing.

ANGEL FOOD CAKE

1 cup sifted cake flour with ¾ cup sugar |
1¼ cups egg whites (10 to 12 approximately) | ¼ teaspoon salt |
1¼ teaspoons cream of tartar | ¾ cup sugar |
¼ teaspoon vanilla or almond extract

Sift flour mixture into mixing bowl. Beat egg whites with salt till foamy, then add cream of tartar while beating with increased speed if using an electric mixer. When stiff but not dry, add sugar gradually while beating till combined. Gradually add flour and sugar mixture after sifting twice, stirring or reducing speed in electric mixer. Fold in flavouring. Turn into a 10-inch tube cake pan and bake for 1 hour at 325° F. or gas mark 3. Invert and let cool 1 hour before removing from pan.

SALLY'S APPLE CAKE

1½ cups flour | 1 teaspoon baking powder | Pinch of salt |
½ cup sugar | ⅓ cup butter or shortening | 1 egg, beaten |
Enough milk to form a ball of dough | 4 cups thin slices of apples |
Dash of cinnamon or nutmeg | Grated rind of ½ lemon

Sift the dry ingredients twice and cut in the butter or vegetable shortening with two knives or a pastry blender. When crumbles have formed, add the beaten egg diluted with a little milk, enough to combine into a ball of dough. Chill an hour in refrigerator before cutting into two sections.

Roll one part of dough into a rectangle to fit the bottom of a well-greased oblong cake pan. Let it come up the sides slightly. Spread the sliced apples evenly, dot with grated lemon rind and sprinkle with cinnamon or nutmeg. Roll out the second ball of dough the same way and cover, fluting the edges as you do a pie if you desire.

Bake at 325° F. or gas mark 3 for 20 minutes then turn up the heat for 10 minutes to 350° F. or gas mark 4. When evenly browned remove from oven. Let cool before removing from baking pan to serving plate.

APPLESAUCE CAKE

1 *cup applesauce (sweetened)* | 1 *teaspoon baking soda* |
Juice and grated rind of 1 *lemon* | 1¾ *cups flour* | ¼ *teaspoon salt* |
½ *teaspoon each cinnamon, allspice* | ¼ *teaspoon nutmeg* |
½ *cup seedless raisins* | 3 *tablespoons shortening, melted*

Dissolve baking soda in applesauce, add lemon rind and juice. Sift together all dry ingredients. Roll the raisins in some of the flour mixture. Combine with first mixture and fold in the hot melted shortening. Turn into a well-greased loaf pan. Bake at 350° F. or gas mark 4 for 40 minutes or till nicely browned. Serve un-iced.

Variation: Turn into individual baking tins for small cakes. Serve plain or with icing on top of cakes. This cake does not dry out for a week. Keep covered.

BANANA CAKE

½ *cup shortening* | 1 *cup sugar* | 2 *eggs* | 2 *cups flour* |
½ *teaspoon baking powder* | ¾ *teaspoon baking soda* | ¼ *teaspoon salt* |
1 *cup mashed bananas* | ¼ *cup sour milk* | 1 *teaspoon vanilla*

Cream shortening and sugar. Add well-beaten eggs and stir till creamy. Stir together all dry ingredients and add alternately with mashed bananas blended with sour milk. Add flavouring. Turn into two 9-inch greased cake pans. Bake at 350° F. or gas mark 4 for 30 minutes. Remove to wire rack. When cool put together with lemon filling and top with white icing flavoured with lemon juice.

COCONUT SNOW CAKE

½ *cup shortening* | 1 *cup sugar* | 2 *eggs* | 2 *cups cake flour* |
3 *teaspoons baking powder* | ¼ *teaspoon salt* | ⅔ *cup milk* |
1 *teaspoon vanilla* | ⅔ *cup shredded coconut* | ⅓ *cup currant jelly*

Cream shortening and sugar. Add one egg at a time and continue creaming. Sift dry ingredients together twice and stir in alternately with milk, beating after each addition. Add flavouring. Turn into two 9-inch greased cake pans and bake for 10 minutes at 350° F. or gas mark 4. Turn up heat to 375° F. or gas mark 5 for an additional 15 minutes. When the layers are cool, put together with currant jelly and ice top and sides with white icing. Spread shredded coconut over top and sides while icing is soft.

DEVIL'S FOOD CAKE

2 cups cake flour | ½ teaspoon baking soda |
1½ teaspoons double-acting baking powder | 1 teaspoon salt |
1½ cups sugar | ½ cup butter or vegetable shortening |
⅔ cup buttermilk or sour milk | ⅓ cup hot milk to melt |
3 squares chocolate | 2 eggs | 1 teaspoon vanilla

Sift together the first five ingredients listed. Add butter and sour milk, stirring lightly. Add milk and chocolate mixture as soon as cool enough. Fold in slightly beaten eggs and flavouring. Beat 2 or 3 minutes and turn into two 8-inch greased layer cake pans. (If using an electric beater, beat at medium speed.) Bake for 30 minutes at 350° F. or gas mark 4, or till evenly browned on top. Put together with white or chocolate filling. Dust top with icing sugar or ice with chocolate or white icing.

BROWN SUGAR FUDGE CAKE

¾ cup shortening | 1¾ cups firmly packed dark brown sugar |
1 egg and 3 additional yolks | 4 ounces unsweetened chocolate |
2¼ cups flour | 1½ teaspoons baking soda | ¼ teaspoon salt |
1½ cups milk | 2 teaspoons vanilla

Cream sugar and shortening and add egg. Beat well and add yolks one at a time, beating well after each addition. Melt chocolate in top of double boiler over hot water and stir into the creamed mixture. Sift together dry ingredients and stir in alternately with the milk. Add vanilla last. Turn into 2 greased 9-inch square cake pans and bake 40 minutes at 350° F. or gas mark 4. Cool before icing or dust with icing sugar. Delicious and easy to serve from the pans after cutting into 1½-inch squares.

FRUIT CAKE (Traditional American Recipe)

1 *cup shortening* | 2 *cups sugar* | 8 *eggs* | 4 *cups flour and* 1 *teaspoon salt* |
1 *teaspoon each cinnamon, nutmeg, cloves* |
3 *teaspoons baking soda, dissolved in* ½ *cup cold water* |
¼ *pound each candied orange, lemon peels* | ¼ *pound citron* |
¼ *pound each candied cherries and pineapple* |
¼ *pound each dried apricots, figs, dates (pitted)* | ¾ *pound chopped walnuts* |
½ *pound cut pecans* | 2 *pounds each seeded raisins, currants* |
1 *cup sherry or rum*

Cream sugar and shortening. Add eggs and continue creaming. When smooth, stir in sifted dry ingredients except baking soda. Dissolve baking soda in cold water and stir in. Combine finely cut or chopped fruits and candied peels, and nuts. Add 2 tablespoons flour to fruits and blend all together, adding sherry last. Turn into 3 well-greased loaf pans or 2 spring-form cake pans. Bake for 1¼ hours at 300° F. or gas mark 1–2, turn heat to 325° F. or gas mark 3 for 1 hour, and again down to 300° F. for ½ hour. Be careful not to let this cake bake too rapidly or it may fall and become sticky. Fruit Cake should be ripened or aged 3 or 4 weeks before cutting. Store in a covered tin or crock.

BLACK FRUIT CAKE

½ *cup shortening* | 2 *cups brown sugar* | 1 *square bitter chocolate* |
½ *cup black coffee* | 2 *tablespoons molasses* | 2 *eggs* | 2 *cups flour* |
3 *teaspoons baking powder* | ½ *teaspoon salt* | ½ *teaspoon cinnamon* |
¼ *teaspoon each cloves and mace* | ½ *cup each seeded raisins and currants* |
¼ *cup each shredded citron, candied orange and grapefruit peel*

Cream shortening and sugar. Beat in melted chocolate. Dissolve molasses in coffee, stir in, add beaten eggs. Sift together all dry ingredients, roll the fruits in this. Combine with first mixture. Turn into well-greased loaf pan. Bake at 250° F. or gas mark ¼–½ for 20 minutes, turn up heat gradually every 10 minutes till 350° F. or gas mark 4 is reached. Cake should be baked in 1 hour and 20 minutes.

HONEY CAKE

3 eggs | 1 cup sugar | 2 tablespoons salad oil |
3½ cups flour (measured after sifting once) | 2 teaspoons baking powder |
1 teaspoon baking soda | ½ teaspoon salt | ½ teaspoon ginger |
¼ teaspoon nutmeg | 1 teaspoon cinnamon | Dash of cloves | 1 cup honey |
1 cup warm coffee | ½ cup chopped English walnuts (or any other nuts)

Beat eggs with sugar till combined and stir in salad oil till smooth.
Sift the measured sifted flour with other dry ingredients twice. Stir
in the egg mixture, alternately with the honey and coffee combined,
till smooth. Then stir in the chopped nuts. The batter will be fairly
soft and easily stirred. Turn into well-greased and floured round cake
pan and bake 50 minutes at 325° F. or gas mark 3. When removed
from the cake pan, dust with icing sugar if the cake is to be served
within a few hours.

To keep this cake for several days, cover top and sides with uncooked icing, made as thick or as thin as desired, by combining icing
sugar with either fruit juice or evaporated milk to the consistency
desired for spreading. Or, soften butter to mix with sugar and
flavour with rum, vanilla extract or lemon juice.

LEKACH (Traditional Honey Cake)

6 eggs, or 4 eggs plus ½ cup coffee | 1 cup sugar | 1 cup honey |
2 tablespoons salad oil or melted shortening | 3½ cups flour |
1½ teaspoons baking powder | 1 teaspoon baking soda |
¼ teaspoon ground cloves | ½ teaspoon each allspice, cinnamon |
½ cup each raisins, chopped nuts | ¼ cup finely cut citron |
2 tablespoons brandy

Beat eggs, adding sugar gradually while beating until light and
creamy. Stir in honey and shortening. (The 6-egg recipe makes a
cake of finer texture.) If using eggs and coffee, dilute honey with
hot coffee before combining. Sift together all dry ingredients and
add nuts and fruit before combining with first mixture. Add brandy
last. Turn into a greased, paper-lined rectangular pan and bake at
310° F. or gas mark 2 for 1 hour. Invert and allow cake to cool before
removing. When ready to serve, cut into squares or diamond shapes.

NUT AND RAISIN HONEY CAKE
(Traditional Holiday Cake)

2 eggs | 1 cup sugar | ½ cup salad oil | ½ pound honey |
2 tablespoons brandy | 2 cups flour | 2 teaspoons baking powder |
½ teaspoon baking soda | ⅛ teaspoon salt | ½ cup seedless raisins |
¼ cup chopped nuts | ½ cup hot coffee

Beat eggs, adding sugar while beating till smooth and creamy. Stir
in oil till smooth, add honey and brandy and beat with spoon till
well blended. Sift dry ingredients together and add raisins and nuts.
Combine with creamy mixture, adding a little coffee while stirring
to a smooth batter. Turn into a wax-paper-lined baking pan
8 × 11 × 2 inches and bake at 350° F. or gas mark 4 for 1 hour. If
browned at edges and light brown on top the honey cake is done.
Test by inserting a toothpick in centre. If toothpick comes out dry,
remove cake from oven to cool. Cut into slices 1½ inches wide, then
diagonally to make diamond shapes.

JELLY ROLL (Basic Recipe)

4 eggs, separated | ¾ cup sugar | 1 cup cake flour |
2 teaspoons baking powder | ¼ cup cold water |
2 tablespoons butter or vegetable shortening | 1 tablespoon flour |
1 cup currant or grape jelly | 2 tablespoons icing sugar

Beat egg yolks and sugar till thick and lemon-coloured. Sift together
flour and baking powder and stir in gradually, adding a few drops of
water alternately till well combined and smooth. Beat egg whites
stiff and fold in lightly. Coat the bottom of a flat baking tin with
butter or shortening and dust lightly with flour. Spread the batter
evenly in the pan and bake in a preheated oven 10 to 15 minutes
at 375° F. or gas mark 5. While hot, loosen the edges of cake with a
spatula and turn out on a double fold of heavy wax paper a few
inches larger than the baking pan. Cut away the crust of cake from
the narrow ends and quickly roll up from the long end. Wrap in the
wax paper and twist edges together at both ends. When cool, unroll
and spread lightly with jelly. Roll up quickly and dust with icing
sugar.
Serves 8.

Variation 1: Chocolate Roll is made by adding 2 tablespoons cocoa to the dry ingredients before combining with egg mixture. Or, stir in 3 tablespoons chocolate syrup before folding in the egg whites.

Variation 2: Omit jelly filling. Spread with 1 cup heavy cream beaten stiff and flavoured with ½ teaspoon vanilla or rum. Spread the cream evenly, reserving about ¼ for topping rolled-up cake. Chill 1 hour before serving. Whipped cream filling may be used with basic recipe or Variation 1. Cream-filled roll must be refrigerated if not served immediately.

LEBKUCHEN (Traditional Recipe)

4 eggs | 1 pound brown sugar | 3½ cups flour | 1 teaspoon baking powder | 2 teaspoons cinnamon | ¼ teaspoon allspice | ¼ cup shredded citron | ¼ cup chopped walnuts or almonds

Beat eggs and sugar till creamy. Sift dry ingredients and stir in. Blend in the chopped nuts and citron. Spread the dough to ½-inch thickness on a wax-paper-lined baking sheet. Bake in a moderate oven (350° F. or gas mark 4) about 30 minutes. Cover with a thin icing made of icing sugar and water before cake is cool. Cut into squares or oblongs. Keep 1 week before serving. Keep in a well-covered jar.

MANDELBRODT 1 (Komishbrodt)

1 cup sugar | 3 eggs | 6 tablespoons salad oil | Grated rind of 1 lemon | 1 teaspoon lemon juice | ¼ teaspoon almond extract | 2¾ cups flour | 4 teaspoons baking powder | ¼ teaspoon salt | ½ cup coarsely cut blanched almonds

Beat eggs and sugar till light and stir in the oil and flavourings. Sift together flour, baking powder and salt. Combine, adding nuts as dough is formed. Knead on a floured board. Form into long rolls about 3 inches wide and an inch thick. Bake 40 to 45 minutes at 350° F. or gas mark 4, or till light brown. Remove to bread board and slice while warm. Half-inch-thick cuts are best. Place slices cut side up on a baking sheet. Either slip under grill for a quick browning, or on the top shelf of oven till browned on both sides.

Yields approximately 36 to 40.

Variation: For chocolate-filled Mandelbrodt, take one quarter of the dough before shaping into rolls and work into it 2 tablespoons cocoa mixed with 1 tablespoon sugar and a dash of cinnamon. Form into roll about ½ inch thick. Wrap remaining rolled and flattened white dough around. Shape into two rolls and bake.

MANDELBRODT 2

3 eggs | ½ cup sugar | 1½ teaspoons baking powder |
1½ cups flour | ½ cup finely chopped blanched almonds

Beat eggs and sugar until thick. Sift the flour and baking powder, and add the almonds. Combine mixtures and pour the batter into a well-greased narrow loaf pan. Bake in a moderate oven 40 to 45 minutes at 350° F. or gas mark 4. When cold, cut into ½-inch slices.

Yields approximately 24.

WHITE NUT CAKE

¼ cup shortening (butter or substitute) | ⅔ cup sugar |
1½ cups cake flour | 1½ teaspoons baking powder | ¼ teaspoon salt |
½ cup chopped pecans, walnuts or almonds | ½ cup milk |
2 egg whites | ½ teaspoon vanilla

Cream shortening and gradually work in the sugar till smooth. Sift together the dry ingredients and add the chopped nuts. Add the dry mixture to the creamed mixture alternately with the milk, stirring till smooth. Beat egg whites stiff and fold in. Add vanilla. Turn the cake mixture into a well-buttered and lightly-floured square cake pan. Bake 40 minutes at 350° F. or gas mark 4, or till firm to the touch in the centre and lightly browned on top. Remove from the pan and dust with icing sugar or finely ground nuts if desired. Cut into 9 squares when serving.

SOUR CREAM WALNUT CAKE

1 cup sugar | 1 cup butter or substitute | 3 eggs, separated |
2 tablespoons grated orange rind | 2 tablespoons grated lemon rind |
2 cups cake flour | 1 teaspoon baking powder | 1 teaspoon baking soda |
1 cup finely ground walnuts | ¾ cup sour cream

Cream sugar and butter. Add egg yolks and grated rind of orange
and lemon. Stir till smooth. Sift together flour, baking powder and
baking soda. Dust some of the dry mixture over nuts and stir into the
creamed mixture alternately with the sour cream. Beat egg whites
stiff and fold in lightly. Turn the mixture into a buttered spring-
form cake pan and bake 1 hour at 350° F. or gas mark 4. Remove
cake from pan while hot. Prick the top of cake all over with a fork
and baste with the following:

SAUCE FOR WALNUT CAKE

2 tablespoons orange juice | 2 tablespoons lemon juice | ¾ cup sugar

Combine and bring to a boil. Baste the cake with this sauce while
hot, spooning it on so that the cake absorbs it rapidly. There should
be about 8 ounces of sauce.

MOLASSES NUT CAKE

1 cup boiling water | ½ cup vegetable shortening |
½ cup dark brown sugar | ⅔ cup molasses | 1 teaspoon baking soda |
1 egg | 2 cups cake flour, sifted | ½ teaspoon salt |
½ cup chopped walnuts | ½ teaspoon lemon extract

Combine boiling water, shortening, brown sugar and molasses in a
mixing bowl and stir in the baking soda till smooth. Beat egg
and combine with salt and chopped nuts. Stir the sifted flour into
the egg and nuts mixture till well combined. Blend the first mixture
and second combination by stirring till smooth and add the lemon
flavouring. Turn into 2 well-greased round cake pans and bake 30
minutes at 350° F. or gas mark 4. Put together when cold with your
favourite filling and icing. Or use the following:

BANANA FILLING AND ICING

3 tablespoons butter or substitute | 1½ cups sifted icing sugar |
1 large banana | 1 tablespoon lemon juice

Cream butter and icing sugar till smooth. Mash banana to a pulp or
put through a sieve and mix with lemon juice. Combine both mixtures and beat till light and the mixture holds its shape. Spread ⅓
the amount between cake layers and top the cake with remainder.

ORANGE CAKE

½ cup butter | 1½ cups sugar | ½ cup orange juice |
Grated rind of 1 orange | ½ cup cream or milk |
2½ cups flour | 2 teaspoons baking powder | 2 whole eggs |
1 teaspoon vanilla

ORANGE ICING

1 cup icing sugar | Juice and grated rind of orange |
½ teaspoon lemon juice

Cream butter and sugar. Add orange juice, grated rind, and cream.
Blend well. Sift flour and baking powder. Add one egg and half the
dry mixture, blending well, before adding the second egg and
remainder of flour. Add flavouring. Bake in 2-layer cake pans at
350° F. or gas mark 4 for 40 minutes. Put together with orange
icing. Shredded coconut may be added to icing.

OREGON PRUNE CAKE

1 cup sifted wheat flour | 1 teaspoon double-acting baking powder |
4 tablespoons sugar | ½ teaspoon salt | 3 tablespoons shortening |
1 egg, beaten | 1 tablespoon milk (approximately) |
12 halved prunes or 10 cooked, seeded, dried whole prunes |
1 tablespoon sugar | ¼ teaspoon cinnamon | ¼ cup butter or margarine |
½ cup walnut meats, broken

Sift together flour, baking powder, sugar and salt. Cut in shortening until well blended. Stir in egg and add milk to make a soft dough. Turn mixture into greased 8-inch square baking pan, press in prunes, dust with sugar, sprinkle with cinnamon, dot with butter, cover with walnut meats. Bake at 375° F. or gas mark 5 for 30 minutes.

CRANBERRY UPSIDE-DOWN CAKE

TOPPING

4 tablespoons butter or vegetable shortening | 1 cup brown sugar | 2 cups cranberries

CAKE

1½ cups sifted flour | 2 teaspoons baking powder | ¼ teaspoon salt | ¼ cup shortening | ½ cup sugar | 1 egg | ½ cup milk | 1 teaspoon vanilla

Grease an 8-inch square pan. Preheat oven to 350° F. or gas mark 4. Melt butter in pan. Add sugar and blend it in thoroughly. Let it almost melt. Add cranberries, spreading evenly. Place pan where topping will keep warm but do not leave over direct heat.

Sift flour, baking powder and salt. Cream shortening, blend in sugar gradually. Add egg and beat until mixture is light and fluffy. Add vanilla to milk. Add dry ingredients to egg and shortening mixture alternately with milk, stirring after each addition until batter is smooth. Do not stir too much. Turn into square pan, distributing batter evenly over cranberries. Bake 35 minutes at 350° F. or gas mark 4 in preheated oven until cake shrinks from sides of pan and is nicely browned. Let stand two or three minutes. Turn on to serving plate or platter.

PINEAPPLE UPSIDE-DOWN CAKE

Follow recipe for Cranberry Upside-Down Cake, substituting canned pineapple slices in topping, using a round cake pan.

Variation : Place maraschino cherries in centres of pineapple slices. Or canned cherries.

TUTTI-FRUTTI UPSIDE-DOWN CAKE

TOPPING

3 *tablespoons butter or vegetable shortening* | ½ *cup brown sugar* |
8 *to* 10 *dried apricot halves* | ¾ *cup canned pineapple cubes* |
Pecan halves | *Maraschino cherries*

CAKE

1¼ *cups sifted flour* | 1½ *teaspoons baking powder* |
¼ *teaspoon salt* | ⅓ *cup shortening* | ½ *cup sugar* | 1 *egg* |
½ *cup pineapple syrup*

Grease an 8-inch round or square cake pan. Preheat oven to moderate, 350° F. or gas mark 4. Prepare topping first. Melt butter or vegetable shortening, blend in brown sugar. Distribute evenly over pan. Arrange fruits neatly in the sugar. Place pan where it will keep slightly warm.

Sift flour. Add baking powder and sift together. Cream shortening, add sugar gradually. Add egg and beat until mixture is light and fluffy. Add dry ingredients alternately with pineapple syrup. Pour over topping, distributing evenly. Bake, until cake shrinks from sides of pan, at 350° F. or gas mark 4 for 45 to 55 minutes. Let stand 5 minutes. Turn on to platter.

PUMPKIN CAKE (Like Granny Made)

½ *cup shortening* | 1¼ *cups sugar* | 2 *eggs* | 2¼ *cups cake flour* |
3 *teaspoons baking powder* | ½ *teaspoon salt* |½ *teaspoon cinnamon* |
½ *teaspoon ginger* | ½ *teaspoon nutmeg* | 1 *cup cooked pumpkin* |
¾ *cup milk* | ½ *teaspoon soda* | ½ *cup chopped nuts*

Cream shortening and sugar thoroughly. Blend in beaten eggs. Sift flour, baking powder, salt and spices. Mix pumpkin and milk together, stir in soda.

Add flour and pumpkin mixtures alternately to creamed mixture. Blend in nuts. Pour into well-greased and floured pans. Bake 50 to 55 minutes at 350° F. or gas mark 4.

SPONGE CAKE (Basic Recipe)

1 cup sifted cake flour | ¼ teaspoon salt | 5 eggs, separated |
1½ tablespoons lemon juice | 1 teaspoon grated rind of lemon |
1 cup sugar

Sift flour and salt four times. Beat egg yolks till thick and creamy. Add lemon juice and grated rind. Beat egg whites stiff but not dry, add sugar gradually while beating till smooth. Combine with the egg yolk mixture and sift one-third of the flour on the surface. Fold in till smooth before adding half of remaining dry mixture. Combine lightly. Fold in balance. Turn into an ungreased tube pan and bake at 300° F. or gas mark 2 for 30 minutes, then turn up heat gradually to 350° F. or gas mark 4 during the next 33 minutes. Remove from oven, invert and let cake cool over a wire rack 1 hour.

BUTTER SPONGE CAKE

6 eggs | 1¾ cups sugar | ½ teaspoon salt | 2 cups cake flour |
2 teaspoons baking powder | ½ cup melted butter |
1 teaspoon vanilla or almond flavouring

Beat eggs and sugar together till light lemon-coloured and thick. Sift together dry ingredients 3 times. Stir in egg and mixture till well combined. Stir in melted butter and flavouring. Turn into an ungreased 10-inch spring form and bake 1 hour at 350° F. or gas mark 4.
Variation 1 : With a sharp knife cut this cake in two horizontally. Fill with pineapple filling and put together.
Variation 2 : Use 1 package of lemon filling or vanilla pudding prepared according to instructions on the package and spread between the two layers of this cake.

HOT WATER SPONGE CAKE

1 cup sifted cake flour | 1½ teaspoons baking powder |
¼ teaspoon salt | 2 eggs, separated | 1½ tablespoons lemon juice
and grated rind | 1 cup sugar | 6 tablespoons hot water

Sift flour, baking powder and salt. Beat egg yolks till creamy and
23

add lemon juice and grated rind, beating till thick. Beat egg whites
stiff but not dry. Fold in a little sugar at a time while beating till
sugar has been thoroughly blended. Combine egg mixtures and
fold in a little of the flour mixture at a time alternately with hot
water. Turn into an ungreased cake pan and bake 1 hour at 325° F.
or gas mark 3. Invert over a cake rack 1 hour before removing cake.

TOMATO SOUP CAKE

*2 tablespoons butter | 1 cup sugar | 1 can condensed tomato soup |
½ can cold water | 1 teaspoon baking soda | 2 cups sifted flour |
2 teaspoons baking powder | 1 teaspoon each cinnamon, nutmeg, cloves |
1 cup seeded raisins, cut fine, or ½ cup each seedless raisins and
chopped nuts*

Cream butter and sugar. Add tomato soup diluted with cold water
in which the baking soda has been dissolved. Sift together flour and
baking powder, add spices and sift again. Stir raisins and nuts into
the dry mixture and then combine with first mixture, stirring till
smoothly blended. Turn into a greased cake pan and bake 45
minutes at 350° F. or gas mark 4. Test by inserting a toothpick in
centre of cake. If dry, remove cake from pan on to cake rack. Cool
away from draughts. This cake is at its best when it is two or three
days old. Just before serving, ice top and sides with your favourite
icing. Or cover with *Cream Cheese Icing* made as follows:

Blend ½ pound cream cheese with 1¼ cup icing sugar and 1 teaspoon vanilla till smooth.

Caution: Cream cheese icing does not keep. Use only if the cake
is to be eaten at once.

VIENNESE MANDELTORTE

*6 eggs, separated | 1 cup sugar | 1 cup finely ground almonds |
½ cup toasted white crumbs | 1 teaspoon grated rind and
1 tablespoon juice of lemon or orange | ½ teaspoon almond extract |
1 teaspoon cinnamon | ¼ teaspoon salt*

Beat egg yolks till creamy, adding sugar gradually till well combined
Add almonds, crumbs, grated rind and juice of lemon, almond
extract and cinnamon. Beat egg whites and salt stiff but not dry.

Fold in lightly. Turn into a spring form and bake 1 hour at 350° F. or gas mark 4. Let cool in the pan. Dust with icing sugar or top with white icing.

Variation: Bake in a loaf pan.

VIENNESE SACHERTORTE

½ cup butter | ⅔ cup icing sugar | 4 ounces sweet chocolate |
6 eggs, separated | 1 cup plus 2 tablespoons fine toasted white crumbs
½ teaspoon cinnamon | ¼ teaspoon nutmeg | Grated rind of 1 lemon |
¼ teaspoon salt | 1½ cups apricot pulp or jam

Cream butter till soft and stir in sugar, beating till thoroughly blended. Melt chocolate in a bowl over boiling water and add one egg yolk at a time, beating thoroughly after each addition. Combine dry bread crumbs with spices and grated rind. Stir in smoothly. Beat egg whites and salt stiff but do not dry and fold in lightly. Turn into 2 greased 8-inch layer cake pans and bake 25 to 30 minutes at 325° F. or gas mark 3. When cool put layers together with apricot pulp and top with chocolate or white icing flavoured with almond extract.

VINEGAR CAKE (Like Granny's)

½ cup butter | 1½ cups sugar | 2 eggs | 1 teaspoon vanilla |
2 squares bitter chocolate, melted | 2 cups sifted cake flour |
1 cup sour milk | 1 tablespoon vinegar | 1 teaspoon baking soda

Cream together butter and sugar until light and fluffy. Stir in eggs. Add vanilla and blend in. Add chocolate. Sift flour with salt and add to creamed mixture alternately with sour milk. Mix together soda and vinegar and add. Pour into two greased 9-inch layer pans. Bake at 375° F. or gas mark 5 for 25 minutes.

ANCIENT GINGERBREAD

½ cup shortening or butter | ½ cup sugar | 1 egg | 1 cup molasses |
1 cup hot water | 1½ teaspoons baking soda | 1 teaspoon each cinnamon
and ginger | ½ teaspoon salt | 2½ cups sifted flour

Cream shortening and sugar. Blend in beaten egg. Mix molasses with hot water and stir in. Sift all dry ingredients together and combine with first mixture, stirring a little at a time and beating after each addition. Line a 9-inch square cake pan with waxed paper and turn in the batter. Bake for 45 minutes at 350° F. or gas mark 4. Cut into squares and serve.

> *Variation:* For a sugarless gingerbread omit sugar and water. Heat molasses to boiling point, add shortening, stir and fold in 1 cup sour milk. Add 1 teaspoon vanilla and ½ cup chopped nuts or dates. Proceed as in basic recipe.

SOYBEAN GINGERBREAD

3 tablespoons shortening | ½ cup sugar | ¾ cup molasses |
1 egg | 1½ cups mashed cooked soybeans (canned) |
2 cups sifted flour | 4 teaspoons baking powder |
½ teaspoon each baking soda, salt, cinnamon, cloves | 1 teaspoon ginger |
½ cup milk

Cream shortening and sugar, add molasses and beaten egg, and blend in soybeans. Sift dry ingredients together twice and stir in alternately with the milk till smooth. Bake in well-greased shallow pan for 30 minutes at 350° F. or gas mark 4. Serve hot with whipped cream.

BABA AU RUM

(This is said to be of Turkish origin. It is very popular in Continental countries.)

2 cups sifted flour | 1 package yeast | ¼ cup lukewarm milk |
3 eggs | ½ cup sugar | ¼ teaspoon salt | ⅓ cup butter

RUM SYRUP

½ cup rum | ⅓ cup honey or light syrup

Place the flour in a deep bowl. Dissolve yeast in warm milk and stir into the centre of flour. Cover with a towel and let stand 10 minutes.

Beat eggs, add sugar and salt. Stir into yeast mixture, combining with the flour till smooth. Beat with a heavy spoon or turn on to a lightly floured board. Melt the butter and work it into the soft dough, tossing and kneading lightly about 5 minutes. Pat the dough into a well-greased fluted pan. Cover with tea towel till doubled in bulk. Brush lightly with melted butter and bake 30 to 40 minutes at 375° F. or gas mark 5, or till nicely browned and crusty. Invert on a cake rack. The cake should be feather-light. When cool, place the cake on a serving plate. Cover with the rum and honey mixture, allowing the cake to soak up the syrup.

Variation: Bake individual babas in individual baking tins or fluted gelatin moulds. Cover with rum syrup 10 to 15 minutes before serving.

CHEESECAKES

CHEESECAKE 1 (With Sour Cream)

CRUST AND TOPPING

1 *package rusk (rolled into crumbs)* | ¼ *cup sugar*
1 *teaspoon cinnamon* | ¼ *pound butter*

CHEESE FILLING

½ *pound cream cheese (or three 3-ounce packages)* |
½ *pound dry cottage cheese* | 2 *eggs* | 1 *cup sugar* |
2 *tablespoons cornflour* | *Pinch of salt* | 1 *cup sour cream* |
1 *cup milk* | 1 *teaspoon vanilla*

Mix crumbs, sugar and cinnamon. Work in the softened butter until well mixed. Line a well-buttered spring form, bottom and sides, with the mixture, reserving ¼ to sprinkle on top. Combine the filling ingredients in the order given:

Beat the cheeses until smooth, then add one egg at a time, continuing the beating till combined. Mix the dry ingredients and add before stirring in the liquids. This makes a very loose batter which should be poured into the crumb-lined pan carefully. Sprinkle top with crumbs and bake at 350° F. or gas mark 4 for one hour, turn off heat and let cake cool in oven one hour. For high altitudes, bake at 325° F. or gas mark 3.

CHEESECAKE 2

CRUST
⅛ *pound butter* | 1 *cup fine crumbs (rusk or biscuits)*

FILLING
1½ *pounds cream cheese* | 1 *cup sugar* | 1 *teaspoon vanilla* | 4 *eggs*

TOPPING
1 *pint sour cream* | 2 *tablespoons sugar* | ½ *teaspoon vanilla*

Melt butter and blend with crumbs, using a fork. Press firmly over bottom and sides of a spring-form cake pan. Combine cheese, sugar and vanilla. Add one egg at a time, beating till well-combined after each addition. Turn into the crumb-lined cake pan and bake at 350° F. or gas mark 4 for 35 minutes, or till firm in centre. Let cake cool in the oven after turning off heat. Leave oven door open. Remove cake when cooled and add the sour cream mixed with sugar and vanilla. Return to the oven, preheated to 425° F. or gas mark 7 and bake 5 minutes, no longer. The sour cream topping congeals when the cake cools.

This recipe is different from the usual ones but makes a most delicious cheese cake.

MOCK CHEESECAKE (A Quick-Easy)

CRUST
1½ *cups crumbs* | 2 *tablespoons caster sugar* | ¼ *cup melted butter*

FILLING
4 *eggs, separated* | 1 *tall can sweetened condensed milk* |
Grated rind of 2 lemons and juice

Blend ingredients for crust and line bottom and sides of a 9-inch pie pan. Beat egg yolks light, stir in milk, lemon juice and rind, fold in stiffly-beaten egg whites. Turn into crust-lined pan and bake 15 to 20 minutes at 375° F. or gas mark 5, or till set.

Variation: Bake the crumb crust first after chilling it. Fill when cool and bake only till centre is firm.

Serves 6.

REFRIGERATOR CHEESECAKE

Crumbed crust of rusk or stale cake crumbs | 3 tablespoons butter |
¼ cup milk | 1 egg plus 2 egg yolks | ⅓ cup sugar | Dash of salt |
1 tablespoon gelatin (unflavoured or lemon) |
¼ cup hot or cold water | 12 ounces creamy cottage cheese |
Grated rind of 1 lemon and juice (less if lemon gelatin is used) |
½ teaspoon vanilla | ½ cup heavy whipping cream |
2 egg whites beaten stiff | ¼ cup sugar

Blend crumbs with butter. Use a deep round cake pan with a
removable bottom if possible. Press the buttered crumbs evenly in
bottom of the pan, reserving 3 tablespoons for the top. Make a
custard of the whole egg and egg yolks, sugar, salt and milk. Use
double boiler. Soften gelatin in water and stir into the custard. Let
cool. Add sieved cheese, lemon juice and rind, and vanilla. Beat
cream stiff and fold in. Beat egg whites with ¼ cup of sugar and fold
into the mixture. Turn into the crumb crust and chill until firm.
    Serves 6 to 8.

COFFEE CAKES

YEAST DOUGH COFFEE CAKE (Basic Recipe)

4½ cups wheat flour | 2 ounces yeast | 1 cup lukewarm milk or water |
½ cup sugar | 1 cup shortening | 3 eggs | 1 tablespoon salt |
Grated rind of 1 lemon |
Sugar, cinnamon, nuts, raisins, citron in quantities to taste

Sift flour. Dissolve yeast in lukewarm liquid and stir in 1 cup flour.
Cover and set sponge to rise in a warm place, about a half hour.
Cream shortening with sugar, beat in eggs one at a time and add
salt and grated lemon rind. Beat into the sponge and stir in sifted
flour. Beat at least 5 minutes. Add raisins, citron, chopped nuts, and
sugar to taste. Cover with a towel and set in a warm place to rise
till double in bulk, approximately 2½ hours. For plain coffee cake
dough, omit nuts and raisins, etc. When ready to shape the dough,
remove to a floured board. Knead lightly. Roll or shape dough as
required.

FILLED COFFEE RING

Pat half the above amount of dough into a ½-inch-thick rectangle. Spread evenly with chopped nuts, raisins, citron or other cut candied fruit, sprinkle with mixed sugar and cinnamon, dot with butter or other shortening. Roll up lengthwise and shape into a ring. Place in a well-greased tube pan and let rise till double in bulk. Brush top with milk or melted butter, or diluted egg yolk. Sprinkle with sugar and chopped nuts or other decoration. Bake 30 minutes at 350° F. or gas mark 4, or till nicely browned.

Variation 1: Twist the filled roll before placing in pan and decorating.

Variation 2: Slash every 3 inches of the roll before twisting.

Variation 3: Omit raisins and other fruit from basic dough recipe. Fill with ½ cup finely ground hazel nuts mixed with ½ cup sugar, 2 teaspoons cinnamon and moistened with ½ teaspoon vanilla or 1 tablespoon sherry.

Variation 4: For *Schnecken,* cut the rolls into 1-inch pieces and bake cut side up. Be sure to place on the baking sheet far enough apart to permit well-browned outer edges on all rolls. Bake 30 minutes at 375° F. or gas mark 5, or till nicely browned.

KUCHEN (Basic Recipe)

1 ounce yeast | ¼ cup lukewarm water | 4 cups flour |
1 teaspoon salt | 2 eggs | ½ cup melted shortening mixed with
1 cup scalded milk | ½ cup sugar | 1 teaspoon vanilla

Let yeast stand in water for 3 to 5 minutes till softened. Sift together flour and salt into a mixing bowl and stir yeast mixture into the centre. Add eggs, melted shortening, milk, sugar and vanilla and stir till combined into a soft dough. Dust lightly with flour and cover with a towel. Let rise till double in bulk. Turn out on a floured board and knead lightly. Let rise at room temperature 1 hour and pat or roll to 1½- or 2-inch thickness. Divide into 12 equal parts by cutting with a knife or pinching off balls of dough. Flatten to 1-inch thickness, brush with melted shortening and arrange on a well-greased baking sheet. Let rise 1 hour or till about double in bulk. Dust with sugar and cinnamon and bake 20 to 25 minutes at 375° F. or gas mark 5, or till nicely browned.

Yields 12 kuchen.

BUTTER KUCHEN
(Basic Recipe for Sour Cream Dough)

¾ cup butter | ¾ cup sugar | 3 eggs | 1 cup sour cream |
1 tablespoon grated lemon rind | 2 ounces yeast | ¼ cup warm milk |
1 teaspoon salt | 5½ cups flour (approximately)

FILLING

1 cup sugar | 1 tablespoon cinnamon | 1 cup raisins |
1 tablespoon cut citron

Cream butter and sugar, add beaten eggs, sour cream, lemon rind, yeast dissolved in the warm milk, then the sifted flour and salt to make a dough. Turn out on a floured board and knead till soft and satiny smooth. Place in a bowl, dust with flour and cover with a towel. Let rise overnight in a place free from draughts. In the morning, knead well and roll out into two large rectangles about a half-inch thick. Brush with melted butter, sprinkle with cinnamon and sugar and dot with raisins and citron. Roll up like jelly rolls and bring ends together to form rings. Place on well-greased baking sheet and let rise about two hours. Brush the tops with a little butter or milk, make several diagonal cuts across the tops and bake at 375° F. or gas mark 5 for 45 minutes or until nicely browned. While still warm, cover with a thin icing and a light sprinkling of chopped nuts if desired.

Variation 1: Use prune butter *(lacqua)* for filling. (see pp. 522)

Variation 2: After rolling up, twist the roll before forming rings.

Variation 3: For small Butter Kuchen, pinch off balls of dough the size of small apples. Roll ½ inch thick, fill with prune butter, chopped raisins and nuts. Bring up the edges and invert. With the points of your kitchen scissors make several cuts to expose fruit centres. Brush with diluted egg yolk of evaporated milk. Let rise till light and bake.

BRAIDED COFFEE CAKE

1 recipe Butter Kuchen dough | ¼ cup chopped peanuts |
¼ cup chopped walnuts | 1 egg yolk diluted with water

Divide dough into 3 parts. With the palms of both hands, roll each into a long, tapered length as thin as desired. Pinch together at one end and braid lightly. Pinch ends together. Place in a well-buttered rectangular baking pan. Let rise 1 to 2 hours at room temperature, or till double in bulk. Combine nuts in a bowl. Brush braided cake with diluted egg lightly and top with nuts. Bake at 375° F. or gas mark 5 for 30 to 35 minutes or till nicely browned.

FRUIT STOLLEN

1 recipe Kuchen dough or Sour Cream dough |
½ cup seeded raisins, cut or chopped | ½ cup walnuts, chopped or slivered |
¼ cup candied fruit, diced fine | 1 tablespoon citron, chopped fine |
3 tablespoons sugar | 3 tablespoons butter

TOPPING

2 tablespoons nuts | 1 teaspoon citron |
3 tablespoons icing sugar | 2 tablespoons water

After the first rising of dough on kneading board, pat or beat well into a rectangular shape. Combine raisins, nuts, candied fruit and citron. Spread over dough and sprinkle with sugar. Roll up and twist into a ring or leave in one length. Place the ring in a buttered round cake pan. Or if baking a long stollen, place the roll in a rectangular pan. Brush top with melted butter. Let rise till double in bulk, approximately 2 hours at room temperature. Bake at 375° F. or gas mark 5 for 30 to 40 minutes or till nicely browned. While the stollen is warm, brush again with melted shortening and sprinkle with chopped nuts or decorate with citron, candied fruit and/or nuts. Drizzle a little thin icing sugar over top.

FRUITED COFFEE CAKES

These may be made by rolling or patting a part of the kneaded dough to ½-inch thickness, round or rectangular in shape, depending on cake pan to be used. If a round cake is desired, brush the round of dough with melted shortening, sprinkle generously with cinnamon and sugar. Cover with a mixture of chopped or shredded apple combined with seedless raisins or currants, a little grated lemon or orange rind and ¼ cup fine crumbs. Bring up the outer part of the round towards the centre, pinch together securely and invert on a well-greased round pie or cake pan. Let rise till light, mark into pie-shaped wedges with the point of a sharp kitchen knife in order to expose the fruit filling, brush with melted shortening and sprinkle with cinnamon and sugar and/or chopped nuts and bake as above till nicely browned. Fluting the edges, pie fashion, adds a professional touch.

JIFFY CINNAMON COFFEE CAKE

1 egg | 1 cup milk | 2 cups sifted flour | ¼ cup sugar | ½ teaspoon salt | 4 teaspoons baking powder | 4 tablespoons melted shortening | ½ teaspoon cinnamon mixed with 2 tablespoons sugar

Beat egg well and add milk. Sift together dry ingredients except cinnamon and sugar mixture. Stir in the egg and milk till smooth and beat in the melted shortening lightly. Spread in a well-greased square pan, sprinkle the sugar and cinnamon evenly over top and bake for 30 minutes at 375° F. or gas mark 5. Best when served hot from the oven.

ALMOND CUP CAKES

¼ pound butter | 1 cup sugar | 3 eggs | 2 cups flour sifted with 3 teaspoons baking powder | ½ cup sweet cream | 2 teaspoons almond extract | Pinch of salt if unsalted butter is used

Cream butter and sugar. Beat eggs and add. Stir in sifted dry ingredients alternately with the cream. Add almond extract last and fill greased individual baking tins half full. Sprinkle chopped or finely slivered blanched almonds on top and add a little sprinkle of sugar to each cake. Bake in a preheated oven at 350° F. or gas mark 4 for 30 minutes or until nicely browned. Remove and let cool on a cake rack covered with wax paper.

FOOLPROOF CHOCOLATE CUP CAKES

1 egg | 5 tablespoons cocoa | ½ cup shortening | 1½ cups flour |
½ teaspoon salt | 1 teaspoon baking soda | ½ cup sour milk | 1 cup sugar |
½ cup hot water | ½ teaspoon vanilla

Combine in the order given and stir or beat till smooth. Turn into
well-greased baking tins and bake at 350° F. or gas mark 4, 15
minutes, or till edges are lightly browned and crisp. Remove and
dust with icing sugar if desired.

KIPFEL (Viennese Style)

1 recipe Butter Kuchen or Sour Cream dough | 2 egg whites |
½ cup currants or light raisins | ¼ cup chopped citron |
¼ cup chopped almonds and 24 almond halves |
1 egg yolk diluted with water

Roll out dough to 1-inch thickness in rectangular shape. Cut into
3-inch triangles and arrange on well-buttered baking sheet, allowing
2 inches between cakes. Let rise 1 hour. Brush with beaten egg white,
top with currants or raisins, citron and chopped nuts. Bring together
the three corners and pinch securely. Brush with diluted egg yolk
and let rise 45 minutes. Press an almond half into the centre of each
cake and bake for 25 minutes at 375° F. or gas mark 5, or till glazed
light yellow and nicely browned on the bottoms.
Yields 24.

KOLATCHEN (Bohemian)

1 recipe Basic Kuchen dough or Sour Cream dough

Toss on a well-floured board and roll out to 1-inch-thick round.
With a biscuit cutter 2¼ inches in diameter, cut rounds of dough.
Place them on a well-greased baking sheet and let rise 1 hour. With
a spoon or fingers press down centres to form a ridge around each
kolatch. Let rise 1 hour, brush with beaten egg white and sprinkle
lightly with sugar or sugar and cinnamon. Bake for 20 minutes at
375° F. or gas mark 5, or till glazed and nicely browned.
Yields 24.

KICHLACH (Basic Recipe)

1¼ cups flour | 2 tablespoons sugar | ¼ teaspoon salt | 3 eggs

Sift together dry ingredients. Make a well in the centre and add eggs. Beat with a fork till combined into a smooth paste or dough and drop from a teaspoon on a slightly greased baking sheet at least 1 inch apart each way. Bake 20 minutes at 325° F. or gas mark 3, or till lightly browned at the edges and puffed.
    Yields approximately 36.
    Variation 1: Combine as in basic recipe, adding ½ cup melted shortening or salad oil. Beat till well combined.
    Variation 2: For *Mohn Kichlach*, add 3 tablespoons fine poppy seed to Variation 1 and follow same procedure.

DROP KICHLACH

3 eggs | ½ cup salad oil | 3 teaspoons sugar | ⅞ cup flour

Beat eggs together with the oil, sugar and flour for about 20 minutes. With the tip of a teaspoon drop bits of this mixture on a baking sheet at least 5 inches apart to permit spreading. Bake 15 to 20 minutes at 300° F. or gas mark 1–2, or till lightly browned at edges and puffed.

DOUGHNUTS AND CRULLERS

RAISED DOUGH DOUGHNUTS (Basic Recipe)

1 ounce yeast dissolved in ¼ cup lukewarm water | ¼ cup scalded milk |
1½ cups flour | ¼ cup sugar | ⅛ teaspoon salt |
2 tablespoons melted shortening | 3 cups flour | ½ cup sugar |
¼ teaspoon cinnamon | 1 egg | 4 tablespoons shortening

Add dissolved yeast to scalded milk and stir till combined. Sift together flour, sugar and salt. Stir together, adding melted shortening. This sponge should be covered with a towel and set aside at room temperature till it falls when touched with the fingers.
    Sift 3 cups flour twice. Add sugar and cinnamon to the sponge by stirring in lightly. Add beaten egg and melted shortening and stir in

the sifted flour gradually to make a dough slightly softer than bread dough. Cover and let rise 2 to 3 hours. Knead lightly on a floured board, adding flour if necessary to make a dough firm enough to roll out ¾-inch thick. Cut with a doughnut cutter and drop into deep hot melted shortening (365° F. or gas mark 5), without crowding. Fry 3 to 5 minutes, turning to brown on both sides. Drain on paper towels. Roll in sugar while hot.
Yields 24 to 30.

Variation 1: Cut rolled-out dough with a 2-inch biscuit cutter. Fry as in basic recipe and drain. When cool enough to handle, slash the side of doughnut and insert 1 tablespoon strawberry jam or currant jelly. Dust with icing sugar.

Variation 2: Cut rolled-out dough into strips 1-inch wide. Cut strips into 3-inch lengths. Twist 2 together. Fry as in basic recipe. Dust with icing sugar before serving.

BAKING POWDER DOUGHNUTS (Basic Recipe)

1 cup sugar | 2 eggs and 1 yolk | ¼ cup melted shortening | 3½ cups flour |
3 teaspoons baking powder | ½ teaspoon salt | Dash of nutmeg |
1 cup sweet milk or 1 cup sour milk with 1 teaspoon baking soda

Combine sugar and eggs till smooth. Add additional yolk and melted shortening and beat lightly. Sift together dry ingredients and stir in alternately with milk or sour milk and baking soda. Toss on a floured board and pat or roll out to ½-inch-thick rectangle. Cut into 1-inch strips and cut strips into 4- or 5-inch lengths. Pinch together ends to form doughnut and drop into hot melted shortening deep enough for cooking or frying for 5 or 6 minutes till nicely browned on both sides. Drain on unglazed paper and dust with icing sugar while warm.
Yields 24 to 30.

BERLINER KRANTZE (Pretzel-Shaped Dainty)

1½ cups butter or other shortening | 1 cup sugar |
Grated rind of 1 orange | 2 eggs | 4 cups sifted flour

Cream shortening well, adding sugar gradually till well combined and smooth. Work in the grated orange rind gradually during the process. Beat eggs till light and stir into creamed mixture. One of the egg whites may be reserved for the brushing of twists. Sift flour, stirring to blend in a little at a time till well absorbed. *Chill dough overnight.*

When ready to bake, break off small bit of dough, roll into thin pencil-shaped lengths, and twist into pretzels. Place on lightly greased baking sheet, working as rapidly as possible to prevent dough from becoming too soft. Should the dough become too soft to shape easily, chill in the refrigerator again. Brush tops of pretzels lightly with beaten egg white and bake for 15 minutes at 400° F. or gas mark 6.

BOWKNOTS (also called *Crushchiki*)

5 egg yolks | 5 tablespoons sugar | 1 tablespoon grated lemon rind |
5 tablespoons sour cream | 1 tablespoon brandy, cognac or rum |
½ teaspoon vanilla | 2½ cups cake flour | 1 teaspoon salt |
Hot melted shortening for frying

Beat egg yolks and sugar till creamy. Stir in grated rind, sour cream, brandy and vanilla. Sift together flour and salt and combine by stirring till smooth. The mixture should be stiff enough to roll out to ⅛-inch-thick rectangle. Cut into strips 2 inches wide. Cut strips into 4-inch lengths and with the point of a paring knife cut a 2-inch gash lengthwise in the centre of each. Put one end of the strip through the gash to form a bowknot and drop into hot melted shortening in a deep frying pan. Fry until lightly browned, turning to brown evenly on all sides. Skim out with perforated spoon and drain on paper towels or unglazed paper. Dust with icing sugar just before serving. May be reheated in a moderate oven and dusted with sugar before serving.

Yields 24 to 30.

COFFEE KISSES

1 cup very strong coffee | 1 cup water | 2 cups sugar | Dash of salt |
5 egg whites (left from above recipe)

Cook coffee, water and sugar till they make a thick syrup. Beat egg whites, adding salt after the first strokes. Add hot syrup, beating continuously till thick. Place over hot water and stir 5 minutes. Cover while preparing baking sheet and preheating oven to 300° F. or gas mark 1–2. Cover baking sheet with unglazed paper or aluminium foil and drop the mixture from the tip of a teaspoon, shaping to a peak with tip of spoon. Bake 45 minutes at 300° F. or till lightly browned at the tip and firm to the touch.

Yields 24.

American Style Shortcake: The most popular shortcake is Strawberry Shortcake. American shortcake is literally biscuit with fruit and whipped cream. It has been called 'poorman's cake', probably because it is made without expensive ingredients that usually compose cakes. Shortcake is made without eggs, for instance. But cream topping of berries or other fruit is an essential part of shortcake. This inconsistency dates back to the time when an agricultural environment placed more value on marketable eggs than on heavy cream. Eggs could be kept for marketing while heavy cream could not wait and was therefore used more freely in the farm home.

Shortcake is characteristically American, much like pie, biscuits and corn bread. Not that other countries do not have eggless, baking powder cakes filled and topped with fruit, but Strawberry Shortcake, the old-fashioned kind, is accented in the United States, especially in New England. It has become a national favourite.

STRAWBERRY SHORTCAKE (Old Fashioned Recipe)

2 cups wheat flour | 4 teaspoons baking powder | ½ teaspoon salt | 2 tablespoons sugar | ½ cup shortening | ¾ cup milk | Strawberries | Whipping cream or heavy cream for pouring over cake

Sift together flour, baking powder, salt and sugar. Cut in shortening as for biscuits. Add milk slowly while combining into a moderately stiff dough. Roll or pat out on a floured board. For individual shortcakes, use a large biscuit cutter on dough 1 inch thick. Arrange cakes on a lightly greased baking sheet. Bake for 12 to 15 minutes at 400° F. or gas mark 6. For a 9-inch shortcake, roll out to ½-inch thickness and divide dough in two parts. Pat or roll out each to fit bottom of a 9-inch layer cake pan, lightly greased. Place 1 round in pan, drizzle melted shortening on top and add second layer. (This helps separate the layers easily.) Bake for 15 minutes at 400° F.

or gas mark 6. Separate and fill with berries. Top with berries and whipped cream or serve with heavy cream for pouring.

PURIM CAKES

Hamantashen. These are three-cornered cakes made of either yeast dough or biscuit dough. They are filled with *mohn* (poppyseed), and honey. Variations of filling are indulged in but the traditional filling of poppyseed and honey is basic, although nuts and raisins are sometimes added. *Lacqua* (thick prune butter, see p. 522) is also traditionally used as filling.

HAMANTASHEN YEAST DOUGH

Use recipe for Refrigerator Rolls, increasing sugar by one half. Form balls of dough the size of a medium apple and roll ¼- or ½-inch thickness, 4 to 6 inches in diameter. Some hamantashen are small and some large, depending on local custom, family tradition, etc. On each round of dough place a ball of filling and bring edges together to form a triangle, pinching the seams together from top down to corners. Let rise at room temperature till double in bulk. Brush tops with diluted egg yolk, evaporated milk or melted shortening. Bake 30 to 40 minutes at 350° F. or gas mark 4, or till lightly browned.

HAMANTASHEN BISCUIT DOUGH

Use recipe for Filled Biscuit Dough.

HAMANTASHEN FILLINGS

POPPYSEED AND HONEY FILLING (Cooked)

2 cups poppyseed | 1 cup water or milk | ½ cup honey | ¼ cup sugar | ⅛ teaspoon salt | 2 eggs (optional)

Combine poppyseed (large seeds should be scalded, drained and pounded or put through food chopper, using fine blade), liquid, honey, sugar and salt in a saucepan. Cook over moderate heat till

24

thick, stirring to prevent scorching. Let cool before adding eggs, beating in thoroughly. If the addition of eggs thins out filling too much, return to heat and stir while cooking 1 to 2 minutes.

Yields filling for 24 small or 12 to 14 large hamantashen.

Variation 1: Add ¼ cup finely chopped almonds or other nuts.

Variation 2: Add nuts and ¼ cup currants or seedless raisins.

Variation 3: Add ¼ cup fine crumbs to basic filling or variations.

Variation 4: Add 1 tablespoon lemon juice and ½ teaspoon grated lemon rind.

LACQUA FILLING
(thick Prune Butter, sometimes called *Providle*)

1½ *cups lacqua (see p. 522)* | ½ *cup ground almonds* |
2 *tablespoons fine cake crumbs* | 1 *tablespoon grated rind of orange or lemon*

Combine ingredients.

DRIED FRUIT FILLING

½ *cup each seeded or seedless raisins, pitted prunes, dried apricots* |
½ *cup dry bread or cake crumbs* | *Dash of salt* | 4 *tablespoons honey*

Combine and heat over boiling water till honey is melted. Stir well and remove from heat. When cold, use as filling. If too thick, add lemon juice. If not thick enough, add more crumbs.

HONEY DOUGH FOR HAMANTASHEN

4 *cups sifted flour* | 1 *teaspoon baking soda* | ½ *teaspoon salt* |
4 *eggs* | 1 *cup honey, warmed* | ¼ *pound butter or vegetable shortening*

Sift the dry ingredients into mixing bowl. Make a well in the centre and add the other ingredients in the order given, mixing thoroughly with a heavy spoon to form a dough thick enough to roll out. Roll out on lightly floured board to ¼-inch thickness and cut into 3- to 4-inch rounds. Follow procedure as for basic yeast dough and biscuit dough, filling with any of the mixtures given. Preheat oven to 350° F. or gas mark 4. Place hamantashen on greased baking sheet. Brush tops and sprinkle with poppyseed, finely chopped nuts or place 3 almond halves with points towards top centre of each. Bake for 25 to 30 minutes or till nicely browned.

Yields 36 to 40.

LITTLE DUTCH HAMANS

⅓ cup shortening | 1 cup brown sugar | 1½ cups black molasses | ½ cup cold water | 7 cups sifted flour | 1 teaspoon salt | 1 teaspoon allspice | 1 teaspoon ginger | ¼ teaspoon cloves | ¼ teaspoon cinnamon | 2 teaspoons baking soda | 3 tablespoons cold water

ICING

1 cup icing sugar | 2 tablespoons water | Few grains of salt | ½ teaspoon vanilla

DECORATIONS

Slivered almonds | Currants

Combine shortening with sugar and molasses, adding ½ cup cold water while stirring. Sift dry ingredients into a mixing bowl, and dissolve baking soda in 3 tablespoons cold water. Combine well, mixing all the above to a ball of dough. Chill dough at least 1 hour in refrigerator. Roll dough on a lightly floured board or pat into a rectangle not more than ⅛ inch thick. Use a gingerbread man cutter. Roll dough remaining after cutting and pat out again or form little men by rolling small bits of dough in the palm and flattening as you form the figures on a well-greased baking sheet. Arrange cut-out men and/or moulded ones on a baking sheet 1 inch apart. Bake for 18 to 20 minutes at 350° F. or gas mark 4.

Mix icing to a consistency thin enough for spreading. When biscuits are cold decorate with icing and press in slivered almonds over currants for eyes. If desired, use points of Brazil nuts for shoes.

POPPYSEED COOKIES

1 cup fine poppyseed | ½ cup milk, scalded then cooled | ½ cup butter | ½ cup sugar | 1½ cups flour | ⅛ teaspoon salt | 1 teaspoon baking powder | ¼ teaspoon cinnamon | 1 cup currants or seedless raisins

Soak poppyseed in milk. Cream butter and sugar. Combine with the other ingredients in the order listed. Drop from tip of teaspoon to greased baking sheet. Bake for 20 minutes at 350° F. or gas mark 4, or till lightly browned at bottom. Slip under grill for a few seconds to brown lightly on top.

Yields approximately 30.

PURIM KICHLACH

1 cup sugar | 1 cup melted shortening or salad oil | 4 eggs | 4 cups sifted flour | 3 teaspoons baking powder | ½ teaspoon salt | ¾ cup lukewarm water or milk | ¾ cup poppyseed

Cream sugar and shortening. Add 1 egg at a time, beating or stirring well after each addition. Sift dry ingredients and add poppyseeds. Combine both mixtures, adding a little of the liquid as you mix to a stiff dough. Roll out on lightly floured board to ¼-inch thickness. Cut with a fluted cutter into triangles 2½ inches in size. If no fluted cutter is available, use a knife for cutting into squares then fold from opposite corners to make triangles. Brush biscuits with diluted egg yolk and sprinkle with a few poppyseeds after arranging them on a greased and lightly floured baking sheet. Bake for 12 to 15 minutes at 375° F. or gas mark 5.

Yields 50 to 60 biscuits.

PURIM POPPYSEED PIE

1 recipe pie pastry (see Pastries)

FILLING

1 cup poppyseed | 1 cup milk | 1 cup sugar | ½ cup honey | Dash of salt | ¼ teaspoon grated lemon rind | 3 tablespoons lemon juice | 5 medium apples, grated

Bake rolled-out pastry in a layer cake pan till lightly browned. Brush inside with milk or slightly beaten egg white to form a coating. Combine ingredients for filling and cook over low heat 12 to 15 minutes, stirring constantly to prevent scorching. Cool and turn into baked pie shell. Return to oven for 2 minutes.

Variation: Use filling for 6 baked tart shells.

MOHN SQUARES (Poppyseed and Honey Candies)

*1 cup honey | ¼ cup sugar | ½ pound poppyseed (ground or pounded) |
1 cup chopped English walnuts | 60 blanched almond halves*

Combine honey and sugar in a saucepan and heat over low heat until sugar is dissolved. Stir in poppyseeds and cook until thick and sticky, stirring frequently for 12 to 15 minutes. Add chopped nuts and stir once or twice. Remove from heat and turn out the mixture on a wet wooden board. Wet hands in cold water and pat mixture down to make a ½-inch round or rectangle. Dip a sharp knife in hot water and cut into ½-inch squares or diamonds. Work rapidly to prevent hardening of this candy before pressing an almond half in the centre of each cut.

To blanch the almonds, place them in a shallow saucepan and pour boiling water over. Let stand a minute and pour off the water. The brown skins will come off easily. Separate the halves.

Yields approximately 60 candies.

TAYGLACH (Holiday Confection)

*3 eggs | 2 cups flour | ¼ teaspoon salt | ½ teaspoon ginger or nutmeg |
Chopped almonds (optional)*

HONEY SYRUP

1 cup honey (1 pound) | 1 cup sugar | 1 teaspoon ground ginger

Beat egg slightly in a mixing bowl. Sift dry ingredients, except almonds, and stir in to form a stiff dough. Turn out on a lightly floured board and knead 1 or 2 minutes. Pat into ½-inch thickness a small ball of this dough and cut into ¼-inch squares. Remove cut squares to a large plate and proceed with the rest of the dough till all of it has been cut. Or, roll small pieces of dough between palms to form ¼-inch-thick rolls, pencil fashion, and then cut ¼-inch pieces. Bring honey, sugar and ginger to a rolling boil in a deep pot and drop the bits of dough in, a few at a time, to prevent lowering temperature of syrup. Cook over reduced heat after all tayglach have been dropped into syrup about 20 minutes, using a wooden spoon to prevent boiling over. *Do not stir* while cooking. Turn out on a wet board and pat with wet wooden spoon to an even thickness – ½ inch is about right. If almonds are desired, spread evenly on wet board before turning out tayglach mixture as evenly as possible without spreading the nuts too far apart. Let cool before cutting into small squares or diamond shapes 1 to 1½ inches in diameter, or finger lengths 1 inch wide. This confection may be prepared long in advance of the holiday and stored in a crock after they become cold.

Variation: Drop individual cuts of dough into boiling honey syrup and cook only a few at a time, skimming out as they rise to the top in about 7 to 8 minutes. Use perforated spoon to lift out and transfer to a platter or board. When cold, store like candy.

22 Biscuits

ALMOND BISCUITS (Basic Recipe)

3 eggs | 1 cup sugar | 1 cup heavy sour cream |
3 teaspoons baking powder | ½ teaspoon vanilla | 1 cup blanched almonds |
Approximately 3 to 3½ cups flour

Beat eggs and sugar till creamy. Add sour cream, baking powder, flavouring and crushed almonds (crush the almonds by rolling with ordinary rolling pin, or putting them through food chopper) and blend in enough flour to make a soft dough. Roll out the dough to ¼-inch thickness and cut into rounds or squares, or 2-inch strips. Sprinkle with some of the almonds. Bake for 10 to 15 minutes at 350° F. or gas mark 4, or until a light brown.
Yields 36 biscuits.

BRAZIL NUT BISCUITS

¾ cup water | ½ teaspoon salt | ⅓ cup farina | 2 cups ground Brazil nuts

Combine water, salt and farina by stirring in a saucepan. Place over moderate heat and stir with a spoon until it begins to thicken and becomes slightly dry, forming a mass in the centre of the saucepan. Remove from heat. When cool, add ground Brazil nuts and mix thoroughly. Place the ball of dough on a sheet of heavy wax paper and cover with another piece of wax paper. Roll with a rolling pin till the dough is ¼ inch thick or thinner if desired. Remove top paper. Cut into 1½-inch rounds, or make diamond-shaped pieces. Transfer while on wax paper to a greased baking sheet using a spatula or very broad-bladed knife. Bake at 325° F. or gas mark 3 for 20 minutes. Remove from baking sheet when the edges of the wafers are nicely browned and crisp.
Yields 24 biscuits.

ALMOND-CHEESE BISCUITS (Basic Recipe)

¼ cup butter | ¼ cup finely ground almonds |
¼ cup finely ground peanuts or peanut butter | ¼ teaspoon salt |
2 egg yolks | ¾ cup sifted flour | 1 egg white |
⅓ cup grated sharp cheese | Paprika

Cream butter till soft and work in the almonds, peanuts, or peanut butter. Add salt, egg yolks. Work with a fork till smooth and blend in flour a little at a time. Turn out on a lightly floured board and roll out to ⅛-inch thickness. Cut with a small biscuit cutter in rounds or crescents. Brush each with beaten egg white and place on a greased baking sheet. Press a little grated cheese into each biscuit, sprinkle with paprika and bake for 10 minutes at 350° F. or gas mark 4, or till nicely browned.

Yields 36.

Variation 1: Cut into 3-inch rounds, brush with beaten egg white, add grated cheese to centres and fold over. Press or pinch edges together. Brush tops with more beaten egg white or milk, sprinkle with paprika and bake for 15 minutes at 350° F. or gas mark 4.

Variation 2: Sprinkle rolled dough with chopped almonds or peanuts. Press lightly with rolling pin. Cut into rounds or small crescents. Bake as in basic recipe.

SUGAR BISCUITS (Basic Recipe)

2 cups sugar | 1 cup butter or vegetable shortening | 3 eggs |
1 tablespoon grated lemon rind | 4 tablespoons brandy or lemon juice |
3 cups flour | 3 teaspoons baking powder | 1 teaspoon salt

Cream the sugar and butter till smooth. Add eggs, one at a time, stirring well after each addition. Stir in grated lemon rind and brandy or lemon juice. Sift together the flour, baking powder and salt. Stir in a little at a time till well-combined and compact enough to roll out. Divide ball of dough into 2 or 4 parts. Roll out 1 part at a time to ⅛-inch thickness (or thinner). Cut into 1½-inch rounds or other shapes. Place biscuits on a greased, lightly floured baking sheet. Bake 10 to 12 minutes at 375° F. or gas mark 5, or till lightly browned at edges. Remove from baking sheet as soon as done using a spatula or pancake turner. When cold, store in a well-covered crock or metal container.

Yields 60 to 72 biscuits.

Variations can be made by sprinkling biscuits with coloured sugar, finely chopped nuts, or a mixture of cinnamon and sugar.

CARROT BISCUITS

⅛ teaspoon baking soda | ½ cup honey | 1 egg, slightly beaten with ½ cup shortening | 1 cup sifted flour | 1 teaspoon baking powder | Dash of salt | 1 cup quick cooking oatmeal | ½ cup chopped nuts | ½ cup grated raw carrot | ½ cup seedless raisins | 1 teaspoon vanilla flavouring

Stir baking soda into honey and add to creamed shortening and egg. Sift together flour, baking powder, salt, and stir into the mixture. Combine oatmeal, nuts, raisins and grated carrot and stir into the mixture until well-blended. Add flavouring last and drop by tea-spoonfuls on a greased baking sheet, flattening each ball of dough with the tines of a fork. Bake for 12 minutes at 350° F. or gas mark 4, or until lightly browned.

Yields 50 biscuits.

CASTLE BISCUITS

3 eggs | 1½ cups light brown sugar (packed down in measuring cup) | ¾ cup flour | ½ teaspoon baking powder | ⅛ teaspoon salt | 1½ cups finely chopped nuts or shredded coconut | 1 teaspoon almond extract

Beat eggs till light and add sugar during the beating process. Sift dry ingredients together and combine. Add nuts or coconut and flavouring last and mix lightly. Drop from the point of a teaspoon on to a well-greased baking sheet at least an inch apart. Bake at once in a preheated oven at 350° F. or gas mark 4 for 12 to 15 minutes.

Yields 48 biscuits.

CHOCOLATE BISCUITS (Basic Recipe)

*1 cup sugar | ½ cup shortening | 3 ounces chocolate, unsweetened |
2 eggs | 1 teaspoon vanilla | 2¼ cups flour | ¾ teaspoon baking soda |
½ teaspoon salt*

Cream sugar and shortening. Melt chocolate over hot water and add.
Beat eggs, add flavouring and stir into other mixture. Sift dry
ingredients together and add, mixing till smooth. Chill until firm.
Roll out ⅛ inch thick on lightly floured board and cut with small
biscuit cutters or into any desired shapes with a knife. Place on
greased baking sheet and bake for 10 minutes at 375° F. or gas
mark 5.
Yields 70 biscuits.

DELCO DELIGHTS

*¼ pound butter | 3 ounces cream cheese | 1 cup flour |
Dash of salt if unsalted butter is used*

Mix butter and cream cheese with a fork, adding a little flour and
continue mixing after each addition. Roll out ⅛ inch thick, cut into
small rounds or diamond shapes. Bake at 350° F. or gas mark 4 for
10 to 12 minutes or till nicely browned.
Yields 18 to 24.

FILLED BISCUITS (Basic Recipe)

*⅔ cup shortening | ½ cup sugar | 1 egg | 3 tablespoons milk or water |
½ teaspoon vanilla | 2 cups sifted flour*

Cream shortening and sugar. Add egg and continue creaming till
smooth. Add liquid and flavouring and stir in sifted flour till a ball of
dough is formed. Chill 2 to 3 hours or overnight. Roll out on lightly
floured board to ⅛-inch thickness. Cut into 2-inch rounds. Place
ball of filling the size of a hazelnut in the centres of half the number
of biscuits. Top with the other biscuits, pressing edges together with
the tines of a fork. Bake on a well-greased baking sheet 10 minutes
at 375° F. or gas mark 5.
Yields 24 to 30 biscuits.

Variation 1 :
   ¾ *cup fruit preserves (see pp.* 518-19*) | 2 tablespoons dry cake or*
      bread crumbs | Dash of grated lemon peel

Combine. Place ½ teaspoon of filling on each round of biscuit dough, fold over and press edges together with fingers or fork. Makes 48 to 60 filled biscuits.

Variation 2: Brush tops of either round or folded over filled biscuits with evaporated milk and bake as in basic recipe.

Variation 3: Bake filled biscuits and top with a thin coating of icing sugar and fruit juice or milk, after biscuits are cool.

FILLINGS FOR BISCUITS

ALMOND AND RAISIN

½ *cup seeded raisins | ¼ cup nuts | 1 tablespoon dry cake or bread crumbs |*
      1 tablespoon lemon juice

Put fruit and nuts through a food chopper. Combine with crumbs and moisten with lemon juice.

DATE AND PEANUT BUTTER

½ *cup finely cut unsugared dates, pitted | ½ cup peanut butter |*
      1 tablespoon honey | 1 tablespoon lemon juice

Combine with a fork, mashing to a smooth pulp.

ICING SUGAR GLAZE FOR BISCUITS

1 *cup icing sugar |*
Milk, evaporated milk or fruit juice to form a thin consistency

Stir with a fork till smooth.

   Yields an amount sufficient for a thin glaze on the tops of 48 biscuits.

   Variations can be made by adding a drop or two of vegetable colouring to all or part of the mixed glaze or thin icing.

DROP BISCUITS

ALMOND DROPS

½ pound almond paste | 3 egg whites |
½ cup each granulated and icing sugar | ¼ cup sifted flour | Dash of salt

Work the almond paste smooth with a wooden spoon and add slightly beaten egg whites, blending thoroughly. Sift dry ingredients together and add, mixing well. Drop from a teaspoon on to a wax-paper-lined baking sheet. Bake for 30 minutes at 300° F. or gas mark 1–2. Remove from paper while warm.
Yields 48 drops.
Variation: Make peanut butter drops by substituting peanut butter for almond paste and increase flour by 1 tablespoon.

BROWN SUGAR DROP BISCUITS

3 eggs | 1½ cups light brown sugar | ¾ cup flour |
½ teaspoon baking powder | ⅛ teaspoon salt | 1 teaspoon almond extract |
1½ cups finely chopped nuts or shredded coconuts

Beat eggs till light and add sugar. Sift dry ingredients together and combine till smooth. Add nuts or coconut and flavouring. Mix lightly. Drop from a teaspoon on a well-greased baking sheet. Bake for 12 to 15 minutes at 350° F. or gas mark 4.
Yields 48 biscuits.

DRY CEREAL CHOCOLATE DROPS

1 pound milk chocolate | ⅛ teaspoon cinnamon | 4 cups puffed dry cereal

Melt chocolate in top of double boiler over hot water. Add cinnamon as soon as melted and stir once or twice before adding dry cereal. Remove from heat and stir lightly with a fork. Drop from a tablespoon on to a wax-paper-lined baking sheet. Chill in refrigerator 2 hours or till chocolate clusters are firmly set.
Yields 36 drops.

Variation 1: Sprinkle with coconut shreds before placing in refrigerator.

Variation 2: Top with chopped nuts before chilling.

COCONUT MACAROONS

4 egg whites | ¼ cup cold water | ⅔ cup sugar | ¼ teaspoon salt | 1 tablespoon flour | 2½ cups shredded coconut

Beat egg whites with water until stiff but not dry and add sugar gradually while beating till combined. Blend in salt and flour carefully and fold in coconut. Drop from a teaspoon on heavy-paper-lined baking sheet. Bake for 25 to 30 minutes at 325° F. or gas mark 3.

Yields 30 macaroons.

ROBINS' NESTS

½ cup shortening | ¼ cup brown sugar | 1 egg, separated | 1 cup sifted flour | 1 cup chopped nuts | Jam or jelly

Cream shortening and sugar and add egg yolk, beating together thoroughly. Stir in flour till well blended. Beat egg white. Shape dough into small balls and dip into beaten egg whites then roll in chopped nuts. Place on a well-greased baking sheet and with the finger make a depression in centre of each ball. Bake at 325° F. or gas mark 3 for 8 minutes, press in the centres again and continue baking 10 minutes longer. Remove to a cooling rack or place on a folded kitchen towel. When cool fill centres with jam or jelly.

Yields 18 to 20 biscuits.

MOLASSES DROP BISCUITS

½ cup shortening | ½ cup sugar | ½ cup molasses | 1 egg | 1 teaspoon baking soda | ½ cup sour milk | 2½ cups flour | ½ teaspoon salt | 1 teaspoon flour | ½ teaspoon each cinnamon, ginger, allspice or nutmeg | ½ cup each chopped seeded raisins and nuts

Cream shortening and sugar and blend in molasses till smooth. Add beaten egg. Dissolve baking soda in sour milk. Sift dry ingredients together and add to creamed mixture alternately with milk combination. Dust raisins and nuts with the spoonful of flour and fold in. Drop from a teaspoon on a well-greased baking sheet and bake for 12 to 15 minutes at 350° F. or gas mark 4.

Yields 40 to 48 biscuits.

NUT NUGGETS

1 cup brown sugar | ⅔ cup shortening | 2 eggs | 1½ cups flour |
2 teaspoons baking powder | ½ teaspoon salt |
¼ teaspoon mixed spice or nutmeg | ¼ teaspoon cinnamon |
¾ cup each coarsely chopped nuts and dates or figs

Cream sugar and shortening, add beaten eggs. Sift together flour, baking powder, salt and spices. Add nuts and fruit to dry mixture. Combine till smooth enough to drop from a teaspoon on a well-greased baking sheet. Bake for 15 minutes at 375° F. or gas mark 5.

Yields 36 nuggets.

Variation: Omit nuts. Press half an almond, point down, into each dropped nugget and bake.

OATMEAL DROPS (Basic Recipe)

⅔ cup sugar | ½ cup shortening | 2 eggs | ¼ cup milk | 1 cup flour |
½ teaspoon salt | 1 teaspoon baking powder |
½ teaspoon each cinnamon, nutmeg | 1 cup quick cooking rolled oats

Cream sugar and shortening. Beat eggs and add milk. Sift together flour, salt, baking powder and spices. Add egg and milk to creamed mixture. Stir in dry ingredients including oats. Drop from a teaspoon on a well-greased baking sheet and bake for 20 minutes at 350° F. or gas mark 4.

Yields 30 to 36 biscuits.

Variation: Add ½ cup each seedless raisins and chopped walnuts. Or press a piece of nut or several raisins into each biscuit. Bake.

EGGLESS OATMEAL DROPS

¾ *cup shortening* | ¾ *cup brown sugar* | 3 *tablespoons dark or light corn syrup* |
1 *cup flour* | ½ *teaspoon salt* | 2 *teaspoons baking powder* |
½ *teaspoon each cinnamon, allspice* | ¾ *cup milk or* 1 *cup liquid cocoa* |
1 *tablespoon soluble cocoa or coffee* | 2 *cups quick cooking rolled oats* |
½ *cup each chopped nuts and raisins*

Cream shortening and sugar. Add syrup. Sift together dry ingredients and add alternately with the liquid till well blended. Mix
oatmeal with nuts and raisins and stir in. Chill for 1 hour. Drop from
a teaspoon on a well-greased baking sheet an inch apart each way.
Bake for 10 minutes at 375° F. or gas mark 5, or till nicely browned.
Yields 30 to 36 biscuits.

PINEAPPLE DROP BISCUITS

1 *cup shortening* | 1 *cup brown sugar* | 1 *cup granulated sugar* |
1 *cup crushed pineapple* | 1 *cup chopped nuts* | 2 *eggs* | 1 *teaspoon vanilla* |
½ *teaspoon salt* | ½ *teaspoon soda* | 4 *cups sifted cake flour* |
2 *teaspoons baking powder*

Cream together shortening and sugars. Add fruit, nuts and eggs,
mixing in thoroughly. Add flavouring. Sift together dry ingredients.
Add to other mixture. Drop from teaspoon on greased baking sheets.
Bake for 10 minutes at 400° F. or gas mark 6.
Yields 100 small biscuits.

RAISIN NUT DROPS

1 *package chocolate chips or* 6 *squares* | ¾ *cup sweetened condensed milk* |
¾ *cup finely crushed plain biscuits* | ½ *cup raisins* |
¼ *cup chopped nut meats* | ½ *teaspoon vanilla*

Heat chocolate in double boiler until melted, stirring constantly.
Remove from heat and add remaining ingredients. Mix thoroughly.
Drop from teaspoon on wax paper. Cool until firm.
Yields 36 biscuits.

SOYBEAN DROP BISCUITS

1 *cup cooked, mashed soybeans* | 2 *cups crushed dry cereal flakes* |
2 *egg whites* | ⅛ *teaspoon salt* | 1 *cup sugar* | 1 *teaspoon vanilla*

Combine mashed soybeans with cereal flakes. Beat egg whites with
salt till foamy and add sugar a little at a time till well beaten and
smooth. Stir into first mixture and add flavouring. Drop from a
teaspoon on wax-paper-lined baking sheet. Bake for 25 minutes at
325° F. or gas mark 3, or till light brown and firm.

Yields 36 biscuits.

23 Exterior and Interior Cake Decoration

Hints for Fillings and Icings

Syrup for cooked icings reaches the soft ball stage or is thin enough to spin a thread at 238° F.

Test for soft ball stage by dropping a little syrup in cold water. It should form a soft ball instantly.

Egg whites will beat stiff sooner if a pinch of salt is added.

Pouring hot syrup into beaten egg whites must be done while egg whites are stiff, and while beating with a fork.

Adding cream of tartar or lemon juice to thickened icing will prevent grittiness. Or, add 1 tablespoon corn syrup to each cup of sugar before boiling.

Flavouring should be added as the icing cools.

If cooked icing does not thicken sufficiently, beat it vigorously over boiling water until it reaches the right consistency.

If syrup hardens prematurely, beat in a little boiling water or a few drops of lemon juice.

Add nuts or raisins, or other ingredients to icing just before spreading to avoid thinning the mixture.

Use a spatula dipped in hot water for spreading icing quickly and evenly.

Pile icing on top of cake and spread quickly around and down.

Icing sugar is the basic ingredient in uncooked icings.

FILLINGS AND ICINGS

BOILED ICING (Basic Recipe)

*2 cups sugar | 1 cup water | 2 egg whites | ⅛ teaspoon salt |
⅛ teaspoon cream of tartar or a few drops of lemon juice*

Dissolve sugar in water and cook without stirring till syrup spins a thread from spoon. Beat egg whites and salt to a froth. Add hot syrup in a thin stream and beat while pouring. Add cream of tartar or lemon juice.

Yields enough to fill and ice a 9-inch 2-layer cake.

Variation 1: Add ½ cup nut meats, ground or finely chopped.

Variation 2: 1 cup finely chopped seeded raisins.

Variation 3: ¼ cup each chopped raisins and nuts, adding 1 teaspoon vanilla, rum or sherry.

Variation 4: 1 cup grated or shredded coconut.

Variation 5: 2 tablespoons orange juice and ¼ teaspoon grated orange rind.

Variation 6: 2 ounces shredded semi-sweet chocolate added to hot syrup.

Variation 7: Add a few drops of peppermint extract to basic recipe. Spread over top and sides of cake and decorate. Add swirls of Chocolate Icing.

Variation 8: Cover one half of cake with Chocolate Icing and the other half with Boiled Icing.

Variation 9: Fill cake with either Chocolate or Boiled Icing and use the other for icing top and sides.

AMBROSIA FILLING AND ICING

*1 tablespoon cornflour | 1½ cups water | ¼ cup each dates and figs |
1 cup seedless raisins | ½ cup sugar | Pinch of salt |
1 teaspoon lemon juice | ½ cup chopped nuts*

Mix cornflour with 1 tablespoon cold water. Chop dates, figs and raisins, add sugar, salt, lemon juice and water. Cook 5 minutes, stir in dissolved cornflour and cook 5 minutes longer. Add nuts and cool. Use half of this mixture for filling. Add the rest to 1 cup of basic Boiled Icing or basic Uncooked Icing for top of cake, letting some of the mixture run down sides.

Yields enough to fill and ice a 9-inch 3-layer cake.

CARAMEL FILLING AND ICING

2 cups brown sugar | ½ cup butter | ½ cup cream | 1 teaspoon vanilla

Combine sugar, butter and cream in top of double boiler over hot water. Cook to soft ball stage, beat till thickened and cool. Add

vanilla and spread filling between layers and over top and sides of a
9-inch 2-layer cake.
Variation: Add a dash of salt and ½ cup chopped nuts.

CRISP CARAMEL COATING

Use a heavy skillet. Cook 1 cup sugar over moderate heat until it
becomes clear and brown. Spread at once over the top of an 8-inch
square cake or torte, using spatula dipped in boiling water for easy
spreading.

CREAMY CHOCOLATE ICING

*2 egg yolks | 1½ cups sugar | 1 tablespoon butter or vegetable shortening |
½ cup milk | 2 squares unsweetened chocolate | 1 teaspoon vanilla*

Beat yolks slightly in top of double boiler. Add sugar, shortening
and milk, mixing well. Cook over boiling water, stirring constantly
until mixture thickens. Remove from heat. Add chocolate, stirring
till melted, then add flavouring. Beat until thick enough to spread.
Yields icing for 9-inch-layer cake.

CHOCOLATE WHIPPED CREAM FILLING

*1 ounce chocolate, shredded | 2 tablespoons cream | 4 tablespoons sugar |
Dash of salt | 1 cup whipping cream | ½ teaspoon vanilla*

Heat in a double boiler all ingredients except whipping cream and
flavouring. When chocolate and sugar are dissolved, beat vigorously
over hot water till ingredients are thoroughly blended. Remove from
heat. Cool. Whip cream stiff, add vanilla and fold in chocolate
mixture.
Yields enough to fill a 9-inch 2-layer cake.

CREAMY CHOCOLATE FILLING

*2 cups sugar | ½ cup dry cocoa | ¼ teaspoon salt | 1 cup milk |
2 egg yolks | 1 teaspoon vanilla*

Cook all except flavouring in a saucepan till it reaches the soft ball stage. Cool and beat until the right consistency for spreading. Stir in flavouring.

Yields enough to fill a 9-inch 3-layer cake.

WHIPPED CREAM AND JAM FILLING

1 cup whipping cream | 1 cup strawberry jam

Whip cream stiff and fold in the jam.

Yields enough to fill a 9-inch 2-layer cake.

Variations can be made by substituting apricot pulp, sweetened to taste. Or, use red raspberry jam with $\frac{1}{2}$ teaspoon lemon juice.

BEATEN FUDGE FILLING AND ICING

1 ounce unsweetened chocolate, shaved fine | 1 cup sugar | $\frac{1}{4}$ cup butter or substitute | $\frac{1}{3}$ cup milk | $\frac{1}{8}$ teaspoon salt | $\frac{1}{4}$ teaspoon vanilla | $\frac{1}{4}$ teaspoon almond extract

Place chocolate, sugar, shortening, milk and salt in a saucepan and bring slowly to a boil over moderate heat. Stir constantly till it comes to a rolling boil. Remove from heat and beat with a fork till lukewarm. Add flavourings and continue beating until thick enough to spread. Should the icing become too thick, add about 1 tablespoon cream or evaporated milk, stirring till smooth.

Yields enough to fill and ice an 8- or 9-inch 2-layer cake.

HONEY FILLING AND ICING

1 cup honey | 2 egg whites

Heat the honey over low heat or in top of double boiler. Beat the egg whites stiff. Pour in hot honey slowly while beating till fluffy.

Yields icing and filling for a 9-inch 2-layer cake.

ORANGE FILLING

¾ cup sugar | 2 tablespoons flour | Grated rind of 1 orange |
4 teaspoons orange juice | 3 egg yolks | ⅛ cup water

Mix together sugar and flour, stir in juice and grated rind. Beat egg yolks, add water and stir into other mixture. Cook till thick and smooth over low heat, stirring constantly. Cool before spreading.
Yields enough filling for a 9-inch 3-layer cake.

ORANGE ICING

1 cup sugar | ¼ cup water | 1 egg white | 1 teaspoon grated orange rind

Boil sugar and water till it spins a thread. Do not stir while cooking. Beat egg white stiff and pour in hot syrup while beating till the right consistency for spreading. Stir in grated rind.

SEVEN-MINUTE ICING AND FILLING

2 egg whites | 1½ cups sugar | Pinch of salt | ¼ teaspoon cream of tartar |
5 tablespoons cold water | 1½ teaspoons light corn syrup (optional) |
1 teaspoon vanilla

Place all ingredients except flavouring in top of double boiler and beat with a rotary or whisk beater till well blended. Place over boiling water and beat constantly for 7 minutes by the clock. Remove from heat, let cool and add vanilla while beating till the right consistency for spreading.
Yields enough to fill and cover a 9-inch 2-layer cake with thick icing. For light icing, divide by half.

LEMON FILLING

2 tablespoons cornflour | ¾ cup cold water | ½ cup sugar |
3 tablespoons butter | Juice and grated rind of 1 lemon | 1 egg yolk

Moisten cornflour with 2 tablespoons cold water. Bring sugar and remaining water to a rapid boil. Add butter, lemon juice and grated rind. Stir in cornflour till smooth. Reduce heat. Cook slowly 10 minutes or till clear and smooth. Beat in egg yolk with a fork. Remove from heat. Spread between cake layers when cool.

Yields enough filling for a 9-inch 2-layer cake.

LEMON CUSTARD FILLING

2 cups milk | ¾ cup sugar | ⅓ cup flour | ¼ teaspoon salt |
4 egg yolks or 2 eggs | ½ teaspoon vanilla | 1 tablespoon lemon juice |
¼ teaspoon grated lemon rind

Combine dry ingredients and stir into scalded milk in top of a double boiler until thick and smooth. Pour over egg yolks or slightly beaten whole eggs. Return to double boiler and cook until eggs thicken. Add flavouring, lemon juice and grated rind. Spread between layers.

Yields enough filling for a 9-inch 3-layer cake.

Variation 1: Add 1 tablespoon sherry or rum.

Variation 2: Add ½ cup finely chopped almonds or walnuts.

Variation 3: Add 2 thinly sliced ripe bananas. Or 1 cup mashed banana.

Variation 4: Sprinkle generously with ¾ cup shredded coconut as soon as filling is spread.

Variation 5: For Lemon or Orange Icing, reduce water to 3 tablespoons and add 2 tablespoons lemon or orange juice and ¼ teaspoon grated rind.

MAPLE SYRUP ICING

¾ cup maple syrup | ¼ cup sugar | 1 egg white

Boil sugar and syrup till it spins a thread. Pour slowly over beaten egg white and beat until thickened to spreadable consistency.

MAPLE SUGAR ICING

2 cups maple sugar | 1 cup cream

Break up maple sugar and heat over a low flame. Add cream as soon as sugar begins to melt. Stir until completely dissolved, then boil until it reaches soft ball stage. Be careful not to let this mixture burn. Remove from heat. Beat until the right consistency for spreading.

SEA FOAM FILLING AND ICING

2 cups brown sugar | ⅔ cup water |
1 egg white, beaten with ⅛ teaspoon salt | 1 teaspoon vanilla

Bring sugar and water to soft ball stage and pour into stiffly beaten egg white, beating while pouring. Keep icing over hot water while beating till thick enough to spread. Add vanilla.

Variation 1: Use 2 egg whites beaten stiff and flavour with almond extract.

Variation 2: Sprinkle icing with ½ cup chopped nuts or shredded coconut.

Variation 3: Make *Mocha Sea Foam Icing* by substituting ½ cup extra strong coffee for water.

UNCOOKED ICINGS

BASIC ICING

1 cup icing sugar | 1½ tablespoons butter | Pinch of salt |
½ teaspoon vanilla or almond extract

Cream butter with sugar till smooth. Add salt and flavouring. Yields enough icing for a 9-inch cake.

CARAMEL ICING (Uncooked)

Melt 6 tablespoons butter till brown and blend in gradually 1½ cups icing sugar. Stir in a little hot water to form consistency for spreading. Add ½ teaspoon vanilla.

CHOCOLATE ICING

Melt 2 squares of semi-sweet chocolate and blend with Basic Icing.

Or, substitute 3 tablespoons cocoa dissolved in 1 tablespoon hot water or milk.

MOCK MAPLE ICING

Dissolve 2 tablespoons instant cereal coffee substitute (can be bought at Health Food shops) with just enough hot water or milk to make a thick syrupy mixture. Stir into 1½ cups icing sugar till smooth. Add 2 tablespoons butter and blend well.

ORANGE ICING (Uncooked)

2 tablespoons butter | 3 tablespoons orange juice | 1 tablespoon lemon juice |
¼ teaspoon each grated orange and lemon rind | Dash of salt |
2 cups icing sugar

Mix ingredients in the order given. Let stand 5 minutes before beating till creamy. Spread in swirls over top and sides of cake.
Variation: Add 1 egg yolk before beating to make icing more yellow. Or add a few drops of yellow vegetable colouring.

ORNAMENTAL BUTTER ICING

2½ cups sifted icing sugar | 2 tablespoons butter, softened |
1 egg white, unbeaten | 1 tablespoon cream | ¾ teaspoon vanilla | Pinch of salt

Add sugar gradually to softened butter, blending by stirring with a fork. Add egg white and beat until the consistency is spreadable. Stir in cream, flavouring and salt. Tint with vegetable colouring to suit the occasion and put through decorator (cone-shaped bag with tube attached) to form designs on top of cake already iced. Use a toothpick for fine tracery in your design. If you have no regular icing cone in your kitchen equipment, make an emergency one by using a rectangle of heavy wax paper or piece of heavy muslin rolled into a cone shape with a small opening at the tip end. An inexpensive thimble punctured with a small nail can serve as a substitute for the professional cone point.

24 Pies and Strudel

Types of Pies

Two-Crust or covered pies are best for juicy fruits and berries.

Single Pastry or Crumb Crusts are used for open-faced pies and tarts which may be prebaked then filled; or filled and then baked.

Deep-Dish Pies are made by filling a deep baking dish or casserole with fruit, vegetable combinations, or meat and vegetables, and topping with pie pastry.

Turnovers are individual small pies made by filling a round or square pastry with fruit, or chopped, cooked and seasoned meat, doubling over and pinching edges together to form half rounds or triangles.

Open-Face Pies are topped with strips of pastry crossed or laced to form a lattice pattern of wheel spokes.

Meringue Pies are open-faced pies, usually custard-filled and topped with stiffly beaten egg whites combined with sugar and baked or slipped under the grill to brown lightly.

Chiffon Pies are made by filling prebaked, cold, pie shells or tarts with gelatin base mixtures which are allowed to cool before topping with whipped cream or meringue.

Tarts are cuplike containers made of pastry baked and filled with fruit or creamy mixtures.

Patty Shells are made of Puff Paste rolled thin, cut into 3- to 5-inch rounds. Remove or cut out centres from some rounds, lay several of these pastry rings in position to form shells and bake. Use for creamed mixtures, compotes, fruits, etc.

Size of Pies: In this section, unless otherwise noted, the ingredients specified are for a 9-inch pie pan. This will yield from 6 to 8 servings depending on the size of the cuts.

Pie Crusts: When the recipe calls for a single crust to be used on the bottom, it will be referred to in the ingredients as a *pie shell*. When a double crust is called for (one on the bottom and one on top), it will be listed as a *pie pastry*.

FLAKY PIE PASTRY (Basic Recipe)

*2½ cups sifted flour | ¾ teaspoon salt | ¾ cup vegetable shortening |
5 tablespoons ice-cold water | Pinch of sugar*

Sift together dry ingredients, measuring accurately amount needed.
Cut shortening into the dry mixture, using a pastry blender or work
rapidly with 2 knife blades until the mixture is reduced to pea-size
particles. Add water, a spoonful at a time, pressing the moistened
particles together lightly with a fork. As some of the mixture begins
to cling together, place the ball of pastry on a sheet of heavy wax
paper or aluminium foil. Wrap and chill 30 minutes before rolling
out. This is sufficient for 1 double crust 9-inch pie or 2 shells the
same size. To prevent soggy undercrust, brush with beaten egg
white before turning in the fruit filling.

Insert a 2-inch piece of large uncooked macaroni in centre of top
crust of juicy fruit or berry pies. This serves as a chimney for rising
juice and prevents bubbling over on top. Or make a small funnel
cut from corner of an envelope and insert in top crust.

PUFF PASTRY (Basic Recipe)

1 cup unsalted butter | 2 cups sifted cake flour | ½ cup ice water

Soften about ¼ cup of butter. Cut remainder into flour with 2 knives
or wire pastry blender. Add ice water a tablespoon at a time, and
only enough to hold ingredients together in a ball. Roll out on a
lightly floured board to ¼-inch thickness in rectangular form. Cut
rectangle into equal thirds. Spread softened butter over 1st
section of rolled-out dough, place 2nd rectangle above 1st, and
spread with butter. Place remaining part of dough over the 2nd, to
make a triple decker of pastry. Roll from narrow end of pastry towards the centre, turn and roll from other end towards centre.
Spread with butter very lightly and fold over to make another
triple decker. Chill 2 to 3 hours in refrigerator. Place pastry on
lightly floured board and roll out to ¼-inch thickness, working from
each end in turn. Work rapidly and roll lightly. Cut into desired
shapes and bake 10 minutes at 450° F. or gas mark 8, reduce heat to
400° F. or gas mark 6 for 5 minutes, then reduce heat to 350° F.
or gas mark 4 for 10 minutes.

Yields 24 small pastries.

ALMOND PASTRY (Near East Recipe)

¼ cup finely ground almonds | 1½ cups sifted flour | ¼ cup sugar |
½ teaspoon salt | ½ cup shortening | 1 egg | Ice water

Mix dry ingredients and cut in shortening. Add beaten egg and just enough water to form a stiff dough. Chill, roll out like plain pastry.
Variation: Substitute ground Brazil nuts. Reduce to ¼ cup shortening.

CHEESE PASTRY

½ cup butter | 1 cup sifted flour | ¼ pound cottage or cream cheese

Cut butter into flour then add cheese. Mix to a smooth dough. Chill 2 hours before rolling out. Makes one 9-inch pastry.

CRUMB CRUSTS

These are made of crushed or rolled soda or water biscuits, vanilla wafers, stale cake, ginger snaps or rusks, combined with shortening and pressed into the bottom and up the sides of a pie pan to form the crust or container for pie filling. Use rolling pin and paper bag for crushing biscuits. Emergency pie shells can be made with finely crushed dry cereal like cornflakes.

CRUMB PIE SHELL

1½ cups fine crumbs | ¼ cup sugar | ½ cup softened butter or substitute

Combine and press an even layer against bottom and sides of 9-inch pie pan. Bake 10 minutes at 400° F. or gas mark 6. Cool and fill.

CONTINENTAL MERBERTEIGE

¼ cup butter | 1 cup sifted flour | 1 tablespoon brown sugar |
Pinch of salt | 1 egg yolk | 2 tablespoons brandy or ice water

Cream butter. Add dry ingredients and work with 2 knives till particles are like sand. Add beaten yolk to liquid and stir in lightly. Roll to ¼-inch thickness and line 9-inch pie pan.

SALAD OIL CRUST

1¼ cups flour | ½ teaspoon salt | ⅔ cup oil | 3 tablespoons cold water

Sift together dry ingredients. Mix oil and water. Stir into dry ingredients with a fork to form dough. Roll out on floured board, or chill about a ½ hour before rolling to ⅛-inch thickness.

SOUTHERN PIE CRUST

1 cup shortening | 2 cups flour, sifted | ½ teaspoon salt | 6 tablespoons ice water

Cut shortening into sifted flour and salt. Add water a spoonful at a time to make a dough. This makes a very rich pastry dough and must be handled deftly. Chill well before rolling out.

Makes 1 double crust or two 9-inch shells.

SUET PASTRY FOR MEAT PIES

2 cups sifted flour | 1 teaspoon baking powder | ½ teaspoon salt | 1 cup finely chopped beef suet | ½ cup cold water

Chill all ingredients. Sift together flour, baking powder and salt. Add suet and stir in water to make a smooth, firm dough. Chill before rolling out.

Makes two 9-inch shells or can be cut and used for meat turnovers.

HOT WATER PASTRY (For Meat Pies or Turnovers)

2 cups sifted flour | ½ teaspoon baking powder | 1 teaspoon salt | ⅓ cup boiling water | ⅔ cup shortening

Sift dry ingredients together. Combine shortening with boiling water, and when creamy, stir in flour mixture to make a dough. Chill. Roll out when ready to bake.

Makes two 9-inch pie shells or 1 double crust.

WHEATLESS PIE CRUST

1 cup white rye flour (obtainable at Health Food shops) |
1 cup potato flour | ½ teaspoon baking powder | ½ teaspoon salt |
½ cup shortening | ¼ cup water

Sift together dry ingredients and cut in shortening. Add water to make a dough stiff enough to handle and roll out to ⅛-inch thickness. Must be handled skilfully in lifting to pie pan as this dough breaks up easily. Prick the crust to prevent blistering. Bake 10 to 15 minutes at 425° F. or gas mark 7.

VINEGAR PIE CRUST

1 cup flour | ¼ teaspoon salt | ¼ cup shortening |
3 tablespoons vinegar | 3 tablespoons cold water

Sift dry ingredients together twice. Cut in shortening. Combine vinegar and water and stir in a tablespoonful at a time to make a dough easy to handle. Some flours require less water. Mix carefully.

PIES

APPLE PIE (Covered)

6 tart apples | ½ cup sugar | ¼ teaspoon salt |
Dash of cinnamon or nutmeg | 2 tablespoons flour or 1 tablespoon tapioca |
1 pie pastry | 1 tablespoon butter or vegetable shortening

Pare and slice apples. Mix dry ingredients together and combine with apple slices. Line pie plate with pastry, fill with apple mixture, dot with butter and top with crust. Bake 10 to 15 minutes at 425° F. or gas mark 7, reduce heat to 350° F. or gas mark 4 and bake 45 minutes longer.

For a glazed crust, brush with evaporated milk or diluted egg yolk.

OPEN-FACE APPLE PIE

Arrange thin apple slices in a pastry-lined pie plate, dot with butter and sprinkle with a mixture of flour or tapioca, spices and sugar. Arrange strips of pastry across top. Bake 30 to 45 minutes at 400° F. or gas mark 6.

DEEP-DISH APPLE PIE

Use 2-inch deep glazed ramekins or other ovenware in which pies may be served. Fill compactly with sliced apples well over the top. Add as much sugar as required for the apples used, a dash of cinnamon or nutmeg, and butter the size of a hazelnut. Sprinkle with flour or fine crumbs. Top with pie shell, press down the rim with a fork and trim off excess pastry. Prick pastry with a fork. Brush with milk or egg yolk and water. Bake at 400° F. or gas mark 6 about 30 minutes or until browned.

APPLE-CHEESE PIE

1½ cups thinly sliced apples | ¼ cup sugar |
¼ teaspoon each cinnamon and nutmeg | A 9-inch pie shell

Combine these ingredients and turn into a pastry-lined 9-inch pie pan. Bake 15 minutes at 425° F. or gas mark 7. Meantime, prepare the rest of the pie filling as follows:

FILLING
½ cup sugar | 2 eggs, slightly beaten | Dash of salt | ½ cup light cream |
¾ cup milk | 1 teaspoon vanilla | 1 cup creamed cottage cheese

Beat sugar, eggs and salt, a few strokes till smooth. Scald combined cream and milk and stir into egg mixture. Add vanilla and cheese, stirring till smooth. Turn in over the baked apple in the pastry shell and bake at 325° F. or gas mark 3 for 20 minutes, then increase heat to 350° F. or gas mark 4 and continue baking 20 minutes longer or till set and nicely browned at edges and on top.

> *Variation:* For *Pineapple-Cheese Pie*, substitute 1 cup well-drained, canned crushed pineapple for prepared apple. Proceed exactly as in recipe.

HOLIDAY APPLE PIE

6 tart apples, slices | 1½ cups grapefruit juice |
1 prebaked Crumb Crust made from a spicy biscuit | 3 tablespoons cornflour |
½ cup sugar | 10 maraschino cherries | 1 teaspoon almond extract

Stew apples in grapefruit juice till tender. Drain apples, reserving
juice, and arrange in baked pie shell. Mix cornflour and sugar. Add
to grapefruit juice and cook till clear and thick. Pour over apples.
Cool and decorate with halves of cherries flavoured with almond.
Top with whipped cream if desired.

APPLE, RAISIN AND ALMOND UPSIDE-DOWN PIE

4 tablespoons butter or vegetable shortening | ⅔ cup chopped almonds and
1 cup seeded raisins | ⅔ cup brown sugar, tightly packed | 1 pie pastry |
2½ to 3 pounds apples, cored, pared and thinly sliced | ½ cup brown sugar |
1 tablespoon flour | ¼ teaspoon salt | Dash of nutmeg or cinnamon

Spread the butter or other shortening evenly over the bottom of a
9-inch glass pie plate. Sprinkle chopped almonds evenly over the
bottom of buttered pie plate and arrange the raisins in a ring close
to the rim. Place raisins in 3 rows across bottom of pie plate, forming
a wheel-spoke pattern. With the bowl of a teaspoon press the nuts
and raisins gently down into the shortening. Sprinkle brown sugar
evenly and press gently into place with bowl of spoon.

Place the 1st layer of pie pastry over the bottom of plate, press the
pastry against side of plate and let the pastry come about ½ inch over
the rim. Fill the pastry with sliced apples. Combine brown sugar,
flour and salt and sprinkle over apple slices. Dust with nutmeg or
cinnamon and cover with top layer of pie pastry. Turn the under
edge of pastry up and flute the edges, pressing firmly against the rim
of plate. Prick the top pastry in several places with the tines of a fork,
or mark with some design. Bake in a preheated oven 10 minutes at
350° F. or gas mark 4. Brush top of pie with diluted egg yolk or any
fruit juice. Continue baking 40 to 45 minutes. Test with a fork to
make sure apples are tender before removing from oven. As soon as
the syrup in bottom of pie plate stops bubbling, place a large serving
plate over pie and carefully invert pie and plate to remove pie with
design intact.

APPLESAUCE PIE

1 *prebaked cheese pie shell (see Pie Crusts)* |
3 *cups sweetened applesauce, fresh or canned* | ¼ *teaspoon nutmeg* |
3 *egg whites* | 3 *tablespoons icing sugar* | ½ *teaspoon vanilla*

Fill shell with applesauce. Sprinkle with nutmeg. Beat egg whites till stiff, fold in sugar, add flavouring and cover pie filling, to pastry rim. Bake 20 minutes at 425° F. or gas mark 7, or until nicely browned.

APPLESAUCE-RAISIN PIE

2½ *cups thinly sliced apples* | 1 *cup sugar* | 1 *tablespoon lemon juice* |
1 *cup seedless raisins* | *A 9-inch prebaked pie shell* | 2 *egg whites* |
2 *tablespoons icing sugar*

Cook apples, sugar and lemon juice 10 minutes in a covered saucepan. Beat with spoon or fork till smooth and add raisins while hot. Turn into baked pie shell as soon as cool. Top with meringue made by beating egg whites and icing sugar till thick. Slip under grill to brown lightly.

APPLESAUCE AND CRANBERRY PIE

2 *cups cranberries* | 1 *cup sugar* | 2 *cups applesauce* | ½ *cup water* |
2 *tablespoons quick cooking tapioca* | *A 9-inch prebaked pie shell* |
Whipped cream for topping

Cook berries in a covered saucepan for 10 minutes over moderate heat. Press through strainer, add sugar, applesauce, water, and return to heat. Stir in tapioca and cook till clear. Cool and turn into baked pie shell. Top with whipped cream just before serving.

BERRY PIES

For a 9-inch pie, use from 3 to 4 cups blackberries, blueberries, currants, loganberries or strawberries. Be sure to pick over, wash and

Strudel:
Sliced Apple
(*page 410*)
Cherry and
Nuts
(*page 411*)

drain thoroughly any berries used. Fill a pastry-lined pie pan with fruit, add sugar mixed with a little flour or fine crumbs, or quick-cooking tapioca. Dot with butter or vegetable shortening. Cover with pastry, insert a paper funnel or macaroni chimney in centre of top crust. Press edges together, flute with a fork or fingers and bake. Berry pies take from 30 to 45 minutes at 375° F. It is best to start at 425° F. or gas mark 7 and turn down the heat to 350° F. or gas mark 4 after the first 10 minutes.

Variation: For open-face or one-crust berry pies, use prebaked pie shells and fill with cooked and seasoned fruit. Add lemon juice mixed with a little flour or cornflour to thicken the juice formed in cooking fruit. Sweeten to taste according to kind of berries used and degree of ripeness. Decorate with strips of pastry in lattice or wheel pattern and bake 10 minutes or till brown on top.

Note: Brush pie shell with egg yolk or beaten egg white before baking and filling with berries. Prevents soggy crust.

CHERRY PIE (Basic Recipe)

1 *quart pitted sour cherries, fresh or canned* | 2 *tablespoons tapioca* | ¾ *cup sugar (approximately)* | *A pie pastry*

Line a 9-inch pie pan with pastry and fill with well-drained cherries. Sprinkle tapioca and sugar evenly over top, cover with pastry strips in lattice form, flute edges and bake 40 minutes at 375° F. or gas mark 5, or till nicely browned.

Variation 1: Cover with slashed or perforated pastry and flute edges. Bake at 400° F. or gas mark 6 for 30 minutes or till browned.

Variation 2: Omit tapioca. Mix 3 tablespoons flour with ½ cup syrup from canned cherries and pour over fruit in pastry-lined pie pan. Top with lattice strips or cover with pastry and insert funnel. Bake till brown.

Variation 3: For a Mock Cherry Pie use 3 cups chopped cranberries and 1 cup seedless raisins. Add 1 cup sugar, ¼ teaspoon salt and 3 tablespoons quick-cooking tapioca. Fill 9-inch pastry-lined pan, top with strips or whole pastry, insert funnel and bake.

26

CHERRY-PRUNE PIE

Line a pie pan with pastry and arrange alternate rounds of pitted, soaked and drained prunes and canned pitted cherries. Dissolve 1 tablespoon cornflour in ¼ cup water. Cook with 1 cup juice from canned cherries till clear. Pour over the fruit and bake at 400° F. or gas mark 6 until rim of pie crust is nicely browned, approximately 30 minutes.

CHERRY-RAISIN PIE

1 crumb pie crust or prebaked shell | 2 cups seedless raisins |
1½ cups drained and pitted canned cherries | ⅔ cup cherry syrup |
¼ cup water | 1 tablespoon cornflour | Dash of salt

Combine raisins and syrup. Mix cornflour with water. Add salt and cook 5 minutes. Add cherries and turn into pie shell. Bake 10 minutes at 450° F. or gas mark 8.

MERINGUE TOPPING (Basic Recipe)

2 egg whites | 4 tablespoons sugar | Few grains of salt |
¼ teaspoon lemon extract

Beat egg whites with a rotary beater till stiff, gradually adding sugar and salt until the mixture holds a peak. Stir in flavouring very lightly and use on puddings or pies as directed, by spreading in swirls or dropping from the spoon to form peaks. In spreading on pies, puddings or tarts, be sure to have the meringue mixture touch the pastry rim or baking dish to prevent shrinking away from edge. Bake 18 to 20 minutes at 325° F. or gas mark 3.

LEMON MERINGUE PIE (Basic Recipe)

1 cup milk | 1 tablespoon butter | Pinch of salt | ¾ cup sugar |
3 tablespoons cornflour | 2 eggs, separated | 6 tablespoons lemon juice |
1 teaspoon grated lemon rind | A 9-inch prebaked pie shell |
3 tablespoons icing sugar

Scald milk in top of double boiler. Add butter, salt and sugar. Mix cornflour with a little cold water and stir in. Cook till thickened and beat till smooth. Remove from heat and add beaten egg yolks. Cook 2 to 3 minutes and add lemon juice and grated rind. Turn into 9-inch baked pie shell as soon as cool. Top with meringue made by beating egg whites and icing sugar. Arrange topping in peaks and slip under grill to brown.

Variation 1: Top with shredded coconut.

Variation 2: Use 4 egg yolks in place of 2 and fold in stiffly-beaten whites of 2 eggs just before turning custard into pie shell. Cover with meringue of 2 egg whites as above and bake 15 to 20 minutes at 400° F. or gas mark 6.

Variation 3: Substitute water for milk. Use vegetable shortening instead of butter. Will not be as rich and creamy, but can be served with meat meals.

Variation 4: Make it Lemon-Carrot Pie by cooking 1½ cups grated raw carrot with the milkless custard. Cook 10 minutes. Top with meringue and brown under grill just before serving.

Variation 5: Add 6 crushed macaroons to cooked lemon custard and beat till smooth. Cool before filling baked shell. Top with meringue and sprinkle some of the macaroon crumbs on top. Brown lightly.

BERRY CHIFFON PIE (Basic Recipe)

1 package raspberry or strawberry gelatin | ½ cup hot water |
1 cup fruit juice | 1 egg white | ½ cup heavy cream, whipped |
½ cup caster sugar | 1½ cups sliced berries |
A 9-inch prebaked pie shell | 1 egg yolk

Dissolve gelatin in water and stir in fruit juice. Chill till partially set. Beat with a rotary beater till light. Beat egg white stiff and fold in whipped cream. Combine the 2 mixtures by stirring lightly. Add sugar to 1 cup of berries and fold into the gelatin and cream mixture. Turn into baked pie shell which has been brushed with egg yolk to prevent soggy crust. Top with remainder of berries and chill until firm.

CHOCOLATE CHIFFON PIE

*1 tablespoon unflavoured gelatin | ¼ cup cold water |
½ cup boiling hot water | 2 squares unsweetened chocolate | 1 cup sugar |
3 eggs, separated | 1 teaspoon vanilla | ¼ teaspoon salt |
A 9-inch prebaked pie shell | ½ cup heavy cream, whipped*

Soften gelatin in cold water and stir in boiling water till dissolved. Melt chocolate over boiling water in top of double boiler, add sugar and beaten egg yolks. Cook 2 minutes. Remove from heat. When cool, add vanilla and egg whites beaten stiff with salt. Fold in whipped cream and turn the mixture into baked pie shell. Chill till firm.

Variation: Turn chocolate and egg white mixture into baked shell, chill till firm and top with swirls of whipped cream just before serving.

LEMON CREAM PIE

*2⅔ cups sweetened condensed milk | ¾ cup lemon juice |
1 tablespoon grated lemon rind | A 9-inch prebaked pie shell |
½ cup heavy cream, whipped with 2 tablespoons icing sugar*

Combine condensed milk, lemon juice and grated rind in a bowl and stir till thoroughly blended. Pour into pie shell. Chill till firm, approximately 1 hour. Spread top with whipped cream and sugar just before serving time.

LEMON PIE

*5 tablespoons sugar | 2 tablespoons water | 3 tablespoons lemon juice |
Grated rind of 1 lemon | 3 egg yolks | Dash of salt | 3 egg whites |
3 tablespoons sugar | A 9-inch prebaked pie shell*

Combine and cook sugar, water, lemon juice, grated rind and beaten yolks in top of double boiler till thick and creamy. Beat egg whites and salt till stiff but not dry and fold in 3 tablespoons sugar. Stir into the cooled custard and turn into pie shell. Bake 10 minutes at 400° F. or gas mark 6, or brown lightly under grill.

ORANGE PIE

3 egg yolks / $\frac{1}{3}$ cup sugar / 3 tablespoons flour / $\frac{3}{4}$ cup orange juice / 2 tablespoons lemon juice / $\frac{1}{2}$ teaspoon grated orange rind / 2 tablespoons water / 3 egg whites / Dash of salt / A 9-inch prebaked pie shell

Combine all ingredients except egg whites and salt. Cook in double boiler. Stir till thick and creamy. Set aside to cool. Beat egg whites and salt until stiff but not dry and fold into cooled custard. Turn into pie shell and brown under grill or bake 10 minutes at 400° F. or gas mark 6.

MARMALADE AND CRANBERRY PIE

1 cup granulated sugar / $\frac{1}{4}$ cup fruit marmalade / $\frac{1}{4}$ cup water / 3 cups fresh cranberries / 2 pears, pared and diced / 1 tablespoon cornflour / Juice and grated rind $\frac{1}{2}$ lemon / $\frac{1}{4}$ cup chopped, cooked, pitted prunes / $\frac{1}{2}$ cup blanched almonds, shredded / Water biscuit crumb crust (see Crumb Crust recipes)

Heat sugar, marmalade and water together. Add cranberries and pears. Cook about 5 minutes till cranberry skins pop open. Blend cornflour with lemon juice, add to hot fruit. Stir and cook for 2 minutes. Cool, stir in lemon rind, prunes and almonds. Turn into crust and chill. Serve garnished with whipped cream cheese.

MOCK MINCE PIE

1$\frac{1}{2}$ cups seeded raisins / 4 medium tart apples, shredded / $\frac{1}{2}$ cup orange juice / $\frac{1}{4}$ cup lemon juice / 1 cup cider / 1 cup brown sugar, tightly packed / $\frac{1}{4}$ teaspoon cinnamon / $\frac{1}{4}$ teaspoon allspice / 3 tablespoons dry bread crumbs / A prebaked 9-inch pie shell

Put raisins and shredded apple through food chopper, medium blade. Simmer fruit juices and cider 5 minutes and add fruit, sugar, cinnamon, allspice and crumbs. Simmer 10 minutes or till apple is

very soft. Cool. Fill pie shell. Bake 20 to 30 minutes at 375° F. or
gas mark 5. Top with meringue made of 2 egg whites if desired.
   Variation: Add ½ cup drained canned crushed pineapple. Omit
allspice. Proceed as in basic recipe.

BANANA-PRUNE MAJESTIC PIE

⅔ *cup honey | ¼ cup butter | 1 teaspoon lemon juice | Dash of salt |*
2 cups soaked, pitted prunes | 2 cups thinly sliced bananas |
A 9-inch prebaked pie shell

Combine honey and butter, beating with a fork. Add lemon juice
and salt, and beat 1 minute before adding to fruit, stirring lightly.
Turn into pie shell. Top with whipped cream.

UNBAKED PERSIMMON PIE

2 *tablespoons lemon juice | ½ cup sugar | ½ teaspoon cinnamon |*
3 *cups mashed and pitted ripe persimmons | A 9-inch prebaked pie shell |*
1 *cup whipped cream*

Cook lemon juice, sugar and cinnamon 5 minutes. Add to persimmon
pulp and turn into a pie shell. Top with whipped cream.
   Caution! Don't attempt to bake persimmon pie. Heat reverts this
fruit to its unripe stage. Unripe persimmons make the mouth pucker!

OLD-FASHIONED PUMPKIN PIE

3 *eggs | ⅔ cup light brown sugar | ¾ cup milk |*
1½ *cups cooked, drained and mashed pumpkin | ¼ teaspoon salt |*
¼ *teaspoon ginger | Dash of nutmeg and cloves |*
1 *tablespoon hot water | An 8-inch pie shell*

Beat eggs till light and creamy. Stir in sugar, milk and pumpkin.
Mix spices with hot water and stir in. Turn into a pastry-lined pie
pan and bake at 450° F. or gas mark 8 for 15 minutes, reduce heat
to 300° F. or gas mark 1–2 for 45 minutes or until custard is set.

RHUBARB PIE

5 cups rhubarb (cut into ½-inch pieces) | 1¾ cups sugar |
2 tablespoons cornflour | 3 tablespoons cold water |
2 tablespoons shortening | A 9-inch pie pastry

Cover the rhubarb with sugar and shake gently to distribute
evenly. Let stand 5 to 10 minutes before arranging in pastry-lined
pie pan (or individual shells). Add the blended cornflour and water
with a spoon, then dot with shortening and cover with rolled-out
pastry. Press down the edges with a fork and pierce the centre of
top crust 3 times with the tines of fork. Bake in a preheated oven at
425° F. or gas mark 7 for 40 minutes.

STRAWBERRY FESTIVAL PIE

2 cups hulled fresh strawberries | ½ cup honey | 2 cups cornflakes |
Pinch of salt | 1½ cups whipped cream | A 9-inch prebaked pie shell |
¼ cup shredded coconut for topping

Crush the berries and combine with honey, cornflakes, salt and ½
cup of the whipped cream, folding the cream in lightly. Turn this
mixture into a pie shell. Spread the remaining whipped cream on
top in swirls and sprinkle with coconut. Chill at least ½ hour before
serving.

DE LUXE STRAWBERRY PIE

A 7-inch prebaked pie shell | 1 cup whipped cream |
A 3-ounce package cream cheese | 1 quart strawberries |
3 tablespoons cornflour | 1 cup sugar

Use enough of the cream to soften cream cheese and spread evenly
over the bottom of baked pie shell. Wash, hull and drain the berries
and place half of them in the cheese-coated pie shell. Wash remaining berries, cover, and bring to a boil. Mix sugar and cornflour and
stir into the hot berries, cooking over reduced heat and stirring until
the juice is clear, approximately 10 minutes. Cool and spread over
the uncooked berries. Chill in refrigerator until 10 minutes before

serving time. Top with sweetened whipped cream or stiffly beaten
egg whites flavoured with a few drops of lemon juice and sugar to
taste. 2 or 3 egg whites will amply cover. Mashing a few uncooked
strawberries into the whipped egg whites for colour adds a festive
touch. A coating of strawberry jam may be used in place of the cream
cheese if you want to use this dessert with a meat or poultry meal.

YAM PIE (Southern Style)

*1¾ cups cooked yams, sieved through soup strainer | ¾ cup light corn syrup |
¼ cup brown sugar | ½ teaspoon nutmeg | ¼ teaspoon ginger |
1 teaspoon cinnamon | ½ teaspoon salt | 2 egg yolks | 1 cup milk |
2 stiffly beaten egg whites | 1 tablespoon molasses | An 8-inch pie shell |
½ cup pecan halves*

Combine well-sieved yams with syrup, sugar and seasonings. Stir
in beaten yolks mixed with milk. Stir molasses into beaten egg
whites gradually until meringue comes to a peak. Fold into the
original mixture and turn into unbaked pie shell. Top with pecan
halves, helter-skelter, and bake 15 minutes at 450° F. or gas mark 8,
then reduce heat to 350° F. or gas mark 4 for the next 30 minutes or
until inserted silver knife point comes out clean, dry.

STRUDEL

Strudel is the pastry that is as Jewish as pie is American. There are
many kinds of strudel, depending on family custom and locale.
Strudel may be made of stretched, paper-thin dough, filled with
sliced apple, cheese, sour milk, marmalade, prune butter (see p. 522),
raisins, generously sprinkled with cinnamon and sugar. This type
of strudel is made by Austrian and Hungarian cooks. Roumanians
pride themselves on tissue-thin stretched dough for strudel filled
with chopped nuts and raisins as well as thinly sliced fruit, sugared
and spiced, and baked to a crisp flakiness.

Polish and Russian cooks use a thinly rolled pastry filled with
finely chopped or shredded cabbage, chopped chicken or cooked
meat, kasha, all seasoned superbly and baked in long rolls then cut
diagonally into 1½- or 2-inch pieces and browned. Sweetened
fillings are also popular and used for special occasions as well as
Sabbath and holidays.

Rolled Strudel Dough is sometimes used for a fruit-filled pudding called a *shalat*. It also is known as a *kugel*. But it can be used for strudel with any of the fillings listed. This dough is rolled as thin as noodle dough but need not be stretched to tissue thinness.

ROLLED STRUDEL DOUGH (Basic Recipe)

2 cups flour | 1 tablespoon sugar | Pinch of salt | 1 egg |
3 tablespoons melted shortening or oil | 1 cup cold water (approximately)

Sift dry ingredients into a mixing bowl. Make a well in the centre and add egg and melted shortening. Stir to combine, then add a little water at a time to make a dough firm enough to handle. Toss on to a lightly floured board and knead 3 minutes. Roll out very thin and evenly. If rolling pin adheres to dough, dust lightly with flour and continue rolling from the edges to the centre, working around the dough instead of from one side.

STRETCHED STRUDEL DOUGH

2 cups flour | 1 tablespoon salad oil or melted shortening | 1 egg |
½ cup lukewarm water (approximately) | ⅛ teaspoon salt

Sift flour into a deep bowl. Combine slightly beaten egg with oil, salt and water. Stir into the centre of flour, working it in with a knife till it forms a ball of dough. Turn out on a lightly floured kneading board and knead till smooth and elastic. Warm the mixing bowl and turn it over to cover the mound of dough while you prepare the filling. Let stand at least 30 minutes before rolling out on a large lightly floured cloth, rolling it as thin as possible.

Brush the surface of dough with melted shortening or oil and begin the stretching process, placing the hands underneath and working from the centre towards the outer edges, all around the table, until the dough is stretched evenly and paper thin. This takes time and patience but it is well worth the trouble. Before spreading the filling, cut away any thick edges that remain.

Now it is ready for filling and rolling. Spread the filling in rows about 2 inches apart if made of apple, cheese, prune or other juicy ingredients. Sprinkle generously with sugar and spice, grated lemon or orange rind, finely rolled dry bread crumbs and a sprinkling of melted shortening or oil over all. By lifting the cloth at one end you can start the strudel rolling up and over as each row of filling is reached. Trim off the ends and cut into lengths to fit the baking pan. Place the rolls on well-greased baking sheet, allowing plenty of space between each length.

Bake at 375° F. or gas mark 5 for 40 to 50 minutes or till nicely browned and crisp. Brushing the top with melted shortening is most desirable but not essential.

STRUDEL FILLINGS

SLICED APPLE

*3 cups thinly sliced (or shredded) apples | ¾ cup sugar |
½ teaspoon cinnamon | Dash of nutmeg | 4 tablespoons melted shortening*

APPLE AND CURRANTS

Add ½ cup currants to above ingredients

APPLE AND RAISINS

*1½ pounds tart apples, shredded (or grated) | ½ cup seeded raisins, chopped |
¾ cup sugar | ¼ cup fine crumbs | ½ teaspoon cinnamon |
1 teaspoon grated lemon or orange rind | 4 tablespoons oil*

DRIED FRUITS

*1 cup finely cut dried apricots | 1 cup finely cut dried prunes |
2 tablespoons lemon or orange juice | 1 teaspoon grated rind of lemon or orange |
½ cup sugar | 2 tablespoons honey, warmed | 3 tablespoons fine crumbs |
½ teaspoon nutmeg (optional)*

Combine fruit with fruit juice and grated rind. Add sugar and honey alternately. Sprinkle with crumbs and nutmeg before rolling up.

CHERRY AND NUTS

2 quarts pitted cherries, fresh or drained canned | ¾ cup dried bread crumbs |
1 cup sugar | ¼ cup chopped almonds or mixed nuts |
¼ cup melted shortening

Combine cherries, crumbs, sugar and nuts. After spreading on stretched or rolled dough, drizzle shortening over and roll up.

CHOPPED NUTS

½ pound blanched almonds, finely ground | 4 egg yolks | ½ cup sugar |
1 teaspoon grated lemon or orange rind | ¼ cup melted shortening, oil

Combine ground almonds, egg yolks, sugar and grated rind to form a paste. Spread in rows on rolled or stretched dough. Drizzle with shortening and roll up.

RAISINS AND CHEESE

½ cup chopped seeded or seedless raisins (or light raisins) |
½ pound dry cottage cheese, rubbed through a sieve |
2 eggs beaten with ¼ cup sugar | 4 tablespoons dry crumbs mixed with
½ teaspoon cinnamon | 1 tablespoon grated lemon rind

Combine the first 3 ingredients. Sprinkle with crumbs and grated rind. Spread and roll up.

KASHA

2 cups prepared, cooked groats (see p. 311) |
1 onion, finely diced and browned in 4 tablespoons melted shortening

Combine and spread over stretched or rolled dough. Roll up and bake, basting with hot melted shortening once or twice during the process.

LIVER

1 pound beef or calf's liver, grilled and chopped fine |
1 onion, finely diced and browned in 4 tablespoons chicken or goose schmaltz |
¼ cup dry bread crumbs or fine matzo meal | 1 teaspoon salt

Combine ingredients in the order listed. Spread and roll up. Bake
and baste with more melted schmaltz once or twice during the
process until nicely browned.

LUNG

3 cups chopped cooked beef or calf's lung | ¼ cup chopped greben |
2 hard-cooked eggs, chopped | 1 tablespoon grated onion

Combine with a fork. Scatter over stretched or rolled dough. Roll
up tightly and bake. Baste once or twice with hot melted shortening,
preferably chicken or goose schmaltz, if a fat strudel is desired.

TARTS

FRUIT TARTS

Roll out chilled Puff Paste (see p. 394) to ½- to 1-inch thickness.
Cut into 3-inch rounds with a floured biscuit cutter. Divide rounds
into 3, and with a 2-inch biscuit cutter cut out centres of ⅔ of
rounds. Moisten each round at edges and place a circle on top.
Moisten the circle with water and adjust second circle of pastry.
Arrange on ungreased baking sheet and bake 10 minutes at 450° F.
or gas mark 8, reduce heat to 350° F. or gas mark 4 and continue
baking 30 minutes. The tarts are ready to fill with fresh sweetened
berries or creamed cottage cheese, sweetened to taste. Top with
whipped cream if desired. Baked small rounds may be added as
topping or served separately.
    Yields 8 tart shells and 16 small pastries.

APRICOT TARTS

½ pound dried apricots | ¾ cup sugar | 1 cup flour | ¼ teaspoon salt |
½ cup shortening | 1 egg | ½ cup whipped cream

Cover apricots with cold water and bring to the boiling point. Cover and simmer 30 minutes till tender. Drain, reserving the liquid (about 1 cup). Make a syrup of liquid and sugar, add apricots and cook 1 minute. Cool.

Sift together flour and salt, and cut in shortening. Beat egg slightly and stir in to make a ball of dough. Roll out on a floured board to ⅛-inch thickness. Cut in rounds a little larger than the tart tins. Fit each round over inverted pans, trim edges or mark with a fork. Be sure to prick the bottoms and sides so dough will not blister. Bake 10 minutes at 425° F. or gas mark 7. Cool before filling with apricot mixture. Top with whipped cream.

Variation 1: Fill with Prune Whip (see Index) and top with whipped cream.

Variation 2: Fill with pitted fresh cherries, or drained canned cherries. Thicken 1 cup canned syrup with 1 teaspoon cornflour and cook 5 minutes, stirring till thick. Add to fruit. Top with whipped cream.

Variation 3: Fill with sweetened applesauce and top with whipped cream.

JAM AND JELLY TARTS

1 recipe of Cheese Pastry (see p. 395) | 1 cup strawberry jam or preserves | 1 tablespoon dry cake crumbs

Roll chilled pastry to ¼-inch thickness. Cut into 3-inch rounds with a biscuit cutter, making 36 rounds. With a 2-inch biscuit cutter, cut out centres from 24 rounds. Moisten the rim of rounds with cold water and place a ring of pastry on top. Moisten ring with cold water and adjust second ring of pastry. Mark edges with the tines of a fork and bake 12 to 15 minutes at 475° F. or gas mark 9. Cool and fill centres with jam combined with cake crumbs or sprinkle cake crumbs on top of jam.

Yields 12 three-inch tarts.

25 Puddings
Sweet and Otherwise

A Kugel in Jewish cuisine is a pudding. There are two types of kugels – those which may be served as a side-dish with the meal (generally made of vegetables), and those which may be served as desserts (sweet kugels).

Puddings or kugels may be served either hot or cold, depending on whether they are baked, steamed, chilled or frozen.

APPLE KUGEL

1 *Merberteige Pastry (see Pie Pastry)* | 6 *cups thinly sliced apples* |
½ *cup fine crumbs* | 1 *cup sugar or honey* | ½ *teaspoon cinnamon* |
¼ *teaspoon nutmeg* | 4 *tablespoons shortening*

Roll out pastry very thin, divide into 3 parts and roll each part separately as needed. Arrange a layer of apple slices on 1 rolled-out pastry fitted into a pudding dish or glass casserole. Scatter crumbs and drizzle some of the honey over or, if using sugar, combine it with cinnamon and nutmeg before scattering ⅓ cupful over apple and crumbs. Roll out the second round of pastry and place it over apples and add second layer of apple slices, crumbs, sweetening and spices. Adjust the rolled-out third layer of pastry and cover with apple slices, crumbs and remainder of sweetening. Heat shortening and drizzle over top of kugel. Press down lightly with a spoon if necessary. Cover and bake 45 to 50 minutes at 400° F. or gas mark 6. Remove cover and bake 10 minutes longer till lightly browned on top.

Serves 6.

KUGEL (Four-Layer Shalet)

*1 recipe of Rolled Strudel Dough (see Index) |
4 tablespoons melted chicken or goose schmaltz | 1 cup thinly sliced apples |
2 tablespoons sugar | Dash of cinnamon |
½ cup chopped seeded or seedless raisins | 1 tablespoon flour |
2 tablespoons sugar | ½ teaspoon grated lemon rind |
¼ cup chopped mixed nuts | 1 tablespoon lemon juice |
2 tablespoons dry bread crumbs*

Divide dough into 4 equal parts. Roll out one to fit inside a greased pudding dish. Drizzle with melted fat and cover with apples. Combine sugar and cinnamon and sprinkle generously over apples. Roll out 2nd layer of dough and fit it over the apples. Roll raisins in flour till coated and arrange over layer of dough. Sprinkle sugar and grated lemon rind over evenly. Roll out 3rd layer of dough and cover raisins. Drizzle a little melted fat over dough and sprinkle with chopped nuts, lemon juice and crumbs. Roll out 4th layer of dough and cover. Brush with remaining melted fat. Let stand 10 to 15 minutes before baking at 375° F. or gas mark 5 for 45 to 50 minutes or till nicely browned. Invert on serving plate while warm. Sprinkle with chopped nuts and sugar if desired.

Serves 4 to 6.

Batter Puddings are sometimes called 'cottage puddings'. They are made of plain batter or with small fruits usually berries added. Or, the berries or thinly sliced dried, fresh or canned fruit (apples, apricots, peaches) are placed in the bottom of a well-greased baking pan and the batter poured over before baking.

Batter puddings are usually served with milk or cream, or with fruit sauce. Preserves may be thinned with fruit juice of any kind and served with batter puddings. Batter puddings may be baked in custard cups.

BATTER PUDDING (Basic Recipe)

*1½ cups wheat flour | 3 teaspoons baking powder | ½ teaspoon salt |
1 egg | ½ cup sugar | ¼ cup shortening | ½ cup milk*

Sift flour, baking powder and salt together into a mixing bowl.

Cream sugar, egg and shortening, beating till thoroughly combined and creamy. Add milk and creamed mixture alternately to the dry ingredients, stirring till well-blended. Turn into a well-greased baking pan and bake 35 minutes at 375° F. or gas mark 5.

Serves 4.

Variation: Grease the bottom of a glass pudding dish. Place a thick layer of sliced fresh fruit or well-drained canned fruit that can be sliced in the bottom of dish and pour pudding batter over. Bake at 400° F. or gas mark 6 for 25 to 30 minutes. Serve from the baking dish. Serve with whipped cream, if desired.

BREAD PUDDING (Basic Recipe)

4 cups milk | 2 cups broken stale bread slices (rye, white, or wholewheat) | 2 eggs | ½ cup sugar (brown sugar if dark bread) | ¼ teaspoon salt | 1 teaspoon vanilla | ½ cup currants or seeded raisins | 2 tablespoons flour

Heat milk to lukewarm and add bread bits. Turn off heat and let stand over warm burner, while you beat eggs, sugar, salt and flavouring, till combined. Stir into the bread and milk. Roll currants or raisins in flour. Combine lightly. Turn the mixture into a buttered pudding dish. Set pudding dish in a larger container with a little water in it, and bake 40 minutes at 325° F. or gas mark 3, or till lightly browned on top.

Serves 4.

Variation: Add 2 ounces semi-sweet chocolate, melted over hot water or added to the warm milk-and-bread combination.

BREAD PUDDING WITH APPLES
(Commonly called 'Brown Betty')

¼ cup melted butter or vegetable shortening | 2 eggs | ½ cup light brown sugar or molasses | ¼ teaspoon salt | 1 cup milk | 2½ cups dry bread crumbs (wholewheat, white or rye) | Grated rind of 1 lemon | 2 cups diced apples or dried mixed fruits | ¼ cup currants or seedless raisins

Melt shortening in baking dish to be used. Beat eggs, sugar and salt till creamy. Or beat eggs and salt and stir in molasses. Add milk.

Banana Fluff (*page 433*)
Banana and Cranberry Dessert (*page 434*)

Arrange a layer of crumbs in bottom of pudding pan, sprinkle lightly with grated lemon rind and cover with a thin layer of diced fruit and raisins. Add a second layer of crumbs, sprinkle with grated rind and add diced fruit. Turn in the egg-and-sugar mixture, top with crumbs and dot with butter. Cover and bake at 300° F. or gas mark 1–2 for 30 minutes. Remove cover and bake 20 minutes longer or till brown.

Serves 4.

Variation: Use vegetable shortening and substitute orange or pine-apple juice for milk. Use thinly sliced unpared apples or pared pears. Or use canned, sliced apples.

Charlottes or Shalets are puddings made with a base of stale bread, plain or toasted. The fruit used is arranged on the bottom layer of bread and topped with more bread. These puddings are served hot with fruit sauce.

APPLE CHARLOTTE (Basic Recipe)

Use ¼-inch-thick stale bread slices, plain or toasted, whole or cut into sections to fit into the bottom of pudding pan.

Grease the bottom and sides of pudding dish, preferably rect-angular in shape, and fit the pieces of bread in as close together as possible. Cover with applesauce seasoned to taste with nutmeg or cinnamon, grated orange or lemon rind, or enriched with finely chopped nuts. Cover with more stale bread slices, buttered on top. Dust with a mixture of sugar and cinnamon and bake 30 minutes at 400° F. or gas mark 6 till well browned. Turn out on a large serving platter while hot. Any fruit sauce makes a welcome accompaniment. *Serve hot or cold.*

Serves 4 to 6.

EMERGENCY CHARLOTTES

Arrange small triangles of sponge cake or halves of small lady fingers upright in sherbet glasses. Fill centres with stewed fresh or dried apples, peaches, pears or apricots. Top with whipped cream or sour cream, or sprinkle generously with shredded coconut or chopped nuts.

27

DANISH PUDDING BALLS

2 cups dried bread or parkin crumbs | 1 tablespoon sugar |
1 cup jam of any tart fruit (plum is excellent)

Mix crumbs with sugar and heat in the oven till very dry. Combine with jam as soon as cool and press into a well-buttered round mould or form into balls. Chill in refrigerator 1 to 2 hours. Top with fruit sauce or cooked custard and serve at once.

Serves 3 to 4.

Crusty Puddings are made of fruit, topped with either a scone dough or a rolled pie pastry, and baked in a very hot oven until the fruit is well done and the crust is nicely browned. They are similar to deep dish pies.

CRUSTY PUDDING (Basic Recipe)

6 cups diced or sliced apples or other fruit | 1 cup sugar, approximately |
Dash of nutmeg or cinnamon | 6 tablespoons cold water |
Biscuit pastry or pie shell to cover (see Index)

Grease a pudding dish or casserole and fill with the fruit. Sprinkle with sugar and seasoning and add the water. Top with either pie or biscuit pastry and press down around the edges and trim, or turn back and flute pastry with thumb and forefinger as for pie. With the point of a knife cut a few 2-inch slashes in centre of topping and turn back the pastry slightly to permit steam to escape while baking. Or, after rolling out pastry, cut one or several small rounds or stars with biscuit cutter. Or use a thimble for cut-outs. Adjust over fruit filling. Bake 35 to 45 minutes at 400° F. or gas mark 6, or till crust is nicely browned.

Serves 6.

FIG PUDDING (Without Shortening)

1 cup finely cut dried figs (unsweetened) | 1 cup boiling water | 1 egg |
⅔ cup sugar | ½ cup chopped nuts (optional) |
1½ cups flour (½ this amount may be wholewheat flour) | 1 teaspoon salt |
2 teaspoons baking powder | 1 teaspoon baking soda | 1 teaspoon vanilla

Add figs to boiling water and let stand, covered, 10 minutes. Drain and reserve the liquid. Beat egg, adding sugar gradually while beating till creamy. Add nuts, if used, to dry ingredients that have been sifted together. If whole wheat flour is used, add after sifting the other ingredients. Add figs to bowl of nuts and dry ingredients and stir once or twice till coated. Stir in egg and sugar mixture alternately with liquid. The mixture should not be thicker than cake batter. A few drops of water may be added if required, to make batter of a consistency to drop heavily into a pudding mould. Cover and steam 2 to 2½ hours in water to come ⅔ of the way up side of mould. Serve with lemon or orange sauce (see Index) if desired.

Serves 4.

FIG AND CARROT PUDDING

*1 cup flour, sifted | 1 cup brown sugar | 1 teaspoon baking soda |
1 teaspoon baking powder | 1 teaspoon cinnamon |
¼ teaspoon nutmeg (optional) | 1 teaspoon salt |
1 cup each grated raw carrots and potatoes |
1 cup chopped or finely cut dried black figs*

Mix ingredients in the order given. Turn into a well-greased pudding dish and bake 1 hour at 350° F. or gas mark 4. Serve hot with lemon or orange sauce.

Serves 6 to 8.

HALPERN'S HOT PUDDING

*1 cup each, grated pared raw potato, pared raw sweet potato,
unpared tart apple and raw carrots | 1 cup brown sugar | 1 cup flour |
1 teaspoon baking soda | ½ teaspoon each cinnamon, nutmeg |
1 cup chopped seeded raisins | ¼ cup chopped nuts |
⅔ cup hot melted vegetable shortening*

Combine grated vegetable and fruit. Add sugar. Sift together dry ingredients, and add raisins and nuts. Combine thoroughly. Heat shortening in casserole. Fold in quickly and turn the mixture into the greased casserole. Cover and bake 1 hour at 375° F. or gas mark 5, then, uncovered, 15 to 20 minutes or till browned.

Serves 6.

INDIAN PUDDING

*1 cup farina | ½ cup cold water | 1 quart milk | ½ teaspoon salt |
¾ cup sugar | 1 teaspoon cinnamon | 2 cups chopped or shredded apples |
¼ cup currants or chopped seeded raisins | 2 eggs*

Moisten farina with cold water. Stir into hot milk in a double boiler,
stirring constantly to prevent lumps. Cover and let cook 30 minutes
or till the mush is thick. Turn into a mixing bowl and add the other
ingredients except eggs. Beat eggs slightly and stir in last. Turn
into a well-greased baking dish not deeper than 3 inches. Bake at
350° F. or gas mark 4 for 45 minutes to 1 hour. Serve with any fruit
sauce or plain, sprinkled with sugar and cinnamon.
Serves 4 to 6.

LOKSHEN KUGEL (Basic Recipe)

*½ pound broad noodles | 2 quarts boiling water | 1 teaspoon salt | 2 eggs |
3 tablespoons sugar | ¼ teaspoon cinnamon or 1 tablespoon lemon juice |
⅛ teaspoon salt | 4 tablespoons shortening | ½ cup chopped seedless raisins |
¼ cup chopped almonds (optional) | 3 tablespoons bread crumbs*

Drop noodles in rapidly boiling salted water and cook till tender.
Drain in a colander, pouring hot water through to rinse well. Beat
eggs with sugar, cinnamon, salt, and add the noodles. Melt shortening in the baking dish and add to mixture. Turn half the mixture
into greased baking dish, sprinkle with raisins and nuts, and add
remainder. Top with crumbs and bake 45 minutes at 400° F. or gas
mark 6.
Serves 4 to 6.

Variation 1: Substitute 1 cup thinly sliced tart apples for raisins,
or combine equal amounts of each.

Variation 2: Use chopped greben (cracklings) and chicken or
goose fat for shortening.

Variation 3: Substitute 1 cup finely cut dried prunes for other
fruit, with or without nuts. Add lemon juice and ¼ teaspoon
grated rind.

GRATED POTATO KUGEL

*6 medium potatoes | 1 onion | 3 eggs | ½ teaspoon salt |
¾ cup flour (approximately) | Dash of white pepper (optional) |
4 tablespoons shortening*

Grate raw pared potatoes, squeeze out excess liquid and grate onion into the pulp. Add eggs, salt and as much flour as necessary to make a batter that will drop from the spoon. Heat shortening in baking pan and fold into batter. Turn batter into greased baking pan. Bake 30 to 40 minutes at 375° F. or gas mark 5, or till nicely browned and crisp at edges.
Serves 4 to 6.

MOCK PLUM PUDDING

*1 cup white or rye flour | 1 teaspoon baking soda |
½ teaspoon cinnamon or nutmeg | ½ teaspoon salt |
1 cup each grated raw potato, carrot and seeded raisins |
1 cup brown sugar | 4 tablespoons chicken or goose fat*

Combine and sift dry ingredients. Add sugar to grated vegetables and raisins. Combine. Heat fat in baking dish. Mix quickly into batter and turn into greased baking dish. Bake 45 minutes at 375° F. or gas mark 5, or till nicely browned.
Serves 5 or 6.

RICE PUDDING (Basic Recipe)

*1 cup long grain or converted rice | 4 cups milk or water | 1 teaspoon salt |
2 tablespoons butter | 4 tablespoons sugar | ½ teaspoon vanilla*

Wash and drain rice. Cook rice, liquid and salt at least 1 hour in double boiler. Add butter, sugar and flavouring. Serve hot or cold with milk or cream.
Serves 6.
Variation 1: Fold in 2 beaten eggs. Bake in a well-buttered pudding dish or 6 buttered individual baking dishes, 15 to 20

minutes at 375° F. or gas mark 5 till lightly browned on top. Serve hot or cold, with milk or cream.

Variation 2: Add ½ cup seedless raisins, diced dried apricots or prunes to basic recipe or variation.

Variation 3: Pack firmly into buttered individual baking dishes. Chill. Turn out and serve with stewed berries or canned fruit.

Variation 4: To serve with meat, steam rice in water as in basic recipe. When rice is tender, fold in beaten eggs, ¼ cup greben and chicken fat, ½ cup seeded or seedless raisins. Add sugar and cinnamon if desired. Turn into greased baking dish and bake at 375° F. or gas mark 5, 20 minutes or till browned on top.

IMPROMPTU CARAMEL RING

1 cup dark brown sugar | 4 tablespoons melted butter or vegetable shortening | 4 cups crushed dry cereal | Pinch of salt | ⅛ teaspoon cinnamon

Cook sugar and shortening over very low heat till melted. Add crushed cereal, salt and cinnamon and stir lightly till blended. Remove from heat and pack mixture into a heavily-greased ring mould. Let stand 10 minutes. Unmould on a large serving plate. Fill centre of ring with fresh berries of any kind and top with whipped cream or ice-cream. Place a few of the berries on top for colour.

Serves 4.

DATE PUDDING

½ pound beef suet | 1 pound pitted unsweetened dates | 3 cups dry bread crumbs | ½ cup honey or ¾ cup brown sugar | 2 eggs | ½ cup fruit juice | 5 tablespoons flour | 1½ teaspoons baking powder | ¼ teaspoon cinnamon (optional)

Chop suet and dates together as finely as possible. Add bread crumbs and stir well. Combine honey and eggs and beat slightly. Add to first mixture, stirring in fruit juice. Sift together dry ingredients and stir in till smooth. Turn into a well-greased pudding mould, cover and steam in boiling water to come ⅔ to top of mould. Use a large, well-covered pot for this purpose. Pudding must be steamed over moderate heat 3 hours or longer. May be steamed overnight over very low heat.

Serves 6.

Variation: Substitute soaked and pitted prunes for dates. Drain well and roll in crumbs. Follow procedure as in basic recipe.

SWEET POTATO PUDDING

4 cups mashed boiled sweet potatoes | 4 tablespoons butter or substitute | ½ cup well-drained canned crushed pineapple | 2 tablespoons brown sugar | 1 teaspoon salt | 4 tablespoons grape juice or red wine

Combine all ingredients and beat thoroughly till creamy. Turn into a well-greased pudding dish or casserole. Bake 45 minutes at 375° F. or gas mark 5, or till lightly browned on top. Serve with pineapple sauce or plain.

Serves 6.

Variation 1: Substitute 1 cup shredded unpared apples for pineapple.

Variation 2: Substitute 1½ cups finely cut pitted dates or figs for other fruit. Use sherry in place of grape juice or wine.

PUDDING SAUCES

APRICOT GLAZE

2½ cups cooked apricot pulp | 1 cup sugar | ⅓ cup boiling water

Combine. Cook over moderate heat, stirring till thick and smooth. Cool. Pour over gingerbread, sweet muffins (see p. 134), or cup cakes just before serving.

Yields enough for 8 servings.

BANANA CREAM SAUCE

1 egg white | 1 cup sugar | 1 cup mashed bananas | Dash of salt

Beat egg white, adding sugar gradually till combined. Fold in mashed bananas and salt.

Variations may be made by susbstituting any crushed fruit or berries. For a richer sauce, fold in ½ cup whipped cream just before serving.
Yields 1¼ cups.

BRANDY SAUCE 1 (American Style)

4 tablespoons caster sugar | 1½ teaspoons butter or substitute |
2 egg yolks | ½ cup boiling water | ½ cup brandy |
Dash of nutmeg and vanilla

Cream butter and sugar in the top of double boiler. Stir in egg yolks slowly while the water boils. Remove from heat. Combine water, brandy and flavouring. Stir well.
Yields 1 cup.

BRANDY SAUCE 2

1 tablespoon butter | 6 tablespoons caster sugar | 1 wineglass brandy |
3 tablespoons boiling water | Nutmeg or any other flavouring

Stir all together in top of double boiler over boiling water. When smooth and creamy, add the flavouring. This is a thin sauce.
Yields ½ cup.

BRANDY SAUCE 3 (English Style)

1 cup milk | 2 egg yolks | 1 tablespoon sugar | Grated lemon peel |
3 to 4 tablespoons brandy

Cook all ingredients except brandy over boiling water till thick and creamy. Remove from heat. Add brandy.
Yields about ¾ of a cup.

BUTTER-VANILLA SAUCE

½ cup butter | 2 tablespoons flour | 4 tablespoons sugar | Pinch of salt |
1 cup water | 1 teaspoon vanilla

Melt butter over a low heat. Mix dry ingredients and blend in. Add water gradually and cook 3 minutes. Add flavouring and serve hot.

Yields 1¼ cups.

CUSTARD SAUCE

2 cups milk, scalded | 5 egg yolks | ¼ cup sugar |
⅛ teaspoon salt | ½ teaspoon vanilla

Beat yolks slightly, add sugar and salt. Stir milk in slowly and return to double boiler. Cook over boiling water till mixture coats a spoon. Remove from heat and stir in flavouring.

Yields 2¼ cups.

Note: Should custard curdle, cool immediately and beat with a rotary beater.

FLUFFY FRUIT SAUCE (Uncooked)

¼ pound butter | ½ cup brown sugar, tightly packed |
1 teaspoon grated orange or lemon rind

Cream the butter till fluffy and add the brown sugar gradually, beating the mixture till light. Stir in the grated fruit rind lightly. Use for pancakes, puddings, waffles or as topping for gingerbread.

Yields approximately 1 cup.

FOAMY SAUCE

1 cup icing sugar | ½ cup softened butter or substitute |
1 egg, separated | 2 tablespoons hot water | ¼ teaspoon lemon juice |
¼ teaspoon vanilla | Few grains of salt

Combine sugar and butter by stirring with a fork. Add egg yolk and continue till smooth. Place bowl over boiling water and stir in hot water, beating till smooth and thick. Stir in lemon juice, vanilla and stiffly beaten egg white. Add salt and beat well for 1 minute.

Yields 1 cup.

HARD SAUCE (Basic Recipe)

1 *cup sugar* | ½ *cup creamed butter* | 1 *teaspoon white wine or brandy*

Work sugar into butter with a fork until creamy and smooth. Add wine or brandy by stirring in a few drops at a time.
Yields 1 cup, approximately
Variation 1: Substitute 1½ cups icing sugar and add rum instead of wine.
Variation 2: Substitute vegetable shortening or margarine for butter in basic recipe. Add a dash of nutmeg.
Variation 3: Use dark brown sugar, tightly packed in cup, and flavour with vanilla.

HONEY SAUCE (Basic Recipe)

1 *egg* | ½ *cup honey with* 1 *cup hot water* | 2 *tablespoons butter or substitute* | 1 *tablespoon lemon juice* | 1 *teaspoon grated lemon rind*

Beat egg and add honey and water, stirring rapidly till combined. Add the other ingredients. Cook in double boiler over boiling water 15 minutes, stirring constantly till smooth.
Yields 1½ cups.
Variation 1: Add 1 cup crushed strawberries to basic sauce when cold, and stir. Or, mash 1 cup quick frozen berries into sauce.
Variation 2: Substitute 2 tablespoons canned unsweetened pineapple juice for lemon juice. Add 1 egg to basic recipe.

LEMON-BUTTER SAUCE

1 *tablespoon cornflour* | ½ *cup sugar* | ¼ *cup lemon juice* | 1 *cup boiling water* | *Few grains of salt* | *Dash of grated lemon rind* | 3 *tablespoons butter or substitute*

Combine cornflour, sugar and lemon juice. Stir in boiling water till smooth. Cook in double boiler over boiling water 20 minutes, stirring till smooth. Add salt, grated lemon rind and butter after removing from heat, and stir or beat with a fork.

ORANGE-BUTTER SAUCE

*¼ cup butter or substitute | ½ cup sugar | ½ cup boiling water |
2 egg whites | ¾ cup orange juice | 1 tablespoon lemon juice*

Cream butter and sugar in a saucepan or top of double boiler. Add boiling water and stir well. Cook over low heat or over boiling water. Beat egg whites and stir in after 10 minutes. Remove from heat immediately and stir in orange and lemon juice. Beat till foamy and light.
Yields 1½ cups.

PINEAPPLE SAUCE

*2 tablespoons cornflour | 3 tablespoons cold water | Few grains of salt |
1 cup canned pineapple juice | 3 tablespoons lemon juice |
2 tablespoons sugar or honey | 2 egg whites*

Combine cornflour and cold water. Add the other ingredients except egg whites. Cook over low heat 5 minutes till clear. Add beaten egg whites when cold.
Yields 1½ cups.

MOCHA SAUCE

*½ cup hot strong coffee | ¼ cup sugar | Few grains of salt |
2 eggs, separated | ½ cup whipped cream*

Add sugar and salt to hot coffee in top of double boiler. Beat yolks well and stir in. Cook over boiling water, stirring till thick and creamy, approximately 15 minutes. Remove from heat. When cool, add stiffly beaten egg whites then whipped cream, stirring well.
Yields 1¼ cups.

MOLASSES-BUTTER-CREAM SAUCE

*1 cup molasses | ½ cup butter or substitute |
½ cup evaporated milk or coffee cream*

Combine in top of double boiler over boiling water. Stir only till
well combined. Remove from heat. Chill before serving.
Yields 1¼ cups.

RAISIN AND ALMOND SAUCE

½ cup seedless raisins | 3 tablespoons sugar or honey | 1 teaspoon lemon juice |
1 tablespoon cornflour | 2 tablespoons cold water |
2 tablespoons butter or substitute | 1 cup hot water |
¼ cup chopped or slivered almonds

Place raisins in a strainer over boiling water for 10 minutes to plump
them. Put them in a mixing bowl and add honey and lemon juice.
Mix cornflour with cold water in top of double boiler. Add butter
and hot water. Cook over boiling water, stirring till thick. Add the
other mixtures and cook 10 minutes, stirring lightly till combined.
Remove from heat and add almonds.
Yields approximately 2 cups.

RUM SAUCE

½ cup sugar | Pinch of salt | 1 tablespoon flour | 1¼ cups milk |
3 egg yolks | 3 tablespoons rum

Combine half the sugar with the flour and salt and stir into milk
gradually. Cook in top of double boiler or over direct heat till it
begins to thicken. Beat egg yolks till thick and light-coloured, adding
remaining sugar while beating. Combine mixtures. Cook over hot
water, stirring till thickened. Let cool. Blend in rum and chill
thoroughly.
Can be used for Batter or Bread Pudding or Milchig Kugels.
Yields 1½ cups sauce.

26 Custards and Kindred Desserts

Custards, although easy to prepare, are delicate and should be baked slowly to permit the egg and milk to solidify smoothly and evenly. Too rapid baking may cause custard to 'run' or separate and be most unappetizing. Plain custard is concentrated nourishment and may be served to convalescents and invalids as well as children.

CUP CUSTARD (Basic Recipe)

2 cups milk | ¼ cup sugar | Dash of salt | 4 egg yolks or 2 whole eggs

Scald the milk in top of double boiler. Add sugar and salt. Beat eggs and stir in the hot milk till well blended. Turn into 6 individual moulds. Place filled moulds in a pan of hot water and bake 40 minutes at 325° F. or gas mark 3, or till set. Test before serving by inserting a silver knife blade or spoon. Custard is done when it does not adhere to the knife or spoon. Remove from oven and serve hot or cold.

Serves 6.

Variations:

Lemon Custard: Omit egg yolks. Beat 4 egg whites stiff, add gradually ¼ cup sugar while beating. Heat the milk, add salt and stir or beat in the egg whites. Flavour with 1 teaspoon lemon juice and a dash of grated rind, or ¼ teaspoon vanilla, or ¼ teaspoon almond extract and ¼ teaspoon grated orange rind. Bake in individual moulds 1 hour at 325° F. or gas mark 3, or till set.

Coffee Custard: Substitute 1 cup strong coffee plus 1 cup light cream for the milk.

Caramel Custard: Line moulds with caramelized sugar, turn in basic custard and bake. To caramelize the sugar in the moulds, put about 1 tablespoon sugar in each, place over heat till the sugar is brown. Turn the moulds to spread the melted, browned sugar over the inside surface. Turn in the custard while hot.

Maple Custard: Substitute ¼ cup maple syrup for sugar. Add ¼ to ½ cup chopped nuts if desired.

Fruit Custard Cups: Butter the inside of each individual mould and line generously with finely chopped nuts. Place in each, half an apricot or peach, round side down, add a drop or two of almond extract or rum, fill to the top with custard mixture and bake. Top with whipped cream if served cold, or turn out and top with fruit juice if served hot.

Serves 8.

BAKED CHOCOLATE CUSTARD

1 tablespoon cornflour | 2 cups milk | 1 cup sugar | 2 ounces chocolate | ⅛ teaspoon salt | 4 eggs (separated) | Dash of salt | ½ cup sugar | 1 teaspoon vanilla

Dissolve cornflour in ¼ cup milk. Scald the rest of the milk and add sugar and chocolate, stirring till dissolved. Add salt and cornflour mixture. Cook over hot water in double boiler till thickened, stirring till smooth. Beat egg yolks and pour the cooked mixture over, beating until well blended. Turn into a baking dish or individual moulds. Beat egg whites and salt stiff, adding a little sugar at a time. Fold in flavouring. Top the custard with meringue and bake at 300° F. or gas mark 1–2, 50 to 60 minutes or till the topping is set. Serve hot or cold, with or without chocolate sprinkles on top.

Serves 6.

HONEY-RICE CUSTARD

2 eggs | 3 tablespoons sugar | 6 tablespoons honey | 1⅔ cups milk, scalded | 1 cup cooked rice | ¼ teaspoon cinnamon

Beat eggs with sugar and honey. Gradually stir into milk. Combine with rice and cinnamon. Turn into a buttered pudding dish. Bake 1 hour at 350° F. or gas mark 4, or till nicely browned on top.

Serves 2.

TAPIOCA CREAM (Basic Recipe)

*1 egg (separated) | 2 cups milk, scalded | 3 tablespoons quick cooking tapioca |
¼ cup sugar | Pinch of salt | ½ teaspoon vanilla flavouring*

Beat egg yolk and add milk. Stir in tapioca, sugar and salt and cook
10 to 12 minutes stirring constantly. Remove from heat. The mixture
will be thin. Beat egg white stiff but not dry, and stir in the hot
tapioca gradually. Cool and add flavouring. Chill and serve plain or
with cream.

Serves 4.

Variations:

Pineapple Tapioca: Increase tapioca to 5 tablespoons. Add ½ cup
drained crushed canned pineapple and substitute almond
extract for vanilla flavouring. Top with whipped cream or
chopped nuts.

Rhubarb-Pineapple Tapioca: Add ½ cup each crushed pineapple and
stewed rhubarb. Use 2 eggs and omit flavouring extract. Top
with meringue made of 1 egg white and 2 tablespoons icing
sugar.

Peach Tapioca: Use 6 tablespoons tapioca for a thicker cream. Add
mashed or flaked canned peaches.

Fruit Tapioca: Add 1 cup crushed fresh or quick frozen strawberries, raspberries, blueberries, or ½ cup stewed berries to the
thicker tapioca cream.

CRANBERRY TAPIOCA DESSERT

*1 pound cranberries | 1 cup sugar | 5 tablespoons tapioca | Dash of nutmeg |
2 tablespoons honey | 2 tablespoons vegetable shortening*

Wash and drain cranberries. Turn them into a deep well-buttered
baking dish or casserole. Add sugar mixed with tapioca and nutmeg.
Pour honey over and dot with butter or shortening. Bake in covered
dish 30 minutes at 350° F. or gas mark 4. Remove cover and brown
under grill. Serve with poultry dinner.

Serves 6.

TAPIOCA CASSEROLE

3 to 4 pounds tart apples, sliced | 2 tablespoons butter |
4 tablespoons tapioca | ¼ cup cinnamon drops or 3 tablespoons red sugar |
3 tablespoons honey | 3 tablespoons lemon juice

Core but do not pare apples. Slice ¼-inch thick. Arrange a layer of
apples in a well-buttered casserole or deep baking dish, sprinkle with
tapioca and cinnamon drops. Repeat for each layer and pour honey
and lemon juice over top. Dot with butter and cover. Bake at 350° F.
or gas mark 4 for 30 minutes. Remove cover and brown under grill.
Serve from the baking dish.
  Serves 6.

BAKED APPLES FOR DESSERT

Core 6 large baking apples. Arrange in baking dish. Fill cavities. Add
1 cup cider or orange juice. Bake 45 to 50 minutes at 350° F. or gas
mark 4.

FILLINGS

Cranberries, honey or sugar.
  Pitted dates stuffed with almond or pecan halves.
  Seedless raisins.

SWEETENING

For baked apples amount depends on the tartness of fruit. Add 1
tablespoon sugar or corn syrup for each large apple. Substitute
honey for sugar or syrup in lesser amount.

TO THICKEN SAUCE

Combine 1 tablespoon cornflour with 1 cup liquid before baking.
Or add to sauce in pan after removing baked apples and stir while
cooking 3 to 5 minutes over moderate heat. Add 1 tablespoon butter
or substitute. One tablespoon rum or brandy may be added to sauce
before or after cooking.
  Variation 1: Pare large apples ¼ way down and dust with flour and
    sugar.
  Variation 2: Bake apples in well-greased large tart tins.

Fruit Dumplings. Use any of the scone dough recipes (see Index) for
the making of apple or other fruit dumplings to be served as dessert.

Roll dough to ¼-inch thickness and cut into squares large enough to cover the fruit and tuck the edges tightly together, allowing 1 square for each apple, peach, apricot, etc.

APPLE DUMPLINGS

These are the most popular. But peaches make excellent fruit dumplings and should rank second in popularity. Pare and core apples to be used. Place an apple in the centre of each square of rolled scone dough. Fill the centre of apple with brown sugar and a dash of nutmeg or cinnamon (or a few cinnamon drops). Cut a few slashes down the sides of filled apple and bring the 4 corners of the dough together at the top. Pinch the edges together from the top down, making 4 seams and moistening slightly to make a neater closing that will stick together. Brush with diluted egg yolk, evaporated milk or diluted orange marmalade. Place the dumplings in a baking pan not too close together; add a ½-inch depth of hot water and bake 40 to 45 minutes at 425° F. or gas mark 7 until crust is nicely browned. Thicken any fruit juice with cornflour, sweeten and flavour with vanilla or sherry and serve as a sauce with baked apple dumplings. (For other sauces, see Index.)

Fruit dumplings are delicious with heavy cream or sour cream as a dessert with milchig meals.

CHERRY DUMPLINGS

Use large sweet fresh cherries or the canned variety. Be sure they are pitted. Place 5 or 6 cherries in the centre of a 4-inch square of rolled pie pastry dough (see Pastries). Bring edges together as for Apple Dumplings, or fold into a ball by placing the seamed side down. Bake 30 minutes at 425° F. or gas mark 7 without liquid. Serve with fruit sauce.

OTHER DESSERTS

BANANA FLUFF

*3 ripe bananas | 3 tablespoons icing sugar | Dash of salt |
1 teaspoon vanilla or 1 tablespoon lemon juice | 1 cup heavy cream |
8 pairs Lady Fingers*

28

Mash bananas with fork or put through sieve. Stir in sugar, salt and flavouring. Whip cream stiff and fold in lightly. Arrange 2 pairs of cut Lady Fingers in each of 4 sherbet glasses and mound up the fluff lightly. Or, make a ring of cut Lady Fingers on a round serving plate and mound up the fluff in centre. Top with more sliced bananas.
  Serves 4.

BANANA AND CRANBERRY DESSERT

*1 cup canned cranberry sauce | 3 bananas, mashed |
1 egg white | 1 teaspoon sugar*

Combine. Use a rotary beater and whip into a light fluffy combination. Serve in stem glasses or sherbet cups and top with stiffly beaten egg white and sugar and a sprinkling of chopped nuts if desired.
  Serves 4.

BAVARIAN CREAM (Basic Recipe)

*1 package fruit-flavoured gelatin | 2 tablespoons water | ½ cup milk, scalded |
½ cup sugar | ⅛ teaspoon salt | 2 cups heavy cream | 2 teaspoons vanilla*

Soak gelatin in cold water and dissolve in the hot milk. Add sugar and salt. Cool. Whip cream stiff and fold in. Stir in flavouring. Turn into cake-lined mould for Ice Box Cake. Can be turned into a ring mould, rinsed in cold water and chilled. Garnish with whole or crushed berries, or serve with stewed fruit.
  Variations:
  Enriched Bavarian: Add 5 egg yolks beaten with the sugar. Fold in stiffly beaten egg whites and 1 cup whipped heavy cream.
  Macaroon Bavarian: Add 6 crushed macaroons to either basic Bavarian or variation.
  Chocolate Bavarian: Add 2 ounces chocolate and 6 tablespoons dry cocoa to hot milk. Use 2 tablespoons unflavoured gelatin.
  Mocha Bavarian: Add 2 tablespoons plain gelatin to 1 cup milk. Dissolve with 1 cup very strong coffee, boiling hot. Add sugar and salt. When cool, fold in 5 stiffly beaten egg whites and whipped cream. Flavour with 1 tablespoon rum.

Nut Bavarian: Add ¾ cup finely chopped almonds or hazelnuts to basic recipe and flavour with 1 teaspoon almond extract or 1 tablespoon rum.

CHESTNUT DESSERT

2 pounds chestnuts | 1 quart milk | 1 cup sugar | 1 cup heavy cream |
2 tablespoons icing sugar | 2 tablespoons brandy or rum

Boil whole chestnuts in salted water to cover, 10 to 12 minutes. Drain and remove shells. Cook hulled chestnuts in milk in top of double boiler until easily pierced with a toothpick. Cook 3 minutes longer. Carefully lift out 6 or 8 whole chestnuts. Put the remaining chestnuts and milk mixture through a sieve or fruit press and let the mixture fall in a mound on a large round serving plate. Put the other chestnuts through a sieve and let it cover first mound lightly. Whip cream stiff, fold in icing sugar and brandy. Cover top of mound, letting cream cascade down sides. Chill well before serving.
Serves 6.

COFFEE SOUFFLÉ

1½ teaspoons instant coffee or substitute | 4 tablespoons sugar | 3 egg whites |
Pinch of salt | 1 teaspoon vanilla | 2 tablespoons flour

Combine coffee and sugar. Beat egg whites with salt till stiff but not dry. Beat in coffee mixture. Stir in vanilla and fold in flour. Turn into a well-buttered quart-size casserole and bake at 300° F. or gas mark 1–2 for 30 minutes or till lightly browned on top. Serve hot with rum sauce (see Pudding Sauces).
Serves 4.

CRANBERRY CONFITURE

1 pint cranberries | 2 cups sugar | 1 cup water | 3 ounces cream cheese |
1 tablespoon cream | 1 teaspoon caster sugar

Pick over and wash the berries. Drain well. Boil sugar and water 5 minutes and add berries. When boiling rapidly, turn off the heat and cover the saucepan with a tight lid. The hot syrup will retain

enough heat to soften the berries and they will remain transparent.
Let stand till cold. Combine cream cheese and cream, work in the
caster sugar and beat till light and creamy. Serve the cranberries in
parfait glasses and top with the creamy mixture. Add one or two
berries.

FRUIT FLUFF

1 *cup heavy cream, whipped with* 1 *cup caster sugar | 2 egg whites |*
Dash of salt | 4 cups sweetened applesauce or 2 cups prune pulp

Chill all ingredients. Beat egg whites and salt till stiff. Fold in fruit
pulp or applesauce. Reserve some for topping. Combine with
whipped cream and sugar. Chill thoroughly before serving in
sherbet glasses.
Serves 4.

FRUIT SOUFFLÉ

1 *cup fruit pulp | Sugar to taste | Few grains of salt | 3 egg whites*

Dried prunes or apricots may be used. Soak several hours or overnight and mash through a strainer. Pulp should not be too soupy.
Sweeten to taste, add a pinch of salt and fold in stiffly beaten egg
whites. Turn into a greased pudding dish, set it in a pan of hot water
and bake 20 to 25 minutes at 375° F. or gas mark 5, or until set.
Serve at once. Serve with cream or lemon sauce.
Serves 3 or 4.
Variation: Turn into individual moulds and bake. Top with a
spoonful of the same fruit pulp.

NEVER-FAIL MERINGUE SHELLS

2 *egg whites | Few grains salt |* 1½ *cups caster sugar |*
⅛ *teaspoon cream of tartar |* ½ *teaspoon vanilla*

Beat egg whites till foamy, sprinkle with salt and continue beating
till stiff but not dry. Use a rotary beater. Sift sugar and cream of
tartar together and sprinkle over the beaten egg whites, about half a

spoonful at a time, beating the mixture until it holds a peak. Add flavouring while continuing to beat. Drop from a spoon on to wax-paper-covered baking sheet, shaping with a spoon as desired. Bake 1 to $1\frac{1}{4}$ hours at 250° F. or gas mark $\frac{1}{4}-\frac{1}{2}$.
Serves 6.

FILLINGS FOR MERINGUE SHELLS

Sugared fresh berries.
Sliced fresh or canned peaches or apricots.
Custard.
Ice-cream.
Meringues should be filled just before serving and topped with whipped cream to which icing sugar and a few drops of almond or vanilla extract has been added. A few drops of rum or sherry makes a specially good flavouring.

PRUNE WHIP

1 cup prune pulp | $\frac{1}{2}$ teaspoon lemon juice | 1 tablespoon sugar |
2 egg whites

Combine pulp with lemon juice. Beat egg whites, adding a little sugar at a time till stiff. Fold into prune mixture lightly with a fork. Serve in sherbet cups or stem glasses, topped with whipped cream.
Serves 4.

EGGLESS PRUNE WHIP

$\frac{1}{2}$ pound dried prunes | $\frac{1}{4}$ teaspoon cinnamon or lemon juice |
2 cups water | $\frac{1}{2}$ cup sugar | 1 tablespoon gelatin |
$\frac{1}{2}$ cup cold prune juice | 1 cup hot prune juice | Dash of salt

Stew prunes and cinnamon or lemon juice in water 30 minutes. Add sugar. Cook 5 minutes longer or till tender. Drain. Remove pits from prunes and put through fruit press or strainer. Soak gelatin in the cold prune juice and dissolve it with the hot prune juice. When cold and thickened, whip with a rotary beater till fluffy. Add salt. Fold in prune pulp and chill the mixture thoroughly.
Serves 6.

27 Appetizers and the Hostess Tray

HELP-YOURSELF TRAYS

Hostess and guests alike enjoy helping themselves to *hors d'œuvres*, or *smorgåsbord* as in the Scandinavian countries, *antipasto* as in Italy or *zakuski* as in Eastern Europe. Sometimes it is called *aperitif*. In Yiddish it is called *forschpeisse*. Everywhere it serves as a welcome prelude to good eating, and a stimulant to conversation.

Suggestions for the Help-Yourself Tray
Use a hostess tray with several fitted-in glass or china compartments. Or, several trays with sections fitted together.

Place the filled trays on a serving table where guests can serve themselves. Arrange salad plates, salad forks, etc., at one end.

Place cocktail glasses at the opposite end. Have cocktail napkins at both ends.

SPREAD-YOUR-OWN APPETIZERS

Cream cheese, beaten with sour cream and seasoned with salt, pepper or celery salt, and heaped lightly to a peak.
Cream cheese, mixed with chopped nuts and icing sugar to taste.
Cream cheese, mixed with chopped ripe or green olives, mayonnaise or salad dressing, and garnished with pimento.
Cream cheese, tinted light green with vegetable colouring and combined with chopped pistachio nuts. Add a few drops of mint flavouring.
Herring salad, tuna fish or salmon salad, garnished with ripe olives, parsley, watercress or mint leaves.
Chopped chicken, goose or calf's liver, moulded and garnished with parsley, watercress or pimento strips.

Have crackers, melba toast, rye, white or wholewheat bread sliced thin and cut into rounds or triangles, on convenient trays.

CANAPÉ SPREADS OR SANDWICH FILLERS

For Canapés or Open-Face Sandwiches, spread any of the following fillings on small squares or rounds of thinly sliced, crust trimmed, rye, white or wholewheat bread. Or use crackers, or matzo squares. If canapés or open-face sandwiches are to be toasted, slip them under the grill just before serving.

For Sandwiches, spread generous portions of filling between thinly sliced bread cut in rounds or other shapes, if for cocktails or parties. Toasted, fried or baked sandwiches can be prepared just before serving. Or, they may be filled in advance and toasted, fried or placed in the oven before they are to be served. Sandwiches for picnics or lunch boxes may be made long in advance, wrapped individually in wax paper, sandwich bags, or aluminium foil and kept in the refrigerator until wanted. Such sandwiches should be very generously filled because they serve as meals. Bread slices may be thicker and crusts left on.

INTERESTING SPREADS

Avocado, mayonnaise, onion juice, mashed and blended in proportions to suit the taste. A good rule is 3 parts avocado to 1 part mayonnaise. Add a dash of paprika.

Avocado, Hard-Cooked Egg Yolks, lemon juice, salt. Mash and combine equal portions of avocado and egg yolks. Moisten with lemon juice and season with salt to taste.

Olives, Nuts and Hard-Cooked Eggs, moistened with salad dressing. Remove pits from ripe or green olives. Or use stuffed olives. Chop together with hard-cooked eggs, add chopped nuts and salad dressing.

Toasted Cheese Canapés are made by placing grated or sliced Cheddar cheese on buttered round, square or triangular slices of bread, sprinkling generously with paprika and toasting 1 minute under the grill just before serving. Any dry sharp cheese may be grated and toasted.

Hard-Cooked Eggs, mayonnaise, minced parsley, chopped green pepper, and/or watercress. Chop hard-cooked eggs fine or mash with a fork. Blend to a paste with mayonnaise. Add minced greens on top.

Hard-Cooked Eggs with Herring Roe, blended with mayonnaise or salad dressing. Top with a thin slice of stuffed green olive.

Peanut Butter, blended with equal amount of chopped green or black olives and moistened with mayonnaise or salad dressing.

Peanut Butter, blended with equal amount of Roquefort or Danish Blue cheese and topped with minced parsley or strips of canned pimento.

Filled Sandwich Variations can be made by blending grated cheese with prepared mustard and a generous amount of butter, seasoning with celery salt, garlic salt, paprika or a dash of cayenne. Fill sandwiches of any size or shape, brush tops with melted butter and bake 3 to 5 minutes at 350° F. or gas mark 4, or till nicely browned on top and the cheese filling melted. Or, spread the filling on thin slices of crust-free bread, roll up, fasten with a coloured toothpick and toast or bake till nicely browned just before serving.

MILCHIG SPREADS AND SANDWICH FILLERS

Anchovy Paste, Cream Cheese and Minced Parsley. Use 1 tablespoon anchovy paste to 3 ounces of cream cheese. Top with minced parsley.

Caviar, Cream Cheese or Unsalted Butter, blended in equal portions and moistened with lemon juice or onion juice to taste. Top with a thin strip of canned pimento or green pepper. Use either black or red caviar.

Cream Cheese, Chopped Walnuts or Pecans, Icing Sugar. Mash cheese with a fork, add an equal amount of chopped nuts, sweeten to taste with sugar. Flavour with a few drops of lemon juice, almond extract, vanilla or grated rind and juice of orange. Top with chopped nuts or halves. Substitute sherry for other flavourings.

Cream Cheese, Stuffed Green Olives, Mayonnaise. Use 6 large olives, minced, to 3 ounces of cheese. Combine with 1 tablespoon mayonnaise. Top with a thin slice of stuffed olive.

Cream Cheese, Sour Cream and Jam. Blend 3 ounces of cheese with 2 tablespoons thick sour cream. Top with a little strawberry or red raspberry preserves or jam. Or top with a tiny strip of canned cranberry sauce. If used for sandwiches, reduce sour cream to half, spread both slices of bread with jam before filling with cheese mixture.

Roquefort Cheese, Cream Cheese and Chopped Nuts, moistened with a few drops of lemon or orange juice. Top with chopped nuts or grated orange or lemon rind.

Sardines, Salmon, Tuna Fish or Chopped Herring, blended with mayonnaise or unsalted butter. Top with diced or sliced hard-cooked egg, or hard-cooked egg yolk rubbed through a strainer and sprinkled on lightly.

FLEISHIG SPREADS AND SANDWICH FILLERS

Chopped Chicken or Goose Greben, with chopped hard-cooked eggs in equal proportion. Season with salt and pepper to taste. Moisten with chicken fat or mayonnaise. Garnish with minced watercress, parsley or green pepper.

Variations can be made by combining chopped cracklings with chopped chicken, calf's or beef liver, with or without adding chopped hard-cooked eggs. Season to taste with celery and/or garlic salt.

Chopped Chicken, white meat preferably, may be combined with any pickle relish, chili sauce, minced black or green olives, minced parsley, green pepper or watercress. Blend with mayonnaise or salad dressing to form a thick consistency for spreading. Garnishes may be parsley sprigs, sliced stuffed green olives, strips of canned pimento or green pepper, sieved hard-cooked egg yolk, thin rings of hard-cooked egg white around minced green olives or green pepper.

Minced Sausage, Salami, Bologna, Corned Beef, Tongue, Roast Beef or Veal. Blend with finely chopped dill pickle, sweet pickle relish, chili sauce, horse-radish mixed with mayonnaise. Garnishes or toppings may be made of minced parsley, watercress or red pepper minced or cut in rounds or strips. Sliced stuffed green olives, sieved hard-cooked egg yolks sprinkled with paprika, caraway or celery seed add a festive note.

ADVANCE NOTICE APPETIZERS

Lox Cornucopias. Cover thinly sliced bread rounds or squares with butter. Place a thin slice of lox (smoked salmon) on top, fold over into cornucopias and fasten with toothpicks. Place a small ball of cream cheese rolled in minced parsley in the opening and press a strip of green pepper in.

Lox Sticks are made by wrapping thin strips an inch wide around 3-inch lengths of pumpernickel or white bread cut into inch-thick and inch-wide fingers. Fasten with toothpicks, leaving room at one end for finger grip.

Cheese-Filled Green Peppers. Remove stem and cut away enough to enable removing seeds. Fill compactly with cream cheese seasoned with mayonnaise, salt, celery salt, and white pepper. Or add chopped green pepper, minced parsley, watercress, mint leaves and a few drops of green vegetable colouring. Chill. Just before serving, cut into wedges from stem end down.

Stuffed Dill Pickles are prepared in advance. Cut away both ends of fairly thick dill pickles. Scoop out centre and fill with cream cheese. Chill and cut into ½-inch-thick rounds. Cucumbers may be used instead of dill pickles. Score with tines of fork before filling.

Smoked Salmon or Lox. Cut thin and into strips 1 inch wide. Wrap around a 2-inch length of cut dill pickle or gherkin, fasten with a toothpick.

Filled Plum Tomatoes must be prepared in advance. Cut away stem ends, scoop out, drain and fill with cream cheese, herring salad or chopped hard-cooked egg moistened with dressing. Chill before serving.

Salami Rolls. Salami or other sausage, sliced thin and spread with sweet pickle relish mixed with mayonnaise, may be rolled up and held together with toothpicks. Or, wrap around dill pickle spears or gherkins.

Boiled or Smoked Tongue Rolls. Wrap thin slices of smoked tongue around thin lengths of dill pickle, fasten with coloured toothpicks.

Hot Speared Tidbits are made by pan frying or grilling inch cubes of sausage, rounds of frankfurters or wieners, 1-inch balls of chopped meat prepared as for Hamburgers. Stick a coloured toothpick into each and serve piping hot.

Cold Speared Tidbits may be cubes of Cheddar cheese; bite-size cuts of boned herring marinated in lemon juice or wine, or dipped in sour cream; snails of lox; ripe or green stuffed olives; anchovies or herring fillets; cheese-filled pickles; cheese-filled cuts of celery; peanut butter balls; cubes or bite-size bits of salami or bologna with an olive, gherkin or pickled watermelon (see p. 490) bit.

CHOPPED CHICKEN LIVER

Combine grilled chicken livers, hard-cooked eggs and greben. Run through food chopper, season to taste with salt, pepper, celery salt or garlic salt, and add chicken or goose fat, or salad oil. Use as canapé spread. Top with tiny bits of pimento or green pepper, minced parsley or watercress, or sliced stuffed olive. Or press into a well-greased mould. Unmould on shredded mixed greens and garnish.

CHOPPED LIVER AND PEANUT BUTTER

Two parts chopped liver to 1 part peanut butter makes a delicious spread.

EGGPLANT 'CHOPPED LIVER'

6 small eggplants or 1 large one (1½ to 2 pounds) | 2 medium onions | 2 eggs, hard-cooked | Vinegar to taste | Salt to taste | Oil for frying

Cut the unpared eggplant into thin slices. Fry on both sides in very hot oil. Fry onions till nicely browned. Add eggs and run all through the food chopper or chop in a wooden bowl to make a smooth pulp or paste. Season with vinegar and salt to taste. Chill and garnish with minced parsley. Serve as an appetizer. Excellent for Sabbath and holiday meals.

GREENBEAN 'CHOPPED LIVER'

1 pound green beans, boiled | 1 green pepper, diced | 2 hard-cooked eggs | Salt and pepper to taste | 2 tablespoons mayonnaise

Run cooked beans through a food chopper with the pepper and hard-cooked eggs. Season to taste and add dressing. Serve as an appetizer or as a salad, garnished with salad greens.

HERRING SALAD IN CUCUMBER BOATS

A nice way to make this delicious appetizer is to use cucumbers or large dill pickles for boats. Cut lengthwise. Scoop out seeds and some of the pulp. Chop scooped part with hard-cooked egg, and an equal amount of pickled herring or chopped herring. Combine with salad dressing and fill the 'boats'. Use thin slices of black radish for sails.

HERRING SALAD AND GRATED APPLE

To each cup of chopped herring add ½ cup grated unpared apple (tightly packed). Moisten with a little mayonnaise or French dressing. A few finely chopped walnuts or almonds makes it specially good.

HOT SANDWICHES may be made easily and served for midnight snacks, by preparing the filling in advance. Bread may be toasted on one side in advance. Biscuits may be baked, split in halves, then toasted when ready to spread and serve. Holland rusks may be heated and used with hot creamed mixtures.

GRILLED BEEF PATTIES
(A Spread for Hot Sandwiches)

Prepare chopped beef as for Hamburgers. Form into patties to fit the rounds of bread, biscuit, rusks or prepared toast. Arrange on a flat plate or platter with wax paper between if more than one layer of patties is required. Store in refrigerator till needed. Press a ¼-inch thick pattie of meat on each round and grill 15 to 20 minutes or until nicely browned. Keep hot in the oven. Garnish with parsley sprigs, slivers of pickle, a slice of pickled green tomato, or pass the ketchup or horse-radish.

BOLOGNA ROLLUPS (Basic Recipe)

3 medium size sweet potatoes, cooked and mashed |
3 tablespoons orange juice | 1 teaspoon grated orange rind |
2 tablespoons minced parsley | 1 tablespoon chicken fat | ¼ teaspoon salt |
1 tablespoon brown sugar | 1 pound thin sliced bologna

Combine all ingredients listed except bologna. Cover each slice of bologna with potato mixture. Roll up and fasten with toothpicks.

Arrange in a shallow pan. Chill. 5 minutes before serving, brown under grill or in a hot oven.

Variation: Substitute dry bread crumbs for mashed sweet potatoes. Combine with 1 slightly beaten egg or 2 egg yolks. Add the other ingredients as listed, spread on bologna slices and roll up. Fasten and arrange as in basic recipe. Brown before serving.

FRANKS-IN-BLANKETS

For a hearty snack, cut frankfurters in 2-inch lengths and wrap a ½-inch strip of pastry dough around. Bake 10 minutes and serve hot, with a toothpick in each piece for easy handling.

RELISHES

Spear maslinas (black olives in brine), stuffed green olives, pickled onions, whole or cut pickles with coloured toothpicks. Arrange separately or together in a compartment dish or tray.

SARDINE SALAD

*½ cup mashed sardines | 1 teaspoon lemon juice |
1 tablespoon mayonnaise | Onion salt to taste*

TUNA FISH SALAD NOUVEAU

To each cup of flaked tuna fish add 1 heaped tablespoon of chopped green pepper, 1 tablespoon mixed sweet pickle relish and 1 tablespoon each mayonnaise and sour cream. Combine lightly with 2 forks just before filling tiny puffs.

TINY PUFFS

*½ cup butter or vegetable shortening | 1 cup boiling water |
¼ teaspoon salt | 1 cup flour | 3 eggs*

Into the top of your double boiler put the shortening, salt and boiling water. Dump the flour in all at once, stirring vigorously (while keeping the water in the under part of the double boiler very hot). When the mixture is thoroughly combined and leaves the sides of the pot, remove from heat. Let cool about 1 or 2 minutes before adding eggs one at a time, beating well after each addition till thoroughly blended. Dip a teaspoon in cold water and drop small amounts of this mixture on a well-greased baking pan, leaving at least $1\frac{1}{2}$ to 2 inches of space between drops to permit ample room for expansion. Shape the drops or mounds with the tip of the spoon till evenly rounded. Bake 10 minutes at 450° F. or gas mark 8 then turn down heat to 400° F. or gas mark 6 for the next 20 minutes or till golden brown and puffed high. The centres of these puffs should be hollow. When cold, cut an opening with the point of a paring knife in the side of each and fill just before serving time with any of the preceding or the following mixtures.

Yields 36 puffs.

TINY PUFFS FILLINGS

$1\frac{1}{4}$ cups grated Cheddar cheese | $\frac{1}{4}$ teaspoon Worcester sauce |
1 tablespoon cream | 1 teaspoon tomato ketchup | Dash of onion juice

Blend together with a fork or spoon. Chill for $\frac{1}{2}$ hour.
Yields filling for 36 tiny puffs.

CHEESE AND NUT FILLING

Combine equal portions of cream cheese, chopped walnuts or almonds, sour cream and red raspberry preserves.

OTHER SWEET FILLINGS

Chocolate or Vanilla Pudding, prepared according to directions on the package, with a spoonful of rum or sherry for additional zip.

Cream Cheese, chopped walnuts, sour cream and a flavouring of rum or sherry with just enough sugar to taste. Mix in advance and fill before serving.

Ice-Cream (homemade or otherwise) makes a delicious filling. Fill just before serving.

Pineapple Fluff makes a good variation. Combine 1 cup of drained crushed pineapple with 1 stiffly beaten egg white and a pinch of salt. Chill 10 minutes before filling.

WHOLEWHEAT CHEESE FINGERS

*1 cup wheat flour | 3 teaspoons baking powder | 1½ teaspoons salt |
2 cups unsifted wholewheat flour | ⅔ cup vegetable shortening |
Ice water | 1 cup sharp Cheddar cheese, shredded | Paprika*

Sift together flour, baking powder and salt. Add wholewheat flour
and stir till well combined. Cut in shortening with knives or pastry
blender. Add ice water a little at a time to form a ball of dough. Pat
out to ½-inch thickness on a lightly floured board. Spread with
shredded cheese and fold over. Pat down lightly to ½-inch thickness
into a rectangle. Cut into strips, 1 inch wide and 2 or 2½ inches long.
Prick each lightly with a fork and sprinkle with paprika. Bake on an
ungreased baking sheet 15 minutes at 400° F. or gas mark 6. Serve
with cocktails or salads.
    Yields 48 to 50 fingers.

CHEESE BEIGELACH (Also called *Rugelach*)

*1 recipe Stretched Strudel Dough (see Index) | 1 pound dry cottage cheese |
2 eggs | 2 to 3 tablespoons sugar (optional) | ¼ teaspoon salt |
2 tablespoons melted butter or substitute*

Cut Stretched Strudel Dough into strips 4 inches wide. Combine
cheese with eggs, sugar and salt, mixing with a fork till smooth.
Place an inch-thick line of cheese mixture along centre of strips, roll
up and place on greased baking sheet each rolled-up length of filled
dough, allowing 2 inches of space between. Cut filled rolls to suit
size of baking pan if desired. With a sharp knife cut rolls into 5-inch
lengths and bend slightly to form crescents or beigels, but do not
pinch ends together. Brush with melted shortening and bake 10
minutes at 425° F. or gas mark 7 to 350° F. or gas mark 4 for 15 to
20 minutes or till nicely browned on top and bottom. Remove from
pan when cool.
    Yields approximately 24 beigelach.

FRIED COCKTAIL ROLLS

Trim away crusts from a whole loaf of bread. Slice lengthwise and roll as thin as possible with a rolling pin. Spread each slice with any of the fillings for Spirals (see following). Roll up tightly and arrange close together on a large plate. Weight with a heavy plate and chill in refrigerator at least 1 hour. Toast under grill till nicely browned on all sides. Cut into ½-inch slices, dip in a thin mixture of 2 eggs and ¼ cup water. Fry in hot melted shortening till brown on all sides. Stick a coloured toothpick in each for easy handling.

COCKTAIL SPIRALS (Basic Recipe)

Roll out any pie pastry to ¼-inch thickness. Spread with cream cheese, sprinkle with paprika or celery salt and roll up lengthwise like a jelly roll. Wrap in wax paper or aluminium foil. Chill thoroughly in refrigerator. Fifteen minutes before serving time, cut into ½-inch pieces and bake 10 minutes at 400° F. or gas mark 6, or till nicely browned.

Variation 1: Spread with grated Cheddar cheese, sprinkle lightly with cayenne and roll up. Chill before baking.

Variation 2: Spread with finely chopped chicken liver and proceed as above.

Variation 3: Spread with mashed sardines sprinkled with lemon juice. Proceed as in basic recipe.

Variation 4: Spread with anchovy or sardellen paste mixed with cream cheese (see Canapé and Sandwich Fillers). Proceed as in basic recipe.

CHICKEN SALAD

Chill cooked chicken to be used for salad before cutting from bones. Dice or chop (not too fine), combine with hard-cooked eggs, celery, green pepper, parsley or watercress, in any desired proportions. Bind with mayonnaise or cooked salad dressing and serve on a bed of lettuce. Garnish with fresh mint, parsley, green pepper rings or strips, sliced cucumber and tomato, red radishes, olives and pickles.

Note: For large quantities, chicken, turkey, goose or capon meat may be combined with ⅓ or ½ the quantity of diced or chopped cooked veal or lamb.

AMOUNTS OF CHICKEN SALAD REQUIRED

6 servings	25 servings	50 servings
1½ cups diced meat	6 cups	12 cups
1½ cups diced celery	6 cups	12 cups
1 cup diced green pepper	5 cups	10 cups
4 hard-cooked eggs	15 eggs	30 eggs
½ cup mayonnaise	4 cups	2 quarts
2 tablespoons cider vinegar	½ cup	1 cup
¼ cup parsley and watercress	1 cup	2 cups

THE SWEETS TABLE

Along with the hot beverages served informally, small cakes, biscuits, fruit tarts and other goodies may be offered in serve-yourself style. For the convenience of hostess and guests, serve only the kind of sweets that can be taken up in the fingers. It makes cumbersome extra plates unnecessary.

Candy, glazed fruits, fondant or nut-filled dates, prunes, etc., are good.

SUGGESTIONS FOR THE SWEETS TABLE (SEE INDEX FOR RECIPES)

Biscuits
Cocktail Cheese Knishes or Spirals
Cup Cakes, small size
Doughnuts or Crullers,
   miniature size
Fruit Fingers
Hamantashen
Meringues
Tiny Puffs, sweet filling
Turnovers

PINEAPPLE CENTRE-PIECE

Choose a large, ripe pineapple. With a sharp knife cut through green spears to stem end in quarter sections or eighths. Remove hard core. Cut close to skin, then down in ½-inch pieces. *Do not remove from skin.* Arrange on a large round plate with spears outward, stem ends meeting in centre. Mound up white and black grapes in centre. May be served for dessert.

STUDDED PINEAPPLE

Spear maslinas, stuffed green olives, ripe olives, pickled small onions,

29

gherkins, watermelon rind pickles (see pp. 490–91), red radish roses or sausage cubes with coloured toothpicks. Stick them into the pineapple. Place on a bed of autumn leaves or watercress in the centre of a mirror plate or other serving plate. Excellent for a dinner table decoration that serves also as *hors d'œuvres*.

GRAPEFRUIT HOLDERS FOR OLIVES

Stick speared stuffed green olives into large grapefruit.

CANTALOUPE BASKETS

Cut ripe cantaloupes in half crosswise. Cut away a small part of each end so halves will stand firmly on a plate. Remove fibre, seeds. From each half cut off a ½-inch round to serve as basket handle. Fasten with toothpicks. Make melon balls with a spoon or special gadget for the purpose. Fill baskets with melon balls and green or tokay grapes. Serve as starters or as dessert. Or use one large cantaloupe or honeydew melon basket as a centrepiece from which melon balls and grapes are served as dessert.

GARNISHES FOR THE DINNER TABLE

FRUIT STARTERS

GRILLED GRAPEFRUIT

Cut grapefruit in halves, remove centres and cut segments free from shell and membrane. Use a grapefruit knife or other sharp-pointed knife. Or cut through skin, scallop fashion. Sprinkle with icing sugar or add 1 teaspoon honey. Slip under grill for 3 minutes or till lightly browned.

Serve a half grapefruit per person.

GRAPEFRUIT BASKETS

Cut grapefruit in half, crosswise. Use a corer or sharp-pointed scissors to remove centres. With a curved grapefruit knife loosen the segments from membrane and skin. Sprinkle with caster sugar and chill. Before serving, use a sharp-pointed knife or scissors to cut a ½-inch rim of shell all around, leaving the segments untouched. Use the rim for basket handle, add a cherry to centre of fruit, arrange a few mint leaves around cherry and serve.

FRUIT CUP

*1 cup diced peeled orange | 1 cup diced segmented grapefruit |
1 banana, diced | ½ cup pitted canned cherries |
½ cup orange juice or grapefruit juice | ½ cup sherry*

Combine, chill thoroughly, and serve in stem glasses or sherbet cups. Top with a whole cherry.
Serves 6 to 8.

FRESH PINEAPPLE AND ORANGE CUP

Cut away outer skin of pineapple. Remove core, dice or cut into small wedges. Add equal amount of diced orange. Add sherry or lemon juice to taste. Serve in sherbet cups or stemmed glasses.

MELON COCKTAILS

*2 cups watermelon balls or cantaloupe balls | 1 tablespoon caster sugar |
2 tablespoons lemon juice | Fresh mint*

With the proper cutter make small balls of melon meat. Sprinkle with sugar, add lemon juice and chill thoroughly. Fill low stem glasses and add fresh mint.
Variation: Add a teaspoonful of sherry, claret or grape juice to each serving.

SUGGESTIONS FOR FRUIT JUICE COCKTAILS

Combinations that Please
Grape juice and ginger ale, equal parts.
Grape juice and unsweetened grapefruit juice.

Unsweetened grapefruit juice and pineapple juice.

Apple juice and ginger ale or lemonade.

Orange-mint cocktail. Juice of oranges to which minced mint leaves, lemon juice and sugar to taste are added. Chill and serve with a sprig of fresh mint and green maraschino cherry. Serve with crushed ice.

A novelty that improves any fruit juice cocktail is to make ice cubes of the same fruit juice combinations, or of one of the juices used. Pour juice into ice-cube tray and freeze.

Another novelty is to place in each cube section of the freezer tray a sprig of fresh mint, and/or a cube or two of canned pineapple, a whole fresh or canned cherry, a strawberry or red raspberry. Fill the tray with water and freeze. Or, fill tray half full of water and add the fruit. Freeze, then add water to fill the tray and freeze solid. The fruit will be fixed in the centre of each cube.

28 Quick-Easies for Home Parties

APPLE SNOW

2 cups shredded unpared apples, tightly packed | 2 tablespoons lemon juice |
2 egg whites | $\frac{1}{2}$ cup sugar (or less)

Combine apple and lemon juice. Beat egg whites, adding sugar gradually. Fold into apple combination. Pile lightly in sherbet glasses.
   Serves 4.

FONDANT BALLS

2 cups icing sugar | 2 tablespoons butter |
Lemon or orange juice, approximately 1 tablespoon |
$\frac{1}{4}$ cup finely chopped almonds or walnuts

Cream butter in a bowl and stir in sugar. Moisten with fruit juice till consistency is easy to mould. Form into balls the size of hazelnuts. Roll candy balls in chopped nuts.

FONDANT FILLING FOR BISCUITS

Moisten fondant, as for Fondant Balls, till a spreadable consistency is reached. Add chopped nuts and spread between 2 biscuits, same size and shape. Put together, pressing lightly. Decorate with a bit of fondant. Press in a little chopped nuts or a slice of maraschino cherry.

FROSTED GRAPE CLUSTERS

Seedless green grapes are best for this. Select small clusters and dip them in slightly beaten egg whites. Place grape clusters on wax paper. When nearly dry, dust with granulated sugar. Arrange on a bed of green leaves – grapevine leaves if available.

HAWAIIAN DAINTY

1 cup brown sugar | 1 cup granulated sugar | ½ cup grated pineapple, drained |
¼ cup cream | 1 tablespoon butter | 1 teaspoon ginger flavouring |
1 teaspoon vanilla | ½ cup coarsely chopped pecans

Boil the sugars, pineapple and cream until mixture forms a soft ball when tested in cold water. Remove from heat. Add butter, flavourings and nuts. Beat with a silver fork until creamy. Pour into a buttered shallow pan. Cut into squares when cold.

NUBIANS (Basic Recipe)

1 cup each pitted dates, pitted, soaked and drained prunes, fresh figs,
seeded Muscat raisins | 1 cup English walnut meats |
½ cup crystallized ginger

Run through food chopper. Form into balls the size of a walnut. Roll in caster sugar and place on wax paper.

ORANGE AND GRAPEFRUIT STICKS

1½ cups sugar | ¾ cup water | ½ teaspoon ginger |
Peel of 2 grapefruit | Peel of 2 oranges

Cut orange and grapefruit peel into strips with scissors. Boil 10 minutes in enough water to cover. Drain. Add cold water to cover and repeat. This removes the bitter taste from fruit peel. Boil sugar and water until syrup threads from the spoon. Add ginger. Cook the strips of peel in this syrup for 20 minutes. Lift out carefully with kitchen tongs or pour entire mass on a large platter and separate when cool enough to handle. Straighten the strips, roll in sugar while they are still warm.

Variation: If a colour scheme is desirable, add vegetable colouring after removing from fire. Shake the pot to distribute colouring but if possible do not stir the strips.

CANDIED WHEAT PUFFS

*2 cups brown sugar | ½ cup water | 1 teaspoon vinegar | Pinch of salt |
Pinch of cream of tartar | 2 tablespoons butter | 8 cups wheat puffs*

Boil sugar, water, vinegar, salt, cream of tartar and butter till syrup
reaches the soft ball stage. Spread puffed wheat in a shallow,
buttered pan and pour the boiling syrup over it, pressing the cereal
down with the back of a spoon. Be careful not to crush the puffs.
When cool enough to handle, butter the palms of your hands and
form into balls. The wheat puffs are delicious served like popcorn.
  Variation: Substitute rice puffs or similar cereal product for wheat
puffs.

MARRON GLACÉ

*2 cups sugar | 1 tablespoon corn syrup | 1 cup water |
⅛ teaspoon cream of tartar | 2 cups peeled chestnuts, boiled and drained*

Dissolve sugar, syrup, water and cream of tartar, then boil without
stirring until slightly straw-coloured. Remove from fire and place
saucepan in a pan of hot water. With a knitting needle or a fine steel
skewer, dip each chestnut into the syrup. Place on wax paper until
cold and glazed.

SUGAR PLUMS

*½ cup sugar | ½ cup butter or margarine | 1½ cups flour, sifted |
½ teaspoon baking powder | ½ teaspoon salt | 2 eggs | ¼ cup milk |
1 teaspoon vanilla | ½ cup chopped walnuts or pecans | 4 dozen pitted dates*

Cream sugar and shortening till fluffy. Combine dry ingredients and
sift twice. Beat eggs and add milk, stirring till smooth. Add dry
ingredients to creamed mixture alternately with the liquid, stirring
till smooth after each addition. Drop from a teaspoon on to the
finely chopped nuts and place each separately on a greased baking
sheet, about 2 inches apart. Press a pitted date (whole or half)
down into the centres, and press together. Bake 15 minutes at 375° F.
or gas mark 5, or till lightly browned. Just before serving dust with
icing sugar.
  Yields approximately 50 sugar plums.

UPSIDE-DOWNIES

1 cup sugar | ½ cup butter or vegetable shortening | 2 eggs, separated |
2 cups flour | 2 teaspoons baking powder | ¼ teaspoon salt |
1 cup brown sugar | 1 cup milk or water | 1 teaspoon vanilla or
¼ teaspoon almond flavouring | 16 large dried apricot halves or 32 prunes |
4 tablespoons shortening

Cream sugar and shortening and add egg yolks. Sift dry ingredients together and add alternately with the milk, beating after each addition. Add flavouring. Soak the dried fruit till soft. Drain well and remove pits from prunes. Cut prunes in halves. Grease 16 individual baking tins and place a teaspoonful of brown sugar in each. Lay a half apricot or 4 prune halves, rounded side down, in each and turn in cake batter to fill not more than ⅔ full. Bake 20 to 30 minutes at 350° F. or gas mark 4, or till nicely browned. Turn out carefully. The fruit bottoms of each Upside-Downie will be glazed when cold.

Yields 16.

POTATO CREAM CANDY (Basic Recipe)

1 medium sized potato | 1½ to 2 cups caster sugar |
½ teaspoon vanilla | ½ teaspoon almond extract | Pinch of salt

Boil and mash the potato. When cool, work in caster sugar with a silver fork till it forms a mass stiff enough to roll. Add flavouring and salt. Knead or work with a fork till blended. Form into balls.

Variation 1: Add chopped nuts and form into balls.

Variation 2: Add ¼ cup finely cut candied fruits; form balls.

Variation 3: Form balls and roll in cinnamon to resemble potatoes.

Variation 4: Form balls and roll in shredded coconut.

Variation 5: Divide into 3 parts, colour each with a different vegetable colouring, and use as stuffing for prunes, dates, figs, adding a nut meat or tiny piece of citron.

Variation 6: Add mint flavouring and a little green colouring; use as filling between apricots that have been prepared by steaming in a little water and cooled separately.

Variation 7: Press a small ball of potato cream candy into centre of black or light figs, add a strip of citron to represent stamen of lily.

PRALINES

4 cups sugar | 1 teaspoon salt | 2 cups cream | 3 cups pecan halves

Make a syrup of 3 cups of sugar, salt and cream. Melt the other cup of sugar slowly in a heavy skillet till it caramelizes. Stir constantly during the process. Stir in cream mixture rapidly till thoroughly blended. Boil this mixture without stirring till it reaches the soft ball stage. Beat till creamy, then add pecans. Pour into a buttered shallow pan and cool before cutting. Or drop by spoonfuls on to wax paper and flatten to form round cakes. Cool and store in a cool place.

STUFFED PRUNES OR DATES

1 cup icing sugar | 1 tablespoon butter | ½ teaspoon vanilla |
½ cup chopped nuts or crisp breakfast cereal |
2 dozen large prunes or dates (soak prunes overnight and drain)

Cream butter and sugar. Add vanilla flavouring, nuts or cereal and combine till well blended. Remove pits from prunes or dates and fill the cavities with balls of the mixture. Roll in icing sugar.

PEANUT BRITTLE

2 cups sugar | 1 cup shelled peanuts | 1 teaspoon butter |
¼ teaspoon baking soda | ¼ teaspoon salt

Butter the bottoms of an oblong baking dish or 2-layer cake pans. Place a heavy iron skillet or other very heavy frying pan over very low heat, put in sugar and stir until it melts and becomes clear and golden-brown. Spread the peanuts evenly over the bottom of greased dish or layer pans and dust with salt. Add the baking soda to the melted sugar, stirring till it bubbles, and pour over the peanuts. It will cool almost instantly. Turn out on a large platter and break into pieces.

MAPLE NUT BRITTLE

1 cup light brown sugar | 1 cup maple sugar | ½ cup water |
2 tablespoons butter | ¼ teaspoon salt | 1 teaspoon vanilla |
1 cup broken nut meats

Boil sugars and water to the stiff ball stage, 246° F., add butter and continue to cook to the brittle stage, 300° F. Add salt and vanilla. Butter the inside of a baking pan and spread the nut meats evenly. Pour on the hot syrup and let stand till cold. Break the candy into pieces.

MARZIPAN

2 egg whites | 1 cup almond paste (about 2⅔ cups blanched almonds
ground and pounded to paste) | ½ teaspoon lemon flavouring |
1 cup icing sugar (approximately)

Beat egg whites and combine with almond paste. Add flavouring and stir in sugar to make paste stiff enough to handle. Let stand overnight. Shape into desired forms, or use as fruit fillings. Colour with vegetable colouring for tiny carrots, apples, cherries, etc.

PENOCHE

1 cup dark brown sugar | 2 cups granulated sugar | 1⅓ cups milk |
2 tablespoons butter | ½ cup coarsely cut pecans | ½ teaspoon vanilla

Boil together the sugars, milk and butter till syrup reaches the soft ball stage. Set aside for 10 minutes then beat till thick. Add the other ingredients and pour into a buttered platter to cool. Cut into squares while still warm, or roll and wrap in heavy wax paper. Cut the roll when cold. Store in a cool, dry place.

TURKISH DELIGHT

2 cups sugar | ½ cup corn syrup | ½ cup water | 2 egg whites |
1 teaspoon vanilla | 1 cup walnut meats, chopped |
½ cup diced, candied fruit (pineapple, cherries, lemon, orange, etc.)

Boil sugar, syrup and water till it reaches the soft ball stage. Pour the mixture slowly into beaten egg whites, beating constantly. When this begins to stiffen, add flavouring, nut meats and candied fruit. Pour into a well-buttered shallow pan as soon as thick and creamy. When cold, cut into squares or strips, 2 inches long and 1 inch wide.

ICE-CREAM FLOWER-POTS (for Children's Parties)

Tie a piece of crêpe paper around each paper cup, using the colours you select for the party. Flute the upper edge of the crêpe paper. This makes the flower-pot. Fill the paper cups with chocolate ice-cream. Arrange coloured gumdrops on coloured toothpicks for flowers.

VANILLA CREAM

*2 eggs | ⅓ cup granulated sugar | ⅓ cup light corn syrup | 1½ cups milk |
1½ cups light cream (or top milk for less rich dessert) |
1 tablespoon lemon juice | 1 tablespoon vanilla*

Beat eggs until lemon coloured. Add sugar gradually and continue beating until thick. Combine with syrup, milk, cream, and lemon juice. Pour into freezing tray. When frozen remove to bowl; add vanilla and beat with electric rotary beater until light and creamy. Return quickly to freezing tray and finish freezing.
Serves 6 to 8.

VANILLA CUSTARD CREAM (Basic Recipe)

*¾ cup granulated sugar | 2 tablespoons cornflour |
1 cup sweet milk, scalded | 2 eggs, separated | 1 pint light cream |
Few grains salt | 2 teaspoons vanilla*

Mix granulated sugar and cornflour. Add scalded milk gradually, stirring constantly. Cook in double boiler 25 minutes. Stir several times during cooking process. Combine with well-beaten egg yolks. Cook for about 5 minutes or until thick, stirring constantly. Cool, add cream and strain. Pour into freezing tray. When frozen remove to bowl, add vanilla and beat with rotary beater until light and creamy. Fold in stiffly beaten egg whites with salt. Return quickly to freezing tray and allow to finish freezing.
Serves 6 to 8.

CHOCOLATE CUSTARD CREAM

Melt 2 squares of bitter chocolate in top of double boiler over boiling water. Add to custard in basic recipe before it is cool and before egg whites are added. Continue method as in the basic recipe.

BANANA CREAM

1 *medium size banana* | ⅔ *cup icing sugar* | 1 *tablespoon lemon juice* |
1/16 *teaspoon salt* | 1½ *teaspoons vanilla* | 1½ *pints light cream*

Slice banana very thin and mash with sugar. Add lemon juice and cream and pour into freezing tray and allow to freeze firm. Remove to ice-cold mixing bowl; add vanilla and beat with electric or rotary beater until mixture becomes very light. Return to freezing tray, freezing without further stirring.
Serves 6.

CARAMEL CREAM

3 *tablespoons granulated sugar* | 1 *cup milk* | ½ *cup caster sugar* |
1½ *tablespoons flour* | 2 *eggs, separated* | ⅛ *teaspoon salt* |
1 *pint light cream* | 1 *teaspoon vanilla*

Caramelize sugar by heating until it is melted and becomes light brown in colour. Stir in milk and cook until sugar is dissolved. Mix caster sugar, salt and flour thoroughly and combine with caramel mixture, stirring constantly and slowly. Cook 15 minutes or until thickened, stirring constantly. Beat egg yolks in double boiler, and combine. Cook slowly for 5 minutes or until thick, stirring constantly. Cool; add salt and cream. Pour into freezing tray. When frozen, remove to bowl; add vanilla and whip with beater until light and creamy. Fold in stiffly beaten egg whites, beaten stiff with salt. Return quickly to freezing tray to finish freezing.
Serves 8 to 10.

CHOCOLATE CREAM

¾ *cup granulated sugar* | 2 *tablespoons cocoa* | *Few grains salt* |
⅓ *cup hot water* | 1½ *pints light cream* | 2 *teaspoons vanilla*

Mix sugar, cocoa, and salt thoroughly. Add hot water. Heat until sugar is thoroughly dissolved. Remove from heat and partially cool. Add cream, pour into freezing tray and allow to freeze firmly. Remove to chilled mixing bowl. Add vanilla and beat with rotary beater until mixture becomes light and creamy. Return quickly to freezing tray and finish freezing.

Serves 6 to 8.

LEMON CREAM

*2 eggs | ½ cup sugar | ½ cup corn syrup | 1 cup milk |
1 cup light cream | ¼ cup lemon juice | 1 teaspoon grated lemon rind*

Beat egg until lemon coloured. Add sugar gradually until the mixture reaches a thick custard-like consistency. Combine with syrup, milk, cream. Add lemon juice and rind. Pour into freezing tray. When frozen, remove to bowl and beat with a rotary beater until mixture becomes light and creamy. Return quickly to freezing tray and finish freezing.

Serves 6 to 8.

MAPLE CREAM

*1 cup maple syrup | 1½ tablespoons flour | ⅔ cup water | 2 egg yolks |
1/16 teaspoon salt | 1 pint light cream | 1 teaspoon vanilla |
1 teaspoon lemon juice | 2 egg whites*

Heat the syrup. Make a paste of the flour and water. Add hot syrup to paste, stirring constantly. Cook for 10 minutes, or until thickened. Add to well-beaten egg yolks in double boiler and cook over boiling water, stirring constantly until it reaches the consistency of thin custard. Cool. Add salt and cream. Pour into freezing tray. When frozen, remove to bowl; add vanilla and lemon juice and beat with rotary beater until light and creamy. Fold in the stiffly beaten egg whites. Return quickly to freezing tray and finish freezing.

Serves 8 to 10.

FRESH PEACH CREAM

*1 tablespoon gelatin | 3 tablespoons cold water | 2 cups fresh peach pulp |
1 cup granulated sugar | 1 tablespoon lemon juice | ½ cup light cream |
1 cup heavy cream, whipped | 1 or 2 drops almond extract*

Soak the gelatin in cold water for 5 minutes. Dissolve over hot water. Add peach pulp, sugar, lemon juice, and place in refrigerator to chill. Add the light cream and fold in the heavy cream which has been whipped to a custard-like consistency. Add almond extract. Pour into tray and freeze. Remove tray and stir once during the freezing process. This stirring can be done in the freezing tray without removing it to the mixing bowl.

Serves 8 to 10.

CANNED PEACH CREAM

2 cups crushed canned peaches | ½ cup sugar |
1½ tablespoons lemon juice | 1 cup milk | 1 cup light cream |
1 or 2 drops almond extract

Crush peaches, then measure 2 cups. Add sugar and lemon juice. Combine with milk and cream, add almond extract, stirring until sugar is thoroughly dissolved. Pour into freezing tray and freeze firm. Remove to chilled mixing bowl and beat with an electric or rotary beater until mixture becomes light and creamy. Return quickly to freezing tray and finish freezing.

Serves 6 to 8.

PEPPERMINT CANDY CREAM

¼ pound or 1 cup crushed peppermint stick candy | 1½ cups milk |
1½ cups light cream | 1/16 teaspoon salt

Dissolve candy in milk over low heat. Add cream and salt. Pour into freezing tray. Freeze until firm, remove to mixing bowl and beat with rotary beater until mixture is light and creamy. Don't whip too much. Return to freezing tray quickly and finish freezing.

Serves 8 to 10.

RASPBERRY CREAM

1 pint red raspberries | ½ cup granulated sugar | 1/16 teaspoon salt |
½ cup light cream | 1 cup heavy cream, whipped

Crush berries and add sugar. Cook 5 minutes and strain. Add salt and cool. Add light cream and fold in whipped cream. Pour into tray and freeze, stirring twice during the freezing process without removing it to the mixing bowl.
Serves 6.

FRESH STRAWBERRY CREAM

1 *pint fresh strawberries, hulled | 1 cup sugar | 1 tablespoon lemon juice | ½ cup milk | ½ cup light cream | ¾ cup heavy cream*

Crush berries and add sugar. Combine with lemon juice, milk, and light cream. Pour into freezing tray. When frozen, remove to bowl and beat with electric or rotary beater until light and creamy. Beat heavy cream and fold in. Return quickly to freezing tray and finish freezing.
Serves 8 to 10.

QUICK STRAWBERRY CREAM

½ *cup strawberry preserves (see p. 519) | 2 cups light cream*

Heat strawberry preserves before putting through strainer. Add cream slowly. Beat with rotary beater. Chill. Pour into tray and freeze firm. Remove to bowl and beat until light and creamy. Return quickly to tray and finish freezing.
Serves 6 to 8.

CIDER FRAPPÉ

2 *cups apple cider | ⅔ cup sugar | ¼ teaspoon cinnamon | 1 cup cream, whipped*

Bring cider and sugar to boiling point. Strain and cool. Add cinnamon. Fold in whipped cream. Freeze in refrigerator tray, stirring several times to ensure smooth consistency.
Serves 6.

Pineapple Centrepiece (*page 449*) with
Frosted Grape Clusters (*page 453*)
Grapefruit Baskets (*page 450*)

EGGNOG FRAPPÉ

5 eggs, separated | 1¾ cups sugar | ¾ cup whisky |
Dash of nutmeg | 2 cups heavy cream, whipped

Beat egg yolks and sugar till light and creamy. Stir in whisky and
nutmeg. Beat egg whites and fold in. Fold in stiffly beaten cream.
Turn into freezer trays and freeze without further stirring. Unmould, cut into squares. Serve like ice-cream if desired. Garnish
with mint leaves, maraschino cherries.
Yields 1¾ to 2 quarts.

MOCHA FRAPPÉ

1¾ cups sugar | 3 cups extra strong coffee | 3 cups light cream |
3 egg whites | ⅛ teaspoon salt | Whipped cream for topping

Dissolve sugar in hot coffee. Cool. Add cream. Freeze 2 hours. Beat
egg whites with salt till stiff enough to hold a peak. Remove partly
frozen mixture to a bowl, beat well and fold in egg whites. Return to
freezer tray, turn cold control to coldest point. Freeze till firm. Top
with whipped cream.
Yields approximately 2 quarts.

MOUSSES

MOUSSE (Basic Recipe)

1 cup heavy cream | ¼ cup caster sugar | ½ teaspoon vanilla |
1 egg white | Few grains salt

Whip cream, add caster sugar and vanilla. Fold in stiffly beaten
egg white to which salt has been added. Pour into freezing tray and
freeze without stirring.
Serves 4 to 6.

PISTACHIO MOUSSE

2 cups heavy cream | ½ cup sugar | ½ teaspoon pistachio flavouring or
1 part almond flavouring combined with 2 parts vanilla |
½ cup pistachio nuts, chopped fine | 3 drops green vegetable colouring |
2 egg whites | Few grains salt

30

Whip cream. Add sugar, flavouring, nuts, and just enough green colouring to give a yellowish green tint. Fold in stiffly beaten egg whites to which salt has been added. Pour into freezing tray and freeze without stirring.
Serves 8.

STRAWBERRY MOUSSE

1 pint strawberries | 1 cup sugar | Salt | 2 teaspoons lemon juice | 2 cups heavy cream, whipped | 2 egg whites | Few grains salt

Wash and hull berries. Add sugar and crush. Heat until sugar is dissolved. Add pinch of salt, strain and chill. Add lemon juice to berry mixture. Fold in whipped cream and stiffly beaten egg whites to which salt has been added. Pour into freezing tray or individual cups. Freeze without stirring. Decorate with whipped cream or whole fresh berries.
Serves 8 to 10.

PARFAITS

ANGEL PARFAIT

1 cup sugar | ¼ cup water | 2 egg whites | 1/16 teaspoon salt | 1 pint heavy cream, whipped, chilled | 2 teaspoons vanilla

Boil water and sugar slowly without stirring until it spins a thread, at 236° F. Combine slowly with stiffly beaten egg whites to which salt has been added. Continue to beat until thick. Cool. Combine with the chilled whipped cream. Add vanilla. Pour into freezing tray. Freeze without stirring. Top with crushed fruit. When served in parfait glasses, top with whipped cream and garnish with cherries or other fruit.
Serves 8 to 10.

BUTTERSCOTCH PARFAIT

⅔ cup brown sugar | 2 tablespoons butter | ½ cup water | 4 egg yolks | 1 pint heavy cream, whipped | 1/16 teaspoon salt | 2 teaspoons vanilla

Combine sugar and butter. Heat until melted. Cook for 1 minute. Add water; cook until butterscotch is melted. Add syrup mixture slowly to beaten egg yolks. Cook in double boiler until light and fluffy. Chill. Add whipped cream, salt and vanilla. Pour into freezing tray or individual cups. Freeze without stirring. Serves 10 to 12.

MAPLE PARFAIT

¾ cup maple syrup | 3 eggs, separated | 1½ cups heavy cream, whipped | 1 teaspoon vanilla | 1/16 teaspoon salt

Heat syrup in double boiler. Add syrup slowly to well-beaten egg yolks and return to double boiler. Beat until mixture is thick and light. Pour into stiffly beaten egg whites. Chill thoroughly. Add whipped cream, salt, and vanilla to custard. Mix thoroughly and pour into freezing tray. Freeze without stirring. Garnish with whipped cream and chopped nuts. Serves 8 to 10.

SHERBETS AND ICES

APRICOT SHERBET

1 cup apricot juice | ½ cup water | ¼ cup sugar | 1 cup apricot pulp | 1½ tablespoons lemon juice | ½ cup light cream | 2 egg whites | Few grains of salt

Cook apricot juice, water and sugar slowly for 10 minutes. Cool. Add apricot pulp and lemon juice to cooled syrup. Chill. Pour into freezing tray and freeze firm. Remove mixture to chilled bowl and beat until light. Beat egg whites with salt. Combine mixtures. Return to tray and finish freezing. If mixture separates after it is partly frozen, remove to chilled bowl and beat again. Serves 8 to 10.

LEMON MILK SHERBET

1¼ cups sugar | ⅓ cup lemon juice | Grated rind of 1 lemon ¼ teaspoon lemon extract | 1 pint milk

Combine sugar, lemon juice, lemon rind and flavouring. Add milk and stir until the sugar is thoroughly dissolved. Pour into freezing tray and freeze firm. Remove to a chilled mixing bowl and beat with rotary beater until light and creamy. Return quickly to freezing tray and finish freezing.
Serves 6 to 8.

ORANGE CREAM SHERBET

¾ cup sugar | ¾ cup water | Grated rind of 1 orange |
1½ cups orange juice | 1 tablespoon lemon juice | ½ cup light cream |
2 egg whites | Few grains of salt

Cook sugar and water slowly for 10 minutes. Add grated rind to syrup and continue cooking for several minutes. Strain. Add syrup to fruit juices. Cool. Pour into freezing tray and freeze firm. Remove mixture to chilled mixing bowl and beat until light. Add cream. Fold in stiffly beaten egg whites to which salt has been added. Pour into tray and freeze. If ingredients separate, stir mixture again with a spoon.
Serves 6.

PINEAPPLE MILK SHERBET

⅔ cup sugar | ½ cup pineapple juice | 1 tablespoon lemon juice |
1 teaspoon grated lemon rind | 1 pint milk

Combine sugar, pineapple juice, lemon juice, and lemon rind. Add the milk and stir until the sugar is thoroughly dissolved. Pour into freezing tray and freeze firm. Remove to chilled mixing bowl and beat until mixture is light and creamy. Return quickly to freezing tray and finish freezing.
Serves 6 to 8.

CRANBERRY ICE

1 quart cranberries | 1 pint water | 2 cups sugar |
1 teaspoon grated rind | ¼ cup orange juice

Heat cranberries and water to boiling and cook for a few minutes or until the berries become soft. Put through sieve. Add sugar. Add grated rind and heat again until sugar is dissolved. Add orange juice. Remove from fire. Cool. Pour into tray and freeze firm. Remove to chilled mixing bowl and beat until mixture is very light. Return to freezing tray and finish freezing without stirring.

Serves 6 to 8.

LEMON ICE

*¾ cup sugar | 1 pint water | ½ cup lemon juice |
2 egg whites | Few grains salt*

Cook sugar and water slowly for 10 minutes. Cool. Add to lemon juice. Pour into tray and freeze firm. Remove to chilled mixing bowl and beat with rotary beater until light and creamy. Beat egg whites with salt. Fold in. This should be done as quickly as possible in order to prevent melting. Return to freezing tray and freeze.

Serves 4 to 6.

LIME ICE

*⅔ cup sugar | 1 pint water | ½ cup lime juice |
2 drops green vegetable colouring | 2 egg whites | Few grains of salt*

Cook sugar and water slowly for 10 minutes. Add to lime juice. Cool. Add green colouring. Pour into freezing tray and freeze firm. Remove to chilled mixing bowl and beat until mixture is very light. Fold in stiffly beaten egg whites to which salt has been added. Return to tray and finish freezing.

Serves 4 to 6.

RASPBERRY ICE

*¾ cup sugar | 1 pint fresh raspberries, crushed | ½ cup water |
2 tablespoons orange juice | 2 egg whites | 1/16 teaspoon salt*

Add sugar to berries. Heat slowly and cook 5 minutes. Add water, strain and cool. Add orange juice. Pour into freezing tray and freeze firm. Remove to chilled mixing bowl and whip until very light. Add stiffly beaten egg whites to which salt has been added. Return quickly to tray and finish freezing.

Serves 8.

STRAWBERRY ICE

1 pint fresh strawberries, hulled | 1 cup sugar |
½ cup water | 1 tablespoon lemon juice

Crush the berries. Add sugar, water and lemon juice. Press through a fine sieve. Pour into freezing tray and freeze firm. Remove to chilled mixing bowl and whip until very light. Return quickly to freezing tray and finish freezing.

Serves 6.

OTHER DESSERTS

CREAM CHEESE MOUND

1 cup heavy cream | 1 pound cream cheese | 4 tablespoons caster sugar |
4 tablespoons light cream | Dash of salt | ½ teaspoon vanilla |
1 quart hulled strawberries or red raspberries | Caster sugar

Whip heavy cream stiff. Mash cream cheese with a fork and fold in caster sugar and light cream, salt, vanilla. Fold whipped cream into this mixture till well combined and light. Turn out in a mound on a large serving plate and surround with berries. Chill 2 hours. Sprinkle berries with caster sugar just before serving.

Serves 10 to 12.

DEVONSHIRE FROZEN SHORTCAKE

6 to 8 slices of white bread, trimmed of crusts |
3 to 4 tablespoons softened butter | 1 quart fresh or frozen strawberries |
¾ cup sugar | 1 cup heavy cream, whipped stiff

Cut bread to fit into bottom of a loaf pan. Brush with butter. Hull, wash and drain fresh berries. Crush them and add sugar. Pour crushed berries on bread slices and top with remaining bread. Place

a flat plate over to weight contents of pan. Chill several hours. Turn out on serving plate and top with whipped cream.
Serves 6.

FROZEN STRAWBERRY SHORTCAKE

2 *cups strawberries, hulled* | ½ *cup icing sugar* |
1 *cup Strawberry Mousse (see Index)* | 1 *cup heavy cream, whipped* |
Sliced sponge cake

Wash berries and drain. Slice and add sugar. Remove mousse from refrigerator freezing compartment. Whip cream. Cut sponge cake slices to fit bottom of freezer tray and fit in snugly. Spread sugared berries over cake. Add a layer of mousse and top with whipped cream. If any sponge cake crumbs remain, scatter them over top. Chill 2 hours, then place in freezer till very cold but not frozen. Serve with additional whole strawberries as garnish if desired.
Serves 8.

FROZEN CRUMB CAKE (Basic Recipe)

2 *cups dry cake crumbs* | 1 *cup heavy cream, whipped* |
½ *teaspoon vanilla* | ¼ *cup chopped almonds*

Combine crumbs, whipped cream and vanilla, using a fork. Add chopped nuts and turn into freezing tray. Freeze without further stirring. Turn out when solid and cut into cubes or slices.
Serves 6.
Variation: Add 6 red maraschino cherries sliced very thin. Substitute 1 teaspoon maraschino syrup for vanilla and add 1 drop of red vegetable colouring. Mix and freeze.

FROZEN DESSERTS MADE WITH EVAPORATED MILK

How to Whip Evaporated Milk: Evaporated milk may be prepared for whipping by three different methods. The method to be used should be determined by the purpose for which the whipped milk is intended.

If the milk must be very stiff and stand up for some time, as for garnishing desserts, use the following method: Pour the necessary quantity of evaporated milk into the top part of a double boiler and heat over boiling water to the scalding point. The scum on top and sediment at bottom of pan should not be discarded. They will blend smoothly with the rest during whipping and will aid in stiffening the milk. When the milk has reached the scalding point, cool quickly by setting the container in cold water. Chill and beat with rotary beater.

For frozen desserts and salads, evaporated milk is prepared by heating the unopened can in an *uncovered* saucepan with cold water to cover. Boil 5 minutes, counting time after boiling begins. Remove from pan and chill quickly. Much of the heat may be removed by placing the can in a pan of cold water or under running cold water. Chill in refrigerator until ready to use.

Or, chill can of evaporated milk in freezer compartment overnight. Open and heat.

BUTTERSCOTCH MOUSSE

½ *cup light brown sugar* | 2 *tablespoons butter* | 6 *tablespoons water* |
1 *whole egg* | 1 *egg yolk* | *Few grains salt* | 2 *tablespoons evaporated milk* |
1 *cup evaporated milk* | ½ *teaspoon lemon juice (scant measure)*

Combine sugar, butter and water. Heat in top of double boiler 45 minutes. Beat eggs. Pour mixture over beaten eggs, stirring vigorously till smooth. Add salt and 2 tablespoons of evaporated milk. Cook in double boiler 5 minutes, stirring continuously to keep smooth. Scrape down sides of pan and beat until smooth. Cool mixture. Chill prepared milk and lemon juice in bowl surrounded by chipped ice and salt. Whip until stiff. Fold cooked mixture lightly but thoroughly into the milk. Pour immediately into cold freezing pan and place in freezing compartment. Requires 3 to 8 hours for freezing.

Yields 6 servings.

FROZEN BANANA SALAD

Two 3-*ounce packages cream cheese* | ¼ *teaspoon salt* | ½ *cup mayonnaise* |
2 *tablespoons lemon juice* | ½ *cup canned crushed pineapple* |
2 *medium size bananas* | ½ *cup coarsely chopped walnuts* |
½ *cup thinly sliced maraschino cherries* | 1 *cup whipped evaporated milk*

Mash cheese in a mixing bowl, adding salt, mayonnaise and lemon juice. Combine with the other ingredients in the order listed, folding in whipped milk last. Turn into freezer tray and freeze till firm. Unmould on a bed of shredded salad greens. Garnish with sliced bananas, maraschino cherries, chopped nuts or fresh berries. Serves 8.

FROZEN PINEAPPLE-CHEESE SALAD

*¼ pound cream cheese | 3 tablespoons light cream |
2 tablespoons lemon juice | 1 cup canned crushed pineapple |
½ cup canned pitted cherries | ½ cup chopped walnuts |
½ cup mayonnaise | 1 cup whipped evaporated milk*

Mash cheese with cream and add lemon juice, stirring till smooth. Combine with the other ingredients, stirring after each addition till smooth. Fold in whipped milk last. Turn into a rinsed ring mould and chill overnight or freeze in freezer tray 4 hours till firm. Unmould on shredded salad greens and garnish with whole fresh strawberries, chopped walnuts or whipped cream. Serves 8.

CREAMLESS FROZEN DESSERTS
(Dry Skim Milk Base)

By using packaged dry skim milk, a number of excellent fat-free frozen desserts can be made in 2 hours in your electric refrigerator. This type of dessert retains a fairly high amount of protein and calcium. The flavour and consistency reaches the equivalent of commercial frozen desserts, with much less fat and sugar content. It can be served like any ice-cream or fruit sherbet.

DRY SKIM MILK TOPPING
(for Fruit Salads, Gingerbread, etc.)

*½ cup cold water | ½ cup dry skim milk | 2 tablespoons sugar |
1 tablespoon lemon juice |
½ teaspoon each vanilla and rum flavouring or 1 teaspoon sherry*

Combine water and dry skim milk in a mixing bowl and beat with rotary beater till thick as cream – 10 minutes by hand or 3 minutes with electric mixer. Add lemon juice and sugar and beat till it holds a peak. Remove beater and fold in flavouring. Turn into freezer tray as for fruit dessert and freeze till firm. Or store in glass covered jar in refrigerator for future use.

SAUCES FOR FROZEN DESSERTS

ORANGE-PINEAPPLE SAUCE

2 *tablespoons cornflour* | ½ *cup sugar* | 1 *cup orange juice* |
1 *tablespoon lemon juice* | 1½ *cups canned crushed pineapple*

Combine cornflour and sugar. Stir in orange and lemon juice. Cook over low heat, stirring till thick and clear, approximately 5 minutes. Cool and add crushed pineapple. Chill.
Serves 6 to 8.

MIXED NUTS SAUCE

¼ *cup butter* | 1 *cup dark brown sugar* | ½ *cup light cream* |
½ *cup finely chopped mixed nuts* | 1 *teaspoon lemon juice* |
¼ *teaspoon almond flavouring* | *Dash of salt*

Combine butter, sugar and cream in a saucepan. Bring slowly to boiling point and simmer 1 to 2 minutes. Remove from heat and stir in nuts, lemon juice, flavouring and salt.
Yields approximately 1½ cups.

RAISIN AND ALMOND SAUCE

¼ *cup chopped seeded raisins* | 1½ *cups water* | ¼ *cup sugar* |
Dash of salt | 2 *tablespoons butter* | 1 *tablespoon cornflour* |
1 *tablespoon cold water* | ¼ *cup finely chopped almonds* |
¼ *teaspoon almond flavouring*

Cook the first four ingredients 5 to 10 minutes over low heat. Add butter and stir in cornflour mixed with cold water. Cook over reduced heat 5 to 6 minutes or till sauce is clear. Remove from heat and add almonds and flavouring.

Yields $1\frac{1}{2}$ cups.

COFFEE

Drip Method: For each serving, place 1 to 3 tablespoons (according to taste) medium ground coffee into the coffee compartment of your coffee maker. Measure and bring to boiling point 1 cup of cold water per serving. Pour into the upper part of coffee maker and cover. Place coffee maker on an asbestos pad over very low heat or in a warm place until the water has dripped through to the bottom section of coffee container. Serve hot.

Vacuum Method: For each serving, place 1 cup boiling water into the lower bowl of coffee maker. Adjust filter on upper bowl, and measure 1 to 3 tablespoons finest ground coffee for each serving into the upper bowl. Place coffee maker over moderate heat and fit upper bowl into position over lower bowl, making sure the seal is air-tight. Reduce heat under coffee maker as soon as the water boils. Allow only a small quantity of water to rise into the upper bowl. Stir mixture in upper bowl and remove from heat. Allow the brew to return to lower bowl. Remove upper bowl and serve coffee hot.

Percolator Method: Use 1 cup cold water for each serving, measuring the water and turning it into the lower section of coffee maker. Adjust the perforated coffee basket and add 1 to 3 tablespoons percolator ground coffee for each cup of cold water. Cover. Place the coffee maker over moderate heat and permit the coffee to brew as the water percolates upward and through the ground coffee, allowing 8 to 10 minutes percolating time over reduced heat. Coffee basket may be removed and the cover adjusted. Serve hot.

Boiled Coffee: Use an old-fashioned coffee pot. Add 1 to 3 tablespoons ground coffee for each cup of freshly boiled water used. Add the ground coffee to boiling water in coffee pot and stir well. Cover tightly and let stand on an asbestos pad over low heat from 8 to 10 minutes. Strain the brewed coffee into a heated serving coffee pot. Serve hot.

Note: For extra strength coffee made by any of the above methods, use 3 tablespoons ground coffee for each serving.

Iced Coffee: Pour left-over coffee made by any of the methods into ice cube tray of electric refrigerator. Freeze till firm. Use 2 to 3 cubes per tall glass and fill with regular strength chilled coffee. Add cream and sugar to taste.

Or, pour extra strength coffee into glass filled with ice cubes or crushed ice. Add cream and sugar to taste.

Or, chill coffee made by any of the above methods by placing the regular strength or extra strength brew in a glass jar; cover tightly and place in the refrigerator. Allow ¾ cup cooled coffee per serving. Add ice cubes or crushed ice and sugar and cream to taste.

White Coffee or *Café au Lait* is made by pouring together equal quantities of scalded milk and either regular strength or extra strong brewed coffee, freshly made. Use 2 pitchers and pour the hot liquid simultaneously into serving cups.

Roumanian Coffee: Combine equal quantities of freshly brewed coffee with scalded milk and let the mixture drip through the coffee basket of coffee maker used for percolating coffee.

Turkish Coffee: Mix 1 tablespoon of finely ground coffee with 1 tablespoon granulated sugar, and add 1 *demi-tasse* of boiling water. Bring to a boil over moderate heat. Remove from heat as soon as it becomes frothy. Wait 2 or 3 seconds before returning the beverage to the fire. Bring to a boil and remove from heat as soon as it becomes frothy. Wait 2 to 3 seconds and then bring to a boil for the third time. The beverage should be thick and foamy at the top. Serve in *demi-tasse* without added cream or sugar as an after-dinner beverage. Or, add 1 teaspoon rum to each *demi-tasse* of hot Turkish coffee just before serving.

Viennese Coffee: Top extra strength coffee with stiffly beaten cream to which pulverized sugar has been added to taste. Sugar may be added if desired. Serve in *demi-tasse* or regular cup.

Instant Coffees are available for making coffee in the cup at the table in the strength desired.

Coffee Substitutes: These are made of roasted grains, combined with malt and molasses or other syrups, and ground or pulverized. The ground cereal coffee may be used like coffee in any of the methods given for brewing coffee. The pulverized cereal coffee is mixed with boiling water, or milk and water, in accordance with instructions given on each container. Coffee substitutes may be served hot or iced.

TEA

Black Teas produce a beverage with a rich amber colour and fruity flavour as well as tempting aroma. They are the fermented or oxidized varieties and contain a small percentage of tannin.

Green Teas are not oxidized and therefore contain a larger proportion of tannin than the black teas. They have a delicate flavour and are light coloured. The beverage made from green tea is light coloured.

Iced Tea: For clear iced tea, fill a tall glass with ice cubes or crushed ice and add boiling double strength prepared tea slowly, stirring once or twice with a long-handled spoon. Serve with lemon wedges or slices and sugar to taste.

> *Variation:* Make double strength tea in the amount desired for serving. Chill in a well-covered glass container. Serve with ice cubes or crushed ice. Add lemon slices studded with 3 or 4 cloves per slice, and sugar to taste.
>
> Or, serve with candied or maraschino cherries, fresh mint leaves or rose petals, or a small rose geranium leaf in each glass of tea.

Tea Bags: These are small packages of tea which are dipped into cups of boiling hot water and left in the cup until the desired strength and colour of tea has been attained. Tea bags are a convenience for serving tea at table.

Instant Teas: These are prepared by stirring as much of the pulverized tea as desired into boiling water at the table or in a serving teapot.

CHOCOLATE AND COCOA

HOT CHOCOLATE

1½ squares unsweetened chocolate (1½ ounces) | ¾ cup water | 2½ tablespoons sugar | Few grains of salt | 2¼ cups milk

Combine chocolate and water in top of double boiler. Cook over boiling water till chocolate is melted. Add sugar and salt. Stir to dissolve and add milk gradually, stirring constantly. Cook 3 to 4 minutes over moderate heat or 8 to 10 minutes over boiling water. Before serving, beat till frothy, using a rotary beater.

Serves 4.

SEMI-SWEET CHOCOLATE DRINK

4 cups scalded milk | 1 cup finely shredded semi-sweet chocolate

Pour milk over chocolate and stir well. Beat with a rotary beater till well combined.
Serves 4.

SPICED CHOCOLATE

4 egg yolks | 4 cups chilled milk | ½ cup malt-cocoa | Dash of nutmeg |
¼ cup heavy cream | 4 teaspoons shredded semi-sweet chocolate

Beat egg yolks and stir in milk and malt-cocoa. Beat with a rotary beater till all ingredients are well combined. Add nutmeg and pour into tall glasses. Whip cream stiff. Top each glassful of beverage with whipped cream and sprinkle with shredded chocolate.
Serves 4.

COCOA

2 tablespoons sugar | 2 tablespoons cocoa | Few grains of salt |
1 cup warm water | 3 cups milk

Combine sugar and cocoa. Add salt and stir in water till blended. Bring to the boiling point over low heat and boil 2 minutes, stirring constantly. Add milk slowly, stirring constantly. Heat but do not boil.
Serves 4.
Variation: Add a dash of cinnamon and ¼ teaspoon vanilla extract. Top with 1 tablespoon of whipped cream per cup.

ICED MALTED MILK

1 cup milk | 2 to 3 tablespoons malted milk

Combine and beat with a rotary beater until well blended. Chill before serving.
Serves 1.

EGG-MILK SHAKE

1 egg | 1 tablespoon sugar or honey | Crushed ice to fill glass |
⅔ glass iced milk

Beat egg with sugar or honey in glass to be used. Add crushed ice
and milk. Stir well with a long-handled spoon, if a tall glass is used.
Serves 1.

Variation 1: Omit sugar or honey. Beat egg in glass and stir in 3
tablespoons fruit juice. Add crushed ice and milk as in basic
recipe.

Variation 2: Beat egg and sugar or honey as in basic recipe. Add
extra strong coffee and crushed ice to fill glass ¾ full. Stir in
2 tablespoons cream and add iced soda water to make the
mixture foam to the top. Sprinkle a few grains of nutmeg on
top. Serve.

FRUIT AND VEGETABLE JUICES

Fruit Juices for cold drinks are available in cans, glass jars and quick
frozen packages, or can be made in a blender. Among the popular
juices are:

Apple Juice
Apple Cider
Apricot Juice
Grape Juice
Grapefruit Juice
Grapefruit and Orange Juice
Loganberry Juice
Orange Juice (in cans and frozen)
Pineapple Juice
Prune Juice

Vegetable Juices
Carrot Juice
Sauerkraut Juice
Tomato Juice
Vegetable, Mixed Juice

See also *Suggestions for Fruit Juice Cocktails* in Chapter 27.

Pickled Peppers (*page 487*)
Dill Pickles (*page 492*)
Ginger Pears (*page 498*)
Spiced Plums (*page 499*)

31 Homemade Pickles and Relishes

Pickling means preserving foods in brine or vinegar. Cucumber pickles are most commonly used in Jewish households, but there are many other vegetables that can be pickled in one form or another. Also, some fruits can be pickled successfully at home.

Types of Pickles. There are many varieties of pickles and relishes, their predominating flavour determining the type, such as sour pickles, sweet, dill, mustard or spiced.

Pickles are made of fruits or vegetables. In general, the whole product or large pieces are used in pickles, and often only one product is used. Fruits are prepared as for bottling and then placed in the pickling solution given in the following recipes. Relishes are more often made of vegetables, especially of a combination of vegetables chopped fine, usually in a sweet and sour solution.

PRESERVATIVES

Vinegar is used in pickling as a preservative, to modify flavour and aroma and to aid in controlling a desired type of fermentation.

Cider Vinegar is good for its mellow, acid taste and aroma, although it has a tendency to discolour light and white vegetables, turning them a reddish brown.

White Vinegar, because of its more harsh and biting taste, is not as appetizing in flavour and aroma as cider vinegar. However, the clear white colour of such vegetables as onions and cauliflower is retained and the green colour of green vegetables is intensified with its use. Thus, for colour use white vinegar and for flavour use cider vinegar. Vinegar of 45 to 50% strength should be used for pickles.

Salt is used in pickling as a preservative, to improve taste and flavour, to harden and make firm vegetable tissues and to control fermentation. Salt may be used in the dry form or dissolved in water as brine.

HONEY VINEGAR

Mix together 1 quart of strained honey and 8 quarts warm water. Allow mixture to stand in a warm place until fermentation ceases. Seal in clean fruit jars. The resulting vinegar is white and of excellent quality.

PICKLING SOLUTIONS

For dill pickles, 1 quart water to ¼ cup salt.
For green tomatoes, 4 quarts water to 2 cups vinegar and ½ cup salt.

SPICES AND SEASONINGS

Bay leaves, 3 to each quart jar.
Fresh or dry dill, 1 bunch per quart jar.
Grape leaves, 2 or 3 medium size leaves per quart jar.
Whole mixed spice, 1 tablespoon per quart of pickling solution.
Garlic is used in any desired quantity, usually 3 cloves per jar.

QUANTITIES AND YIELD

Because it is difficult to estimate by weight the amount of cucumbers required per quart of pickles, it is best to approximate the size of cucumbers as 3½ inches long and expect about 1 quart jar of pickles for each pound of cucumbers.

In making chopped or sliced pickles, the following recipes will indicate proportions as well as yield in pints or quarts.

Vegetables to be Pickled must be scrubbed in plenty of clear water and given a preliminary soaking in a mild salt and water solution. Using ⅛ to ¼ cup of salt to a quart of water is the usual proportion. Some vegetables should be soaked for a few hours or overnight. Other vegetables should be parboiled in salted water before placing them in the pickling solution. Salt helps draw the water from vegetable tissues. They are then prepared to absorb the brine or pickling solution without becoming limp.

HELPFUL HINTS

Don't let the bubbling of pickles scare you into throwing them away.

It's only fermentation. It should stop in 3 to 5 days, after which time you should clamp down the cover of jar.

Use coarse salt and not the refined table variety for pickling vegetables. It makes a less scummy brine.

Do your pickles turn soft? They won't if you remember to use ½ cup of coarse salt to a quart of water as the standard brine solution. Dissolve the salt in boiling water and let it cool before using.

Use only a high grade pickling vinegar or your best recipes will disappoint you.

Don't substitute ground spices when the recipe calls for whole spice. The pulverized variety will turn the product dark enough to frighten away appetites.

Tie whole spices in a muslin or cheesecloth bag and save your temper.

A bit of alum added to the scalding hot pickling liquid will ensure crispness – that is if you don't object to using alum.

PICKLED BEETS

3 pounds beets | 1 pint vinegar | ½ cup sugar |
1 tablespoon stick cinnamon | 1 teaspoon whole allspice | 6 whole cloves

Cook beets in water until tender. Slip off skins. Dice or slice. Bring to boil the vinegar, sugar, spice mixture in a bag. Add beets. Boil 5 minutes. Remove spice bag. Fill jars. Seal, store.

Yields 2 pints.

PICKLED PUMPKIN

3 pounds pumpkin | 1 cup brown sugar | ½ cup pickling vinegar |
½ teaspoon cloves

Cut pumpkin into wedges. Remove seeds and inside fibrous part. Pare and cut into ¼-inch-thick slices from tip to tip of each wedge. Or, cut into ¼-inch cubes. Make a syrup of sugar and vinegar by boiling 8 to 10 minutes. Add prepared pumpkin and cloves and bring to a boil. Turn into sterilized jars and fill to the top. Cover and invert to make certain there are no bubbles or air pockets. Store at least 2 weeks before using.

Yields approximately 2 pints.

WILMA'S SLICED CUCUMBER PICKLES

12 cucumbers (5- to 6-inch lengths) | 1 tablespoon salt | ¾ cup white vinegar |
½ cup granulated sugar | ½ cup water | 1 large clove garlic |
4 white pickling onions (1 inch diameter) | 8 bay leaves |
4 small sticks cinnamon | 4 teaspoons mustard seed |
2 teaspoons prepared horse-radish

Select tender cucumbers about 1½ to 2 inches in diameter. Pare and slice lengthwise into quarters. Remove seeds and sprinkle lightly with salt. Let stand 2 hours. Bring to a boil vinegar, sugar and water when ready to pack cucumber slices. Pack sliced cucumber lengthwise into pint jars, allowing approximately 3 cucumbers per pint. Into each jar tuck ¼ cut of garlic clove, 1 onion, cut or left whole, 2 bay leaves, 1 stick of cinnamon, 1 teaspoon mustard seed and ½ teaspoon horse-radish. Pour in the boiling hot vinegar and sugar solution and seal at once. These pickles may be eaten after 8 hours.
Yields 4 pints.

WILMA'S PICKLE SLICES

10 to 12 medium size young cucumbers (1½ inches thick, 5 inches long) |
¾ cup white vinegar | ½ cup sugar | ¼ teaspoon salt |
1 green pepper, chopped fine | ½ cup celery, chopped fine |
2 white pickling onions, sliced thin | 4 bay leaves | 4 small sticks cinnamon

Slice unpared cucumber ⅛ inch thick. Combine vinegar, sugar and salt in a deep pot and bring to a quick boil. Add the cucumber slices, chopped green pepper, chopped celery, sliced onions and cook over moderate heat till the liquid bubbles over the top of cucumber slices. Remove from heat. Pack quickly into pint jars. Add 1 bay leaf and 1 stick of cinnamon to top of each filled jar and seal while hot.
Yields 4 pints.

CHOWCHOW

4 quarts chopped or cut green tomatoes | 6 diced cucumbers |
4 large onions, diced | 4 red peppers (sweet), chopped |
4 red peppers (hot), cut fine | 2 cups diced celery | 3 cloves garlic, minced |
1 cup salt | 1 quart pickling vinegar | 1½ cups brown sugar |
2 tablespoons dry mustard | ½ teaspoon cinnamon | ½ teaspoon ground allspice

Combine vegetables, garlic and salt. Let stand overnight in a crock or wooden bowl. In the morning, drain off all liquid. Add vinegar, sugar and seasonings. Cook until vegetables are tender, stirring occasionally. Pack in sterilized pint jars and seal.

Yields 10 to 12 pints.

ECONOMY CHOWCHOW

1 medium sized cabbage | 1 pint small onions | 2 green peppers |
2 tablespoons salt | 1 quart vinegar | 1 cup brown sugar |
¼ cup mustard seed | 1 tablespoon ground mustard | 1 teaspoon celery seed

Chop the vegetables separately, combine and add salt. Let stand an hour. Drain in a cheesecloth bag for 3 hours or overnight. Boil together the vinegar, sugar and seasonings for about 1 minute; add the drained vegetable mixture; bring to a boil and turn into hot pint jars. Seal.

Yields 4 to 5 pints.

AUTUMN MEDLEY

2 quarts green tomatoes | 1 quart ripe tomatoes | ½ head of cabbage |
3 green peppers, seeds removed | 3 stalks of celery | 3 red peppers |
3 large onions | 1 cucumber, peeled | ½ cup salt | 2 cups brown sugar |
3 pints vinegar | 1 teaspoon dry mustard

Put vegetables through food chopper and place in layers in a large bowl. Sprinkle with salt. Cover; let stand overnight. Drain; press out all the liquid. Add remaining ingredients. Cook 1 hour, or until transparent. Pour into hot sterilized jars and seal.

Yields 4 quarts.

APPLE AND RAISIN CHUTNEY

4 quarts apples, peeled | 2 onions, peeled | 1 clove of garlic |
1 cup seeded raisins | 5 cups vinegar | ¼ cup white mustard seed |
2 tablespoons ground ginger | 1 pod hot red pepper | 1 cup brown sugar

Chop apples, onions, garlic and raisins. Add half of the vinegar. Cook until soft. Add remaining ingredients. Cook until thick, stirring occasionally. Pour into hot sterilized jars and seal at once.

Yields 8 to 9 pints.

CRANBERRY CHUTNEY

3 cups canned whole cranberry sauce | ¾ cup seedless raisins, chopped |
½ pound pitted dates, chopped | ½ cup sugar | ½ cup vinegar |
¼ teaspoon ginger | ¼ teaspoon cinnamon | ¼ teaspoon allspice |
⅛ teaspoon cloves | ⅛ teaspoon salt

Combine ingredients and cook slowly until thick, about 20 minutes, stirring occasionally. Pour into hot sterilized jars and seal immediately.

Yields 1 quart or four 8-ounce jelly glasses.

ENGLISH CHUTNEY

3 green peppers, seeded | 1 medium sized onion | 13 tart apples, peeled |
1½ cups seeded raisins | 1 tablespoon salt | 3 cups vinegar |
1½ cups sugar | 1½ tablespoons ginger | 1½ cups tart grape jelly |
¾ cup lemon juice | Grated rind of 1 lemon

Chop peppers, onions, apples, raisins. Place all ingredients in large saucepan and simmer about 1 hour, or until quite thick. Turn into hot sterilized jars and seal.

Yields 4 pints.

PICKLED ONIONS

4 quarts small white onions | 3 pints boiling water | 1 cup salt |
3 tablespoons whole allspice | 3 tablespoons whole white mustard seed |
¼ cup grated horse-radish | 1 quart white vinegar |
3 tablespoons peppercorns | ¼ cup sugar

Peel onions. Pour boiling water and salt over onions and let stand 24 hours. Drain, cover again with boiling water for 5 to 10 minutes.

Drain and pack jars. Boil vinegar, water, sugar and spices for 3 minutes. Remove allspice and peppercorns. Add a bit of red pepper to each jar. Fill jar with liquid. Seal, store.

PEPPER HASH

1 *small head cabbage* | 12 *peppers (red and green)* | 6 *onions* |
1 *large bunch celery* | 1½ *cups sugar* | 1 *pint vinegar* |
2 *teaspoons salt* | 1 *tablespoon mustard seed*

Put vegetables through food chopper and pour boiling water over them. Let stand till cool. Drain well. Add sugar, vinegar, salt and mustard seed and cook slowly for 15 minutes. Fill pint jars and seal while hot.

Yields 4 pints.

PICKLED PIMENTO PEPPERS

8 *to* 10 *large pimento peppers* | 1½ *cups vinegar* |
¾ *cup sugar* | ¼ *teaspoon salt*

Wash peppers, remove stems and seeds. Cut into strips. Cover with boiling water and let stand 3 minutes. Drain well. Pack into sterilized jars. Boil sugar, vinegar and salt 5 minutes and pour over pepper strips to fill jars. Seal at once.

Yields 2 pints.

PICKLED PEPPERS (Roumanian Style)

Grill sweet green peppers or hold them against a high flame till skins blister. Plunge into cold water and remove the skins. Drain well. With the point of a paring knife make a slit in the side of each pepper and remove seeds. Pack peppers into quart jars. Boil together 1 part water to 2 parts vinegar, or any solution to suit the taste. Cover peppers with the solution as soon as cool. To each quart jar add 10 slices of raw carrot, 2 cloves of garlic, 2 bay leaves, 1 small hot red pepper, 10 peppercorns, ½ teaspoon salt and 1 tablespoon brown sugar. Cover and let stand 1 hour before serving. Will keep for a week or longer.

PICCALILLI

6 *large onions* | 6 *green peppers* | 12 *pounds green tomatoes, cut* |
1 *cup salt* | 2 *quarts vinegar* | 4 *cups brown sugar* |
1 *cup prepared horse-radish* | 1 *teaspoon each, cinnamon, allspice and ginger* |
2 *tablespoons mustard seed* | 1 *tablespoon celery seed*

Peel onions. Remove seeds and stems from peppers. Put all vegetables through food chopper, using coarse blade. Or chop in a wooden bowl. Sprinkle with salt. Let stand in a crock or wooden bowl overnight. Drain well. Add the other ingredients and bring to a quick boil. Turn down heat and simmer 45 minutes, stirring occasionally. Turn into hot sterilized jars and seal.

Yields 12 pints.

Variation: Use 6 pounds green tomatoes, 4 pounds cabbage. Prepare as above. Omit mustard seed and celery seed. Add 1 teaspoon dry mustard and 1 teaspoon turmeric.

OLD-FASHIONED MUSTARD PICKLES

1 *quart large cucumbers, cubed* | 1 *quart gherkins (whole, 1 to 2 inch)* |
1 *quart small white onions, whole* | 1 *quart green tomatoes, cut or
chopped coarse* | 2 *red sweet peppers, chopped fine* |
2 *green sweet peppers, chopped fine* | 1 *large cauliflower, cut into small flowers* |
1 *quart water* | ½ *cup salt* | 6 *tablespoons dry mustard* |
1 *tablespoon turmeric* | 1 *cup flour* | 2 *cups brown sugar (packed tight)* |
2 *quarts cider vinegar*

Rinse the vegetables, drain, and cover with brine solution made of the salt and water. Let stand 24 hours in a crock or glass container. Drain well.

Make a dressing by mixing the mustard, turmeric, flour, sugar and vinegar. Cook over moderate heat till thick. Stir in the pickles, cover and bring to a boil. Fill sterilized glass jars and seal while hot.

Yields 6 quarts.

OLIVE OIL PICKLES

50 *small cucumbers (4-inch)* | 6 *small onions* | 8 *cups vinegar* |
1 *cup water* | 8 *cups sugar* | ¼ *cup whole black pepper* |
½ *cup mustard seed* | ½ *cup celery seed* | 2 *cups olive oil*

Wash and slice cucumbers and onions. Soak overnight in a brine made of 2 pints salt to 2 gallons cold water. Drain, but do not rinse the vegetables. Mix vinegar, water, sugar and spices and boil 1 minute. Add cucumbers and onion. Simmer 5 minutes. Add oil and simmer until cucumbers change colour. Pack hot into jars and seal at once.
Yields 16 pints.

UNCOOKED OLIVE OIL PICKLE SLICES

24 small cucumbers (4-inch) | 3 medium size onions | ¾ cup salt |
½ cup olive oil | 4 cups vinegar | 1 cup mustard seed |
1 tablespoon celery seed

Wash cucumbers. Slice very thin, and sprinkle with salt. Let stand 3 hours in a crock or bowl. Prepare the onions about 15 minutes before rinsing and draining the sliced cucumbers. Combine oil and vinegar, and shake well in a covered jar. Add sliced onions and shake once or twice. Mix this with the sliced cucumbers, add mustard and celery seeds, and turn into hot, sterilized pint jars (zinc top or bail variety). Seal and let stand 2 to 3 weeks before using.
Yields 8 pints.

EMERGENCY RELISH (Uncooked)

8 small white onions | 6 green peppers | 1 red pepper | 6 tart apples |
8 green and 8 red tomatoes, medium size | 1 tablespoon salt |
2 tablespoons sugar | 1 cup vinegar |
¼ teaspoon each celery and mustard seed

Peel onions and dice or chop. Remove seeds and stems from peppers and cut fine or put through food chopper. Grate unpared apples. Cut tomatoes fine or put through food chopper, using coarse blade. Combine all ingredients. Cook salt, sugar, vinegar, 3 minutes and add celery and mustard seed. Combine. Can be used immediately.
Yields approximately 6 pints.

RED RELISH (Uncooked)

1 *quart chopped or diced boiled beets* | 1 *quart finely chopped cabbage* |
1 *cup chopped or diced onion* | 1 *cup grated horse-radish (plain or
beet coloured)* | 2 *cups sugar (brown preferred)* | 1 *teaspoon salt* |
1 *teaspoon celery seed (optional)* | ½ *teaspoon white pepper (optional)* |
Vinegar to cover

Combine chopped or diced ingredients in a large bowl or crock,
add seasonings and enough vinegar to cover the mixture. Stir until
sugar is dissolved and seasonings well distributed. Turn into hot,
sterilized pint jars (zinc or bail tops only), and seal. Can be used in a
few days but flavour improves after a week.

Yields 6 pints.

SENFGURKEN

4 *to* 5 *large yellow cucumbers* | 3 *pints water* | ⅔ *cup salt* |
2 *cups cider vinegar* | 4 *cups water* | ¾ *cup brown sugar*

TO BE ADDED TO EACH JAR

1 *clove garlic* | 2 *teaspoons grated horse-radish* |
1 *teaspoon mustard seed* | 2 *small hot red peppers*

Wash and pare cucumbers. Slice lengthwise into halves. Scoop or
scrape out seed section. Cut into strips 1 inch thick by 2 inches in
length. Cover with brine made of water and salt in above proportions. Let stand in bowl or crock overnight. Drain. Bring vinegar,
water and brown sugar to a boil and add sliced cucumber. Simmer
5 to 8 minutes till tender. Drain and pack sliced cucumber into pint
jars. Add to each jar garlic, horse-radish, mustard seed and hot red
peppers. Bring vinegar syrup to a boil and add to jars, filling to top.
Cover and seal while hot.

Yields approximately 8 pints.

PICKLED WATERMELON RIND 1

8 *pounds watermelon rind, diced* | ½ *cup salt* | 4 *quarts cold water* |
5 *pounds brown sugar* | 1 *quart vinegar* | 3 *sticks cinnamon* |
1 *teaspoon whole cloves* | 1 *pint maraschino cherries*

Trim off the green skin from watermelon rind and cut into small cubes. Soak overnight in brine made of salt and water. In the morning drain and cover with fresh cold water. Cook till tender, and drain. Make a syrup of brown sugar and vinegar, add the rind, spices (tied loosely in a bag) and the cherries. Boil 2 minutes and let stand 6 to 8 hours (or overnight). Bring again to a boil and pour into sterilized jars. Seal while hot.

Yields approximately 8 pints.

PICKLED WATERMELON RIND 2

8 pounds watermelon rind | 1 quart vinegar | 4 pounds sugar |
½ cup mixed whole pickling spices | 4 small sticks cinnamon | Salt

Use thick watermelon rind. Pare away the outer green and inner red portion. Cut into 1-inch cubes or ¼-inch slices. Make a solution of ¼ cup coarse salt to 1 quart cold water, sufficient to cover the cut rind. Let stand overnight and drain. Cover with boiling water and cook till tender enough to pierce with a toothpick. Drain. Boil vinegar, sugar, cinnamon and pickling spice (tied in a muslin bag) 5 minutes. Remove spice bag. Add drained watermelon rind and cook until transparent. Let stand overnight and then bring to boiling point. Pack in hot sterilized jars. Seal at once.

Yields approximately 8 pints.

EASY METHOD PICKLES

FOR EACH JAR

Cucumbers (3 to 3½ inches in size) | 1 tablespoon coarse salt |
1 teaspoon brown sugar | 1 tablespoon vinegar | 3 cloves garlic |
3 bay leaves | Dry dill

Pack cucumbers into quart jars. Add spices to each jar in the amounts listed. Pour into each jar as much boiled water, slightly cooled, as is required to fill to the top. Adjust rubber rings and covers but do not seal. Keep jars at room temperature until fermentation stops and the liquid in jars becomes cloudy. Tighten covers and store in a cool place. Fermentation period is hastened if jars are placed in the sun. Pickles are ready to eat within 10 days.

Variation: For a spicy pickle, add 1 small red hot pepper to each jar and ¼ teaspoon whole mixed spice at top before adding water.

DILL PICKLES (Kosher Style)

50 *medium cucumbers (approximately* 3½ *inches long)* |
3 *quarts pickling solution*

FOR EACH JAR

2 *or* 3 *bay leaves* | ¼ *teaspoon celery or mustard seeds* |
½ *teaspoon whole mixed spice* | 1 *tablespoon vinegar* | 2 *cloves garlic* |
Bunch of dry dill | 2 *vine leaves*

Wash and drain cucumbers and pack into quart jars. To each jar add bay leaves, mustard seeds, mixed whole spice, vinegar and garlic in the quantities listed. Bring pickling solution to a boil and fill packed jars. Top each jar with small bunch of dried dill and vine leaves. Adjust covers and seal at once. Can be used after 8 or 10 days.

Yields approximately 6 to 7 quarts.

SALT DILL PICKLES

10 *pounds cucumbers (* 1 *peck, approximately)* | 4 *quarts water* |
4 *cups salt* | 1 *pound dry dill* | 3 *heads garlic* | ½ *cup whole mixed spice* |
¼ *cup bay leaves* | *Vine leaves*

Wash and drain cucumbers. Arrange in a crock in layers. Bring water and salt to a boil and cool quickly. Add the other ingredients and pour in liquid to cover. (If necessary add more of the brine solution.) Place vine leaves on top, adjust a heavy plate or wood cover to fit inside the crock and place a weight on to hold cucumbers submerged. Skim when scum forms during the fermentation period. When bubbles disappear, the pickles are ready to use – approximately 4 to 5 weeks. Before serving salt pickles, soak them for 1 hour in lukewarm water, drain and chill.

SWEET GHERKINS

After washing tiny gherkins (cucumbers) in plenty of cold water, drain well and place in a glass or glazed crock. Cover with a salt solution – ½ cup salt to 4 quarts water – and let stand, covered with a muslin cloth, for 24 hours. Drain thoroughly, rinse in hot water and drain again or wipe dry with a tea towel.

Make a pickling liquid of 3 pounds brown sugar to 1 quart cider vinegar and bring to the boiling point. Add 2 tablespoons whole mixed spice tied in a muslin bag to the vinegar solution while hot and turn in the dried gherkins. Remove from heat and let gherkins remain in the pickling solution till cold. Turn into pint jars or quart jars placing the gherkins in first as compactly as possible, then adding strained vinegar to cover. Add 1 or 2 bay leaves or a few mustard seeds to each jar if desired. Or, add 1 or 2 hot peppers for variation.

MUSTARD MIXED PICKLES

1 large cauliflower | 2 quarts small green tomatoes | 6 red bell peppers | 12 small gherkins, whole | 1 quart white pickling onions, whole | 1 cup salt

MIXTURE FOR THICKENING

3 tablespoons flour | 3 tablespoons mustard | 1 teaspoon turmeric | 1 cup water | 4 cups vinegar | 2 cups sugar

Cut vegetables into small pieces, leaving onions whole unless larger than 1 inch in diameter. Add salt and cover with cold water. Let stand overnight. Bring to a quick boil and cook 3 minutes. Drain. Prepare the mixture for thickening by making a paste of the first 3 ingredients blended smooth with water. Stir in vinegar and sugar and bring to a boil. Add all the vegetables and simmer 5 to 6 minutes. Pack into hot sterilized jars and seal.

Yields approximately 7 pints.

PICKLED HOT PEPPERS

2- to 3-inch hot red and green peppers | 1 pint cider vinegar | 1 cup tightly packed brown sugar | ¼ teaspoon salt

Wash and drain peppers well. Pierce each with a knitting needle or toothpick. Arrange compactly in pint jars. Bring cider vinegar and brown sugar to a boil. Add salt and stir. Add 1 or 2 cloves of garlic to each jar and pour in enough hot vinegar solution to cover peppers. Seal. Can be used in a few days.

GREEN TOMATO CHILI

24 green tomatoes | 6 large green peppers, chopped |
6 large onions, chopped | 6 small red peppers, chopped |
4 cups cider vinegar | 8 tablespoons brown sugar | 2 teaspoons cinnamon |
2 teaspoons mixed spice | Salt to taste

Wash the tomatoes and dry them. Cut into quarters and run through the food chopper, using the medium cutter. Boil with the other ingredients 30 minutes. Salt to taste after mixture comes to a boil. Seal in pint jars while hot.

Yields 6 pints.

GREEN TOMATO DILL PICKLES

FOR EACH JAR

1½- to 2-inch green tomatoes | 2 bay leaves | 1 teaspoon mixed whole spice |
1 large clove of garlic | 2 small red peppers (elongated, sweet variety) |
Dill (fresh or dried)

PICKLING SOLUTION

4 cups water | 2 cups mild vinegar | ½ cup salt

Wash tomatoes. Remove stems and drain. Pack tightly into quart jars. Fill spaces with quartered tomatoes. Add spices in the amount listed and 2 red peppers to each jar. Place a head of fresh or dried dill on top of each jar. Bring pickling solution to a boil quickly. Pour while hot into filled jars through a small funnel at one side of jar. Seal at once.

Solution fills 6 to 8 quart jars of green tomatoes. However, size of tomatoes and method of packing varies and this can only be approximate quantity.

Note: When jars are filled and sealed, keep at room temperature for 1 week before storing in a cool, dark place. To hasten pickling process, keep jars exposed to the sun. They are ready to use when the liquid in jar becomes slightly cloudy. For long storage, store as soon as cool.

FRUIT PICKLES

PICKLED CRAB APPLES

12 pounds large crab apples | 5 pounds sugar | 3 cups cider vinegar |
2 sticks cinnamon | 1 teaspoon cinnamon drop candy

Use only perfect crab apples, ripe but firm. Wash thoroughly. Do not remove stems. Bring sugar, vinegar and cinnamon sticks to a quick boil, stirring till sugar is dissolved. Add cinnamon drops. Add crab apples and cook over moderate heat 1 hour, pushing fruit down as it rises to the top. Test apples with a fork or toothpick. If not tender, continue cooking 15 to 20 minutes. Lift with a perforated spoon into wide-mouthed jars. Cook syrup 10 minutes after filling jars with fruit. Pour over fruit in jars and seal.

Yields 6 to 8 quarts.

GINGER APPLES

1 quart diced tart apples | 2 cups brown sugar | 1 lemon (rind and juice) |
½ cup orange juice | Ginger root (1-inch piece)

Pare and quarter apples before dicing. Grate rind of lemon and extract juice. Boil sugar and juices 2 minutes, add ginger. Boil 5 minutes and add diced apple. Cook slowly till thick and the apples are golden-brown. Seal in sterilized jars while hot.

Yields 2 pints.

CANTALOUPE PICKLES

1 cantaloupe | 4 cups water | 4 cups sugar | 1 cup vinegar |
1 tablespoon cinnamon | 1 tablespoon allspice | 1 tablespoon cloves

Select under-ripe cantaloupe. Cut into sections and remove rind. Soak for 3 hours in salt solution (4 tablespoons of salt to 1 quart of water). Drain off brine and add the well-drained rind to the pickling syrup compounded by the ingredients itemized above. Boil the rind rapidly in this syrup for 10 minutes. Let stand overnight. Drain the syrup from cantaloupe rind and boil until it coats a spoon. Add cantaloupe rind and cook until clear (about 1 hour). Seal immediately in hot fruit jars.

PICKLED CHERRIES

Wash, stem and remove pits from large sweet cherries. Large sour cherries may be used, but the meatier sweet varieties are best for this purpose. Weigh pitted cherries. Allow ¾ pound sugar to 1 pound fruit. Place a compact layer of cherries in a large bowl or crock, sprinkle generously with sugar and repeat the layers, making the top one sugar. Let stand overnight. In the morning, stir to thoroughly dissolve sugar and drain off the syrup. Boil the syrup until reduced by half. (Mixed whole spices, stick cinnamon and a piece of ginger root may be tied in a muslin bag and cooked with the syrup if desired.) If spices are omitted, add a few rose geranium leaves. Pack cherries into sterilized jars and cover with the hot syrup. If cherries are very sweet and the syrup thick, add 1 tablespoon wine vinegar to each jar before pouring in the syrup. Seal while hot. Store away from strong light. Can be used after 2 weeks.

GRAPE KETCHUP

*6 pounds seedless grapes | 3 teaspoons whole allspice |
1 small stick cinnamon | 2 teaspoons whole cloves | 3 cups vinegar |
3 pounds sugar | ¼ cup brown sugar | 1 tablespoon salt*

Wash and stem grapes. Cook over a slow fire in a covered pot until soft. Rub through a sieve. Tie spices in a muslin bag, add, and cook with the other ingredients 15 to 20 minutes over a slow fire. Pour into hot sterilized jars and seal.

Yields 3½ to 4 pints.

ginger. Combine and simmer 15 minutes. Pour into sterilized glasses. Seal immediately with melted pure paraffin.

Yields approximately four 8-ounce glasses.

DAMSON PLUM CONSERVE

2 quarts Damson plums | 4 cups sugar | ½ teaspoon cinnamon |
2 tablespoons lemon juice | 3 tablespoons orange juice |
½ teaspoon each grated lemon and orange rind |
1 cup chopped English walnuts (or mixed nuts)

Wash plums. Cut into small bits, removing pits. Add the other ingredients except nuts and cook in a covered saucepan approximately 20 minutes or until thick. Stir in chopped nuts and remove from heat. Pack in hot sterilized jelly jars. Cover with a thin layer of melted pure paraffin.

Yields approximately six 6-ounce glasses.

PLUM CONSERVE

5 pounds purple plums | 2 large oranges | 5 pounds sugar |
1 pound seedless raisins | 1 pound English walnuts, chopped

Wash, peel and pit the plums. Remove seeds from oranges and cut pulp into thin pieces. Rinds may be chopped very fine and added to the pot if desired. Add sugar and raisins. Stir carefully and bring mixture to boiling point over moderate heat. Cook until orange peel is tender. Remove from heat and stir in chopped walnuts. Pour into sterlized jelly jars and seal.

Yields approximately 6 pints.

RHUBARB CONSERVE

4 cups finely diced tender rhubarb | 1 orange | 1 lemon | 1 cup water |
3 cups sugar | 1 cup blanched, shredded almonds

Rhubarb need not be peeled. Cut orange and lemon in two, squeeze and reserve juice. Boil the peels in water 5 minutes, discard water
33

and slice the peel very thin or put through a food chopper using the coarse blade. Combine rhubarb, orange and lemon juice and chopped peel. Add sugar and stir to dissolve. Cook rapidly, stirring constantly for 15 to 20 minutes or till thick. Add shredded almonds and boil until thick, approximately 15 minutes. Turn into hot sterilized jars and cover with melted pure paraffin.

Yields four 6-ounce jars.

MARMALADES

Marmalades are made of whole fruit or small pieces of fruit cooked in a syrup until clear and transparent. The shape of the fruit is retained and should be evenly distributed throughout the juice, which is of a jelly-like consistency, though not firm enough to hold its shape when turned out on to a plate.

Marmalades are made of pulpy fruits, usually one, but more than one fruit may be used. The fruit should contain a moderate amount of both pectin and acid to obtain the characteristic jelly-like consistency. One-fourth slightly under-ripe fruit may be used. A basic rule is $\frac{3}{4}$ pound of sugar to 1 pound of fruit for marmalades.

Steps in Making Marmalade

Pick over and clean fruit, then prepare for cooking, usually cut in thin slices or small pieces.

Weigh or measure fruit and sugar. Make 2 or 3 quarts at one time.

Cook fruit until tender and excess liquid is evaporated.

Add sugar and dissolve it, then boil as rapidly as possible without scorching, until done.

Test when done – thick enough to remain in place without spreading on cool plate and the syrup gives the jelly or sheet test (see JELLIES). Skim, partially cool, stir occasionally as it cools to distribute the fruit evenly so that it may remain suspended throughout the mass, not come to the top.

When partially cooled, but not yet thickened, fill containers, seal with hot pure paraffin and lid.

Wipe containers, label, and store in a cool, dry place.

APRICOT AND PINEAPPLE MARMALADE

1 pound dried apricots | 2½ cups canned crushed pineapple |
¾ cup sugar for each cup pulp and juice | 4 tablespoons lemon juice

Soak dried apricots in cold water to cover overnight. Bring to boil slowly and cook 3 minutes. Put through a sieve. Add crushed pineapple and juice. Measure and add ¾ cup sugar for each cupful. Add lemon juice and cook over moderate heat 45 minutes or till thick. Stir frequently during the cooking process.

Yields approximately ten 8-ounce jars.

Variation: Add 1 orange and 1 lemon, put through the food chopper after cutting and removing seeds. Omit lemon juice.

CANTALOUPE AND PEACH MARMALADE

2 cups finely diced cantaloupe | 2 cups diced peeled peaches |
2 oranges, seeded | 1 lemon, seeded | 3 cups sugar

Cook cantaloupe and peaches in a covered saucepan 2 minutes. Put oranges and lemon through food chopper and add to the hot mixture. Stir in sugar and cook over moderate heat until the mixture thickens. Stir frequently to prevent scorching. Fill jars, cover with pure paraffin.

Yields approximately 4 cups.

Variation: To the above add 12 maraschino cherries and juice and proceed as in basic recipe. The cherries may be sliced thin.

CARROT MARMALADE

2 cups thinly sliced lemon | 2 cups shredded carrot, raw |
4 cups water | 4 cups sugar

Combine sliced lemon, carrot and water. Let stand overnight. Cook in a covered saucepan approximately 25 minutes or till carrot bits are tender. Add sugar, stir and cook rapidly until it gives the sheeting test as for jellies. Pour into hot sterilized jars and add a thin layer of melted pure paraffin to cover. When cold, wipe top edges of jars, add more melted pure paraffin, tilting the jars to make a complete seal. Adjust covers, wipe outside of jars and label. Store in a cool, dark place away from possible dampness.

Yields approximately 5 cups.

CITRUS MARMALADE

½ grapefruit | 2 oranges | 1 lemon | 4 cups water | 4 cups sugar

Squeeze juice from fruit and store in the refrigerator. Slice the peel very thin, add water and let stand overnight. Bring slowly to a boil in a covered saucepan and cook over moderate heat 30 minutes or until tender. Add sugar and boil 10 minutes. Add juices and boil the mixture until it gives the sheeting or jelly test, approximately 10 minutes. Pour into hot sterilized jars and add a thin layer of melted pure paraffin to cover. When cold, wipe top edges of jars, add more melted pure paraffin, tilting the jars to make a complete seal. Adjust covers, wipe outside of jars and label. Store in a cool, dark place away from possible dampness.

Yields 6 cups.

TOMATO AND APPLE MARMALADE

*2 pounds ripe red tomatoes | 2 cups diced apples | 1 lemon |
3 cups sugar | 3 tablespoons chopped candied ginger*

Scald and skin tomatoes. Cut, let stand 5 minutes and drain. There should be approximately 2 cupfuls. Put diced apples through food chopper or chop fine. There should be approximately 2 cupfuls of apple. Slice lemon very fine, removing seeds. Combine and cook 15 minutes over moderate heat. Add sugar and cook till thick. Add chopped candied ginger and cook 5 to 10 minutes longer over reduced heat. Stir frequently. Turn into jars and cover with melted pure paraffin.

Yields approximately four 6-ounce jars.

PRESERVES

Preserves, jams, marmalades, conserves and fruit butters are various classes of preserves. All are similar in that they are preserved with enough sugar to form a thick consistency. All are cooked by the open-pot method in much the same way. The main difference between the products is the way the fruit is prepared.

Preserves are made usually of one fruit, but more than one may be used. The fruit is whole or cut into large pieces and cooked in a syrup until clear and transparent, tender, firm and well plumped. The shape of the fruit is retained. The juice is of a thick, syrupy consistency and sufficient to surround the fruit.

In general, ¾ pound of sugar to 1 pound of fruit is used for preserves. Hard fruits, such as pears, quinces, apples and melon rind, may be cooked in water until tender, using the water they are cooked in to make syrup.

Steps in Making Preserves

Sterilize containers and assemble equipment – broad-bottom aluminium or enamel pan or pot, long-handled spoon and a smaller pot.

Sort, pick and clean fruit. Prepare whole or cut into desired pieces for cooking.

Weigh or measure fruit, sugar and liquid. Cook only a small quantity at a time – 2 to 3 quarts.

Sugar down fruit or make a syrup of sugar and liquid (water or fruit juice).

If fruit is sugared down for several hours, bring slowly to boil. If not sugared down, add the fruit to cooled syrup, then bring slowly to boil and boil rapidly (for bright colour, natural flavour and good texture) until done.

Test when done – fruit is clear, tender and retains a heavy coating of thick syrup.

CHESTNUT PRESERVE

3 quarts shelled uncooked chestnuts | Cold water to cover |
½ teaspoon salt | 3 cups sugar | 6 cups honey |
3 cups water | 1 tablespoon vanilla

Bring chestnuts and water to a brisk boil. Reduce heat and simmer 30 minutes or till chestnuts are tender. Drain. Remove brown skins. Sprinkle with salt. Combine sugar, honey and water and cook 10 minutes over moderate heat. Add chestnuts to this syrup and simmer 20 minutes, covered. If more water is necessary, add ¼ cupful at a time. The syrup must not be completely absorbed. Test chestnuts for tenderness. Additional cooking over low heat may be necessary till chestnuts are tender enough to pierce with a toothpick but not cooked apart. Add vanilla and remove from heat. Pack into pint jars and seal while hot.

Yields approximately 8 pints.

SOUR CHERRY PRESERVES

4 cups pitted sour cherries, tightly packed | 3 cups sugar

Let cherries stand for 30 minutes after pitting. The juice will be sufficient in which to cook cherries over moderate heat until tender, approximately 10 minutes. Add sugar, stir well and bring to a boil. Cook 5 minutes. Cover and remove from heat. Let stand 2 to 3 minutes. Stir well and turn into hot sterilized jars. Seal while hot.

Yields three to four 6-ounce jars.

SWEET CHERRY PRESERVES

4 cups pitted cherries, tightly packed | 3 cups sugar

Crush some of the cherries to start the juice flowing. Let stand 5 minutes before bringing to a boil. Cook 10 minutes over moderate heat or till tender. Add sugar, stir well and cook 5 minutes. Cover the hot preserves after removing from heat and let stand 2 minutes. Stir well and turn into hot sterilized jars. Seal.

Yields 3 to 4 cups.

PEACH PRESERVES

4 cups sliced, peeled peaches | ½ cup water | 3 cups sugar

Cook peaches in water 10 minutes or till tender. Add sugar, stir well and cook approximately 10 minutes or till peaches are clear and the syrup thick. Let stand 3 minutes, stir well and turn into hot sterilized jars. Seal.

Yields 4 to 5 cups.

PEAR PRESERVES (Basic Recipe)

4 cups thinly sliced pears | ½ cup water | 3 cups sugar

Bring pears and water to a quick boil. Add sugar, stir and cook
10 minutes or till the pears are clear and the syrup thick. Cover and
let stand 2 minutes. Stir well and turn into hot sterilized jars. Seal.
Yields 4 cups.
Variation: Bring sugar and water to a brisk boil and add 2 tablespoons chopped crystallized ginger. Add pears and cook as in
basic recipe, till clear and thick.

STRAWBERRY PRESERVES (Basic Recipe)

4 cups hulled strawberries | 3 cups sugar

Add sugar to berries and let stand 30 minutes. Bring to a boil,
stirring till sugar is dissolved. Cook 3 to 5 minutes or till berries are
tender. Let stand overnight. Next morning bring the mixture to a
boil and cook 1 minute. Cover preserves and let stand 2 minutes
before stirring and turning into hot sterilized jars. Seal while hot.
Yields 3 cups.
Variation: Cut berries in halves. Add 1 cup canned crushed pineapple that has been well drained. Add sugar and let the mixture
stand 15 minutes. Bring to a boil and cook 10 minutes, stirring
constantly to prevent sticking to the bottom of the pan. Let the
preserves stand, covered, 2 to 3 minutes. Stir and turn into hot
sterilized jars. Seal.
Yields approximately 4 cups.

TOMATO PRESERVES

*5 pounds red or yellow plum tomatoes | 5 pounds sugar |
½ cup lemon juice | ½ cup pineapple juice (canned) |
1 tablespoon ginger or 2 ounces finely cut crystallized ginger*

Scald and skin tomatoes. If tomatoes are small, do not cut them. If
larger ones are used, cut into quarters. Cover with sugar and let
stand overnight. Strain the juice and combine with lemon and

pineapple juices. Bring juices to a boil, add tomatoes and simmer 35 to 45 minutes. Add ginger and cook till syrup is thick enough to drop from a spoon in a single heavy drop. Turn into hot sterilized jars. Cover with a thin layer of melted pure paraffin. Seal.

Yields approximately eight 6-ounce jars.

FRUIT BUTTERS

Fruit butters are smooth, even, fine-grained mixtures of medium soft consistency, without seeds or distinct pieces of fruit and with no juice as a separate liquid. Butters are less sweet than jams, preserves, marmalades or conserves – usually ½ to ⅔ pound sugar to 1 pound of fruit.

Steps in Making Fruit Butters
Pick over and clean fruit (cook small amount at one time – 2 to 3 quarts).

Weigh fruit and sugar.

Chop or cut the larger and harder fruits.

Do not pare.

Cook until tender with very little or no liquid.

Run pulp through sieve to remove seeds and skins. (Pulp left from extraction of juice for jelly may be used.)

Place over heat, bring gently to boil, stirring to prevent scorching. When mixture begins to thicken (sputter), add sugar and thoroughly dissolve it. Then cook as rapidly as possible without scorching, until done.

Fill sterilized containers, seal.

Wipe sealed containers, label and store in a cool, dry place.

APPLE BUTTER

8 pounds apples | 4 cups apple cider or water | 3 cups sugar |
4 tablespoons lemon juice | 1 tablespoon grated lemon rind |
1 tablespoon allspice | 1 tablespoon cinnamon

Select well-flavoured apples for making Apple Butter. Quarter apples without paring. Cover with cider or water and cook over moderate heat till soft. Press through sieve. Add sugar, lemon juice, grated rind and spices. Cook over moderate heat as direct in *Steps in Making Fruit Butters.*

Yields approximately 6 pints.

PEACH BUTTER

10 pounds peaches, sliced unpared | 2 cups cider vinegar or water | Sugar as required | Cinnamon or allspice

Cook over moderate heat till soft. Put through a sieve and measure. To each cup of thick pulp add $\frac{2}{3}$ cup sugar, 1 teaspoon cinnamon or $\frac{1}{2}$ teaspoon allspice. Cook till thick, stirring to prevent scorching.

Yields approximately 6 pints.

COMBINATION FRUIT BUTTERS

Follow basic procedure for preparing pulp, putting through sieve, measuring pulp and adding sugar and spices. Cook as in general directions.

Combinations that please are
Equal parts apple and apricot pulp, allspice – $\frac{1}{2}$ teaspoon per cup.

Equal parts apple and blueberry pulp, allspice – $\frac{1}{2}$ teaspoon per cup.

Equal parts apple and plum pulp, cinnamon – $\frac{1}{2}$ teaspoon per cup.

DRIED APRICOT BUTTER

3 pounds dried apricots | Cold water to cover | Sugar as required | 1 teaspoon cinnamon

Wash apricots in several waters and drain well. Cover with cold water. Let stand overnight. Bring to a boil and simmer 15 minutes or till very soft. Put through a sieve or fruit press. Measure the pulp. For each cupful add a $\frac{1}{2}$ cup sugar. Stir well, add cinnamon. Cook over moderate heat, stirring constantly to prevent scorching. The mixture should be thick in approximately 30 minutes.

Yields approximately 3 pints.

POVIDLE OR PLUM BUTTER (Also called *Lacqua*)

4 pounds purple plums / Sugar – 1 cup for each cup of fruit purée

Wash plums, remove stems and cut into halves. Remove pits. The water that clings to plums will be sufficient moisture in which to cook the fruit over moderate heat until very tender. Put through a sieve. Measure the pulp. Add sugar in equal portions and stir well. Cook over moderate heat, stirring continuously, until the mixture becomes very thick. Povidle is of a denser consistency than the usual fruit butters. It keeps well in glass containers or glazed crocks, covered with muslin.

Povidle is used for filling Purim Hamantashen as well as in making other filled small cakes and cookies.

Yield depends on the ripeness of fruit and length of cooking. 4 pounds of purple plums should yield about 3 pints of Povidle.

34 Quick Frozen Foods in the Home

If you grow your own or can buy fresh fruits and vegetables cheaply during the height of their season, it will be to your advantage to preserve them by the *Quick Freeze Method*. Quick frozen foods have come to stay. They are practical. They rate high in palatability and vitamin content because they can be preserved at just the right moment of their tender ripeness.

Another point in favour of quick frozen foods is that they can be prepared in a minimum of time with a minimum of effort. Storage space is reduced. Automatic refrigerators are being equipped with quick frozen food compartments and special freezer cabinets are on the market that will fit into the average kitchen or pantry.

There are a few basic rules for *home freezing of foods:*

Freeze firm, well-ripened fruits and tender vegetables.

If foods must be kept for a day after picking, keep them as cool as possible before freezing.

Select the proper type of freezer carton or wrapping required for the special food product to be frozen. Various types of containers are on the market. Plastic containers to hold small quantities come with covers and do not require other moisture-proof wrapping.

Label each container indicating contents, date packed, and your name and locker number if stored outside your home.

PACKAGING FOR THE FREEZER

Packing Fruits in Dry Sugar: Mix fruit and sugar until all sugar is dissolved and sufficient syrup formed to cover fruit when packed. If necessary press fruit down in package until syrup covers the fruit.

Packing in Syrup: Leave 1 inch head space.

Citric Acid Solution: ¼ teaspoon citric acid dissolved in 1 quart water, to be used only when recommended to prevent discoloration. Or, *Ascorbic Acid Solution:* ¼ teaspoon to each 1 to 1½ cups syrup.

THAWING FROZEN FRUITS

Thaw only enough for immediate use, cutting package of frozen fruit in half or in thirds. Keep unused part wrapped and frozen. Thaw fruit on the refrigerator shelf, allowing 6 to 8 hours for 1 pound package. Allow 2 to 3 hours at room temperature. To thaw fruit quickly, place package in cool running water 30 minutes to 1 hour.

Serve berries while they still contain a few ice crystals. DO NOT REFREEZE fruits after thawing. Cook first then store in refrigerator.

AVAILABLE QUICK FROZEN COOKED FOODS

The list of prepared foods that require only a minimum of 'finishing' in the home kitchen is steadily growing. Customary Jewish items are increasing in number.

To be sure that food is prepared under strict observance of Jewish Dietary Laws, see that it carries the stamp of the London Beth Din or of a recognized Rabbinate. If in doubt, consult your own Rabbi. For preparation, follow directions on the package.

HOME FREEZING DIRECTIONS

Syrup is made by stirring sugar in boiling water till dissolved.

$$30\% - 1 \text{ quart water to 2 cups sugar}$$
$$40\% - 1 \text{ quart water to 3 cups sugar}$$
$$50\% - 1 \text{ quart water to 4 cups sugar}$$

HOME FREEZING OF FRUITS

Fruit	Preparation	Syrup or Sugar Pack
Apples	Pare, core, cut in sections of uniform size. Steam or scald 1½ to 2 minutes. If syrup is to be used, slice apples directly into it.	Pack by weight – 1 part sugar to 3 or 4 parts fruit. Or 40–50% syrup to cover.

Fruit	Preparation	Syrup or Sugar Pack
Apricots	Blanch, halve, pit and cut into sections. To prevent discoloration dip 1 to 2 minutes in citric acid solution. $\frac{1}{4}$ teaspoon citric acid to 1 quart water. Or, add $\frac{1}{4}$ teaspoon ascorbic acid to each cup syrup.	Cover with 40% syrup.
Berries (except Strawberries or Raspberries)	Stem, wash, handle lightly. Remove hulls without crushing.	Cover with 40–50% syrup. Mix lightly.
Cherries, Sour, pitted	Wash and chill.	1 pound sugar to 3–4 pounds, or cover with 40% syrup.
Sweet, whole or pitted	Wash and chill.	Pack like sour cherries.
Cranberries	Stem, wash, drain.	50% syrup to cover.
Grapes, ripe, firm	Stem and wash.	40–50% syrup to cover.
Melons, ripe, firm	Pare, cube or cut in balls.	Cover with 40% syrup, or 1 pound sugar to 5 pounds fruit.
Nectarines	See Apricots.	
Peaches	See Apricots.	
Pears, firm, mature	See Apples	
Pineapple, matured	Pare, remove eyes, cut away core, cube or slice.	Cover with 40% syrup.
Plums	Sort, wash, halve and pit.	Cover with 40–50% syrup. Add $\frac{1}{4}$ teaspoon ascorbic acid to each cup of syrup.
Strawberries, Red Raspberries	Sort, hull, wash, drain. Pack whole or slice.	40% syrup to cover, or 1 cup sugar to 5–6 cups berries.

HOME FREEZING OF VEGETABLES

Vegetable	Preparation	Blanching* Time (Use Boiling Water)	
Asparagus tips	Wash, drain	Small size	2 min.
		Large size	3 min.
Green Beans, cut or sliced long	Wash, drain.		2½ min.
Green Limas or white	Wash, drain.	Small size	2 min.
		Large size	3 min.
Broccoli	Remove large leaves and stalks. Wash well and soak heads down in salted water. Cut into 2½-inch widths.		4 min.
Cauliflower, white, compact	Break into flowerettes 1 inch across. Wash, drain.		3 min.
Corn-on-Cob, fresh, tender	Husk, remove silk and trim ends.	Under 2 ins. in diam.	5 min.
		2 ins. or over	7 min.
Eggplant, mature, tender (but not soft)	Peel and slice. Cover with hot citric acid solution – ¼ tsp. citric acid to 1 quart water. Drain. Chill.		4 min.
Mushrooms, white	Wash, trim, sort according to size.	Small	3 min.
		Large	4–5 min.
Peas, tender	Shell, sort sizes.		1 min.
Soybeans, green, young	Pre-cook in pods 5 min. Chill. Shell.	No blanching required.	

Packing: In cartons or bags – when packed without liquid, leave ½ inch head space for vegetables that pack tightly such as peas and beans. No head space is needed for vegetables that pack loosely such as broccoli, cauliflower.

* *Blanching:* To blanch, place a wire basket or colander containing the vegetables into a pot or bowl and submerge in boiling water for time indicated.

For altitudes of 5,000 feet or over, blanch vegetables 1 minute longer.

COOKING FROZEN VEGETABLES

Cook frozen vegetables like fresh ones, except that less time is required for cooking. Use as little water as possible and cook rapidly until just tender. Most vegetables can be cooked without thawing. Bring lightly salted water to a boil, add frozen vegetables, cover. Bring to a boil and cook only as indicated in the chart. Start counting cooking time after bringing to a boil.

APPROXIMATE TIME CHART

Asparagus	7 minutes
Beans, green	12–15 minutes
Beans, lima	7–15 minutes
Broccoli	7 minutes
Cauliflower	5 minutes
Corn-on-Cob	5 minutes
Peas	7 minutes
Soybeans	10–15 minutes

Note: Consult book of instructions that comes with your particular freezer cabinet for information on freezing as well as cooking quick frozen vegetables.

GUIDE FOR BOTTLING FRUITS

Fruits bottled sliced or whole lose little of their original flavour and practically none of their rich food content. In many cases, the natural syrups added in the bottling process greatly enhance the nutritive values of the fresh fruits. See page 508 for *Sugar Syrup for Bottling Fruit.*

Product	Yield		Preparation	In Boiling-Water Bath	Pressure Cooker
	Raw	Bottled			
Apples	1 bushel	20–25 qts.	Pare, core, quarter or slice. Steam or precook in thin boiling syrup 5 minutes. Pack in jars and cover with thin syrup, boiling hot. Process at once.	20 min.	10 min. at 5 lbs. pressure
Green Apples			Windfall or green apples may be made into sauce. Pack boiling hot and process immediately.	5 min.	5 min. at 5 lbs. pressure
Apricots	20 lbs.	12 qts.	Wash, halve, pit, pack in jars and cover with thin syrup, boiling hot. Process immediately.	20 min.	10 min. at 5 lbs. pressure
Berries: Blackberries Blueberries (*See* Strawberries)	22 lbs.	12 qts.	Pick over, wash, drain, hull. Pack in jars and cover with syrup, boiling hot. Process. To prevent floating of berries because of shrinkage, precook before filling containers. Boil with sugar 3 to 4 minutes, allowing $\frac{1}{4}$ to $\frac{1}{2}$ lb. sugar per pound of berries. Pack boiling hot and process same as above.	20 min.	10 min. at 5 lbs. pressure
Cherries: With pits Pitted	15–20 lbs. 60–80 lbs.	10 qts. 20 qts.	Wash, stem, pit or prick with a pin. Pack into jars and cover with medium or heavy syrup, boiling hot. Process at once. *Or,* add sugar to cherries as needed and boil 2 minutes. Pack boiling hot and process at once.	25 min. 10 min.	10 min. at 5 lbs. pressure 10 min. at 5 lbs. pressure

SPICED GRAPES

10 pounds stemmed grapes | 8 cups sugar | 2 cups vinegar |
1 teaspoon each nutmeg, ginger, cinnamon |
½ teaspoon ground cloves (optional)

Use Tokay grapes, cut in halves and with seeds removed. Boil sugar,
vinegar and spices 5 minutes. Add grapes and cook until thick. Turn
into hot sterilized jars and seal.
  Yields 8 to 10 pints.

PICKLED GOOSEBERRIES

6 pounds gooseberries | 6 pounds sugar | 1 pint vinegar

Remove blossom points from gooseberries. Add half the amount of
sugar listed and stir in vinegar. Cook over moderate heat 20
minutes. Add remainder of sugar and cook 20 to 25 minutes. Seal in
pint jars while hot.
  Yields approximately 6 pints.

SPICED CITRON MELON

Two 5- to 5½-pound citron melons | Water to cover | 8 cups sugar |
4 cups cider vinegar | 2 cups water | 2 tablespoons whole spice |
Four 3-inch sticks cinnamon

Cut melon and remove seeds. Pare and dice. Cover with water and
bring to a boil. Simmer 30 minutes. Drain. Make a syrup of sugar,
vinegar and water, adding spices and cinnamon tied in a bag. Add
melon and cook 10 to 15 minutes over moderate heat. Let stand in
syrup overnight. Drain. Pack into sterilized jars. Bring syrup to a
quick boil. Pour into packed jars to overflowing. Adjust covers and
process in boiling water 30 minutes. Tighten covers to complete
seal.
  Yields 4 to 5 pints.
  32

PICKLED PEACHES

18 medium size clingstone peaches | 36 whole cloves | 2 cups sugar |
2 cups cider vinegar | 3 sticks cinnamon

Blanch and peel peaches. Stick 2 cloves into each. Cook sugar,
vinegar and stick cinnamon in a large pot, dropping in the peaches
one at a time as soon as the syrup begins to boil. Boil slowly 10
minutes. Pack in hot sterilized quart jars. Add syrup to within ½
inch of top. Seal.
Yields 2 quarts.

SPICED PEACHES

3 pounds clingstone peaches, under-ripe | Water | 1 cup sugar |
¾ cup cider vinegar | 1 teaspoon whole mixed spice | 3 bay leaves |
Stick cinnamon | Cloves (as desired)

Pare peaches and insert 2 or 3 whole cloves in each. Add enough
cold water to come half-way up the side of pot in which they are to
be cooked. Bring to a boil quickly, then turn down heat and cook,
covered, till tender enough to pierce with a toothpick. The liquid
should be reduced by half. Add sugar, vinegar, bay leaves, and stick
cinnamon and the whole mixed spice tied in a piece of cheese-cloth.
Bring to a quick boil and cook 3 to 5 minutes, uncovered. Turn into
wide-mouthed glass jars. Seal while hot.
Yields 2 to 3 pints.

GINGER PEARS

8 pounds semi-ripe pears | 4 lemons |
½ pound preserved ginger or crystallized ginger | 4 pounds sugar

Pare and core pears. Cut into thin slices or dice. Cut ginger into
tiny bits. Cut lemons, remove seeds and extract juice. Put rinds
through food chopper. Combine all ingredients and let stand overnight. Simmer over low heat until thick and the fruit clear. Turn
into sterilized jars and seal while hot.
Yields 4 quarts.

SPICED PLUMS

8 *pounds firm-meated purple plums | 7 cups sugar | 2 cups vinegar |*
1 teaspoon nutmeg | 1 small stick cinnamon | 1 tablespoon whole allspice

Pierce plums with knitting needle. Boil sugar, vinegar, and spices tied in a muslin bag, 5 minutes. Cool. Add plums and simmer 5 minutes or until heated through. Let stand overnight. Cook 15 minutes over low heat or until plums are tender. Pack in hot sterilized jars and seal.
Yields 8 to 10 quarts.

SPICED SECKEL PEARS

5 *to 6 pounds Seckel pears | 1 pint vinegar | 1 cup water |*
3 pounds light brown sugar | Stick cinnamon | Whole mixed spice

Select small, hard Seckel pears. Pare and remove blossom end, leaving stems on. Parboil 10 minutes in water to barely cover. Drain. Make a syrup of vinegar, water and sugar. Cook till thick. Add a small bag of stick cinnamon and whole mixed spice to taste, if desired. Lift out bag of spices after 5 minutes of rapid boiling. Add well-drained cooked pears. Cook 10 to 15 minutes over moderate heat and turn into hot sterilized jars. Seal while hot.
Yields approximately 1 pint for each pound of pears.

RELISHES FOR IMMEDIATE USE

BEET RELISH

2 *cups cooked diced beets | 1 cup finely cut celery | 1 cup shredded cabbage |*
¾ *cup mild vinegar, or 1 cup lemon juice | 3 tablespoons brown sugar |*
½ *teaspoon salt | 1 tablespoon each prepared horse-radish and salad dressing |*
¼ *teaspoon ginger (optional)*

Prepare vegetables. Bring vinegar and brown sugar to a boil. Add the other ingredients, stir well with a wooden spoon. Cover and let stand 5 minutes. Chill before serving.

PICKLED BEET RELISH

Chop pickled beets. Add 1 tablespoon prepared horse-radish to each cupful. Add lemon juice and brown sugar to taste. Let stand a ½ hour before serving.

CABBAGE AND GREEN PEPPER HASH

*1 sweet red pepper | 2 green peppers | 1 tablespoon onion juice |
2 cups shredded cabbage | ¾ cup vinegar | Brown sugar to taste |
1 teaspoon salt | 1 teaspoon whole mixed spice | 1 clove garlic*

Hold peppers near flame to blister skins. Plunge into cold water. Remove skins, seeds and stems. Chop or shred and combine with onion juice and cabbage. Bring vinegar, sugar and salt to a boil. Add spice and garlic. Cover till cold. Strain over vegetables. Chill before serving.

CARROT AND GREEN PEPPER RELISH

*½ cup vinegar | 2 tablespoons brown sugar | 1 tablespoon onion juice |
Dash of salt | 1 cup shredded raw carrot |
½ cup chopped green pepper | 3 tablespoons salad oil*

Bring vinegar and sugar to a quick boil. Add onion juice and salt. Add to chopped pepper and carrot. Mix well and stir in salad oil as soon as cold. Chill before serving.

CORN AND PEPPER RELISH

*2 cups cooked corn (cut from cob) | 2 large green peppers | ½ cup vinegar |
2 tablespoons brown sugar | ¼ cup water | ¼ teaspoon salt |
1 tablespoon onion juice | ¼ teaspoon each celery and mustard seed*

Canned corn, whole kernels, may be used. Chop green peppers or dice very fine. Boil vinegar, sugar, water, salt, and onion juice 2 minutes. Add the other ingredients and let stand in a glass jar or bowl till cool. Chill before serving.

CRANBERRY AND APPLE RELISH

*3 tart apples, unpared | 1 orange | 2 cups cranberries |
1½ cups sugar | ⅛ teaspoon salt*

Cut apples in halves and remove cores. Remove seeds from orange.
Put all fruits through coarse blade of food chopper. Add salt and
sugar, mix well and let stand about half an hour before serving.
Variation: Make it *Cranberry and Orange Relish* by substituting 2
    oranges for apples. Add 2 tablespoons mayonnaise before
    serving.

DELHI RELISH

*1 large Spanish onion | 8 boiled potatoes | 1 large green pepper |
3 tablespoons fresh dill or parsley | 4 tablespoons lemon juice or vinegar |
1 tablespoon brown sugar | ¼ teaspoon salt*

Skin onion. Remove seeds and stem from pepper. Dice or slice boiled
potatoes, onion and pepper. Combine with the other ingredients and
chill before serving.

CANNED RELISHES

CELERY RELISH

*4 sweet red peppers | 4 sweet green peppers | 2 quarts chopped celery |
2 cups chopped white onions | 2 cups shredded cabbage |
1 tablespoon salt | 3 cups vinegar | 2 cups sugar |
1 tablespoon mustard seed | 3 cloves garlic*

Remove seeds and stems from peppers. Chop or cut fine. Bring all
the vegetables to a boil in enough water to cover. Add all seasonings,
vinegar and sugar. Cook slowly 20 minutes or until celery is tender.
Remove garlic and turn into hot sterilized jars. Seal while hot.
    Yields approximately 3 pints.
    Note: If a toothpick is used to spear garlic cloves, it will be easy to
identify and remove.

CRANBERRY RELISH

2½ pounds cranberries | Vinegar to cover | 2¾ cups sugar |
1 tablespoon cinnamon | 1 teaspoon cloves (optional)

Cook the cranberries in enough vinegar to cover. Let boil till the
berries burst. Put through a sieve. Add the other ingredients and
bring to a boil. Reduce heat and simmer until thick. Stir occasionally.
Process should not take more than 1½ hours. Seal in hot sterilized
6-ounce jelly glasses.

Yields 4 to 5 glasses.

CUCUMBER RELISH

12 large cucumbers | 6 green peppers | 3 large onions | ½ cup salt |
1 cup horse-radish | 1 cup sugar | 1 tablespoon mustard seed |
1 teaspoon celery seed | Vinegar

Peel and remove the seeds from the cucumbers. Put the cucumbers,
green peppers and sliced onions through coarse food chopper or chop
in a large wooden bowl. Add the salt, mix well and let stand overnight. In the morning, drain, add the horse-radish, sugar, mustard
and celery seeds and enough vinegar to cover. Mix thoroughly and
pack in sterilized pint jars. Seal at once. Makes a mild relish.

Yields 4 to 5 pints.

RHUBARB RELISH (New England Style)

2 quarts diced rhubarb | 1 quart chopped white onions |
4 cups brown sugar | 1 cup cider vinegar | 2 teaspoons salt |
1 large clove garlic | 1 tablespoon each cinnamon, ginger |
1 tablespoon whole spices

Do not skin rhubarb but cut into ½-inch slices up to 2 inches below
leaves. Tie spices and garlic in a muslin bag. Cook all ingredients
together till rhubarb is tender but not cooked apart. Turn into hot
sterilized jars and seal.

Yields approximately 3 pints.

TOMATO RELISH

*12 firm green tomatoes | 4 sweet red peppers | 2 green peppers |
2 cups cider vinegar | 1½ cups brown sugar | 1 tablespoon salt |
½ cup prepared mustard*

Dice tomatoes. Remove seeds and stems from peppers, cut or chop.
Bring vinegar and sugar to a boil, add salt and mustard and pour
over the vegetable mixture. Bring to a quick boil, turn down heat
and simmer 20 to 30 minutes. Stir occasionally. Turn into hot
sterilized jars and seal.

Yields 4 pints.

RELISH SAUCES

KETCHUP (Early American)

*1 peck ripe tomatoes | 2 cups vinegar | 2 tablespoons salt |
2 teaspoons pepper | 1 teaspoon allspice | 1 teaspoon cloves | 1 clove garlic*

Wash tomatoes, scald and remove skins. Put through a wire sieve.
Strain through a jelly bag. Use the pulp for ketchup and save the
juice for other purposes. Add vinegar to the pulp, season with salt,
pepper, allspice and cloves. Crush the garlic and add to the mixture.
Turn into sterilized bottles and seal. This method of ketchup making
retains the taste of fresh tomatoes and can be used to flavour soups
and sauces.

Yields 4 quarts or 8 pints.

HINTS ON HOME BOTTLING

Successful home bottling depends largely upon the efficiency and type of equipment used, as well as following the correct methods. Bottling equipment need not be elaborate or expensive. It should be easy to handle, of convenient size, serviceable, light in weight, and easy to clean.

All vegetables other than rhubarb and tomatoes are referred to as *low-acid* vegetables. If not properly bottled, low-acid vegetables are more frequently subject to spoilage than fruits.

Use pint jars for bottling low-acid vegetables in a pressure cooker. Consult the directions which accompany your type of pressure bottler for processing time.

TYPES OF BOTTLERS

The type of bottler used depends upon the product to be bottled. A large preserving pan can be used for preserves, conserves, marmalades, and jams, since these require cooking in an open vessel. For fruits and vegetables, another type of bottler is necessary.

HOT WATER BATH

This may consist of any container which can be fitted with a suitable rack for holding jars and which allows for a free circulation of boiling water under and around the jars. It should be equipped with a tight-fitting lid, and the container should be deep enough to permit 1 inch of water to cover the jars. The commercial Water-Bath Canner is fitted with a wire rack, and equipped with handles for lifting the jars in and out of boiling water. In a Hot-Water Bath Canner the product is processed at boiling temperature.

STEAM PRESSURE COOKER

Recommended for processing low-acid vegetables and meats, the Steam Pressure Cooker is a vessel especially designed for obtaining temperatures higher than can be reached in the hot-water bath. It consists of an aluminium vessel with a tight-fitting cover, equipped with a petcock, safety valve, and pressure gauge. The reading of the pressure gauge is affected by altitude. The pressure and time specified for processing apply from seal level to 2,000 feet. One additional pound of pressure should be added for each additional 2,000 feet elevation.

CONTAINERS

In selecting a container, be sure to select a jar that gives a perfect seal, is easy to clean, easy to pack, easy to open, and of a practical size for your family. Select a standard jar for which you can get new lids. There are several good types of jars on the market with glass top, screw top, or automatic seals.

FOOD SPOILAGE

Natural decay of fruits and vegetables can be prevented only by prompt bottling.

Home economic experts in the government laboratories make it a rule to can all products the day they are gathered from the garden.

The second great cause of food spoilage is a hidden one – the microscopic bacteria which are always in the air and water about us. Bacteria can be killed only by heat. Thus, the high temperatures applied to fruits and vegetables in the bottling processes are the most essential step in food preservation.

But it is not enough merely to destroy these tiny, dangerous organisms. After the killing application of heat the foodstuffs must be tightly sealed and not exposed to the air again until opened for consumption.

FERMENTATION

This type of spoilage is caused by yeast plants which form gas bubbles in the jar. The product is usually soft, sour, discoloured, and has an offensive odour.

TO PREVENT FERMENTATION

Have the packed jar for processing free from air bubbles and leakage.

Process the right length of time at the right temperature.

Have a perfect seal.

BOTULINUS

The growth of this organism in food produces a poisonous product which often proves fatal to the consumer of such food.

Its resistance to heat makes bottling of low-acid vegetables safer when bottled in the pressure cooker. In acid foods the organism is destroyed at a comparatively low temperature. This type of spoilage is not easily detected; thus, it is a safeguard to *boil for 10 minutes all low-acid bottled food before eating*.

TEMPERATURES

In killing bacteria by heat, both the degree of temperature and the length of time it is applied must be considered. A very high temperature may produce a sterile product that will keep well, but this may be at too great a sacrifice of flavour and texture. Therefore the *temperature applied should ordinarily be the lowest necessary to accomplish the desired result*, varying with the acidity and other conditions of the food.

No growing or vegetative forms of bacteria will survive for any length of time at the temperature of boiling water (212° F.); but the spore form is killed at boiling temperature only by long continued heating, especially if the fruit or vegetable has juice that is nearly neutral or only very slightly acid.

When the juices are acid, as in fruits and tomatoes, both the vegetative and spore forms of bacteria are killed more quickly at the temperature of boiling water. The bacteria that require long continued heating at boiling temperature may be killed quickly at higher temperatures, such as are obtained in a pressure cooker.

BOTTLING IN JARS

Before bottling in jars, carefully examine the jars to see that the screw tops fit, that there are no nicks or chips around the rim of the glass, and that the bails are tight.

To detect nicks, rough spots, or dents, run the finger around the top of the jar and the edge of the lid. Use a file to remove rough bits of glass and discard all jars that are not in perfect condition.

To detect loose or bent screw-top lids, tap the lid with the finger, or shake. If the lid rattles, press down in the centre with the thumb. Screw the lid on the jar without the rubber. A good top should not permit the thumb nail or a knife to be inserted. If the edge of the lid is bent, lay it flat on the table and straighten with a hammer or heavy knife.

To determine the tightness of the bail on glass-top jars, place the lid on the jar without the rubber. The bail should go into position with a snap. If it does not, tighten by bending the bail in the centre. If the bail around the jar is loose, tighten with pliers.

Test for leakage by filling the jar with water, placing the rubber, tightening the lid and inverting.

Always use new rubbers. A rubber should be pliable, one-twelfth of an inch thick and should be wide enough to come beyond the jar rim. It should be free from spongy or porous places and should stand boiling. It is good if it returns to its original size after being stretched and does not crack when folded or pressed between the fingers.

GENERAL DIRECTIONS FOR BOTTLING
LOW-ACID VEGETABLES

Have plenty of boiling water ready before starting to bottle. Prepare vegetables to be bottled as directed in the accompanying chart. Blanch freshly gathered vegetables by plunging them into boiling salted water to cover, then bring the water to a full rolling boil. Pack the hot vegetable loosely in the jar to within $\frac{1}{2}$ inch of top. Cover the vegetable with boiling liquid and add salt as required. Use a silver knife blade to work out bubbles in the jar. Wipe sealing surfaces of jars with a clean cloth. Cover and seal jars as directed for the type of jar and cover used. Place each filled container in the pressure canner for processing. Make certain the petcock is open and that a steady flow of steam escapes for 7 minutes before petcock is closed. Start counting processing time when pressure reaches recommended point for product. Keep the pressure steady as a sudden drop causes loss of liquid in the jars.

In the boiling-water bath, count time from the instant the water returns to the boiling point after jars have been placed in the bath.

Allow full time listed in the Chart for both methods of bottling.

Remove jars when processing time has been completed. In the *pressure canner*, when the gauge registers zero, allow the cooker to stand 2 minutes then slowly open the petcock before loosening the cover. In the *boiling-water bath*, jars may be removed immediately.

Let jars stand away from drafts, preferably on racks or boards, or on several layers of paper or towel. A cold surface may cause jars to crack. Invert jars to make certain there are no leaks.

Store in a cool, dry, dark place.

SUGAR SYRUP FOR BOTTLING FRUIT

Kind of Syrup	Amount of Sugar	Amount of Water
Light	1 cup	3¼ cups
Moderately light	1 cup	2 cups
Medium	1 cup	1⅓ cups
Moderately heavy	1 cup	⅞ cup
Heavy	1 cup	½ cup

To make the syrup, boil sugar and water approximately 5 minutes. Remove scum that forms on top. Pour syrup boiling hot over fruit packed in jars. Allow approximately ¾ cup to 1 cup syrup for each pint of fruit after it is packed in jars.

SUGAR SUBSTITUTES FOR BOTTLING

FOR A LIGHT SYRUP FOR FRUITS

1 cup honey with 1 cup sugar equals 2 cups sugar |
1 cup corn syrup with 2 cups sugar equals 3 cups sugar

FOR JELLIES

1 cup honey with 1 cup sugar equals 2 cups sugar
1 cup dark or light corn syrup with 2 cups sugar equals 3 cups sugar |
When using substitutions for sugar, cook jelly a little beyond usual
time allotment

FOR BUTTERS, JAMS, CONSERVES AND PRESERVES

Substitute equal weight of corn syrup or honey for half the sugar in
recipe when measuring pound weight of fruit and sugar |
1 pound sugar equals 2 cups | 1 pound corn syrup or honey equals 1⅓ cups |
When using substitutions for sugar, cook a little beyond the usual
time allotment

Note: See pages 528–31 for guides to bottling fruits and vegetables.

33 Jellies and Jams

JELLIES

A good jelly is clear, sparkling, free from sediment or crystals, is of a tender texture and has the natural colour and flavour of fresh fruit. When turned from the glass, it is firm enough to hold its shape, but quivers, and is tender enough to cut or break easily, leaving a clean, clear, sharp cleavage.

Essentials for a Good Jelly

Fruit juice containing both pectin and acid in the right proportion.
Sugar in the right proportion to pectin and acid.
Proper cooking.
Proper equipment and containers.
Not all fruit juices can be made into good jelly nor is the juice of a given fruit identical in strength year after year. This makes it difficult to have a set rule or recipe for making jelly.

CHART FOR MAKING JELLIES

Fruit	Water per Pound of Fruit	Approximate Boiling Time	Sugar per Cup of Juice
Apples	1 cup	20 minutes	¾ cup
Crab Apples	1 cup	20–25 minutes	1 cup
Blackberries	When ripe, none	5–10 minutes	¾ to 1 cup
Black Raspberries	When ripe, none	5–10 minutes	¾ to 1 cup
Currants	¼ cup, approx.	5–10 minutes	1 cup
Grapes	¼ cup, approx.	5–10 minutes	¾ to 1 cup
Plums, Purple	½ cup, approx.	15–20 minutes	¾ cup
Quince	2 cups, approx.	20–25 minutes	¾ to 1 cup
Raspberries	When ripe, none	5–10 minutes	1 cup

Variations:

Apple Jelly, Mint Flavoured – add a few drops peppermint extract and a few drops of green colouring after jelly stage is reached.

Crab Apple, Spiced – tie in a bag two 1-inch sticks cinnamon and
6 to 8 cloves for each 8 pounds fruit. Cook with sugar and fruit
juice.

In general, the juice of slightly under-ripe fruit contains more
pectin and acid but is lacking somewhat in flavour. Ripe fruit gives
the best flavour. It is often advisable to use about ¾ ripe and ¼ slightly
under-ripe fruit. If over-ripe fruit is used 1 tablespoon of lemon
juice to each cup of fruit juice is advisable.

Juice of fruits difficult to make into good jelly because of in-
sufficient acid or pectin or both, can be made into good jelly by
combining with an equal quantity of a juice rich in the substance
lacking; for example, blueberries are rich in pectin but lacking in
acid, and should be combined with tart apples or some other tart
fruit juice. Tart apple juice is usually used because it is rich in both
acid and pectin and affects the colour and flavour least.

Commercial pectin today is made from apple pulp after the juice
has been removed, or from the white inner peel of citrus fruits that
are rich in it.

Test for Jelly Stage can be made as follows: Drop 1 teaspoon jelly
on a saucer. If it sheets from the spoon, that is, drops in one mass, the
jelly stage has been reached. This occurs at about 220° to 222° F.

Filling of Jelly Jars: Sterilize jars by filling them ¾ full with cold
water and place them in a container of cold water. Place the covers
in the container. Bring to a boil. Remove from heat. Use a pair of
tongs for lifting out jars and covers. Invert to drain on a rack. Pour
jelly into jars while hot, filling within ¼ inch of top.

Pure Paraffin from the chemist, melted in a small pitcher over
boiling water, is easier to pour on top of jelly as soon as cold and set.

JAMS

Jams are usually made of one fruit. The whole small fruits or small
pieces of larger fruit are crushed or jammed together into a mass of
an even, soft consistency thick enough to spread and easily divided
into portions with a spoon. The fruit is evenly mixed with the juice
which is not separated from the fruit and is of a jelly-like consistency.

In general a little less sugar can be used for jams than for preserves – from ½ to ¾ pound of sugar to 1 pound of fruit. About ¼
under-ripe fruit may be used in jams to obtain pectin.

Steps in Making Jam
Prepare and measure fruit. Slightly crush a part of it. Place in a pot over moderate heat.

Bring slowly to boiling, adding none or very little water. When mixture begins to thicken, add sugar, thoroughly dissolve it, then cook as rapidly as possible without scorching until done. Test when done – fruit remains heaped on the spoon or thick enough to remain in place without spreading when tested on a plate. The juice will give the sheet jelly test and should not separate from fruit when cooled.

Skim, partially cool, stir occasionally to prevent froth.

Fill containers and seal with hot paraffin and lids.

Wipe containers, label and store in a cool, dry place.

KUMQUAT JAM

Slice the kumquats. Cook until tender in just enough water to keep from burning. Measure. Add equal parts of sugar with a little lemon juice. Cook all together until the consistency of jelly. Seal in small fruit jars.

CONSERVES

Conserves are a jam-like product made of two or more fruits. They may or may not contain nuts or raisins. They are made of very small whole fruit or fruit cut into small pieces, cooked until crushed or jammed together into a mixture of an even, soft consistency. The liquid is slightly jelly-like in character. The name and flavour of the conserve is that of the dominant fruit.

Steps in Making Conserves
Pick over and clean fruit.

Weigh or measure fruit and sugar. Cut fine or put the harder fruits through a food chopper. Slightly crush softer fruits to start juice. Make only a small quantity at a time – 2 to 3 quarts.

Place in pot and heat slowly to start juice, then bring to a boil, add little or no water.

When mixture begins to thicken, add sugar, dissolve thoroughly, then cook rapidly; stir to prevent scorching.

If nuts are added, add just before removing from fire. (Almonds should be blanched and English walnuts dipped in boiling water to freshen.)

Test when done, same as for jam. The fruit remains in a mound in spoon and the juice gives the jelly test and does not separate from the fruit when cooled.

Skim, partially cool, stir occasionally.

Fill containers and seal with hot paraffin and lids.

Wipe containers, label and store in cool, dry place.

APRICOT CONSERVE

2 pounds fresh apricots | 1 cup light raisins |
1 cup blanched, shredded almonds | Sugar to equal by weight

Cut apricots in halves and remove pits. Crack 6 pits and add the kernels to almonds, after blanching and shredding. Combine apricots, raisins and nuts and weigh the mixture. Add an equal amount of sugar, stir well and cook in a saucepan over moderate heat until thick. Stir frequently to prevent scorching. Turn into hot sterilized jelly glasses, cover with melted pure paraffin and cover when cold.

Yields approximately eight 6-ounce glasses.

Variation: Omit apricot kernels. Add 4 tablespoons brandy 2 minutes before removing from heat.

CHESTNUT AND CRANBERRY CONSERVE

½ pound chestnuts | 4 cups cranberries | 1 cup water | 2½ cups sugar |
¼ cup orange juice | 2 tablespoons grated orange rind |
½ teaspoon cinnamon | ½ teaspoon ginger

The chestnuts need not be cut into for boiling, but it does help to remove shells and brown inner skins if one or two cuts are made before cooking them in cold water to cover about 30 minutes. Remove shells and skins from chestnuts while boiling the cranberries. Chop chestnuts, or put through food chopper using medium blade. Cook cranberries in water till skins burst and put through a sieve. Add sugar, orange juice and grated rind, cinnamon and

	lbs.	qts.	Directions	Time	Pressure
Figs			Use only firm figs. Sprinkle with 1 cup baking soda for each 6 qts. figs and add 1 gallon boiling water. Let stand 5 minutes. Drain, rinse. Cook figs in boiling hot medium syrup 1 hour. Remove fruit to containers, cover with boiling hot syrup and process immediately.	5 min.	5 min. at 5 lbs. pressure
Fruit Juices			Crush ripe fruit, berries, cherries. Heat slowly and simmer 2 minutes. Strain, add sugar and water to taste in amounts desired. Heat juice and fill jars. Seal and process at once.	30 min.	
Peaches	40 lbs.	20–25 qts.	Blanch 1 minute in boiling water. Slip skins, cut in halves or slices. Cover with medium syrup, boiling hot. Process immediately.	25 min.	10 min. at 5 lbs. pressure
Pears	50 lbs.	20–25 qts.	Pare, cut into halves, core. Precook in light syrup 4 to 8 minutes. Pack, cover with syrup and process at once.	30 min.	10 min. at 5 lbs. pressure
Pineapple			Peel, remove eyes, cube. Pack into jars and cover with light syrup, boiling hot. Process at once.	30 min.	10 min. at 5 lbs. pressure
Plums	50 lbs.	28–30 qts.	Wash, stem and prick with pin. Pack in jars and cover with medium syrup, boiling hot. Process at once.	20 min.	10 min. at 5 lbs. pressure
Rhubarb			Wash, trim off leaves, 2 inches of stalks. Cut into ½-inch pieces. Pack in jars and cover with heavy syrup. Process at once. For use in pies, precook 3 minutes in very little water with a little sugar added to suit the taste. Pack and process as above.	15 min.	10 min. at 5 lbs. pressure
Strawberries	22 lbs.	8–10 qts.	Wash, stem and add 1 cup sugar to each 1 qt. of berries. Let stand 2 hours, or overnight. Simmer 5 minutes. Pack into jars, with syrup and process.	5 min.	5 min. at 5 lbs. pressure
Tomato Juice			Same as Fruit Juices.		

34

GUIDE FOR BOTTLING VEGETABLES

| Product | Yield | | Preparation for Bottling | Pressure Cooker | | | Boiling-Water Bath |
	Raw	Bottled		10 lbs. pints min.	10 lbs. quarts min.	15 lbs. pints min.	pts. qts.† hours
Asparagus	1½ lbs., 1 crate (1 doz. bunches)	1 pt., 8 qts.	Wash thoroughly, using brush. Remove coarse scales, tough ends, and fibrous surface from lower stalks. Tie stalks into bundles or cut into short pieces. Pre-cook for 3 minutes. Pack hot. Add ½ teaspoon salt* per pint. Cover with boiling liquid.	30	35		2
Beans Dry Soy†	¾ cup	1 pt.	Sort and wash beans. Soak overnight. Drain from soaking water. Bring water to a boil, add beans and bring to boil. Pour into jars. Add 1 teaspoon salt per pint.	55	60		3
Beans Green Soy† Sprouted Soy	1½-2 qts. in pods	1 pt.	Place pods in boiling water and boil five minutes to make shelling easy. Pre-cook 3 minutes. Pack loosely. Add ½ teaspoon salt* per pint. Cover with boiling liquid. Pre-cook sprouted soy beans and proceed as for green soy.	50	55		3
Beans Lima and Shell†	1½-2 qts. in pod, 1 bushel	1 pt., 9 qts.	Pre-cook shelled beans 3 minutes. Pack loosely, while hot. Add ½ teaspoon salt* per pint. Cover with boiling liquid.	50	55		3
Beans Snap	¾ lb., 1 bushel	1 pt., 20 qts.	Wash. Remove tips; cut into pieces, if desired. Pre-cook 3 minutes. Pack loosely. Add ½ teaspoon salt* per pint. Cover with boiling liquid.	30	35		3
Beets, Baby	1-1½ lbs., 1 bushel	1 pt., 15-20 qts.	Boil or steam washed beets until the skins slip easily. Skin. If large, dice or slice. Pack hot. Add ½ teaspoon salt* per pint and 1 tablespoon vinegar, if desired. Cover with boiling water.	30	35		2

Broccoli	1½-2 lbs.	1 pt.	Wash, trim off tough portions. Cut broccoli in pieces. Pre-cook for 3 minutes. Pack loosely while hot. Add ½ teaspoon salt per pint. Cover with boiling water.	30	35	3
Carrots	1¼ lbs. / 1 bushel	1 pt. / 20 qts.	Wash and brush carrots. Slice or dice, if desired. Pre-cook 3 minutes. Pack hot. Add ½ teaspoon salt* per pint. Cover with boiling liquid.	30	35	2
Corn, whole cream†	4-6 ears (Golden Cross) / 1 bushel	1 pt. / 12 qts.	Husk and brush off corn silks. Cut corn from cob. (For cream style, scrape cob.) Cover with boiling salted water (1 teaspoon salt per pint of water). Bring to boiling point. Pack loosely.	60	70 / 75 (cream style)	3
Greens†	1-1¼ lbs. / 1 bushel	1 pt. / 7-9 qts.	Wash greens thoroughly. Blanch by steaming or boiling until leaves are wilted (2 to 4 minutes). Pack loosely. Cut crosswise to bottom of jar with knife. Add ½ teaspoon salt* per pint. Cover with boiling liquid.	95	105	3
Peas†	2 qts. in pod / 1 bushel	1 pt. / 8 qts.	Pre-cook shelled peas for 3 minutes. Pack loosely. Add ½ teaspoon salt* per pint and cover with boiling liquid.	45		3
Pumpkins,† Marrow†	2 lbs. in shell	1 pt.	Steam or bake pumpkin or squash until tender. Remove from shell. *Or* peel and cube vegetable and boil in salted water until tender. Pack while hot.	85	105	3
Tomatoes	1¼-1¾ lbs. / 1 bushel	1 pt. / 18-20 qts.	Scald tomatoes 10 seconds and peel. Remove white core. Pack whole or cut up. Press down until juice fills jar. Add 1 teaspoon salt per quart. *Or* pre-cook peeled tomatoes. When boiling, pour into hot jars. Add 1 teaspoon salt per quart .... {35 min. pts. / 45 min. qts.} .... 10 min. qts.		60	3

* If salted blanching water is used in packing, omit additional salt.
† Because of slower heat penetration, pint containers are recommended.

Product	Preparation
Sweet Apple Cider	Wash fully ripened fruit. Remove stems and blossom ends. Crush with hand power press or electric press to extract juice. Fill jars, adjust covers loosely without rubbers, and place jars in a deep pot on a rack. Add a few inches of warm water and steam 1 hour. Remove a jar, lift cover and adjust rubber, seal while hot. Proceed likewise with the other jars. Cider made in this way will remain sweet indefinitely.
Boiled-Down Cider	Proceed as for making Sweet Apple Cider. When the juice has been extracted, cook in an open pot over moderate heat until the cider has been reduced by one half. Skim frequently. Fill jars while hot and seal.

35 Magic Meals Out of Cans

THE EMERGENCY SHELF

There should be a special emergency shelf or part of a shelf in every well-ordered home. The home may be a kitchenette apartment or a spacious residence equipped with pantries and storage rooms, but a handy homemaker at some time or other finds need for last minute meals. That occasion may be when unexpected guests stay to luncheon or dinner. Or, when weather conditions unavoidably postpone a trip to the grocery, meat market or delicatessen shop. Or, when illness of the cook makes emergency meals necessary.

Thanks to the canning industry, every type of essential food from soup to nuts is available in neat cans or glass containers. Directions for using, plainly printed on each container, help even a novice in the quick preparation of nourishing meals. Even 'company' meals can be prepared out of cans with no sacrifice of essential nutritional or aesthetic values.

Another great 'assist' to the emergency cook is the ever increasing number of ready-to-heat, bake or fry *quick frozen foods*, plainly marked with the approved label for use in the Kosher kitchen.

There are also a number of frozen desserts on the market. These include the following:

Fruit Ices or Sherbets.
Fruit Juices.
Ice-Cream.
Peaches (sliced).
Pears (sliced).
Strawberries and other berries (sliced or whole).

WHAT THE EMERGENCY FOOD SHELF SHOULD WEAR

To meet the necessity for quick, nourishing meals-out-of-cans, jars and packages, it is well to stock the emergency shelf with at least one of each of the following ready-to-heat-and-serve items:

SOUPS

Beet borsht, for cold soup (may be heated)

Schav, for cold soup (may be heated)

Gumbo soup (to be heated)

Mushroom, cream of (to be heated)

Mushroom and barley (to be heated)

Pea, cream of green (to be heated)

Tomato, cream of (to be heated)

Vegetable, condensed (to be heated)

BASIS FOR SOUPS

Corn, cream style

Mushrooms

Peas

Potatoes (canned, whole)

Tomatoes

Vegetables, mixed

SOUP ACCESSORIES

Crackers, several varieties

Dry cereal, flaked or puffed

Matzo, several varieties

Noodles, fine (8-minute cooking)

BASIS FOR MAIN DISHES

Baked beans with tomato sauce

Chicken, semi-boned

Corned-beef loaf

Roast beef in gravy

Gefilte fish

Goulash

Hamburgers

Kishke

Meat balls

Peanut butter

Soybeans

Tongue

Veal and gravy

FISH

Gefilte fish

Herring, pickled and in wine sauce, kippered

Salmon

Sardines

Tuna fish

VEGETABLES

Asparagus, tips and cuts

Beans, lima, navy, soy

Beets, diced, Julienne, sliced, whole (small)

Carrots, diced

Carrots and peas

Corn-on-cob kernel

Peas

Potatoes, white and sweet

Pumpkin

Tomatoes

Mixed vegetables

Tomato and Vegetable Juices

MEAL ACCESSORIES AND GARNISHES

Biscuit and muffin mixes (packaged)

Olives, pickles, relishes (in cans and jars)

Potato mix for mashed potatoes (packaged)

Potato pancake mix (packaged)

BASIS FOR DESSERTS

Canned and packaged cake, biscuit mixes

Coconut, shredded

Custard and pudding mixes

Fruits (in cans and jars)

Fruits, dried (packaged)

Gelatin, fruit flavoured

Milk, evaporated, condensed

(canned) dry skim and whole milk (packaged)

Nuts, various kinds shelled or whole

Puréed fruit (apricot, prune – for fruit whip)

Jams, jellies, marmalades, preserves

Raisins and almonds

SOLUBLE INSTANT BEVERAGES, HOT OR ICED

Chocolate

Cocoa

Coffee, and coffee substitutes

Dry skim milk, or whole milk

Sweetened condensed milk

Evaporated milk

Tea

FRUIT JUICES, SWEETENED AND UNSWEETENED
TOMATO JUICE

SAMPLE EMERGENCY MENUS OF
CANNED AND QUICK FROZEN FOODS

WARM WEATHER MENUS

1

Chilled beet borsht (sour cream, boiled or canned potato)

Kippered herring in tomato sauce (parsley garnish)

Tossed green salad (lettuce, celery, cucumbers, peppers)

Crackers

Sliced peaches (canned or quick frozen)

2

Tomato juice cocktail (with crackers or matzo wafers)

Cheese blintzes (quick frozen), serve with sour cream

Asparagus salad (canned, drained). Serve with French dressing, lettuce or other greens

Fresh or canned apricots, peaches, pears, plums

3
Orange juice (canned or frozen)
Herring tidbits in wine sauce or
with sour cream dressing
Canned whole potatoes
(browned in butter)
Tomato and cucumber salad,
French dressing
Ice-cream
Iced beverage (instant coffee or
substitute, with evaporated
milk)

4
Schav, sour cream thickening
with crackers or matzo wafers
Salmon with hard-cooked egg
garnish
Diced celery and green pepper
salad on lettuce with mayonnaise dressing
Fresh or canned pineapple
Iced tea, coffee or substitute,
topped with dry skim milk
topping

5
Grapefruit juice
Soybeans, heated with tomato
sauce, crackers or rye bread

Tomato salad, French dressing
Frozen or canned peaches
Iced beverage (instant coffee or
substitute, tea or cocoa with
evaporated milk)

6
Tomato juice cocktail
Tuna fish with tomato and
cucumber garnish
Celery, green pepper, parsley in
salad or as garnish
Canned or quick frozen straw-
berries
Iced beverage (chocolate, cocoa,
tea, coffee or substitute)

7
Vegetable juice cocktail with
crackers or matzo wafers
Gefilte fish, chilled with horse-
radish or pickle relish
Canned potatoes, drained and
browned in butter or oil
Canned diced beets in lemon
sauce
Frozen fruit or canned mixed
fruits
Iced beverage (instant coffee or
substitute, tea)

COLD WEATHER MENUS

1
Chicken noodle soup (packaged)
Pot roast (quick frozen)
Kasha-Varnitchkes (quick
frozen)

Tossed green salad
Frozen fruit ice
Hot tea or black coffee

COLD WEATHER MENUS – continued

2

Chicken noodle soup (packaged)
Holishkes (quick frozen, chopped meat in cabbage)
Mashed potatoes (packaged – few minutes' preparation)
Salad of canned carrots on lettuce, salad dressing
Canned or quick frozen sliced peaches
Hot beverage (instant tea or black coffee or substitute)

3

Hot beet borsht (egg yolk thickening or sour cream)
Baked beans with tomato sauce, rye bread
Waldorf salad
Hot beverage (with evaporated milk)

4

Barley and mushroom soup (parsley garnish)
Creamed salmon with peas (or tuna fish) with toast or crackers
Salad of canned Julienne beets
Stewed dried fruit
Hot beverage with evaporated milk

5

Hot vegetable soup, packaged or canned, with crackers
Potato pancakes with sour cream and pot cheese
Salad of canned or quick frozen fruit, mayonnaise dressing
Hot beverage with evaporated milk

6

Hot tomato soup, canned
Gefilte fish, horse-radish or dill pickles
Potato knishes (quick frozen – baked, brown in oven)
Diced beets, in lemon sauce
Shredded cabbage salad
Hot beverage with evaporated milk

7

Hot tomato soup (canned) with crackers or egg drops (5 minutes' cooking)
Scalloped salmon or tuna fish, using sliced potatoes between layers and matzo meal topping
Salad of canned green beans, mayonnaise dressing
Frozen strawberries
Hot beverage (instant tea or coffee) with evaporated milk

WEIGHTS AND MEASURES
(All measurements are level and standard)

The measures used in this book are American measures. The cup measure is 8 fluid ounces (the Standard British Measuring Cup is 10 fluid ounces); the tablespoon measure is $\frac{1}{2}$ fluid ounce (the Standard British Measure for tablespoons is $\frac{2}{3}$ fluid ounce).

1 teaspoon	equals	1 teaspoon
2 teaspoons		1 dessert spoon
1 tablespoon		$\frac{1}{2}$ fluid ounce
4 tablespoons		$\frac{1}{4}$ cup
8 tablespoons		1 gill
2 cups		1 pint
4 cups		1 quart
4 quarts		1 gallon
16 ounces		1 pound
1 tablespoon butter		1 ounce
2 cups butter		1 pound
4 cups flour		1 pound
2 cups granulated sugar		1 pound
$2\frac{2}{3}$ cups brown sugar		1 pound
$3\frac{1}{2}$ cups icing sugar		1 pound
1 square baking chocolate		1 ounce
7–8 egg whites		1 cup

Kosher Meats. In accordance with the Rules of Kashrut, only the forequarters of beef, lamb and veal are used in Jewish cuisine. The meat is sectioned in several cuts from the neck to and including eight ribs. Following is the order of cut sections and their general uses:

Cuts	*Used for*
Neck of Beef	Soups, stews (unboned), boned and chopped – for meat patties, hamburgers, etc.
Chuck to Short Ribs	Boned and rolled for pot roasts, stews, also with vegetables
Chuck Steaks	Braising, potting, stewing
Shoulder of Beef	Thin sliced for steaks, boned or whole for roasts, pot roasts
Brisket of Beef	Boned for making corned beef; under shoulder and leg sections used for braising, potting, also with vegetable combinations
Flank Cuts and Corner Piece	For tzimmes, pot roasts, also soups and stews
Plate, below Ribs, around Middle	For tzimmes, stews
Rib Cuts	Steaks, roasts (boned and rolled or standing)
Neck of Lamb	Stews
Breast of Lamb	Cut up for stew; whole, unboned for roast with dressing
Shoulder of Lamb	Boned or whole, pot roast, roast, or cut up for stew
Rack of 8 ribs with part of upper section	Cut into and fastened for crown roast with stuffing
Ribs, Shoulder Chops	Grilling, pan frying
Shank	Whole, braising, pot roast, or boned and chopped for patties
Veal Breast	With pocket for stuffing, roasting; pot roast

Cuts	*Used for*
Rib Chops and Shoulder Chops	Pan frying
Shoulder	Boned or whole for pot roast; roasting whole or boned and rolled
Shank	Same as lamb

TIME CHART FOR COOKING VEGETABLES

Vegetable	*Top of Stove Cooking – Minutes*	*Pressure Cooker Method** *Amount Water*	*Minutes*	*Pounds Pressure*
Asparagus (cut or spears)	Uncovered, 15–20	¼ cup	2 min.	15 pounds
Green Beans, Wax, Limas	Covered, 10–15	⅛	3	10–15
Beets, sliced	Covered, 25–30 Uncovered, 30–45	½	6	15
Beets, small, whole	Covered, 30–50	¾	12	15
and large, whole	Covered, 50–60	¾	18	15
Broccoli	Uncovered, 15–30	¼	2	15
Brussels Sprouts	Uncovered, 8–12	½	5	15
Cabbage, shredded,	Covered, 8–12	½	3	15
wedges	Uncovered, 15–20	¾	8	15
Carrots, sliced	Covered, 10–15	¼	2½	15
whole	Covered, 20–25	¼	4	15
Cauliflower, pieces	Uncovered, 8–10	½	3	15
whole	Uncovered, 15–20	½	6–8	15
Corn, on cob	Covered, 5–7 (in boiling water)	½	5	15
cut	Covered, 10	¼	3	15
Kale, trimmed	Covered, 20	½	4	15
Okra, sliced	Uncovered, 15–20	¼	3	15
Onions, whole	Uncovered, 20–30	½	7–10	15
Parsnips, whole	Uncovered, 20–30	½	7	15
Green Peas	Covered, 10–12 (in boiling water)	¼	2	5
Potatoes, cut up	Covered, 12–15	¾	8	15
whole	Covered, 20–30	1	15	15
Sweet Potatoes, medium, whole	Covered, 20–30	½	10	15
Spinach	Covered, 5–6	¼	1½	15
Tomatoes, whole	Covered, 5–10	¼	2½	15
Turnips, small whole,	Uncovered, 20–35	½	7	15
white, yellow, cut (Rutabagas)	Uncovered, 25–45	½	5	15
Zucchini, sliced	Covered, 5–8	¼	2½	15

* Consult directions for your type of Pressure Cooker.

TIME AND TEMPERATURE FOR COOKING, FRYING, BAKING

Food	Temperature	Gas Mark	Time
Beef Roast (uncovered)	300° F.	1–2	20–25 min. per lb.
Biscuits	350°–375° F.	4–5	12–15 min.
Bread (yeast)	375° F.	5	45–60 min.
Cakes			
Angel Food or Sponge	325° F.	3	1 hr.
Butter, Layer	375° F.	5	25 min.
Coffee	375°–400° F.	5–6	20–30 min.
Fruit	275° F.	¾	2 to 3 hrs.
Loaf	325°–350° F.	3–4	45–60 min.
Chicken, roasted whole	350° F.	4	30 min. per lb.
Chops			
Lamb (shoulder), broiled, sautéed			15–20 min.
Veal (shoulder), broiled, sautéed			20–30 min.
Custard, baked (water surrounded)	350° F.	4	30–40 min.
Duck	325°–350° F.	3–4	25 min. per lb.
Fish, Fillets, Smelts			
Fried			10–15 min. (including turning)
Baked	350° F.	4	25–30 min.
Chopped, boiled			30–40 min. per lb.
Goose	325°–350° F.	3–4	25 min. per lb.
Lamb, shoulder roast (uncovered)	325° F.	3	30 min. per lb.
Muffins	375°–400° F.	5–6	25–30 min.
Pie Shells	425°–450° F.	7–8	12–15 min.
Fruit filled, 2 crusts	425° F.	7	40–50 min.
Potatoes, baked whole	425°–450° F.	7–8	45–60 min.
Scalloped, with cheese	350° F.	4	45–60 min.
Puddings			
Baked (rice, etc.)	325°–350° F.	3–4	50–60 min.
Steamed	400° F.	6	1 hr.
Scones	425°–450° F.	7–8	
Soufflés (water surrounded)	375° F.	3	20–30 min.
Squash, all varieties	350° F.	4	30–45 min.
Turkey	325°–350° F.	3–4	25 min. per lb.
Veal, shoulder roast (uncovered)	325° F.	3	25–30 min. per lb.

Index

Desserts—*continued*
  cherry dumplings, 433
  chestnut, 435
  chocolate Bavarian, 434
  coffee soufflé, 435
  cranberry confiture, 435
  cranberry tapioca, 431
  custards, *see* custards
  doughnuts, *see* doughnuts
  eggless prune whip, 437
  enriched Bavarian, 434
  fondant balls, 453
  fondant filling for biscuits, 453
  fritters, *see* fritters
  frosted grape clusters, 453
  frozen, 460–476
    banana cream, 461
    caramel cream, 461
    chocolate cream, 461
    chocolate custard cream,
      460
    cream cheese mound, 470
    crumb cake, 471
    Devonshire shortcake, 470
    frappés, 464
    ice cream flower pots, 459
    lemon cream, 462
    maple cream, 462
    mousses, 465–6
    parfaits, 466–7
    peach cream, canned, 463
    peach cream, fresh, 462
    peppermint candy cream,
      463
    raspberry cream, 463
    sherbets, 467–8
    strawberry cream, fresh,
      464
    strawberry cream, quick,
      464
    strawberry shortcake, 471
    vanilla cream, 460
    vanilla custard cream, 460
    with evaporated milk, 471
  fruits, *see also* individual fruits

fruit fluff, 436
fruit soufflé, 436
gelatins, *see* gelatins
Hawaiian dainty, 454
Israeli, 119–21
macaroon Bavarian, 434
marron glacé, 455
meringue shells, fillings for,
  437
meringue shells, never-fail,
  436
mocha Bavarian, 434
nubians, 454
nut Bavarian, 435
orange and grapefruit sticks,
  454
pastry, *see* pastry
pies, *see* pies
prune whip, 437
pudding, *see* puddings
soufflé, *see* soufflé
sugar plums, 455
tapioca casserole, 432
tapioca cream, 431
tarts, *see* tarts
upside-downies, 456
dessert salads, 328–31, *see* salads
devilled eggs, 149
devil's food cake, 343
Dill pickles
  salt, 492
  stuffed, 442
dolma, 114
dough, methods of preparation,
  123–4
doughnuts and crullers, 365
doughnuts, baking powder, 366
doughnuts, raised dough, 365
  variations, 366
Dressing
  dessert salad 1, 330
  dessert salad 2, 331
  for lamb, 249
  for veal, 252
  poultry, *see* poultry dressings